KNOWLEDGE-BASED AND EXPERT SYSTEMS SERIES

Series Editor: **Alex Goodall,** *Expert Systems International Ltd., Oxford, England*

Approaches to
Knowledge Representation:
An Introduction

Approaches to Knowledge Representation: An Introduction

Edited by
G. A. Ringland
and
D. A. Duce
Rutherford Appleton Laboratory, England

RESEARCH STUDIES PRESS LTD.
Letchworth, Hertfordshire, England

JOHN WILEY & SONS INC.
New York · Chichester · Toronto · Brisbane · Singapore

RESEARCH STUDIES PRESS LTD.
58B Station Road, Letchworth, Herts. SG6 3BE, England

Marketing and Distribution:

Australia, New Zealand, South-east Asia:
Jacaranda-Wiley Ltd., Jacaranda Press
JOHN WILEY & SONS INC.
GPO Box 859, Brisbane, Queensland 4001, Australia

Canada:
JOHN WILEY & SONS CANADA LIMITED
22 Worcester Road, Rexdale, Ontario, Canada

Europe, Africa:
JOHN WILEY & SONS LIMITED
Baffins Lane, Chichester, West Sussex, England

North and South America and the rest of the world:
JOHN WILEY & SONS INC.
605 Third Avenue, New York, NY 10158, USA

Library of Congress Cataloging in Publication Data

Approaches to knowledge representation: an introduction/edited by
G. A. Ringland and D. A. Duce.
    p. cm. — (Knowledge-based and expert systems series; 1)
    Bibliography: p.
    Includes index.
    ISBN 0 471 91785 0 (Wiley)
    1. Expert systems (Computer science)   2. Artificial intelligence.
I. Ringland, G. A. (Gordon A.)   II. Duce, David A.   III. Series.
QA76.76.E95A669   1988
006.3'3—dc19   87-32331

British Library Cataloguing in Publication Data

Approaches to knowledge representation: an
   introduction.—(Knowledge-based and
   expert systems series).
   1. Expert systems (Computer science)
I. Ringland, G.A. II. Duce, David A.
III. Series
006.3'3   QA76.76.E95

ISBN 0 86380 064 5   **02318242**
ISBN 0 471 91785 0 Wiley

ISBN 0 86380 064 5 (Research Studies Press Ltd.)
ISBN 0 471 91785 0 (John Wiley & Sons Inc.)

Printed in Great Britain by SRP Ltd., Exeter

Preface

Knowledge Representation is the keystone of the Artificial Intelligence enterprise, and systems utilizing AI techniques. Any project with a knowledge based content must choose some way of representing that knowledge, yet too rarely is this choice informed or even conscious.

This book originated from a series of lectures on Knowledge Representation given by the authors at Rutherford Appleton Laboratory. The aim is to explain and analyse a wide range of approaches to Knowledge Representation to assist in the process of rational design for knowledge based systems. The book is divided into three parts.

- The first is a discussion of the standard approaches to knowledge representation: logic, semantic networks, frames and rule based systems.

- The second is a discussion of how we, as humans, appear to represent knowledge.

- Finally a selection of more advanced topics is presented - the representation of time, meta-knowledge, conceptual graphs, issues of computational tractability, and functional approaches.

The intended audience is final year undergraduates, first year graduate students and computer professionals who are beginning to work in the areas of Knowledge Engineering and Artificial Intelligence.

Acknowledgements

Special thanks are due to Bob Hopgood for reading and commenting on the first draft of this volume and to Ronald Brachman of AT&T for his very perceptive comments on parts of the first draft.

We are particularly indebted to Amanda Hopgood and Charlie Kwong for producing a large number of the diagrams, to Alex Goodall of ESI Ltd. (Series Editor) and Veronica Wallace of Research Studies Press for their patience and help during the preparation of this book.

Credits

Chapter 3. Figure 1 adopted from M.R. Quillian "Semantic Memory" in M. Minsky (Editor) *Semantic Information Processing* (1968) with permission from MIT Press. Figure 2 reproduced with permission from McGraw-Hill Book Company from P.H. Winston *The Psychology of Computer Vision* (1975). Figure 3 adapted with permission from *Computer Models of Thought and Language* by R.C. Schank and K.M. Colby, copyright 1973 W.H. Freeman and Company. Figure 7 reproduced with permission from Elsevier Science Publishers B.V. from L.K. Schubert "Extending the expressive power of semantic networks", *Artificial Intelligence* **7**(2), pp.163-198, 1976. Figure 8 is used by permission of the International Joint Conference on Artificial Intelligence, Inc. from P.J. Hayes, "On Semantic Nets, Frames and Associations", *Proc. 5th IJCAI* 1977. Copies of the Proceedings are available from Morgan Kaufmann Publishers, Inc., 95 First Street, Los Altos, CA 94022, U.S.A. Figure 9 is reproduced with permission from R.J. Brachman and J.G. Schmolze "An overview of the KL-ONE knowledge representation scheme", *Cognitive Science* **9**(2), pp.171-216, 1985.

Chapter 6. Figure 1 is reproduced with permission from the American Association for the Advancement of Science from R.N. Shepard and J. Metzler "Mental rotation of three-dimensional objects", *Science* **171**, pp.701-3, 1971. Figures 2 and 4 are reproduced with permission from Academic Press from L.A. Cooper and R.N. Shepard in *Visual Information Processing*, ed. W.G. Chase (1973) and R.N. Shepard and C. Feng "A chronometric study of mental paper folding", *Cognitive Psychology*, **3**, pp.228-243, 1972, respectively. Figure 5 is reproduced with permission from L.R. Brooks "Spatial and verbal components of the act of recall", *Canadian J. Psychology*, **22**, pp.349-368, 1968.

Chapter 7. Figures 10 and 11 are reproduced from J.F. Sowa, *Conceptual Structures: Information Processing in Mind and Machine* (1983), with permission from Addison-Wesley Publishing Co. Inc.

Chapter 10. Figure 4 is reproduced with permission of the Institute of Electrical and Electronic Engineers from J. Mylopoulos, T. Shibahara and J.K. Tsotsos, "Building Knowledge-based Systems: the PSN experience", *IEEE Computer*, **16**(10), copyright © IEEE 1983.

Gordon A. Ringland
David A. Duce

14 October 1987

Table of Contents

All authors are located at the Rutherford Appleton Laboratory, Chilton, Didcot, OXON OX11 0QX, U.K.

1 Background and Introduction

David Duce and Gordon Ringland

1.1 Background

There is a sense in which every computer program contains knowledge about the problem it is solving. A program for solving differential equations, for example, certainly contains knowledge about that particular problem domain. The knowledge is in the particular algorithms the program employs and the decision procedure which determines which algorithm to employ in a particular set of circumstances. However, it is a characteristic of most computer programs that the knowledge they contain is not represented explicitly and cannot be readily expanded or manipulated. Knowledge is in a sense projected onto the program, like a 3-Dimensional image being projected onto a 2-Dimensional surface, and cannot be reconstructed. Given a "traditional " payroll program it would be only possible to make fragmentary deductions about, say, statutory sick pay legislation, yet this is a part of the knowledge on which the program is based and which was used in the construction of the program.

This scenario is to be contrasted with the field of Artificial Intelligence (AI) where the concern is to "write down descriptions of the world in such a way that an intelligent machine can come to new conclusions about its environment by formally manipulating these descriptions" (Brachman and Levesque, 1985a). As Sloman (1979) remarks, "work in Artificial Intelligence, whether aimed at modelling human minds or designing smart machines, necessarily includes a study of knowledge. General knowledge about how knowledge is acquired, represented and used, has to be embodied in flexible systems which can be extended, or which can explain their actions. A machine which communicates effectively with a variety of humans will have to use information about what people can be expected to know in various circumstances".

Jackson (1986) in his excellent book *Introduction to Expert Systems* gives a very succinct overview of AI. He identifies three periods in the development of AI, the Classical Period, the Romantic Period and the Modern Period. He identifies the Classical Period with the game playing and theorem proving programs that were written soon after the advent of digital computers. The game playing (for example, chess) programs of this era were based on the notion of searching a state space. Problems were formulated in terms of a starting state (e.g. the initial state of a chess board), a test for detecting final states or solutions (e.g. the rules for checkmate in chess), and a set of operations that can be applied to change the current state (for example, the legal moves in chess). In any but the simplest of cases, an exhaustive search of the state spaces was infeasible and the trick then was to find some means of guiding the search. This led to the use of rules of thumb or heuristics, that could be used to guide the search in specific domains. Chess-playing programs constructed according to this paradigm cannot be said to explicitly represent the knowledge the chessmaster has about the game and the strategies he uses to reason about this knowledge.

Similar considerations apply to theorem proving systems of this era. Jackson describes the most important discoveries of this period as the twin realizations that (a) problems of whatever kind could, in principle, be reduced to search problems providing that they could be formalized in terms of a starting state, an end state and a set of operations for generating new states, but (b) that the search had to be guided by some representation of knowledge about the domain of the problem. In most cases it was felt necessary to have some explicit representation of knowledge about the objects, properties and actions associated with the domain or to have a global problem solving strategy.

The Romantic Period is identified with the research in computer understanding that went on between the mid-1960's and mid-1970's. Whatever beliefs one may hold about the possibility of a computer understanding anything, the ability to represent knowledge about real or imaginary worlds and reason using these representations is certainly a prerequisite for understanding. Much research was devoted in this period to the development of general frameworks for encoding both specific facts and general principles about the world, and although the whole enterprise turned out to be a very nontrivial exercise, many of the approaches to knowledge representation to be described in this book have their origins in this period.

The Modern Period covers the latter half of the 1970's to the present day. There has been a growing conviction that the power of a problem solver lies in the explicit representation of knowledge that the program can access, rather than in a sophisticated mechanism for drawing inferences from the knowledge. This period has seen the development of a number of expert systems which perform well on non-trivial tasks. These programs generally have two components, a *knowledge base* which contains the representation of domain specific knowledge, and an *inference engine* which performs the reasoning. Jackson observes that these systems tend to work best in areas where there is a substantial body of knowledge connecting situations to actions. Deeper representations of the domain in terms of spatial, causal or temporal models are avoided, but these are problems that a general knowledge representation system cannot side-step quite so easily.

1.2 The Knowledge Representation Problem

Brachman and Levesque in their introduction to *Readings in Knowledge Representation* (1985a) remark that the notion of knowledge representation is essentially an easy one to understand. It simply has to do with writing down, in some language or communications medium, descriptions or pictures that correspond in some salient way to the world or a state of the world. As in other areas of computer science, it is also necessary to consider the ways in which the representation is to be manipulated and the uses to which it is to be put. As remarked earlier, the primary reason for wanting to represent knowledge is so that a machine can come to new conclusions about its environment by manipulating the representation.

The first ingredient of the knowledge representation problem is to find a *knowledge representation language*, that is some formal language in which domains of knowledge can be described. Most systems of practical interest then need to be able to provide their users with access to the facts implicit in the knowledge base as well as those stored explicitly, and thus it is necessary to have a component of the knowledge representation that can perform automatic *inferences* for the user. The third component of the knowledge representation problem is how to capture the detailed knowledge base that represents the system's understanding of its domain. This latter problem is beyond the scope of this book, however.

David Israel characterized the knowledge representation problem as follows:

> All parties to the debate agree that a central goal of research is that computers must somehow come to "know" a good deal of what every human being knows about the world and about the organisms, natural or artificial, that inhabit it. This body of knowledge - indefinite no doubt, in its boundaries - goes by the name "common-sense". The

problem we face is how to impart such knowledge to a robot. That is, how do we design a robot with a reasoning capacity sufficiently powerful and fruitful that when provided with some subbody of this knowledge, the robot will be able to generate enough of the rest to intelligently adapt to and exploit its environment? We can assume that most, if not all, common-sense knowledge is general, as is the knowledge that objects fall unless they are supported, that physical objects do not suddenly disappear, and that one can get wet in the rain.

The following simple example, given by Minsky, points out that knowledge representation is not a simple problem:

> The only time when you can say something like, "if *a* and *b* are integers, then *a* plus *b* always equals *b* plus *a*", is in mathematics. Consider a fact like "Birds can fly". If you think that common-sense reasoning is like logical reasoning, then you believe there are general principles that state, "If Joe is a bird and birds can fly, then Joe can fly". Suppose Joe is an ostrich or penguin? Well we can axiomatize and say if Joe is a bird and Joe is not an ostrich or a penguin, Joe can fly. But suppose Joe is dead? Or suppose Joe has his feet set in concrete?

It is worth exploring this theme a little further. Some domains of knowledge, for example mathematical knowledge, are well-behaved in a certain sense, and are relatively straightforward to deal with. For example, a triangle is a 3-sided polygon, or the sum of the interior angles of a triangle is 180°. These facts are true of all triangles and can be used as definitions of the concept of a triangle.

For other domains of knowledge, it is not quite so straightforward. Some concepts, for example *bachelor*, have an explicit definition "a man who has never married" (at least that is true when the terms are used strictly!). However, the majority of names do not have simple definitions of this form. An important class of objects are *natural kinds* (naturally occurring species), for example *lemon*, and *elephant*. The book *Naming, Necessity and Natural Kinds* (Schwartz, 1977) contains a fascinating collection of papers on this subject which is well worth studying, if only to remind oneself that the problems of knowledge representation did not arise with the advent of digital computers, but have long been studied by philosophers whose writings ought not to be ignored by computer scientists.

Putnam in his paper "Is Semantics Possible?" in the above volume, looks in detail at natural kind objects. In the traditional philosophical view, the meaning of, say, "lemon", is given by specifying a conjunction of *properties*, akin to the definition of triangle. A lemon is something that has all of the properties in the definition. Putnam and the other authors in (Schwartz, 1977) challenge this traditional view. Suppose the defining characteristics of a lemon are "colour lemon", "tart taste" etc. The problem is that a natural kind may have abnormal members, for example there are green fruits that everyone would agree are lemons, and elephants with three legs are still elephants. It is argued that nouns meant to designate natural kinds do not have their extensions (the set of things to which they refer) determined by a finite number of concepts.

Suffice it to say in this chapter, that it is important when choosing a knowledge representation scheme for a particular domain of knowledge, to consider the types of objects in the domain.

Some of the issues that arise in knowledge representation are summarized below to give more of a feeling for the problems.

(1) *Expressive adequacy.* Is a particular knowledge representation scheme sufficiently powerful? What knowledge can and cannot particular schemes represent?

(2) *Reasoning efficiency.* Like all representation problems in computer science, a scheme that represents all knowledge of interest and is sufficient to allow any fact of interest to be inferred by no means guarantees that it will be possible to perform the inference in an acceptable time. There is generally a tradeoff between expressive adequacy and reasoning efficiency.

(3) *Primitives.* What are the primitives (if any) in knowledge representation? What primitives should be provided in a system and at what level?

(4) *Meta-representation.* How do we structure the knowledge in a knowledge base and how do we represent knowledge about this structure in the knowledge base?

(5) *Incompleteness.* What can be left unsaid about a domain and how do you perform inferencing over incomplete knowledge and revise earlier inferences in the light of later, more complete, knowledge?

(6) *Real-world knowledge.* How can we deal with attitudes such as beliefs, desires and intentions? How do we avoid the paradoxes that accompany self-referential propositions?

The remainder of the first part of this book describes four approaches to the knowledge representation problem which have acquired some degree of acceptability amongst researchers in the field. The four approaches are: logic, semantic nets, frames, logic and rule based systems. Subsequent chapters deal with each of these approaches in turn. The second part of the book covers some current research directions, and problems common to all of these basic approaches, for example the representation of time and the trade-off between expressive power and the computational efficiency of inferencing.

The next section gives a brief introduction to the four basic approaches.

1.3 Overview of the Basic Approaches

1.3.1 Logic

Mathematical logic is an attempt to make rigorous the reasoning process involved in mathematics. The starting point is the introduction of a symbolic language whose symbols have precisely stated meanings and uses. The next step is to define the rules by which these symbols can be combined and manipulated and then the properties of the resulting formal system are explored. Chapter 2 gives a detailed introduction to various systems of mathematical logic and their application to knowledge representation. In this introduction, we will give a flavour for the approach in a very informal style.

A recent paper by Sergot *et al.* (1986) describes the use of a certain system of logic to describe a large part of the British Nationality Act, 1981. The system of logic is known as definite Horn Clauses, which are essentially rules of the form:

$$A \text{ if } B_1 \text{ and } B_2 \text{ and } \cdots B_n$$

which have exactly one conclusion A, but zero or more conditions B. A simple example of a Horn clause is the following:

(Socrates is mortal) if (Socrates is a man)

The first clause of the British Nationality Act is as follows:

1.-(1).A person born in the United Kingdom after commencement shall be a British citizen if at the time of birth his father or mother is
(a) a British citizen; or
(b) settled in the United Kingdom.

Clause 1.-(1)(a) is represented as a first approximation by:

(x is a British citizen)
if (x was born in the U.K.)
and (x was born on date y)
and (y is after or on commencement)
and (z is a parent of x)
and (z is a British citizen on date y)

The symbols x, y and z are variables.

Using a slight extension of this mathematical apparatus, a major part of the British Nationality Act was represented. Having obtained such a representation, it can then be manipulated using the rules of logical inference, appropriate to this system of logic, so that answers to queries such as "is Peter a British citizen on 16 January 1984 given that he was born on 3 May 1983 in the U.K. and is still alive and his father William ...", can be given.

1.3.2 Semantic Networks

The study of semantics is an attempt to describe the concepts behind word meanings and the ways in which such meanings interact. It is such a description which semantic networks were designed to provide. A network is a net or graph of nodes joined by links. The nodes in a semantic network usually represent concepts or meanings (e.g. BOOK, GREEN) and the links (or labelled directed arcs) usually represent relations (e.g., a book IS COLOURED green).

Semantic networks may be loosely related to predicate calculus by the following substitution: *terms* are replaced by *nodes* and *relations* by *labelled directed arcs*.

A large number of semantic networks have been developed as variations on this simple pattern since Quillian (1968) first used one in a computer system. These networks share few assumptions, although they nearly all represent the relations between concepts using a semantic representation consisting of a network of links between nodes, a set of interpretative processes that operate on the network, and a parser. They also show a general commitment to parsimony.

The most often used link in semantic networks was introduced in Quillian's system to show that one concept is an example of another (e.g. canary IS-A bird). More recent systems have chosen their link and node types on the basis of epistemelogical concerns about how the knowledge will be used. These have shown that even the apparently simple IS-A relationship is more complex than had been previously believed.

Recent developments in semantic networks together with work on the theoretical underpinnings of this approach are reviewed in the chapter by Mac Randal.

1.3.3 Frames

The use of nodes and links to represent concepts and relations seems straightforward, but contains many pitfalls.

Some designers of network systems were not too careful about the way in which they assigned meanings to nodes. Thus, a type node labelled "elephant" might well stand for the concept of elephant, the class of all elephants, or a typical elephant. Similarly token nodes labelled elephant were open to interpretation as a particular elephant, an arbitrary elephant etc. Different interpretations support different sets of inferences and so the distinctions are important. There was thus a sense in which semantic network formalisms were logically inadequate in that they could not make many of the distinctions that can be easily made in mathematical logic, for example between a particular elephant, all elephants, no elephant etc.

Frames are ways of grouping information in terms of a record of "slots" and "fillers". The record can be thought of as a node in a network, with a special slot filled by the name of the object that the node stands for and the other slots filled with the values of various common attributes associated with such an object. Frames are particularly useful when used to represent knowledge of certain stereotypical concepts or events. The intuition here is that the human brain is less concerned with defining strictly the properties that entities must have in order to be considered as exemplars of some category, and more concerned with the salient properties associated with objects that are typical of their class.

Frame systems reason about classes of objects by using stereotypical representations of knowledge which usually will have to be modified in some way to capture the complexities of the real world, for example that birds can fly, but emus cannot. The idea here is that the properties in the higher levels of the system are fixed, but the lower levels can inherit values from higher up the hierarchy or can be filled with specific values if the "default" fillers are known to be inappropriate.

1.3.4 Rule Based Systems

A classic way to represent human knowledge is the use of IF/THEN rules. The satisfaction of the rule antecedents gives rise to the execution of the consequents - some action is performed. Such production rule systems have been successfully used to model human problem-solving activity and adaptive behaviour.

More recently, substantial knowledge-based systems have been constructed using this formalism, for example the R1/XCON computer configuration system, implemented in the OPS5 production rule language. Chapter 5 describes the basic operations of a production system and the problems which arise in systems involving large numbers of rules, as well as considering the suitability of this formalism as a general knowledge representation.

1.4 Psychological Studies of Knowledge Representation

The second part of the book is a review of how we, as humans, appear to represent knowledge.

In this chapter the schemes which have been suggested as being those used to represent knowledge in human memory are reviewed. These include the use of frames, schema, semantic nets and production rules described in the earlier chapters. Instantiations of these are described for which both the representations and processes acting on them are specified in sufficient detail to enable experimentally testable hypotheses to be drawn. Experimental evidence is presented which supports an argument that schemes using only one of these representation mechanisms are inadequate to account for the full range of phenomena exhibited in human performance, although individual models can account for the specific sets of phenomena which they are intended to address.

A class of analogical representations is introduced which has not been described in earlier chapters but which are capable of supporting the phenomenon of visual imagery. Evidence is presented as to the use of imagery by humans and the nature of the representations which would have to support it. This suggests that although it is possible to account for visual imagery by processes acting on a propositional representation, it seems more likely that some form of analogical representation is used by humans.

One use of analogical representations is to form models of situations so that reasoning can be performed on them. Johnson-Laird's (1983) suggestions as to how such *mental models* could be used to support inference are described, along with findings which suggest the use of both propositional and such analogical representations by humans. As well as describing the limitations of suggested representation schemes and providing evidence that supports the use of multiple forms of representation, this chapter provides a set of phenomena for which any representation scheme will have to account if it is to address the range of human performance.

1.5 More Advanced Topics in Knowledge Representation

The third part of the book reviews a selection of more advanced topics.

1.5.1 Conceptual Graphs

In Chapter 7 Jackman and Pavelin give an overview of the basic concepts of the conceptual graph knowledge representation language. This includes the concept of the conceptual graph, the type hierarchy, the basic operations that may be performed on conceptual graphs, and logical deduction. Reference is also made to the "maximal join" - one of the fundamental derived operations in the language. This operation would appear to be equivalent to the graph equivalent (with a type hierarchy) of unification.

1.5.2 The Explicit Representation of Control Knowledge

Production systems have been used in many knowledge-based systems to model human expertise in classification. For example, the MYCIN family of expert systems can identify which microbial organisms are producing symptoms of disease in a patient. Important criticisms of such systems have been made by Clancey and others. Although the systems effectively "do the job" of the expert physician, much of the knowledge has been compiled, which is to say that it has been compressed and restructured into effective procedures. Bainbridge in Chapter 8 shows this makes it difficult to re-use the knowledge in explanation and knowledge acquisition subsystems, since the knowledge is implicit and therefore unavailable.

An important research area involves reconstructing these systems to make the knowledge explicit and available for use, and from these implementations extracting general principles for making better expert systems which more effectively represent the knowledge in their domain.

1.5.3 Representing Time

One of the most fundamental, and deceptively simple, representations that humans have is that of time. A great deal of effort has been expended on attempting to formulate temporal representations for use by knowledge-based systems. Chapter 9 considers first the basic issues in the representation of time, such as the choice of point or interval representations, the treatment of fuzziness and granularity, and the problem of persistence. A number of approaches are then presented, with reference to the systems in which they have been used or the contexts in which they are appropriate. State-space modelling, date-based methods and before/after chains are all covered, along with temporal logics, which have attempted to place representations of time on a formal foundation.

1.5.4 Functional Approaches

An important approach to knowledge representation is the functional approach pioneered by Levesque and Brachman. There is a relation to mainstream computer science in that a knowledge base is regarded almost as an abstract data type with a set of operations defining the services it provides. The approach is motivated by the misuses or misinterpretations of knowledge representation formalisms which can occur when the user is allowed unrestricted access to representational structures: for instance, the nodes and links of a semantic net. Chapter 10 discusses some early work, and then describes Levesque's formalization in which he defines operators TELL and ASK for interacting with a knowledge representation system. Finally, the KRYPTON system is dealt with. It is the most advanced implementation of functional ideas, and it also incorporates multiple representations in having a taxonomic component for defining absolute relationships and an assertional component for making statements.

1.5.5 Expressive Power and Computability

There is a fundamental difference between a knowledge representation system and a database: the former will in general perform inferencing of some kind in order to answer queries about what is represented, while the latter is limited to retrieving the facts it contains. Databases cannot therefore represent incomplete information, for everything must be stored explicitly. Knowledge representation systems are more expressive, and their inference capabilities mean that they can act on incomplete knowledge. Indeed, when there is incomplete knowledge, queries to a database concern no more than what the database happens to contain; only a knowledge representation system can go further and attempt to deal with the world it represents. Of course the price to pay is in the computational effort needed to answer queries - the trade-off between the two factors is discussed in Chapter 11 by Williams and Lambert.

It is well-known that full first-order logic is not decidable, that is, a theorem prover cannot be guaranteed to terminate. Restricting the expressive power of the representation language results in systems that exhibit various degrees of tractability: though decidable, some are NP-complete, while others, less expressive, admit inferencing algorithms that operate in polynomial time. A number of the knowledge representation schemes described earlier in the book are discussed in these terms. It is not yet understood precisely how the tractability of a knowledge representation system depends on its expressiveness though there are some indications, but the trade-off may have important implications for our view of what service is expected of such systems.

2   Logic in Knowledge Representation

Cliff Pavelin

If your thesis is utterly vacuous
Use first-order predicate calculus
   With sufficient formality
   The sheerest banality
Will be hailed by the critics: "Miraculous!"

(Henry Kautz, from Canadian Artificial Intelligence, 9, 1986)

2.1 Introduction

Logic was originally developed to formalize the principles of valid reasoning. It has been studied since the time of Aristotle, although what is now regarded as Classical Logic was invented by Frege in the last century. His notation was diagrammatic and cumbersome; the current symbolic notation was introduced by Peano and perfected by Russell and Whitehead in 'Principia Mathematica'.

Logic attempts to make rigorous the reasoning process involved in science or mathematics; indeed Principia Mathematica was an attempt to reduce mathematics to Logic. It thus arises naturally in areas where deductive proof is required - for example proof of a geometrical theorem or proof that a computer program has the effect expressed by its specification. But Knowledge Representation problems typically relate not to formal domains but to ordinary discourse, to problems of everyday life, which are solved by informal reasoning often difficult to characterize. It is in such domains that the role of logic is not so clear.

An introduction to Moore's paper (1985a) in 'Readings in Knowledge Representation' observes 'an often furious debate over the proper role of formal logic in Knowledge Representation has raged almost unabated since the very beginnings of the field'. Moore's paper is in fact a prominent representative of the 'logicist' position, as is Hayes (1977a), while well-known expressions of the 'non-logicist' viewpoint are given in the Appendix to Minsky (1975) and Newell (1980). McDermott (1987) presents an account of the logicist position from the point of view of someone who has become less convinced. The two sides are respective subsets of the 'neats' and 'scruffies' identified by Bundy (1982).

What is it all about? Like many debates the issues become confused. Israel in a good analysis of some of these confusions (Israel, 1983) believes that failure to sort them out is one of the reasons for the inconclusive nature of the arguments. Not least of the problems is a lack of a consistent definition of 'logic'. In AI, it is likely to mean one of the following:

(a)   First Order Logic (FOL) summarized in the next section.

(b)   Some development of FOL which maintains its notation, its notion of a formal language, a deductive proof theory and a well defined model theory.

(c)   Any *formally defined* method of representing knowledge and making inferences about it.

The alternative to all these is to have reasoning techniques that are embodied inside a computer program, non-explicit and without any general principles.

In this chapter we assume definitions (a) or (b) and examine the benefits and deficiencies of logic, in these terms, for the representation of knowledge. We do not take sides in the debate; indeed the cynic may suggest it is a somewhat contrived polarization which came about to give stimulus and sparkle to the development of the subject. However, long may it continue.

Logic is, by definition, formal, while this chapter, in an attempt to give an insight into the basic principles, is informal throughout. There are numerous modern textbooks on formal logic available and it should also be noted that many books on Artificial Intelligence (e.g. Nilsson, 1982; Frost, 1986) give substantial introductions to logic.

2.2 A Brief Introduction to First Order Logic

The modern basis of logic is 'First Order Logic' (FOL) - also known variously as Classical Logic, Predicate Calculus (PC), Lower PC, FO functional calculus and general logic. Most of the other logics being studied in AI are developments (in some cases supersets) of FOL and they inherit at least some of its notation, limitations and advantages. This section gives a very brief introduction to those elements of FOL which are most relevant to the discussion on Knowledge Representation.

2.2.1 Basic Elements

FOL attempts to abstract the essential features of deductive reasoning and express them in what could be called an algebra of propositions. Propositions are statements which can be regarded as either TRUE or FALSE - no half measures are allowed. For example:

> 144 is a square number
> the internal angles of triangle ABC total 180 degrees
> Puccini wrote 10 operas

are three propositions (the last is false).

FOL is defined on two quite distinct levels. At one level it is a formal language with formation rules to generate sentences ('well-formed formulae') in the language. At this level propositions are typically denoted by symbols like p,q,r etc. A correspondence can then be set up between the symbols of the language and objects or values in some domain - which may be arithmetic or Euclidean geometry or the 'real world' or whatever. The sentences in the language then map on to statements about the objects in the domain. Mapping on to a domain is known as *interpretation*. For example a sentence in the language might simply be:

> p

Under a particular interpretation this may map onto the TRUE proposition that Puccini wrote 13 operas. If under a particular interpretation each of a set of sentences is TRUE, the interpretation is termed a *model* of those sentences.

It is important to maintain this distinction between language and interpretation. To say 'p is TRUE' is really nonsense as p is a symbol that cannot be true or false. The statement is just a shorthand either for 'p is asserted or can be proved' or sometimes 'under an interpretation currently being assumed, p maps onto a predicate that is deemed to be TRUE'.

Connectives

The next stage is to build up more complex expressions in the language by use of a further set of symbols known as 'connectives'. These correspond (under interpretation) to well known Boolean operators. Typically the ones used in logic are ∧ (and), ∨ (or), ¬ (not) and → (implies).

> p ∧ q   is TRUE only if both p and q are TRUE
> p ∨ q   is TRUE if at least one of p and q are TRUE
> p → q   is TRUE unless p is TRUE and q is FALSE
> ¬ p   is FALSE if p is TRUE and vice versa

∧, ∨ and → can be termed 'Dyadic' operators - they act on two truth values and produce a third. Since each proposition can have two possible values (TRUE or FALSE), there are four possible combinations of values, and the result of a connective must define a TRUE or FALSE for each, there are sixteen (four squared) possible connectives that could be defined (some are well known as basic electronic operations like NOR, NAND etc). The choice made in classical logic is somewhat arbitrary: those given above are traditional and make sentences easy to understand. There is redundancy - for example ∨ can be defined in terms of ¬ and ∧:

> p ∨ q is equivalent to ¬ (¬ p ∧ ¬ q)

It is possible to define all the connectives in terms of one carefully chosen one (for example ¬ (p ∧ q)) and this is often done in formal mathematical logic in order to minimize the basic concepts - but expressions and proofs are then obscure to the human reader.

It is important to realize that 'implies' is just another logical connective.

> p → q

does not, under an interpretation mean there is a causal link between whatever p and q map onto. For example:

> 144 is a square number → Puccini wrote 13 operas
> 30 is a prime number → Puccini wrote 10 operas

are both TRUE in FOL although there is no causal link in either and neither the antecedent nor the consequent is true in the second (see section 2.5.2).

Using the connectives (and brackets) as above, expressions can be built up of arbitrary complexity, for example:

> (p ∧ q ∧ r) → ((p ∨ q) ∧ (p ∨ r))

and there is an elementary algebra of these symbols which allows simplification of expressions etc. As an example:

$\neg$ (p $\wedge$ q) is equivalent to ($\neg$ p) $\vee$ ($\neg$ q)

such transformations being easily checked by a 'truth table' which gives all possible assignments to p and q.

2.2.2 Predicates and Quantification

It is possible to construct a logic purely on the basis of representing propositions as above - generally known as 'propositional', 'primary' or 'sentential' logic'. But it is very limited in what it can express. First Order logic goes a very significant stage further in the refinement by which it can represent propositions by being able to represent statements about members of classes of objects. Take as example two of the propositions given previously:

> The angles of triangle ABC total 180 degrees.
> Puccini wrote 10 operas

These might be generalized by writing

> The angles of triangle x total 180 degrees
> y wrote z operas

As written, with the 'variables' x, y, z, these sentences mean nothing, but the statements acquire a meaning if the variables are *quantified*. In FOL, two quantifiers are introduced: $\forall$ (meaning 'for all'...) and $\exists$ (meaning 'there exists' ..).

Thus the following are first order sentences:

> For all x, the angles of triangle x total 180 degrees

> There exists an x, y such that x wrote y operas
> > (i.e. someone wrote some operas).

In the notation of FOL the above statements would be represented as:

> $\forall$ x p(x)
> $\exists$ x,y q(x,y)

p(x) represents the incomplete proposition 'the angles of triangle x total 180 degrees'; p and q are *predicate symbols*; x and y are known as *variable symbols* which must be quantified either by $\exists$ or $\forall$.

A predicate thus (under interpretation) represents the set of objects for which a certain property is true. In this case p represents *all* triangles. q is true for all pairs of people and numbers such that the person wrote the given number of operas.

It is this ability to make statements about all objects or assert the existence of objects, without necessarily mentioning the individuals, which gives FOL its power.

The language of FOL also has constant symbols which represent specific objects, and function symbols which map onto functions:

$$\exists\ x\ q(x,c) \quad \text{where c is a constant symbol}$$

Under an interpretation in which q had the meaning above and c mapped onto the number 10, this would mean:

Someone (i.e. some x) wrote 10 operas.

There is an algebra which allows some simplification of expressions and transformation into certain canonical forms. A simple example (which shows the redundancy in $\exists$ and $\forall$) is

$$\exists\ x\ (p(x)) \text{ is equivalent to } \neg\ (\forall\ x\ \neg p(x))$$

Example

$$\forall\ x,y\ \ g(x,y) \rightarrow$$
$$s(x,y) \vee (\exists\ z\ s(x,z) \wedge g(z,y))$$

(For all x and for all y, g(x,y) implies either s(x,y) or the existence of some z such that s(x,z) and g(z,y)).

One interpretation of this is in the domain of integers where

g(x,y) means $x > y$
s(x,y) means $x = y + 1$ (x is the successor of y)

Then this sentence means for any choice of integers x and y, if $x > y$ then either $x = y + 1$ or there is some number z which is greater than y and one less than x. This is plainly true and therefore this interpretation is a model of the sentence.

Another interpretation is the domain of people: g(x,y) means 'x is an ancestor of y', s means 'is a mother of'. This says that if x is an ancestor of y then x is a mother of y or a mother of some ancestor of y. This interpretation makes the sentence FALSE; it would be a model if 'mother' were replaced by 'parent'.

2.2.3 Interpretations and Models

The term 'interpretation' has been used as a mapping from the language (the syntactic level) onto some domain in which 'TRUE' and 'FALSE' have some meaning. This does not necessarily imply that an interpretation has any real-world connotations. A proposition p may correspond to an infinity of statements but *all that is relevant to Logic* is whether it is TRUE or FALSE - it has just TWO essentially different interpretations. A sentence in propositional logic (i.e. no variables) involving n distinct propositions has just 2^n interpretations - corresponding to an assignment of TRUE or FALSE to each proposition. The sentence:

$$(p \lor q) \land (p \lor r)$$

has just eight interpretations - the meanings of p and q and r in the normal sense, are irrelevant.

The same principle applies in predicate logic where there are variables, but the range of values of the variables must be specified and since this may be an infinite domain, the number of interpretations is typically infinite:

$$\exists x \, p(x)$$

To give an interpretation of this sentence means giving the domain of the variable - and then specifying the subset for which p is going to be designated TRUE. There is thus an infinite number of interpretations and all those for which p is designated true in at least one instance are 'models'.

An interpretation is thus rigorously defined, but it is concerned with no more of the content of a proposition than simply 'truth' or 'falsity'. This definition of truth and falsity by mapping from the language onto a domain is known as giving the logic a *semantics* (after Tarski). However, one should not necessarily equate 'semantics' with 'meaning' in the real world.

2.2.4 Deductive Reasoning

Deductive reasoning consists of taking a set of sentences, inferring from it new sentences which can form the basis of further inferencing and so on until some 'interesting' conclusion is reached.

In this way an edifice of theorems is built up upon a few assumptions, the system of Euclidean geometry being the exemplar. Each step in this process is the application of one of a few simple rules of inference. The aim of logic is to formalize and automate this process of reasoning; an ideal might be the mechanical generation of the whole of Euclid from his simple postulates.

Deductive reasoning is applied to sentences of the FOL languages without reference to what they mean in any interpretation. Some scheme of inference (variously rules of inference, 'axiom schema' or sometimes a diagrammatic method) is defined which effectively gives transformation rules which can be applied mechanically to sentences to form new sentences.

An example of a simple rule of inference is as follows. If

    $A \rightarrow B$
    A

are given, then

    B

can be derived as a theorem. In this rule (the well-known '*modus ponens*'), A and B may stand for any well formed formulae. Other (fairly obvious) examples might be:

    If $A \wedge B$ is proved, then A can be derived.

    If $\forall x\ p(x)$ is proved, then $p(c)$ can be derived
                     where c is any constant symbol.

Any scheme of inference must preserve truth in any model (i.e. in any interpretation which makes the assumptions true). In the cases above this is obvious by the definitions of the connectives.

A proof starts from a set of 'axioms' and that proof will then be relevant to any model of these axioms. (A set of axioms, plus all the FOL rules etc. is sometimes called a 'theory'.) Since the same set of axioms may characterize many models, theorems in different domains may have a single proof when the abstraction into logic is made. For example, from the statements:

    All men are mortal
    I am a man

it follows:

    I am mortal.

Another argument might run:

All AI professors are mad	(1)
Professor X. is an AI professor	(2)
Therefore (theorem) Professor X. is mad	(3)

In first order logic, both these arguments are represented by:

$\forall x\ p(x) \rightarrow q(x)$	(1)	assumption
$p(c)$	(2)	assumption
$p(c) \rightarrow q(c)$	(2a)	from (1)
$q(c)$	(3)	from (2) and (2a)

There are many schemes of inference for FOL - they are all equivalent in terms of what can be proved from a given starting point. An FOL proof scheme should have the following properties:

(a)   It should be SOUND - any theorem must be true in any model of the axioms.

(b)   It should be COMPLETE. If some sentence is TRUE under *every* model of its axioms, then it should be derivable from the axioms.

If (a) were not true, we could prove theorems which were false in a model - equivalent to showing both p and $\neg$ p.

If (b) were not true, we have two definitions of a theorem: (i) a sentence derivable from the axioms, (ii) a sentence which is true in all models. In higher order and other logics they are not necessarily the same - there are for example 'truths' in arithmetic which cannot be proved from the normal axioms of arithmetic. However FOL is complete in this sense.

2.2.5 Validity and Consistency

It is possible to construct sentences which are *inconsistent* - which no interpretation can possibly make true. Examples are

$$p \wedge (\neg \, p)$$

or

$$\neg \; p(10) \wedge \forall \, x \; (p(x))$$

The second, for example, is saying (under any interpretation) that some property is false of some object 10 but is also true for all possible objects. The inconsistency is obvious in these simple examples but in general will not be so. A set of sentences for which a model does exist is known as *consistent*.

Conversely a sentence can be a *tautology* - this means it is true in *every* interpretation. Examples are:

$$(p \wedge q) \rightarrow (p \vee q)$$
$$p(c) \rightarrow \exists \, x \; p(x)$$

Sentences like this are known as *valid*.

Since the rules of inference preserve truth under interpretation, a model of a set of sentences is still a model for all sentences derived under the rules of inference, i.e. for all theorems. Everything it is possible to prove from a set of consistent axioms forms a consistent set.

If the axioms are inconsistent, the whole system breaks down - in fact anything can be proved. If the axioms are valid, nothing can be proved other than more tautologies which can be proved anyway using the rules of inference and starting with nothing!

Proving a theorem can easily be seen as equivalent to checking a set of sentences for validity. Suppose A, B and C are a set of axioms and we wish to know whether a theorem T can be derived from them. If it can, then T must be TRUE under any interpretation which makes A, B and C TRUE. In other words no possible interpretation could make:

$$A \wedge B \wedge C \wedge (\neg T)$$

true. The proof of T is thus equivalent to showing this set of sentences is inconsistent - there is no model. It is also equivalent to showing that its negation:

$$(\neg A) \vee (\neg B) \vee (\neg C) \vee T$$

is always TRUE, i.e. the expression is valid.

How does one go about checking for validity? In propositional calculus, it is obviously always possible since the value of the expression can be calculated for every possible assignment of truth values (although in practice this may be a huge number). It is not so obvious for FOL, but in fact there are decision procedures which guarantee to terminate if an expression is valid. This is equivalent to the remark above that FOL is complete.

It can be shown there is no procedure which can be guaranteed to complete if the set is non valid - FOL is said to be semi-decidable for this reason. In other words it is not in general possible to prove that a sentence is *not* a consequence of some theory.

2.2.6 Theorem Proving in FOL

We have said that rules of procedure can be devised which are sound and complete for FOL, i.e. can, in principle, be used to derive any theorem. Devising such rules is unfortunately not the difficult problem. The difficulty which gives rise to most of the research into theorem proving is devising rules which are *efficient* for the typical problems which arise in practice. Issues of decidability are of little concern if proving a simple theorem takes millions of years of Cray time. Much research into computer methods of theorem proving was stimulated by a uniform method, suitable for automated inference, known as 'resolution'. Theorem proving in FOL is a very active research area although it is unfortunately still the case that some logical puzzles which may be very simple for an intelligent human to solve are quite stringent tests of state-of-the-art theorem proving.

2.3 FOL in the Representation of Knowledge

The semantics of FOL gives the basis of a powerful mechanism to represent knowledge of the real world in logic. As will be seen, however, this is much easier in 'formal domains'.

2.3.1 Formal Domains

To map a domain onto FOL, it must be possible to regard the domain as consisting of objects plus properties of, or relations between, the objects which in any particular case can be designated as TRUE or FALSE. In 'formalized' domains - for example mathematics, the law, the information represented in a computer database - this is likely to be the case and a mapping into FOL or some extension of it is normally a natural one.

A relational database can be regarded as already in FOL form: each relation type corresponds to a predicate and each relation to a proposition expressed with this predicate. Thus one may have an office-building database storing information about room numbers, occupants and telephones in each room. Suppose there are two relations: OCCUPANT (giving room numbers and occupants) and TELEPHONE (giving telephone numbers and occupants):

OCCUPANT		TELEPHONE	
person	room	number	room
D.Owen	1	345	1
D.Steel	1	123	1
M.Thatcher	2	639	2
N.Kinnock	3	639	3

Messrs. Owen and Steel share a room but it has two telephones in it, while Thatcher and Kinnock each have their own room but have a party line. Each relation can be viewed as a FOL predicate with an obvious interpretation in the real (or perhaps pretend) world represented by the database. Thus the FOL sentences would be:

occupant(D.Owen,1)
telephone(639,2)

etc.

The interest in logic database systems is to add *rules*, which can be expressed as logical implications, to such systems. The traditional use of relational databases often assumes implicit rules, e.g.:

(a) Objects have unique identifiers: room 1 and room 2 cannot stand for the same thing.

(b) If a relation does not exist, one can assume its negation: there is no telephone 639 in room 1 (this is known as the Closed World Assumption).

(In fact neither of these implicit rules can quite be expressed in FOL.)

Logic Databases can introduce *explicit* rules written in FOL, e.g.:

(c) $\neg \exists x \, occupant(x,4)$
Room 4 is empty

(d) $\forall x,r \, occupant(x,r) \wedge even(r) \rightarrow nonsmoker(r)$
Even numbered rooms contain non-smokers

This allows the construction of 'deductive databases' - one can infer much more than those facts which are directly stored in the initial relations. However, there are a number of theoretical problems, for example databases get updated. If a relation is added giving a definition of an occupant in room 4, the database is inconsistent with the rule (c) given above. Once implications are allowed, there are problems in avoiding inconsistency with the implicit rules given above. Particularly (b) becomes tricky even to define because a relation can be inferred from the rules rather than given explicitly in the database. Such problems are an active research area (Gallaire and Minker, 1978; Flannagan, 1986).

The issues are of much more than theoretical interest; if full FOL deduction is allowed, anything at all can be deduced from inconsistent data. However the problems are about consistency and proof in logic rather than about Knowledge Representation itself. It should be noted that the mere existence of a relational database assumes that the knowledge is highly structured already.

2.3.2 Non-formal Domains

In mapping formal systems like the database onto logic, the database system itself is a model of a logical theory and there is likely to be a straightforward mapping between the facts in the database and the real world. However in the case of real-world knowledge of an unformalized type, the mapping is not so obvious.

Take the example as a piece of 'knowledge':

John gives a book to Mary

This is a proposition, but simply representing it by a predicate p would be totally unhelpful. One would have as many predicates as ideas that could be expressed and no way of analysing their content. The constituent concepts that appear to be basic here are 'John', 'Mary', 'book' and 'give'. A natural approach may be to take 'John', 'Mary' and 'book' as objects and 'gives' as a relation between them. The import of the above sentence is presumably that John and Mary are specific individuals but that the book is some unspecified book.

> $\exists$ x book(x) $\wedge$ gives(John, x, Mary)
> i.e. there is some x which is a book and John gives x to Mary

One may say in addition that John and Mary are human beings:

> human(John)
> human(Mary)

However this representation will make it impossible to treat this act of giving as an object about which one may want to specify information - the time it took place (or does one want a special predicate for 'gave'?), the place etc. A more basic formulation can specify a 'giving event' and then associate other predicates with this, e.g.:

> giving (e1)   e1 is a giving 'event'
> agent(e1,John)   John was the giver
> recip(e1,Mary)   Mary was the recipient
> $\exists$ b, book(b) $\wedge$ object(e1,b)   A book is the object of giving

The act of 'giving' is then an individual in the domain just as are John, Mary, etc. Temporal information could be added:

> time(e1,T)   the giving was at time T

This would seem to be a reasonable FOL formulation of the sentence. However one will presumably want to express also more general ideas about 'giving' which would allow reasoning about the situation. For example:

> $\forall$ e1,y,t,x giving(e1) $\wedge$ recip(e1,y) $\wedge$ time(e1,t) $\wedge$ object(e1,x) $\rightarrow$
> ($\forall$ t1, t1 > t $\rightarrow$ owns(y,x,t1))

This is saying that if y was the recipient of x at time t then he becomes the owner for all time after this. (Notice that > signs have slid in here - let us assume they can be defined as a predicate.)

Of course this rule is not always true in the real world; in practice it is difficult if not impossible to write universal rules about the real world unless they be true by definition ('all dogs are mammals', for example). However, such a rule as above might be taken as true in some idealization of the world which a certain application can assume. In representing the real world as a logical model one has two problems - first idealizing the world and then selecting the best FOL formulation.

2.3.3 Semantic Networks

Various network and structured object representations described elsewhere in this book have been developed specifically for dealing with knowledge about the real world and it is very instructive to investigate the extent to which they are equivalent to logic.

A semantic network can be mapped into FOL by taking its nodes as corresponding to terms and its arcs to relations. Since all arcs link two nodes, the predicates will be binary. As pointed out in Deliyanni and Kowalski (1979), the semantic network representation draws attention to the advantages of using only unary and binary predicates in a logic formulation (as above). Some care must be taken because (typically) the nodes of a semantic network may be individuals or types. Figure 1 adapts an example from Deliyanni and Kowalski (1979), representing the example given in the previous section. Here the links from Mary and John to Human are 'instance-of' relations and are probably best represented by a predicate 'human' and statements of the form:

> human(Mary)
> human(John)

The 'isa' relation is often used in semantic networks to denote the subset (subtype) relation, as well as the instance-of relation given above.

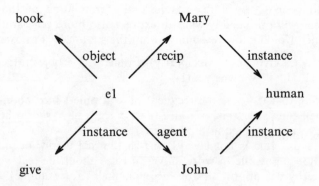

Figure 1

$$human \xrightarrow{\text{ isa }} animal$$

This means 'all humans are animals'; a translation into logic would read:

$\forall$ x human(x) → animal(x)

One can treat these links like any others, by having predicates 'instanceof' and 'isa', but this would be introducing predicates for concepts that are already built in to FOL and an additional set of axioms about these predicates would have to be introduced.

In the 'conceptual graph' representation of Sowa (1984), there are two types of node: concepts and relations (arcs are unlabelled apart from direction). Relations take the place of arcs in the normal semantic network. The previous sentence is represented by the diagram in Figure 2. A common confusion between 'isa' and 'instance-of' is removed in Sowa's system by maintaining a type hierarchy external to the network. Thus the fact that:

$$human \xrightarrow{\text{ isa }} animal$$

is not represented in the graph itself - indeed Sowa claims that being a different 'order' of link from those given, it should not be.

The 'instanceof' relation is similarly specially treated: the 'John' attached to the 'human' box is a referent which says that the individual John is of type 'human'. Sowa gives a formal mapping from conceptual graphs into FOL; this one would be:

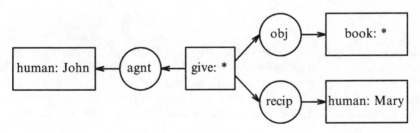

Figure 2

$\exists$ e1,b1   human(John) $\wedge$ agnt(John,e1)
$\wedge$ recipient(Mary,e1) $\wedge$ gives(e1)
$\wedge$ obj(b1,e1)
$\wedge$ human(Mary) $\wedge$ book(b1)

Notice the concepts of Give and Book were not given individual referents and so existential quantification appears in the FOL formulation. Fuller details are given in Chapter 7.

These 'isa' and 'instance-of' relations map into particular cases of quantification in FOL. But there is no generally accepted notation for quantifications, disjunctions ($\vee$s) and implications in semantic networks although there have been a number of proposals (see Deliyanni and Kowalski, 1979; Sowa, 1984).

2.3.4 Frames

Mapping properties of frames (see Chapter 4) into FOL demands some assumptions about what they mean. Hayes (1979) makes assumptions but then proceeds to show that an FOL mapping is, on the whole, straightforward. A frame type represents some generic concept; an instance of the frame type, with appropriate values in the slots, represents an instance of this concept. Suppose C is a frame type and x is an instance, then C(x) can be taken as the predicate corresponding to 'the object x is a concept of type C'. Thus if C is the 'house' frame, and '10 Downing Street' an instance, then in FOL we would assert:

C('10 Downing Street')

interpreted by the fact that '10 Downing Street' is a type of house. The properties of 'slots' correspond to two sorts of logical implication. The first says that frame instances have slots with appropriate values:

$\forall$ x C(x) $\rightarrow$ $\exists$ y1   RC1(x,y1)
$\forall$ x C(x) $\rightarrow$ $\exists$ y2   RC2(x,y2)
. . .

The yn represent slot values. The RCn predicate represents the relation between a frame and its nth slot; thus RC1(x,y1) would mean that the value of the first slot of the frame x is y1, and furthermore it is appropriate for that slot. If C is the house concept with the first slot giving the number of rooms, then a model of RC1(x,y1) would check that the y1 was a number in the right range.

The second mapping is slightly more subtle: some applications of frames assume that if some object has all its slots filled with appropriate values for a certain type of frame, then indeed it is taken as an object of that type.

$$\forall\ x,y1,...,yn\quad RC1(x,y1) \wedge ... \wedge RCn(x,yn) \rightarrow C(x)$$

In like manner the typing and inheritance characteristics of frames can be largely mapped onto FOL. Suppose we wish to say that the frame type 'bungalow' is a 'house' with its 'number of floors' slot constrained to contain the number one:

$$\forall\ x\ bungalow(x) \rightarrow RB1(x,1)$$
$$\forall\ x\ bungalow(x) \rightarrow house(x)$$

(It is assumed that the first slot gives the number of floors.) The second implication would show, together with the axioms given formerly, that the 'bungalow' is constrained by properties of slots in the 'house' frame.

One common characteristic of frames - inheritance of default values where no current values are given in the slot of a subtype - raises the same issues in mapping onto FOL as those addressed by 'non-monotonic logic'. We return to this in section 2.6.1. A general discussion of Hayes' 'Logic of Frames' is given in section 4.4.

2.3.5 An Advantage of Network Systems

If semantic networks and structured object representations, designed *a priori* to represent *ad hoc* knowledge, can map onto FOL or some extension of it, what advantages do these somewhat ill-defined formalisms have over the precise and well analysed language of logic?

The crucial advantage is practical rather than theoretical and is best shown by examples.

In a semantic net, all the predicates about Mary will have a link to the node Mary. A theorem-prover working on such a network and operating on this node may naturally follow links from it: compare this with looking at the set of predicates which contain Mary somewhere in them - an unlikely operation for an FOL theorem-prover.

Similarly the 'isa' link (or type hierarchy in the Sowa formulation) is explicit. In logic, to find out that Mary inherits the characteristics of a human, a theorem-prover has to stumble across statements of the form:

$$human(Mary)$$
$$\forall\ x\quad human(x) \rightarrow some\text{-}property(x)$$

One further example (taken from Reiter, 1985) is where a network representation is used to show mutual exclusiveness (see Figure 3). In some systems the diagram shown would be an is-a hierarchy which was meant to imply

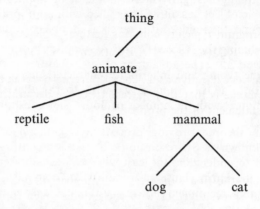

Figure 3

that reptile/mammal/fish are mutually exclusive classes. Although it is easily expansible into logic, the formulation is messy and the reasoning to discover that, say, a dog is not a reptile, is cumbersome.

This is all summed up by saying that a network representation embodies as *primitives* certain important relations or reasoning steps which in a *theoretically equivalent* logic representation may be deeply buried. The network may thus be clearer to understand and easier to reason with.

2.3.6 Logic Programming

Any computer program is a representation of knowledge and some mention must therefore be made of that programming paradigm known as 'logic programming'. In a logic program - the current manifestation being the now widely used Prolog language - the statements of the program can be regarded as assertions of a logical theory. The ability to make the equivalent of quantified logical statements, e.g. *all* of a set of objects have a certain property, gives a programming language of remarkable power. The aim of the program is to exhibit relevant inferences. Running the program is equivalent to proving a theorem in a sequential manner which makes predicates the analogue of procedures in a traditional programming language. The differences between running a program in Prolog and expressing a problem and solving it in FOL are:

(i)   A Prolog program cannot express the whole of FOL; the particular restriction (to 'Horn clauses') is equivalent to disallowing implications which have disjunctions on the right hand side:

$$A \rightarrow B \vee C$$

(ii)   A Prolog program typically contains features which are not equivalent to FOL (including the 'Closed World Assumption') or in some cases are not 'logical' at all. The advantage of such features is that they allow Prolog to be very effective as a general purpose programming language. The disadvantage is that they detract from the declarative character of the logical statement of the problem.

(iii) The built-in theorem-proving procedure is constrained to a specific technique (known as SL resolution). It is a straightforward one for a programmer to understand (at least when expressed in terms of implications given the Horn clause restriction) but, combined with the non-logical features mentioned above, can make answers dependent on statement ordering.

Current research into logic programming is attempting to design languages nearer to logic which will thus increase the declarative nature. At present however a typical logic program will combines features of pure logic with *ad hoc* representation or reasoning steps typical of any computer program.

2.4 Benefits of Logic

Before we discuss the deficiencies of logic in knowledge representation, it is as well to summarize its very cogent benefits.

2.4.1 Precision and Analysis

The great feature of FOL is its precisely defined and well understood notation, with a model theory (semantics) which gives precision to the mapping between the sentences of logic and some domain.

Thus the constructs:

$$P \xrightarrow{\text{isa}} Q \quad \text{(semantic net)}$$

$$p \quad \text{is a} \quad Q \quad \text{(English)}$$

are made unambiguous when given a logical formulation:

$$\forall x\ P(x) \rightarrow Q(x)$$
$$Q(p)$$

If a representation can be expressed in FOL (or any of its derivatives) it is clarified not only to the reader but to the author. Subtle questions about the interpretation of a 'frame' can be seen to be quite unsubtle when expressed in logic.

It is difficult to think of any other ways than logic to explain precisely what a particular network or structured object formalism is supposed to denote. Sowa (1984) is careful to give all his constructs an expression in FOL other than when they go beyond what FOL can express.

2.4.2 Expressiveness

FOL is *expressive* in the sense that its notions of quantification and negation are not easy to represent unambiguously in network and structured data form. The difficulties of deciding what a frame formulation is meant to suggest will be returned to several times in this book - some of these problems amount to the differences between existential and universal quantification.

Expressiveness is discussed in Moore (1985a) where he observes that problems of reasoning and representation involving incomplete knowledge are typically solved only by systems of formal logic. Figure 4 shows his well-known example. Is there a green block next to a non-green block? The answer is clearly yes - but the statement of the problem and the reasoning required for the solution are difficult to give in many knowledge representation systems and require precisely the constructs of FOL.

2.4.3 Proof Theory

The triumph of FOL is its proof theory - in particular the completeness theorem that everything that is true in all models of a theory can be proved. There is a continuing large amount of work in developing wholly automated or computer-assisted proof mechanisms in FOL and its derivatives (some of which do not have the completeness property).

| GREEN | ? | BLUE |

Figure 4

This feature is of course one of reasoning rather than representation. and one of the criticisms of logic below will be the extent to which deductive proof is relevant to common-sense reasoning in a non-formal domain.

2.5 Limitations of Logic in Knowledge Representation

Any discussion of the limitations of Logic in knowledge representation must take into account what function logic is expected to play. It can be used to *represent* and *analyse* knowledge; it can also be used for (indeed was invented for) *deductive reasoning* over this knowledge. It will be seen that the limitations in representation have or are being successfully tackled by the development of more advanced logics than FOL. But the deficiences of logic in 'common-sense' reasoning (see sections 2.5.1, 2.5.3 below) appear to be more fundamental and have led some critics to deny a role for logic in representation. Israel (1983) analyses such criticisms; he concludes that although logical proof is but one tool to be used in reasoning, this is not at all a deficiency of logic in a representational role but an indication that one must clearly distinguish between logic and reasoning. Notwithstanding, we present here all the traditional arguments against logic.

2.5.1 Limitations of Deductive Reasoning

The major objection to Logic in knowledge representation applies only to its role in reasoning - this is the fact that most reasoning about the real world is not deductive. This is eloquently argued in McDermott (1987); that the argument is not new is shown in the following passage from Bertrand Russell (1945):

> The Greeks in general attached more importance to deduction as a source of knowledge than modern philosophers do. In this respect, Aristotle was less at fault than Plato; he repeatedly admitted the impor- tance of induction, and he devoted considerable attention to the ques- tion: how do we know the first premises from which deduction must start? Nevertheless, he, like other Greeks, gave undue prominence to deduction in his theory of knowledge. We shall agree that Mr Smith (say) is mortal and we may, loosely, say that we know this because we know that all men are mortal. But what we really know is not 'all men are mortal'; we know something rather like 'all men born more than one hundred and fifty years ago' are mortal, and so are almost all men born more than one hundred years ago. This is our reason for thinking Mr Smith will die. But this argument is an induction, not a deduction. It has less cogency than a deduction, and yields only a probability, not a certainty; but on the other hand it gives *new* knowledge, which deduction does not. All the important inferences outside logic and pure

mathematics are inductive; the only exceptions are law and theology, each of which derives its first principles from an unquestionable text, viz. the statute books or the scriptures.

It should be noted that even in mathematics, real proofs are not really checked, let alone designed, using FOL. Establishing a proof is typically by vague intuition or by mental leaps; checking it is by a 'consensus of the qualified' (see Davis and Hersh, 1981). The mechanization of proofs on high speed parallel computers may well extend the domains in which formal proof is practicable - but real problems take a lot of logic. It requires 362 pages to show that $1 + 1 = 2$ in Principia Mathematica.

2.5.2 Implications and Modal Logic

FOL is an *extensional theory*; it is described in terms of models which are sets (the extension of a predicate is the set of entities which make it true). Many of the ideas one may wish to express in knowledge representation involve *intension*: the qualities implied by a concept, rather than the set of objects it describes. An example from Sowa (1984):

All unicorns are cows
$\forall$ x unicorn(x) $\rightarrow$ cow(x)

Any model of the real world makes this implication TRUE, as there are no unicorns, whereas even in the real world we know that unicorns are mammals with one horn and certainly not cows. It was mentioned in section 2.2.1 that the FOL definition of implication (known as material implication or the 'Philonian' conditional) does not represent the normal 'causal' interpretation. This (again from Sowa, 1984) would be TRUE in FOL:

If elephants have wings then $2 + 2 = 5$

There are logics which are designed to overcome some of these representational deficiencies; the most well known are a series of 'modal' logics originally presented by Lewis (1932). They were initially based on a new form of implication ('strict implication') where

$p \Rightarrow q$

was true only if q 'could be deduced' from p. This concept is unrelated to the truth or falsity of p; it is saying that if p *were* true, then q would follow. This gives rise to 'modalities' of 'possibility' and 'necessity' that can be attached to predicates (see section 2.6.2).

2.5.3 Non-monotonicity and Defaults

'Monotonicity' is a feature of FOL which has come to be seen as a deficiency of FOL both in representation and reasoning, and which has been responsible for perhaps the greatest amount of work in logic in AI. If we have a domain defined by a set of logical axioms (a theory), then any additional axiom must be consistent with the original theory. Otherwise the whole system breaks down - anything can be proved. Having said:

$$\forall \, x \; bird(x) \; \rightarrow \; flies(x)$$
$$bird(ostrich)$$

we cannot then add:

$$\neg \; flies(ostrich)$$

A new axiom cannot invalidate any of the previous conclusions. This property does not map onto the real world. The fact that 'Janet has no children' may be true now, false next week. An axiom that 'all birds fly' may be established in good faith before an exception is found. If someone parks his car outside, he will later reason on the assumption that it is still there - until he finds it has been towed away.

One can of course accept that a logical theory applies to a situation as exists (or is believed) at a certain point, and when anything changes all the necessary axioms change and one starts again. There are 'truth maintenance' systems which attempt to keep track of valid inferences in a changing situation. However, default assumptions do seem to be a necessary and basic part of common-sense reasoning and, this being so, any representation should itself include the fact that they are being made.

Changes in time can be incorporated by having an additional 'time' parameter in every predicate, although this in fact gives rise to need for many more default assumptions of exactly the above type (see section 2.6.1). Many 'temporal' logics are being designed to try and cope with the problem of time (see Chapter 9).

Section 2.6.1 discusses 'non-monotonic' logics which have been developed in an attempt to handle the representation of, and reasoning with, defaults.

2.5.4 Truth and Falsehood

Classical logics are based on the concept of a proposition which is either TRUE or FALSE. Propositions in the real world are not like that. There are degrees of uncertainty, degrees of judgement to be made, and these will be reflected in the inferences that can be drawn. From the statement that 'a man had large feet', one can make inferences about his shoe size, but they will be of the form 'he is almost certainly at least size 10, probably 11'. A representation which is constrained to truth or falsehood is not flexible enough to deal with much of the vagueness of the real world.

There are many schemes for representing and reasoning with uncertainty but many of them could probably not be described as 'logics' under our informal definition in section 2.2.1. Multi-valued logics have been developed within FOL - changing the semantics to allow values other than TRUE and FALSE in an interpretation. The most well known is a more radical departure known as 'fuzzy' logic where a predicate can take any real value between zero and one. Fuzzy logic was developed by Zadeh (e.g. 1974) and has influenced many expert system developments.

Some 'uncertain' logics are based on probability, some on numerical 'weights' whose interpretation in the real world may be as vague as the concepts they are expressing. Others represent uncertainty in some qualitative way. The success of these systems is only possible to assess in real life applications.

2.5.5 Reference to Predicates and Propositions

In FOL there is no way of referring to propositions or predicate names in other propositions.

One requirement is to quantify over predicate names. An example is a definition of 'equality'. FOL is often defined with equality as a special additional 'built-in' predicate. If it is not, one can define some of the properties, for example the reflexive property of equality:

$$\forall \ x,y \ \ equals(x,y) \rightarrow equals(y,x)$$

But what about substitution:

$$\forall \ x,y \ \ p(x) \wedge equals(x,y) \rightarrow p(y)$$

We wish to say that if $p(x)$ is true and $y = x$, then $p(y)$ is true *no matter what* the predicate p is. We cannot put a $\forall$ p on the front in FOL. This would be a statement of *second-order* logic. The statement: 'there is a set of people in this department whose members do not talk to anyone else' refers to the existence of a *set* with certain properties and is thus a second order statement. Second and higher order logics are well defined but the proof theories do not have the nice properties of completeness etc.

Perhaps a more common requirement in knowledge representation is the need to represent statements about *propositions*. One class arises from the modal logic mentioned previously:

It is necessary that ... some proposition.
It is possible that ... some proposition.

There are many circumstances in which propositions need to be referenced and many other logics which have been and are being developed to try and cope with them. Examples are:

X knows that ...	(epistemic logic)
It was true that ...	(temporal logic)
It was always true that ...	
It is permissible that ..	(deontic logic)

It might be thought superficially that such expressions can easily be incorporated in FOL by expressing the modalities by a predicate. Thus one may represent 'John knows the proposition P' by:

knows(John,P)

But we wish simultaneously to analyse P as a proposition; one may want to say:

knows(John,P) → P
∀ x knows(John,Q(x))

and so on. Making propositions into objects is not defined in FOL and its interpretation would become paradoxical. Modal logics introduce additional notation for 'modalities' like 'necessary that', 'knows that' etc., together with new rules of inference and semantics - a short discussion is given in section 2.6.2.

2.6 Non-standard Logics

Section 2.5 mentioned some of the many non-standard logics on which work is being pursued vigorously and which have found application in AI as well as other areas of computer science. Turner (1984) and several chapters of Frost (1986) survey advanced logics in this field. We discuss here two flavours of non-standard logic which have had the greatest influence in knowledge representation - non-monotonic and modal logics. Section 9.3.4 gives some discussion of temporal logic.

2.6.1 Non-monotonic Logic

As mentioned in section 2.5.3, non-monotonic logics have developed in an attempt to deal with representation and reasoning using default assumptions - which appear to be a ubiquitous characteristic of 'common-sense reasoning'. There are various formulations - notable are McDermott and Doyle (1980), McCarthy (1980) and Reiter (1985). Although the theoretical bases are very different, the difficulties are very similar and can be explained easily, if in an entirely non-formal way.

We wish to incorporate the idea of:

P normally-implies Q

i.e. if P is true we want to assume Q unless for some reason we *know* Q is not true.

Thus:

∀ x (bird(x) normally-implies flies(x))

If bird(ostrich) we wish to assume flies(ostrich) unless we can *deduce* that an ostrich cannot fly, for example there may be a statement:

¬ flies(ostrich)

Such a concept is not so easy to formalize in FOL. One obvious reason is that finding out that ¬ flies(ostrich) is not the case may not be decidable. A much worse problem is that having introduced such an abnormal implication we have to decide whether the inferences we make using it are allowed to be used in determining whether further abnormal implications can be made. An example with a simple model makes this clear:

1. P(gingko)   a gingko is a conifer
2. R(gingko)   a gingko is broad-leaved
3. ∀ x P(x) normally-implies Q(x)   conifers are evergreen
4. ∀ x R(x) normally-implies ¬ Q(x)   broad-leaves are deciduous

P(gingko) and R(gingko) are given and not much that is useful can be deduced with FOL reasoning. But since we cannot prove ¬ Q(gingko), we can assume (by 3) that Q(gingko). This presumably blocks the application of 4. But if we start again, we might choose to make 4 the abnormal inference we start with, thus proving ¬ Q(gingko). Whether we prove Q(gingko) or R(gingko) depends on whether our reasoning starts with 3 or 4. This is totally against the philosophy of logic where the set of theorems is not dependent on the proof procedure. Non-monotonic logics get around this problem by defining a theorem as that which is common to all the theories - i.e. is always proved. In the above example nothing new could be proved, but if 4 was not present, Q(gingko) would be provable.

Hanks and McDermott (1986) claim that in practice such logic is likely to be very limited. Their example is very instructive as it not only demonstrates this problem, but shows how non-monotonic argument naturally arises when arguing about time due to the 'frame' problem (nothing to do with frames). The example is thus worth presenting here, although in a much simplified notation.

Their problem concerns John and a gun which can be loaded or shot, and a succession of states. States change when something happens. Predicates are:

alive(s)	John is alive in state s
loaded(s)	The gun is loaded in state s

and functions:

result(load,s)	the state which results if the gun is loaded in state s
result(shoot,s)	the state which results if the gun is shot in state s
result(wait,s)	the state which result if we wait for a minute in state s

The axioms are:

alive(s0)   John is alive at s0   (1)

∀ s loaded(result(load,s))   (2)
If someone loads the gun when in any state s
it becomes loaded in state result(load,s).

∀ s loaded(s) → ¬ alive(result(shoot,s))   (3)
If someone shoots a gun when it
is loaded, John is not alive in the
resulting state

One cannot deduce very much without 'frame' axioms. We wish to say that, for example if the gun is loaded at state s, it is loaded at whatever the next state is, unless we can prove otherwise. Otherwise, for every possible change of state in the world (for example someone walking into the room), we will have to define that it does not change the effect on the loading of the gun. This is the same as the 'car-park' assumption mentioned previously - the car is there unless there is some statement that it has been moved. The exact formulation of the non-monotonic axioms depends on which of the logics is adopted; in our informal notation we will say:

∀ s,a loaded(s) normally-implies loaded(result(a,s))   (4)
∀ s,a alive(s) normally-implies alive(result(a,s))   (5)

Guns stay loaded and people stay alive unless we can prove otherwise.

Suppose: result(load,s0) is denoted by s1
result(wait,s1) is denoted by s2
result(shoot,s2) is denoted by s3.

We can deduce loaded(s1) from (2). We cannot prove directly loaded(s2) but by the frame axiom (4) we can assume it since we cannot prove ¬loaded(s2). Now from (3) with s = s2, we see John is *not* alive at s3. This is all consistent and expected.

But even for such a simple problem, there is another solution, obtained by doing the proof in a non-intuitive direction. Since we cannot prove directly ¬ alive(s1), we can assume (by 5) alive(s2). A further application shows alive(s3). Then (3) shows that the gun was not in the state 'loaded' at s2. This may seem strange as it was loaded at s1, but everything is consistent. The only 'abnormal' inferences common to both scenarios are alive(s1) and alive(s2). This small example appears to show that non-monotonic logics as normally defined are not likely to be very useful.

2.6.2 Modal Logics and Possible Worlds

Many modern logics being studied in Knowledge Representation are derived from 'modal logic' developed by Lewis (1932). Hughes and Cresswell (1968) is a standard contemporary work. Modal logic was originally based on a concept of 'strict implication' (see section 2.5.2). Just as a language and theory of FOL can exist independently of its semantics, modal logic did not have a generally accepted model theory until Kripke formulated the 'possible world' semantics. This gave not only a precise model of various formulations of modal logic; it seems to be one which is relevant to the world that we wish to represent in an 'intelligent agent'. A logic of Knowledge and Belief, originally due to Hintakka, can be defined as an extension to the same semantics and this is formulated by Moore (1985b) - one of the most prominent attempts to apply modal logic in AI.

The basic notions introduced in Lewis' Modal Logic were 'necessity', 'impossibility', 'contingency', and 'possibility'. Any of these can be expressed in terms of the others so in fact only one need be defined as primitive - generally this is either 'possibility' or 'necessity'. Intuitively, 'necessity' is interpreted as 'could not fail to be true'. This obviously has no place in FOL where under an interpretation a proposition is either true or false; there is no other quality about it. In modal logic an interpretation embodies a parallel set of scenarios (see below) which could (for example) correspond to different hypotheses about the world.

The apparatus of modality is added to existing FOL. Thus a proposition p can still be asserted (and correspond to TRUE under interpretation) but one can also assert:

Lp

saying 'it is necessary that P'; and

Mp

saying 'it is possible that P'. The relationship between them is that p is possible if and only if it is not necessary that ¬ p:

Mp is equivalent to ¬ L (¬ p)

The strict implication (which was originally the primitive from which modal logic was defined) is normally defined as:

p⇒q is equivalent to ¬ M(p and ¬ q)

i.e it is not possible that p should be true without q being true.

Additional rules of inference or axiom schema must be added to the normal FOL ones in order that deductive reasoning using these new modalities can take place. All modal logics would contain the following:

LP → P

(i.e. if P - which can be any well-formed formula - is necessary, it is true) and:

L(P→Q) → (LP→LQ)

Also any logical axioms (these are valid sentences in FOL) are necessary:

L(p→p) would be an example

A variety of modal logics can be defined by adding other rules of inference, of greater or lesser intuitive meaning, to the basic system (which is known as system T). For example:

Lp → LLp if p is necessary, then it is necessarily necessary

Quantification gives more room for varieties of axiomatic system, for example:

∀ x Lp(x) → L(∀ x p(x))

The semantics of modal logic (without which the whole theory may seem rather obscure) can be regarded as an extension of that for FOL. Rather than having a single domain, an interpretation of a modal logic theory specifies a *set* of domains (possible worlds), of which one is distinguished - the *actual* world. This (say W0) acts as the model of the theory in the FOL sense, i.e. the non-modal propositions of the theory are interpreted in this world. An *accessibility* relation is defined over the possible worlds:

r(W1,W2)

defines W2 to be *accessible* from W1. Intuitively this means that an agent in

W1 can imagine a world as described in W2. The relation r is normally reflexive, and there may be other constraints on it (transitive, symmetric etc.) - it is the type of these constraints that precisely determines which of the various classes of modal logic is defined.

In each possible world various assignments may be made to the values of propositions just as with FOL interpretations (a complication is that the domains in possible worlds may be different also). An interpretation is a model of Lp just if p is TRUE in all worlds accessible from W0 (intuitively in all scenarios that someone in W0 can imagine). It is a model of Mp if p is TRUE in at least one accessible world.

By extension, the interpretation is a model of LLp if Lp is TRUE in all worlds accessible from W0, i.e. p is TRUE in all worlds accessible from these.

Moore (1985b), following Hintakka, developed a modal theory of knowledge.

Kap

means agent a knows proposition p. If a is kept fixed this becomes equivalent to the 'necessity' modality. (This means that another and perhaps better intuitive interpretation of Lp in ordinary modal logic could be 'I know that'; and the axiomatic structure may be much easier to follow.) The semantics is as above with the additional feature that an accessibility relation must be defined for each agent. A model of an agent's knowing a proposition must make that proposition TRUE in all the worlds accessible from W0 *for that agent*. Moore expresses the semantics itself in FOL; thus a formal translation can be made from the modal logic of knowledge into FOL, proofs undertaken and a translation made back.

2.7 Summary Comments

Logic is now widely studied not just by philosophers and mathematicians but by computer scientists and AI workers; the number of new logics being proposed is too great even to reference in this short chapter. The debate mentioned at the beginning of this chapter is but a continuation of argument about logic in the representation of knowledge which has continued for over two thousand years.

It might be thought that the development of mathematically sound semantics not just for FOL but (for example) for quantified modal logics, should have lessened the arguments, as much of the field becomes a part of uncontroversial mathematics rather than controversial philosophy. However this would be a mistake; the arguments are not about the soundness of models but about the extent to which they represent the world that we wish to reason about.

This remains to some extent a philosophical question and it is not clear whether the argument will ever be settled. But whatever the eventual role of logic, a firm grounding in it would be advisable for any student of knowledge representation, if only to understand and analyse the numerous other recondite representation schemes which will no doubt emerge.

3 Semantic Networks

Damian Mac Randal

3.1 Introduction

The study of language is usually divided into four fields: phonology, syntax, semantics and pragmatics. Phonology investigates the mapping of words onto sound. Syntax addresses the ordering of words and speech parts, often involving a grammar which specifies the criteria for acceptable sentences. Semantics is the study of the meaning of the individual concepts used in the language. Pragmatics maps these meanings and the other aspects of language onto the speaker's intentions behind an utterance (e.g. when crying out "the house is on fire" to someone standing in it, the intention is for them to leave, although this is not stated in the exclamation). The study of semantics is therefore an attempt to describe word meanings (and the usage of words where their meaning is ambiguous) and the conditions under which such meanings can interact to be compatible with the other aspects of a language. It is such a description which semantic networks were designed to provide.

A network is a net or graph of nodes joined by links. The nodes in a semantic network usually represent concepts or meanings (e.g. BOOK, GREEN) and the links usually represent relations (e.g., a book IS COLOURED green). Networks of this type not only capture definitions of concepts but also inherently provide links to other concepts. A large number of semantic networks have been developed as variations on this simple pattern. Some of these networks have been proposed as models of human memory and meaning representation, while others are used as components of language understanding and reasoning systems. The psychological validity of semantic networks will be discussed in Chapter 6. The development of semantic networks for computational purposes will be described here.

The origins of semantic networks lie in Aristotle's associationism (behaviour is controlled totally by associations learned between concepts) and reductionism (concepts are built of more elementary concepts; e.g. "bachelor" is built from "unmarried" and "man"). Much later associationism was extended and refined by philosophers and psychologists. Around 1869 James Mills showed that the use of a single concept term to refer to any occurrences of a concept leads to an ambiguity if that concept arose more than once (e.g. a representation of BOOK would not distinguish between "John's book" and "Mary's book"; one representation is required for each book). However, he did not specify the currently dominant solution to this problem of distinguishing between "types" (e.g. the concept BOOK) and tokens (individual occurrences of the concept; there are four tokens for "book" in the previous sentence, although "book" is just one type). Thomas Brown (c. 1820) contributed the notion of labelling links with semantic information (e.g. the book BELONGS TO John) instead of just giving them associative force (e.g. the book IS ASSOCIATED WITH John; the bird IS ASSOCIATED WITH green). Otto Selz in 1926 further added to the complexity of semantic networks by suggesting that paths between nodes across the network could be used for reasoning. All of these ideas were taken up by Quillian (1966) who proposed the first major computer system using semantic networks.

Since Quillian (1966) a large number of semantic networks have been proposed which share few features in common. A recent review of networks (Johnson-Laird, Herrmann and Chaffin, 1984) could only discern four assumptions which are common to the networks reviewed. These were:

(1) Network theories are designed to elucidate relations between concepts (intensional relations), in particular between the meanings of words. They embody no general principles concerning the relation between the concepts and the real world objects (extensional relations).

(2) A corollary of this: semantic networks are constructed on the assumption that intensional relations can be considered independently from extensional ones.

(3) Network theories are based on a formalism containing three components: a parser, a semantic representation consisting of a network of links between nodes, and a set of interpretative processes that operate on the network.

(4)   There is a general commitment to parsimony.

Since there are so few assumptions which a set of semantic networks share, it is necessary to describe the details of several systems in order to investigate the differences and follow the direction of developments in semantic networks.

3.2 Outline

In section 3.3, two of the earliest and most influential systems, Quillian's and Winston's, are described in some detail. As the inaugural systems in the field, they tackled most of the basic components of semantic networks and supplied the framework upon which a lot of later systems were built. In section 3.4, the work on *case frames* leading up to Schank's conceptual dependency is described. Section 3.5 describes the work carried out in the mid to late 70's on the epistemological and logical basis for semantic network representations of knowledge. This work placed the whole field of semantic networks on a much sounder theoretical base and led to the development of the KL-ONE system. This is, perhaps, the most influential semantic network system that has been produced and has been the foundation upon which a lot of current research in Knowledge Representation is based.

Although in section 3.6 the quintessential features of some later systems are described, by this time, the mid eighties, single knowledge representations were not capable of handling the variety of knowledge structures that had to be manipulated. As a result, hybrid systems, using multiple representations, started to appear, and the work on semantic networks became more enmeshed with that on other representations. One such hybrid system is described in more detail in Chapter 10.

3.3 Early Developments

Ross Quillian is generally acknowledged to have been the first to apply the semantic network ideas in the AI field or, more specifically, in the field of natural language translation/understanding. In his PhD thesis in 1966, the central theme was "What sort of representational format can permit the *meanings* of words to be stored, so that humanlike use of these meanings is possible?". Towards this end, he proposed an associational model of human memory which he called *Semantic Memory* (Quillian, 1968). His idea was to capture the "objective" meanings of words in an encoding scheme of sufficient power to reflect the structure and capabilities of human memory, but simple and uniform enough to be implemented in a computer. These two goals conflict; implementation considerations require a small number of simple node and link types, while the representation of human knowledge, even "objective" knowledge, requires a complexity of representation approaching that of English itself. Figure 1 shows a fragment of Quillian's semantic memory, corresponding to two meanings of the word PLANT, which will be used to illustrate his model. Each meaning is defined in a "unit" bounded by a dotted line.

The other main, independent, example of the use of semantic networks was Winston's work on *Structured Descriptions* (Winston, 1975). He was working in the field of machine learning and was concerned with the learning-from-example of concepts behind common structures which he took from the blocks world, for example, pedestals, arches, tents, etc. built from rectangular blocks and wedges. The classical example used is his structured description of an arch, shown in Figure 2.

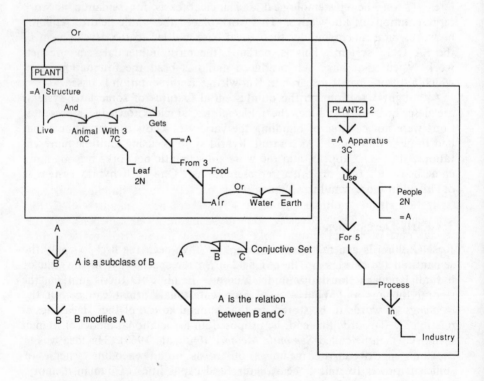

Figure 1 Quillian - Fragment of semantic memory for the word "PLANT"

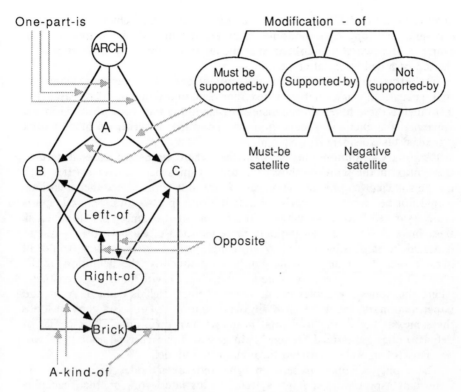

Figure 2 Winston - Structural description of an ARCH

The main part of Winston's work was on scene understanding and generalization from multiple instances. However, he recognized that the representation of knowledge, or scene description, as he called it, was the crucial part of the program. Like Quillian, Winston tried to develop a knowledge representation that was similar to the way humans apparently represented the concepts. The motivation for this was so that the examples and counter examples that would seem most natural for teaching these concepts to humans could be used to provide suitable input for his program.

3.3.1 Nodes

Quillian's model consisted of a mass of nodes, interconnected by different kinds of associative links. Each node basically corresponds to an English *Word Concept*, and represents the meaning of this "word" either directly or indirectly. For direct representation of meaning, a *type* node is used. These can be considered as the definition of the Word Concept, having associative

links to other nodes (words) which *define* its meaning. Obviously, there is one, and only one, type node for each Word Concept in the model. For example, the two words contained in boxes in Figure 1, i.e. that appear at the top of a definition, are type nodes.

In contrast, a *token* node is used simply as part of a type node definition. In Figure 1, all words not in a box represent token nodes. The reason for introducing these token nodes, instead of using the type node itself, becomes apparent if a dictionary definition of one word in terms of other words ("tokens") is considered.

Dictionary definitions include sentences where words are ordered so that the syntax of the sentence shows the relationships between them. It would not be sufficient to present the words in a random order since their relations would not be known. Similarly, in a definition expressed in a semantic net it is necessary to have links between the nodes for the concepts. However, if these links existed between the only representation of each word in a system it would be impossible to follow any single definition since they would all involve links through the same words. Consequently, the definition of the type "plant" is a collection of nodes (e.g. "live") with links between them, where the nodes are copies of the node when it itself is defined. As in the paper dictionary, the word "live" in the definition "plant" is a copy (it looks the same) as the word "live" that heads its own definition. These copies of defined nodes are termed "tokens". In general for each type node there will be many token nodes scattered throughout the model.

The explicit distinction between type and token nodes was one of the important aspects of Quillian's system. In his later work on the Teachable Language Comprehender (TLC), he eliminated the explicit copying of type nodes to token nodes and used pointers (a type of link meaning "a copy of" rather than "is associated to") to the type node instead. The conceptual distinction remains while a reduction is gained in storage space. He also adapted the idea of Word Concept node to introduce "attribute values" to denote the strength of properties rather than simple association or its absence. This provided a mechanism for handling negation (an attribute with a value of 0) and quantification. For example in Figure 1, the token node "ANIMAL" in the definition of "PLANT 1" has a value 0C, underneath it. This indicates that the attribute ANIMAL is to be applied with a value (or precisely C for Criteriality) of "not at all" (0), i.e. the structure is not an animal. This introduction of values to properties was accompanied by a third important modification, the introduction of property inheritance. This mechanism allows a type node to inherit properties from superclass nodes in definitions. That is, if "PLANT" has a superclass of "LIVE", then it inherits the properties of "LIVE". This use of inheritance further reduces storage and is an illustration of the commitment to parsimony in semantic nets.

Quillian's work was directly taken up by J. R. Carbonell (1970), who used it to represent geographical knowledge for his computer aided instruction system, SCHOLAR. This provided students with a mixed initiative question and answer interface to a database about South America.

While building on the ideas in TLC, Carbonell introduced two further refinements to Quillian's idea of a node. Firstly, he drew a distinction between *Concept* nodes (e.g. latitude) and *Example* nodes (e.g. Argentina). This, of course, is the basis of instantiation. Secondly, he allowed Lisp functions to be attached to nodes to work out (infer?) properties that were not explicitly stated. This facility is the basis of the slot daemons used in frame systems.

Winston, in his system, also had two basic types of nodes. The first were nodes for those concepts corresponding to the physical objects in the scene. These were organized as a hierarchy, so that most of these nodes had a collection of other nodes as constituents. For example, a brick would be represented as a node, as would each of the faces that defined it.

The other type of node that Winston used was for concepts that corresponded to relationships that existed in the scene between the physical objects in the example being considered. For example, in an arch, the top block must be supported by the uprights, so the relationship "supported-by" was represented as a node. The reasoning behind this was that the nodes alone should contain all the information extracted from the scene. This simplified the comparison of different scenes for points of similarity or dissimilarity.

One consequence of the use of nodes to represent relationships was the ability to create new nodes (or "satellite nodes") to represent new relationships derived from old relationships. Since a node representing "supported-by" could be used in the representation of a counter-example to a concept, the concept learned from this ought to include the relation "not-supported-by". Therefore a negation of a relationship should be derived creating a new node. Similarly, if all the examples contained a relationship, then the learned concept should contain some modal necessity for this relationship (e.g. "must-be-supported-by"). Therefore a necessity modification had to be added to a relationship, creating a new node. Thus from the basic concept "supported-by" would be created a small collection of related nodes.

3.3.2 Links

Without offering any justification other than that they were needed to cope with the complexity of English definitions (but see below), Quillian introduced a number of different kinds of associational links. One of the most important link types is his *Special* link, where a token node "points" to its type node. For example, in the definition of PLANT 1, a link, drawn as a dashed line, points from the token node FOOD to the type node for this word concept. These Special links form the backbone of the Semantic Memory structure, linking related knowledge fragments into a graph. All other links occur inside a type node definition, and fall into one of six categories.

Four of these are:

Subclass links, used to indicate that the type node is a subclass of another word concept (which, of course, is represented in the definition by a token node). For example, in Figure 1, PLANT 2 is a subclass of APPARATUS. This link permits the construction of taxonometric hierarchy.

Modification links, used to show that the word concept represented by a particular token node is modified by the presence of another word concept, e.g. the concept APPARATUS is modified by the requirements of the USE structure.

Disjunction/conjunction links, to indicate that two or more token nodes must, or must not, be applied at the same time. For example, food can be obtained from AIR, WATER or EARTH, so these token nodes are connected by a multi-arc link labelled "or", while a plant is a structure satisfying the token nodes LIVE, WITH leaves "and" not ANIMAL.

Relationship links, used when a token node actually describes a relationship that must hold between two other token nodes. For example, the USE concept relates the user, PEOPLE to an object " = A".

One of the reasons for the poor performance of Quillian's later program, Teachable Language Comprehender, was that it did not take the semantic meaning of the links into account. Later Carbonell, in his system, introduced the idea of labelling the links.

In Winston's system, each link denotes a particular relationship between two Concepts. As there are many different relationships possible between Concepts, there are many varieties of link. However, not all relationships are represented as links, some being represented as Concept nodes. This creates two basic types of links, those conventional links which are themselves the relationship, e.g. in Figure 2, the "one-part-is" link, and those which are just associations between the object nodes and a relationship node which relates the objects, e.g. the "supported-by" link. This hints at the later separation, more fully developed by the case frame advocates, of relationships into syntactic ones (i.e. the grammar of the sentence) and semantic ones (i.e. the words of the sentence). Unfortunately, Winston is rather inconsistent about link types, the "supported-by" relationship sometimes being shown by a simple link, sometimes, as in Figure 2, by a Concept node. The only apparent criterion used to decide which link type to use is whether the relationship will be required to discriminate between the given examples and counter-examples. It can be seen in Figure 2 that the labelled links refer to relationships between nodes, while the relationship nodes refer to relationships between the concepts the nodes represent.

3.3.3 Discussion

Quillian's *Semantic Memory* model introduced, in some form or another, nearly all the important aspects of semantic networks. His model is based very heavily on the organization and layout long used by dictionary and thesaurus compilers, and he claimed to be able to express *anything* that could be expressed in natural language. Though in a sense this is true, the problem is that the concept definitions rely very heavily on the reader's human intuition, obviously not available to a program, as to the meaning of the nodes and, particularly, the links. Also, he recognized the apparent conflict between the associative and schema memory models, but claimed that the two could be handled in parallel by a sufficiently sophisticated program.

Quillian's notion of units contains the basis of a concept hierarchy, complete with an inheritance mechanism. Unfortunately, the notation is not sufficiently rich to distinguish between the different epistemological levels of the concepts that are represented by the same type of nodes and links. For example, the same interchangeable node type is used for a class, an instance, an event and a relation. The other interesting feature of Quillian's units was the later definition of a concept by a property (attribute/value) list.

Though Winston's semantic network was relatively successful for his purposes, it shares a lot of the failings of Quillian's. It contains both the idea of a concept hierarchy, related by "has-part" and "kind-of" links, and the distinction between class and instance nodes, although via the same "kind-of" link used between classes. It also demonstrates quite clearly that the representations of relationships as typed links and as Concept nodes are interchangeable, though at the expense of notational obscurity and computational complexity,

However, like Quillian's semantic memory, it also fails to identify the vital distinction between the links used as part of the representation, e.g. the "kind-of" link used to build the concept hierarchy, and the domain specific links, e.g. "supported-by". This lack of distinction rather obscures the concept hierarchy and forces the application, here a learn-by-example program, to have this information built in.

3.4 Linguistic Influences: Case Grammar and Conceptual Dependency

Whereas Quillian and Winston based their knowledge representations on psychological models of memory, other representations have been developed based on models developed in linguistics. One of the most influential models has been that of Case grammar, originally developed by Fillmore (1966) in the light of the questioned validity of the relations of "subject" and "object" found in the influential linguistic text by Chomsky (1965: 63-73). In Fillmore's grammar "case relations" were semantic relation primitives linking verb (and some other) structures to the nominal elements of sentences. The relations for each verb can therefore be specified by a set of cases. The set of cases which characterize a verb is called the "case frame" for that verb.

Fillmore originally suggested six case relations (Agentive, Instrumental, Objective, Dative, Factitive and Locative) as a "set of universal, presumably innate, concepts". However, it has been a recurring problem for Case grammarians to define a comfortable set of cases, and even Fillmore himself allowed the number and nature of cases to grow. A recently proposed set (Sparck-Jones and Boguraev, 1987) involves 28 cases.

A large number of successful computational systems have been developed which incorporate some aspects of Case grammar (e.g. the general purpose language front-end of Somers and Johnson (1979); Marcus' (1980) English parser; Binot *et al.'s* (1980) French parser; van Bakel and Hoogeboom's (1981) Dutch parser; Nash-Webber's (1975) speech understanding system; the medical expert system of Kulikowski and Weiss, 1971; Bobrow and Winograd's (1977) KRL). Simmons (1973) was the first to develop a semantic network using the set of cases as the set of possible link types. This provided a firm theoretical foundation and a clearly specified semantics for each link type, rather than choosing them on an *ad hoc* basis. In his system verbs were represented by nodes and the case links connected them to nodes for other concepts in order to represent sentences.

In contrast to these language oriented systems are others which claim to capture some deeper cognitive aspect (e.g. the long term memory model of Rumelhart and Norman, 1973; Norman *et al.*, 1975; and more deeply, Schank's (1972) "Conceptual Dependency"). Conceptual Dependency is different from other case-like systems since it is intended to be a language-free representation of concepts whereas the others are language dependent. Consequently both the set of cases used to describe relations and the representation chosen for actions and objects had to use language-free semantic primitives.

3.4.1 Conceptual Dependencies

Schank's (1972) conceptual dependency captures the underlying meaning of utterances as "conceptualizations" by reducing them to combinations of primitive "predicates" chosen from a set of twelve "actions" plus state and change of state, together with the primitive "causation", and seven role relations or "conceptual cases".

Schank attempted to express all verbs as some combination of his primitive actions. These included TRANS (transfer of possession); INGEST (the taking in of an object by an animal); PTRANS (the transfer of physical location of an object) and ATRANS (the transfer of an abstract relationship such as possession, ownership and control). It can clearly be seen from this subset of actions that a large number of verbs can be built up from them given the appropriate relations. However, some of these appear weak when considered. For example, walk can be defined as: PTRANS of x by x through MOVEing the feet of x in the direction of y.

Surprisingly, the cases in conceptual dependency are no more primitive than those of case systems which are more surface oriented. They are Object (in a state), Object (change of state), Object (of action), Actor, Recipient/Donor, From/To, and Instrument. This selection of high level cases suggests that their nature may vary depending on which predicate they are attached to (for example, is there a difference in Actor of "dance" and Actor of "hit"?). However, since there is such a small set of primitive acts, even if this were so, there would only be 37 relations, which is comparable to the number in some other Case systems. Each case is given a graphic representation designed to make illustrations of the semantic nets more readable. Figure 3 shows an example of a conceptual dependency incorporating primitive acts, conceptual cases (using this graphical representation) and objects to describe a state in which "Joe is drinking some soup with a spoon".

Schank's proposals are unsurprisingly inadequate to fulfil his objective of a universal language-free conceptual reasoning system. Conceptual dependency has been criticized by linguists since it is not a theory of language (although it was not intended to be); by psychologists since it requires an unrealistically precise definition of concepts and provides no mechanism to analyse pragmatics; by logicians since it does not capture the relative scope of existential and universal quantifiers; and by computer scientists because it is not described exactly enough to be understood and implemented.

Despite these failings conceptual dependency is important for two reasons. Firstly, it enabled the development of an inference engine for Schank's memory structures which was able to handle a much larger and wider range of language than any of the earlier systems. Secondly, it was the first major attempt to derive both the conceptual nodes and the relational links in a system from an abstract theoretical position.

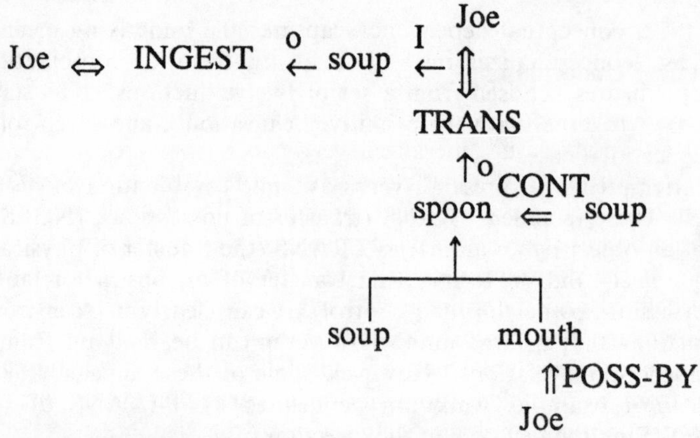

$$\text{Joe} \Leftrightarrow \text{INGEST} \overset{o}{\leftarrow} \text{soup} \overset{I}{\leftarrow} \overset{\text{Joe}}{\Updownarrow}$$

$$\text{TRANS}$$

$$\overset{o}{\uparrow}\text{CONT}$$

$$\text{spoon} \Leftarrow \text{soup}$$

$$\uparrow$$

$$\text{soup} \qquad \text{mouth}$$

$$\Uparrow\text{POSS-BY}$$

$$\text{Joe}$$

Figure 3 Schank - A conceptual dependency

There have been many attempts in formal semantics to define sets of semantic primitives which can be used to build the concepts with which we reason (e.g. Wierzbicka, 1972; Miller and Johnson-Laird, 1976) and attempts such as Case grammar to define the relations that hold between concepts. Conceptual dependency brought these together with a computational approach to knowledge representation and reasoning into a single system. It showed that we do not have an adequate theoretical knowledge to develop systems capable of universal reasoning, but it illustrates a methodology which can be applied in a structured manner to smaller domains.

3.4.2 Discussion

One of the things that made case structures so important in semantic networks was the success they had in natural language understanding. The impression is given, however, that a great deal of this was because the cases were chosen with great care to match the language style, the number and scope of the concepts were quite restricted, and the inference engines using the representations were hand crafted to suit the particular domain.

On the other hand, their development firmly shifted the emphasis of semantic networks away from the associative memory mould of the earlier work. One aspect of this shift is the move away from what Brachman calls the implementational level of semantic networks, where the network is interpreted simply as a data structure, to the conceptual level, where the links have a well-defined semantic content representing conceptual relationships. Another aspect was the attention they paid to the structure of the knowledge they were trying to represent, as opposed to the structure of the domain containing the knowledge.

3.5 Theoretical Underpinning

Nearly all systems developed before 1975, including those described above, and several after that date, generalized very badly from their test examples to real world situations. In most cases, it was the attempt to build natural language understanding systems that prompted the use of semantic networks, mainly because they fit so neatly onto the way humans verbalize their knowledge. As the subject matter grew more complex, the notation became less tightly defined and the more it was left to the user, or the application program, to ensure that the correct interpretation of the notation was made. As a consequence, the simple network formalism was extended to handle knowledge from a particular domain, or a particular subset of natural language, without much thought being given to the semantics of the structure used to represent the knowledge. This had several consequences, besides making the applications very brittle (for example, Quillian's Teachable Language Comprehender only worked on a handful of sentences).

The obvious problems were the logical and expressive inadequacy of most of the proposed notations. Though this could be, and was, tackled in an incremental manner, a large part of the difficulty was due to the lack of understanding of the semantics of the semantic network itself. These problems were tackled by a number of people during the mid to late 1970s, in particular Woods, Schubert and Brachman. They, among others, started addressing the epistemological issues raised by these knowledge representations and laying the foundations for an adequate theory of semantic networks. In this section, the work which led to semantic networks being placed on a sound footing will be described, together with the context in which it was carried out.

3.5.1 The Semantics of Semantic Networks

Woods (1975) was really the first to tackle head-on the major epistemological problems that beset earlier semantic networks. He strongly challenged the logical adequacy of previous notations, focusing on the need for care in the choice of conventions for representing facts as semantic networks, and on the need for an explicit definition of the meaning of the links and arcs used.

Firstly, however, Woods tried to clarify the meaning of the word "semantics". He identified in the literature three independent and conflicting usages of the term, covering the translation of natural language into a formal representation of its meaning(s), the meaning (truth value) of the formal representation, and the procedures that operate on the formal representation.

Woods himself holds the view that all three stages are necessary, and had earlier described such a mechanism based on *procedural semantics*, i.e. where the semantics of an entity is defined by the procedures that operate on it. He pointed out two common misconceptions of "semantics", firstly in extending the term to cover the retrieval and inference mechanisms of the semantic network, secondly, at the other extreme, in denying a fundamental distinction between syntax and semantics.

Having defined "semantics", Woods went on to examine "semantic networks". His target was a formal notation which will accurately and unambiguously represent any (humanly) possible interpretation of a natural language sentence. This he referred to as the *logical adequacy* of the semantic representation. As well as this, he required that the representation facilitate the translation from natural language and the subsequent use of the knowledge by an inference engine. One task he places outside semantic networks is the reduction of all equivalent propositions to their canonical form, i.e. the conversion of all sentences with the same meaning to the same internal form, even though this could resolve paraphrases without a combinatoric search. This is partly because he believes it impossible for full natural language, but mainly because he believes that normally paraphrase is not one of full logical behaviour, but only of logical implication in one direction. For example consider the two phrases, "he is my mother's brother" and "he is my uncle", where the first implies the second but not *vice versa*. Hence, the mechanism for searching for equivalent propositions is still required. Of course, on efficiency grounds, a certain amount of canonicalization might still be beneficial.

3.5.2 What's in a Link

As well as the semantics of the compete network, it is necessary to have a clear idea of the semantics of the components of the network, i.e. of the links and nodes themselves. One characteristic of the early semantic network systems was that a lot of the "meaning" of the links depended on the user's intuitive understanding of the labels on the link. Of course, given a user who was not totally familiar with the representation scheme, or attach the representation to an automated retrieval/deduction system, and the whole edifice collapses. Several people had considered this before Woods addressed it in his 1975 paper.

One of the earlier efforts to remedy these problems was the semantic network model developed by Shapiro (1971) to act as the database for a question answering machine. Although, as usual, nodes represented conceptual entities and the links the relations that held between them, he insisted, for obvious pragmatic reasons, that anything about which information can be

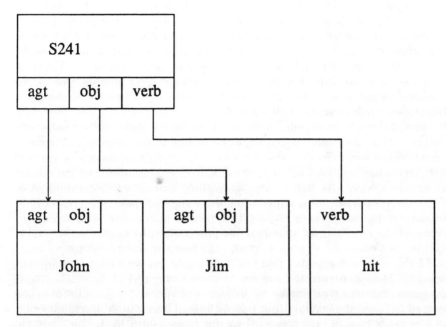

Figure 4 Shapiro - system relations for sentence components

given or questions asked, had to be represented by an item, i.e. a node. For example, in Figure 4, the statement S241 "John hit Jim" can be believed, discussed, and otherwise referred to, and therefore it must be represented as an item. Thus most relationships between items may also be required to be held as items. Shapiro claimed that eventually, if this requirement were adhered to rigorously, there would be some relations that were not conceptual but were merely used by the system to tie a fact-like item to the terms taking part in it. These could be represented as system relations, i.e. links.

Shapiro's system relations were not part of the semantics of the domain, but purely a part of the knowledge representation structure. This separation of the epistemological structure from the semantic structure was a major step forward towards networks that were logically and semantically sound. It was also a belated recognition that epistemology - the study of knowledge and the methods used in that study - should be distinguished from the subject of study. At the epistemological level, provision was made for different types of system relations. Unfortunately, though his examples show several different types, mainly linguistic cases such as object, agent, verb, etc., he does not discuss the semantics of a system relation, or what properties the set of system relations would have. In his quest for generality, he tries not to restrict the number or type of system relations, leaving it to the application developer in the hope that many different semantic networks could be built using his system.

Woods considered the links themselves from a more philosophical viewpoint and identified two different types of link, structural and assertional. An assertional link establishes a relationship between two existing nodes, while a structural link is one which exists only to provide meaning to a node, For example, in Figure 5, the link from "John" to "Mary" connects two nodes which have an existence beyond the concept of the link "hit" and the link makes an "assertion" about a relationship between them. However, the node "S1234" only exists as a focal point for the links "VERB", "AGENT", "RECIP", etc., and the sole function of these links is to provide the "structural" support for the node "S1234" (which otherwise would not exist). This is just the distinction that Shapiro made but his solution was to eliminate assertional links, representing them as relational nodes, rather than complicate the network by mixing the epistemological and semantic structure. Of course, this just relocated the problem in the semantic interpretation of the node, once again confusing semantics with epistemology.

At this point, it is worth jumping forward to Brachman's paper (Brachman, 1983) on taxonometric links in semantic networks. One of the major problems in earlier nets was the confusion they allowed between the subclass type of link and the instantiation type of link. This occurred mainly because in English both may be represented by the pseudo-word IS-A. For example "Tweety is a canary" and "A canary is a bird". Since these links form the taxonometric backbone of any semantic network and provide the inheritance mechanism that is the *raison d'être* of most implementations, it is important to have a clear understanding of the epistemological role of these links.

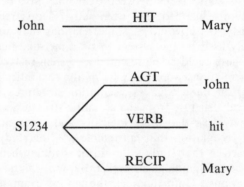

Figure 5 Woods - Assertional vs Structural links

Also, in order to consider the relationship of semantic networks to other knowledge representations, especially first order predicate logic, it is necessary that the function, or functions, of the IS-A link be clearly defined.

Brachman firstly divides IS-A links into two groups according to the type of participating nodes, either *generic*, i.e. a description applicable to many individuals, or *individual*, i.e. a description or representation of one individual. He then goes on to enumerate the different meanings that IS-A takes with these node types, including subset, superset and set membership, generalization, specialization and instantiation, etc. The more common of these are shown Table 1 below.

From this, Brachman identifies two basic types of IS-A, those that take one concept and form another out of it, and those that convey some sort of information about the relation between two sets, or between the arguments of two predicates. The latter category needs to specify: its *assertional force*, i.e. whether it is a statement of fact or not; its *modality*, i.e. whether it is part of the definition of the concept; its *quantifier*, whether it is universally quantified, i.e. always true, or just a default, i.e. true unless cancelled; its *content*, usually a set inclusion/membership or material conditional (if..then..)/predication.

He points out in passing that a number of these requirements, for example modalities and defaults, raise severe difficulties for standard predicate logics.

3.5.3 What's in a Concept

Having teased out a number of insights relating to the semantics of a link, the next step is obviously to tackle nodes. Like links, the early semantic networks relied on the user's intuition for the correct specification and use of nodes. They had been used to represent "facts", "events", "classes",

Generic	to similar Generic	to Individual
Set	**Subset**	**Member**
Predicate	**Univ. Material conditional**	**Predication**
Structured description	**Conceptual containment**	**Description (falls under)**
Prototype	**Sharing typical property**	**Similarity to prototype**
Role	−	**Specifies filler**
Predicate	−	**Abstraction**

Generic	to different Generic	gives
Set	*prototype/predicate*	*Characteristic of set*
Role	*prototype/predicate*	*Constraint on filler*

Table 1 Brachman - Summary of IS-A link flavours

"predicates", "relations" and even "meaning of sentences". Usually they are represented as groups of features, but again the structure of the grouping, and even of the features, left a lot to the imagination.

Woods, once again taking a deeper philosophical approach, pointed out the intensional nature of a lot of the concepts that semantic networks have to represent. The classic example is Frege's Morning star/Evening star, two phrases with different meanings (intensions) but denoting the same planet (extension). Handling extension (or denotation), i.e. representing the set of objects satisfying the concept, is straightforward, but can be computationally infeasible. Handling intension (or meaning), i.e. the concept itself, which may or may not be true of a particular entity, is more difficult. For example, as shown in Figure 6, representing the sentence "John's height is 1.82m" is straightforward: a link Height between an extensional node John and an extensional node 1.82m. If the sentence "John's height is greater than Sue" is added, it becomes clear that an intensional node representing John's_height is required. The main problem that intensional nodes raise is how the program distinguishes between the two types of node, ensuring the correct type is created when building the semantic network, and that inferences on these nodes are performed correctly. The solution Woods proposed was to make all nodes intensional, and add a specific predicate of existence where necessary. This also solves the problem of nodes which represent concepts which do not or cannot have a real world instantiation.

There is also the need to distinguish those links to an intensional node that are part of its definition, e.g. the Height link to John in Figure 6, and those which are assertional, e.g. the Is link to 1.82m. Woods introduced the idea of an "EGO" link, which was used by nodes to indicate their defining links. Thus, following the EGO link from a node such as John would get the information "I'm the guy whose name is John Smith, who works down

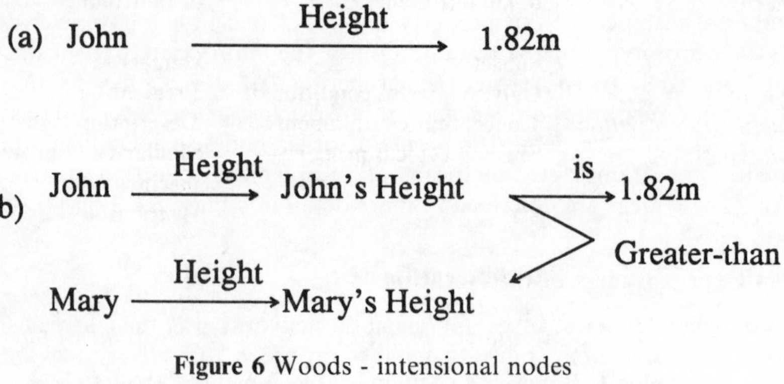

Figure 6 Woods - intensional nodes

the corridor, etc.", whereas the EGO link from John's height would give "the height of the John described by that node over there".

Later, Brachman (1977) addressed the epistemology of *Concept nodes*. In a similar vein to Woods' division of nodes into extensional and intensional categories, he divided nodes into two main types, those which represent particular things in the world, and those which represent a class of particular things. Examples of the former are nodes that represent *objects*, e.g. John, *factual assertions*, e.g. "John's height is 1.82m" or *events*, e.g. "John hit Mary". Nodes representing a class usually have links to instances of the class and to subclasses/superclasses. Unfortunately, this notion of class is frequently extended to try to capture the *Concept* behind the class, i.e. what it means to be a member of this class, as well as representing the set of class members. This is normally achieved by considering the node to be a collection of properties or predicates that somehow "define" the concept desired.

Apart from re-emphasizing the problems discussed by Shapiro, i.e. the distinction between structural and relational links, and Woods, i.e. the distinction between intensional and extensional nodes and between assertional and descriptional links, Brachman pointed out several other sources of confusion connected with nodes. Firstly, unlike properties of an individual which refer to the individual itself, properties of a class node refer to the *members* of the class, and not to the class itself. Of course, a way of talking about the class as a class is still required. A second problem is that the value of a property can either specify a particular value that holds for every member of the class, for example, "elephants are grey", or specify a class of values of which one must hold, for example, "John's height is greater-than 1.82m".

Brachman's solution to these problems was to remove the definitional properties of the Concept node to separate nodes called *role descriptors*. The role descriptor then holds all the information about the function of this definitional property, such as what class the property values belong to, the number of instances of this property that this Concept can have, etc. It also acts as a prototype for the instantiation of the appropriate part of the Concept. As well as specifying the properties, or Roles, the relationships between the properties are specified in a *Structural Description*. Thus, concept nodes could be defined in terms of other nodes, c.f. Quillian's planes, Schank's case frames, etc., by means of an organized collection of structured links. These ideas are described in more detail in section 3.6.2 on KL-ONE.

3.5.4 Expressiveness of the Notation

Woods' main criticism of extant semantic networks was their logical inadequacy, that is, their inability to express precisely, formally and unambiguously all the interpretations that a human listener would place on a sentence. He was most concerned with the rather *ad hoc* way that quantification was handled.

Schubert (1976) addressed the problems that semantic networks have with logical connectives, quantifiers, and modal operators. He approached this from the viewpoint of Predicate Calculus, which he considers to be almost isomorphic with semantic networks. Firstly, he developed a propositional notation in which the basic unit of information is the atomic proposition. This consists of a *propositional* node, a mandatory PRED link to a *predicate* node and links to the concept nodes serving as arguments of the predicate. This is simplified by replacing the propositional and predicate nodes with the predicate name. Figure 7 shows, for monadic and triadic predicates, both an atomic proposition and its simplified version, together with its predicate calculus equivalent. One of the more interesting features is that it is unnecessary to coerce monadic predicates into dyadic form, so that this need for an IS-A link is eliminated; at least in Brachman's *generic* sense.

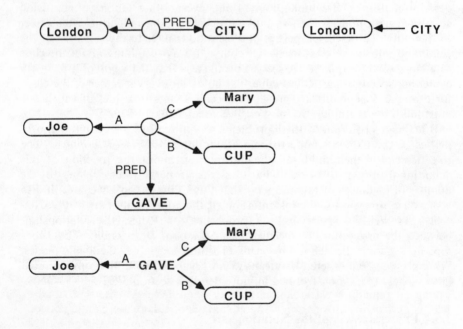

Figure 7 Schubert - Atomic propositions

Schubert also compared his notation to Schank's conceptual dependencies (see section 3.4.1). Although, as a semantic network, conceptual dependencies can mostly be translated into Schubert's notation, he claims that case-structured action propositions lack expressive power and are anyway at a semantically higher level than necessary, and are therefore not primitive.

Quantification

Woods discussed quantification, linguistic (definite and indefinite) as well as numerical and logical (universal and existential). He pointed out the need, not only for definite entities, which exist in the real world, and indefinite entities, which do not have to exist, but also for definite and indefinite variable entities, whose instantiation depends on the instantiation of those other entities to which they are related. For example, the system has to be able to deal with sentences such as "Every boy loves his dog" where "dog" is a definite variable entity whose instantiation exists but is different for each instantiation of "boy", and such as "Every boy needs a dog", where the node "dog" is an indefinite variable entity.

Woods also brought up the problems of numerical quantification using the sentence "three men saw two boats". He insisted that the three possible interpretations of this sentence had to be representable separately in the semantic network. Obviously, explicitly representing this with three nodes for the men and two for the boats, though acceptable here, is not generally possible, e.g. "50 million frenchmen ...". He also brought up the problem with universal quantification of ensuring that future nodes of the same type were created with the correct links. For example, after processing the sentence "Every boy has a dog", all new "boy" nodes must have a "has a dog" proposition added to them.

Woods proposed three methods for dealing with quantification. Firstly, quantifiers were added explicitly as higher order operators, represented in the network as a special node with assertional links to the quantification type, range, variable and proposition. This adds several extra indirections to the representation of the three men/two boats sentence, to hold the set of three men with a "for-all" link, etc. This is the method used by Shapiro (see above). Secondly, a standard resolution theorem proving technique was used to remove all existentially quantified variables from the expression, leaving all remaining variables universally quantified. This is reversible, so there is no loss of information. The advantage of this in a semantic network is that it is only required to indicate which nodes are universally quantified. The problem with it is that, whilst the process is reversible, it is not easy. Thirdly, a quantifier can be converted into a relation between the set of instances of the quantified variable and a predicate containing the rest of the proposition. For example, "All men are mortal" is converted into a relation between a set (all men) and a predicate (mortal). This can also be applied to existential quantification. Putting this into the network would require the predicate to be held as a special type of node that has to have a link to a "set" node.

Schubert in his system also addressed the issue of quantification, and came up with a scheme very similar to the second one above. One further enhancement, however, is that time is handled as quantification over the *moments* at which the proposition holds. A number of notational abbreviations were introduced to simplify the network and make knowledge input easier.

3.5.5 Discussion

The importance of Woods' paper was that it focused attention on the epistemology of semantic networks. Although the paper was rather negative, concentrating on pointing out what was wrong with existing systems, and the new ideas he put forward were rather weak, he did have a major impact on the evolution of semantic networks. By challenging the logical adequacy of previous systems, and clearly identifying the problems, he changed the development of semantic networks from a series of implementations of assorted psychological models of human memory into a serious knowledge representation methodology with an emerging strong theoretical foundation. The questions he raised were the focus for most of the work on semantic networks over the following few years.

Schubert provided a strong, predicate calculus-based foundation for semantic networks, which to a large extent satisfies Woods' point about logical adequacy. However, he does not give much help in representing knowledge in terms of his pseudo predicate calculus. Schubert himself admits this, and when referring to the problems with conceptual dependencies he suggests that higher order constructs, along the lines of the case structure, may be needed to handle real natural language. This contains the seeds of Brachman's five-level structure for semantic networks.

3.5.6 Inheritance and Defaults

Before moving on to discuss the KL-ONE system, there is one other issue that was raised and which had a major influence on the evolution of semantic networks. This is the whole matter of inheritance and defaults, which have an important role in the frame structures developed by Minsky. These are dealt with in greater detail in Chapter 4, but as they have been shown to be useful, not only in handling subset/superset and part/whole relations, but also in controlling search and delineating contexts, their impact on semantic networks will be mentioned here.

Hayes (1977b), developed a higher level structure, along the lines of a frame, but built and interlinked with a more conventional semantic network. This was one of the earlier attempts to merge the frame representation and semantic networks. These structures, called *depictions*, are really just subsets of a larger semantic network, but with a definite, generic head node, the *depictee*, which is connected to the rest of the conceptual hierarchy via IS-A links. Inside the depiction is a collection of other generic nodes called *depicters*, which are related to the depictee by PART-OF or CONNECTED links. Figure 8 shows a typical depiction, with the depictees being the solid nodes and the dashed lines indicating the extent of the depictions. Links leaving the depiction are "inside"; links entering are not. This allows the depiction to be viewed as an archetype, with the depictee universally

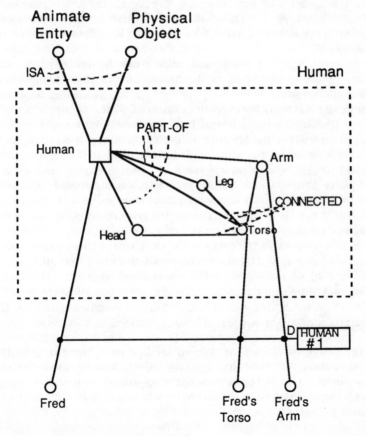

Figure 8 Hayes - An instantiation of a depiction of a human

quantified and the rest existentially quantified within its scope. Upon instantiation, a *binder*, e.g. the D-HUMAN#1 in Figure 8, creates an instance node bound to the depicters and inheriting their connectivity structure. Not all depicters need be instantiated: for example, there is not an instance for head in the Fred instance. If needed, these other depicters can be instantiated later.

The binder/depiction has a number of interesting features. It provides a context mechanism capable of handling referents and resolving ambiguities. For example, given an instantiation, Fred, of "human", "his head" would be instantiated as Fred's head, rather than the head of another person, of a hammer, etc.

Inheritance can be handled by making the depicters instantiations of depicters in a higher level depiction, e.g. dog-leg and human-leg are instances of creature-leg. Hayes recognized that these instantiations were fundamentally different from normal instantiation and had a different type of binder to handle them.

Inherited properties (links and nodes) can be cancelled or augmented without affecting the parent - the binder, in the child depiction, does the instantiation. Also, since the same node name can be re-used, search up through the hierarchy for defaults is fairly efficient.

Depicters can have numerical modifiers that specify the number of instance nodes that the binder can link to them, e.g. a human can have two arms represented by the same depictee. The different instances can optionally be modified by *distinguishers*, e.g. to distinguish right and left arms.

Depicter nodes can be defined further down the conceptual hierarchy by their own depiction. Thus the same node can act as a depicter and a depictee, i.e. it acts as a *role* specifier in the encompassing depiction and as an entity in its own right in its own defining depiction.

Since in some cases the role cannot exist without its depictee, e.g. an arm requires a human, SQN links are provided to ensure that all necessary superiors are instantiated when a subpart is instantiated.

The most important feature of Hayes' notation is his use of a frame-like construction to control instantiation. This, in common with most frame systems, provides a convenient, and easily controlled, mechanism for structuring knowledge, A second important feature is the distinction drawn between the use of a node in its own right to act as a prototype for an instance, and its use to specify a role that needs to be filled in order to create another prototype's instance. Hayes' attempt to capitalize on the work going on into related representations was one of the first examples of the recent trend towards hybrid systems.

Brachman (1983), in his paper on IS-A links, notes that one important use of IS-A in previous semantic networks was to give a default, i.e. a statement that holds unless explicitly cancelled. This is important because it permits exception handling, an essential for real world problems (this becomes clear if an attempt to define "elephant" is made), and was one of the reasons for the development of Frames. The difficulty with cancellable defaults is that they negate the usefulness of a concept hierarchy; for example if "Clyde IS-A elephant", then he has all the inherited elephant properties by default. However, if "Gerry" has all the elephant properties, it cannot be assumed that he is an elephant - he could be a giraffe with all giraffe properties cancelled and a few elephant-like properties added. Thus the node "elephant" does not represent the concept of an elephant any more, but merely acts as a placeholder for a bundle of typical elephant properties. A semantic network which permits the arbitrary use of cancellable defaults seriously jeopardizes its utility as a knowledge base for an inference engine.

3.6 An Epistemologically Adequate Semantic Network, KL-ONE

The work described in the last section highlighted a number of problems with the existing semantic networks. Although the problems were tackled and potential solutions suggested or demonstrated, this was predominantly carried out piecemeal and in isolation. Though they are all built on the same basic associational structure, the various network formalisms described above are all quite different from each other.

Following this period of exploration, Brachman produced his seminal paper identifying five independent levels at which semantic networks can be understood. This paper was a watershed in the development of semantic networks, providing an integrating framework in which the emerging ideas on logical adequacy and expressive power could be investigated. In it he gathered together under one overall umbrella most of the ideas and trends that had emerged from earlier systems. The epistemological framework was the basis of the knowledge representation used in the KL-ONE system. Since it first appeared, KL-ONE has been used in a number of applications, ranging from natural language understanding, to question answering systems, to the modelling of office automation.

In this section, firstly, Brachman's five-layer model will be examined, along with his proposed criteria for evaluating the "correctness" of semantic networks, and then the implementation of these ideas in the KL-ONE system will be described.

3.6.1 Conceptual Levels

Brachman, by examining the various representational primitives used, shows that these differences are a reflection of deeper and quite fundamental philosophical differences (Brachman, 1979). Four of Brachman's five layers concern the conceptual *levels* or viewpoints into which the various network primitives could be categorized. These levels are:

Implementational. This level is the most basic form of semantic network, where links are merely pointers and nodes are merely destinations for links. At this level, the network is simply a data structure, with no real semantic content.

Logical. A semantic network can be understood as a set of logical primitives with a structured index over those primitives. It bears a strong relationship to predicate calculus, with the extra feature of the network topology, and thus provides at least a basic method for factorizing and organizing knowledge. Nodes represent predicates and propositions and links represent the logical relationships between these nodes, such as "and", "subset", "there-exists" etc. This level deals with questions of logical adequacy, including quantification. It is best exemplified in the work of Schubert, and was also obviously influential in the work of Shapiro, Woods and Hendrix.

Conceptual. At this level, the real semantics becomes very obvious, and the relationship with natural languages is strong. Nodes represent word-concepts, i.e. language independent object, action and event types, e.g. GRASP, INGEST, PTRANS etc., while links represent the *case structure*, out of which all expressible concepts can be constructed, e.g. AGENT, INSTRUMENT, RECIPIENT etc. This level deals with the issue of expressive power, in that the types of node and link provided dictate what language expressions can be handled. The champion of this approach is Schank, though it has been adopted by many others, for example, Rumelhart and Norman, Simmons, Rieger.

Linguistic. The top level is really natural language itself. The example given by Brachman is the OWL system which, apart from the implementation level, has no structuring primitives other than those of English. The nodes in this scheme are words, and have context-dependent meanings, e.g. "fire" changes meaning when attached to "man", and the links represent real world relationships, e.g. Colour, Hit, etc.

In the above, each level is a self-contained network representation, more or less independent of the levels above and below it. By separating out the primitives like this, Brachman shows clearly that the primitives of different levels, e.g. there-exists, AGENT and Colour, are fundamentally and philosophically different from each other. This variety of primitive types had been implicitly recognized by the developers of some of the networks mentioned above, although it was not formalized as clearly as here. A lot of the problems that arose in the earlier networks were due to the mixing of primitives from several levels. The four level scheme described above does not quite cover all the notational features of previous semantic networks. For example, the binders of Hayes, and even the ubiquitous inheritance, are not logical primitives, and even though they are generally assumed by the case structure, they are not represented in it.

Brachman proposed introducing a fifth level, the *epistemological* level, to handle this formal structuring. The primitives of this level are for representing *knowledge-structures* and their interrelationships as knowledge-structures, independently of the knowledge contained within them. For example, an intensional entity has to be defined from lower level primitives, and has to be related as a unit to other entities, using epistemological links.

This paper has had a major impact, partly because it tied together a number of strands that were emerging in isolation, that is, it reconciled the work on logical adequacy which was driving towards a variant of formal logic, the conceptual dependency work which was driving towards more expressive power and the epistemological work that was starting to examine knowledge-structures as structures. A second reason for the impact was that the five level structure put forward was the basis for the KL-ONE system, and this, until recently, was the foundation for a large number of important semantic network research projects.

3.6.1.1 Criteria for Assessing Semantic Networks

Since each level represents a particular type of semantic network, Brachman explores the capabilities of the levels, and specifically the epistemological level, against the three criteria, *neutrality*, *adequacy* and *semantics*. By neutrality he means that each particular type of semantic network must not constrain the choice of primitives for the next level up. For example, the logical level must not contain features, such as inheritance links, that will affect the design or operation of the epistemological level. This offers the usual advantages of modularity. Nearly all previous semantic networks violated this criterion, and therefore not only were less flexible for building on top of, but were confusing to use. However, some of the logical networks, for example Schubert and Woods, go a long way towards this goal.

By adequacy he means that the each level must provide the facilities required to implement the next level up. For example, a conceptual level should be able to support any possible linguistic system of knowledge. Conceptual adequacy has been addressed in particular by Schank and Rieger. Logical adequacy has already been relatively successfully tackled by Woods and Schubert. The trend towards logical networks is partly explained by the extra difficulty in achieving adequacy in a mixed level network.

By semantics he means the provision of a formal specification of the *meaning* of each element and the operations that can be performed on them. Here, he considers the meaning of a primitive to be specified by the procedures that operate on it. For the logical level, if a mapping to predicate calculus is established, then the semantics is defined. At the conceptual level, Schank and Rieger have specified the inferencing operations for each primitive act. This is only possible since they have a fixed number of primitives. At the linguistic level, a formal semantic specification of natural language is next to impossible.

3.6.2 Overview of KL-ONE

Firstly, it should be pointed out that KL-ONE is more than just a representational language, as it includes facilities for the building, storing, querying etc. of the network. KL-ONE is an evolving system with new ideas constantly being added, and thus it is difficult to pin down. However, the main interest is in its capabilities to explicitly represent conceptual information as a *structured inheritance network*, a feature that has been fairly consistent over the various implementations. The system described here is a fairly recent implementation, and some of the elegance of Brachman's earlier ideas has been lost as new problem areas emerged (Brachman and Schmolze, 1985c). Although the various aspects of the system will be considered in some detail in later sections, an overview of the complete system will be given here.

KL-ONE is primarily an epistemological level network which provides the necessary primitives with which to describe and handle knowledge. The primitives are knowledge independent, in that they can be used to describe the internal structure of a broad spectrum of concepts. Briefly, the primitives used to represent the internal structure of a *Concept* are *Roles*, which represent the attributes associated with the Concept. A Role not only holds the information about the function of the attribute, that is, the intension of the attribute, but also acts as a description of the potential fillers, that is, the instances of the attribute. These Roles indicate the type and number of the instances permissible for this attribute. The interrelations between the Roles are handled by a *Structural Description*, which contains a set of relationships between the Roles that must hold between the Role fillers when the Concept, and hence the Roles, is instantiated.

Given this notion of a Concept, the epistemological level primitives there-fore consist of the relationships between Concepts, Roles and Structural Descriptions, and the internal relationships of Roles and Structural Descriptions. As well as this, the relationships between two Concepts, and indeed between two Roles and between two Structural Descriptions, need to be addressed. These relationships are the basis of the inheritance mechanism, which, at its simplest, requires the Roles and Structural Descriptions of the parent Concept to be linked to the child Concept. Obviously, a mechanism must be provided to allow modification of the Role or Structural Description being inherited.

3.6.3 Concepts

KL-ONE *Concepts* correspond to conceptually primitive pieces of domain knowledge, and are either *primitive Concepts* or *defined Concepts*. Primitive Concepts are used for domain concepts that are atomic, i.e. have no internal structure, or that cannot be defined in terms of necessary and sufficient properties. However, primitive Concepts can still specify necessary properties, though they may not be able to define all of them. Defined Concepts are built up from primitive Concepts and other defined Concepts and have their necessary and sufficient properties defined. For example, the Generic Concept (see below) for a natural kind such as "elephant" cannot be defined by necessary and sufficient properties, so it is primitive. However, in Figure 9, the Generic Concept URGENT-MESSAGE is a defined Concept since it is completely defined in terms of REPLY-REQUESTED-MESSAGE and the "less than 1 hour" modification. Most Generic Concepts fall into the primitive category.

The most important type of KL-ONE concept is the *Generic Concept*, i.e. an intensional description of a class of domain objects, e.g. person, message, date etc. Generic Concepts are either primitive, or are defined, using *SuperC* links, in term of other Generic Concepts. This creates a basic tax-onomy formed of those Concepts that *subsume*, or are subsumed by, other Concepts. The subsumption criterion allows multiple SuperConcepts, and the taxonomy is actually a lattice. By subsumption, Brachman meant that an instance of the lower Concept would always, by definition, be an instance of the higher Concept. Thus, a Concept gets its meaning from its Super-Concepts, possibly modified locally either by additional specific properties, or by restrictions on the SuperConcept's properties. As an example of this, in Figure 9 the Generic Concept URGENT-MESSAGE is subsumed by REPLY-REQUESTED-MESSAGE since it is completely defined by adding the local property "within one hour" to those properties of its SuperCon-cept, REPLY-REQUESTED-MESSAGE. KL-ONE provides a method of

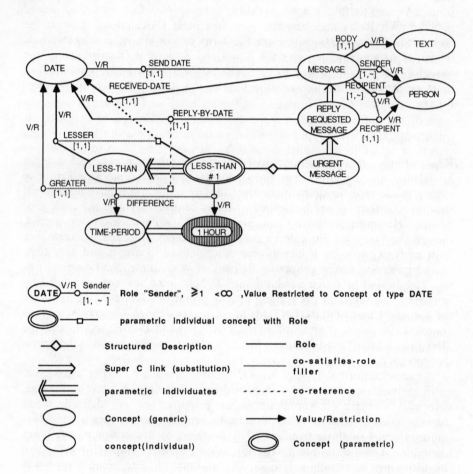

Figure 9 Brachman - Fragment of KL-ONE network

deciding if one Concept subsumes another, and this is the basis of the *Classifier*, which automatically places new Generic Concepts into their correct place in the taxonomy.

3.6.4 Roles

Before considering other types of Concept the internal structure of a Generic Concept will be discussed. The primitives used to represent the internal structure of a Concept are *Roles*, which represent the attributes associated with the Concept. Roles not only hold the information about the function of the attribute, i.e. the intension of the attribute, but also act as a description of the potential fillers, i.e. the extension, or instances, of the attribute. Since several different types of entities could satisfy these functional requirements, a set of Roles, called the *Roleset*, is needed to identify the different types of filler allowed for this attribute, e.g. the sender of a message could be a machine or a person. This identification is achieved by having a link, *Value/Restriction*, point to the Concepts that satisfy the functional requirements. Similarly, the function might permit multiple instances, for example, a message could have several recipients, so again the Role has to identify the number of instances allowed. As an example of this, in Figure 9 the Concept MESSAGE has a Role "Sender" whose Value/Restriction link is to the type PERSON and whose number is shown (under the Role symbol) as having a minimum of 1 and no maximum number of senders. Early versions of KL-ONE also allowed the Role to be optional, and provided a modality flag to indicate whether the role was a necessary part of the Concept, or was a derivable or optional attribute. However, as Brachman pointed out earlier, default cancellation destroys the logical adequacy of a semantic network, so in later versions Roles were restricted to necessary attributes of the Concept.

3.6.5 Structural Descriptions

As well as specifying the Roles that define a Concept, the relationships that must exist between the Role fillers have also to be specified. For example, the sent-date must be before the received-date, the recipient of a message might need to be the sender's supervisor etc. This is a function of the *Structural Descriptions*. These relate two or more Roles in terms of another Concept. For example, in Figure 9, an URGENT-MESSAGE is defined as a REPLY-REQUESTED-MESSAGE, with a Structural Description which relates the Reply-By-Date Role to the Received-Date Role via a particular version of the LESS-THAN Concept. This version is isomorphic with the Generic Concept LESS-THAN, but is a *parametric individual Concept*, parameterized by the URGENT-MESSAGE context. (There is also a shorthand notation for the common parameterized Concepts of equality and subset.) The required Roles of the LESS-THAN parametric Concept, identified by links to the corresponding Roles in the Generic Concept, are *co-referenced* to the Roles in the URGENT-MESSAGE Concept being related. Not all Roles of the Generic Concept have to be co-referenced, and can be instantiated in any appropriate fashion.

3.6.6 Individuation and Individual Concepts

All KL-ONE Concepts are intensional, so there are no Concepts to directly represent extensional objects, that is, objects in the real world. Individual objects are *denoted* by *Individual Concepts*, which are *individuations* of the appropriate Generic Concept. Brachman reserves the word *instantiation* for the association between the Generic Concept and the real world object. Individual Concepts individuate a specific Generic Concept, but describe at most one individual. As the Concept is intensional, there is no implication of existence of the individual being described. For each Role in the Generic concept, there is a Role filler in the Individual Concept. As well as matching Roles and Role fillers, the Individual Concepts pointed to by the Role fillers must accord with the relationships specified in the Structural Description.

3.6.7 Inheritance

Individuation can be considered as an example of one aspect of inheritance. In general, inheritance is the passing down of the properties of the parent Concept to the child Concept. To do this in KL-ONE requires not only an indication of the link between the parent and child Concept, that is the subsumption link described earlier, but also, for each Role in the SuperConcept, an indication of what, if any, restrictions are to apply. In the case where no restrictions apply, there is no Role shown for the child Concept, and the Role shown in the parent Concept is deemed to apply. If, as is usually the case, the child is to be a specialization of the parent, the Role in the child Concept has the new number of fillers or type of entity shown, along with a *restricts* link to the corresponding Role in the parent Concept. For example, the Concept REPLY_REQUESTED_MESSAGE inherits the Role Recipient from its SuperConcept MESSAGE, but restricts the number of Recipients to 1. Structural Descriptions, on the other hand, must be inherited intact.

Another controversial issue hinted at earlier was that of default values and cancellation. Brachman's stance, mentioned above, is that allowing cancellable defaults in the definitional, or description formation, aspect of a semantic network undermines the logical adequacy of the representation. He therefore insisted that Roles represent only necessary attributes of a Generic Concept, and thus, from his definition of subsumption, they are not cancellable. Non-necessary properties, which may need to be cancellable, are dealt with outside the taxonomy in the Assertion Language. The use of Reiter's default reasoning mechanism for this was suggested but no details of how this could be done were given.

3.6.8 The Conceptual Coat Rack

Brachman, and later Woods (1983), give an analysis of *procedural attachment* in KL-ONE, i.e. the mechanism by which the user of a semantic network can access the implementation code (interpreter) directly to attach a procedure to an entity. One reason for these procedural attachments is to represent metaknowledge, for example, about a Concept as an entity. This, called a *metahook*, is really a means for one level to perform functions of the next higher level. A second reason is to attach special interpreter code to an entity, for example, to short circuit, for efficiency, the normal code sequence the interpreter follows when handling a specific Role. This, called an *ihook*, is really a means for a level to modify the level below. (The hooks form a "coat rack" upon which to hang auxiliary knowledge.) Both these *escape* mechanisms are not philosophically necessary, and, if needed, demonstrate inadequacies in the semantic network, either at the current level or the one below (the interpreter). Brachman warns against abuse of these hooks.

3.6.9 Discussion

The main criticism of KL-ONE is the complexity of the Role and Structured Description, due in large part to the evolutionary nature of their development, which makes the system hard to use. However, there are also some more fundamental weaknesses which appeared in use. It should be noted that a number of these weaknesses are complementary, and the tradeoff between them necessarily fails to eliminate both, or either, of the problems.

The most serious of these is the incomplete treatment of Roles, in that they derived their semantics via other constructs, the Concept and its Structural Description. This lack of an adequate formalization led to the grafting on of such kludges as Rolesets, and even then the system could only cope with primitive Roles. Another shortcoming was the inability of the hierarchy to handle Concepts unless their necessary conditions could be specified. This arose from the desire to ensure that the representation, and especially the classifier, was demonstrably complete and sound, i.e. obtained all and only all the right results. However, the tradeoff for this was less expressive power, which did make the system less useful in practice. Finally, there was a lack of support for such things as representing exhaustion or exclusion among a Concept's subsumees or indication sequence in Role fillers. Most of these issues were tackled by one or another of the later systems that were built on or around KL-ONE, some of which are described in the next section.

3.7 Recent Systems

As well as acting as a representational language for application systems, KL-ONE has also been the foundation for some basic research in knowledge representation. KL-ONE was extended and refined over a number of years, with a number of new ideas being introduced. Most of these were application oriented and thus were more interested in being usable than in addressing the theoretical issues. One such system is NIKL, described below. One idea, that was raised but not fully developed in KL-ONE, was the separation of the description formation aspects of the knowledge representation from the assertion making aspects, and this led to the development of the KRYPTON system described in Chapter 10. In parallel with this work, several other unrelated systems were being produced. One example of this is the Conceptual Graph system of Sowa, which was biased towards the logical representations to about the same degree as KL-ONE was biased towards the schema representations. This is described in outline below and in detail in Chapter 7.

3.7.1 NIKL

NIKL (a New Implementation of KL-ONE) is one of the many offshoots from KL-ONE (Kaczmarek, 1986). As a new implementation, it follows its parent system fairly closely. However, as well as improved efficiency, there are some significant differences between the two systems and, interestingly, a number of similarities with KRYPTON. The major change is in the representation and use of Roles. Roles were now thought of as representations of conceptual Relations which are 2-place relations in the same way as Concepts are 1-place relations. They could then be organized in a separate taxonomy and given a domain and a range, i.e. restricted to a particular set of Relations and particular range of values of each Relation. For example, the Concept "parent" could have a Role "child" which is restricted to the Relations "daughter" or "son" and with a numerical range " > 0". This gives the advantages that the user, or system, can define and refer to Roles in an analogous manner to Concepts.

Another of NIKL's enhancements was the provision of better support for reasoning, in particular classification-based reasoning. Unlike KRYPTON, the emphasis was placed on efficiency, forgoing completeness in favour of expressiveness. Firstly, facilities were provided to allow the user to specify that a set of Concepts was disjoint, i.e. mutually exclusive in the real world, or covered another Concept, i.e. every extension of the covered Concept is described by at least one of the set of Concepts. Secondly, support for partial orderings of Roles is provided in the shape of Relations that allowed sequences to be described. For example, an initialization phase can be forced to come before the main phase, which in turn precedes the terminal phase. Thirdly, the ability was provided to specify, as a Relation, a set of Roles that are sufficient conditions for a Concept - the necessary conditions having been defined by the Concepts position in the taxonomy. In coping with these extra features, the classifier, which automatically classifies Concepts in terms of Concepts already existing in the Concept hierarchy, is actually carrying out quite sophisticated classification-based reasoning. This greatly reduces the load on the user specifying the Concept hierarchy as well as on the application program's reasoning ability.

3.7.2 Conceptual Graphs

One modern semantic network not based on KL-ONE is the Conceptual Graph system of Sowa (1984). Sowa was interested in natural language processing and his system reflects this, though it is based strongly on logic and was designed to support logical inference. A Conceptual Graph is a mini-semantic network representing a sentence. A Concept node represents entities, attributes, states or events, while a Relation shows how the Concepts are interconnected, i.e. the semantic relationship between two Concepts. Links have no meaning in themselves, other than to indicate the Concepts dealt with by each Relation. The Concepts and Relations have referents, i.e. refer to either a specific individual, an unspecified individual or a set of individuals. For further details see Chapter 7 of this book.

3.8 Conclusions

The various "extensions" that are currently being grafted onto semantic networks seem to indicate that they are not sufficient in themselves to be an adequate knowledge representation language, though they provide a powerful and flexible base on which more complex hybrid systems can be built. However, there is a trend for the more philosophically sound of these extensions to be subsumed into the network notation, e.g. Minsky's notion of schema was first tagged onto the network as KL-ONE Roles / Structured Descriptions and then in NIKL became part of the infrastructure connected with Relations. Certainly semantic networks appear to be a very intuitive representation, but this very intuitiveness can lead to logically unsound systems unless a lot of care is taken with the notation. In common with most other representations, the main outstanding problems are how to describe natural kinds, how to handle defaults and negation and how to deal with incomplete, or incorrect, information.

4 Structured Object Representation - Schemata and Frames

Gordon Ringland

4.1 Introduction

In this chapter we discuss the representation scheme called frames or schemata. Though this representation has been attacked as adding nothing
really new to the tools of AI (Hayes, 1979) it remains widely popular both in
practical applications and in research. The reason for this popularity lies in
the fact that much knowledge has a structure, arising either out of the structure apparent in the domain to be represented, and/ or the structures we
have to impose to be able to deal *usefully* with large amounts of knowledge.
To the extent that structured object representations (afterwards called
frames or *schemata*) can reflect the structure natural to given sets of
knowledge then it will be advantageous to use them. Even in the cases
where frames are logically equivalent to representation by randomly ordered
sequences of clauses in first order logic, it does not follow that the readabil-
ity and expressive power of the two representations are equivalent.

In the next section we discuss Minsky's original paper on frames (Minsky,
1975). The hope here is to give some help to those who will read this rather
difficult paper, and to motivate the discussion.

In section 4.3 we present examples of the use of frames which bring out
their usefulness in representing structure. Section 4.4 gives a presentation of
the influential paper by Hayes (Hayes, 1979) which argues there is little new
in the frame idea. Though we defer to the clarity and scope of the paper,
our conclusion is that Hayes' claims are too strong. Section 4.5 reviews the

most recent important contribution to the frames literature, that of Brachman (Brachman, 1985). Broadly speaking, Brachman shows that the use of frames for 'common-sense' reasoning is, if not impossible, at least fraught with traps for the unwary. In section 4.6, we review other approaches to default reasoning and note that the problem of 'common-sense' reasoning is still a major research issue and at the time of writing this problem cannot be definitely asserted to be solved.

4.2 Minsky's Paper (Minsky, 1975)

The notion of organizing perception into some kind of unitary whole dates back as far as Kant's Critique of Pure Reason, first published in 1781 (Kant, 1787) and is represented in this century by the work of Bartlett (Bartlett, 1932). Minsky squarely acknowledges his debt to Bartlett and observes that similar ideas were in the air in AI two or three years before the publication of the first version of his frame paper in 1975. However it cannot be denied that the paper by Minsky has had great influence on the enterprise of Knowledge Representation and is probably the most widely referenced contribution to the field. For this reason alone it would be right to devote a section to the paper, but it is also worth some discussion to allow us to compare Minsky's hopes with their realization.

The opening section of Minsky's 1975 paper captures much of what has been influential. He begins by asserting that most theoretical work on AI and in psychology has been too fine-grained, local and unstructured to account for effective common-sense thought. At this stage it is appropriate to make explicit a significant part of Minsky's argument. By linking work on AI and psychology he has staked out a definite and contentious position on AI: essentially that though artifact is unavoidable we should try to represent the real thing (human intelligence) as effectively as we can. For an extensive discussion of human knowledge representation see Chapter 6. This should be contrasted with McCarthy's position which emphasizes the A(RTIFICIAL) in AI and consequently makes psychological reality a subordinate or even irrelevant issue (Kolata, 1982).

Next, his opening emphasizes 'common-sense thought' as a process that AI must capture. There are two important issues here. The first is plain and should not be contentious, namely the necessity for any satisfactory AI system to display the sense and reasonability tests most humans apply most of the time as a part of their 'common sense'. For definiteness let us consider a simple case. Suppose you, the reader, a human intelligence, accept, along with a great many other things (the preceding qualification really is important), that P implies Q and also accept the antecedent P. Are you then forced to accept the consequence Q? Should you accept it? The answer "not necessarily" is a display of common-sense. Clearly you could have excellent reasons for believing not-Q, and if so you might cease to accept either the conditional P implies Q, or the antecedent P. The point here is that while rules of proof sanction the conclusion Q, the rules are local to the relation P implies Q, and the antecedent P, and apply to those individual syntactic forms. But the *overall* excellent reasons for not accepting Q may be global, involving reasoning and judgement over all 'the great many other things' you accept. This is the reason for Minsky's complaint against locality.

The second and less obvious point is the use of 'thought' in the desideratum 'common-sense thought'. I believe that using 'thought' rather than 'reasoning' in this term is significant and is an example of a confusion on the part of the anti-logicist school as exemplified by Minsky, and also the logicist school as represented by McCarthy and Hayes (Hayes, 1977a). We distinguished, quite deliberately, rules of proof as in logic from the more general 'reasoning'. There has been a tendency to equate the two terms, leading to a view that if one uses logic as a representation one is inevitably committed to a particular formal deductive machinery and, to avoid such a machinery, one must avoid logic as a representation. We shall return to this point in discussing Hayes' critique of frames (Hayes, 1979) in the following section.

Minsky asserts that "chunks" of reasoning and the representation of language memory and perception should be larger and more organized than, say, production rules, and frames are the device to provide the structure. This structured representation and the interaction of these structures is generally taken to be the essence of frames or schemata, and is surely the aspect of Minsky's essay which has had the most practical effect.

A simple example of a frame might be the frame for a domestic pet

FRAMENAME	PET
SLOT 1	DISPOSITION: FRIENDLY
SLOT 2	HAS: OWNER
SLOT 3	HAS: A HOME

Minsky's original idea is that the upper levels of the frame are fixed and represent unalterable truths about the object or situation, while lower levels consist of 'terminals' or 'slots' (the usual notation) which are filled with specific instances. In practice this distinction between upper and lower levels is not much used, except for the name of the frame itself.

No particular originality was claimed for the notion of frame and he acknowledges the parallel work of others in attempting to move away from representing knowledge as 'collections of separate simple fragments'. More novelty is claimed for the notion of 'frame systems', which are collections of related frames which are linked together by the sharing of slots. This sharing allows lower level frames to inherit the properties of higher level frames -

the implementation of this mechanism is not very explicitly discussed, but the idea is that the linkage mechanism is some sort of 'information retrieval network' using a 'matching' process.

Consider the two linked frames in Figure 1 to see what results are expected. Through the retrieval network the two frames are compiled to produce a new explicit frame for DOG shown at the bottom of the figure. Here the first three slots of the new frame for DOG are inherited from the MAMMAL frame via a matching of the frame name MAMMAL with the IS-A slot value MAMMAL.

Though some slots (higher level) are presumed to be inherited without exception, Minsky required that a frame's slots would usually be filled with 'default' and that these default assignments should easily be replaced by values which better represent the situation. This requirement arose from Minsky's view of cognitive memory and he believes that much of the power of the theory stems from these default assignments. He held that on considering a new situation a frame is selected from memory, and this remembered framework is adapted to the actual situation by changing details (slot values) as necessary. Indeed he asserts that this is the essence of the theory. The role of the frame in memory (and knowledge representation) is to represent stereotypical situations.

We illustrate this notion with the following very simple example of a stereotype of elephant:

FRAMENAME	ELEPHANT
SLOT 1	IS: A MAMMAL
SLOT 2	LEG: CARDINALITY: 4

Here the first slot is to be inherited without exception - an elephant must be a mammal. But the second slot is a default of the stereotype elephant, in that most people conjuring up the notion (frame?) elephant would attribute four legs, but any specific elephant, inheriting the ELEPHANT frame might have lost a leg and therefore have 3 for the second slot value. This slot then has a default value which should be easily replaced according to circumstance. Stereotypes will usually have many (perhaps most) slot values which are not strictly entailed by the top level node or frame name.

In summarizing what Minsky takes to be the essentials of frames and frame theory, at least one thing should be clear - a snappy one line description is not appropriate. So two definitions of frames from the literature

● 'A generalized property list' (Winston and Horn, 1984)

● 'An example of a structured object' (Bonnet, 1985)

hardly capture what Minsky was advocating. Sowa comes closest to capturing some of the essence of Minsky with his one line description

FRAMES & INHERITANCE

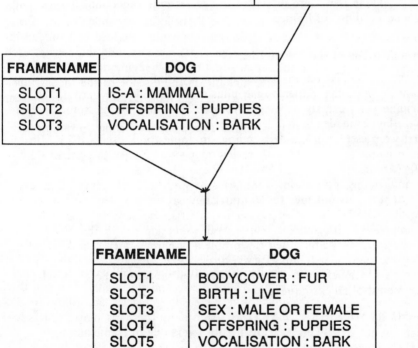

Figure 1

'Prefabricated patterns assembled to form mental models' (Sowa, 1984) but clearly much is left out.

Another notion which Minsky wished to have embodied in 'frames systems' was what he called 'view changing'. This could be the changes of view a vision system experiences from relative rotation of the viewed scene, or in language systems 'procedures which in some cases will change the contextual definitional structure to reflect the action of a verb'. No real idea was given of how such a 'view changing' facility might be implemented. However the notion appears to have been influential in the use of 'viewpoints' and 'Kee worlds' in the ART and KEE commercial knowledge-based systems.

Minsky's paper concludes with a criticism of logic in knowledge representation. I believe that in this he was partly right in spirit, but mostly wrong in letter. These issues are discussed in the sections concerning Hayes' and Brachman's critique of frames.

4.3 Applications of the Frame Idea

In the preceding section we discussed Minsky's influential paper with some difficulty - since the rather vague allusive style makes it hard to clearly understand what exactly is being advocated. We now discuss some applications of the frame idea.

First we present story understanding, an application discussed by Minsky in his original paper. Then we review a medical diagnosis system: CENTAUR (Aikins, 1983).

An interesting application of frames is to story understanding. I am concerned that as an outsider to natural language work I may give a wrong impression to other outsiders. This concern arises because the results do not look impressive. Presumably the moral to be drawn is that, since the researchers are very able, then the problem is hard. Our example is taken from work on understanding news stories (De Jong, 1979) about earthquakes. The frame construction anticipates what would be expected in a short account of an earthquake:

FRAMENAME	EARTHQUAKE
SLOT 1	PLACE: LOWER SLABOVIA
SLOT 2	DAY: TODAY
SLOT 3	FATALITIES: 25
SLOT 4	DAMAGE: 500,000,000
SLOT 5	MAGNITUDE: 8.5
SLOT 6	FAULT: SADIE HAWKINS

The slot values are filled as above from the following news story.

"Earthquake Hits Lower Slabovia

Today an extremely serious earthquake of magnitude 8.5 hit Lower Slabovia killing 25 people and causing $500,000,000 in damage. The President of Lower Slabovia said the hard-hit area near the Sadie Hawkins fault had been a danger zone for years".

Having obtained the slot values from the news story these are inserted into the Earthquake Summary Pattern:

"Earthquake Summary Pattern

An earthquake today occurred in *value in location slot value in day slot* There were *value in fatalities slot* fatalities and $ *value in damage slot* in property damage. The magnitude was *value in magnitude slot* on the Richter scale, and the fault involved was the *value in the fault slot*."

This produces the following summary after instantiation:

"An earthquake occurred in *Lower Slabovia today*. There were *25* fatalities and *$500,000,000* in property damage. The magnitude was *8.5* on the Richter scale, and the fault involved was the *Sadie Hawkins*".

Now that seems quite good, though one might be worried about a news story which mentioned 25 *injured*. Wouldn't the system kill them off in the summary? A cruder problem is what happens to a story concerning earthquakes but not actually reporting one. Take the following news story:

"Earthquake Study Stopped

Today the President of Lower Slabovia killed 25 proposals totalling $500,000,000 for research in earthquake prediction. Our Lower Slabovia correspondent calculates that 8.5 research expenditures are vetoed for every one approved. There are rumours that the President's close adviser, Sadie Hawkins, is at fault".

This would produce an identical summary to the earthquake story. The solution, in principle, was stated by Minsky - namely give the frames sufficient information and procedures for them to recognize when to act - the solution in practice can be rather elusive.

The expert system PUFF (Kunz *et al.*, 1978) for lung function test is of considerable interest. Though not nearly so well known as MYCIN (Shortliffe, 1976), it is in widespread everyday use, whereas MYCIN has only ever diagnosed one patient 'in anger'. Another reason for interest is that Aikins, prompted by its deficiencies, produced CENTAUR (Aikins, 1983) which makes extensive use of frames to improve upon PUFF. PUFF is a clear descendant of MYCIN, using simple unstructured rules to represent knowledge, strategy and control. This modular, uniform representation was at one time held to be a positive advantage. In analysing PUFF, Aikins noted that though PUFF was adequate as a problem solver it had important shortcomings which she traced to the flat knowledge representation of rules. The problems found were:

(1) It was hard, or impossible, to represent typical sorts of patient and disease patterns.

(2) During a consultation it was difficult to modify the order in which questions were asked since these questions were generated by rule firings controlled by the interpreter, and much of the control information was implicit, buried in the rules themselves.

(3) Maintainability and modifiability were problems because of unanticipated side effects of rule changes or additions.

Frames provide, as Minsky intended, a suitable mechanism for representing stereotypical uses and also for embedding the specific stereotype in a more general stereotype. So, for instance, Aikins has a frame for OBSTRUCTIVE AIRWAYS DISEASE with lower order frames representing ASTHMA, BRONCHITIS and EMPHYSEMA, and also a set of four frames representing the degree of severity of the disease.

The issue of control as a problem for flat rule based systems had also been recognized by Clancey (1983) and Szolovits (1983). Szolovits noted that the overall strategy of MYCIN - try the most probable cause first - is nowhere explicitly represented, but is instead encoded separately and implicitly in each of the rule sets representing the 26 blood infections considered by MYCIN.

In CENTAUR Aikins solved this problem by using frames to give an explicit representation of how reasoning was to be controlled and to keep this separate from inferencing from data. Hence the name CENTAUR - the head is of different type to the body. The control of question asking mainly resides in the stereotypical frames - which may contain sets of production rules for inferring a required value - if the rule set does not instantiate a value then the user is questioned.

A related benefit from grouping production rules in sets of frame slots is that the rules are explicitly organized in relation to the stereotype being matched to data. This makes for ease of understanding, maintenance and modifiability. Though CENTAUR was no better as a problem solver than PUFF, it was argued that the representation of knowledge for both disease stereotypes and strategy greatly improved intelligibility and maintenance. These benefits, both for the expert and knowledge engineer, are clearly much more than symbol level implementation issues; they are of importance at the knowledge level.

Apart from Aikin's original paper, a thorough discussion of CENTAUR is given in Jackson's excellent book (Jackson, 1986). Jackson also discusses another medical expert system, INTERNIST, where frames were found necessary to organize the knowledge comprehensibly.

4.4 The Backlash - Hayes' 'Logic of Frames'

Some four years after Minsky's paper, Hayes (1979) analysed what frame representation had achieved. His conclusions were mostly negative. He held that with the exception of 'reflexive reasoning' no new insights had been achieved from work based on frame representations. Though we record this view as overly harsh, and indeed believe some of Hayes' assertions to be wrong, the paper is important in that it was the first attempt to subject frame structures and theories to a systematic logical analysis.

In his introduction, concerned with representation and meaning, Hayes loses no time in expressing a distaste for the lack of tight analysis in Minsky's paper and some subsequent work. "Minsky introduced the terminology of 'frames' to unify and denote a loose collection of related ideas on knowledge representation: a collection which, since the publication of his paper has become even looser. It is not clear now what frames are, or were ever intended to be."

He opens by discussing three different views of frames:

(1)   as a formal language for representing knowledge, to be compared with, say, predicate calculus (representational);

(2)   as a system which presupposes that a certain kind of knowledge is to be represented - this he calls the 'metaphysical' interpretation;

(3)   as an implementation issue - frames are to be viewed as a computational device for the organization of memory, retrieval and inference.

Though he observes that Minsky seems to speak to the 'metaphysical' and implementation (or heuristic) interpretations, he largely bases his analysis on the representational interpretation. He notes that it has been common - and still is - to confuse these views, particularly the representational language in that it has a semantic theory which defines the *meanings* of expressions in the language. It is the semantic theory that changes a formal language into a representational language, and this theory must explain the way in which expressions carry meaning.

Having discussed the meaning of meaning, Hayes is ready to address the meaning of frames. To motivate his discussion he first considers a frame representing a typical house and then specializes to an instance of a particular house by giving (some) slots values. This example he then rewrites as a set of assertions in predicate calculus.

He concludes that, used in this way, stereotypical frames are bundles of properties expressible in predicate calculus, and particular instances are simply instantiations. This, then, suggests to him that frames are merely an alternative syntax for predicate logic - i.e. expressions about the relationships between individuals. However he notes that though the meanings appear to be the same, the inferences allowed by frames may be different from those sanctioned by logic, in some important way. It is then suggested that we must examine how frames are used to get a better insight into their meaning. Here "use" is plainly meant to mean what inference rules are used. This is a rather strange path given Hayes' representation - Hayes' prime focus is at least partly separate from inference. In particular, commitment to a representation does not automatically require commitment to a particular inference mechanism. Indeed, commitment to logic as representation does not commit one to deductively sound rules of proof. The reader is strongly encouraged to read the article by Israel (1983) for an excellent account of the distinctions (and confusions) between representation and reasoning.

Nonetheless, we shall follow Hayes' discussion of the *use* of frames. He considers a form of inference suggested by Minsky - 'criteriality'. The idea is simply that if we find values for all the slots of a frame, then we can infer that an appropriate instance of the concept represented by the frame exists. So if 'Dunroamin' has the appropriate slot fillers for kitchen, bathroom etc., then, by virtue of possessing these attributes, 'Dunroamin' satisfies the necessary and sufficient conditions to be a house. Hayes simply takes this example and maps it onto first order logic, where such slot names as kitchen become the function kitchenof. This example reinforces Hayes' belief that frames are just another syntax for first-order logic, with the defect that it is unclear whether criteriality is being assumed, whereas in clausal form this is obvious.

Hayes now considers a third form of frames reasoning - *matching* as made concrete by Bobrow and Winograd (1977). If we have an instance of a concept frame, say John Smith as an instance of Man, we can regard John Smith as an instance of another concept frame, say Dogowner. Hayes observes that a match may be established if the man frame had a slot for *pet* and this was filled by an object known to be a dog, or if the Dogowner frame had a slot for owner name and dog and name was filled by John Smith, and dog filled by anything. Either would be sufficient for the instance John Smith to be matchable to Dogowner. He points out that the knowledge is expressible in first order logic, and the result is obtained through the standard inference rules of logic. He leaves out entirely the situation where 'matching' fails - Minsky envisaged this as a trigger to seek alternative frames, or construct new ones. Hayes allows that more profound use of the matching process might be envisaged, but would probably be only expressible as in higher-order logic, and remarks that it may not be possible to implement such schemes.

This hints at a tendency which becomes more marked in the discussion of defaults and stereotypes - choosing examples which are expressible in first order logic, or if they are not so expressible ignoring them.

Take first stereotypes, which Minsky asserts to be a very significant component of the frame notion. Hayes distinguishes three ways in which stereotypes may be used.

The first is simply filling in details - this may result in the satisfaction of criteriality or in matching - in either case expressible in predicate calculus.

The second is as the *correct* way of looking at a single thing. Once again this can amount to criteriality - but there can be a difficulty - a single thing may have apparently contradictory properties or be seen from different points of view. He takes an example of someone who is unfriendly at work but friendly at home. This again is dismissed as a non-problem with three sketched possible solutions; which, unless the solution is translated into assertions with consequent contradiction, he has no theory for. There does appear to be a solution at least partly in the spirit of Minsky; namely, the "Viewpoints" of ART or the 'Kee worlds' of KEE. This allows for the maintenance of internally consistent hypothetical worlds which may contradict each other, and for drawing inferences between these worlds. Though Minsky appears to have some of the idea of this mechanism, and presumably influenced its development, his suspicion of inference apparently did not allow him to discuss consistency in each separate viewpoint. Nevertheless this seems evidence against Hayes' assertion that no new insights resulted from the frame movement.

His third view of stereotypes is to understand them as representing a metaphor or analogy. Frame-like structures were used for analogical reasoning in MERLIN (Moore and Newell, 1973) and Minsky acknowledges this as a major influence. The example considered is 'pig' as an (unkind) metaphor for man.

Hayes seems to make heavy weather of metaphor, noting at some length that a man cannot literally be a pig. This means, in the jargon, that matching of a metaphor should never establish criteriality. But if matching does establish criteriality, as it may to Bobrow and Winograd (1979) - but not to Minsky - then frames have a problem in that they cannot distinguish a metaphor (or 'mere caricature' to Hayes) from a real assertion. Hayes does note however that the bundling of the appropriate properties in the frame used in metaphor would be a criterion for pig-likeness as distinct from pig-hood. Having scented 'criterial' he then notes that a systematic vocabulary translation could allow logic to do all (and more) than is claimed for the frame as metaphor. Though he allows that logic itself does not provide the syntactic machinery for this translation, an analogy is sketched to an unreferenced use of analogy in mathematics. It is claimed that if a caricature frame contains the translation information then all is reducible to first order logic. Surely the point here for frame aficionados is that once they are allowed to characterize a frame as a metaphor, matching then validates the metaphor as a metaphor and not a true assertion - so no translation is needed.

The weakest of all the discussion in 'Logic of Frames' concerns defaults. One has the feeling in this section that Hayes' considerable, but incomplete, success in showing a correspondence between frames and first order logic has now convinced him that all aspects of frames are expressible in first order logic. He defines a default as the slot value in the absence of contrary information, but does not add that with such contrary information the value should be replaced. He does not say that defaults take us out of first order logic - but only that they *seem* to do so. This apparent unequivalence is asserted to be a consequence of a *naive* mapping of default reasoning onto assertional reasoning. After discussing an example he concludes that what is required for default reasoning is some process which subtracts previous beliefs or assertions. The trouble is that classical logic does not allow this - it is monotonic - beliefs can only be added and conclusions increase monotonically. Hayes simply disagrees - he asserts that no new logic is needed - merely some new primitives and the ability to "talk about the system itself". This is firmly disputed by at least some of the workers cited as producing such a system. Etherington and Reiter (1983) state "... common sense reasoning about exceptions is non-monotonic, in the sense that new information can invalidate previously derived facts. It is this feature which precludes first order representations, like those used for taxonomies, from formalizing exceptions". We should conclude that Hayes fails completely to establish an equivalence between first order logic and frame defaults. The situation is clearer now (1987) than at the time of Hayes' paper (1979) and it appears that most workers in the field agree with the quote from Etherington and Reiter.

For exceptionless hierarchies - which are representations of universal set inclusion - it should come as no surprise that first order logic *can* represent the knowledge as can frames and there is a mapping/transformation between the two. This of course does not show frames are 'merely' first order logic. It is hard to believe that anyone who has seen a frame representation for a taxonomic hierarchy could fail to believe, whatever the logical equivalence, that for this case frames are a superior representation to an unstructured sequence of clauses. An example from physics - cartesian and spherical polar coordinates are equivalent - but cartesian coordinates are far superior for solving problems about particles in cubic boxes, spherical coordinates superior for solving the hydrogen atom. So I would claim the 'bundling' aspect of frames, even for those cases where there is a mapping onto predicate calculus, is by no means the triviality Hayes makes it out to be - and has been one of the major practical attractions of the frame idea.

Just because replaceable defaults cannot be handled by predicate calculus does not mean that frames do not have problems and in the next section Brachman's concerns (Brachman, 1985) are discussed.

In the final section of 'The Logic of Frames' it is argued that one positive product of the frames movement is the idea of *reflexive reasoning*. Reflexive reasoning is that in which the reasoner thinks about himself, in particular about his own reasoning process. Interestingly, the possibility of this knowledge level activity arose in part out of an implementation (or symbol) level issue. In some, but not all, frame systems the frames are implemented as structured objects in the sense of Object Oriented Programming (OOPS) - see for instance (Bobrow and Winograd, 1979) and (Bobrow and Stefik, 1983). This implementation, at least in principle, allows for the possibility of reflexive reasoning. So far there are only two or three pioneering examples in the literature, and these suffer from a somewhat *ad hoc style*; however, work is being pursued to put the basis of reflexive reasoning on a firmer foundation - see (Maes, 1986).

Summarizing, then, Hayes set out to show that almost all of frames is equivalent to some of first order logic, and so the movement had produced no new insights. Although he did some of the job, he did not complete it . His dismissal of the use of frames as stereotypes, their use for 'seeing as', is unconvincing, and his section on defaults, where he asserts that no new logic is required, is wrong. Still, the paper is important, and beautifully written - whether or not one agrees with Hayes there is usually no doubt what he is saying and why he says it - not something that can be said of Minsky's paper.

4.5 Problems with Defaults and their Cancellation - Brachman's Elephant Joke

In the discussion of Hayes' 'Logic of Frames' we observed that though Hayes was wrong to say that no new logic was needed to handle defaults, this did not mean that all was well for every, or perhaps any, frame representation of default reasoning. Brachman, in a superb essay (Brachman, 1985) which sets depressingly high standards for just what can be achieved in a popular account, brings out the problems of replaceable defaults in frame (or semantic network) representations.

Very crudely summarizing, though Hayes argued that most of the frames idea is equivalent to predicate logic, Brachman makes a case that none of the default aspect of frames is logic, and indeed they let you do very little consistently. Refining the above caricature a little, Brachman's main point is that once overrideable defaults are used uniformly then definitional (or criterial) conditions cannot be used, and without definitional power frames cannot express simple composite descriptions such as 'polygon with four sides'.

The argument is organized as follows: first it is shown that the use of cancellable defaults forces us to represent everything in terms of defaults, and this does not allow us to represent universal truths. Then comes the really great problem - this means that even the simplest of composite descriptions cannot be constructed - so every description must be a primitive.

Now one might think that the first problem is terrible - being unable to represent universal truths - like 'every rhombus is a quadrilateral'. But that is not so, for two reasons. First, if you stick to the 'ideal' world of geometry no default cancellation is needed, and frames, logic etc. work fine. But much more importantly, if you do not stick to 'ideal' worlds but try to deal with the real world as the frames movement wants to do, then you have to recognize that 'natural kind' concepts like elephant cannot be defined (Putnum, 1977). So it could be argued that the loss of definitional capability is no great loss after all if our main goal is to represent the real world and the real world is not amenable to definition. Similarly, classical logic is inadequate, in the sense that 'natural kind' concepts cannot be represented by a finite number of necessary and sufficient conditions. Now what is devastating about Brachman's argument is that though you can define 'polygon' and you cannot define 'elephant' you surely should be able to conclude that an ELEPHANT-WITH-THREE-LEGS is an elephant just as you can conclude that a THREE-SIDED-POLYGON is a polygon. But, argues Brachman, with cancellable defaults you cannot - ELEPHANT-WITH-THREE-LEGS is not a composite description, it is a new primitive because we have lost all definitional capacity.

Before wrapping up, he addresses the question of what frames in systems with cancellable defaults might be, discussing various meanings of the IS-A link.

A word of caution - before deciding you will never (again) have anything to do with frames, keep in mind that Brachman's argument bears on frame systems with " .... a uniformly applicable facility to cancel properties". Brachman himself notes that it is possible to have systems where some defaults are explicitly uncancellable whereas others are explicitly cancellable and notes that thus explicit marking of defaults may also have expressive value. So frames are not necessarily bad for you, but badly (or not at all) thought out knowledge representation frameworks are.

Now to the argument. Brachman takes frames with inheritance to mean that subframes inherit all the properties of their parent frame. The specific example considered is the frame for elephant which is a subframe of the parent mammal frame. This could be represented as:

FRAMENAME	ELEPHANT
SLOT 1	SELF: A MAMMAL
SLOT 2	TRUNK: A CYLINDER
SLOT 3	COLOUR: GREY
SLOT 4	LEGS: CARDINALITY: 4

Now what does this mean? The first possible meaning discussed is essentially that put forward by Hayes. If the inference mechanism of frame systems is inheritance, and no defaults are cancellable, then one could argue that the elephant frame is stating the necessary conditions for class membership. So if CLYDE is an elephant by virtue of some kind of IS-A link to the ELEPHANT frame then CLYDE necessarily is a mammal, has a cylindrical trunk, is coloured grey and has four legs. In this interpretation Hayes would be quite right to interpret the slots of the frame as right-hand sides of conditionals.

This interpretation simply will not do for the 'natural kind' concept elephant. It is entirely thinkable that a given elephant would have none of the properties specific in our frame, apart from being a mammal. Brachman conceives of an unfortunate elephant suffering from hepatitis which is consequently yellow not grey. (Honestly it won't affect the argument if elephants stricken with hepatitis do not go yellow, or even if elephants are immune to hepatitis.) To handle this problem of exceptions most frame systems allow the overriding or cancellation of a property that would normally be inherited. Now once this is so we cannot use the Hayes interpretation of the colour slot - 'every elephant is grey'. Instead there has to be an interpretation such as 'the typical elephant is grey' and grey is a *default* value - in the sense originally suggested by Minsky.

Brachman observes that typical has nothing to do with frequency - one is not saying most elephants are grey (though probably they are) or even that grey is the most frequently observed elephant colour. Instead, the force of the statement is "in the absence of any evidence to the contrary, assume that any given elephant is grey". This interpretation is consistent with Minsky's paper - though he does not give it - and also with subsequent more or less formal approaches to default reasoning (Reiter, 1978).

At this stage we ask what has been given up to talk about conceivable real elephants. If the mechanism is the *uniform* (my emphasis) possibility of default cancellation then we have lost the possibility of representing necessary universal truths like the truths of geometry or arithmetic. Of course we might puzzle over why someone would like to represent and reason about the abstractions of plane geometry in the same system that considers real elephants. Remember there is a subtle difference between the statement that 'all quadrilaterals are polygons' and 'all elephants are mammals.' The first is true by definition and cannot in principle be otherwise, the second is a matter of scientific discovery - we *could* have been wrong.

A slightly less obvious problem is that abandoning 'every' means that we cannot represent contingent universal facts with a single statement. This is definitely a nuisance. One might well observe that *all* the vehicles in the parking lot are cars - there are no vans, motorcycles etc. Having a true every, as in predicate calculus, allows us to capture this without even knowing, as one need not, how many cars there are, still less representing each one. This is clearly a loss compared with predicate calculus - but not, as Brachman brings out - the most severe loss.

The worst problem concerns that of description. The essence of the problem is simply represented - once we have the concept elephant, never mind how we came by it, then we should be able to construct an indefinite number of composite concepts, each of which is related to the parent concept ELEPHANT by definition - i.e. necessity and sufficiency. So consider the concept of an elephant with three legs - the frame for this might be called 'ELEPHANT-WITH-THREE-LEGS'. This concept is just the composition of two attributes, each necessary and both together sufficient. We require that it is impossible to have an elephant with three legs that is not an elephant, and that it is impossible for something that was both an elephant and had three, and only three, legs not to belong to ELEPHANT-WITH-THREE-LEGS. Stating the problem in a slightly different way, ELEPHANT-WITH-THREE-LEGS should stand in the same relation to ELEPHANT as POLYGON-WITH-THREE-SIDES stands in relation to POLYGON. Now the 'natural kind' concept 'elephant' is very different from the mathematical idealization 'polygon' in that the latter is a well and simply defined concept, whereas the former has no definition at all. But still we must, without fail, infer that an elephant with three legs is an elephant just as we conclude that a polygon with three sides (the primitive triangle) is a polygon. The crunch is that in allowing the *uniform* (my emphasis again) overrideability of defaults we have lost the definitional capability to do this - and cannot represent that ELEPHANT-WITH-THREE-LEGS and similar compositions are more like POLYGON-WITH-THREE-SIDES than they are like ELEPHANT. The analogy to natural language is clear - it is as if we had given up the possibility of noun phrases and were just left with simple nouns - since now all frames are primitives.

At this point Brachman rather goes overboard and tells us that frame systems cannot deduce that a rhombus (a polygon with four equal sides) is also a quadrilateral with four equal sides, and that the concept of a three-sided rhombus would be just as acceptable. It must be noted that (most) frame systems allow inheritance without cancellation, and that is just what is wanted for completely definitional representation. Indeed the construction of a frame system which never lies about plane geometry is a standard tutorial exercise used by the makers of one commercial AI-toolkit.

One of Brachman's parting shots concerns IS-A links. He observes that the informal practitioners of knowledge representation often confuse different meanings of IS-A. He gives three different meanings of IS-A:

(1)   the *concept* of a *kind* of thing (e.g. elephant);

(2)   a generic *description* specifying the properties that *typically* apply to instances of a kind of thing;

(3)   a *"stereotypical"* (he says prototypical) *individual* somehow typifying the kind.

Confusing these different meanings is evidently no way of going about knowledge representation - but it has happened. One might, in mitigation of the informal school observe that the verb 'to be' has given philosophers a lot of trouble - see, for instance Russell's History of Western Philosophy (Russell, 1945). The prosecution might argue that, not knowing the relevant literature, particularly from another field, is a frequent failing in AI. Sowa (Sowa, 1984) has made this point with many telling examples.

Brachman's conclusion is that the very proper desire to represent 'natural kind' concepts had led to naive mechanisms that admit arbitrariness and force ignorance of crucial facts. As he notes, when *all* rules (of inheritance) are made to be broken, then no rules are left. But the rule that elephants with three legs are elephants is not to be broken. As he pithily remarks "(some) AI systems have thrown out the compositional baby with the definitional bathwater".

As we have hinted, though Brachman's argument is convincing, it does not close the door on an effective and useful frame representation. What is needed is a representation where some properties and property values (slot values) are inherited without exception ('sacred') and others are explicitly marked as replaceable. These 'sacred' markings should also distinguish between the slot value being uncancellable and the slot name (or attribute) being uncancellable. As he notes, the presence of an *explicit* cancel link adds to the representations' expressiveness. A cancelled attribute could give information about the property's history and applicability. This is clearly an area for more research and Brachman and friends have been active. One apparently promising approach used in the system KRYPTON (Brachman, Fikes and Levesque, 1983b) is to separate as completely as possible definitional and factual information. Lambert discusses this work in Chapter 10.

Finally we should note that though the 'informal' school of knowledge representation has suffered some well-aimed blows (and others not so well aimed) as reviewed in these last two sections, the 'formal' school appears to be having considerable problems with formalizing 'common-sense' reasoning. We give a short account below.

4.6 The Problems of Formalizing Default Reasoning

Hayes' analysis of default reasoning in 1979 (Hayes, 1979) mentioned work in progress by McDermott and Doyle and also by Reiter which it was hoped would give a formally satisfactory account of default reasoning. This is also referred to as work on the problem of non-monotonic logic. Classical logics are monotonic in the sense that assertions once made cannot be retracted, and so the numbers of conclusions increase monotonically with the number of assumptions. In default reasoning one is allowed to retract assertions in the light of evidence - the conclusions of a logic which allows this is non-monotonic with respect to assertions.

The enterprise of formally representing default reasoning looked very promising (see McCarthy, 1980; McDermott and Doyle, 1980 and Reiter, 1980). But prior to 1986 problems have surfaced in the work of Reiter and Doyle and McDermott.

The problem is that the non-monotonic extensions to predicate calculus seemed to allow only weak, or even no, conclusions be drawn. McCarthy's more elaborate formalism was not known to suffer from these problems until the analysis of Hanks and McDermott (1986). In this paper they claim to show by a detailed example that McCarthy's approach also, in some circumstances, yielded no useful conclusions in the sense that the system yielded two contradictory conclusions, and gave no guidance in selecting one of them. At the time of writing this is still recent work and we cannot claim any final conclusion. However there is at least some evidence that formal methods may not be able to handle the sort of default reasoning required for representing common-sense reasoning. Since this is one of the key issues in AI we should expect much work and lively debate on these issues.

4.6.1 The 'Frame Problem' - a Brief Note

Since Hanks and McDermott mention the 'frame problem' it is worth noting that this problem has nothing specifically to do with frames as discussed in this chapter. The frame problem recognized by McCarthy and Hayes (McCarthy and Hayes, 1969) concerns the problem of expressing information about what remains unchanged by an event. The essential assumption is that a state persists between events. This is discussed at greater length in Chapter 9.

4.7 Comparisons and Conclusion

The use of frames to represent knowledge about structured domains or structured knowledge continues to increase in popularity, particularly as systems get larger. The wide variety of hopes (explicit and implicit) in Minsky's paper (Minsky, 1975) are unlikely to be fulfilled completely - in particular 'common-sense' or default reasoning cannot be effectively represented by the cancellable inheritance of defaults.

Though Hayes (Hayes, 1979) showed a logical equivalence of a particular use of frames to first order predicate logic, this does not diminish the utility of the frame approach, since the additional structure which can be represented or imposed by frames has considerable value.

One demonstration of this is the reconstruction of knowledge bases originally expressed in unstructured production rules into frame systems and the consequent improvement in system understanding and ease of maintenance.

Frames have some similarity to semantic networks - a frame system whose frames consist of the framename and top relation slot is just a semantic network of nodes joined by relation arcs defined in the relation slot. The issue of inheritance and cancellable defaults arises in exactly the same way for semantic networks, though the argument may be a little less clear.

5 Rule Based Systems

Tony Williams and Brian Bainbridge

5.1 Introduction

The knowledge representation that may be already familiar to the general reader is the production rule formalism. In this chapter, the origin and development of production rule systems will be examined, applications will be described and an evaluation of the formalism will be made.

5.2 Basic Components and a Simple Model

In general, production systems have three main components: working memory, rule memory and the interpreter. The architecture and execution cycle of a simple production system comprising these three components is given in Figure 1.

The *working memory* is a store containing objects defined by attribute-value lists. These objects represent facts about the world, either given, observed or inferred. As we shall see, they may also represent working hypotheses, rather than real facts. These working hypotheses may be modified or withdrawn in the light of subsequent information. The term *fact* is used loosely in this chapter to refer to all kinds of object in working memory.

For example, using a Lisp-like notation:

```
(        (Patient-ID  12345)
         (Patient-name Smaug)
         (Complaint Bad-breath)
)
...
(        (Patient-ID 12345)
         (Skin-condition  Green-scaly)
)
...
```

This set of objects includes the information that a patient named Smaug has complained of bad breath. The physician has observed that the patient has green scaly skin. The system has assigned an identifier for this patient, and no doubt has other information stored.

The *rule memory* contains rules governing the system's behaviour. These rules have the form

IF   condition(s)   THEN   action(s)

At first sight, these rules appear similar to conditional statements in conventional programming languages, such as the logical-if statement in Fortran. The differences will be discussed later. The conditions govern the premises for selection of this rule, and are sometimes referred to as *antecedents* or left-hand sides. A condition defines a pattern to be matched against the content of the working memory. Such a pattern can match one or more objects whose attributes conform to requirements expressed in the pattern.

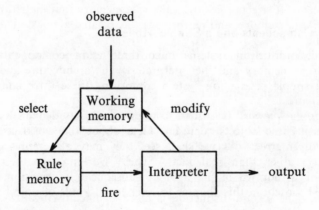

Figure 1 Production system execution cycle

An action defines modifications or additions to the working memory, and may include side-effects, such as output. The resultant changes to working memory play the role of inferences in an expert system. Actions are sometimes referred to as *consequents* or right-hand sides of the rule.

Contrived examples of rules might be:

```
IF     (Complaint Bad-breath)
AND   (Patient-species dragon)
THEN (assert (remedy mouthwash))
```

```
IF     (remedy ?x)
AND   (no-side-effects ?x)
THEN (print "Take" ?x "and see me in a month")
```

(?x signifies a variable)

The first rule states that the way to cure bad breath in dragons is for them to gargle with mouthwash. The second rule states that if a remedy has been inferred (as indicated by the presence of a remedy attribute in working memory) and there are no unwanted side-effects, then the patient can be given the prescribed remedy.

Rules have a readily understandable form, provided that the condition part does not become too complex. They can be used in explaining to the user why the system made a particular deduction, because they directly state the information on which the deduction was based, and the reason why the deduction holds.

The *interpreter* (also called the inference engine) is the active component of the system. It selects rules from the rule memory that match the contents of the working memory, and performs the associated actions. This is termed *firing* a rule.

Two factors distinguish rules from conventional conditional statements:

(1)   the conditional part is expressed as a (possibly complex) pattern rather than a boolean expression;

(2)   the flow of control (as found in conventional languages) does not pass from one rule to the next in lexical sequence but is determined entirely separately, by the interpreter.

The first distinction can be seen as mere syntactic sugaring, as an equivalent pattern matching function can be called from within a boolean expression. The second distinction is more significant. It allows separation of the knowledge from control of how the knowledge is applied. Knowledge bases can be expressed as sets of rules, each of which can be validated independently of the control structure. Each rule expresses a relationship between antecedents and consequents which must hold in a static way: the "truth" of the rule must hold independently of when it is applied. This implies that the antecedents of the rule must adequately determine the context in which the consequents apply.

5.3 Survey of Production Systems

Post (1943) used production systems in symbolic logic and invented the name. In mathematics they first showed up as Markov algorithms (Markov, 1954), and they have been used in linguistics under the name of rewrite rules (Chomsky, 1957). Later, the formalism was used in programming languages such as SNOBOL (Farber, Griswold and Polonsky, 1964), and in compiler translation languages (Floyd, 1961).

An illustration of the use of production systems in linguistics is in expressing a context-free grammar. For example, an insult grammar (a favourite of introductory AI texts) could be expressed by these rules (after Bundy *et al.*, 1980):

> insult   = > suggest 'you misname
> suggest = > 'buzz 'off
> suggest = > 'go 'jump 'in 'a 'big 'hole
> misname = > 'nasty 'fellow
> misname = > 'little 'toad
> (a quote signifies a literal)

This will generate such marvels as

> "go jump in a big hole you little toad"

The first use of production systems in knowledge-based systems seems to be in 1965, when Herbert A. Simon and Allen Newell at Carnegie-Mellon University used them in a chess analysis program (Simon and Newell, 1965). Since 1954, these researchers have worked on aspects of human problem-solving (Newell and Simon, 1972). They have studied the performance of intelligent adults on short (half-hour) tasks of a symbolic nature, tasks not centrally concerned with perception or motor skill. Three main problem areas have been used - symbolic logic, chess problems and algebra-like puzzles. Test subjects are asked to perform the task, and to "think aloud" as they do so. These protocols are recorded and transcribed to form the data to be represented in a production rule formalism. The resultant system behaves in a similar way to the human problem-solver, and this can be interpreted as being a result of the similarity of the two information processing systems.

These studies have typically not been concerned with learning and age-related differences or development. Later applications of production systems have been more concerned with such areas, and have dealt with such domains as seriation (putting physical objects in order) and learning arithmetic operations (Young, 1976, Young and O'Shea, 1982, Evertz, 1982).

In these types of research, the production system is regarded as being a psychological model of human knowledge and skills. It is possible to model adaptive behaviour by using rules which modify rule memory (seen as akin to human long-term memory) and/or the working memory (seen as akin to human short-term memory). For example, it has been suggested that user interfaces to computer systems could be built which would adapt to the user, and accelerate the more common interaction sequences (Hopgood and Duce, 1980). Conway and Wilson discuss this approach to modelling human procedural knowledge in Chapter 6 of this text.

The other main approach has been technological in thrust rather than psychological. Whatever their significance for psychological modelling, it can be said that production systems offer a useful *ad hoc* programming formalism. However, there are problems in using them for realistic knowledge-based systems applications, some of which are touched on in succeeding sections. Useful work has been done to improve efficiency and representational power, and commercial quality tools such as the OPS languages (Forgy, 1981, 1982) and ART (Laurent *et al.*, 1986) are now available. Large applications such as R1 (McDermott, 1982b) and MYCIN (Buchanan and Shortliffe, 1984) have been developed. Finally production system architectures are being designed, such as the RISC machine based on gallium arsenide technology proposed by researchers at Carnegie-Mellon University (Lehr and Wedig, 1987).

5.4 Extensions to the Simple Model

The simple model of production systems described in section 5.2 is inadequate for implementing commercial quality knowledge-based systems. In the first instance, problems arise concerning rule selection, control strategy and permissible actions.

5.4.1 Rule Selection

The first problem with rule selection is *conflict resolution*: determining which rule to fire when more than one set of conditions match the working memory. The simple solution is to fire the first rule whose conditions match. However, this strategy means that the designer of the system has to ensure that the rules are in the correct order. For example, it might be required to deal with exceptions or unusual cases first. This means that rules with more antecedent clauses, ones with more conditions and which are therefore more specific in their application, would have to be at the beginning of the rule set. If a new rule were added, it would have to be inserted into the rule set at the 'correct' position. One of the advantages of production rules, that the rules are modular and represent a separate chunk of knowledge, only weakly coupled to other rules, has been lost if ordering has to be done. More sophisticated production systems, e.g. the OPS family of languages, provide explicitly for a conflict set: the set of instantiations of rules that match the current contents of working memory. The user is allowed to choose a particular conflict resolution strategy, such as giving preference to rules that operate on the most recent information (this provides focus), or giving preference to those rules that match the most items (to implement the strategy described previously). As a last resort, if the conflict resolution cannot indicate which rule should be selected, a rule is chosen arbitrarily.

A second problem arises with large rule sets: there may be many rules to choose from, only some of which lead to the desired result quickly. In this case, some systems use heuristics, perhaps encoded as metarules, to perform more sophisticated conflict resolution. (Metarules are rules which control the use of domain rules.) The metarules could refer to particular domain rules, either by name or by pattern matching their conditions and/or actions. The conflict resolution strategy is thus embodied in the metarules. Figure 2 shows the schematic architecture of a production system with metarules.

An example might be a financial expert system which could contain the metarule:

> IF   the company is seeking finance
> THEN   first consider rules that conclude medium-term finance

(possibly because experience has shown that medium-term finance is the best candidate as a source of company finance). This is an instance of the more general metarule which states that the most likely candidates should be tried first. An example of the more explicit use of metalevel control is the latest version of the ROSIE production rule language (Sowizral and Kipps, 1986), a much augmented successor of the earlier RITA system (Anderson and Gillogly, 1976). ROSIE has become its own metalanguage, in that in the language itself it is possible to define the action of the inference engine and the conflict resolution strategy.

5.4.2 Control Strategy

The simple model given in section 5.2 describes a forward-chaining data-directed production system. The system starts from observed data, and proceeds to infer all possible consequences (at least in principle). Particularly for usefully large rule sets, this may lead to a combinatorial explosion

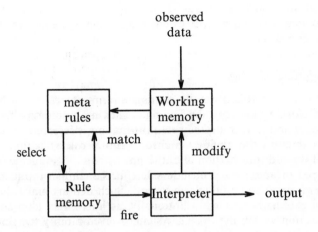

Figure 2 Production system with metarules

in the working memory, and in the conflict set.

An alternative control strategy is known as backward-chaining, or goal-directed search. In this model, the system is given some goal to achieve. The interpreter selects rules that may lead to that goal, and infers the subgoals required to satisfy those rules. The subgoals are then put into working memory, and the cycle continues until all subgoals are satisfied. The intent is that the system will perform more efficiently and in a more focused way, because the rules are being selected in a sequence which is proceeding towards the desired goal. Again, conflict resolution is required, and heuristics or metarules may be applied. The MYCIN series of medical expert systems use a goal-directed control strategy to implement the classification strategy of a doctor treating microbial disease, and are described in Chapter 8 by Bainbridge (and see Buchanan and Shortliffe, 1984).

The forward-chaining production system architecture can be viewed as one particularly suitable for dealing with data opportunistically, as it arrives. It is also suitable for dealing with synthetic tasks, such as configuration of computer systems or flexible manufacturing systems where there are very large numbers of possible goal states and there is really no choice but to be driven by the data to a suitable goal.

The possibility of backward-chaining and a goal-directed strategy represents a considerable extension to the power of a production system. Often a subtask will involve a small number of pre-enumerated goals. For example, a medical diagnosis system dealing with microbial infections might have only 20 candidates. Backward-chaining gives a focused and efficient way to deal with such a situation. Recent systems, such as ART, offer hybrid strategies, with both types of chaining. Such systems have to be used with care, as noted below.

5.4.3 Permissible Actions

The action part of a rule normally contain a series of actions to modify the contents of working memory, by adding, removing or altering facts. Facts are added to working memory as new information is inferred. Facts can be retracted, to prevent their being matched in future rule selection. Facts can be modified, to add information about them.

Other types of action may include side-effects such as output to the user of the system, or to some other subsystem. Such actions make the effect of a rule firing externally visible. Additionally, actions might alter some global state information within the overall system, or even modify the rule memory itself. Such assertion and retraction can cause problems, particularly with hybrid control strategies. Such a strategy may find a rule sequence by backward-chaining in an attempt to prove a goal. If in the course of this chaining a rule fires forward, side-effects may destroy the justifications of the current state, since facts (and rules) may be retracted or asserted that invalidate that state. If it is desired to use such non-monotonic reasoning, the programmer will have to be very careful indeed to ensure adequate control of side effects. ART recognizes this problem by offering an assumption-based truth maintenance system (known as Viewpoints). It would be fair to say that this area is still not understood well.

Other possible forms of interference are global side-effects which alter conflict-resolution strategies or heuristics. Again, it is the job of the programmer to deal with this in a principled way.

5.4.4 Improved Representation of Domain Knowledge

First, a production system provides an empty 'shell' in which domain knowledge can be embedded. It can be used to implement any system you want - a credit-card authorizer, a chemical spill disaster system, an assistant to help intelligence analysts to deal with international terrorism, or whatever. At least, that is what the vendors tell you.

Real-life experience serves to modify this simplistic view. Any given domain will have specific representation requirements. For example, the spill system might require the representation of a drainage system as some sort of graph which can be searched. The international terrorist system could involve the representation of a taxonomy of terrorist organizations. It would be convenient if such representations were easily implementable and easy to manipulate.

Second, a production system is not really an empty shell. The interpreter contains proceduralized metaknowledge about how to deal with rules. It would be useful if this metaknowledge were available for use and manipulation (Clancey, 1983).

We will now consider these two factors in detail.

5.4.5 Complex Domain Knowledge

The simple way in which facts about domain objects are recorded in a classical production system makes it difficult to represent complex information, such as:

(1)   a cluster of facts about a given object;

(2)   complex relationships between objects, such as taxonomies;

(3)   information about prototypical objects;

(4)   exception information about object classes or instances.

Logic-based representations, semantic networks and frames are often more convenient representations. For example, in a frame system, it would be possible to define a frame to represent the class of small companies and to create instance frames to represent individual companies. It would then be possible to deal with

```
(frame   ABC_ltd
          (instance-of small-company)
          (capitalization  100000)
          (market-sector double-glazing)
          (created 1984))
```

rather than the facts:

```
(small-company ABC_ltd)
(capitalization ABC_ltd 100000)
(market-sector ABC_ltd double-glazing)
(created ABC_ltd 1984)
```

Examples of additional representational power added to production systems are CENTAUR (Aikins, 1983), which uses frames to represent knowledge about the form of a consultation and the taxonomy of lung diseases (see Chapter 8), and AM (Lenat, 1982), which uses frames to represent "interesting" mathematical concepts.

Other areas where there are particular representational problems are the representation of uncertain knowledge and knowledge about time (temporal knowledge). The latter is treated by Kwong in Chapter 9.

5.4.6 Domain-related Control Knowledge: R1 as a Case Study

One of the advantages of production systems is that the control knowledge is simple and is embedded in the interpreter. But often we have a great deal of domain-derived knowledge concerning control, and find some difficulty fitting this into the Procrustean bed provided. We wish to use our own metaknowledge, rather than that supplied.

As a case study, it is useful to consider the control aspects of the R1 system used by DEC to configure VAX and PDP11 minicomputers (McDermott, 1982b; Bachant and McDermott, 1984). (R1 is known within DEC as XCON. The original name, according to McDermott, came from his realization in 1982 that "Four years ago I couldn't even say knowledge engineer, now I ...").

The implementation language of the present version is OPS5. The syntax of OPS5 is similar to the simple system described in section 5.2. The language has been optimized for maximum efficiency of the computationally expensive process of pattern matching. It uses a mechanism known as Rete match (Forgy, 1981, 1982) which avoids the repetition of attempted matches, as a collection of production rule antecedents are matched with a collection of working memory elements.

OPS5 is a general-purpose production system language - it "knows" nothing of the configuration task. However, it is used in R1 to represent the knowledge used in configuration. The interesting question is how good, in some sense, is the representation?

The task itself is complex, and divides into two subtasks:

(1) check that the order from the customer for the set of items that make up a VAX (or PDP11) minicomputer system is complete, and correct it if it is not;

(2) determine the spatial arrangement of the components.

The output is a correct component list and a set of diagrams specifying the cabinets required, the position of the units within the cabinets, the control panels, the cabling and the floor plan.

What is required is a satisfactory solution, with no missing or unwanted components, and without excessive unused space within the cabinets.

A sample rule, to illustrate the type of knowledge used, is:

RULE VERIFY-SBI-AND-MB-DEVICE-ADEQUACY-3
>   IF   the most current active context is verifying
>   SBI and Massbus adequacy
>   AND   there are more than two memory controllers on the order
>   THEN mark the extra controllers as unsupported
>   (i.e. not to be configured)
>   AND   make a note to the salesperson that only two memory
>   controllers are permitted per order.

(Rendered into near-English from OPS5)

The meaning of this rule is reasonably obvious (even though what SBI and Massbus mean might have to be guessed by the reader). What is not apparent is the nature of the configuration strategy.

There are not a small number of configurations which can be recorded or generated and then tested for suitability. There are a very large number of possible configurations, and it is simply not possible to search the solution space blindly. The search has to be massively constrained. Part of the knowledge elicitation process was to get the technical editors (the domain experts) to expose these constraints. McDermott determined that the experts:

(a)   have a highly reliable, if sparse, picture of their task domain, which they describe in terms of the subtasks involved and the temporal relationships between these subtasks.

They describe 6 major subtasks:

1.   determine gross errors in the order;

2.   put the appropriate components in the cpu cabinets;

3.   configure the boxes and the components in the boxes in the unibus expansion cabinets;

4.   put the panels in the expansion cabinets;

5.   lay out the system on the floor;

6.   do the cabling.

(b)   have a great deal of detailed knowledge about how unconfigured components (ones that have not yet been assigned positions etc.) and particular partial configurations can be extended in particular ways.

He found that it was relatively easy to express this task knowledge as rules. Originally there were about 100 concerned with which subtask was to be initiated and about 400 rules concerned with situations in which some partial task was to be extended. The design process did contain a certain amount of backtracking as a state was transformed into the succeeding state. What McDermott did was to slightly redesign the process of transforming from state to state (from partial configuration to slightly less partial configuration) so that a possible solution is always available at any stage and it will never be necessary to undo that solution and retry. This seems to be possible since certain features of the domain are not too closely constrained. For example, a power supply does not have to be fully loaded; a panel does not have to be totally filled up, and nor does the space in a box; a data bus does not have to have the maximum number of devices attached to it. Search can be eliminated by providing a generously wide path.

The major stages of configuration are known in R1 as contexts. The word "context" has been used with a variety of meanings in knowledge engineering. It usually refers to some mechanism which provides some degree of focusing of rule use, and involves metalevel knowledge, which might be explicit or implicit. In R1, this metalevel knowledge is about configuration stages. In other systems, it may be about other aspects of the problem. As is explained in Chapter 8, the MYCIN medical system contains metalevel knowledge about the types of objects relevant to a consultation about a patient with a microbial infection, and this knowledge is represented in a "context tree". As far as the present discussion goes, the important points are that both the types of knowledge elicited from the domain experts have been represented in the R1 system, and that different expert systems may have different architectures depending on their application domains.

R1 is a successful system, and has to date processed about 90000 orders, each one taking about 2.5 minutes, including the printing of the results. Its success has been facilitated by the careful design of OPS5, particularly by the fast matching provided by the Rete algorithm. However, a great deal of its success is due to McDermott's knowledge engineering skill. His elicitation and redesign of the experts' heuristics have made it a realistic system - not the rather limited representational power of OPS5.

R1 has now grown to 6200 rules, of which approximately 50% change every year (Soloway *et al.*, 1987). Its performance continues to be satisfactory, but it is becoming increasingly difficult to change. It seems that the problems of updating this large piece of software are growing more than linearly. Soloway and his research partners at DEC attribute this to:

(1) the dynamic properties of rules. To obtain the required sequencing, "tricks" have been used to override the domain-independent conflict resolution strategy of OPS5. This explicit domain-dependent control knowledge is encoded as extra clauses to rules, and can be hard to

understand by the different programmers working on the rule-base.

(2)   the static properties of rules. The action part of an OPS5 rule can be almost anything. As pointed out in section 5.4.3, great care is needed to avoid unwanted side-effects. When a new device is available from DEC, what has happened is that the programmers have often created a new rule to represent the system's knowledge of that device by editing a pre-existing rule for a similar device, possibly without always being sure what the rationale for all the functions is.

This implies that what software engineers call a "degradation in integrity" is occurring in R1's rule-base. Parnas (1985) reports:

> That example is always the same − a program designed to find configurations for VAX computers. ... Recently I read a paper that reported that this program had become a maintenance nightmare. It was poorly understood, badly structured, and hence hard to change.

What Soloway *et al.* are proposing is a design for a re-implementation of R1 (XCON). The knowledge base is to be re-expressed in a language called RIME, which will then be compiled into a runnable OPS5 form. It will be possible in RIME to make domain knowledge more explicit, both in structuring the rules themselves and in controlling rule firing, in a similar way to that suggested and implemented by Clancey (1983) with respect to the knowledge in the MYCIN systems. The new system (XCON-IN-RIME) will be built with the help of the rule developers from DEC (by metaknowledge engineers?)

The reader might find it of value to compare this short case study with that done in Chapter 8 of MYCIN. Similar problems of metalevel control and the encoding of different types of knowledge within a homogeneous rule syntax seem to have come to light. At a lower level, the Rete algorithm of OPS5 is paralleled by fast hashing algorithms underlying EMYCIN (van Melle, 1981) and Interlisp (Kaisler, 1986).

5.5 Summary

5.5.1 Advantages of Production Systems

(1)   Production systems exhibit useful modularity, in that rules are independent of each other, and of the rest of the system. Each rule encodes a 'chunk' of independent domain knowledge.

(2)　The explicit representation of rules permits the system to allow enquiries about rules, such as what rules would indicate a particular conclusion.

(3)　The straightforward if-then form of a rule often maps well into English, for purposes of explanation.

(4)　Simple chaining methods can be used to implement inference procedures which are not unlike those used by humans. Production rule systems can be built which seem to model closely human problem solving in some domains.

(5)　Very large rule-based systems can be built which model expert behaviour in narrow domains, e.g. medical diagnosis and computer system configuration.

5.5.2 Disadvantages of Production Systems

(1)　For each rule, information has to exist in the system somewhere as to its context of use. This can result in overlarge rule antecedents, or in implicit knowledge, such as that contained in rule order. Either way, control knowledge is often not clear.

(2)　Rule sets have no intrinsic structure, which makes management of large knowledge bases difficult.

(3)　Not all human problem-solving methods are easily represented in the production method formalism.

(4)　The matching involved in the match-select-fire is an inherently inefficient computational process. This has serious implications for realistic applications.

(5)　Because of the independence of the rules from each other and from the control strategy, it is all but impossible to determine rigorously properties of the system's behaviour by static analysis. It is necessary to test the system with the data of interest to see what it will do. Since realistic production systems cannot be exhaustively tested, they cannot be used in safety-critical applications.

5.5.3 Further Reading

Introductory texts

Young (1987) gives a simplified account of the field with various clearly-explained examples. Hasemer (1984) fully describes a Lisp implementation, with special reference to matching and conflict resolution.

Research texts

There is a noteworthy collection of papers (Waterman and Hayes-Roth, 1978), now rather dated. Brownston *et al.* (1985) and Buchanan and Shortliffe (1984) describe recent research.

Human problem-solving and its modelling

Simon and Newell's work is well-documented (Newell and Simon, 1972). A more recent reference is Klahr *et al.* (1986).

Applications

One of the largest users of production systems technology is Digital Equipment Corporation (DEC). See Kraft (1987) and Polit (1985).

New architectures

Both hardware and software architectures are being designed. See Lehr and Wedig (1987) and Rosenbloom *et al.* (1985).

5.6 Concluding Remarks

Production systems have a long and respectable history as a knowledge representation formalism. They have been used for the modelling of human cognitive processes and as an implementation language for knowledge-based systems. It has been possible to abstract from the implementations guidelines and metrics which are being used to design new hardware and software architectures to embody problem-solving strategies.

6 Psychological Studies of Knowledge Representation

Tony Conway and Michael Wilson

6.1 Introduction

The only model we have for a working intelligent system which uses and represents large amounts of knowledge is the human. This chapter describes psychological studies which investigate some of the knowledge representation schemes suggested as structures for representing human knowledge. By including a psychological viewpoint on knowledge representation it is being argued neither that the human should be a model for machine representation, nor that artificial intelligence studies should be the model on which psychological descriptions should be based. It is, however, assumed that an exchange of ideas would be fruitful between two fields where an understanding of knowledge representation is desired, both to examine possible representations and to identify phenomena against which to evaluate them.

The first section of this chapter will outline the motivations and concerns that guide psychological studies, so as to provide a background in which to place the remainder of the chapter. The second section describes various forms of representation that have been suggested for human knowledge of procedures, semantics and images which specify control and representation to different degrees. The third section then describes the use of reasoning by humans and the representation formulated as *mental models*. This approach illustrates how more than one type of representational format can be combined to represent the knowledge required to support the inferencing demanded by a variety of tasks.

6.1.1 Methodology in Cognitive Psychology

Common-sense psychology provides explanations for people's actions in terms of motives and desires. In contrast, explanations in cognitive psychology, are phrased in terms of the mental processes and representations drawn on during the performance of tasks such as problem solving and comprehension. Unlike explanations in common-sense psychology, explanations in cognitive psychology are presented as theories and models which can be tested experimentally.

Experiments designed to test hypotheses about knowledge representation do so by testing differences in the performance of tasks when some aspect of those tasks is manipulated. Since such experiments are performed by measuring behavioural phenomena, models are described in terms of the constraints of the experimental situation as well as the theoretical mental processes and representations. For example, experiments that test the representation of conceptual relationships such as 'DOG is a MAMMAL' will actually test subjects' performance on tasks involving the confirmation of statements such as 'a dog is a mammal' and the disconfirmation of statements such as 'a dog is a fish'. For models of performance on such tasks to yield testable hypotheses, they must include accounts of the decisions and the responses which are made, as well as the representation of knowledge. Therefore, it is these models of task performance, rather than the theories of knowledge representation, which are actually being experimentally tested. Consequently, much of the psychological debate about knowledge representation will be a debate about details of the models of experimentally testable performance, rather than abstract representation schemes themselves. It has even been forcefully argued (Anderson, 1978) that it is impossible to evaluate any claim for a particular sort of representation unless the processes that operate on that representation are specified in the theory. In the descriptions which follow, these issues of task performance will be avoided as much as possible, but it should be borne in mind that they provide the basis for any statements that are made about knowledge representation.

Different experimental tasks offer different views of the underlying knowledge representation. Therefore, models developed for different techniques will be models of the cognitive system from different viewpoints. Theories will, consequently, also be presented from different viewpoints on knowledge representation. If these theories use different terms, it does not follow that they are incompatible, merely that they focus on different aspects of the cognitive system. In cognitive psychology (as in other sciences) there can, of course, be more than one theory that explains the data: no observations can ever establish definitely that a single unique theory is the correct one, although the converse is, of course, true.

6.1.2 Levels of Description

In order to interpret psychological theories it is necessary to understand the level of description they offer, not only of the data, but also of the cognitive system.

When providing explanations of psychological phenomena there are at least four possible levels of description. Firstly, there is a general competence level. Descriptions at this level include linguistic theories of grammar that describe the knowledge which an individual may tacitly hold about a language, but do not describe how an individual puts that knowledge to work in speaking and understanding. An example of an explanation at this level in the field of computer science would be the theory of possible database structures. Secondly, there is an algorithmic level of description. A computational example at this level would be a specification of the algorithm for a relational database. Thirdly, there is an implementational level description. This would describe the details of the algorithm as implemented in a particular program. Fourthly, there is an implementational description which includes details of the substrate in which the implementation is made. In a computational example, an explanation of the structure of the circuitry on which a particular algorithm for a database is implemented would be at this level. A psychological example of this level of explanation would be a theory of visual perception which specifies the neurophysiological structures that perform the required computation. Newell (1982) has also argued that a theory of cognition in a particular domain first demands a theory of the domain itself, which he calls the *knowledge level*. This is not a level on the same dimension as the four levels of description of process or representation, but is a requirement for a theory of content. In Newell's terms, the levels distinguished here are all at the *symbol level* since they appertain not to the content of the information that is represented but the form of representation described.

Most theories in cognitive psychology are described at the algorithmic level, in that they draw functional distinctions between mental processes and explanations, without giving details of the exact implementation or the neurophysiological structures. For example, three forms of mental representation are generally posited. The first is a propositionally based approach in which knowledge is assumed to be represented as a set of discrete symbols or propositions. The second is to use an analogical representation in which the correspondence between the represented world and the representation is as direct as possible, traditionally using images and other analogical representations. The third form is a procedural representation in which knowledge is assumed to be represented in terms of active processes or procedures, directly interpretable by action systems. This distinction is one at the algorithmic level, since at the implementational level everything could undoubtedly be reduced to a common code in the language of the brain, just as the data structures of high level programming languages can be reduced to patterns of bits in the machine code of a computer. There has recently been great interest in the proposal for a common code of representation (McClelland, Rumelhart and the PDP Research Group, 1986) in terms of parallel distributed processing. It is an issue of debate (see Broadbent, 1985; Rumelhart and McClelland, 1985) whether this description lies at the algorithmic or the implementation level; however, it will not be discussed further here. Within the algorithmic level of description, most theories in cognitive psychology are built on the view that the human is an information processing device.

6.1.3 The Human Information Processing Paradigm

The currently dominant view of cognitive processing is that it proceeds in a linear, sequential fashion through a series of stages (Norman and Bobrow, 1976). Details of the stages vary from one author to another, but the general assumption is that processing in task performance proceeds from the perception of cues; the processing of these cues in a short-term memory to retrieve action plans from long-term memory and then the execution of plans by effector systems responsible for the articulation of sounds or physical movement.

A more detailed description of the working model would be that signals (auditory, visual, tactile) are received by transducers, which transform them into a form which can be stored in a temporary sensory information store. Pattern recognition processes then attempt to identify the physical signals by matching them against stored patterns in long-term memory. If a match is found, then a word or concept which identifies that pattern will be stored in short-term memory (STM). Without this information being actively maintained in STM (by methods such as its rehearsal) it will be lost within a few seconds. The concept will be processed to construct a description which will be used to retrieve items from long-term memory. After processing, a plan will be passed to effector systems where it will become an action. The perceived concept and a record of processing may themselves be encoded and stored more permanently in long-term memory than in STM.

There are several memory systems used by the general human information processor. The perceptual memory systems are very short term stores of the transducers' output. The short-term memory is more complex. Early experiments (Miller, 1956) illustrated that educated adults can repeat back about seven digits, words or letters. This storage could be increased if there was a structure to the items which permitted their chunking into categories. For example, twenty words could be remembered instead of seven, if there were five words from each of four categories. This initial description of a device with a limited capacity which can apparently be increased by the imposition of categorization has been developed so that contemporary theories (for example, the working memory model of Baddeley, 1983) include not only the main short-term memory (or central executive) but also limited capacity stores for verbal material (an articulatory loop), and spatial imagery (a visio-spatial scratchpad). Similarly, it has been suggested that the long-term memory store can be divided. Tulving (1972; 1984) has suggested that in our long-term memory we have both a memory for procedures and a declarative memory which is further split between episodic knowledge and semantic knowledge. Episodic knowledge concerns temporally dated episodes or events, and temporal-spatial relations among them, whereas semantic knowledge is information which a person possesses about words, their meaning, and rules for the manipulation of symbols, concepts and relations.

Much of the research on the representation of knowledge in short-term memory has focused on issues about the sensory form in which that information is perceived and processed. In contrast, most of the research on long-term memory has focused on how it is encoded, indexed and retrieved. Some of these studies and the models that result from them will be discussed in the remainder of this chapter.

6.2 Suggested Knowledge Representation Schemes

Several forms of knowledge representation will be described along with the arguments as to their relevance to the general model of the human information processor outlined above. It was noted above that, at the algorithmic level of description, there are generally suggested to be three forms of representation: procedural representation; propositional representation; and analogical representation. A complementary distinction between forms of knowledge representation is in the way that the control of the representation is handled. The first form of representation discussed focuses on the control of the representation while specifying a very general structure for that representation itself. The second form discussed is a procedural representation which combines the control and representation into a single form. The other forms use: propositional representations with other levels of more abstract content patterns to organize and index the propositional information (schemata and frames); lower level propositional representations of concepts (semantic nets and semantic feature models); and analogical representations. The focus of these forms of representation is on the structure of the representation rather than on their control. The later sections will describe an approach which suggests how a combination of these approaches can be used to represent the knowledge used to make inferences in a variety of tasks.

6.2.1 Headed Records

The Headed Records approach to memory has been proposed as a powerful framework within which a wide range of data and observations can be encompassed (Morton, Hammersley and Bekerian, 1985). In particular, the framework is aimed at encompassing observations of day to day remembering and forgetting. The model of memory suggested is very simple in principle. It consists of a set of discrete records into which our experience has been divided by some means. Each record is associated with a heading. The heading is made up of a number of distinct elements, not necessarily related or of the same kind. Thus, the heading for a record about a particular individual may include his name, a representation of his face, and his relationship to the owner of the record. Single events may be encoded in more than one record, but there are no explicit pointers from one record to another to indicate a relationship or continuation.

These records are accessed much as a file is accessed in a filing cabinet. To locate a file of which a description is known, a drawer is searched by reading the headings on the files until a heading is found which matches that description; then that file is retrieved for further examination. Within the headed records framework, the demands of a specific task are turned into a retrieval specification. This is an intermediate stage in which relevant material is assembled. The specification can include the purpose for which the information is required, such contextual information as one has concerning the conditions under which the information sought was originally encoded, and a more or less complete description of the information being sought. Unlike other theories where descriptions have direct access to record contents (e.g. Norman and Bobrow, 1979; Williams, 1978), in the headed records framework the description is used to match with only the headings of memory records. Not all the elements in the heading need be matched by the description, nor all the description be found in the heading. When the heading is matched, the consequence is that the record is accessed. The information in the heading will not be made available for further processing; the heading is solely a means of accessing the record. When a record is accessed it has to be evaluated for suitability according to criteria established with the retrieval specification. As a result of this evaluation, the record may be judged to be the one sought. Alternatively, information in the record may be used to refine the description or the verification process; then the record will be rejected, and the cycle recommenced.

One feature which distinguishes the headed records approach from most other attempts to describe complex remembering using semantic nets or frames (e.g. Norman and Rumelhart, 1975; Anderson, 1976) is that there are no direct connections between records. When the system is operating to narrate a story which covers several records, each record will provide the information required to produce a suitable description for the next one in the sequence. This information will always be content based, and never a direct internal pointer. There are two further principles of the headed records framework which make it unusual. Firstly, unlike many other theories that demand overwritable or decaying records (e.g. Loftus and Loftus, 1980), once a record has been laid down there will be no loss or change to it other than what might be called 'physiological decay'. Secondly, unlike several other accounts, in the headed records framework, when memory is being searched for a record, headings are scanned strictly in sequence from the most recent backwards in time.

This simple model of memory and knowledge representation is able to account for many of the phenomena associated with remembering and forgetting information. A full description of these phenomena cannot be given here, but an account of one may make the operation of the memory model more clear.

It has been suggested that memory representations for scenes and events can be altered by subsequent presentations of misinformation concerning what had been presented. In one study (Loftus, 1975), subjects were presented with a filmed car accident. Later they were told that a barn had appeared in the film. Although the barn had not appeared in the film, over 17% of the subjects, when questioned a week later, agreed that they had indeed seen a barn. This compared to 3% of agreement by subjects who had not been given this piece of misinformation. This result may be explained by a representation scheme which permits the overwriting of the record of the original event by the misinformation. It can also be explained in the headed records framework by assuming that when the misinformation is given, a new record is laid down describing the accident. When the subjects are later questioned, they search their memory starting at the most recent events and locate the record containing the misinformation before the original record of the accident. A second study (Bekerian and Bowers, 1983) using a similar technique and materials has shown that when sufficient cues are given during the questioning to facilitate subjects' access to the original memory, that memory is retrieved instead of the misleading information. This evidence is consistent with the original record being maintained, and inconsistent with the view that the original record is updated. This example also illustrates two general mechanisms for forgetting in this framework. Firstly, that new records are laid down after an event with headings that satisfy descriptions which would be created to access the original record, and yet the new records do not contain the detail in their bodies that the originals did. Secondly, that the description used at a second retrieval may not be as rich as that used at the retrieval that illustrated that the knowledge was encoded, and subsequently could not access the relevant record.

6.2.2 Procedural Knowledge

Most of our knowledge is declarative, in that it makes statements about the world. For example, a statement of the form "This chapter was written by two authors" is a typical declarative statement. Knowledge about how to change gear when driving a car is a typical piece of procedural knowledge. We can generally describe our declarative knowledge, as it tends to be accessible, but procedural knowledge is rarely accessible or describable. Thus, although we can change gear in our cars when driving, in order to describe how we do it, we have to imagine the movements of the foot on the clutch and the hand on the gear stick, and enact the procedure. Then we can describe this enactment. We do not have access directly to the knowledge we use when performing the task. One can obviously represent a procedure for performing a task as a declarative sequence of propositions. Therefore, the feature of procedural knowledge that distinguishes it from declarative knowledge is that it cannot be retrieved in the same form as declarative knowledge. This distinction is therefore one concerning the control of the representation as well as the representation itself.

One can separate the control and the representation mechanism for procedural knowledge to give rise to the required effects. For example, one could represent procedural knowledge in the headed records framework by having headings to the records for procedural knowledge that were inaccessible to descriptions produced for the task of describing the contents of those records. Alternatively, one could allow access to procedural knowledge by the process that verbalizes descriptions, but those records would be written in a code that this process could not interpret. However, the major form of representation suggested for procedural knowledge is the production system (Newell, 1973) which uses a procedural representation rather than a separation of representation and control. Productions are active data structures that sit above a database (or 'working memory') waiting for patterns relevant to them. Whenever such conditions occur for a production, it will be 'triggered', and perform its actions. These actions usually involve writing something to working memory, deleting or changing items in working memory. These actions will set up conditions which will allow other productions to 'trigger'. A production therefore contains a procedure to be enacted and a representation of a control structure, thereby containing a combination of the two elements required to differentiate procedural from declarative knowledge. The common data structure in a production system is usually called the 'working memory', and the 'condition → action' relation is stated within each production (or production rule) and commonly has the following structure:

IF *condition-for-triggering* → THEN *do-these-actions.*

The architecture of production systems with a working memory and a body of production rules is argued to match that of human processing. Consequently, various models of human processing have been proposed which incorporate production rules (e.g. Anderson, 1983; Kieras and Polson, 1985). Three properties of production systems in particular have been equated with aspects of human processing. Firstly, working memory may correspond to short-term memory, but the unlimited size of working memory in such models, and the actual size of working memory required to get production systems to work correctly, far exceed estimates for human short-term memory. Secondly, production rules are modular, which can permit their addition and deletion from carefully structured systems without affecting other knowledge or control structures in the system. This property has been employed to model learning and the acquisition of new skilled procedures (e.g. Anderson, 1983). Thirdly, the control mechanism of production systems permits a conflict between rules with the same conditions, or subsets of one another's conditions, as to which should act. This conflict has been used to model the failures in skilled behaviour exhibited by humans when we select the wrong skill routine. For example, when one hears the door bell and the telephone ring at the same time, picks up the telephone and says "Come in". Such action sequences can be described by the firing of a production rule to lift the telephone and then another to respond to the door, because its conditions appear to be met, although the resulting actions are inappropriate. There are various conflict resolution procedures that can be used by production systems to order the operation of rules which give rise to, or avoid, such conflicts (e.g. the computer language OPS5). However, to be experimentally testable a particular production system must have such details exactly specified. There is a body of research which investigates particular production systems (e.g. Anderson, 1983) but this does not bear on the potential of production systems in general for representing knowledge. The major limitation on production systems in general as models of human knowledge representation remains the lack of a limitation on the size of working memory. Until this fundamental inconsistency is overcome, production systems remain a form of representation which alone cannot represent the architecture of cognition, but must be incorporated with other mechanisms and forms of representation. The most obvious forms of representation which must be included are those which will account for declarative, verbally describable knowledge, such as schemata or semantic nets.

6.2.3 Schemata and Frames

Schemata and frames are discussed at length in Chapter 4 of this volume: in this chapter, they will only be discussed as possible forms of human knowledge representation. Although the idea of schemata has roots which go back as far as Kant (1787), its introduction to psychology was through the work of Bartlett. In one of his most famous studies (Bartlett, 1932) he used a story based on a North American Indian Legend 'War of the Ghosts'. He gave this story to people to read and then tested their recall for it after various time intervals. Bartlett was concerned with the systematic errors which non-Indians made in recalling the story (he deliberately chose a story which did not fit with the cultural pre-conceptions of the subjects in his experiment). His subjects forgot aspects of the story which were incompatible with their knowledge.

To account for his findings, Bartlett proposed that when the story was read, subjects recruited abstract representations of knowledge which are generally used for encoding and retrieval. These abstract representations are not tied into any specific event knowledge; they are called schemata. Secondly, he proposed that they created a schematized representation of the story. In this version, the "irrelevant" event-specific information will have been lost and schematic default information will have been assumed to apply and be stored as being present. To be confusing, this schematized representation of an event is also called a schema (e.g. Bartlett, 1932; Rumelhart and Ortony, 1976). In general, it is the deduced schematized representations of an event which are cited as evidence for the existence of schemata. There is evidence that schematized representations exist (Bransford and Franks, 1971; Bartlett, 1932; Owens, Bower and Black, 1979; Friedman, 1978; Galambos, Abelson and Black, 1986). However, schematized representations could arise through the type of post-event restructuring of knowledge suggested in the headed records approach. The more problematic and significant issue is whether abstract schemata exist.

The most influential introduction of schemata into the AI community has been as frames (Minsky, 1975), which were developed to show how knowledge should be interrelated so that computational systems could use knowledge efficiently. However, the form which has resulted in most psychological study is that of scripts (Schank and Abelson, 1977). These were developed to account for the ability of readers to fill in information required to understand the simplest text. For example, to understand the two sentences 'Tony sat down in the restaurant. The waiter took his order.' we need to have a lot of knowledge about restaurants. We need to know the role of the waiter, and that 'ordering' refers to a request for food prepared in restaurants. Schank and Abelson referred to such social knowledge frames, or schemata, as 'scripts'. Scripts represent performed, ordered sets of knowledge about stereotyped cultural events. There would therefore be a script for visiting the restaurant, the doctor or the dentist. The possession of a script allows a speaker to leave many things unsaid with the certainty that a listener will fill them in by default. If enough is stated to elicit the appropriate script then it can be used to fill in unstated detail. Since scripts only describe stereotyped events, a separate mechanism was envisaged which would create plans of less usual events.

Among the psychological studies following this work, Bower, Black and Turner (1979) demonstrated that when people read a story about a visit to a dentist and a story about a visit to a doctor they were confused in their later recognition of which events were in which story. They found that such confusions were situated within similar scenes across different scripts. This led Schank to reform the notion of scripts so that they describe smaller units, such as the paying scene, which would apply to various situations, or the waiting room scene which would apply to visits to both doctors and dentists. Schank (1980) proposed that, instead of scripts, we have many general scenes in memory called MOPS (Memory Organization Packages) which are dynamically assembled into higher level structures. These are built into structures that resemble scripts, but also account for the memory confusions found experimentally. However, the main limitation on scripts remains that they only specify knowledge about events that are stereotyped, whereas knowledge is also used to understand events and discourse which are *not* stereotyped.

One area of knowledge where stereotyping is less problematic is the representation of word meaning. Berlin and Kay (1969) asked native speakers of twenty different languages to select coloured chips which represented the best examples of each of their language's basic colour terms. They also asked their subjects to select chips which delineated the boundaries between colour terms. There was very little consistency in the choice of boundary chips; however, there was a reliable consensus about the choice of the best exemplars of a colour. Indeed, this agreement extended across many of the twenty languages. This, and subsequent studies by Rosch (e.g. Rosch, 1976), have been used to argue that many natural categories are mentally represented by *prototypes*. These prototypes are schemata of a category's most characteristic members: in the way that a robin is a prototypical bird, whereas other birds have a greater distance from the schema, e.g. a chicken. Although this approach has been developed for 'kind' notions (like *dog, bird,* and *animal*), 'artifact' notions and simple descriptive notions (e.g. 'triangular'), it has not been extended to intricate concepts such as *belief, desire,* and *justice* and it is an open question whether or not the theory can be extended to cover these cases. The second problem with prototype theory lies in the mechanism for conceptual combination. Methods such as fuzzy logic have been suggested for the combination of prototypes, but these seem to result in as many new problems as they solve (see Osherson and Smith,

1981).

Schemata offer high level representations and rules about representation-specific processes. It is argued by their proponents that these are required to supplement the descriptions of processes and representations which are derived from a small number of general principles. The experimental evidence from psychological studies of schemata supports the view that representations are constructed which appear to be schematized. However, there is little evidence for the existence of abstract schemata themselves. Although there are effects which are best explained by stereotyping and the use of defaults, the size of the units that are stereotyped is not certain. Although such problems still exist with the suggested human use of schemata to represent knowledge they do not detract from the potential of schemata as a form of representation for machine use. The problem of the combination of concepts which are represented as schemata or stereotypes and the use of stereotypes to represent non-stereotypical concepts are problems both for the psychological representation of stereotypes and machine representation. These issues are discussed in Chapter 4 of this volume.

Schemata and frames have been suggested as top-down mechanisms to represent general high level knowledge, and prototypes have been used to represent concepts. A second class of representations which use bottom-up processes to represent concepts and word meanings includes the semantic net, and semantic feature models.

6.2.4 Semantic Nets and Semantic Feature Models

The 'semantic net' was developed by Quillian (1966) and others both as an exercise in artificial intelligence and as a possible psychological model of human associative memory. Semantic nets are an extension of the well established idea in psychology of associations. In behavioural psychology these took the form of associations between stimuli and responses, but the best known example is that of word association. Quillian argued that among the properties of concepts were several special property relations that are commonly found. They are special because they permit certain kinds of inferences to be made. A frequently used kind is the *superset* or superordinate relation (e.g. a mammal is an animal). These superset relations will chain like: dog → canine → mammal → animal → living thing → object. Each item in such a structure is termed a 'unit' which can have properties attached to it. A property represents some descriptive feature of a unit, such as would be represented by an English verb phrase. Thus the unit MAMMAL might be linked with a number of properties, such as *has hair, provides milk* and so forth. Each property is stored in the highest level to which it applies. Hence *has hair* is stored with MAMMAL rather than with each individual instance, thereby reducing the amount of storage space. All properties of a superset can also hold for the instances of that superset unless otherwise indicated. In the case of an exception, the fact that the property does not apply is stored with the unit itself. Therefore, to determine a property of a concept a simple three-step procedure can be applied which avoids conflicts which could arise from inconsistent data in a network:

Step 1. In determining properties of concepts, look first at the node for the concept.

Step 2. If the information is not found, go up one node along the relation and apply the property of inheritance.

Step 3. Repeat step 2 until either there is success or there are no more nodes.

This work attracted little attention until a series of experimental studies by Collins and Quillian (1969). The model was tested by presenting subjects with a series of sentences and measuring the time taken to decide whether they were true or false (reaction time). The model predicts that reaction time should depend, first, on the number of levels of the hierarchy that must be traversed (e.g. *a dog is an animal*) and, second, on whether or not a property must be retrieved (e.g. *a dog has hair*). As predicted, reaction time increases linearly with the number of levels of the hierarchy that must be traversed, in that it takes longer to decide that *a canary has feathers* than that *a canary is yellow*. Although this evidence supports the network representation, there is evidence against this simple view of processing. In a hierarchical representation of the sort suggested, the decision that *a pine is not a flower* would be made by finding that there was no path joining the two items. This would imply that the nature of the negative instance should be unimportant, so long as no legitimate path exists. However, as Schaeffer and Wallace (1969) and Wilkins (1971) showed, it takes longer to decide that a *pine* is not a flower, than that a *chair* is not a flower, suggesting that some sort of discrimination takes place, even though no permissible path exists. The more features a negative instance has in common with a category, the longer it will take to reject. A second body of evidence against a hierarchical model is that it fails to predict differences within categories, while such differences have often been found. Subjects can verify a dominant or typical member of a category consistently more rapidly than they can in the case of a less typical one. That is to say, it takes less time to verify that a *robin* is a bird, than that a *chicken* is. A third problem for the simple hierarchical model comes from a study by Rips, Shoben and Smith (1973), who showed that subjects took longer to decide whether some items were members of the class MAMMAL than to decide if they were 'animals' despite the fact that MAMMAL is a subset of the class ANIMAL. This probably reflects subjects' greater familiarity with the concept of an ANIMAL than the concept of a MAMMAL, since these judgements correlate with the rated semantic distance between an instance and its category.

Two alternative classes of representations arose to account for this evidence against the early hierarchical networks as models of human representation. Firstly, more complex theories of processing were developed for semantic network representations themselves which would be capable of representing sentence meaning as a network of labelled associations rather than just being a simple hierarchy supporting inheritance. Secondly, Smith, Shoben and Rips (1974) proposed a 'feature comparison' model as an alternative to a hierarchical structure, using inheritance as a model of the representation which supports performance in the class of tasks investigated.

The basic representational assumption of this model is that words representing categories can be represented by a set of features that vary in their relationship to the formal definition of the category. Features are of two types: 'defining features', must be true if an item is a member of a category; 'characteristic features' usually apply, but are not necessary for a definition. Thus 'has feathers' is a definitional feature for the concept BIRD, whereas 'can fly' is a 'characteristic feature' (although most birds fly, it is not part of the definition since some birds do not show this characteristic). They suggested that category membership was not a pre-stored attribute, but was computed by a comparison of a set of features. They proposed a two-stage model of the verification of category membership. The first stage involved a quick comparison of all the features, both definitional and characteristic. If the comparison was good enough, the statement would be confirmed. If the comparison was poor enough, the statement would be rejected. Intermediate comparisons would result in a slower comparison process using only definitional features. This model accounts for the basic experimental results in that: true statements using items typical of categories are quickly confirmed; false statements involving typical items are quickly rejected; decisions on less typical items take longer.

Although feature models offer good accounts of the experimental data, they are almost always limited to nominal concepts, and it is not clear how such models could represent propositions. Although semantic feature models were intended to account for propositions, this inability is a limitation when compared to recent semantic networks.

The second development following the early hierarchy representations of concepts was to add more complex processing mechanisms to semantic networks in order to enable them to be able to represent sentence meaning as a network of labelled associations. The major processing mechanism proposed was a development of Quillian's notion of 'spreading activation' (Collins and Loftus, 1975).

The semantic network is a highly interconnected structure with relations connecting together nodes, very much like the transport links connect together towns and cities. 'Activation' is an abstract quantity which represents how much processing is taking place in the structure. If a network representing the structure of animals were used to answer the question "Does a dog have hair?", the nodes for DOG and HAIR would both become activated. The activation could then spread down the links connected to these nodes, and onto the nodes at the ends of these relational links. Activation would then spread on down the links from these nodes, and so on. If one imagines spreading rings of activation originating from each starting point, like the ripples extending away from the sites where two pebbles are dropped in a pond, these rings will eventually meet. When the activation patterns meet, a path has been established between the two nodes. The path can be found by following the activation traces, and given the nature of the path, the question can be answered.

There are several properties of activation theories of semantic network processing which have led to empirical investigation. Most research has focused on the time course of activation (e.g. Neely, 1976), or have used one aspect of activation called 'priming' as a tool to examine the details of representation (e.g. Meyer and Schvaneveldt, 1971). The theoretical assumption behind priming is that, once a node has been activated, it will take some time for that activation to decay. Therefore if a second node is accessed the spread of activation will be faster than if the first item had not been activated. This has given rise to many studies where items are presented together or in succession and the reduction in time for some decision on items is used as an indicant of the relation between them. For example, subjects may be asked to read two strings and decide if they are words or not (e.g. "nurse" "plame"). When the two words are related, (e.g. "bread" "butter"), the judgements are considerably faster than if they are not related (e.g. "bread" "nurse"). Sophisticated experiments have used stimuli with multiple meanings (e.g. "bank" with "money" or "river") or embedded words with related meanings (e.g. "cot" "ton" "cotton" "wool" "cottonwool") to investigate the interrelationships of items in memory. Using a similar method, Collins and Quillian (1970) showed that decisions are made more quickly when they require the traversal of recently used paths across the network than when the required paths have not been recently used as evidence for their hierarchical model of memory.

A second aspect of the spreading activation model which has received much investigation has been termed the 'fan effect'. This has been particularly investigated in relation to the detailed model of cognition proposed by Anderson (1976, 1983). This model makes the processing assumption that the activation that crosses a link is inversely proportional to the number of links that "fan out" from, or leave, that link. This results in the prediction that the more nodes that are connected to an item, the harder it will be to retrieve information about that item. A series of experiments (summarized in Anderson, 1983) show that when subjects are shown a number of sentences to learn, and then tested on their ability to recognize test sentences, they are slower to recognize sentences involving concepts about which they have learned other information, than those which contain items which do not occur elsewhere. These studies support the prediction derived from the processing assumption: that the more the facts, the slower the recognition time.

When semantic networks are used to represent sentences, a distinction has to be drawn between 'tokens' and 'types'. That is to say, between BOOK representing any book (the type) and 'book' referring to a particular book (the token). This distinction is required to prevent a confusion about which book is being referred to when two books occur in the same text. For example, to represent the sentence 'John picked up a book and Mary threw a book at John', there must be a node representing each of the books. A variety of mechanisms have been devised to overcome this problem, but a common one (e.g. Norman and Rumelhart, 1975) is to use general identifiers as nodes (e.g. numbers) with links to the type concept. However, this mechanism does not overcome a fundamental problem with semantic networks as models of human memory: that they deal with the connections between concepts rather than their connections with the world. This problem was well summarized by Johnson-Laird, Herrman and Chaffin (1984: 306): "Any psychological theory of meaning should account for these phenomena [the relations among intensional relations, ambiguity, anomaly, instantiation and inference]; semantic networks contain mechanisms designed to do so, but nevertheless fail to deal with them adequately, a failing that also applies to theories based on semantic features or on meaning postulates."

A variety of semantic network theories has been developed (e.g. Quillian, 1968; Anderson and Bower, 1973; Norman and Rumelhart, 1975; Glass and Holyoak, 1974; Collins and Loftus, 1975; Anderson, 1976; 1983; Sowa, 1984). Each of these theories makes specific predictions, some of which have been empirically investigated, and a few of which have been described above. But these studies relate to specific aspects of individual theories. What can be said of semantic network theories as a class? There are few features which all network theories share: they are designed to elucidate the relations between words (intensional rather than extensional relations); they assume that the evaluation of intensional relations can be considered separately from those of extensional relations; they are based on a framework composed of: a parser, a semantic memory consisting of a network of links and nodes, and a set of processes that operate on, and interpret, the network; they have a general commitment to parsimony. These four features in themselves restrict the class of network theories very little. Anderson (1976) has shown that his ACT network system is equivalent in power to a Universal Turing Machine (i.e. the processes it invokes are capable of computing anything that can be computed at all), and it is likely that this equivalence could be proved for other network theories. Although individual network theories may have testable properties, and when used in conjunction with other forms of representation and processing may overcome the problems of extensionality, as a class, they offer no theory which can be assessed in terms of psychological validity. An extreme expression of this position is provided by Johnson-Laird, Herman and Chaffin (1984: 305): "We have no quarrel with the formalism or notation of networks: A commitment to them is little more restrictive, and no more open to criticism, than is a commitment to a particular programming language such as LISP." Consequently, semantic networks remain only a form of computer implementation, as discussed by Mac Randal in Chapter 3 of this volume.

6.2.5 Analogical Representations: Imagery

The representations discussed so far employ symbolic representations of the world. In contrast, there is a class of analogical representations which are much closer to the world being represented. One of the major sources of support for the existence of this class of representation comes from the phenomenon of mental imagery. The study of *imagery* has had a chequered history in psychology, but unlike the representational forms discussed so far, the analogical representation suggested to support it has hardly been addressed as a computational form of representation in AI.

6.2.5.1 What is Imagery and Why Study it?

People, when asked to describe what they experience when they think, often say that they have the sensation of "pictures in their heads". These images are reported as varying in intensity, in the degree of detail present and in their manipulability. Generally there is no difficulty in distinguishing them from the reality of perception; i.e. these images are distinct from hallucinations. If asked to imagine say a cat, specific characteristics of the images (such as colour of fur, length of tail, size relative to an image of a mouse, whether the cat is sitting upon a mat? ...) can often be given. Frequently there is the impression of "zooming-in" on part of the image to obtain more detail.

This human ability to form images has been known and utilized for many years: for example it is the basis of the method of loci as an aid for orators (formalized by the Greek poet Simonides: where a speech is remembered as a trip through the rooms of a familiar building, and the objects in the various rooms act as cues to the next topic). Various mnemonic techniques rely upon imagery ability; and some of these have been explored by psychologists

(Paivio suggested that this accounts for the advantage of concrete words over abstract words in memory tasks, and Bower has investigated the use of bizarre associations as a memory aid). It is also likely that imagery is used routinely, and perhaps unconsciously, in problem-solving. In some of these problem-solving situations there may be practical implications: consider studies of "common-sense" or naive assumptions about physical processes (for example: Caramazza *et al.* (1981), diSessa (1982), Shanon (1976)).

However there seem to be wide individual differences in imagery ability: from spectacular examples such as those claimed for Nikola Tesla (e.g. O'Neill (1980)) to those people who report not having experienced images at all. There are also developmental complications arising chiefly from the slippery area of eidetic imagery ('photographic memory', see Haber, 1979) and its apparent relationship to verbalization (e.g. Glanzer and Clark (1964)).

Other internal vehicles for thought (such as some form of internal speech, symbolisms related to mathematics) are also reported but imagery is currently of great interest within cognitive science because:

(i)   it seems to suggest a form of (knowledge) representation that is **analogical** rather than propositional in nature (and thus presents an interesting problem to workers in artificial intelligence as well as to psychologists), and

(ii)   it suggests, to some psychologists, that there may be **more than one central representation** underlying cognitive processing.

6.2.5.2 Does Imagery Exist as a Real Process?

To the extent that people report such experiences, "imagery" exists as a psychological phenomenon, and is therefore worthy of investigation. It is, however, difficult to experiment on such mental processes and to produce acceptable behavioural data for sceptical colleagues.

At one stage in psychology it was hoped that physiological approaches to psychology might come to the rescue by providing correlates between the electroencephalogram (EEG) and various psychological traits. This followed closely from the hopes of such pioneers of the EEG as Berger (1929), in one of the first papers on the human EEG, that the techniques would prove useful for psychiatric diagnosis.

One exploration attempting to relate "imagery types" to EEG alpha rhythm (electrical activity in the range 8-12Hz: tending to dominate the occipital scalp when the subject is relaxed with eyes closed) was carried out by Golla *et al.* (1943). They classified their subjects into groups as (self-reported) visualizers or non-visualizers and into three EEG-categories: persistent-alpha (those subjects who produced alpha when relaxed with their eyes open or closed), responsive (subjects producing the 'normal' responses of alpha when their eyes closed but not when their eyes were open), and alpha-minus types (those subjects who produced no alpha during the experiment). The report indicated a large number of visualizers in the alpha-minus category and non-visualizers in the persistent-alpha category. However (as shown by Oswald (1957)) very few people produce no alpha (if allowed sufficient time to relax in the experimental situation). Oswald's visualizers, when allowed to settle down, produced almost as much normal (responsive-category) alpha as his non-visualizers. Further, there is a close relationship between alpha rhythm and the activity of the visual system (as suggested by Lippold (1970) and Wertheim (1974, 1981)). This might suggest that any correlations found between some aspects of EEG and differences in cognitive style might be more correctly attributed to differences in habits of visualization.

At present psycho-physiological measures offer little evidence which can be drawn upon to support or reject hypotheses concerning high-level cognitive representations and processes: in the same way as data concerning the voltages across components in a digital computer are not appropriate to describe the current (high-level) program operation.

Psychologists are chary of subjective (introspective) reports as primary evidence, which leaves the major experimental attack upon imagery relying upon the behavioural consequences of tasks in which subjects may use "imagery" (and perhaps subjects pre-selected for such ability, trained and encouraged in its use in the experimental situation).

6.2.5.3 Pre-history of Recent Work on Imagery

In the early days of scientific psychology, imagery was a major area of study for those interested in cognition. For Wundt (1904) **introspection** was seen as the "*sine qua non* of any psychology"; although this was introspection as a controlled experimental technique with highly trained observers. However, a major problem for the introspectionist position was the description and theoretical justification of the distinction between thought involving images and 'imageless thought'.

However with the emergence of **Behaviourism** (e.g. Watson (1913)) and the predominance of a logical-positivist inspired methodology, at least in the United States, through to the 1960s, the study of such mental phenomena declined. Imagery was viewed essentially as epiphenomenal to visual processing, in much the same way that 'imageless thought' was reduced to sub-vocal movements of the throat and larynx. An interesting example of the change in approach at this time is Warden's (1924) report on the relative efficiency of using imagery, verbal coding or motor memory in human maze learning. It is also an early example of **protocol analysis** (the analysis of verbal accounts of tasks while they are being performed) which has since become an important technique in many 'ecologically-valid' (real-life) experiments. Against this general background there were only a few examples of a 'mentalistic' approach to the area before the "Cognitive Revolution" of the early 1960s. However, imagery did feature (as Spatial Visualization) in a number of aptitude tests (e.g. Army Air Force test battery constructed by Guilford *et al.* (1952)).

With the re-emergence of a cognitive psychology (ushered in by such books as Miller, Galanter and Pribram (1960)) it again became respectable to experiment on such mental processes as imagery. This was backed up in 1964 by Holt's paper in the American Psychologist - "Imagery: The return of the ostracized." Within ten years of this paper a number of major texts on imagery had been produced (e.g. Horowitz (1970), Paivio (1971), Sheehan (1972)) and a new range of experimental strategies to tackle these difficult problems had been developed (see, for example, Chase (1973)). With the emphasis within cognitive science on **representation** it has assumed an importance perhaps equal to that it had achieved around 1900. A number of earlier experiments have essentially been re-interpreted within a more cognitive frame, for example, the study by Carmichael *et al.* (1932) where there were distortions in the reproduction of line-drawings from memory after the drawings had been associated with a verbal label. From this it is suggested that images held in memory might be more malleable than perceptions. Interestingly, some of the same problems are recurring: imageless thought, the relationship to self-awareness and the problem of infinite (mental) regress.

6.2.5.4 Experimental Findings: What Do We Know of the Nature of Imagery?

The following are brief descriptions of a selection of psychological studies on imagery. They have been selected as typical examples of the work in the area. For more comprehensive reviews of the area: see Kosslyn's (1980) "Image and Mind" or Pinker's (1985) "Visual Cognition" (which integrates considerations of the mechanisms supposedly underlying imagery with work on visual perception).

6.2.5.5 Mental Rotation

Shepard and his colleagues have been performing experiments on mental rotation from around 1970. In one of their early studies (Shepard and Metzler, 1971) subjects were presented with two drawings of three-dimensional objects (examples of the type of drawing are shown in Figure 1). The experimental task was to report if the represented objects were identical except for orientation. Subjective reports suggested that subjects attempted to match by mentally rotating one of the shapes until it fitted with the other. The decision-time for matching pairs suggested that the process being used seemed to be an analogue of physical rotation of the object because the greater the angular disparity between objects the longer it took subjects to give a decision. The speed of rotation seemed uniform at about 50°/second (although there are differences between subjects). A similar finding was found by Cooper and Shepard (1973) using rotated letter and mirror-image letters (see Figure 2). The subjects' task here was to decide if the letter was well-formed or backward. Again the result suggested that a mental analogue of rotation was being performed. A faster, though still uniform, rotation speed of 300°/second was found, possibly because less complex and more familiar shapes were being used. There is some suggestion from Metzler (1973) (also discussed in Metzler and Shepard, 1974) for the process being continuous. She used an image as an aid to a subsequent perceptual match task. However, there are some difficulties in her technique owing to subject variability.

Schwartz (1979), using a version of a technique pioneered by Cooper and Podgorny (1976), produced some results that, whilst generally supporting the earlier rotation studies, suggest that some refinements may be needed. The experimental design is shown in Figure 3. The results again showed that a greater rotation needed a longer time to carry out. With larger angles of rotation larger patterns needed more time to rotate than small ones but it takes no longer to rotate complex patterns than to rotate simpler ones.

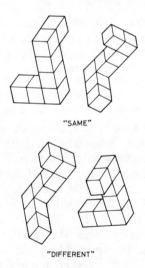

"SAME"

"DIFFERENT"

Figure 1

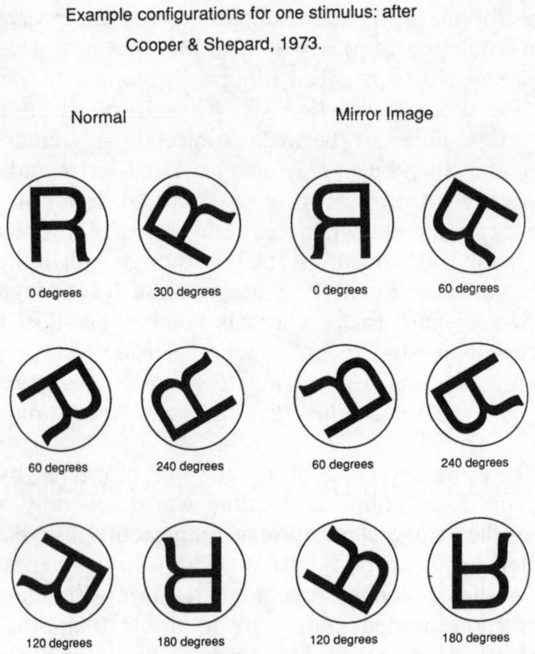

Example configurations for one stimulus: after
Cooper & Shepard, 1973.

Figure 2

There was some confirmation, that subjects were actually rotating an image, from results of a template-matching task where subjects had to match their images against an actual "probe" pattern: in that responses were faster when the probe and image had the same orientation.

6.2.5.6 Mental Paper Folding

Shepard and Feng (1972) used a task in which subjects were required to make judgements about paper cubes which had been unfolded to make patterns of six squares. Some examples are given in Figure 4. The task was to determine from the two-dimensional pattern if the heads of the two arrows marked on the pattern would or would not meet if the squares were folded into a cube. Shepard and Feng found that there was an approximately linear function between the number of folds required to test for a meeting and the time taken to make a decision. That the function was linear rather than exponential in nature would be expected from the nature of the search space. This was congruent with their subjects' reports that they were mentally refolding the squares in order to solve the problem.

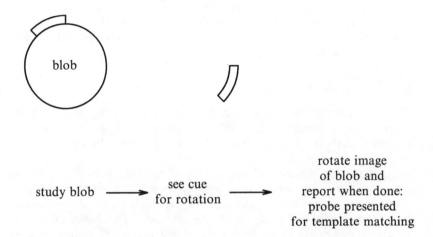

study blob $\longrightarrow$ see cue for rotation $\longrightarrow$ rotate image of blob and report when done: probe presented for template matching

Figure 3 Schwartz (1979) experimental procedure

Do the heads of the arrows meet when the patterns are folded into cubes?

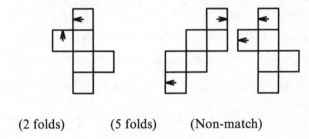

(2 folds)   (5 folds)   (Non-match)

Figure 4 Examples of diagrams used by Shepard and Feng (1972)

6.2.5.7 Scanning Mental Images

Kosslyn, Ball and Reiser (1978) attempted to investigate the amount of movement on, or of, an image. Subjects were given a map of a fictitious island. The island had a number of features (including a hut, a rock, areas of sand). Subjects were trained on the map until they could reproduce the drawing with great accuracy. The main experimental task consisted of the following sequence. An object on the map was named. Subjects were asked to imagine the map and focus upon that object. A second object was named five seconds later. Subjects were instructed to scan the map for this second object and to press a button when they had mentally focused upon it.

Analysis of the data supports the view that the time needed to perform this task increases linearly with the distance apart of the objects (on the real map and presumably on the image). Again this suggests that imagery is a process similar to a physical operation: an analogue.

6.2.6 The Uses of Imagery?

The examples of processes described above relate specifically to imagery rather than to the use and possible relationship of imagery to other forms of cognitive activity. Imagery can take the form of photographic recall of images, but it can also involve the mental construction, representation and manipulation of images of diagrams, and figures. With the acceptance of imagery as a phenomenon and of processes which operate on imagery, two parts of the argument that imagery is an example of an analogical representation being used in human reasoning have been established. The third part of this argument is to attempt to establish the representation upon which imagery is based and to confirm that this representation is indeed analogical in nature. To do this we need to consider the relationships between this form of representation and others which have been described in earlier sections of this chapter.

6.2.6.1 Analogue Representation, Imagery and Inference

There are examples in the psychological literature of tasks which may be helped by the formation of appropriate images. There are also examples where an incorrect image can be misleading. Additionally some operations which may be easy to perform on a picture seem hard for most people to perform on an image. (McKim (1980) is a useful source of examples in this area.)

As an example of the former:

A Buddhist monk visits a shrine at the top of a sacred mountain. It is a difficult climb. He leaves on Monday at 08.03h, reaching the top at 16.30h (with a 15 minute lunch break sharp at noon). At 08.03h the next morning he descends the mountain using the same path. He makes good time in the descent arriving at the bottom of the mountain at 13.05h on Tuesday afternoon.

The question is: Is there any time of day (you do not need to say what time) when the monk was at exactly the same point on the path on Monday and Tuesday?

In this case one can attempt to solve the problem by imaging a saffron robed monk climbing a hill, or a time-distance graph of the movement. The former image does not aid the solution whereas the second image of a graph rather than a picture can lead to a solution.

A number of psychologists working on problem solving in the 1930s and 1940s made extensive use of imagery-like processes as explanatory concepts. For example, a typical study in Maier's (1931) experimental series is the "two-string problem". Two strings hanging from the ceiling have to be tied together, but the strings are positioned so far apart that the subject cannot grasp both at once. The room contains a number of objects, including a chair and a pair of pliers, that may be used to find a solution to the problem. Maier found that subjects tried various solutions involving the chair but these did not work. The suggested solution is to tie the pliers to one string and set that string swinging (like a pendulum), then to get the second string and bring that to the centre of the room, to wait for the first string to swing close enough to grasp and then to tie the strings together. Only 39% of Maier's subjects were able to see the solution within ten minutes. In this problem the difficulty does not arise because subjects view a picture of the situation rather than constructing a diagram, but when they construct either, they do not perceive the pliers as a weight that can be used as part of a pendulum, but as a tool for gripping objects. This difficulty is called functional fixedness (fixity): so named because subjects are fixed on representing the object according to its conventional function and fail to represent the novel function.

Similar results can be found in Duncker's (1945) studies. One task that he posed for subjects was to support a candle on a door, ostensibly for an experiment on visual perception. Materials supplied for the task were a box of drawing-pins, matches and a candle. The suggested solution here is to fasten the box to the door with drawing-pins and then to use the box as a platform for the candle. This task is apparently difficult for subjects because they see the box as a container not as a support or platform. Subjects have greater difficulty with the task if the box is filled with drawing-pins, reinforcing the perception of the box as a container.

The following problem, it is suggested, is relatively difficult to solve using an image but is easy using a picture (adapted from Simon (1978)):

Imagine (but do not draw) a rectangle 2″ wide and 1″ high, with a vertical line cutting it into two 1″ squares. Imagine a diagonal from the upper-left-hand corner to the lower-right-hand corner of the 2″ x 1″ rectangle. Call this line Diagonal A. Now imagine a second diagonal from the upper-right-hand corner to the lower-left-hand corner of the right hand square. Call this line Diagonal B. Consider where Diagonal A cuts Diagonal B.

What is the relationship of the length of B above the cut to the length of B below the cut?

The above problems also give good examples of the wide range of individual differences found in this area. Some people report using images ("like a drawing"), to others it is "just obvious". A number of people find it difficult to solve such problems without resort to external means (such as pencil-

and-paper). It is not clear that these differences relate well to measures of intelligence, personality or 'cognitive style'.

6.2.6.2 Imagery and Interference

Brooks (1968) conducted a series of experiments on processing of visual images contrasting performance here with performance on non-visual tasks reckoned to be of equal difficulty.

For the Visual task subjects had to scan imagined diagrams such as Figure 5. Scanning round, starting at the * and moving in the direction of the arrow, subjects were asked to categorize each corner as a point at the extreme top or bottom ("yes") or a point in between ("no"). For the figure below the correct sequence of responses should be YYYNNNNNNY. The Non-visual task was to hold a sentence, with the same number of words as there are corners in the diagram, in memory (such as " A bird in the hand is not in the bush "), and then to classify each word as a noun or not. The correct sequence of response for the example sentence is NYNNYNNNNY. Three response conditions were used (a) say "yes" or "no", (b) tap with the left hand for "yes" and the right hand for "no", and (c) point to successive Ys and Ns on a sheet of paper.

The following table gives the mean classification time in seconds:

	OUTPUT CONDITION		
	Pointing	Tapping	Vocal
Visual Imaging task	28.2	14.1	11.3
Non-visual task (sentence)	9.8	7.8	13.8

This pattern of results suggests that scanning a sheet for the responses interfered with the scanning of a mental image. The interpretation, again, is that subjects are scanning a representation that is an analogue of a physical display.

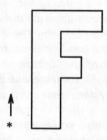

Figure 5 Example of diagram to be imagined and scanned: after Brooks (1968)

It has been suggested that Brooks' result was caused by the interference generated from having to do a visual pointing task and at the same time scan a visual image. Later results (such as Baddeley and Lieberman (cited in Baddeley, 1976)) would suggest that the problem was at a more abstract level than a visual one: that is, the interference is spatial. This latter result also points to the image being an analogue of a physical structure.

6.2.6.3 Distortions of Cognitive Maps

One topic of interest to people from a variety of areas has been how mental (cognitive) maps of the environment are formed and used. Many people report having some form of mental map, and the geographic information that would be encoded in such maps is obviously drawn on in everyday navigation around the world. However, when people are asked to draw such maps, systematic distortions of reality are often produced. For example, Boston Common is usually drawn as a square although in reality it has five sides; the standard New Yorker's view of the United States or Londoner's view of the United Kingdom distort the geography so that the part of the world the author inhabits is overly large, and other areas are reduced. This anecdotal evidence is supported by an experimental study (Milgram and Jodelet, 1976) which shows that Parisians' view the Seine as making a rather gentler arc through Paris than it does. This results in some Right Bank districts being placed (mentally) on the Left Bank. These effects could be due to a greater familiarity, recency or frequency of experience with one area than another (a useful summary of some of the work on mental maps can be found in Gould and White, 1985).

Many mental maps are based on information derived from printed maps rather than directly from experience. The persistence of distortions found in such sources accounts for some people's belief that Greenland is much larger than it actually is, because the Mercator projection used to produce flat maps of the earth distorts its size (a belief usually dispelled when Greenland is viewed on a globe). The persistence of such information is in itself of little interest, however, yet more pronounced distortions can be found in diagrammatic maps such as those of the London Underground. The London Underground map has been found to be very satisfactory for its role, and has been emulated in many similar situations. Since these descriptions are spatial in nature, they are often assumed to represent geographic distance relations. However, they actually represent the connectivity in a network. Consequently, Bayswater station is a third of the map away from Queensway on the London Underground map, whereas, spatially, it is only 50yd away. Here a spatial representation is being used to represent information which is itself not spatial. A similar translation may underly many of the distortions found in cognitive maps.

Stevens and Coup (1978) collected a set of misconceptions about American geography. They analysed their results in terms of the influence from more abstract facts about the relative locations of large physical bodies (such as individual states) producing distortions on the finer detail. They then repeated their experiment and analysis with a set of simplified maps and found the same error patterns, thereby supporting a view that the knowledge of abstract facts results in the distortions in mental maps.

Thorndyke and Hayes-Roth (1978) investigated how mental maps are developed through experience rather than from paper maps. They studied secretaries working in the maze-like Rand Building (Santa Monica, California). They found that 'route-maps', for example how to get from one's office to the photocopying room or to the lunch room, were acquired fairly easily but that it took much longer to develop 'survey-maps', which would enable accurate decisions as to the direction of the lunch room from the photocopying room (a potential route that was not used). It was suggested that secretaries had typically to have ten years' experience of the building before they developed such 'survey-map' knowledge! This finding is supported by developmental evidence (Hart and Moore (1973)) which suggests that children develop from using *route-maps* to *survey-maps*.

Although many of these studies appear to suggest that subjects are using an image (equivalent to a paper map) and can produce a drawing of such an image, backed by subjective report: there are again differences of opinion. For example: Hintzman *et al.* (1981), investigating the way that people orient themselves in somewhat familiar environments, suggest that subjects use propositions not mental images. Reed (1974) has examined the relationship between structural descriptions and mental images, emphasizing the limitations of visual images. Consequently, when information is held as a route-map, a route may be mentally represented and not a two- or three-dimensional representation of geography. These are only produced as drawings when requested by experimenters. Although maps may be viewed as images, they may be constructed from propositions rather than being stored as images themselves. Further, although mental maps are viewed in a spatial manner, the information represented is not always itself spatial in nature.

6.2.6.4 Imagery and Visual Perception: Constructed Analogues or Recalled Pictures?

As described above, a number of authors have investigated the relationship of visual imagery to other cognitive processes: e.g. problem solving (Kaufman, 1979), learning (Fleming and Hutton, 1973), and memory and cognition (Richardson, 1980, Yuille, 1983). These have shown that images that have been seen can be recalled, but also that representations can be developed to aid problem solving and reasoning. Since imagery is easiest to characterise as a phenomenon similar to vision, the most obvious process to compare it to is perception. Although there is a similarity between imagery and perception, some of the evidence as to the nature of imagery is persuasive that images are rather different from perceptions.

For example: Yuille and Steiger (1982), using a modification of the Metzler and Shepard (1974) mental rotation task, described above, have been able to find effects resulting from the complexity of the concepts imaged. This is in contrast with earlier investigations such as Cooper and Podgorny (1976), and suggests a piecemeal (feature analysis) processing system rather than an holistic process.

However, a number of workers in the area still suggest that images take on some of the properties of objects. The idea that images are just (faint) echoes of perceptions has been around for years. There have been attempts to investigate this directly. For example, Perky (1910) found that her subjects confused a faint projection with their own images although there are some methodological problems with this study.

One attempt at a direct test as to the dependence of imagery upon access to 'visual perception processes' was carried out by Mamor and Zaback (1976). They investigated mental rotation by blind subjects using a tactile analogue of the Shepard and Metzler (1971) task. One inspiration for this work appears to be an interview study of dreaming by Jastrow (1888). Mamor and Zabach describe Jastrow's study as indicating that those blind after seven years old reported experiencing visual imagery in their dreams, whereas those blind before five years old made no such claim. The Mamor and Zabach task used tear-drop-shape wedges with a "bite" taken out of the left- or the right-hand side of the wedge. The left-hand wedge was always presented upright, the right-hand wedge was presented at a rotation of 0°, 30°, 60°, 120° or 150° in a clockwise sense. The subjects had to decide if the wedges presented were the same or different. Analysis of these decision times were interpreted by Mamor and Zabach as indicating rotation rates of 54°/sec for their early-blind (before five years old) subjects, 114°/sec for their late-blind subjects, and 233°/sec for the control group of blindfolded, sighted subjects. This study would seem to offer some support for the facilitation of imagery-based tasks, such as mental rotation, by visual processing. However, there is some suggestion in the paper that a verbal strategy may have been used by some subjects.

As a supporter of the view that imagery closely resembles visual perception, Finke has carried out a number of experiments that attempt to use the formation of an image as a potential help or hindrance to a subsequent perceptual task. His experiments tend to support the position that there are some mechanisms that are used both by imagery and by perceptual processes. Some of his studies indicate that imagery can influence perceptions. (This is perhaps not unreasonable if one's view of perception is close to the idea of the brain forming hypotheses about the world outside (one held by Richard Gregory or by the late David Marr and his co-workers).) Finke has a paper in the Psychological Bulletin (1985) which discusses these issues and the related theories: a more accessible source for the non-psychologist reader might be Finke (1986).

In direct contrast to the position that imagery resembles visual perception, Pylyshyn (1984) offers an account of the data from imagery experiments that does not involve analogue representations by drawing on four assumptions. Firstly, that the instructions in imagery experiments lead subjects to recreate as accurately as possible the perceptual events that would occur if they were observing the situation. Secondly, subjects draw on their tacit knowledge of both the environment and human perceptual processes in order to decide how to behave in the experiment. Thirdly, that subjects have the skills necessary to simulate the performance that would arise if they were using a spatial medium. Fourthly, that no special processes are recruited to perform 'as though one were using a spatial medium' when simulating such performance using a representation composed only of propositions. This account is not experimentally falsifiable since tacit knowledge "could obviously depend on *anything* the subject might tacitly know or believe concerning what usually happens in the corresponding perceptual situations" and that "the exact domain knowledge being appealed to can vary from case to case" (Pylyshyn, 1981: 34). Consequently, an assessment of this position depends on whether one can accept that subjects could both possess and apply the tacit knowledge capable of simulating visual perception to the extent experimentally observed.

The influential interpretation of the psychological evidence on imagery favoured by Kosslyn (and his co-workers) seems to be as follows. Imagery (to include the generation, inspection, and transformation of mental images together with their role in fact retrieval) is more than a simple mirror of the equivalent perceptual or physical processes. Because the underlying psychological processes are analogue in nature they are easily performed on an analogue representation and are not easily realized for a propositional representation. He considers it unlikely, given the limited degree of conscious control and access to such processes, that subjects are merely trying to behave as if they were carrying out the equivalent physical tasks. The level of theory specified (for example in Kosslyn and Schwartz, 1978) to emphazise the (cognitive) representation is considered both appropriate and better specified than alternatives such as those offered by Pylyshyn (1984) and Johnson-Laird (1983). He feels it inappropriate, at this stage, to specify the processes at the level of nerve-cell activity. He assumes that these analogue mental representations are actually processed when we have an experience of mental imagery and that processing differences are reflected in external behaviour. These analogue processes are better suited to certain types of data manipulation than propositional forms of representation: and it is in this context that Kosslyn suggests the usefulness of psychological work on imagery for workers in the area of artificial intelligence.

There are still differences of opinion as to the interpretation of many of the experimental results in the area of imagery. A number of authors (e.g. Johnson-Laird, 1983) still see the results as not discriminable from the predictions derived from a propositional model, whereas others (e.g. Kosslyn, 1980) interpret the results as convincing evidence for a unique, analogical processing system - visual imagery. (Discussion on these points can be found in Kosslyn *et al.*, 1979, and in Hilgard, 1981.) It should be remembered that most of the work on imagery has been in the area of 'visual imagery' and not concerned with equivalent processes related to other sensory modalities. One problem that still remains to be solved in the area of imagery, and one in which computer science and other disciplines may be of assistance, is the lack of a suitable formalism for representation.

6.3 Reasoning with Concepts

The use we associate with human action that gives it an advantage over those of machines is that of thinking, or reasoning. The process of reasoning depends on principles that establish some sort of relation between premises and conclusions. There have been several suggestions as to the identity of this set of principles.

Logic specifies the principles of valid reasoning (in certain domains). Most psychologists have assumed that there is a form of mental logic that enables us to reason. According to this *doctrine of mental logic* an inference is made by translating its premises into a mental language, drawing on the relevant general knowledge from long-term memory, and then applying formal rules of inference to these conclusions to derive an inference from them. The doctrine suggests that valid inferences are encountered by children, in the same way as well-formed sentences, and the formal rules of inference are derived in the same way as rules of syntax. The question that follows from this doctrine is: *what logic does the mind contain, and how is it represented there?*

Jean Piaget argued that the formal reasoning which children are supposed to master in their early teens is "nothing more than the propositional calculus itself" (Inhelder and Piaget, 1958: 305). (For an explanation of the propositional calculus and other terms from logic used in this section, see Chapter 2.) One of the major difficulties with this suggestion that the mental logic is the propositional calculus is that the rules of inference would hold true no matter what the content of the propositions. However, there is a body of psychological research to support the argument that the difficulty with which inferences are drawn by humans is dependent on the content of the propositions in the premises. Some of the most dramatic examples of this dependence occur in a task which has been used by a number of researchers. The task seems quite simple; the experimenter lays four cards in front of a subject displaying the following symbols:

E	K	4	7

The subject already knows that each card has a number on one side and a letter on the other. The experimenter then presents the following generalization:

If a card has a vowel on one side then it has an even number on the other side.

The subject's task is to select those cards which have to be turned over to determine if this statement is true or false. The order in which cards would be turned over is not considered, merely the question as to which would determine the truth of the generalization. The problem seems easy; try it before continuing.

In a study by Wason and Johnson-Laird (1972) nearly every subject chose to turn over the card showing a vowel; if it reveals an even number, the generalization is unaffected, if it reveals an odd number then the generalization is false. Similarly, most subjects appreciate that turning over the card with a consonant on would be irrelevant to the generalization. Some subjects chose to turn over the card showing an even number; if it shows a vowel, it would be consistent with the generalization, but would not either prove it true or false; if it shows an odd number it would not affect the generalization since nothing is stated about what should be on the other side of cards that have an even number. To select this card is an error of commission, since it is not relevant, but it does no harm. However, very few subjects select to turn over the card which presents an odd number. If this were to have a vowel on the other side it would disprove the generalization; therefore this error of omission is more serious. Selecting this card, as in selecting the card showing a vowel, might demonstrate a card bearing a vowel and an odd number which would refute the generalization.

If the same test is performed with cards showing a different content by using more realistic materials, there is a change in subjects' selections. With cards showing the modes of transport and place names:

Manchester	Train	Sheffield	Car

and the general rule:

Every time I go to Manchester I travel by car

over 60% of subjects chose to turn over the card with 'car' on it, whereas with the abstract materials only 12% did (Wason and Shapiro, 1971). The finding that performance on this task is different when abstract materials are used from when realistic materials are, has been consistently replicated by many researchers (see Evans, 1982, for a review of studies using this task). This task illustrates that the content of the premises to an inference has an effect on the difficulty of a deduction. This is inconsistent with the principles of the propositional calculus, which suggests that the semantics of the propositions is irrelevant to the inference. This is strong evidence that the propositional calculus is not the mental logic used by humans to perform inferences.

There are two further arguments against the propositional calculus being the mental logic. The first is that it requires the inference of all valid conclusions when it is obvious that only non-trivial conclusions are drawn by people. The second is that inferences that hinge on quantifiers such as 'all' and 'some' cannot be captured within this calculus. They require a quantificational calculus, which includes an additional apparatus for quantifiers.

This requirement suggests first order predicate calculus as a candidate for the mental logic. Johnson-Laird (1983) has pointed out five problems with this suggestion.

The first difficulty that such a suggestion must overcome is that some inferences are more difficult than others. This is easy to illustrate. In a study by Johnson-Laird and Steedman (1978), subjects could readily formulate a valid conclusion that follows from premises of the type:

Some of the children are scientists
All of the scientists are experimenters

whereas hardly any could formulate a valid conclusion from the following:

All of the bankers are athletes
None of the councillors are bankers

From the first problem there are two equally valid, if converse, conclusions: *Some of the children are experimenters; Some of the experimenters are children.* For the second problem the only valid conclusion is *Some of the athletes are not councillors.* For this problem, the converse (*Some of the councillors are not athletes*) is not valid, as would be the response that 'there is no valid conclusion of interest'.

Several theorists have suggested sets of rules of inference within a first order logic which attempt to capture differences in the difficulties of inferences (e.g. Rips, 1983). However, such attempts still suffer from the four other reasons which Johnson-Laird argues prevent first order logic from being the method of human reasoning.

Firstly, that although there are algorithms that will determine that an inference is valid for first order logic, there can be no such procedure to discover that an inference is invalid (Boolos and Jeffrey, 1980). This lack of a decision procedure prevents it from being used to produce the response often given to inferential problems that 'there is no valid deduction that can be made'.

Secondly, that as for the propositional calculus, the semantic content of premises should be irrelevant from processing, which it is not in the case of humans (as was demonstrated above).

Thirdly, that in first order predicate calculus all valid conclusions should be drawn whereas humans only draw non-trivial conclusions. This problem could be overcome by some form of relevance testing filter operating on the products of the logical inference, but this would be sufficiently complex to construct to leave the logic as a minor part of the inferencing system.

The fourth problem for first order predicate calculus is that, although it accounts for quantifiers which the propositional calculus does not, there are still quantifiers such as 'more than one' across which it cannot be used to draw inferences, while humans easily can.

This last problem could be overcome by a higher order calculus that can cope with more complex quantifiers. Although second order predicate calculus can operate over such quantifiers, there is no way to specify the formal inference rules by which the complete set of valid deductions can be derived with it. Because of this lack of specification, it would appear that appealing to higher and higher order calculi will not provide the mental logic required.

Looking elsewhere than logical calculi for a mental logic, there are several candidates. Euler circles have been suggested. However, although there is a complexity in expressing different problems in Euler circles, this complexity does not relate to the difficulty people have in making inferences. Another difficulty with them is that, like the propositional calculus, they cannot give rise to the answer 'no valid conclusion'. A second graphical alternative would be Venn diagrams, but these offer no way of predicting the errors that are made in human inference. There are also several candidates available in goal-directed programming languages. These allow rules of inference to be formulated with a specific content, with every general assertion taking the form of such a rule (such as the production rules discussed above). Although these overcome the problem of the effect of propositional content on inference, they go too far, and provide absolutely no machinery for general inferential abilities. There is a need for the sensitivity to content which they offer, in conjunction with the general inferential ability offered by the logical calculi.

One suggestion which attempts to combine this sensitivity and ability into a single approach is that of *mental models,* proposed by Johnson-Laird (1983). In contrast to the syntactic method of the formal rules of inference this method is semantic in nature. The general spirit of the suggestion is that the reasoner imagines a situation which would be described by a set of premises. Then, after drawing a conclusion from the situation, which would not be stated in the premises, an attempt is made to construct another situation from the premises in which this conclusion would be false. The reasoner can reach any deduction by applying a three-step procedure for this process (from Johnson-Laird and Bara, 1984: 5):

Step 1: construct a mental model of the premises, i.e. of the state of affairs described.

Step 2: formulate, if possible, an informative conclusion that is true in all models of the premises that have so far been constructed. An informative conclusion is one that, where possible, interrelates terms not explicitly related in the premises. If no such conclusion can be formulated, then there is no interesting conclusion from syllogistic premises.

Step 3: if the previous step yields a conclusion, try to construct an alternative model of the premises that renders it false. If there is such a model, abandon the conclusion and return to step 2. If there is no such model, then the conclusion is valid.

What complicates this procedure is that there are usually alternative situations which are compatible with the truth of the premises. Given a premise, such as:

All the scientists are experimenters

how is one to build a single model that captures its content? The answer is to draw on some simple assumptions which can be revised later. Therefore, one can imagine a set of scientists which will be consistent with the word 'all' but as small as possible; for example, three. The information that all the scientists are experimenters can now be added to the model. This would give the resulting model :

scientist =   experimenter
scientist =   experimenter
scientist =   experimenter
                (experimenter)

where the item in brackets represents an experimenter who is not a scientist. Although the premise and the reasoner's general knowledge do not require such an individual, they allow for the possibility of one.

If this were turned into a syllogism with the addition of another premise:

None of the children are scientists
All the scientists are experimenters

the deductive procedure can be applied to yield the conclusions. Firstly, the model would be expanded by the use of the first step of the procedure, to include this premise too, incorporating a barrier to represent set boundaries:

child
child
child
_____
scientist =   experimenter
scientist =   experimenter
scientist =   experimenter
                (experimenter)

Applying the second step of the procedure to this model suggests the conclusion: *None of the children are experimenters,* or its converse that *None of the experimenters are children.* Most subjects erroneously report these conclusions without continuing to apply the third step of the rule (Johnson-Laird and Bara, 1984) which results in a second model:

child
child
child =   (experimenter)
_____
scientist =   experimenter
scientist =   experimenter
scientist =   experimenter
                (experimenter)

which falsifies these conclusions. Applying the second step of the procedure again, the two models together yield the conclusions: *Some of the children are not experimenters* and *Some of the experimenters are not children* which by the application of the third step again, gives rise to a third model:

```
  child  =    (experimenter)
  child  =    (experimenter)
  child  =    (experimenter)
scientist =    experimenter
scientist =    experimenter
scientist =    experimenter
             (experimenter)
```

which eliminates the first of the previous pair of conclusions, leaving the valid conclusion that: *Some of the experimenters are not children.*

The solution of this syllogism has required three mental models. The theory suggests that the greater the number of models required to draw a valid deduction, the harder the task will be. The results of experiments which show the comparative difficulty of reaching valid conclusions from syllogisms in both adults (Johnson-Laird and Bara, 1984) and children (Oakhill, Johnson-Laird and Bull, 1986) can be accounted for by a combination of the number of models called for by this theory and effects of the ordering of the items in the syllogisms (or more formally, the figure of the premises).

It should also be noted that this theory can also account for the types of quantification that the first order predicate calculus could not. For example, given the two premises:

> *more than half the experimenters are scientists*
> *more than half the experimenters are children*

a mental model can be constructed:

```
scientist =    experimenter
scientist =    experimenter    = child
               experimenter    = child
  scientist                      child
```

which yields the valid conclusion: *at least one scientist is a child.*

These examples of the use of mental models are limited to logical syllogisms involving quantifiers of various forms. However, models can also be used to represent and draw inferences across spatial relationships. This use is best illustrated by a particular problem. Given a problem where 12 individuals are seated equally spaced around a circular table, and a description of the relationships between them:

> A is on B's right
> B is on C's right
> C is on D's right
> ...
> K is on L's right

the transitive inference that A is on F's right is unacceptable, since A is close to being opposite F. The criterion for the validity of a conclusion to such a problem is purely semantic, depending on the impossibility of constructing a model of the premises and their context in which the conclusion is false. The application of syntactic inference rules as formalized in the quantificational calculi would not yield it. This example illustrates how spatial problems can be solved by the construction of a model, where other techniques would fail. It has been argued that similar examples of the usefulness of mental models for reasoning can be found not only for quantificational and spatial relationships but also for temporal and other continuous relationships.

6.3.1 The Representation of Mental Models

This evidence suggests that mental models are a realistic mechanism for human reasoning, but how is the information they draw on represented? Johnson-Laird suggests that "discourse can be represented either in a propositional form close to the linguistic structure of the discourse, or in a mental model that is closer to the representation of the state of affairs [...] than to a set of sentences" (Johnson-Laird, 1983: 160). The evidence to support this claim comes from a series of experiments which show that subjects tend to form mental models of a spatially determinate descriptions, while relying on propositional representations for indeterminate descriptions consistent with more than one spatial layout. In one study (Mani and Johnson-Laird, 1982), subjects heard a series of spatial descriptions, such as :

> The spoon is to the left of the knife
> The plate is to the right of the knife
> The fork is in front of the spoon
> The cup is in front of the knife.

After each description they were shown a diagram such as:

spoon   knife   plate
 fork   cup

and they had to decide if the diagram was consistent or inconsistent with the description. Half the descriptions presented to the subjects were spatially determinate (in that they described only one possible arrangement of the objects) and half were indeterminate (in that they described more than one possible arrangement). After the subjects had judged the descriptions and diagrams, they were given an unexpected test of their memory for the descriptions. On each trial, subjects had to rank four alternative descriptions in terms of their similarity to the original. These four were: the original description itself; an inferable description; and two descriptions with a different meaning as confusion items. The inferable description for the example contained the sentence:

The fork is to the left of the cup

in place of the sentence relating the spoon and knife. The inferable description is therefore not a paraphrase of the original, but it can be inferred from the layout of the original description. Mani and Johnson-Laird argue that this inference is only likely to be made if subjects construct mental models, and not if they maintain a propositional representation of the sentence. Further, the model they create would have to be symmetrical, since if they construct an asymmetrical model they will probably fail to consider the fork to be on the left of the cup. An asymmetrical model of the above example will illustrate this point:

    spoon   knife   plate
    fork

        cup

   The results show that subjects remember the gist of the determinate descriptions much better than that of the indeterminate ones, but they tend to remember the verbatim detail of the indeterminate descriptions better than that of the determinate descriptions. This cross-over effect requires the existence of at least two sorts of representation. Models do not encode the surface linguistic form of the sentences they represent, and when using them, subjects confuse inferable descriptions with the original. Propositional representations, however, do encode the surface form of the sentences. This result therefore suggests that subjects use a representation such as mental models to represent determinate descriptions and a propositional representation for indeterminate ones. One motivation that has been suggested for this change in representation is that, because models require a greater amount of processing for their construction than propositions, they are easier to remember, although they cannot express indeterminacy when it is noticed. It is possible that the introduction of propositional elements into mental models (such as the bracketing notation used in the models above) could also be used to represent alternative models of indeterminate descriptions, but it does not appear to be drawn upon in this study.

Further evidence for the construction of mental models is provided by a study of continuous and discontinuous descriptions by Ehrlich and Johnson-Laird (1982). In this study, subjects listened to three sentences describing the spatial relations between four common objects, e.g.:

> The knife is in front of the spoon
> The spoon is on the left of the glass
> The glass is behind the dish

and then attempted to draw a diagram of the layout of the objects thus described. If subjects attempt to construct a mental model of the layout the task should be easier if a single model can be progressively constructed from the assertions (as in the above example), than if the description is discontinuous where the first two statements refer to no item in common, e.g.:

> The glass is behind the dish
> The knife is in front of the spoon
> The spoon is on the left of the glass

In this case subjects may either construct a mental model for each of the first two assertions which must then be combined, or else represent the information in propositional form until some point after all the sentences have been heard. If the effect were one caused by the continuity of the sentences themselves rather than the construction of a single mental model, then a 'semi-continuous' description where the third sentence had no items in common with the second, but did with the first, should also prove difficult to recall, e.g.:

> The spoon is on the left of the glass
> The glass is behind the dish
> The knife is in front of the spoon.

However, if a mental model is being constructed from a description such as this, it should prove no more difficult than the continuous example, since there is no requirement to construct two models because the third assertion refers to the spoon which has already been introduced in the first assertion. The results confirm this prediction of difficulty, since significantly more of the diagrams based on continuous descriptions were correct than those based on discontinuous descriptions, while the semi-continuous condition was not reliably different from the continuous.

These experiments support the view that mental models are used to represent various spatial knowledge, and may be used to represent the premises used to reason without the rules of logic, as described above. Although mental models have an analogical structure, they are not the same as images. The relationship between images and mental models can be seen as one where images can be described as views on the represented mental model. It is this dimensional nature of the representation of mental models that allows them to be manipulated in ways that can be controlled by dimensional variables and give rise to the performance described.

However, there are classes of representation which are currently problematic for mental models. One case is that of infinite regresses which can be exemplified by the representation of the mutual knowledge (Lewis, 1969; Schiffer, 1972) of two participants in a conversation or event. For example, if two people are standing in full view of one another amidst a downpour, then the fact that it is raining is mutual knowledge between them. In general, if the observers are X and Y, and the fact p, then it follows that X and Y mutually know p. This may be described in terms of the concept 'know', by the following series of statements:

    X knows p
    Y knows p
    X knows Y knows p
    Y knows X knows p
    X knows Y knows X knows p
    Y knows X knows Y knows p
        .
        .
        .
        etc. *ad infinitum*

There are two classes of solutions to the apparent paradox of this infinite regress. The first class requires the choice of a stage in the series at which to cut it off, either at a fixed point, or at a point which is selected as a function of the inferential or memory limits of the agents. The second class involves the use of a recursive notation in possible worlds or other advanced logics (e.g. Cohen, 1978). The same apparent paradox can exist in a mental model notation. Then, there will be an infinite number of models representing the situation, as there are an infinite number of statements in the series above. It would be possible to select a cut-off point in the sequence, but the decision as to where to place that point is no easier in a mental-models representation than for the series above. Although it is possible to represent recursiveness in diagrammatic or model form without using an infinite number of models (see Power, 1984), this representation requires the introduction of more

special conventions and notations (like the horizontal bar and brackets in the models above) that make the models look more like expressions in higher order logic. This consequently reduces at least the face validity of mental models as representations to support reasoning which can be attributed to the simple models given above.

6.4 Conclusion

Representations and the processes which operate on them must both be specified for a system to be testable (Anderson, 1978). As a class, semantic networks and possibly the other major classes of representation (e.g. schema, frames) do not specify the processes which operate in them in sufficient detail to be testable. Individual models employing different representations are testable, and there has been found evidence which supports different aspects of many of them:

> People do appear to produce schematized representations of events, although there is little evidence for the existence of base schemata themselves. People do appear to produce successive records of events they experience, of which the most recent is retrieved (unless the description used for searching is specific enough to locate earlier records), as described by the headed records framework. People do seem to use a two-stage checking process based on the typicality of concepts to determine if statements such as 'a dog is an animal' are true as the semantic feature models suggest. People do find it easier to verbalize some knowledge (declarative) than other (procedural), as is accounted for by the use of production systems. People do retrieve information in regard of its connections to other information so as to give rise to the counter-intuitive 'fan effect', as predicted by some semantic networks (e.g. Anderson, 1976; 1983). People do solve some syllogisms with greater ease than others, as is consistent with the use of mental models.

However, there are few data that can be used to decide which of these phenomena arise because of the representation used to store information, rather than the processes which operate on them. There has been a debate as to whether information is stored procedurally or declaratively. The outcome for most theorists (e.g. Anderson, 1983) has been to produce models which contain procedural representations (production rules) for skilled procedures and declarative representations (semantic networks) for other factual information with processes to translate declarative information into procedures to model skill acquisition. There has been a debate about whether information is represented analogically (see Kosslyn, 1981) or whether it is always represented propositionally, but is processed to give rise to the effects of imagery and analogical reasoning (see Pylyshin, 1981). Again, most theorists (e.g. Johnson-Laird, 1983) have compromised and proposed the use of propositional representations to account for the surface effects found in recall and analogical representations (i.e. mental models) to account for analogical reasoning effects.

This chapter has summarized various phenomena and models composed of representations and processes which have attempted to account for them as parts of theories of human knowledge representation and reasoning. A model which claims to be a model of human processing must account for all of these phenomena. AI models which claim to offer the range of representation and reasoning exhibited by humans must also use these phenomena as tests. But what have these psychological studies to offer as criteria by which to assess and select representations for AI systems which are not intended to have any psychological validity? Simon (1978) has suggested that the informational and computational equivalence of representations should be the core criteria. *Informational equivalence* is achieved when the information inferable from one representation is also inferable from another. *Computational equivalence* is only achieved if two representations not only have informational equivalence but also the processes used to draw inferences for a task from one representation can be performed as 'easily' as for another. This introduces two important notions: firstly, that the computational equivalence of two representations can only be judged in the light of a particular task, or set of tasks; secondly, that there is some measure of 'ease' of drawing inferences which may be measured in time and effort to program, as well as time and resource usage at point of computation.

Models of human performance must be capable of accounting for the phenomena listed above, and use representations as close to those that humans do. They must also use the range of processing available to the human, to perform the large range of tasks that humans can. Most recent theories attempt to include such a range (e.g. Anderson, 1983; Johnson-Laird, 1983; Sowa, 1984). However, when producing computational AI programs, it should be possible to define both the tasks to be performed and criteria for 'ease of computation' which are independent of the tasks performed by humans. If the task is one involving the use of images, the computation may be 'easier' if both the processes operate on spatial units and the representation is more analogous to a picture than is a set of propositions. We know that humans have processes which can quickly draw inferences from pictorial representations since they quickly respond to changes in their visual environment (e.g. when driving). It is therefore reasonable to suggest that analogical representations may be more computationally efficient for the performance of some tasks by humans - especially when people draw external diagrams as aids to solve problems (see Larkin and Simon, 1987). However, for the computation to be more efficient using an analogical than a propositional representation for computational AI, there must be machine processes which operate on such representations. Without these, if the task is to solve propositional syllogisms, the 'easier' representation from which to compute may be one which is itself propositional despite the evidence supporting the applicability of the mental-models approach to human syllogistic reasoning.

In a similar way, for different tasks with different criteria for 'ease of computation', any of the representations discussed in this chapter may be the most suitable for computational AI (see Sloman, 1985). What psychological studies have to offer the writer of computational AI programs is an example of one (or more) ways in which the task can be achieved. The other chapters in this book describe specific tasks and the representations which appear most suited to them for the computational purposes of AI.

6.5 Further Reading

Although some aspects of cognitive psychology have been described in this chapter, many have been omitted. The interested reader may wish to consult a standard introductory text to cognitive psychology which covers more of these (e.g. Lindsay and Norman 1977; Anderson, 1985). The details of experiments which have led to the contemporary view of human memory are particularly well described in Baddeley (1976). There are also two more recent books which present individual authors' views of the cognitive system from a cognitive science perspective (Anderson, 1983; Johnson-Laird, 1983). Two issues have been deliberately omitted from this review since their inclusion would have considerably lengthened it: firstly, connectionist theories of representation which are currently a focus of much research (McClelland, Rumelhart and the PDP Research Group, 1986) and secondly, the psychology of language (see Garnham, 1985).

7 Conceptual Graphs

Michael Jackman and Cliff Pavelin

7.1 Introduction

The *Conceptual Graph* is a graph based notation for the representation of knowledge. It was developed by Sowa in his encyclopaedic work (Sowa, 1984) and subsequent papers (Sowa and Way, 1986; Sowa and Foo, 1987; Fargues *et al.*, 1986) and investigated by numerous workers in knowledge engineering applications (Garner and Tsui, 1985). As a representation scheme it draws on and integrates ideas from much previous work and, although there may be little new, the result is arguably a more flexible, more extensive and more precisely defined knowledge representation system than any of its predecessors. The notation gives the full representational power of first-order logic and the mapping onto logic is precisely defined. The notation can also cope with higher order and modal statements.

It is not enough simply to *represent*; the aim of a representation language is to be able to permit computer-based *reasoning* also. Sowa defines operations on conceptual graphs which are useful in reasoning. The most important is the "maximal join" which looks for the greatest match (appropriately defined) between two conceptual graphs; it is a substantial generalization of the unification operation under a suitable mapping. A methodology for performing first-order deductive reasoning on conceptual graphs is developed at length in (Sowa, 1984). There are also proposals about how conceptual graphs can be used in 'common-sense' reasoning although the ideas are far from fully developed.

Clancey (1985) writes: "every AI and cognitive science researcher should study the conceptual graph notation and understand its foundation in logic, database, and knowledge representation research." We are following that advice in this book and giving a summary of the essential facts of the conceptual graph formalism as an example of a contemporary knowledge representation scheme whose essentials can be grasped fairly easily.

The theory as originally described in (Sowa, 1984) begins from a psychological model of perception, but an understanding of this model is not at all necessary to appreciation of conceptual graphs and the scheme is described here purely in analytical terms. It is emphasized that this account can only be a selective summary and the interested reader should consult the substantial works referenced.

7.2 Types, Concepts and Relations

The primitives of the theory are *concept-types* (which comprise a *type-hierarchy*), *concepts* which are individuals (instantiations of concept-types) and *conceptual relations* which relate one concept to another.

7.2.1 Concept-types

Concept-types represent classes of entity, attribute, state and event. Examples may be: CAT, SIT, READ, PRICE, JUSTICE - they broadly correspond to nouns, verbs, adjectives etc. in language. It is assumed that in any conceptual graph (cg) system there is a pre-defined set of such types. A relation < is defined over the set to embody the notion that some concept-types are wholly subsumed in others. (Technically this is a *partial ordering* relation - like the set inclusion relation or the 'less than' in arithmetic, it is transitive and antisymmetric.) For example if PHYSICAL-OBJECT, ANIMAL, MAMMAL and CAT were concept-types, the relations

$$CAT < MAMMAL < ANIMAL < PHYSICAL-OBJECT$$

would exist. The meaning would be that every cat (i.e. instance of CAT) is also a mammal, every mammal is an animal etc. CAT is said to be a *sub-type* of MAMMAL, mammal a *super-type* of CAT. The *type-hierarchy*, as it is called, need not be tree-like. For example, one might have a hierarchy in which:

$$ELEPHANT < MAMMAL$$
$$ELEPHANT < WILD-ANIMAL$$
$$RATTLESNAKE < WILD-ANIMAL$$
$$TIGER < MAMMAL$$
$$TIGER < WILD-ANIMAL$$

The hierarchy must form the mathematical structure known as a *lattice* - this implies that every two types must have at most one maximal common sub-type and one minimal common super-type. In the above example the fact that ELEPHANT and TIGER are sub-types both of MAMMAL and WILD-ANIMAL would necessitate the definition of a somewhat artificial WILD-MAMMAL as a separate concept in order to maintain the lattice. The lattice property is difficult to defend in cognitive terms but essential to some of Sowa's cg algorithms.

Although a type-hierarchy is taken as pre-existing in a system, there are also facilities for new type definitions to be given in conceptual graph form - for example, one may define a type 'WILD-CAT' to be a sub-type of CAT which has certain specified qualities, in this case those of being wild. Sowa calls this an 'Aristotelian' definition of a new type. But many concept-types will not have such a precise definition: Wittgenstein (1953) in a well known example, pointed out that the concept of 'game' has no precise definition; various types of game have family resemblances to each other. The concept-type GAME might well be a sub-type of ACTIVITY in a type-hierarchy but it would be impossible to give it a type definition which would specify the properties which define a game. The cg representation supports such problematic concepts as well as Aristotelian type definitions.

The type-hierarchy represents the subsumption relation between concept-types, sometimes represented by IS-A links in semantic networks. Sowa objects to mixing the higher order relationship represented by IS-A, a relation between *types* of individuals, with other relations such as 'agent of' etc. between *individuals* themselves.

7.2.2 Concept

A concept is an instantiation of a concept-type. In the cg notation it is written as a rectangle with the name of the concept-type inside. Thus Figure 1 represents an (unnamed) object of type CAT. A concept on its own like this forms the simplest type of conceptual graph. It has a meaning 'there exists a cat'.

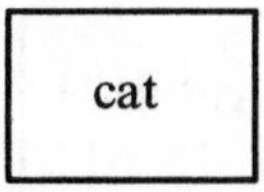

Figure 1

To refer to specific individuals a *referent field* is added. So Figure 2 represents the particular cat #123 (the referent is a name unique in the system). Interpreted as a conceptual graph this would mean 'the individual #123 is a cat'. Referent fields can also indicate much more complicated instantiations, e.g. a set of, one of a set of, etc.

For clarity we will denote referents here by names in quotes (e.g. cat:'fred') although names actually have a special treatment in the conceptual graph scheme.

7.2.3 Conceptual Relations

Conceptual relations show the roles that concepts play in relation to each other. Typical examples are as follows.

ATTR	BIG is an *attribute* of MAN
AGNT	MAN is an *agent* of DRINK
OBJ	WHISKY is an *object* of DRINKing
MANR	SLOW is a *manner* of DRINKing
LOC	An EVENT takes place in a *location*

In language, conceptual relations are indicated by word-order, case endings, prepositions etc. As with concepts there will be a pre-defined set of relation-types in any given system.

Normally a conceptual relation specifies the link between *two* concepts although there are some unary relations (see sections 7.3.3, 7.3.4) and Sowa defines ternary examples like BETW; this links three concepts which are physical objects, one of which lies between the other two.

Each relation will be constrained as to the concepts it can connect to. Thus an AGNT - which is a relation connecting the instigator or agent of an action to that action itself - will link to two concepts one of which is a sub-type of ANIMATE and one which is a sub-type of ACT.

cat:#123

Figure 2

7.3 Conceptual Graph

7.3.1 Definition

A conceptual graph is a connected graph formed from concept and relation nodes. Each relation is linked (only) to its requisite number of concepts, each concept to one or more relations - apart from the special case of a graph consisting of a single concept.

Figures 3 and 4 give examples of simple cgs, with an English interpretation. Note that the arcs have a direction but its significance is minor - the most important use is to increase computational efficiency. There is an elaborate 'linear' notation to facilitate input and output of cgs on alphanumeric devices, but all examples here are given in graphical form.

7.3.2 Assertions

A basic cg, such as those given above, represents an *assertion* about individuals which exist in the domain being described. A precise mapping is defined from a cg into first-order logic; it gives a conjunction of predicates, one corresponding to each node of the graph. A concept C with no explicit referent will map onto the assertion that there exists an individual of type C:

$$\exists \, x \; C(x)$$

while if there is an explicit referent 'fred', it simply maps onto the assertion C('fred'). A binary conceptual relation R linking the concepts C(x) and D(y) would map onto R(x,y). Thus, for example, Figure 4 would correspond in logic to:

$$\exists \, x,y \;\; man('john') \;\land\; agent('john',y) \;\land\; look(y)$$
$$\land \; object(y,x) \;\land\; foot(x) \;\land\; partof(x,'john')$$

x and y respectively denote a foot and a 'looking event'.

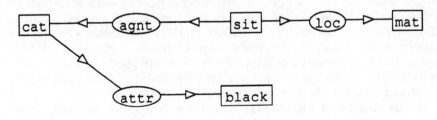

Figure 3 A black cat sits on a mat

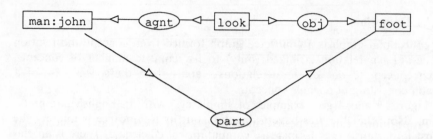

Figure 4 The man 'John' looks at his foot

It should be noted that the type hierarchy embodies obvious logical implications. If MAN is a sub-type of PERSON, then by definition the following is implicitly assumed:

$$\forall\ x\ man(x) \rightarrow person(x)$$

(in particular the above 'john' is a person.) If the type hierarchy is regarded as complete, it is possible to make other inferences; for example if concept-types A and B have *no common sub-type*:

$$\forall\ x\ A(x) \rightarrow \neg\ B(x)$$

Because these relatively complex logical assertions are implicit in the type hierarchy, the reasoning operations on conceptual graphs (see section 7.4 below) are likely to be more efficient than theorem proving methods based directly in logic (see Chapter 2, section 2.3.5 where a similar general point is made).

7.3.3 Negation and Quantification

To give assertions the full power of first-order logic (and allow extensions to higher order and modal logics) demands an extension of this notation above. Effectively a new concept-type 'PROPOSITION' is introduced. PROPOSITION can take one or a number of conceptual graphs *as a referent*. A concept of this type then asserts the conjunction of the graphs in the referent. In the graphical notation, a concept of type PROPOSITION is denoted by a box drawn round all the graphs in the referent as shown below.

The simplest use of PROPOSITION is the notation used to specify negation. A NOT operator (regarded as a unary conceptual relation) is applied to the proposition. The graph inside the box in Figure 5 asserts 'there exists a person with a mother'. Applying the NOT relation denies this proposition.

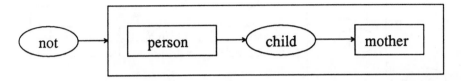

Figure 5

Propositions can be nested indefinitely in this way, and concepts at different levels in this nesting can be identified as referring to the same individual (they are joined by a dotted line known as a *coreferent link*). This enables full first-order logic to be represented. An example is given in Figure 6 - it corresponds to the denial of 'there exists a person and this person does not have a mother', i.e. the graph asserts 'every person has a mother'. However, Sowa uses an extension of the referent notation to make such universally quantified statements more simply (see Figure 7). The graphical notation with boxes indicating 'negative context' etc. derives from one originally introduced by C.S.Peirce who devised an elegant and complete deduction system for first-order logic based on simple operations on graphs of this type.

7.3.4 Modalities and Tense

An advantage of the above notation is the ease by which it can be extended by a range of relations to indicate possibility, necessity, tense, knowledge, etc. These are equivalent to the *modalities* of case grammars (e.g. Simmons, 1973). An example is given in Figure 8.

7.3.5 Abstract and Definition

We have seen that a conceptual graph represents an *assertion* - generally about individuals in the world. There is another class of information to be represented - information about typical objects or classes of objects in the world. (There is a rough correspondence between this information and the Tbox of KRYPTON (Brachman *et al.*, 1983b) which is used for constructing structured definitions as distinct from the Abox, the assertion language - see Chapter 10.) The type hierarchy is one element of this information, but conceptual graphs themselves are also used to define new concepts in terms of old, give default information about a concept, give the constraints on concepts which relations can attach to, etc. It is assumed that, like the type hierarchy, these 'definition' graphs are pre-existing in any system - they are said to form a *canonical basis* for the domain.

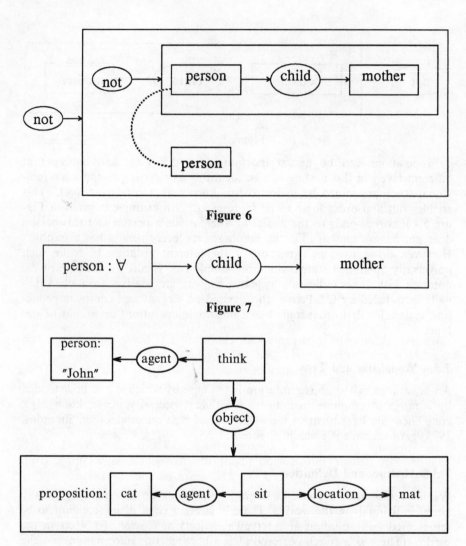

Figure 6

Figure 7

Figure 8 John thinks that a cat sits on a mat

A *Canonical Graph* is an example of one of these. It is a template for a concept or conceptual relation; it defines and puts constraints on the sort of links that can occur. For example a canonical graph associated with the concept-type TEACH may be as Figure 9. This says that the TEACH concept may be associated with AGNT (the agent), RCPT (the recipient, i.e. whoever is being taught) and OBJ (the object or subject matter); if so the

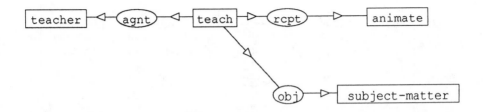

Figure 9

attached concepts must be the same as, or sub-types of, those given in the conceptual graph. The assumption is that all assertions must be derived from a starting set of canonical graphs according to certain rules (see section 7.4.1).

Canonical graphs are incorporated into a number of special types of definition known as 'abstractions' (Sowa gives a mapping from them onto lambda expressions in logic). Examples of two important types are given here.

A *Type Definition* defines a new concept-type in terms of an existing one with the additional properties which characterise it being expressed in conceptual graph form. This is the 'Aristotelian' definition of section 7.2.2. Thus a concept of a KISS may be defined as a sort of TOUCH done by a person with their LIPS in a TENDER manner; this would be expressed in cg form as shown in Figure 10. The 'generic' referent x-x is used to link the defining concept TOUCH with the new one KISS. If KISS appears in another cg, it can be 'expanded' by an operation described below.

A *Schematic Definition* of a concept-type is a canonical graph which gives *plausible* or *default* information about that concept. An example (from (Sowa, 1984)) is given in Figure 11. The set of all such schema for a given type is called a *schematic cluster*. A schema is supposed to act rather like a generalized frame giving typical properties and default values, but its use is far from precise in the current documents. A concept like GAME, impossible to define precisely (see section 7.2.2), would exist in the system as a schematic cluster giving a set of typical usages.

Various other categories of definition (e.g. prototypes, individuals) using conceptual graphs are proposed in (Sowa, 1984).

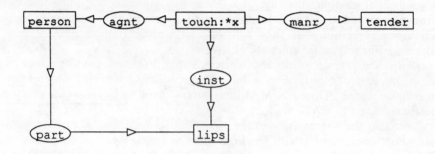

Figure 10

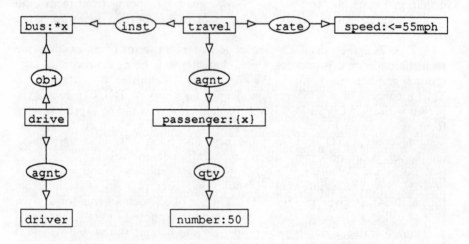

Figure 11

7.4 Fundamental Operations

A number of operations are defined on conceptual graphs. They are all *formation* rules by which one can derive allowable (not necessarily meaningful) conceptual graphs from a canonical basis.

7.4.1 Canonical Formation Rules

Canonical formation rules act as a generative grammar for allowable cgs from the canonical basis. Such graphs will not necessarily have any meaningful interpretation but they will at least obey certain selectional constraints. The important rules are as follows.

Restriction takes a graph and replaces any of its concept nodes either by changing the concept-type to a sub-type or adding a referent where there was none before. Thus ANIMAL may be restricted to CAT, which may be restricted again to CAT: 'fred'.

Note that the system assumes the existence of a predefined set of individuals whose conformance with concepts must be checked on such operations. For example if 'rover' were an individual DOG, the restriction of ANIMAL to CAT: 'rover' would be disallowed.

Joining takes two graphs with a common concept, and joins them over this concept, linking up the arcs from both graphs to form a single graph. Joining may also join a graph to itself, i.e. merge two concepts within the graph.

Simplifying removes any duplicate relations between two concepts - these can arise after a join.

Deduction

A graph that is canonically derived from others in this way is termed a *specialization* of any of the originals. In logical terms, existential variables may have been instantiated, predicates replaced by more constraining ones (i.e. sub-types) or additional constraints added by conjoining with further predicates. If graph g1 is a specialization of g2, then g2 is a *generalization* of g1. It should be fairly obvious that a graph representing an assertion when translated in logic will *imply* any generalization of it (i.e. generalization preserves truth). If the girl Susan eats soup quickly, then certainly a girl eats soup.

It is possible to use these operations and properties of conceptual graphs to perform logical deduction using methods similar to resolution (see Fargues, 1986; Rao and Foo, 1987). In particular making two graphs identical by restriction is equivalent to unification in sorted logic.

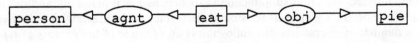

Figure 12(i)

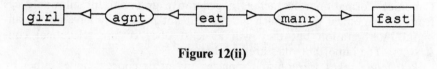

Figure 12(ii)

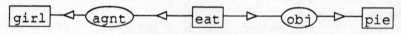

Figure 12(iii) Restriction of (i)

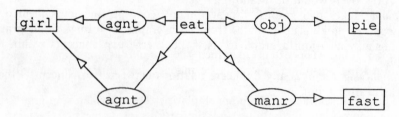

Figure 12(iv) Joining (ii) with (iii)

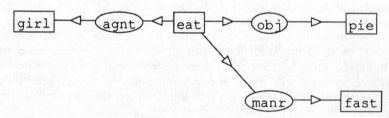

Figure 12(v) Simplification of (iv)

7.4.2 Maximal Join

The sequence of examples in Figures 12(i) to 12(v) form what is known as the *maximal join*: a join of two graphs followed by a sequence of restrictions, internal joins and simplifications so that as much matching and merging of the original graphs as possible is performed. The maximal join is used in a number of operations; the following is an example of the process of *type expansion* where an assertion containing a concept defined by a type definition is expanded by incorporating the type definition. Figure 13(i) is an assertion containing the concept KISS which is expanded using the definition given in Figure 10.

We equate a concept KISS with its super-type TOUCH in the type definition (Figure 10) and then, working out from here, match relation and join concepts restricting the common sub-types if possible. In this case MAN: 'john' joins with person after restriction to give Figure 13.

A *schematic join* is very similar but uses the maximal join to link in default information defined in a schema. This could be a first stage in a common-sense reasoning process.

If two graphs g1 and g2 have a maximal join G, then it is clear that g1 and g2 are generalizations of G, i.e. if g1 and g2 represent assertions, then each is implied by the assertion represented by G. G itself cannot be deduced from g1 and g2 but in certain circumstances it may be a plausible deduction based on matching concepts which are compatible, i.e are the same or have some common restriction.

Thus if a graph declares that Mary loves a man John and Mary loves a Scots person, the maximal join will result in the assertion that Mary loves a Scotsman John. The extent to which the default assumptions of typical common-sense reasoning can really be mapped into this form can only be guessed.

As has been said above, there are similarities between matching graphs by making appropriate restrictions and the process of unification familiar in automated theorem proving and Prolog. The maximal join can be regarded as a generalized unification operation (see Jackman, 1987, 1988).

7.5 Summary

The conceptual graph notation, many features of which could not even be touched upon in this account, is a flexible, consistent and precisely defined notation for the representation of knowledge. A number of operations are defined which are related to the sort of inferences that can be made by using the 'type hierarchy', the conformance of concepts with the names of individuals, and the standard principles of first-order logic. Potentially this may be useful for efficient deductive reasoning and (perhaps more important) methods of plausible reasoning in real-world problems.

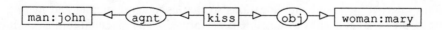

Figure 13(i)

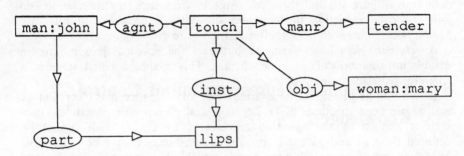

Figure 13(ii) Type expansion of KISS in (i) using type definitions in Figure 10

Clancey (1985) was perhaps going too far when he described the cg scheme as embodying 'the unification of logic, plausibility, and meaning constraints, setting a formal notation with four definitions, proofs, and algorithms for plausible reasoning'. The representation notation is very fully worked out but the reasoning processes require much research. However, there is sufficient world-wide interest in the cg formalism that the ideas are being developed and tested in real systems.

8 The Explicit Representation of Control Knowledge

Brian Bainbridge

8.1 Introduction

It has often been suggested (Bundy, 1983, Jackson, 1986) that a suitable strategy in knowledge-based systems research is to view some working program from a higher level of abstraction in order to see what has been learned from its implementation. A way to proceed is then to perform a 'rational reconstruction' to achieve its ends in a more principled way and to increase the performance of the original program.

The history of the MYCIN experiments of the Stanford Heuristic Programming Project provides good material to illustrate this approach. Chapter 5 gives an overview of the programming formalism employed. In this chapter, some features of expert systems control knowledge which MYCIN well exemplifies will be discussed.

Originally MYCIN formed the subject of E. Shortliffe's Ph.D. thesis (Buchanan and Shortliffe, 1984). The program was designed to aid a physician on the diagnosis and treatment of blood infections. It decides on the basis of clinical and laboratory tests:

(1) whether the infection is significant;

(2) what organisms are involved;

(3)   what are the potentially useful drugs;

(4)   what drug regime is best for the given patient.

These goals are expressed as antecedents in the top-level rule used by the backward-chaining MYCIN system, viz.

RULE 092

IF   1) There is an organism which requires therapy, and
      2) Consideration has been given to the possible existence of additional organisms requiring therapy

THEN 1) Compile the list of possible therapies which, based upon sensitivity data, may be effective against the organisms requiring treatment, and
      2) Determine the best therapy recommendations from the compiled list.

The main objects (contexts) to be reasoned about in the MYCIN domain are:

(1)   the patient;

(2)   cultures prepared in the laboratory from samples taken from the patient;

(3)   organisms identified as present in these cultures;

(4)   drugs suitable for dealing with these organisms;

(5)   prior operations, and drugs associated with these operations.

These are organized into a data structure termed the context tree (see Figure 1). The reasoning process in MYCIN instantiates the context tree by exhaustive backward-chaining of an AND/OR tree, dynamically generated by the application of the inference engine to the rules whose top goals are expressed in rule 092 (above).

As well as obtaining a list of recommended therapies, the user can ask general questions about the knowledge base, for example 'What rules mention meningitis?'. This facility is not a full 'natural language' front-end - it is implemented by key-word scanning. It is also possible for the user to ask 'how' and 'why' at points in the consultation when the system is requesting information. 'Why' is interpreted as 'why is it important that you have this information?', which inevitably results in the printing-out of the rule currently being considered. Another 'why' will produce information about rules referencing the current rule, and so on - up to the top-level goal. The goal-tree is ascended. Similarly, a 'how' question asked in response to the system's statement of some conclusion produces a trace of how the

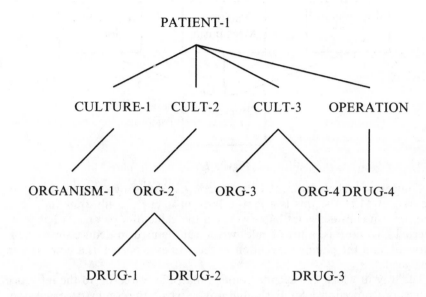

Figure 1 Domain of Mycin (Context Tree for Sample Patient)

information was inferred - it involves a descent of the goal tree.

The simple backward-chaining used in MYCIN was found to give rise to a reasoning process at expert level. The chaining mechanism focuses requests for data, is simple to implement and is also easy to explain to the expert involved in the knowledge elicitation process. It also has the advantage that the description of this line of reasoning can form the basis of an explanation subsystem.

The context tree, in the first place, literally provides rule context, in that it enables the system to relate one object to another. For example, in Figure 1, the tree indicates that organism-4 came from culture-3 and not from culture-1 or culture-2. However, the need to build up the context tree also provides constraints which focus the dialogue with the user, and gives an extra degree of focus to that provided by the depth-first search of the AND/OR goal tree. A fairly natural dialogue results ((Buchanan and Shortliffe, 1984) has examples).

Figure 2 is an attempt to generalize MYCIN's control structure, and could also be used to describe a variety of expert systems, e.g. a blackboard system as in (Aeillo, 1983).

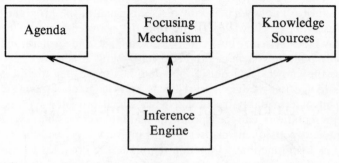

Figure 2

Control is mediated through the agenda - a list of tasks to be done. In the case of MYCIN, this is a first-in last-out queue. To illustrate its operation, we can consider what happens when the value of a parameter has to be inferred. To do this, a list of rules which can be used to deduce the value is retrieved, and the planned execution of these rules is posted as a new task on the agenda.

The way in which the agenda is manipulated is 'wired-in' to the inference engine as a procedure. Similarly, the way in which the context tree is instantiated is represented procedurally. There is no way in which the action of the inference engine can be changed (unlike other systems such as OPS5 (Brownston *et al.*, 1985)). The strategy for rule use is, as noted above, 'wired-in' and is not available for examination, changing or reasoning by the consultation, explanation and knowledge elicitation subsystems. As mentioned in Chapter 5, knowledge about knowledge - metaknowledge - is needed for higher performance expert systems.

8.2 Metaknowledge

To illustrate this point, let us consider the problem of knowledge acquisition in MYCIN. In the original system, the knowledge acquisition system was little more than an editor which could be used to edit the Lisp data structures representing the rules, lists and tables of the knowledge base. R. Davis in his Ph.D. thesis expanded this system and made it knowledge-based (Buchanan and Shortliffe, 1984). The system uses some of the methods used by the knowledge engineer when modifying the knowledge base. When the knowledge engineer peruses the knowledge, perhaps with a view to adding a new rule, he already knows a lot about the form and contents of the rules and facts. He is able to criticize any suggested new rule and to ensure that it can be incorporated into the knowledge base with no unforeseen side-effects.

TEIRESIAS uses such knowledge about knowledge - metaknowledge. It could be said to 'know what it knows'. This enables the program to make multiple uses of its knowledge. The domain knowledge is not only used directly by the system, but can be examined and generalized about (abstracted), and the system can direct precisely how it is used.

Because the knowledge acquisition system has to be able to add new data structures to the knowledge base, it needs knowledge about syntax. Davis' approach involves a data structure schema which provides a framework in which representations can be specified. Taking rules as an example, the antecedent and consequent clauses of the internal representation of a rule are coded as Lisp functions. Function templates are provided which indicate the order and generic types of the arguments in a typical call of that function. For example, the function SAME has as template

(object attribute value).

An instance of its use might be

(SAME CNTXT INFECT PRIMARY-BACTEREMIA).

The system is thus able to examine its own data structures.

Besides representation-specific knowledge about data structure syntax, i.e. about encoding, TEIRESIAS also has knowledge about the contents of rules. This knowledge is specific to the domain of application. Examples would be information about the possible uses of a piece of knowledge (e.g. information about the seriousness of an illness) and its requirements for time and space. Thus information about patterns and trends in object-level knowledge can be represented and used. This metaknowledge is held as rule models - abstract descriptions of rulesets built from empirical generalizations about the rules. The system examines the ruleset and builds up clusters of knowledge about rule patterns. The central idea is the characterization of a typical member of the ruleset (a prototype). This idea is, of course, used in other systems, such as the CENTAUR system of (Aikins, 1980), and usually involves some sort of frame representation.

A use of such a rule model could be when a new rule to categorize an organism is being formulated by the knowledge engineer. If the engineer suggests a rule with no clause concerning the morphology (shape) of organisms, the system can offer some useful criticism, since the rule models suggest that most rules of this type would include such a clause. TEIRESIAS actually offers to write such a clause, and will even include a plausible value for the type of morphology, e.g.

'The morphology is rod'

since it also knows that rod is a typical value of morphology.

Besides these metadata (function templates and rule models), TEIRESIAS also has metarules which guide the use of knowledge and decide what rules and methods are to be applied. At the implementation level, their effect is to modify the list of relevant rules retrieved when an attempt is made to evaluate an antecedent of a rule.

There are two types of metarules. First, a pruning metarule can fire. The effect of this is to exclude particular rules from consideration. In terms of the goal tree, this amounts to a decision not to explore a given branch. It amounts to a judgement on the overall utility of a rule, as to whether it is any use at all in a specific context. The other type of metarule used by Davis encodes knowledge on the relative importance of object-level rules. At the implementation level the metarule acts to reorder object-level rules relevant to some goal before invoking them.

An example:

METARULE 004

IF   1) There are rules which are relevant to positive cultures
AND   2) There are rules which are relevant to negative cultures

THEN It is definite that the former should be done before the latter.

This amounts to a less drastic decision about restructuring the goal tree. The branches are reordered rather than pruned.

At any node expansion, Davis' system chooses complete expansion (exhaustive search), reordering of goals or pruning of goals, and thus allows several types of metaknowledge. Together with the prototypical knowledge of rule models and function templates, it gives rise to a pattern of search which is not 'blind' but which is guided by heuristic knowledge. Only one level of metaknowledge has been described, but the scheme could be extended to indefinite metalevels. The inference engine used is still simple and a number of extensions are possible. For example, metalevel rules could select different types of inference mechanism (such as forward- or backward-chaining) at appropriate points in the search process.

In the past the system performance has been enhanced by adding large quantities of domain-specific knowledge. However, there seems no reason to believe that performance is linearly related to the number of rules. Indeed, it might well be that performance will 'flatten out' - although there are more rules, there is also a harder problem of search. Building the high perfor-mance systems of the future could need strategies for acquiring metalevel knowledge which would guide the use of other, lower-level, knowledge. TEIRESIAS is an important implementation which gives guidelines as to how such additional knowledge and mechanisms can increase functionality.. It also demonstrates how knowledge can be reused - the MYCIN medical knowledge base is used as a knowledge source from which function templates, for example, can be abstracted.

8.3 Classification of Metaknowledge

Davis' work indicates that metaknowledge is not uniform. It can, for example, be held as rules or data. It can be applied at various levels. It can be used by different subsystems. Clancey (1983, 1986) has suggested an interesting classification of metaknowledge. He has certainly raised the level of abstraction in this research field by providing a useful metaknowledge taxonomy and suggesting how we can elicit and use such knowledge.

Clancey points out that MYCIN-style systems are often described in terms of the language of graph search - we use terms such as rules, goals and chaining. He argues that we need a vocabulary which is independent of the implementation language, whatever it may be. The description language should be at the knowledge level and should embody a more psychological and human-oriented approach.

This interest in metalevel description derives from Clancey's Ph.D. work, in which he developed a tutoring system called GUIDON by using the MYCIN knowledge base together with additional knowledge about teaching. It was hoped to develop a tutoring 'shell' which could be used to teach a variety of subjects by using different domain knowledge bases.

By using system-derived knowledge about rules in a similar way to that developed by Davis, Clancey's system abstracts patterns from the domain rules. These rule models are descriptions of typical groups of factors in the rules. By doing this, it becomes possible to annotate a rule with a reference to the corresponding rule model. At a slightly higher level, rule schemas were used to represent abstractions from the object-level rules of descriptions of different kinds of rules. For example, a rule schema description could designate a rule to a type that provided identification ('covers') for a specific disease (say meningitis) and could describe the context of its application (say clinical). Knowing what is typical for a given rule, the system can then determine what is untypical by 'subtracting' the rule antecedents common to all rules of this type, leaving a 'key factor' description. This key factor forms another annotation which is of use to the explanation and tutoring system. The knowledge engineer can provide other annotation, e.g. literature citations, which can prove useful as support knowledge for explanation.

Some knowledge is made explicit and therefore available by these methods. However, Clancey found many glaring examples of implicit knowledge.

Consider the following example :

RULE 123

IF   1) The age of the patient is greater than 17, and
      2) The patient is an alcoholic

THEN Diplococcus might be causing the infection.

The medical knowledge contained in this rule is that the diplococcus organism is associated with alcoholism. What, then, is the function of the first clause? It is to guide the application of the rule in that it prevents the system asking a patient whose age is 17 or less about alcoholism. A 'hidden' rule is being applied, viz.

        IF   The age of the patient is 17 or less
        THEN The patient is not an alcoholic.

The problem is that in the course of a tutoring dialogue, the student user might proffer the relation between alcoholism and diplococcus, but since this item of medical knowledge is not recorded explicitly, the system will not be able to record that the student has offered some possibly relevant and valuable evidence. It seems that as well as knowledge about rule use and form, we also need to unpack a whole range of knowledge which has been encoded into the knowledge representation language. Further examples abound - for instance, consider the effect of rule order. A purported advantage of production rule systems is that each rule is an independent 'chunk' of knowledge. Rule order is seen to be unimportant because the rules are essentially uncoupled. In fact, rule order can govern the order in which rules are applied, and this can cause the focus of the questioning to jump around, to be defocused. If we start tuning rule order to achieve a more satisfactorily focused dialogue, we are effectively embedding a strategy of rule selection and of knowledge use. Clancey terms this embedding *proceduralization* and points out how this makes knowledge unavailable to the system.

This proceduralization enters many areas of computing. Consider what happens when a programmer using a low level language, say assembly code, decides at some point in the program to initialize a variable to zero, and at some later point to increment that same variable and if the result is less than 100 to perform a branch to a prior address. The programmer's intent is to loop 100 times, although this is not explicit in the program.

A higher level language might allow the programmer to achieve the same effect by stating :

```
repeat 100
    .....
    .....
    .....
end-repeat.
```

Here the 'repeat' is explicit - the programming style has become slightly more declarative (and the execution possibly slightly less efficient). As in the other examples, the writing of an efficient procedure tends to hide the intent of the programmer. Clancey advocates unpacking or decompiling procedural knowledge. In particular, he wishes to represent explicitly domain-independent problem-solving knowledge in the medical and tutoring domains and thus to reveal the bases of medical diagnostic strategy. He has developed a framework that (as so often happens) seems to be useful not only in description of medical knowledge but also in the process of eliciting knowledge from the domain expert.

The divisions of his taxonomy are:

(1) Heuristic knowledge, e.g. associations between patient data and therapies or diagnoses.

(2) Strategic knowledge - control knowledge - how to apply rules.

(3) Structural knowledge - the taxonomy of domain objects, e.g. therapies, diagnoses, cultures, organisms.

(4) Support knowledge - knowledge used in justifying rules, ranging from 'deep' (causal) knowledge to reference citations.

In NEOMYCIN, a reimplementation of GUIDON developed with these principles in mind (Clancey, 1983, 1986), Clancey concentrates on structural and strategic knowledge to supplement the object-level knowledge. He points out that there can be problems with the use of support knowledge in explanation. If we have rules which encapsulate a causal model, for example, we need to use these rules in appropriate situations. For example, it might be useful to explain the action of a virus by following the causal chain associated with the viral infection. However, there are instances where this is an inappropriate way to explain a conclusion. For example, a system might decide not to prescribe tetracycline for a young patient because this drug can cause permanent blackening of developing teeth. If the user of the system queries this decision and asks for some justification, an explanation of the causal chain which leads from the administration of the drug to the blackened appearance of the teeth is probably *not* appropriate. It would be better to form an explanation based on the general medical principle that therapies which have socially undesirable side-effects should be avoided. If the system is able to reason about general principles, it will also be able to override them when necessary. For example, if no other drug were available or usable in the case described and the patient's life were at risk, it might be expedient to prescribe tetracycline, since saving life is a high order goal for all medical systems.

In NEOMYCIN, the strategic metarules encode general diagnostic strategy. The structural knowledge is organized as explicit representations of disease taxonomies, taxonomies which represent patient types (old, young, alcoholic) and taxonomies of goals relating to patients (save life, restore to normal physical state).

Clancey claims that his implementations decouple the perceived high-level inferencing procedure from the system's reasoning with domain knowledge and data. The original MYCIN program used, as stated above, exhaustive depth-first search. Clancey's later work seems to involve a more data-directed style. Clearly, the guidance provided by metalevel knowledge is sufficient to focus the consultation as well as providing a good basis for explanation facilities.

8.4 The CENTAUR Implementation

It is of interest to examine in some detail some work which illustrates in a particularly lucid way the abstraction of strategic and structural knowledge suggested by Clancey. Aikins (1980) has implemented a 'rational reconstruction' of PUFF, a system used to diagnose pulmonary (lung) disease which was originally implemented in the EMYCIN shell (i.e. the inference system remaining when the domain knowledge is removed from MYCIN). CENTAUR was discussed by Ringland in Chapter 4. Here we will examine it in more detail.

CENTAUR uses prototypical knowledge, viz. descriptions of typical lung diseases and a typical consultation, to guide the consultation and explanation process. Effectively, the prototypes choose which rules to use - they provide the broad context of action and the rules themselves provide the finer detail. Input data are matched to the prototypical data and this enables the system to classify the data and identify untypical patterns. The prototypes provide the focusing, facilitating clear control and grouping of data.

Control knowledge is represented by rules attached to prototype 'control' slots. This gives the knowledge context and separates it from other system knowledge. Aikins' general strategy is to represent explicitly the various types of knowledge possessed by the system. She criticizes the 'flat' rules of the original MYCIN. The problem is that their structural uniformity and seeming independence hide groupings which exist. Rules have different uses in different stages of a consultation, depending on the particular situation which has come about in response to input data. Domain rules to infer new information should not look similar to rules which control other rules and rules which set default values.

Frame systems (Minsky, 1975) have been put forward as an appropriate way to provide the required grouping, and are used by CENTAUR to organize rule-groups and hence to bring rules into play where appropriate.

The prototypes are organized into a hierarchy whose structure is related to the taxonomy of lung diseases (Figure 3). At the root of the tree is the consultation prototype. This has control slots whose values represent the various consultation stages. A consultation starts by the choosing of this prototype, which represents a primitive plan of the consultation. The user is allowed to set built-in options, for example the selection strategy for the current list of prototypes. A strategy which could be chosen is to pursue the disease prototype with the highest certainty measure (a scoring factor) first. Aikins comments that the explicit representation of the consultation stages means that they can be reasoned about by the system and, for example, could be re-ordered. (This was not actually done by the implemented system.)

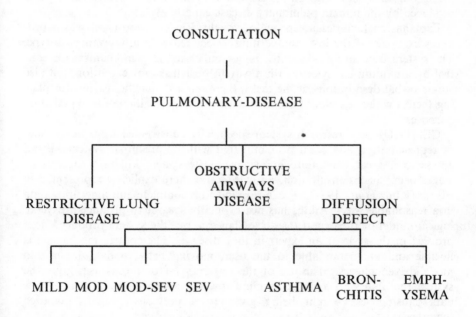

Figure 3 CENTAUR Prototype Tree

The next prototype chosen is the Pulmonary Disease prototype, which controls the acquisition of initial data. This data entry triggers other prototypes. Each triggered prototype is given a certainty measure, similar to the certainty factors used in MYCIN.

A summary of the prototypes which have been triggered is now printed out and the system chooses the ones to be followed up. In considering these active prototypes, the system takes into account all the data (including negative evidence) and so modifies the certainty measures. Since plausible values and possible error values are stored, other values are regarded as 'surprise' values and are printed out by the system for the information of the user.

After considering all the triggered prototypes, the system orders the hypothesis list and indicates the current best prototypes. The next stage is one of refinement, instigated by refinement rules stored with the relevant prototypes, and further questions are asked.

Next the 'summary' rules of the relevant prototypes are executed, which prints out a summary of the information that has been obtained in filling in the prototypes, i.e. the main inferences the system has made.

Lastly, the 'actions' slots of the confirmed prototypes are executed, which prints out the main data and conclusions in the same style as the reports produced by the human pulmonary disease experts.

Explanation facilities are provided by the Review prototype, which produces a review of the instantiated data associated with any given prototype. The system uses an agenda which is not only used as a mechanism for control by providing the system with a way to post tasks for execution, but also stores verbal descriptions of the tasks, their origins, and the reasons for placing them on the agenda. This information is thus available for explanation purposes.

CENTAUR is a research system specifically constructed to explore issues of representation and control. Compared with its precursor systems, it has access to a great deal more knowledge. The system knows what sort of stages occur in a consultation, knowledge nowhere explicitly represented in PUFF (Kunz *et al.*, 1978). It can respond to incomplete and inaccurate data in a reasonable way. Aikins has not explicitly set out to produce a psychological model of the expert (as does Clancey), but the system produced does proceed in the style of an expert in lung disease. The control mechanism is flexible and understandable to the user, moving between data-driven and model-driven phases. The use of the certainty factor mechanism gives the system the ability to 'change its mind' by, for instance, the arrival of new data causing less weight being given to a previously highly favoured hypothesis.

Certainly a great deal of the knowledge in PUFF has been 'unpacked' and made available, together with some new knowledge elicited from the expert. An indication of the greater knowledge is given by the number of rules, which have risen from 50 in PUFF to 300 in CENTAUR, and this does not take into account the wealth of prototypical knowledge.

8.5 Comments on CENTAUR and Conclusion

Jackson (1986), in his critique of Aikins' work, points out that a larger system built in the style of CENTAUR could have much larger numbers of triggered prototypes and that this could give rise to difficult scheduling and focusing problems, of the type encountered in the INTERNIST internal medicine system (Pople *et al.*, 1975). No attempt is made in CENTAUR to let the system itself derive metaknowledge, as was implemented in TEIRESIAS and GUIDON (Clancey, 1983). Clancey (1983) comments on knowledge of various sorts which was not made explicit by CENTAUR. For example, the control steps that specify on each level what to do next, e.g. "after confirming obstructive airways disease, determine the subtype of obstructive airways disease", are compiled into the prototype hierarchy.

However, CENTAUR can certainly be said to exhibit the explicit representation and use of a wide variety of metaknowledge and to be a significant pointer to what might be called the 'second' generation of expert systems. Whether the specific architecture is of much general use can be argued about. At least one system has been implemented with a similar architecture (Gale, 1985). Possibly it is unwise to take too much account of the specific architecture, but instead we should attempt to abstract the essential feature - the explicit representation and use of a wide variety of metaknowledge. Clancey (1983) comments that the metalevel analysis which the 'second generation' of expert systems will require will impose on the expert (and the knowledge engineer) the extra burden of becoming a knowledge taxonomist. This task will require considerable assistance, patience and tools.

9   Representing Time

Charlie Kwong

9.1 The Need for a Temporal Representation

We understand the world around us with relationships between the entities. When we consider something, an elephant for example, we know that it is an animal. Furthermore, we retrieve other identifying attributes to give a picture of a large four-legged creature with a greyish colour, big ears, etc. When told that John gave Mary a book, there is an automatic attachment of attributes to the entities within the discourse: gender to the named persons, perhaps that the book is made of paper leaves bound within covers.

To build AI systems, representations of these entities and their attributes need to be generated. These representations have to be easily manipulated, stored and retrieved. Other chapters in this book have looked at how it is possible to do this, and have discussed the issues involved. Here we examine temporal representation, the time aspect of relationships between universal entities.

First of all one might ask the difficult question - "What is TIME?" and try to think of an answer in the general everyday context. This is highly philosophical and I should not even try to touch upon the answer here. The reader is referred to an in-depth study of Time by van Benthem (1982).

How is time represented in general? We can take an analogue watch and say that it represents the passage of time by the rotation of its hands at a certain rate and it expresses the current time by the positions of its hands. A more appropriate question we should ask is "How do we humans represent time?''. Humans can hold time representations in a variety of ways, by visualizing a pair of clock hands or the numbers of a digital time display to represent an instant or an angle for an interval of some minutes, for example. But our representations are more complex than that. We do not use angles to represent weeks or months. We reason about different time intervals and their relationships, possibly converting between different representations to achieve this. To express different time instances or intervals we use language embedded with ways to express temporal knowledge. In addition to pure temporal representations that we hold, it is more often the case that we associate temporal knowledge with other knowledge, i.e. that they are often intermingled.

The aim of AI is to build systems that will automate processes like problem solving, planning, natural language understanding/ translation and medical diagnosis, to name but a few. One important criterion is that these systems should employ intelligent means to tackle the problems given. A large number of experimental systems built to try out ideas have identified that modelling physical relations between entities is difficult, and have tended to concentrate on solving that problem using different physical models, ignoring the temporal aspects altogether.

In the domain of general problem solving many early implementations concentrated on physical relationships. The laws of 'physics' gave a seemingly better foundation for testing knowledge acquisition, storage and application theories. Certainly this was necessary so that the program controlling a robot did not request it to do physically impossible things. For example, trying to place a spherical object on top of a pyramid shape or to move some shapes from one side of a low wall to the other without lifting them over the wall. However, dealing with the temporal relationships is equally important in many areas of AI applications. Problem solving methods require sophisticated world models that can capture change over time within them.

Early attempts at building a medical diagnosis system examined ways of diagnosing a patient's symptoms to produce a set of possible diseases. Doctors do not stop there. They prescribe medicine to combat the diseases and apply a monitoring procedure to check the effects of the medication over some period. Time is sometimes quite an important factor in this process. If the course of the disease is not significantly stemmed by the medication the doctor may alter the medication to increase the dose or change it. A medical diagnosis system must be able to encapsulate time in a manner that allows it to reason about the progress of diseases and the effects of medication on them.

Temporal reasoning systems, like truth maintenance systems, are limited now by the models of the world that they manipulate. One commonly cited example problem for truth maintenance systems is keeping a fact that there is an ice-cube on a table. Excepting extraordinary conditions, the ice-cube melts at a given rate and hence the fact about the ice-cube being on the table has to be altered into facts about the diminishing size of the cube, its eventual disappearance and an expanding pool of water on the table. If the world model that the truth maintenance system resides in, is a world model without any representation of time the quality of the truth maintenance is doubtful. Temporal representations must be included for there to be an acceptable quality of truth maintenance.

Planning generally involves choosing from a selection of available resources and arranging them so that their use is maximized to solve a given problem. Sometimes a problem can be solved only with certain arrangements of some of the resources, and planning involves finding what that arrangement is. Examples of resources that come under consideration are space, time, money and even people. The earliest planning systems like STRIPS (Nilsson and Fikes, 1971) had no built-in notion of time whatsoever. Actions in the world model took an insignificant amount of time to execute; hence, changes in the world took place instantaneously. Where this has been applied to real robot arms that exhibit the strategy of those planning systems, the time intervals of the actions are modelled by the robot arm receiving a command, executing it and then signalling that it has completed the request. This is all very well when the object of the exercise is to test the planning strategy or the interface to the robot's arm. Later planners used temporal world models (see Allen, 1981; Allen and Koomen, 1983) in which there were explicit time intervals, and the planner tried to fit them together.

Natural language processing has to cope with a lot of tense and temporal information in its input. Linguistics as a subject of its own has produced much formal study into the temporal aspects of language. Dowty (1979) has identified a number of temporal phenomena. From the sentence "John was leaving on Thursday yesterday." there are:

> Past/Future relations
> Deictics - (now, yesterday,Thursday)
> Vague event durations
> Alternate worlds and times
> Adverbial phrase interval bounds
> Expectation/uncertainty

Any true generalized natural language understanding system must be capable of handling all these aspects. Some of them have been quite extensively exercised in "story understanding systems" and "question and answer" systems like "BORIS" (Lehnert *et al.*, 1983) and "CHRONOS" (Bruce,

1972).

Many representations in working systems are a side-effect of modelling the main application domain, although there has been work on producing systems that provide reasoning and representation on time alone. Some of these time reasoning systems were designed to test out methodologies, others were meant as part of other larger applications which needed a 'specialist' to handle temporal information. We shall see examples of these later when we examine the different approaches.

9.2 Characteristics of Temporal Modelling

What characterizes the representation of time? When we are examining a model that uses time what do we have to look for? Temporal information that is received can be absolute or relative to another referenced point in time. It can be an interval that is microseconds long or decades. Separate events can relate to each other in uncertain terms. What about persistence? Let us look at 'now' and what issues this brings up. We also do not want to be limited to retrieving data solely by their temporal references.

9.2.1 Temporal Determinism

Some information is timeless. The statement '3 is a prime number' is an example. It poses no relevant problem as there is no time information that can be meaningfully attached. Any general knowledge representation technique that incorporates a form of temporal representation should be able to handle timeless information with ease.

Statements can have two types of temporal information attached. The first of these is a date or time attached to the non-temporal part of the statement. Instances of these are:

> "The atom bomb was first used in warfare on 6th August 1945"
> "Karl Marx was born on May 5th 1818"
> "At 8:45am this morning, I was driving to work"

These statements all give an absolute reference of time that is either a calendar date or a time. In contrast to the explicitly stated times or dates, a relative reference can be used:

> "Yesterday was a rainy day"
> "The workers will go on strike tomorrow"

In addition to whether the time expression within any statement is relative or absolute, the whole statement can be temporally definite or indefinite.

The time that the statement is made is important in determining whether the statement is temporally indefinite. The truth value of a definite statement is unaffected by the time that the statement is made. The definite statement can be stated at any different time and still hold the same truth value. The following statements illustrate this:

"It is always sunny in Barbados"
"It rains every Sunday in Athens"

Both these statements are false because it does sometimes rain in Barbados and sometimes the sun does shine on Sunday in Athens.

The truth values of temporally indefinite statements are not independent of the time of their assertion. Take the statements

"It is now raining outside"
"It was raining outside yesterday"

The first will hold true if it is factually true that at the time of the assertion it is raining. If it rained on Monday but not on Tuesday then the second statement is true if asserted on Tuesday and false if asserted on Wednesday.

9.2.2 Granularity

Representations of time must be capable of encapsulating large timespans depending on the context. This can range from microseconds in the world of digital computer circuit design to millions of years in the subject of palaeontology. In everyday life the span probably ranges from decades to hundredths of seconds. Within narrower domains this span may be reduced even further. It may well be that not many systems need to be able to hold representations of time of such a wide range granularity. Perhaps it might be sufficient to have a representation that can be easily adjusted to cope with different kinds of granularities.

9.2.3 Points or Intervals

Do we represent time as a set of points or a set of intervals? Perhaps this is one of the most prominent conflicts in representing time. If we see a set of intervals then it is possible that something might be lost within the interval. If we see time as a set of points then we could have very large sets of points to represent long durations, each one representing every instant of the smallest granularity that we care to go down to.

9.2.4 Fuzziness

Often, fuzzy time information is given because it is unnecessary to expand in detail. It would not be useful to do more processing than necessary to try and remove the fuzziness. Words and phrases like 'yesterday', 'tomorrow', 'three weeks ago' often introduce fuzzy intervals.

When uncertain information is given, the representation must be able to handle this. If given two statements

"Yesterday, I went swimming"
"Yesterday, I went shopping"

The representation should be able to hold both of these without imposing any order on the events.

9.2.5 Persistence

Many situations in the real world require us humans to model persistence. I switch on a light in a room and then leave the room. I would normally continue to believe that the light was switched on until told or observe for myself otherwise. Several things could have happened. For instance, someone else switched it off or the bulb might have blown. Whether the light is in reality still on, or off, without any reason to believe otherwise I normally hold to the belief that it is as I left it.

The notion of persistence or truth maintenance is currently an area of intense research. Given a sequence of events at times as denoted by the times of their assertion t(n):

t(0): I (now) pick up a loaded gun.
t(1): I unload it.
t(3): I point the gun at my head.
t(4): I pull the trigger.

Any deductive system should give negative answers to the questions "Was there a noise?", "Am I alive?" asked at time t(5). The temporal representation must be able to denote that, from that time t(1) onwards, the gun that I picked up is unloaded. It would be no good if, at a time later than t(1), the representation did not contain the information that the gun was still unloaded. The default deduction from the action of pulling a trigger might be that there is a loud noise and a bullet projected at what the gun points at. If this is so, then the deductive system would answer that there was a loud noise at t(5) from the given facts. This is a major problem in AI which has been coined the FRAME problem.

Persistence is usually easily gained in a modelling system. Any facts asserted to the system should remain there until explicitly contradicted or removed. This leads to the point of historical representationality. Consider the gun scenario. The immediate known history of the gun is that before t(1) it is loaded and not after. It is possible to have persistence in that at t(now) the gun is still unloaded, but there is no way of telling what time the gun was unloaded. What is needed is the representation of the history. When the assertion is made at t(1), simply replacing 'fact(the gun is loaded)' by 'fact(the gun is unloaded)' in our world state model does not maintain a history. Replacing it with 'fact(the gun is unloaded, t(1)) & fact(the gun is loaded, < t(1))' will represent the history more accurately.

9.2.6 What is Between the Past and Future

In the last paragraph we saw, briefly, a notation t(now) to indicate a particular instant. The dimensionality of time is such that there is a boundary between what has already happened and what is yet to come. This boundary is not simply a separation of the past and future. It often has a duration of its own right we call the present. Furthermore the present illustrates one of the qualities that makes modelling time difficult: it is a dynamic interval, constantly shifting in the direction of the future.

The present can take up different durations dependent on some context. Perhaps it is our human model of time that gives us the view of the present as it is. Time travel can be seen as simply the ability to shift the present that we exist in freely along the time dimension. But whatever it is, the present has a varied duration as shown by our language. Natural language allows different meanings for the word 'now' and we use it to express different things. In the following two sentences this is illustrated:

> "I will clean the floor now."
> "I am cleaning the floor now."

The first is normally used to express the intention of starting the action of cleaning the floor. That is, the interval of time which contains this action starts shortly AFTER the utterance of the sentence, whilst the second utterance usually occurs WITHIN this time. It may be used to refer to the instant or small interval in which an assertion using it is made:

> "Now, I take the knife and slice through ......"

Also there is often an implied 'now' that is used in reference to events of the past or future. Take the scenario:

Mary says to me, "I am setting off NOW, so I will see you in twenty minutes".

Later, I meet John at the cinema entrance and say to him, "Mary said she was setting off THEN so she should be here any minute".

In my communication to John I am implying that Mary said something to the effect of "I am leaving NOW ...".

9.2.7 Co-existence of Time and Other Knowledge

So far, we have mostly concentrated on the characteristics that have to be taken into account when modelling time. Many temporal logics and temporal representation schemes have time as the central concept on which other knowledge is hinged. The temporal aspect of knowledge representation should lie orthogonal to the representation of other knowledge. It should not be restricted to knowledge manipulation using the temporal part of a fact only.

To illustrate what I mean here take the statement 'I was watching the 9 o'clock news on BBC1 last night'. The temporal part of the information conveyed here is the time (9pm) of the night before the sentence was uttered. The non-temporal information is the fact that I was watching the news on BBC1, if the only index used to store and retrieve this fact is the time I did it. The query of what channel I was watching cannot be answered directly without reference to the time index.

Very often the temporal factor in some knowledge is very insignificant or irrelevant compared to some other aspect. Some things are done just for the sake of doing them, others out of necessity. Often some other factor takes higher precedence in the order of things and then WHAT rather than HOW LONG is more important.

9.3 The Alternative Approaches

Having looked at some of the characteristics that exist in temporal representations and modelling, let us take a look at how these are exhibited in past and existing systems, whether explicitly or implied.

9.3.1 State Space Modelling

This method of space representation is an example where the temporal representation is implied. In state space modelling, a state is a snapshot of the current world state. Take an early planning system like STRIPS (Nilsson and Fikes, 1971) for example. It planned the sequence of actions necessary to achieve a requirement for a set of blocks to be in given positions. A typical statement giving a world state might be:

world-state(on(A,B),on(B,C),on(C,table),on(D,table))

Actions are functions which map between states:

move(block,dest)
    if clear-top(block)& clear-top(dest)
    then delete(on(block,X)) & add(on(block,dest))

Because each state is a snapshot, it is taken to represent the world at that instant in time (i.e. point-based representation).

In general we have a series of world states {(S1), (S2), (S3),...} to represent the passage of time as a sequence of instants. There are different temporal semantics that we can apply here.

One is that each state is an instant and there exists an interval between these instants during which the function which maps from one state to the other is active.

Alternatively, we can say that the states are the intervals during which the facts are known to be true. The functions which map between the worlds now are the instants between the intervals and it is during these instants that some of the world facts change from true to false, some disappear or others appear. What is wrong in this interpretation is that the functions take place instantly and that does not reflect the real world closely enough. In addition, there are events as McDermott (1982) pointed out which are not factual changes. He used the example of a person running around a track 3 times. How would a state space modelling representation cope with this?

Using either of the two interpretations above, there is still the problem that there is no distinction of different time interval durations. In the first one, all the operations take the same length of time to execute, whilst in the second there is one common denomination of time for the facts that exist in any world (the duration of each state, which is identical). Therefore in this weak representation we need to store explicitly, in the state, information about how long the function took or how long a state persists. This makes the temporal representation in state space modelling explicit.

In general, state space systems keep copies of old states as new ones are created. This requires a large amount of storage capacity if the worlds get large. Keeping copies of states, however, facilitates history and allows the answering of questions like

"What was the red block on before it was last moved?"

Because the mapping functions only need to change the relevant world objects, and copy the rest into the new state, this provides a very neat way of handling persistence. It demonstrates causality where "things only change when cause exists to change them".

These models, however, have a big disadvantage when it comes to handling tensed information. Consider the assertion "Sue said yesterday morning that she would come tomorrow". The state that represents the world 'yesterday morning' will have to be altered to fit in the new information. This would then have to be propagated through all the intervening states between then and now. It is arguable that changing the world model in this way is altering the belief model and is actually wrong. Because, if we take the view that a world state model like this represents a person's belief about the world around her/him, then doing modifications like these is akin to changing history. We are changing the fact that that person did not know what Sue said prior to the instant of the assertion of the statement above.

STRIPS was typical of the early AI systems which chose to ignore the temporal aspect of solving any given problem. They concentrated on the 'physical' side of things. Later however, some systems took a more direct approach and just concentrated on the temporal aspect of a problem solution. The system by Kahn and Gorry (1977) employed two different types of representation within the same system. Their system was designed to take temporal statements and then answer questions on the temporal part of the information given.

9.3.2 Date Based Method

Intuitively, every event/occurrence starts at a certain time. Using the date based method, these events are stored using this time as the index. Information with relative temporal content is resolved to a fixed time and this is used as the key. Cross referencing tables are needed here, one to hold the times and dates, another to hold the factual information. This or some other mechanism is needed to facilitate the accessibility from the temporal and non-temporal information.

However, there is a need to distinguish between the end time of an event and the start time of the event immediately following. If a switch is activated to turn on a light for example, the model should not allow there to be an instant when the light is both on and off. Figure 1 shows the analogy to the real number line in mathematics for representing ranges of reals.

There is the question of which time is used as the key. The choice is between the time of assertion or the temporal information in the sentence. If the first is used, any relative temporal information within the assertion can be resolved to an absolute time. However, some information may be changed in this transformation. Take, for example, the sentence "The bullion delivery will take place at dawn tomorrow" asserted at 3pm on December 31st 1988.

December 31	3pm	bullion delivery dawn tomorrow	(1)
December 31	3pm	bullion delivery dawn January 1st 1989	(2)

$$f(x) = 1: x < 3$$
$$f(x) = 2: x \geq 3$$

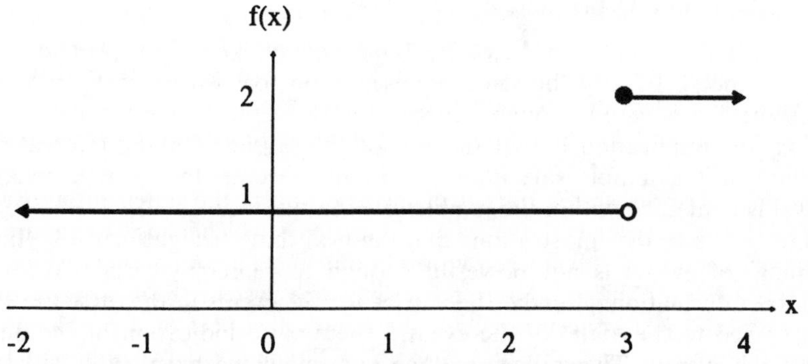

Figure 1 Real line representation of $f(x)$

In the second entry (2), it is not stored that the word tomorrow was actually used in the statement.

If we choose to use the implicit or explicit temporal information as the access/store key, then relative temporal references have to be resolved to a time or date. Again, this loses information (unless the time of assertion is also kept):

> January 1   dawn   bullion delivery [3pm 31/12/88]   (3)

The big drawback with this method is that disjunctive temporal knowledge cannot be stored if we choose to index it on the contained temporal data. For example, the two assertions are made on the 1st of January:

> "Yesterday, there was a demonstration of sausage making"
> "Yesterday, there was a jumble sale"

The 'yesterday' will have to be resolved to the date 31st December. This will be placed in the events table.

> December 31   sausage making demonstration, jumble sale   (4)

Care must be taken to ensure that the textual ordering or the order of the utterance of the sentences is not taken as an ordering of the events. This however can be interpreted more broadly in that there is an ordering based on the times of the assertions of the statements. However, can we really imply this sort of ordering based simply on the sequence of utterance of two statements? In addition, if we have the statements also asserted on the 1st of January:

"Yesterday, there was a demonstration of sausage making
    followed by a jumble sale"
"Yesterday, there was a demonstration of sausage making
    during the jumble sale"

We can have an entry in the events table exactly like that of (4) above for both sentences. Clearly the same representation for two distinctly different statements is not good enough. In the first case the two intervals do not overlap; the implication is that the end of the sausage making interval was the start of the jumble sale interval. In the second, the sausage making interval is contained within the jumble sale interval.

Here we see the illustration that shows that straightforward 'time-stamping' of events is not powerful enough to represent certain kinds of temporal information. Firstly, the entries for the events in the table are simply attached to the 'date' of the event. There is no indication of the duration of the events. The sausage making and sale could have taken 24 hours or 12 hours. They may have different durations. How would it be possible to use time-stamping to obtain default durations for jumble sales? How would that be fitted into the event entry of the table?

So far, some of the relative temporal information like 'dawn', 'yesterday' and 'tomorrow' has been converted to a date. Most often we use general terms to describe a time rather than specifically stating the exact time because there is no need to divulge additional information. Therefore if a system has to be more specific than necessary there is no harm. Sometimes, however, we are uncertain of the exact time of things we are referring to. So we intentionally use fuzzy time intervals or boundaries. This is especially true when talking about the future. In a purely time-stamping system fuzzy time will be extremely difficult to handle:

"Three and a half weeks ago I was ill"
"In four months' time I will be a millionaire"

It would be inaccurate to resolve the temporal information in these sentences to a date or time. If the times of assertion of the sentences are used as the indices for storage, there would be no need to resolve the fuzzy time.

9.3.3 Before/After Chains

Many events naturally fall into a sequence. By linking them together using pointers, we have a representation for the temporal relations of these events. The simplest method would just have bi-directional pointers between events (Figure 2):

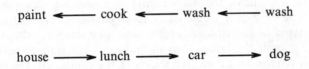

Figure 2 Events connected into a chain

This now forms the basis for building a chain of events (Figure 3a):

paint ◄─── cook ◄─── wash ◄─── wash

house ───► lunch ───► car ───► dog

Figure 3a A simple chain

These chains do not explicitly represent the durations or any time units. These have to be incorporated into the nodes which hold the information about the event. If Xh means that associated activity took X hours, we thus have an interval based representation (Figure 3b):

paint(3h) ◄─── cook ◄─── wash ◄─── wash(30min)

house ───► lunch(1h) ───► car(1h) ───► dog

Figure 3b A chain with events containing their durations

If instead we have the start time of the activity associated, then we have a point-based representation. Simply by looking at the time of the activity after the current one, the duration of the activity can be computed (Figure 3c):

paint(0800)◄─── cook ◄─── wash ◄─── wash(1345)

house ───► lunch(1200) ───► car(1315) ───► dog

Figure 3c A chain with events containing their start times

This allows the mixing of events of varying duration alongside each other in a chain. Parallel events can be modelled by a splitting node with two pointers to its successor events. At the end of these two separate chains they merge again.

Chains, however, can get long, and to search for an event will require starting at the head of the chain and traversing all the way down the nodes until it is found. This can be overcome by abstractions of time intervals and/or event information. For example, at a higher level abstracted chain, there would be a chain of the main events in a working day and the sub-chains of these main events would carry more detail. There will have to be two different types of information abstraction, one temporal the other non-temporal. If we omit the latter, then to find out what time something happened will still require an exhaustive search of the chain. By abstracting the non-temporal information, it may be possible to search only the relevant sub-chains.

The time specialist was implemented and used to gain experience on the problems of having a time specialist integrated with specialist(s) of other domains for general problem solving and to see if this approach of trying to segment temporal information from non-temporal information is feasible.

The final conclusion of this work depended on the actual implementation of other specialist problem solvers which could interact with the time specialist and testing this out on some real problems. On its own, the time specialist produced interesting results when given stories of time travelling to understand.

More recently, the emphasis in temporal representations and reasoning systems has shifted towards the more formal and rigorous approach.

9.3.4 Formal Temporal Logics

These are often based on standard Predicate Logics. Formal Logics are very powerful and expressive for representations. In their book "Temporal Logic" (Rescher and Urquhart, 1971) Rescher and Urquhart give a clear and understandable introduction to a simple temporal logic based on a topological logic. They then go on and develop this further, including incorporation of more than two truth values.

In topological logic there is a positional realization operator, p. Applied to a proposition $P(x)$, the predicate then reads that $P(p)(x)$ is true at that place p. In Rescher and Urquhart's simple system R of Temporal Logic there is a temporal realization operator, t. This operator says that its associated predicate is true at that time and it is denoted as $R(t)(A)$ where t is a time and A is a statement. For example, R(December 25)(it is Christmas day) says that, on December the 25th, it is Christmas day. To represent the important case of 'now' the symbol n is used. Therefore the statement

R(n)(the sun is shining) reads as "the sun is now shining".

There are axioms of R:

(T1) $R(t)(\neg A) = \neg R(t)(A)$

(T2) $R(t)(A \wedge B) = [R(t)(A) \wedge R(t)(B)]$

(T3) $R(n)(A) = A$

(T4) $R(t1)[(\forall t)A)] = (\forall t)[R(t1)(A)]$

(T5) $R(t1)[R(t)(A)] = R(t)(A)$

(T6) $R(t)(n = t1) = t = t1$

(T7) $R(t)(t1 = t2) = t1 = t2$

(T8) $(\forall t)A > A \wedge t/n$

The rules of inference, in addition to *modus ponens*, are:

(R1)   If |- A then |- $\forall(t)R(t)(A)$

(R2)   If |- A = B then |-(..A..) = (..B..)

The proof theory of this system of logic is given in (Rescher and Urquhart, 1971).

What is of most interest to us here is the model theory of this temporal logic. The main idea of the development of the model theory is that the truth or falsity of the statements within the logic can be determined for any time.

As temporally definite statements have constant truth value over time they can be set aside. Whilst conventional Propositional Logic utilizes a Truth Table, Temporal Logic uses a Truth Cube. This simply has a third axis to represent a set of times. Then for each 'time-slice' of the cube, we have a table and this is treated in the conventional way. The exception is the treatment of "n". The interpretation of "n" is that it takes the value of the time at which it is being evaluated.

Since Rescher and Urquhart there have been many more approaches to Formal Logic time representation. Of the latest examples, Ladkin is in the process of implementing a system which uses an interval-based formalism. He has developed a formalism (Ladkin, 1986a, Ladkin, 1986b) based on Allen's work (1983). McDermott (1982a) presents a point-based one.

Alongside the development of formal logic as temporal representation, formal logic as temporal reasoning mechanisms is undergoing heavy research. So far there has been no mention of temporal reasoning, mainly because this book concentrates on the representation side of things. Some understanding of the complexity of reasoning with time is needed to see why the more formalized approaches are necessary.

McDermott (1982a) designed a temporal logic to take into account continuous change and the indeterminacy of the future. He shows how it is necessary to be able to model different futures. Just as in applying different functions that alter the physical world model, different events happening cause different possible futures. To be able to model branching futures is crucial in supporting reasoning about planning for the future. If there is only one future then any reasoning mechanism sees only one outcome of anything that it schedules. (If it were really intelligent, it would see the futility of its actions and give up altogether!!)

Continuous change modelling is supported to allow reasoning about things that change over time, for example, the level of water which rises during the action of filling the bath-tub. A more practical need to model a changing value is for the temperature of the bath water. If the water temperature is rising above a comfortable threshold before the required water level is reached then perhaps the cold tap should be turned on more or the hot one turned down. Furthermore, normally some adjustment of the taps is done and we decide upon a rough estimate of a time lapse after which we will check the water.

9.4 Concluding Discussion

As with most issues in computing, there is a question to be asked about the trade-off between expressibility and tractability. How tractable are temporal representation systems? The time specialist described by Kahn and Gorry (1977) is intended as a representation/reasoning system that handles temporal information. It is designed to operate alongside other 'specialists' to be a general reasoning system. How large will the final system be? Is it fast enough?

Sceptics of AI in the computing world are querying the necessity for all the complex techniques for modelling, planning and expert systems, to name but a few. Their arguments point out that many of the so-called AI systems are very large in terms of size, amount of processing power required and manpower to build, and, despite all this, seem to have very little practical impact. Why not use conventional programming languages, conventional computers?

Applying this argument to the more specific domain of time representation, why not just time-stamp something else that is representing the information that we want to attach a temporal reference to? Indeed, why not? As we saw earlier, time/ date-stamping is one of the methods of temporal representation but we also looked at it's drawbacks. In the naive simple way that time/ date-stamping works, it falls short in supporting deep reasoning about temporal relations.

Really, the question that has to be addressed is why do we want a good representation and how important is it to the application that requires some form of temporal reasoning capability. It may be that time-stamping is sufficient for the purposes so "why use a mainframe when a micro will do?". We cannot let ourselves be content that, when a simple temporal representation works, we stop looking for better ones.

10 Functional Approaches to Knowledge Representation

Simon Lambert

10.1 What is a Functional Approach to Knowledge Representation?

The word 'functional' has a number of usages in computer science. In system design, for example, a *functional specification* is a statement of how the components of a system will behave without reference to how they are to be implemented: their interfaces are defined but their internal operations are of no concern outside themselves. A similar idea is found in the development of programming languages, formalized as the *abstract data type* and described in for example (Liskov and Zilles, 1974), 'What we desire from abstraction is a mechanism which permits the expression of relevant details and the suppression of irrelevant details. In the case of programming, the use which may be made of an abstraction is relevant; the way in which the abstraction is implemented is irrelevant... An *abstract data type* defines a class of abstract objects which is completely characterized by the operations on those objects.'

The usual example of an abstract data type is the stack with its operations of Push and Pop. The practical development of abstract data types has perhaps reached its zenith in Ada, with its packages and ideal of reusable code (see for example (Freedman, 1982), 'A package is a collection of data types and allowable operations between objects defined from these types.'). We shall see, however, that in knowledge representation it is a whole knowledge base with associated operations that may be regarded as an abstract data type.

At this point it is worth mentioning that some work has been done on the application of functional *languages* to the needs of knowledge-based systems. Thus SYNTEL (Reboh and Risch, 1986) is a knowledge representation 'programming language' designed to suit the development of expert systems, and is functional in nature (by which the authors mean that there is no variable assignment as such but only function definition). Languages of this sort are not, however, the concern of this chapter. Our interest is in the knowledge base as abstract data type, and the ideas which have become associated with it. Work in the area has centred around the figures of Hector Levesque and Ronald Brachman. Levesque's remarks from (Levesque, 1984) set the scene:

> '... a knowledge base... interacts with a user or system only through a small set of operations... The complete functionality of a KB is measured in terms of these operations; the actual mechanisms and structures it uses to maintain an evolving model of the domain are its own concern and not accessible to the rest of the knowledge-based system.'

Some interesting results and powerful systems have appeared within the compass of this definition. But their roles are not as restricted as the succinctness of the definition might at first suggest, for there are other themes which have become bound up with the functional approach in various ways. They include procedural semantics - in this context, the definition of behaviour by means of programs attached to entities in a knowledge base - and hybrid representation schemes, the latter being an important feature of KRYPTON, the most highly developed of the systems to be considered. The following sections discuss these related topics in roughly the order they were developed; first, though, we consider why a functional approach to knowledge representation should be desirable.

10.2 Why a Functional Approach?

The definition given in the last section of what it means for a knowledge representation scheme to be functional made clear its links with software engineering principles. Here lies some of the motivation for investigating functional approaches. One should not be over-literal and claim that there is any connection with programming 'style', or that thirty years of high level language design are having a direct influence on knowledge representation, for the concerns of the two areas do not coincide. However, the principle behind the abstract data type, that the user should be prevented from interfering where he should not, from making assumptions about implementation and taking advantage of them, is very applicable to knowledge representation schemes, and in quite a precise way.

What is it that the user of a knowledge representation scheme is to be distanced from? The answer, of course, is the ubiquitous frame or semantic network, and for two reasons: firstly that the interpretation of the links in semantic nets (or slots in frames) is not well defined, so that different users are liable to put different interpretations on them, sometimes confusing levels of abstraction or imparting their own private interpretations; and secondly - though related - that frames/semantic nets are susceptible to treatment as mere data structures for manipulation. We turn to a paper by Woods for a starting point in the analysis of these issues.

One of the major contributions of Woods' famous paper 'What's in a link.....' (Woods, 1975) is the distinction drawn between structural and assertional links in semantic nets (for the purpose of this chapter, there is no real difference intended between semantic nets and frames - both are regarded as means of organizing knowledge for representation purposes). Structural links simply describe, whereas assertional links are intended to make a positive statement: Woods' example is of a representation of 'telephone' which has a link to (or slot containing) the colour 'black', of which he asks whether the resulting structure is a description of a black telephone or an assertion that telephones are black. The distinction is an important one, and Brachman takes it up in, for instance (Brachman *et al.*, 1983a), where he observes that Hayes assumed the assertional interpretation when reducing frames to first order logic (Hayes, 1979). (See Chapter 4 in this volume for a fuller discussion of Minsky's original idea of frames and Hayes' response to it.) Brachman goes on to point out that the assertional interpretation is a limited one for two reasons. First, instantiation (i.e. slot filling) is inadequate for representing incomplete knowledge. A slot must be filled with a definite value, and no progress can be made if the value is not known precisely, but is subject to some known constraints. Second, there is no distinction between essential and incidental properties. This point is of great importance because the drawing of such a distinction is a vital feature of the KRYPTON system described in section 10.5. For the moment let us say that an assertional interpretation sees no distinction between sentences such as 'Every triangle is a polygon with three sides' and 'Every car is red [in the restricted world represented]'.

Having pointed out the limitations of the assertional interpretation of frames, Brachman considers the purely structural alternative. In such systems (exemplified by KL-ONE (Brachman and Schmolze, 1985c)) the frames do not state facts but just create descriptions like 'a car with a steering wheel'. It comes as no surprise to find that the great drawback is precisely the inability to make assertions; or rather, because there is a need to do so but no mechanism available, that the structures are often misused and given assertional interpretations. As Brachman says, 'even if the structures of a frame system are taken non-assertionally, their presence or absence can still be misread assertionally and used to encode facts about the world.'

The fact is that frames, especially with the structural interpretation, are crying out to be manipulated as data structures. The standard notation, with its Lisp-like syntax, makes this all too apparent:

```
(CAR
        (IS-A VEHICLE)
        (OWNER person)
        (WHEELS 4)
        ...
)
```

The user (by which is meant whoever employs the frame package to inter-face to another part of the system or directly to the outside world) may well feel at liberty to treat the slots/links as he likes, pursuing IS-A chains (for instance) with happy disregard for what they really mean. This is another problem that has taxed Brachman: in (Brachman, 1983) he analyses some of the many interpretations that have been put on the overworked IS-A. An example will show just how far frames can go in becoming mere data struc-tures for manipulation, and what effects this can have on the representation of *knowledge*. Consider Figure 1, a classification of students at a hypotheti-cal university. Intuitively, the classes are all on the same 'level', and one feels happy answering the question 'How many kinds of student are there?' with 'Three'. But suppose we throw caution to the winds and attempt to represent students in more detail as in Figure 2. The result is incoherent confusion, and the question of how many kinds there are becomes

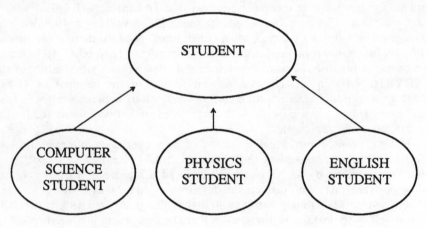

Figure 1 Kinds of Student

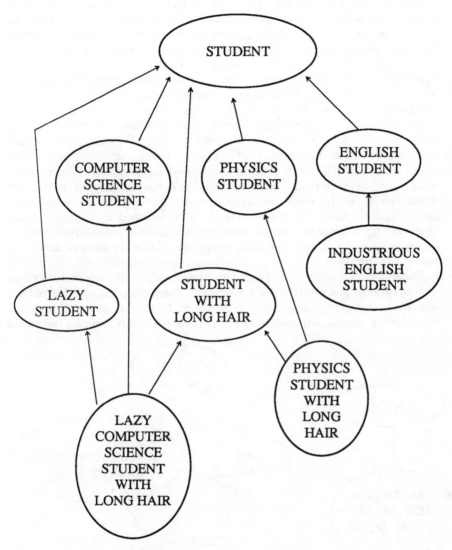

Figure 2 More Kinds of Student

meaningless. Yet one could make a case that all the links shown in the figures are IS-A links. All that seems to have been achieved is an arbitrary encoding without any logical structure. Clearly, many different arrangements of nodes and links could have been chosen, and any inference engine out to use such representations would be on very uncertain ground. In fact,

Brachman gives a definite example of the dangers of uncontrolled use of net-works in considering two definitions of 'bachelor': one sees a bachelor as being a person, with the qualifications of male-ness and being unmarried (two slot values), while the other regards him as a conjunction of a 'man' and an 'unmarried-person', themselves both kinds of person (Figure 3). As Brachman points out, the 'conceptual distance' from person to bachelor is different in these two representations, and 'spreading activation theories of processing in semantic nets might consider this distance to be significant.'

As well as his analysis of IS-A links, Brachman has also considered the nature of semantic nets in general (Brachman, 1979). He gives a comprehensive overview of the history and development of semantic nets, and provides an analysis of the levels of primitive employed, ranging from 'implementational' up to 'linguistic'. What all his work has done is to show how dangerous it is to allow direct access to the structures representing knowledge, for there are almost bound to be unstated assumptions made about the significance of slots or links, and the cause of knowledge representation in general will not have been advanced. Hence the need is seen for a functional approach.

The above discussion was based on Brachman's work, which led to the development of KRYPTON in an attempt to eliminate some of the problems described. Levesque's more formal work on functional approaches has a more formal justification, in terms of bringing out the full implications of a

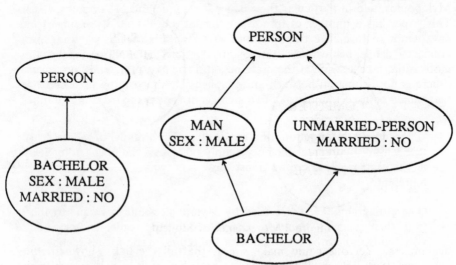

Figure 3 Two Definitions of a Bachelor

set of beliefs - what he calls 'competence'. Ultimately, though, his work needs little justification; like mathematics, its interest lies in the very fact of being able to prove results.

10.3 The Procedural Semantics of Mylopoulos and Levesque

It was mentioned in section 10.1 that one idea associated with functional approaches to knowledge representation is procedural semantics, or at least one manifestation of it, for the term has a wider applicability beyond the scope of this chapter. The time has now come to examine it, for the work of Levesque and others predates the work on functional approaches but possesses its important characteristics. Woods uses the term in his paper (Woods, 1975) introducing the structural/assertional distinction; though he says that his interpretation 'differs slightly from that which is intended by other people who have since used it', his definition, though very vague, conveys some of its later meaning:

> '...a specification of truth conditions can be made by means of a procedure or function which assigns truth values to propositions in particular possible worlds. Such procedures for determining truth or falsity are the basis for what I have called "procedural semantics".'

For something more concrete, we turn to the work of Levesque and Mylopoulos, and in particular their paper (Levesque and Mylopoulos, 1979). This paper has a number of important themes, but essentially springs from an attempt to formalize the semantics of semantic networks by using programs to define behaviour. In the introduction the authors express this motivation, take a swipe at the usefulness of logic as a representation scheme ('there is no distinction between an inference rule that *can* be used and one that *should* be used'), and make two significant statements from our point of view:

> 'To interpret this diagram [of a semantic net] as a model of a data structure within a computer memory simply postpones the problem [of what it really means] since we must now ask what the data structure represents.'

> 'These diagrams [i.e. those used by Mylopoulos and Levesque to illustrate their scheme] should be understood by the reader as convenient visual aids, not to be confused with the representation itself (defined by the operators of a formalism) or a possible implementation of this representation (defined by an interpreter of the formalism).'

The first of these points is precisely the justification for a functional approach that we have seen in the previous section; the second states the essence of that approach.

Mylopoulos and Levesque begin by taking the usual semantic net primitives (in their terminology, *objects* are instances of *classes* and have *relations* between them), and they determine to associate programs with them to permit inferencing in an efficient and modular way. There are eight operations which the programs implement, four on relations and four on classes:

> to assert that a relation holds between two objects;
> to assert that a relation no longer holds between two objects;
> to fetch all objects related to another by a given relation;
> to test whether a given relation holds between two objects;
> to create an object as an instance of a class;
> to destroy an instance of a class;
> to fetch all instances of a class;
> to test whether an object is an instance of a class.

Here we have our functional interface, the interface to the knowledge base by means of TELL and ASK operators which Levesque was later to formalize.

Mylopoulos and Levesque go on to discuss hierarchies within their model, specifically IS-A (taking account of the assertional/structural distinction) and PART-OF. They introduce metaclasses, unifying the whole representation scheme and making the handling of inheritance more consistent. Finally they consider the nature of the programs attached to classes (which now include classes themselves and relations). There is some divergence of interest from the purely functional approach here, but the idea of having operators defining behaviour is exactly right.

Procedural semantics in the sense of Mylopoulos and Levesque came to fruition in the system unimaginatively called PSN, developed at Toronto since 1976 (Mylopoulos *et al.*, 1983). The system is based very closely on the ideas described above. Instances of classes are now called tokens; relations are defined between classes and are instantiated to form links between tokens (Figure 4). Programs specify operations on classes and relations, exactly as above. There are three primitive relations for creating hierarchies: INSTANCE-OF (relating tokens to their classes), IS-A (with inheritance) and PART-OF ('aggregation', using slots to represent parts of a concept). The attached programs are themselves objects, and have their own class with slots (for parameters, prerequisites and actions). A new idea in PSN is the *similarity link*, which suggests other classes to be tried when a match fails, and may owe something to Minsky's suggestion of 'sharply localized knowledge that would naturally be attached to a frame itself for recommending its own replacement' (Minsky, 1981).

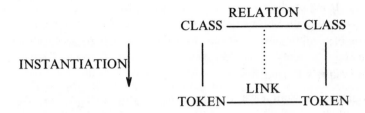

Figure 4 Entities and Relationships in PSN

A number of applications have been developed using PSN. Mentioned in (Mylopoulos *et al.*, 1983) are two in the domain of cardiology.

Before going on to look at Levesque's later work, when he abandoned the procedural aspect and considered the functional interface alone, it is worth mentioning some work by Rich, described in (Rich, 1982). Here we see another theme of importance in our area, that of mixed representations. Rich was working on the Programmer's Apprentice at MIT, for which a representation scheme called *plan diagrams* had been devised to suit the type of knowledge being represented. 'During this period we took a fairly *ad hoc* approach to the semantics of our knowledge representation. This is not to say that we did not know what plan diagrams meant, but just that ultimately the meaning of the representation was implicit in the procedures we were writing to manipulate it.' Rich began to develop a formal semantics for plan diagrams using predicate calculus, and found that the two representations could co-exist in the system implementation. It is a hybrid representation, in which both levels of language are used for various levels of reasoning in the application domain, depending on which is appropriate. A mixed representation scheme, though on a more formal footing, is an important of feature of KRYPTON, described in section 10.5.

Procedural semantics played an important part in the evolution of functional approaches to knowledge representation, but ultimately it is rather limited because it is not suitable for theoretical amplification. Rich makes no bones about this:

'Before going any further it is crucial to understand that this paper is about pragmatic rather than philosophical issues in knowledge representation.'

His concluding remarks are couched as advice for representation designers. Similarly, the procedural semantics of Mylopoulos and Levesque, though undoubtedly fruitful, seems unlikely to lead to any new directions. Defining behaviour by means of programs is clearly advantageous for efficiency of search, but there is not much one can say about it. The programs seem to be at too low a level, despite attempts to impose structure on them. It is not clear how the approach can be extended beyond the pragmatic. Indeed, Levesque realized this when he came to investigate the functional interface in isolation, and it is to his work that we now turn.

10.4 Levesque's Formalization

In the preceding section we have seen that Mylopoulos and Levesque's procedural semantics attached programs to classes and relations in a knowledge representation scheme in order to perform basic operations on those classes and relations. It is these operations that constitute the functional interface, and Levesque's next step was to abandon the procedural aspect and investigate what could be said in the abstract about a knowledge base with such an interface. In a lengthy and important paper (Levesque, 1984) he describes his results.

Levesque begins by specifying the interface by means of two operators TELL and ASK, the former asserting that a statement (made in some language L) is true in the knowledge base, the latter querying whether this is the case:

TELL: KB $\times$ L $\rightarrow$ KB;
ASK: KB $\times$ L $\rightarrow$ {yes, no, unknown}.

He goes on to discuss the requirements on the language L, paying particular attention to the need to represent incomplete knowledge. Arguing that 'it must be possible for the KB to find out about the world in an incremental way', he maintains that TELL and ASK must permit weak statements about the world: saying what something is not, for instance, or giving a range of possible things it might be. A formal discussion of the semantics and proof theory of the language L follows; then Levesque outlines some of the problems arising from the use of L (roughly speaking, if it is possible to make weak statements to the KB, it may return unhelpfully weak answers). He introduces an operator which applies to a sentence of L and returns 'true' if the sentence is currently known in the knowledge base, 'false' if not, and he defines an extended language KL incorporating this operator. Making assumptions of 'competence' (that every consequence of what is known is itself known) and 'closure' (that a pure sentence is true exactly when it is known), semantics is defined for the extended language, and the operators TELL and ASK are redefined.

The argument then takes another dive into formalism: Levesque considers what sort of knowledge (in a formal sense) is representable in his language, and having established it, asks what effect a TELL operation has, and how ASK works. The result is a 'Representation Theorem', which states in essence that communication with the knowledge base in the language KL may be achieved completely in first order terms, just as with the original L.

Having surfaced from the proof of his Representation Theorem, Levesque considers possible extensions to the theory he has established. The most immediately interesting concerns default reasoning. Levesque proposes two possible lines of attack by extending respectively the ASK and TELL operators to take defaults into account. He introduces an operator which, applied to a one-place predicate, yields a predicate of being a 'typical example'. It is possible to assert that 'typical birds fly' and 'typical birds have two legs and two wings' using the operator - and these are necessary properties of typical birds, not just typical properties. In Levesque's words, 'all of the "content" of the default is put into knowledge about the properties of typical instances of the predicates'. The 'is known' operator is now the key, for the representation language can express that if an entity is not known to be atypical then it should be treated as typical - hence default reasoning.

As a final aside, Levesque mentions the possibility of defining new terms from existing ones. His formalization is complete, and we can consider the system which embodies much of it. KRYPTON has a functional interface with TELL and ASK operators, a powerful inferencing mechanism, and a separation of definitions from assertions about the world, and we go on to examine it now.

10.5 KRYPTON

KRYPTON is an experimental knowledge representation system, chiefly the work of Brachman and Levesque (Brachman *et al.*, 1983a, 1983b, 1983c, 1985b). Its origins lie in KL-ONE (Brachman and Schmolze, 1985c) which is a highly influential representation system founded on a formalization of the ideas of frames and semantic nets and intended to allow the formation of complex structured descriptions. Manifesting Brachman's interest in the semantics of such terms, KL-ONE pays particular attention to 'concepts', 'descriptions', 'attributes' and the like. It has undergone several implementations in a variety of languages, and has been used in a number of applications. Its emphasis is very much on the description of concepts by structured inheritance networks at the expense of an assertional capability, and although the distinction was gradually recognized and some account was taken of it, the two have never been on an equal footing. We have already seen how a purely descriptive approach is defective, and KRYPTON is an attempt to combine it with an assertional approach, clearly defining the responsibilities of each and their interrelation.

KRYPTON also has a functional interface with TELL and ASK operators like those of Levesque's work described in the last section. Published reports on the work differ in the emphasis they place on the functional interface and the mixed representation scheme: the papers (Brachman *et al.*,

1983a, 1983b), for instance, are entitled 'KRYPTON: a functional approach to knowledge representation', whereas (Brachman *et al.*, 1983c) is 'KRYPTON: integrating terminology and assertion' and (Brachman *et al.*, 1985b) is 'An essential hybrid reasoning system'. In fact the two ideas are orthogonal, but it is perhaps natural that they should be associated, for the interface between assertional and definitional components is certainly the kind of semantic minefield that Brachman would like to see guarded by a firm functional interface.

KRYPTON's representation involves two components called the TBox and the ABox, intended respectively for structured definitions ('terminology') and for making assertions. The ABox assertions refer to terms defined in the TBox in order to make their statements. Before examining the operators available for communicating with a KRYPTON knowledge base, we shall look briefly at the TBox and ABox in turn.

The TBox language is essentially that of frames, with an important difference. There are concept expressions which correspond roughly to frames and role expressions which are the equivalent of slots. Importantly, there is no direct access to the value of a slot, and hence no danger of these frames becoming data structures; rather, new concepts and roles are formed by combining or restricting others. A range of operators is available for this purpose (not to be confused with the operators defining the functional interface to the system as a whole). Some examples will illustrate this. One of the operators is ConGeneric, which yields a concept which is the conjunction of the concepts which are its arguments. Thus a bachelor might be defined as

(ConGeneric man unmarried-person)

where 'man' and 'unmarried-person' are pre-existing concepts. Another operator is VRGeneric, whose arguments are a concept, a role and another concept, and which returns the first concept restricted so that all specified roles are instances of the second concept.

(VRGeneric paper author scientist)

yields the concept of a paper all of whose authors are scientists. A third operator is RoleChain.

(RoleChain child child)

would yield a 'grandchild' role. Other operators are described in the earlier papers, but it appears that only these three have been fully implemented. It can be seen that considerable power is available for making structured descriptions, but in a form very different from usual frame systems.

Another interesting feature of the TBox is in its handling of 'primitive' concepts and roles. Obviously the construction of concepts and roles has to start somewhere, and the basic ones chosen may be entirely independent of each other. However, it is possible to declare a new concept or role to be a primitive specialization of an existing one, meaning that any instance of the new type is necessarily an instance of the old, but there are no sufficient conditions for determining membership of the new type. Thus an elephant might be declared to be a primitive specialization of a mammal: all elephants will be mammals, but the system will not be able to deduce that anything is an elephant unless explicitly told so. This is KRYPTON's rather defensive answer to the problem of 'natural kinds' - it favours safety and simplicity at the expense of expressiveness.

The ABox is a language for making assertions about the world. It is in fact standard first order predicate calculus, but the basic non-logical symbols are not mere atoms but refer to the terms of the TBox. Because the language is a logical one, incomplete knowledge may be expressed using the usual operators of disjunction, negation and existential quantification.

Operators are provided to define the functionality of a knowledge base from a user's point of view. The ABox has the expected TELL and ASK, the former asserting that some sentence is true, the latter querying it. The corresponding operators for the TBox are called DEFINE and SUBSUMES. DEFINE is used for setting up definitions of concepts and roles, as in the examples above, while SUBSUMES queries whether one TBox term is subsumed by another (as for instance 'bachelor' is subsumed by 'unmarried-person'). There are in fact other TBox operators which return sets of symbols rather than just a truth value.

The two representation schemes of KRYPTON are tightly integrated, meaning that there is no simple translation from one to the other (as, for instance, TBox definitions might be re-expressed as logical sentences indistinguishable from ABox statements). Rather, the two are kept separate and their interrelation is closely defined. There is a requirement for *competence* in deriving conclusions from given definitions and assertions, in that using the definitions and their relationships together with its (incomplete) knowledge in the form of ABox assertions, KRYPTON can answer correctly quite general queries. The structure of the whole system is shown diagrammatically in Figure 5. The principle of having ABox sentences refer to TBox terms seems straightforward enough, but as Brachman *et al.* (1985b) observe:

'It is not enough to say that KRYPTON has a frame-style description language for forming terms and a first-order predicate language for forming sentences - we must explain how the interpretations of the sentences by the theorem prover depend on the definitions of the terms.'

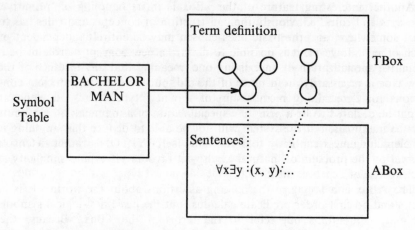

Figure 5 The Structure of KRYTON

Some effort is expended on formalizing the hybrid semantics of the two components, and the TELL and ASK operations are then defined in terms of it. It is possible to prove certain simple results about these operations that are clearly desirable, for instance that a term subsumes any ConGeneric involving it.

The implementation issues of KRYPTON are complicated and this is not the place to discuss them in detail, involving as they do unification algorithms taking account of the hybrid representation scheme. However, there are some points worth making. Because of the functional interface, the way in which reasoning is implemented is irrelevant as long as it yields the required behaviour as defined by KRYPTON's semantics. The ABox incorporates a specialized theorem prover, Stickel's Connection Graph theorem prover, for drawing its inferences, but there is no reason why it could not be replaced by an equivalent mechanism, or why performance could not be improved by preceding use of the theorem prover with an efficient database lookup. In the TBox, the relation of subsumption between terms is of great importance, and a classifier may be used (as in KL-ONE) to place newly defined terms in their correct places in the taxonomy, but the details of how it works are independent of the semantics it implements.

KRYPTON is very much a research tool. It would almost certainly not be possible to develop large applications in its current state. In some areas it is not complete - the theorem prover is only partially integrated with the terminological component. There is no doubt that KRYPTON has been a valuable experiment in representing incomplete knowledge, in functional interfaces and in responding to the fact that 'an intelligent system has more than one kind of representation need'. Its distinction between definitions and assertions, which have no definitional import even if expressed as 'universally quantified biconditionals', is attractive. Yet such a distinction may not always be appropriate for representing certain kinds of knowledge: it may be suitable for an abstract domain like geometry in which one can define a triangle precisely and then state properties of particular triangles, but when one comes to look at natural kinds the situation is less clear. We enter the domain of stereotypes, defaults and redundancy in definitional knowledge, and the structural/assertional distinction begins to look unsure. However, a full discussion is well outside the scope of this chapter, and we can conclude by remarking that KRYPTON is the most advanced implementation of functional ideas, though whether the principle has a future, and how it will resolve with such issues as mixed representation schemes, it is not yet possible to say.

11 Expressive Power and Computability

Tony Williams and Simon Lambert

11.1 Introduction

It should not be forgotten that all the knowledge representation formalisms introduced in previous chapters are intended for implementation on a computing machine, however ulterior their origins. That is how AI proves itself, and is the *raison d'être* of this book. Logic sprang from the head of Aristotle, while Newell and Simon looked into the heads of those around them and saw production rules. Semantic networks too have been proposed as 'models of cognition'. Yet all are amenable to encoding and manipulation within a computer program. The variety of manipulations permitted is of great importance, for a knowledge representation system must do more than just represent; it must be able to respond to queries about what it represents. Algorithms are needed to act upon it: and the study of their properties leads us into one of the provinces of mathematics. It may be that there is no algorithm guaranteed to terminate for a particular task, or that its intrinsic resource requirements are hugely expensive. The complexity of the tasks will depend on how much is expected of the knowledge representation system: there is a trade-off between computability and expressive power, and it has been explored by Levesque and Brachman in their paper (Levesque and Brachman 1985). This chapter serves as an informal introduction to their work, and attempts to relate it to some of the subjects described elsewhere in this book.

11.2 Setting the Scene: What's in a Knowledge Base

Levesque and Brachman start from the Knowledge Representation Hypothesis formulated by Brian Smith (Smith, 1982). It states that an intelligent system has components that:

(a)   appear to contain a propositional representation of the knowledge that the system as a whole possesses;

(b)   cause the system to behave in a way that manifests that knowledge.

A knowledge-based system satisfies this hypothesis by design. Its knowledge representation component is the subsystem that maintains knowledge in some explicit representation, called the knowledge base. (The separation of the knowledge representation component from the rest of the system is very characteristic of Levesque and Brachman's work. It is the essence of the 'functional' approach to knowledge representation described in Chapter 10.) The knowledge representation subsystem is in general more than just a database manager, for it has inference mechanisms enabling it to answer queries whose results are not explicitly stored as facts in the knowledge base. Logic has its rules of inference, while semantic networks lend themselves to operations which we would think of graphically, such as the pursuit of IS-A links.

According to Levesque and Brachman, the knowledge representation system should be capable of accepting new knowledge and incorporating it into the knowledge base; and they mention too the possibility of having it contain reasoning tactics separate from the declarative domain knowledge. Compare the definition of 'ancestor' as the transitive closure of 'parent' with the reasoning tactic that says that to determine the truth of

X ancestor-of Y

it is better to search up from Y rather than down from X. Levesque and Brachman are unsure how such reasoning tactics may be represented, suggesting that in practice they will tend to be implicit, or else take advantage of the sort of pragmatically motivated features that cause Prolog to differ from first-order predicate calculus. There has, however, been some work on the control of reasoning within rule-based systems, described in Chapter 8.

Given that the knowledge representation component is seen as a subsystem, it should be dependable. That is to say, it should respond to queries with results that are 'correct' according to the knowledge it contains. Furthermore, its resource consumption, such as the time taken to respond to a query, should not grow unmanageably as the size of the knowledge base increases.

11.3 First Order Logic

A good place to start our exploration of expressiveness and computability is with first order logic (FOL, see Chapter 2). It permits statements of very unrestricted scope, and its expressive power lies not so much in the propositions that can be expressed directly as in those that need not be explicitly stated. The rules of inference enable the knowledge representation system to generate the implicit information when it is required. As an example, consider,

$$\forall x \ Friend(George,x) \Rightarrow \exists y : Child(x,y)$$

which states that all George's friends have children, without stating who those friends are or even that there are any. Given that $\forall x \ \neg \ Child(Harry,x)$, one can deduce (in FOL) that $Friend(George,Harry)$ is false, without any explicit knowledge of who George's friends are. Similarly, the sentence

$$Child(Ian, \ Anne) \ or \ Child(John, \ Anne)$$

asserts that Anne is the child of Ian or John but without specifying which. This property of providing expressive power through the use of implicit information is not unique to FOL, but is used (perhaps in weaker form) in any knowledge representation system that will perform inference. As we shall see, it appears to be a major cause of computational intractability.

A fundamental property of first order logic is that the question of whether or not a statement is implicit in the knowledge base is equivalent to whether the corresponding sentence is a theorem. Answering a query becomes theorem proving: the statement to be queried is expressed as a proposition, and the system attempts to prove it from the axioms ('facts') it contains. There is a problem, though, in that provability in FOL is 'semi-decidable', meaning that, although a suitable procedure can always prove the theorem-hood of a sentence that does follow from the axioms (see e.g. (Bundy, 1983) for a proof of the soundness and completeness of resolution theorem proving), it cannot be guaranteed to terminate when presented with one that does not. In other words, for some queries the knowledge representation system might simply not respond. The problem of undecidability of FOL is related to Gödel's famous results for formal arithmetic. However, any system whose power is equivalent to or greater than arithmetic is not only undecidable but also incomplete, in that there are sentences that can be neither proved nor disproved. See, for example (Rosser, 1939), or for a more entertaining account including relations to many other phenomena (Hofstadter, 1979).

Even when the query is answerable (i.e. it represents a theorem in FOL), the computational expense of proving it may be too great. An interesting example of a problem which is effectively intractable for a standard FOL system is Schubert's Steamroller. In English, it is stated as follows:

> Wolves, foxes, birds, caterpillars and snails are animals, and there are some of each of them. Also there are some grains, and grains are plants. Every animal likes to eat either all plants or all animals much smaller than itself that like to eat some plants. Caterpillars and snails are much smaller than birds, which are much smaller than foxes, which in turn are much smaller than wolves. Wolves do not like to eat foxes or grains, while birds like to eat caterpillars but not snails. Caterpillars and snails like to eat some plants. Therefore there is an animal that likes to eat a grain-eating animal.

The problem may be easily axiomatized in FOL, using predicates for 'is-wolf', 'is-fox', etc., and 'is-animal', 'is-plant', 'likes-to-eat' and 'is-much-smaller-than'. It is possible to prove the final proposition by hand, but it has utterly defeated all resolution theorem provers because the search space is just too large. Many-sorted logics do permit a solution (Walther, 1985), as does the KRYPTON system described in Chapter 10.

It seems therefore that knowledge representation systems with expressive power equivalent to FOL are not dependable in the sense given above, though it should be noted that the intractability represents worst case behaviour, and that many queries will terminate quickly. One might question whether FOL-equivalent systems are useless: the answer must be that it depends on the problem the system is designed to solve. For example, if one were trying to find a proof for Fermat's Last Theorem, one might be happy to leave a FOL system running for several months, looking periodically to see if it appeared to be making progress and perhaps redirecting it if not. On the other hand, a robot must not get bogged down trying to prove or disprove a low-level subgoal, because it must come to a decision about what to do within a defined amount of time. Aeroplanes and nuclear power plants will not wait.

One could ensure that the knowledge representation system returns some answer within a definite time limit, returning 'unknown' if the decision procedure has not terminated. But if this solution is adopted, it becomes difficult to characterize the class of queries the system can answer. Attempting to make the system dependable in resource consumption by this means will compromise its 'correctness'.

11.4 Limiting Expressive Power

Levesque and Brachman distinguish between queries about the information so stored ('Is Harry included in the list of George's friends?') and queries about the world which the knowledge base is supposed to represent ('Is Harry a friend of George?'). The distinction is important when the knowledge base does not explicitly store complete information about the world; database form is completely incapable of expressing incomplete information, but retrieval of what it does contain is computationally inexpensive. An alternative to the arbitrary termination of queries after a time limit is to achieve termination with a valid answer by restricting the inferential capability of the knowledge representation system. This of course limits the range of queries that can be made of it. It is possible to circumscribe the computational complexity of the inference procedure by limiting the degree of unstated information that can be used in inference. Instead, such information must be explicitly present in the knowledge base. An extreme case is the database form, where all information that is to be retrieved must be explicitly stored.

Databases and full first order logic are two widely separated points on the trade-off between computability and expressiveness. Levesque and Brachman consider three other formalisms in the same context: logic programming, exemplified by Prolog; semantic networks; and frame systems. In each case they are careful to point out their logical foundations, explicit and implicit (Prolog's Closed World Assumption, for example). This preoccupation with clearly defined semantics is very characteristic of Brachman's work; indeed he and Levesque are rather dismissive of inference mechanisms suggested by the knowledge representation formalisms themselves and lacking such a foundation. Of semantics networks, they say (*op. cit.*),

'For better or worse, the appeal of the graphical nature of semantic nets has led to forms of reasoning (such as default reasoning) that do not fall into standard logical categories and are not yet very well understood. This is a case of a representational notation taking on a life of its own and motivating a completely different style of use not necessarily grounded in a truth theory. It is unfortunately much easier to develop algorithms that appear to reason over structures of a certain kind than to justify its reasoning by explaining what the structures are saying about the world.'

And of frames,

'Like semantic networks, frame languages tend to take liberties with logical form and the developers of these languages have been notoriously lax in characterizing their truth theories'.

Though they mention three of what many people would regard as major features of frame systems - default values, restrictions on slots, and attached procedures - it is only to dismiss them when formalizing their own system for the purposes of exploring expressiveness and computability, as we shall see in section 11.5. This does not affect their argument, for the services they expect from their system would probably have to be satisfied by any frame system, and indeed the restrictions are necessary to allow precision in establishing criteria for comparison. One might feel that frames have lost something in the process; but the important conclusion is that when the semantically doubtful accretions have been jettisoned all the above formalisms can be seen as restrictions of first order logic, exhibiting various degrees of expressiveness and computational tractability.

11.5 An Illustration of the Trade-off

In the context of frame systems, Levesque and Brachman have constructed an example to illustrate the trade-off. They define a 'frame description language' similar to that provided by KRYPTON's TBox (see Chapter 10), which allows the user to build composite type definitions from existing types and attributes, starting from some set of primitives (a 'type' defines a set of frames; an attribute corresponds to a slot in a frame). To be specific, a type may either be an atomic symbol or take one of the following forms:

> (AND type-1 type-2 ... type-n)
> (ALL attribute type)
> (SOME attribute).

An attribute can itself be an atom or have the form:

> (RESTRICT attribute type).

(AND type-1 ... type-n) is a type denoting the set of frames which are members of all the types listed. That set is the intersection of the sets denoted by the individual types. (AND doctor male) denotes the set of male doctors.

(ALL attribute type) is a type which denotes the set of things for which, if they have the given attribute, its value is of the given type. For example, (ALL friend doctor) denotes the set of frames whose 'friend' attributes (if any) all have type 'doctor'.

(SOME attribute) is a type which denotes the set of frames which have that given attribute, whatever its value might be. For example (SOME friend) is the set of frames that have any 'friend' slot.

(RESTRICT attribute type) defines a new attribute from the old one by requiring its values to be of the stated type. (RESTRICT friend doctor) defines an attribute 'friend who is a doctor'. Forms using RESTRICT are appropriate for use in constructing type expressions in the above compound forms, particularly ALL. For example, (ALL (RESTRICT friend male) doctor) denotes everyone all of whose male friends (if any) are doctors. Nothing is determined about friends who are not male. (SOME (RESTRICT friend male)) denotes everyone with at least one male friend, irrespective of the types of their other friends. The RESTRICT operator therefore provides a way of qualifying expressions leaving certain information unspecified.

The above constructs can be used to create complex descriptions of frames:

```
(AND person
        (ALL   (RESTRICT   friend male)
             (AND doctor
                   (SOME  speciality)
             )
        )
)
```

denotes the set of frames of type 'person' for which each 'friend' attribute of type 'male' (if any) is of type 'doctor' and has an attribute 'speciality', i.e. every person whose male friends are all specialist doctors. There may be frames in the resulting set that have friends who are not doctors with a speciality, but those friends will not be male.

One might well ask what on earth this little language has to do with the frames of Minsky and those who followed him, as described in Chapter 4. The point is that Levesque and Brachman have to be precise about what they mean by expressiveness and computational complexity. They admit that the frame description language is highly restricted, but at least it meets some of the possible requirements on a general frame system. They are able to furnish it with a formal semantics, and to define the idea of 'subsumption' between two types, which they use in their analysis of complexity. Subsumption is a simple idea, and is essentially set inclusion: one type subsumes another if all instances of the second type are necessarily instances of the first. For example, (AND doctor male) subsumes (AND doctor (ALL friend female) male).

The language defined above with its operators AND, ALL, SOME and RESTRICT is called FL. Levesque and Brachman denote by FL^- the language without the RESTRICT construction. Not surprisingly, the loss of RESTRICT means that there are some frame descriptions that can be expressed in FL but not in FL^-: so FL is more expressive. To show this in some more detail, we can examine the forms in which RESTRICT can be used. To take the earlier example, (ALL (RESTRICT friend male) doctor) would have to be written without RESTRICT as something like

> (ALL friend   (OR
>
> (AND male doctor)
> (NOT male)
>)
>)

requiring negations and disjunctions (with suitable definitions). (SOME (RESTRICT friend male)), by contrast, has no obvious representation even using OR and NOT.

But there is a price to pay. For they show that the operation of determining whether one type subsumes another is perfectly tractable in FL^- (being $O(n^2)$) but not in FL, in which it is technically co-NP hard (for an introduction to the complexity of algorithms, including the significance of NP-complete and NP-hard problems, see for instance (Machtey and Young, 1978)). Levesque and Brachman prove their results by, in the first case, producing an algorithm and analysing it, and in the second case by showing equivalence to the problem of deciding logical implication, whose complexity is strongly believed to be intractable (detailed proofs are given in the augmented paper (Levesque and Brachman, 1987)). These two methods of proof are unrelated and so do not together show why the addition of the RESTRICT operator causes the threshold of intractability to be crossed, but some light is shed on the matter by examining the algorithm for computing subsumption in FL^-. (The authors are indebted to Ronald Brachman for discussing this line of work, currently in progress. Any errors in this discussion are the fault of the authors, not of Brachman.)

The algorithm proceeds by converting an expression into a 'flattened' form, by combining nested AND expressions and collecting together ALL expressions that have the same attribute. For example,

> (AND (ALL friend (AND male
>
> redhead
> athlete
>)
>) -- people whose friends are all male redheaded athletes
> doctor
> (ALL friend (AND ambidextrous
>
> blind
>)
>) -- people whose friends are all blind and ambidextrous
>)

denotes doctors whose friends are all blind male redheaded ambidextrous athletes. This can be rewritten as

```
(AND doctor
     (ALL  friend  (AND male
                        redhead
                        athlete
                        ambidextrous
                        blind
                   )
     )
)
```

We can see that the above expression is subsumed by

```
(AND doctor (ALL  friend  redhead))
```

by determining that the ALL expressions refer to the same attribute and that 'redhead' subsumes the AND expression. It can be shown that the conversion to flattened form can be performed in $O(n^2)$ time, and that subsumption of flattened forms can be determined in the same time complexity. The subsumption algorithm is recursive in the case of ALL expressions, as (ALL a1 t1) subsumes (ALL a2 t2) if and only if a1 = a2 and t1 subsumes t2. The flattened form ensures that, at each level of recursion, the size of the problem is reduced.

We now consider the example modified as follows:

```
(AND (ALL (RESTRICT  friend  male)
          (AND  redhead
                athlete
          )
     ) -- people whose male friends are all redheaded athletes
     doctor
     (ALL  friend  (AND ambidextrous
                        blind
                   )
     ) -- people whose friends are all blind and ambidextrous
)
```

This denotes doctors all of whose friends are blind and ambidextrous, but only the male ones need be redheaded athletes. The restriction on the friend attribute means that the ALL expressions cannot be combined, and the subsumption algorithm must examine these attributes separately for each such expression. Subsumption of the modified expression by

```
(AND doctor (ALL  friend  redhead))
```

can only be determined by establishing whether there are any doctors with non-male friends. This type of determination could potentially be as complex as the original problem, and so the problem does not necessarily reduce in complexity with each recursion.

11.6 Conclusion

Knowledge representation formalisms may be viewed as forming a spectrum of varying inferential power. Databases fall at the low end, and the scale goes through frame languages, logic programming and other schemes up to first order logic and beyond. As one moves along this scale the computational complexity of answering queries about the knowledge base increases, and eventually the problem becomes intractable. It is not yet known how to categorize a knowledge representation scheme into its position on the scale until it is completely specified. It appears that the ability to use information not explicitly stored, but inferrable from other information, adds to the expressive power, but is a major contributor to the computational complexity.

There are two implications. Firstly, it remains useful and interesting to develop knowledge representation formalisms which are subsets of FOL in order to explore this dimension of computability. There may be knowledge representation systems which are computationally tractable, and sufficiently expressive to be useful in some domain. Secondly, if such studies show that inference becomes intractable for any useful knowledge base, the Knowledge Representation Hypothesis would have to be reconsidered. It may be that intelligent systems which can operate in real time will be composed of some number of simpler, tractable representation and reasoning components, with some sort of overseer which arbitrates among them and endows the system as a whole with apparently intelligent behaviour.

If the provision of a full inferencing capability is liable to be intractable, perhaps some restricted capability should be offered. In the words of Levesque and Brachman (*op. cit.*),

> 'Instead of automatically performing the full deduction necessary to answer questions, a knowledge representation system could manage a *limited form of inference* and leave to the rest of the knowledge-based system (or to the user) the responsibility of intelligently completing the inference.'

Of course, what is meant by this is not at all clear. Just as they shy away from those features of frames that have not (yet) been given a clear semantics, so Levesque and Brachman are hesitant when faced with this prospect:

> 'First of all, it is far from clear what primitives should be available... Finding such a service that can be motivated *semantically* (the way logical deduction is) and defined independently of how any program

actually operates is a non-trivial matter, though we have taken some steps towards this...'

Collected References

Aeillo, N. (1983), "A comparative study of control strategies for expert systems : AGE implementation of 3 variations of PUFF", *Proceedings of the Third National Conference on Artificial Intelligence*, pp.1-4.

Aikins, J.S. (1980), "Prototypes and production rules : A knowledge representation for computer consultations", Ph.D. dissertation, Stanford University. (Also Stanford Report no. STAN-CS-80-814.)

Aikins, J.S. (1983), "Prototypical Knowledge in Expert Systems", *Artificial Intelligence* **20**(2), pp.163-210.

Allen, J.F. (1981), "An interval-based representation of temporal knowledge", *Proc. 7th IJCAI*, Morgan Kaufmann: Los Altos, CA.

Allen, J.F. (1983), "Maintaining Knowledge about Temporal Intervals", *Commun. ACM* **26**(11), pp.932-843.

Allen, J.F., and Koomen, J.A. (1983), "Planning using a temporal world model", *Proc. 8th IJCAI*, Morgan Kaufmann: Los Altos, CA.

Anderson, J.R., and Bower, G.H. (1973), *Human Associative Memory*, Winston and Sons: Washington, DC.

Anderson, J.R. (1976), *Language, Memory and Thought*, Lawrence Erlbaum and Associates: Hillsdale, NJ.

Anderson, J.R. (1978), "Arguments concerning representations for mental imagery", *Psychological Review* **85**, pp.249-277.

Anderson, J.R. (1983), *The Architecture of Cognition*, Harvard University Press: MA.

Anderson, J.R. (1985), *Cognitive Psychology and its Implications*, Freeman: New York.

Anderson, R.H., and Gillogly, J.J. (1976), "Rand Intelligent Terminal Agent (RITA): Design Philosophy", R-1809-ARPA, Rand Corporation, Santa Monica, CA.

Bachant, J., and McDermott, J. (1984), "R1 revisited: four years in the trenches", *AI Magazine* **5**(3), pp.21-32.

Baddeley, A.D. (1976), *The Psychology of Memory*, Harper and Row: New York.

Baddeley, A.D. (1983), "Working Memory", *Philosophical Transactions of the Royal Society London B* **302**, pp.311-324.

van Bakel, J., and Hoogeboom, S. (1981), "Eksperiment met een Kasus-Grammatika", pp. 1-57 in *Verslagen Computerlinguistiek 2 (Katholieke Universiteit Nijmegen)*.

Bartlett, F.C. (1932), *Remembering*, Cambridge University Press: Cambridge.

Bekerian, D.A., and Bowers, J.M. (1983), "Eyewitness Testimony: Were We Misled?", *Journal of Experimental Psychology: Learning, Memory and Cognition* **9**(1), pp.139-145.

van Benthem, J.F.A.K. (1982), *The Logic of Time*, D. Reidel Publishing Co.: Dordrecht, Holland.

Berger, H. (1929), "Uber das Ellektrenkephalogramm des Menschen", *Archiv für Psychiatrie und Nervenkrankheiten* **87**, pp.527-570.

Berlin, B., and Kay, P. (1969), *Basic Colour Terms: Their Universality and Evolution*, University of California Press: Berkeley and Los Angeles, CA.

Binot, J.L., Graitson, M., Lemaire, P., and Ribbens, D. (1980), "Automatic processing of written French language", pp. 9-14 in *COLING 80 (Proceedings of the 8th International Conference on Computational Linguistics)*.

Bobrow, D.G., and Winograd, T. (1977), "An Overview of KRL", *Cognitive Science* **1**, pp.3-46.

Bobrow, D.G., and Winograd, T. (1979), "KRL: Another Perspective", *Cognitive Science* **3**, pp.29-42.

Bobrow, D.G., and Stefik, M. (1983), *The LOOPS Manual*, Xerox Corporation.

Bonnet, A. (1985), *Artificial Intelligence: Promise and Performance*, Prentice-Hall: New York.

Boolos, G.S., and Jeffrey, R.C. (1980), *Computation and Logic, 2nd Edition,* Cambridge University Press: Cambridge.

Bower, G.H., Black, J.B., and Turner, T.J. (1979), "Scripts in memory for text", *Cognitive Psychology* **11**, pp.177-220.

Brachman, R.J. (1977), "What's in a concept: Structural foundations for semantic networks", *International Journal of Man-Machine Studies* **9**, pp.127-152.

Brachman, R.J. (1979), "On the epistemological status of semantic networks", pp. 3-50 in *Associative Networks: Representation and Use of Knowledge by Computers,* ed. N. V. Findler, Academic Press: New York.

Brachman, R.J. (1983), "What IS-A is and isn't: an analysis of taxonomic links in semantic networks", *IEEE Computer* **16**(10), pp.30-36.

Brachman, R.J., Fikes, R.E., and Levesque, H.J. (1983a), "KRYPTON: a functional approach to knowledge representation", Technical Report No. 16, Fairchild Laboratory for Artificial Intelligence, Palo Alto, CA.

Brachman, R.J., Fikes, R.E., and Levesque, H.J. (1983b), "KRYPTON: a functional approach to knowledge representation", *IEEE Computer* **16**(10), pp.67-73.

Brachman, R.J., Fikes, R.E., and Levesque, H.J. (1983c), "KRYPTON: integrating terminology and assertion", *Proc. AAAI-83*, Morgan Kaufmann: Los Altos, CA.

Brachman, R.J. (1985), "'I Lied About the Trees' Or, Defaults and Definitions in Knowledge Representation", *AI Magazine* **6**(3), pp.60-93.

Brachman, R.J., and Levesque, H.J. (1985a), *Readings in Knowledge Representation,* Morgan Kaufmann: Los Altos, CA.

Brachman, R.J., Pigman Gilbert, V., and Levesque, H.J. (1985b), "An essential hybrid reasoning system: knowledge and symbol level accounts of KRYPTON", *Proc. 9th IJCAI*, Morgan Kaufmann: Los Altos, CA.

Brachman, R.J., and Schmolze, J.G. (1985c), "An overview of the KL-ONE knowledge representation system", *Cognitive Science* **9**(2), pp.171-216.

Bransford, J., and Franks, J.J. (1971), "The abstraction of linguistic ideas", *Cognitive Psychology* **2**, pp.331-356.

Broadbent, D. (1985), "A Question of Levels: Comment on McClelland and Rumelhart", *Journal of Experimental Psychology: General* **114**(2), pp.189-192.

Brooks, L.R. (1968), "Spatial and verbal components of the act of recall", *Canadian J. Psychol.* **22**, pp.349-368.

Brownston, L., Farrell, R., Kant, E., and Martin, N. (1985), *Programming Expert Systems in OPS5,* Addison-Wesley: London.

Bruce, B.C. (1972), "A Model for Temporal References and its Application in a Question Answering Program", *Artificial Intelligence* **3**, pp.1-25.

Buchanan, B.G., and Shortliffe, E.H. (1984), *Rule-Based Expert Systems : The MYCIN Experiments of the Stanford Heuristic Programming Project,* Addison-Wesley: London.

Bundy, A. (1982), "What is the well-dressed AI educator wearing now?", *AI Magazine* **3**(1).

Bundy, A. (1983), *The Computer Modelling of Mathematical Reasoning,* Academic Press: London.

Bundy, A., Burstall, R.M., Weir, S., and Young, R.M. (Eds.) (1980), *Artificial Intelligence: An Introductory Course: 2nd Edition,* Edinburgh University Press: Edinburgh.

Caramazza, A., Mc.Closkey, M., and Green, B. (1981), "Naive beliefs in 'sophisticated subjects': Misconceptions about trajectories of objects", *Cognition* **9**, pp.117-123.

Carbonnell, J.R. (1970), "AI in CAI: An artificial intelligence approach to computer-aided instruction", *IEEE Transactions on Man-Machine Systems* **MMS-11**(4), pp.190-202.

Carmichael, L., Hogan, H.P., and Walter, A. (1932), "An experimental study of the effect of language on the reproduction of visually perceived form", *Journal of Experimental Psychology* **15**, pp.73-86.

Chomsky, N. (1957), *Syntactic Structures,* Mouton: The Hague.

Chomsky, N. (1965), *Aspects of the Theory of Syntax,* MIT Press: Cambridge, MA.

Clancey, W.J. (1983), "The Epistemology of a Rule-Based Expert System - A Framework for Explanation", *Artificial Intelligence* **20**(3), pp.215-251.

Clancey, W.J. (1985), "Review of *Conceptual Structures in Information Processing in Mind and Machine*", *Artificial Intelligence* **27**(1), pp.113-124.

Clancey, W.J. (1986), "From GUIDON to NEOMYCIN and HERACLES in Twenty Short Lessons: ORN Final Report 1979-1985", *AI Magazine* **7**(3), pp.40-60.

Cohen, P.R. (1978), "On knowing what to say: planning speech acts", Technical Report no. 118, Dept. Computer Science, University of Toronto.

Collins, A.M., and Quillian, M.R. (1969), "Retrieval time from semantic memory", *Journal of Verbal Learning and Verbal Behaviour* **8**, pp.240-247.

Collins, A.M., and Quillian, M.R. (1970), "Facilitating retrieval from semantic memory. The effect of repeating part of an inference", *Acta Psychologica* **33**, pp.304-314.

Collins, A.M., and Loftus, E.F. (1975), "A spreading activation theory of semantic processing", *Psychological Review* **82**(6), pp.407-428.

Cooper, L.A., and Shepard, R.N. (1973), "Chronometric studies of the rotation of mental images", in *Visual Information Processing*, ed. W.G. Chase, Academic Press: New York.

Cooper, L.A., and Podgorny, P. (1976), "Mental transformations and visual complexity processes: Effects of complexity and similarity", *Journal of Experimental Psychology: Human Perception and Performance* **2**, pp.503-514.

Davis, R., Buchanan, B., and Shortliffe, E. (1977), "Production Rules as a Representation for a Knowledge-Based Consultation Program", *Artificial Intelligence* **8**(1), pp.15-45.

Davis, P.J., and Hersh, R. (1981), "Latakos and the Philosophy of Dubitability", in *The Mathematical Experience*, ed. P.J. Davis and R. Hersh, Harvester Press: Chichester, U.K.

De Jong, G. (1979), "A New Approach to Language Processing", *Cognitive Science* **3**(3).

Deliyanni,, and Kowalski, R.A. (1979), "Logic and Semantic Networks", *Commun. ACM* **22**(3), pp.184-192.

diSessa, A. (1982), "Unlearning Aristotelian physics: a study of knowledge-based learning", *Cognitive Science* **6**, pp.37-75.

Dowty, D.R. (1979), *Word Meaning and Montague Semantics,* D. Reidel Publishing Co.: Dordrecht, Holland.

Duncker, K. (1945), "On problem solving (transl. L.S. Lees)", *Psych. Monog.* **58**(5).

Ehrlich, K., and Johnson-Laird, P.N. (1982), "Spatial descriptions and referential continuity", *Journal of Verbal Learning and Verbal Behaviour* **21**, pp.296-306.

Etherington, D., and Reiter, R. (1983), "On Inheritance Hierarchies With Exceptions", *Proc. AAAI-83*, pp.104-108, Morgan Kaufmann: Los Altos, CA.

Evans, J.St.B.T. (1982), *The Psychology of Deductive Reasoning*, Routledge and Kegan Paul: London.

Evertz, R. (1982), "A Production System Account of Children's Errors in Fraction Subtraction", Computer Assisted Learning Research Group Technical Report No. 28, Open University: Milton Keynes, U.K.

Farber, D.J., Griswold, R.E., and Polonsky, I.P. (1964), "SNOBOL, a string manipulation language", *J. ACM* **11**(2), pp.21-30.

Fargues, J., Landau, M.C., Dugourd, A., and Catach, L. (1986), "Conceptual graphs for semantics and knowledge processing", *IBM Journal of Research and Development* **30**, pp.70-79.

Fillmore, C.J. (1966), "Toward a modern theory of case", pp. 361-375 in *Modern Studies in English: Readings in Transformational Grammar.*, ed. D.A. Reibel and S.A. Schane, Prentice-Hall: Englewood Cliffs, NJ.

Finke, R.A. (1985), "Theories Relating Mental Imagery to Perception", *Psychological Bulletin* **98**, pp.236-259.

Finke, R.A. (1986), "Mental Imagery and the Visual System", *Scientific American* **254**(3), pp.76-83.

Flannagan, T. (1986), "The Consistency of Negation as Failure", *Journal of Logic Programming* **2**, pp.93-114.

Fleming, M.L., and Hutton, D.W. (1973), *Mental Imagery and Learning*, Educational Technology Publications: Englewood Cliffs, NJ.

Floyd, R.W. (1961), "An algorithm for coding efficient arithmetic operations", *Commun. ACM* **4**(1), pp.42-51.

Forgy, C.L. (1981), "OPS5 Reference Manual", CMU-CS-81-135, Carnegie-Mellon University : Pittsburgh, Pennsylvania 15213, U.S.A.

Forgy, C.L. (1982), "A Fast Algorithm for the Many Pattern / Many Object Match Problem", *Artificial Intelligence* **19**(1), pp.17-37.

Freedman, R.S. (1982), *Programming Concepts with the Ada Language*, Petrocelli Books: New York.

Friedman, A. (1978), "Framing Pictures: the role of knowledge in automatic encoding and memory for gist", *Journal of Experimental Psychology: General* **108**, pp.316-355.

Frost, R.A. (1986), *Introduction to Knowledge Base Systems,* Collins.

Galambos, J.A., Abelson, R.P., and Black, J.B. (1986), *Knowledge Structures,* Lawrence Erlbaum Associates: Hillsdale, NJ.

Gale, W. (Ed.) (1985), *Artificial Intelligence and Statistics,* Addison-Wesley.

Gallaire, H., and Minker, J. (1978), *Logic and Databases,* Plenum Press: New York.

Garner, B.J., and Tsui, E. (1985), "Knowledge Representation from an Audit office", *Australian Computer Journal* **17**(3), pp.106-112.

Garnham, A. (1985), *Psycholinguistics: Central Topics,* Methuen: London.

Glanzer, M., and Clark, W.H. (1964), "The verbal loop hypothesis: Conventional figures", *Amer. J. Psychol.* **77**, pp.621-626.

Glass, A.L., and Holyoak, K.J. (1974), "Alternative conceptions of semantic memory", *Cognition* **3**, pp.313-339.

Golla, F., Hutton, E.L., and Walter, W.Grey (1943), "The objective study of mental imagery. 1. Physiological concomitants", *J. Ment. Sci. (cont. as Brit. J. Psychiat.)* **89**, pp.216-223.

Gould, P., and White, R. (1985), *Mental Maps,* Allen & Unwin: London.

Guildford, J.P., Fruchter, B., and Zimmerman, W.S. (1952), "Factor analysis of the Army Air Force's battery of experimental aptitude tests", *Psychometrika* **17**, pp.45-68.

Haber, R.N. (1979), "Twenty years of haunting eidetic imagery: where's the ghost?", *The Behavioural and Brain Sciences* **2**, pp.583-629.

Hanks, S., and McDermott, D. (1986), "Default Reasoning, Nonmonotonic Logics and the Frame Problem", *Proc. AAAI-86*, pp.328-353, Morgan Kaufmann: Los Altos, CA.

Hart, R.A., and Moore, G.I. (1973), "The development of spatial cognition: A review", in *Image and Environment,* ed. D. Stea, Aldine: Chicago, U.S.A..

Hasemer, A. (1984), *A Beginner's Guide to Lisp,* Addison-Wesley: Wokingham, U.K.

Hayes, P.J. (1977a), "In defense of Logic", *Proc. 5th IJCAI*, pp.559-565, Morgan Kaufmann: Los Altos, CA.

Hayes, P.J. (1977b), "On semantic nets, frames and associations", *Proc. 5th IJCAI*, pp.99-107, Morgan Kaufmann: Los Altos, CA.

Hayes, P.J. (1979), "The Logic of Frames", in *Frame Conceptions and Text Understanding*, ed. D. Metzing, Walter de Gruyter and Co: Berlin.

Hendrix, G.G. (1975), "Expanding the utility of semantic networks through partitioning", pp. 115-121 in *Proc. 4th IJCAI*, Morgan Kaufmann: Los Altos, CA.

Hilgard, E.R. (1981), "Imagery and Imagination in American Psychology", *Journal of Mental Imagery* 5(1), pp.5-65.

Hintzman, D.L., O'Dell, C.S., and Arndt, D.R. (1981), "Orientation in Cognitive Maps", *Cognitive Psychology* 13, pp.149-206.

Hofstadter, D.R. (1979), *Gödel, Escher and Bach: An Eternal Golden Braid*, Harvester Press: Chichester, U.K.

Hopgood, F.R.A., and Duce, D.A. (1980), "A Production System Approach to Interactive Graphic Program Design", in *Methodology of Interaction*, ed. R. A. Guedj, F.R.A. Hopgood, P.J.W. ten Hagen, H. Tucker and D.A. Duce, North-Holland: Amsterdam.

Horowitz, M.J. (1970), *Image Formation and Cognition*, Appleton-Century-Crofts: New York.

Hughes, G.E., and Cresswell, M.J. (1968), *An Introduction to Modal Logic*, Methuen: London.

Inhelder, B., and Piaget, J. (1958), *The Growth of Logical Thinking from Childhood to Adolescence*, Routledge and Kegan Paul: London.

Israel, D. (1983), "The Role of Logic in Knowledge Representation", *IEEE Computer* 16(10), pp.37-42.

Jackman, M.K. (1987), "Inference and the Conceptual Graph Representation Language", in *Research and Development in Expert Systems IV*, ed. Moralee, S., Cambridge University Press: Cambridge, U.K.

Jackman, M.K. (1988), "The Maximal Join for Conceptual Graphs", in *Conceptual Graphs for Knowledge Systems*, ed. Sowa, J.F., Foo, N.Y. and Rao A.S., Addison-Wesley: Reading, MA.

Jackson, P. (1986), *Introduction to Expert Systems*, Addison-Wesley: London.

Jastrow, J. (1888), "The Dreams of the Blind", *The New Princeton Review* 5, pp.18-34.

Johnson-Laird, P.N., and Steedman, M.J. (1978), "The psychology of syllogisms", *Cognitive Psychology* 10, pp.64-99.

Johnson-Laird, P.N. (1983), *Mental Models,* Cambridge University Press: Cambridge.

Johnson-Laird, P.N., and Bara, B.G. (1984), "Syllogistic Inference", *Cognition* **16**, pp.1-61.

Johnson-Laird, P.N., Herrman, D.J., and Chaffin, R. (1984), "Only Connections: A Critique of Semantic Networks", *Psychological Bulletin* **96**(2), pp.292-315.

Kaczmarek, T.S. (1986), "Recent developments in NIKL", *Proc. AAAI-86,* pp.978-985, Morgan Kaufmann: Los Altos, CA.

Kahn, K., and Gorry, G.A. (1977), "Mechanizing Temporal Knowledge", *Artificial Intelligence* **9**, pp.87-108.

Kaisler, S.H. (1986), *INTERLISP: The Language and its Use,* Wiley: New York.

Kant, I. (1963, Originally published 1787), *Critique of Pure Reason 2nd Edition, N.K. Smith trans.,* Macmillan: London.

Kaufmann, G. (1979), *Visual Imagery and its Relation to Problem Solving: A Theoretical and Experimental Enquiry,* Universitetforlaget: Bergen, Oslo en Tromso.

Kieras, D.E., and Polson, P.G. (1985), "An approach to the formal analysis of user complexity", *International Journal of Man-Machine Studies* **22**, pp.365-394.

Klahr, D., Langley, P., and Neches, R.T. (1986), *Production System Models of Learning and Development,* MIT Press: Cambridge, Maryland.

Kolata, G. (1982), "How Can Computers Get Common Sense", *Science* **217**, pp.1237-1238.

Kosslyn, S.M., and Schwartz, S.P. (1978), "A simulation of visual imagery", *Cognitive Science* **1**, pp.265-295.

Kosslyn, S.M., Ball, T.M., and Reiser, B.J. (1978), "Visual images preserve metric spatial information: Evidence from studies of image scanning", *Journal of Experimental Psychology: Human Perception and Performance* **4**, pp.47-60.

Kosslyn, S.M., Pinker, S., Smith, S.E., and Schwartz, S.P. (1979), "On the demystification of mental imagery", *The Behavioural and Brain Sciences* **2**, pp.535-581.

Kosslyn, S.M. (1980), *Image and Mind,* Harvard University Press: Cambridge, MA.

Kosslyn, S.M. (1981), "The Medium and the Message in Mental Imagery: A Theory", *Psychological Review* **88**, pp.46-65.

Kraft, A. (1987), "Artificial Intelligence: Next Generation Solutions", in *Intelligent Knowledge-Based Systems: an Introduction,* ed. T. O'Shea, J. Self and G. Thomas, Harper and Row: London.

Kulikowski, C., and Weiss, S. (1971), "Computer-based models of glaucoma", Report CBM-TR-3, Deptartment of Computer Science, Rutgers University: New Brunswick, NJ.

Kunz, J., Fallat, R., McClung, D., Osborn, J., Votteri, B., Nii, H., Aikens, J., Fagan, L., and Fiegenbaum, E. (1978), "A Physiological Rule Based System for Interpreting Pulmonary Function Test Results", Working Paper Human Perception and Performance-78-19, Heuristic Programming Project, Dept. of Computer Science, Stanford University.

Ladkin, P. (1986a), "Primitives and Units for Time Specification", *Proc. AAAI'86* **1**, pp.354-359, Morgan Kaufmann: Los Altos, CA.

Ladkin, P. (1986b), "Time Representation: A Taxonomy of Interval Relations", *Proc. AAAI'86,* pp.360-366, Morgan Kaufmann: Los Altos, CA.

Larkin, J.H., and Simon, H.A. (1987), "Why a Diagram is (Sometimes) Worth Ten Thousand Words", *Cognitive Science* **11**, pp.65-99.

Laurent, J.-P., Ayel, J., Thome, F., and Ziebelin, D. (1986), "Comparative Evaluation of Three Expert System Development Tools: KEE, Knowledge Craft and ART", *Knowledge Engineering Review* **1**(4), pp.18-29.

Lehnert, W.G., Dyer, M.G., Johnson, P.N., Yang, C.J., and Harley, S. (1983), "BORIS - An Experiment in In-Depth Understanding of Narratives", *Artificial Intelligence* **20**, pp.15-62.

Lehr, T.F., and Wedig, R.G. (1987), "Towards a GaAs Realization of a Production-System Machine", *IEEE Computer* **20**(4), pp.37-48.

Lenat, D.B. (1982), "On automated scientific theory formation: A case study using the AM program", in *Knowledge-Based Systems in Artificial Intelligence,* ed. R. Davis and D.B. Lenat, McGraw-Hill: New York.

Levesque, H.J., and Mylopoulos, J. (1979), "A procedural semantics for semantic networks", in *Associative Networks: Representation and Use of Knowledge by Computers,* ed. N. V. Findler, Academic Press: New York.

Levesque, H.J. (1984), "Foundations of a functional approach to knowledge representation", *Artificial Intelligence* **23**(2), pp.155-212.

Levesque, H.J., and Brachman, R.J. (1985), "A Fundamental Tradeoff in Knowledge Representation and Reasoning", in *Readings in Knowledge Representation*, ed. R.J. Brachman and H.J. Levesque, Morgan Kaufmann: Los Altos, CA.

Levesque, H.J., and Brachman, R.J. (1987), "Expressiveness and Tractability in Knowledge Representation and Reasoning", *Computational Intelligence* **3**(2).

Lewis, C.I., and Langford, C.H. (1932), *Symbolic Logic,* Dover Publications.

Lewis, D.K. (1969), *Convention: A Philosophical Study.,* Harvard University Press: Cambridge, MA.

Lindsay, P.H., and Norman, D.A. (1977), *Human Information Processing: 2nd Edition,* Academic Press: New York.

Lippold, O.W.J. (1970), "Origin of the alpha rhythm", *Nature* **226**, pp.616-618.

Liskov, B., and Zilles, S. (1974), "Programming with abstract data types", *SIGPLAN Notices* **9**(4), pp.50-59.

Loftus, E.F. (1975), "Leading questions and the eyewitness report", *Cognitive Psychology* **7**, pp.560-572.

Loftus, E.F., and Loftus, G.R. (1980), "On the permanance of stored information in the human brain", *American Psychologist* **35**, pp.409-420.

Machtey, M., and Young, P. (1978), *An Introduction to the General Theory of Algorithms,* North-Holland: New York.

Maes, P. (1986), "Introspection in Knowledge Representation", *Proc. ECAI'86*, pp.256-269, Brighton, U.K.

Maier, N.R.F. (1931), "Reasoning in humans: II. The solution of a problem and its appearance in conciousness", *J. Comparative Psychol.* **12**, pp.181-194.

Mamor, G.S., and Zaback, L.A. (1976), "Mental rotation by the blind: does mental rotation depend on visual imagery?", *Journal of Experimental Psychology: Human Perception and Performance* **2**, pp.515-521.

Mani, K., and Johnson-Laird, P.N. (1982), "The mental representation of spatial descriptions", *Memory and Cognition* **10**(2), pp.181-187.

Marcus, M. (1980), *A Theory of Syntactic Recognition for Natural Language*, MIT Press: Cambridge, MA.

Markov, A.A. (1954), "Theory of Algorithms", National Academy of Sciences, Moscow, U.S.S.R..

McCarthy, J., and Hayes, P.J. (1969), "Some Philosophical Problems from the Standpoint of Artificial Intelligence", pp. 463-502 in *Machine Intelligence 4*, ed. B. Meltzer and D. Michie, Edinburgh University Press: Edinburgh.

McCarthy, J. (1980), "Circumscription - A Form of Non-monotonic Reasoning", *Artificial Intelligence* 13(1, 2), pp.27-39.

McClelland, J.L., Rumelhart, D.E., and The PDP Research Group (1986), *Parallel Distributed Processing: Explorations in the Microstructures of Cognition*, MIT Press: Cambridge, MA.

McDermott, D. (1982a), "A Temporal Logic for Reasoning about Processes and Plans", *Cognitive Science* 6, pp.101-155.

McDermott, D. (1987), "A Critique of Pure Reason", *Journal of Computational Intelligence*, (In press).

McDermott, J. (1982b), "R1: A Rule-Based Configurer of Computer Systems", *Artificial Intelligence* 19(1), pp.39-88.

McDermott, D., and Doyle, J. (1980), "Non-monotonic Logic I", *Artificial Intelligence* 13(1, 2), pp.41-72.

McKim, R.H. (1980), *Experiences in Visual Thinking, 2nd Edition*, Brooks and Cole: Monterey, CA.

van Melle, W. (1981), *System Aids in Constructing Consultation Programs*, UMI Research Press: Ann Arbor, Michigan.

Metzler, J. (1973), "Cognitive analogues of the rotation of three-dimensional objects.", Unpublished Doctoral Dissertation, Stanford University.

Metzler, J., and Shepard, R.N. (1974), "Transformational studies of the internal representation of three-dimensional objects", in *Theories of Cognitive Psychology: The Loyola Symposium*, ed. R.L. Solso, Lawrence Erlbaum Associates,: Hillsdale, NJ.

Meyer, D.E., and Schvaneveldt, R.W. (1971), "Facilitation in recognising pairs of words: Evidence of a dependence between retrieval operations", *Journal of Experimental Psychology* 20, pp.227-234.

Milgram, S., and Jodelet, D. (1976), "Psychological maps of Paris", in *Environmental Psychology*, ed. Revlin, L.G., Holt, Rinehart and Winston: New York.

Miller, G.A. (1956), "The magical number seven, plus or minus two: some limits on our capacity for processing information", *Psychological Review* **63**, pp.81-83.

Miller, G.A., Galanter, E., and Pribram, K.H. (1960), *Plans and the Structure of Behavior*, Holt: New York.

Miller, G.A., and Johnson-Laird, P.N. (1976), *Language and Perception*, Cambridge University Press: Cambridge.

Minsky, M. (1975), "A Framework for Representing Knowledge", pp. 211-277 in *The Psychology of Computer Vision*, ed. P.H. Winston, McGraw-Hill: New York.

Minsky, M. (1981), "A framework for representing knowledge", in *Mind Design*, ed. J. Haugeland, MIT Press: Cambridge, MA.

Moore, J., and Newell, A. (1973), "How Can MERLIN Understand", pp. 201-310 in *Knowledge and Cognition*, ed. L. Gregy, Lawrence Erlbaum Associates Hillsdale, NJ.

Moore, R.C. (1985a), "The Role of Logic in Knowledge Representation and Commonsense Reasoning", in *Readings in Knowledge Representation*, ed. R. J. Brachman and H. J. Levesque, Morgan Kaufmann: Los Altos, CA.

Moore, R.C. (1985b), "A Formal Theory of Knowledge and Action", in *Formal Theories of the Commonsense World*, Ablex Publishing Co.

Morton, J., Hammersley, R.H., and Bekerian, D.A. (1985), "Headed records: A model and its failures", *Cognition* **20**, pp.1-36.

Mylopoulos, J., Shibahara, T., and Tsotsos, J.K. (1983), "Building knowledge-based systems: the PSN experience", *IEEE Computer* **16**(10), pp.83-89.

Nash-Webber, B., Bobrow, D.G., and Collins, A. (1975), "The role of semantics in automatic speech understanding", pp. 351-382 in *Representation and Understanding: Studies in Cognitive Science*, Academic Press: New York.

Neely, J.H. (1976), "Semantic priming and retrieval from lexical memory: Evidence for facilitatory and inhibitory processes", *Memory and Cognition* **4**(5), pp.648-654.

Newell, A. (1973), "Production Systems: Models of Control Structures", in *Visual Information Processing*, ed. W.G. Chase, Academic Press.

Newell, A. (1980), "The Knowledge Level", *AI Magazine* **2**(2).

Newell, A. (1982), "The Knowledge Level", *Artificial Intelligence* **18**, pp.87-127.

Newell, A., and H.A.Simon, (1972), *Human Problem Solving,* Prentice-Hall: Englewood Cliffs, NJ.

Nilsson, N.J., and Fikes, R.E. (1971), "STRIPS: A new approach to the application of theorem proving to problem solving", *Artificial Intelligence* **2**, pp.189-205.

Nilsson, N.J. (1982), *Principles of Artificial Intelligence,* Springer-Verlag: New York.

Norman, D.A., and Bobrow, D.J. (1976), "On the role of active memory processes in perception and cognition", in *The Structure of Human Memory*, ed. C.N. Cofer, Freeman: San Francisco.

Norman, D.A., and Bobrow, D.J. (1979), "Descriptions: a basis for memory acquisition and retrieval", *Cognitive Psychology* **11**, pp.107-123.

Norman, D.A., and Rumelhart, D.E. (Eds.) (1975), *Explorations in Cognition,* Freeman: San Fransisco.

O'Neill, J.J. (1980), *Prodigal Genius: The Life of Nikola Tesla,* Grafton: London.

Oakhill, J.V., Johnson-Laird, P.N., and Bull, D. (1986), "Children's Syllogistic Reasoning", *Quarterly Journal of Experimental Psychology* **38A**, pp.35-58.

Osherson, D.N., and Smith, E.E. (1981), "On the adequacy of prototype theory as a theory of concepts", *Cognition* **9**, pp.35-58.

Oswald, I. (1957), "The EEG, visual imagery and attention", *Quarterly Journal of Experimental Psychology* **9**, pp.113-118.

Owens, J., Bower, C.H., and Black, J.B. (1979), "The 'soap opera' effect in story recall", *Memory and Cognition* **7**, pp.185-191.

Paivio, A. (1971), *Imagery and Verbal Processes,* Holt, Rinehart and Winston: New York.

Parnas, D.L. (1985), "Software Aspects of Strategic Defense Systems", *Commun. ACM* **28**(12), pp.1326-1335.

Perky, C.W. (1910), "An experimental study of imagination", *Amer. J. Psychol.* **21**, pp.422-452.

Pinker, S. (1985), *Visual Cognition: Reprints from Cognition: International Journal of Cognitive Psychology Volume 18, 1984*, MIT - Bradford Books: Cambridge, MA.

Polit, S. (1985), "R1 and beyond: AI technology transfer at DEC", *AI Magazine* **6**(4), pp.76-78.

Pople, H.E. Jr., Myers, J.D., and Miller, R.A. (1975), "DIALOG : A model of diagnostic logic for internal medicine", *Proc. 4th IJCAI*, pp.848-855, Morgan Kaufmann: Los Altos, CA.

Post, E.L. (1943), "Formal reductions of the general combinatorial decision problem", *American J. Mathematics* **65**, pp.197-268.

Power, R. (1984), "Mutual Intention", *Journal for the Theory of Social Behaviour* **14**, pp.85-102.

Putnam, H. (1977), "Is Semantics Possible?", in *Naming, Necessity and Natural Kinds*, ed. S.P. Schwartz, Cornell University Press: Ithaca, NY.

Pylyshyn, Z.W. (1981), "The imagery debate: Analogue media versus tacit knowledge", *Psychological Review* **87**, pp.16-45.

Pylyshyn, Z.W. (1984), *Computation and Cognition: Toward a Foundation for Cognitive Science*, MIT Press: Cambridge, MA.

Quillian, M.R. (1966), "Semantic memory", Unpublished Ph.D. dissertation, Carnegie Institute of Technology: Pittsburg.

Quillian, M.R. (1968), "Semantic Memory", pp. 216-270 in *Semantic Information Processing*, ed. M. Minsky, MIT Press: Cambridge, MA.

Rao, A.S., and Foo, N.Y. (1987), "Congres: Conceptual graph reasoning system", *Proc. IEEE 87*, pp.87-92.

Reboh, R., and Risch, T. (1986), "SYNTEL(TM): knowledge programming using functional representations", *Proc. AAAI-86*, Morgan Kaufmann: Los Altos, CA.

Reed, S.K. (1974), "Structural descriptions and the limitations of visual images.", *Memory & Cognition* **2**, pp.329-336.

Reiter, R. (1978), "On Reasoning by Default", *Proceedings TINLAP-2*: University of Illinois at Urbana-Champaign.

Reiter, R. (1980), "A Logic for Default Reasoning", *Artificial Intelligence* **13**(1,2), pp.81-132.

Reiter, R. (1985), "On Reasoning By Default", in *Readings in Knowledge Representation*, ed. R. J. Brachman and H. J. Levesque, Morgan Kaufmann: Los Altos, CA.

Rescher, N., and Urquhart, A. (1971), *Temporal Logic*, Springer-Verlag.

Rich, C. (1982), "Knowledge representation languages and predicate calculus: how to have your cake and eat it too", *Proc. AAAI-82*, Morgan Kaufmann: Los Altos, CA.

Richardson, J.T.E. (1980), *Mental Imagery and Human Memory*, St. Martin's Press: New York.

Rips, L.J., Shoben, E.J., and Smith, E.E. (1973), "Semantic distance and the verification of semantic relations", *Journal of Verbal Learning and Verbal Behaviour* **12**, pp.1-20.

Rips, L.J. (1983), "Cognitive Processes in Propositional Reasoning", *Psychological Review* **90**(1), pp.38-71.

Rosch, E. (1976), "Classification of real world objects: origins and representation in cognition", in *La Mémoire Sémantique*, ed. E. Ehrlich and E. Tulving, Bulletin de psychologie: Paris.

Rosenbloom, P.S., Laird, J.L., McDermott, J., Newell, A., and Orciuch, E. (1985), "R1-Soar: An Experiment in Knowledge-Intensive Programming in a Problem-Solving Architecture", *IEEE Transactions on Pattern Analysis and Machine Intelligence* **7**(5), pp.561-569.

Rosser, B. (1939), "An Informal Exposition of Gödel's Theorems and Church's Theorem", *The Journal of Symbolic Logic* **4**(2), pp.53-60.

Rumelhart, D.E., and Norman, D.A. (1973), "Active semantic networks as a model of human memory", pp. 450-457 in *Proc. 3rd IJCAI*, Morgan Kaufmann: Los Altos, CA.

Rumelhart, D.E., and Ortony, A. (1976), "The representation of knowledge in memory", CHIP Report 55, University of California: San Diego, CA.

Rumelhart, D.E., and McClelland, J.L. (1985), "Levels Indeed! A Response to Broadbent", *Journal of Experimental Psychology: General* **114**(2), pp.193-197.

Russell, B. (1945), *A History of Western Philosophy*, Simon and Schuster: New York.

Schaeffer, B., and Wallace, R. (1969), "Semantic similarity and the comparison of word meanings", *Journal of Experimental Psychology* **82**, pp.343-346.

Schank, R.C. (1972), "Conceptual Dependency: A theory of natural language understanding", *Cognitive Psychology* **3**, pp.552-631.

Schank, R.C., and Abelson, R.P. (1977), *Scripts, Plans, Goals and Understanding*, Lawrence Erlbaum Associates: Hillsdale, NJ.

Schank, R.C (1980), "Language and Memory", *Cognitive Science* **4**, pp.243-284.

Schiffer, S.S. (1972), *Meaning*, Clarendon Press: Oxford.

Schubert, L.K. (1976), "Extending the expressive power of semantic networks", *Artificial Intelligence* **7**(2), pp.163-198.

Schwartz, S.P. (1977), *Naming, Necessity, and Natural Kinds*, Cornell University Press: Ithaca, NY.

Schwartz, S.P. (1979), "Studies of mental image rotation: Implications for a computer simulation of visual imagery", Unpublished Doctoral Dissertation, Johns Hopkins University. (Mentioned in Kosslyn *et al.*, 1979)

Sergot, M.J., Sadri, F., Kowalski, R.A., Kriwaczek, F., Hammond, P., and Cory, H.T. (1986), "The British Nationality Act as a Logic Program", *Commun. ACM* **29**(5), pp.370-386.

Shanon, B. (1976), "Aristotelianism, Newtonianism and the physics of the layman", *Perception* **5**, pp.241-3.

Shapiro, S.C. (1971), "A net structure for semantic information storage, deduction and retrieval", pp. 512-523 in *Proc. 2nd IJCAI*, Morgan Kaufmann: Los Altos, CA.

Sheehan, P.W. (1972), *The Function and Nature of Imagery*, Academic Press: New York.

Shepard, R.N., and Metzler, J. (1971), "Mental rotation of three-dimensional objects", *Science* **171**, pp.701-3.

Shepard, R.N., and Feng, C. (1972), "A chronometric study of mental paper folding", *Cognitive Psychology* **3**, pp.228-243.

Shortliffe, E. (1976), *Computer Based Medical Consultation: MYCIN*, Elsevier, New York.

Simmons, R.F. (1973), "Semantic networks: Their computation and use for understanding English sentences", pp. 66-113 in *Computer Models of Thought and Language*, ed. K. M. Colby, Freeman: San Francisco, CA.

Simon, H.A. (1978), "On the forms of mental representation", in *Minnesota Studies in the Philosophy of Science. Vol. ix: Perception and Cognition: Issues in the Foundations of Psychology*, ed. W.C. Savage, University of Minnesota Press: Minneapolis.

Simon, H.A., and Newell, A. (1965), *Computer Augmentation of Human Reasoning,* Spartan Books: Washington, DC.

Sloman, A. (1979), "Epistemology and Artificial Intelligence", in *Expert Systems in the Micro-electronic Age*, ed. D. Michie, Edinburgh University Press: Edinburgh.

Sloman, A. (1985), "Why we need many knowledge representation formalisms", in *Research and Development in Expert Systems*, ed. Bramer, M., Cambridge University Press: Cambridge.

Smith, E.E., Shoben, E.J., and Rips, L.J. (1974), "Structure and process in semantic memory: A featural model for semantic decisions", *Psychological Review* **81**, pp.214-241.

Smith, B.C. (1982), "Reflections and Semantics in a Procedural Language", Technical Report MIT/LCS/TR-272, MIT: Cambridge, MA.

Soloway, E., Bachant, J., and Jensen, K. (1987), "Assessing the Maintainability of XCON-in-RIME: Coping with the Problems of a VERY Large Rule-Base", *Proc. AAAI-87*, Morgan Kaufmann: Los Altos, CA.

Somers, H.L., and Johnson, R.L. (1979), "PTOSYS: An interactive system for 'understanding' texts using a dynamic strategy for updating dictionary entries", pp. 85-103 in *The Analysis of Meaning: Informatics 5*, ed. M. MacCafferty and K. Gray, Aslib: London.

Sowa, J.F. (1984), *Conceptual Structures: Information Processing in Minds and Machines,* Addison-Wesley: Reading, MA.

Sowa, J.F. , and Foo, N.Y. (Eds.), *Conceptual Graphs for Knowledge Systems*, (To be published).

Sowa, J.F., and Way, E.C. (1986), "Implementing a Semantic Interpreter Using Conceptual Graphs", *IBM Journal of Research and Development* **30**(1), pp.57-69.

Sowizral, H.A., and J.R.Kipps, (1986), "ROSIE: A Programming Environment for Expert Systems", in *Expert Systems: Techniques Tools, and Applications*, ed. D.A.Waterman, Addison-Wesley.

Sparck-Jones, K., and Boguraev, B. (1987), "A Note on a Study of Cases", *Computational Linguistics* **13**(1-2), pp.65-68.

Stevens, A., and Coup, P. (1978), "Distortions in judged spatial relations", *Cognitive Psychology* **10**, pp.422-437.

Szolovits, P. (1983), "Toward More Perspicuous Expert System Organization", pp. 7-12 in *Report on Workshop on Automated Explanation Production, SIGART Newsletter*, ed. W. Swartout.

Thorndyke, P.W., and Hayes-Roth, B. (1978), "Spatial knowledge acquisition from maps and navigation", Paper presented to the Psychonomic Society Meeting: San Antonio, Texas, U.S.A.

Tulving, E. (1972), "Episodic and semantic memory", in *Organisation of Memory*, ed. W. Donaldson, Academic Press: New York.

Tulving, E. (1984), "Precis of Elements of episodic memory", *The Behavioural and Brain Sciences* **7**, pp.223-268.

Turner, R. (1984), *Logics for Artificial Intelligence,* Ellis Horwood: Chichester, U.K.

Walther, C. (1985), "A Mechanical Solution of Schubert's Steamroller by Many Sorted Resolution", *Artificial Intelligence* **26**(2), pp.217-224.

Warden, C.J. (1924), "The relative economy of various modes of attack in the mastery of a stylus maze", *Journal of Experimental Psychology* **7**, pp.243-275.

Wason, P.C., and Shapiro, D. (1971), "Natural and contrived experience in a reasoning problem", *Quarterly Journal of Experimental Psychology* **23**, pp.63-71.

Wason, P.C., and Johnson-Laird, P.J. (1972), *Psychology of Reasoning: Structure and Content,* Harvard University Press: Cambridge, MA.

Waterman, D.A., and Hayes-Roth, F. (Eds.) (1978), *Pattern-Directed Inference Systems,* Academic Press: New York.

Watson, J.B. (1913), "Psychology as a behaviorist views it", *Psychological Review* **20**, pp.158-177.

Wertheim, A.H. (1974), "Oculomotor control and occipital alpha activity: a review and a hypothesis", *Acta Psychologica* **38**, pp.235-256.

Wertheim, A.H. (1981), "Occipital alpha activity as a measure of retinal involvement in oculomotor control", *Psychophysiology* **18**, pp.432-439.

Wierzbicka, A. (1972), *Semantic Primitives,* Athenäum Verlag: Frankfurt.

Wilkins, A.J. (1971), "Conjoint frequency, category size, and categorisation time", *Journal of Verbal Learning and Verbal Behaviour* **10**, pp.382-385.

Williams, M.D. (1978), "The process of retrieval from very long term memory", Technical Report no. 75, Center for Human Information Processing: San Diego, CA.

Winston, P.H. (1975), "Learning Structural Descriptions from Examples", pp. 157-209 in *Psychology of Computer Vision,* ed. P.H. Winston, McGraw-Hill: New York.

Winston, P.H., and Horn, B.K.P. (1984), *LISP: 2nd Edition,* Addison-Wesley.

Wittgenstein, L. (1953), *Philosophical Investigations,* Blackwell: Oxford.

Woods, W.A. (1975), "What's in a link: foundations for semantic networks", pp. 35-82 in *Representation and Understanding: Studies in Cognitive Science,* ed. D.G. Bobrow and A.M. Collins, Academic Press: New York.

Woods, W.A. (1983), "What's important about knowledge representation", *IEEE Computer* **16**(10), pp.22-27.

Wundt, W. (1904), *Principles of Physiological Psychology (transl. E.B. Titchener),* Swan Sonneschein & Co.: London.

Young, R.M. (1976), *Seriation by Children: an Artificial Intelligence Analysis of a Piagetian Task,* Birkhauser Verlag: Basel.

Young, R.M., and O'Shea, T. (1982), "Errors in children's subtraction", *Cognitive Science* **5**, pp.153-77.

Young, R.M. (1987), "Introduction to Production Systems", in *Intelligent Knowledge-Based Systems: an Introduction,* ed. T. O'Shea, J. Self and G. Thomas, Harper and Row: London.

Yuille, J.C., and Steiger, J.H. (1982), "Non-holistic processing in mental rotation: some suggestive evidence", *Perception & Psychophysics* **31**, pp.201-209.

Yuille, J.C. (1983), *Imagery, Memory and Cognition: Essays in Honor of Allan Paivio,* Lawrence Erlbaum Associates: Hillsdale, NJ.

Zadeh, L.A. (1974), "Fuzzy Logic and its application to approximate reasoning", *Information Processing 1974,* pp.591-594, North-Holland: Amsterdam.

Index

Scheu.

AFGESNEDEN

Sebastian Fitzek
Michael Tsokos

AFGESNEDEN

Vertaald uit het Duits door
Sander Hoving

Uitgeverij Mistral, Amsterdam 2014

Oorspronkelijke titel *Abgeschnitten*
Copyright © 2012 by Droemersche Verlagsanstalt Th. Knaur Nachf.
GmbH & Co. KG, Munich, Germany
The book has been negotiated through AVA international GmbH,
Germany

Nederlandse vertaling © Sander Hoving en Uitgeverij Mistral,
Amsterdam
Omslagontwerp Riesenkind
Omslagbeeld © Mariesol Fumy/Trevillion Images
Typografie en zetwerk Perfect Service

ISBN 978 90 488 1993 5
ISBN 978 90 488 1994 2 (e-book)
NUR 332

www.uitgeverijmistral.nl
www.twitter.com/Mistral_boeken
www.facebook.com/uitgeverijmistral
www.sebastianfitzek.de

Mistral is een imprint van Dutch Media Books bv.

Zoals eerder bericht, had de arrondissementsrechtbank de 61-jarige man tot **twee jaar voorwaardelijke gevangenisstraf** veroordeeld nadat hij had bekend zijn dochter 282 maal seksueel te hebben misbruikt. In het voordeel van de dader werkte dat het slachtoffer pas na vele jaren in staat was over haar ervaringen te spreken. Bovendien waren de feiten '13 tot 18 jaar geleden gepleegd', aldus de rechtbank. Toen het misbruik in 1992 begon, was het meisje 7 jaar oud.

Bron: *Der Tagesspiegel* van 16 april 2010

De arrondissementsrechtbank te Hamburg heeft de van beursfraude beschuldigde heer Rüdiger Beuttenmüller veroordeeld tot een vrijheidsstraf van **vijfenhalf jaar**. De zakenman had miljoenen goedkope aandelen (zgn. pennystocks) aangekocht en de koers daarvan vervolgens door middel van misleidende informatie omhooggedreven, om de aandelen daarna snel weer van de hand te doen voordat de waarde zou kelderen.

Bron: *Frankfurter Allgemeine Zeitung* van 17 april 2009

'Waar zit je nou?'

De stem van haar moeder paste bij de vrieslucht. De oortelefoontjes van Fiona's mobieltje leken een magnetische aantrekkingskracht te hebben op de kou. Haar oren waren al zo verkleumd dat ze de dopjes nauwelijks nog voelde.

'Ik ben zo thuis, mama.'

Haar fiets slingerde even toen ze door een ondiepe kuil met ijs reed. Zonder zich om te draaien controleerde ze of haar schooltas nog goed in de mand op de bagagedrager zat.

'Wat betekent *zo*, jongedame?'

'Over tien minuten.'

Het achterwiel draaide door, en ze overwoog of ze voor de bocht niet liever zou afstappen. Met haar flikkerende lamp zag ze de hindernissen op het bochtige pad pas op het laatste moment. In elk geval lag hier niet zoveel sneeuw als op het fietspad naast de Königsallee.

'Tien minuten? Je had al een uur geleden thuis moeten zijn voor het avondeten.'

'Ik heb Katrin woordjes overhoord,' loog Fiona. In werkelijkheid had ze de middag bij Sandro doorgebracht. Maar dat hoefde ze haar moeder niet aan haar neus te hangen. Die was er toch al van overtuigd dat Sandro een slechte invloed op haar had, alleen omdat hij meerderjarig was en een piercing in zijn wenkbrauw had.

Ze moest eens weten.

'De telefoon piept, mama. Mijn batterij heeft nog maar twee procent.' Dit keer sprak ze de waarheid.

Haar moeder zuchtte. 'Maak een beetje voort, maar je moet niet de korte weg nemen, hoor je?'

'Ja, mama,' zei Fiona hijgend en ze rukte onder het rijden geergerd het stuur omhoog om haar voorwiel over een boomwortel te wippen. *Jezus, ik ben dertien en geen baby meer!* Waarom behandelden haar ouders haar altijd als een klein kind? 's Nachts was het bos de veiligste plek ter wereld, had Sandro haar verzekerd.

Logisch. Welke moordenaar gaat hier staan kleumen in de hoop dat er toevallig een slachtoffer langsfietst?

Statistisch gezien werden er veel meer misdrijven bij daglicht en in verlichte binnenruimtes gepleegd dan in het donker, en toch geloofde iedereen dat het gevaar vooral in de duisternis loerde. Dat was net zo achterlijk als die eeuwige waarschuwingen voor vreemden. Meestal waren zedendelinquenten familie of vrienden, meer dan eens zelfs ouders. Maar natuurlijk waarschuwde niemand je ervoor bij papa en mama in de auto te stappen.

'Schiet op, Fientje,' waren de laatste woorden van haar moeder, toen liet de batterij het met een langgerekte pieptoon afweten.

Fientje. Wanneer hield ze nou eens op met die idiote koosnaam?

Jezus, ik kan die stomme ouders van me wel schieten. Kon ik maar vast het huis uit.

Woedend trapte ze op de pedalen.

Het pad voor haar werd smaller, beschreef een U-bocht tussen dicht op elkaar staande dennen en ging over in een bosweg. Zodra Fiona uit de beschutting van de bomen kwam, sloeg haar een snijdende wind tegemoet en haar ogen begonnen te tranen. Daarom zag ze de achterlichten van de auto eerst nog vaag.

De stationwagen was groen, zwart of blauw. Iets donkers. De grote auto stond met draaiende motor naast een stapel omgezaagde boomstammen. De achterklep was open, en Fiona kon in het zwakke licht van de achterbak zien dat er iets in bewoog.

Haar hart begon te bonken, zoals altijd als ze opgewonden was.

Kom op, je bent toch geen mietje. Je hebt wel vaker gevaarlijke situaties meegemaakt. Waarom ben je toch steeds bang bij zoiets?

Ze reed weer sneller, aan de uiterste rand van de weg. Toen ze nog maar een paar meter van de auto vandaan was, gebeurde het. Er viel een arm uit de achterbak.

Tenminste, zo zag het er in het onnatuurlijke licht van de auto op het eerste gezicht uit. Inderdaad slingerde de arm over het vuile nummerbord, de rest van het lichaam lag nog op de laadvloer.

'Help me!' hoorde Fiona de man in de achterbak steunen. Hij was oud, in elk geval naar Fiona's maatstaven, voor wie iedereen boven de dertig in de categorie schijndood viel. Hij praatte zo zacht dat hij bijna werd overstemd door het geluid van de dieselmotor.

'Help.'

Fiona's eerste impuls was gewoon verder te rijden. Maar toen tilde hij zijn hoofd op, *zijn bloedige hoofd*, en strekte zijn arm naar haar uit. Fiona moest denken aan een affiche in Sandro's kamer met een grafheuvel waar de klauw van een zombie uitstak.

'Niet weggaan, alsjeblieft,' kraste de vreemde, nu iets luider.

Ze remde, stapte van haar fiets en keek hem aarzelend van een veilige afstand aan.

Zijn ogen waren opgezet en zaten dicht, bloed druppelde uit zijn mond en zijn rechterbeen lag in een onnatuurlijke stand.

'Wat is er gebeurd?' vroeg Fiona. Haar stem vibreerde in hetzelfde tempo als haar razende polsslag.

'Ik ben overvallen.'

Fiona kwam dichterbij. Bij de binnenverlichting van de achterbak kon ze niet veel onderscheiden, behalve dat de onbekende een trainingspak en hardloopschoenen aanhad.

Toen viel haar blik op het kinderzitje in de achterbak en dat gaf de doorslag. *'Trap er niet in. Echte psychopaten zien er altijd uit als slachtoffers. Ze maken misbruik van je medelijden,'* had Sandro haar ingeprent. En die wist meer van het leven dan haar moeder.

Misschien was die vent echt kwaadaardig. Hij had het beslist verdiend zo in elkaar geslagen te worden.

En wat dan nog, dat zijn mijn zaken niet. Daar moet iemand anders zich maar mee bezighouden.

Fiona ging weer op haar zadel zitten, en toen begon de man te huilen. 'Blijf toch hier, alsjeblieft. Ik doe je toch niks.'

'Dat zeggen ze allemaal.'

'Kijk dan naar me! Zie je dan niet dat ik hulp nodig heb? Ik smeek je, bel een ziekenauto.'

'De batterij van mijn telefoon is leeg,' antwoordde Fiona. Ze trok de oortjes van haar mobieltje uit haar oren, die ze in de opwinding helemaal had vergeten.

De man knikte uitgeput. 'Ik heb er ook een.'

Fiona tikte op haar voorhoofd. 'Ik raak je met geen vinger aan.'

'Hoeft ook niet. Hij ligt voorin.'

De man lag krom, alsof hij maagpijn had. Hij leek te krimpen van de pijn.

Shit, wat moet ik nou doen?

Fiona klemde haar vingers om het stuur. Ze droeg dikke leren handschoenen, toch waren haar vingers koud.

Zal ik? Of zal ik niet?

Haar adem vormde dampende wolken.

De zwaargewonde man probeerde overeind te komen, maar zonk weer krachteloos terug op de laadvloer.

'Alsjeblieft,' zei hij nog eens. Fiona vermande zich.

Ach, wat maakt het uit. Zal wel weer misgaan.

Haar fiets bleef niet op de standaard staan op het ongelijke wegdek, dus legde ze hem plat op de grond. Fiona lette op dat ze niet binnen de reikwijdte van de man kwam toen ze langs zijn auto liep.

'Waar?' vroeg ze toen ze het linkerportier had geopend.

Ze zag een telefoonhouder van een handsfreeset, maar er zat geen mobieltje in.

'Hij ligt in het handschoenenkastje,' hoorde ze hem zeggen.

Ze dacht even na of ze om de auto heen zou lopen, maar besloot toen over de stoel naar de andere kant te reiken.

Fiona boog zich voorover de auto in en opende het handschoenenvak.

Geen telefoon.

Natuurlijk niet.

In plaats van een mobiele telefoon viel er een aangebroken doos met latexhandschoenen en een rol verpakkingstape uit. Haar hart sloeg nu razendsnel.

'Heb je hem gevonden?' hoorde ze de stem van de man, die ineens veel dichterbij klonk. Ze draaide zich om en zag dat hij zich had omgedraaid en op de laadvloer tegen de achterbank aan knielde. Eén enkele sprong van haar vandaan.

Toen ging alles heel snel.

Fiona negeerde de latex handschoenen, die van haarzelf waren goed genoeg. Toen greep ze onder de stoel. Het wapen lag precies op de plek die Sandro had aangegeven. Geladen en op scherp.

Ze tilde de loop op, kneep haar rechteroog dicht en schoot de man in het gezicht.

Dankzij de geluiddemper klonk het schot alsof ze een kurk uit een wijnfles had getrokken. De man viel terug in de achterbak. Fiona gooide het wapen zoals afgesproken met een wijde boog het bos in. Toen zette ze haar fiets weer rechtop.

Stom dat haar batterij leeg was, anders had ze Sandro even een sms'je gestuurd dat alles was gelukt. Het had een haar gescheeld of ze had de hele zaak afgeblazen, alleen omdat ze opeens medelijden met die klootzak had gekregen. Maar beloofd was beloofd. Bovendien had ze het geld nodig als ze eindelijk het huis uit zou gaan. 'De hufter heeft het verdiend,' had Sandro gezegd toen ze vertrok. En dat het de laatste keer was dat ze zoiets voor hem moest opknappen, wat ook wel logisch was.

Volgende week word ik namelijk veertien. Dan ben ik strafrechte-

lijk aansprakelijk en kan ik voor zoiets de bak in draaien. Als ze me *vandaag te pakken krijgen, komt er hoogstens een of andere maat-* *schappelijk werker aan mijn kop zeuren.*

Te gek rechtssysteem, Sandro had echt een hoop verstand van wetten, juridische dingen en zo. Hij wist gewoon echt meer van het leven dan haar moeder.

Fiona glimlachte toen ze eraan dacht hoe ze hem alles precies zou vertellen als ze hem morgen weer zou zien. De verpakkings-tape had ze helemaal niet nodig gehad om die loser van tevoren vast te binden. Maar nu moest ze voortmaken. Tenslotte stond het avondeten allang op tafel.

I

Dat bloed bevalt me niet!

Linda wierp een vermoeide blik op het slachtoffer. Ze was al uren op de man aan het zwoegen. Met het mes in de behaarde buik was ze tevreden, ook met de uitpuilende darmen en glazige ogen, waarin de moordenares werd weerspiegeld.

Maar het bloed ziet er niet realistisch uit. Ik heb het weer eens verpest.

Woedend scheurde ze het papier van het tekenblok, verfrommelde het en gooide het op de grond naast haar bureau bij de andere mislukte pogingen. Ze trok de dopjes van haar koptelefoon uit haar oren en verruilde de sombere rockmuziek voor het ruisen van de zee. Toen schonk ze zichzelf nog eens een kop warme koffie uit de thermosfles in. Ze hield haar verkleumde vingers tegen de beker, voor ze in gedachten verzonken de eerste slok nam.

Verdomde geweldsscènes.

Met het weergeven van de dood had ze altijd grote moeite gehad, en dat terwijl het daar juist om draaide. Haar comics werden voornamelijk door vrouwelijke tieners gelezen en om een of andere reden had uitgerekend het zwakke geslacht een voorliefde voor expliciet geweld.

'Hoe harder de comics, hoe liever vrouwen ze lezen,' zei haar uitgever altijd.

Zelf hield ze meer van onderwerpen uit de natuur. Geen suikerzoete Rosamunde Pilcher-motieven, geen weilanden met

13

bloemen of golvende korenvelden. Ze was door de oerkracht van de planeet gefascineerd. Door vulkanen, steile klippen en toren-hoge golven, door geisers, tsunami's en cyclonen. En precies zo'n adembenemend onderwerp had ze nu onder handbereik. Vanuit het kleine atelier onder het dak had ze een grandioos uitzicht over de kolkende Noordzee voor Helgoland. Het smalle houten huis van twee verdiepingen was een van de weinige vrijstaande gebouwen op de rotsen aan de westkust van het eiland. Het stond aan de rand van een van de ontelbare kraters die de Engelse bommen na de Tweede Wereldoorlog in het midden van het eiland hadden geslagen. Terwijl Linda de punt sleep van haar blauwe potlood waarmee ze altijd de eerste omtrekken van een tekening aangaf, keek ze door het in ruitjes verdeelde raam naar de zee.

Waarom betaalt niemand me ervoor dit uitzicht vast te leggen, vroeg ze zich af, niet voor het eerst sinds ze hiernaartoe was ge-vlucht.

De schuimende zee en laaghangende wolken oefenden een grote zuigkracht op haar uit. Het leek alsof het eiland de laat-ste dagen verder de zee in was geschoven. Het overloopbekken naast de zuidelijke haven was volgelopen en van de vierarmige be-tonblokken die ter verdediging van de kust in zee waren gestort, staken alleen de punten bij het strand nog boven het water uit. Ondanks de weerswaarschuwing had Linda het liefst haar rub-berlaarzen en outdoorjas aangetrokken en een wandeling naar het strand gemaakt om de koude regen tegen haar gezicht te laten waaien. Maar daarvoor was het te vroeg. Nu tenminste nog.

Je moet eerst de grote storm afwachten voor je hieruit mag, wees ze zichzelf terecht.

Er ging geen dag voorbij zonder dat de stormwaarschuwings-dienst er via de radio op aandrong Helgoland te verlaten, voordat de orkaan met de onschuldige naam Anna het eiland zou berei-ken. En intussen hadden de extreme weersvoorspellingen resul-taat gehad. Eerst geloofde bijna niemand de berichten dat het eiland dit jaar van het vasteland zou worden afgesneden. Maar toen rukte een voorbode van de storm het dak van de zuidvleugel van het ziekenhuis. Al regende het in de andere gebouwen niet in, toch liep de medische zorg nu gevaar, want de elektriciteit was deels uitgevallen, waardoor er bijna brand was uitgebroken. Toen daarna zelfs de aanvoer van levensmiddelen niet meer kon worden gegarandeerd, begonnen vooral ouderen eraan te twijfelen of ze wel op het eiland moesten blijven.

Vervolgens werden de weinige toeristen geëvacueerd; de meeste eilandbewoners met kinderen sloten zich bij hen aan, en wanneer vanmiddag de laatste veerboot vertrok, zou het aantal inwoners van Helgoland tot een kleine zevenhonderd zielen zijn gehalveerd. Die trotseerden het slechte weer en de nog slechtere voorspellingen, en hoopten dat er niet zoveel schade zou ontstaan als de meteorologen verwachtten. De harde kern kwam elke dag bijeen in Bandrupp, het restaurant van de gelijknamige burgemeester, om de toestand te bespreken.

De achterblijvers wilden hun huizen en bezittingen niet zonder slag of stoot prijsgeven en zagen het als hun plicht ook in moeilijke tijden op hun post te blijven, maar Linda bleef om een heel andere reden op het eiland. Waarschijnlijk was ze de enige die naar de orkaan en alles wat die kon aanrichten uitzag, ook al zou ze dan nog heel wat langer van blikvoer en leidingwater moeten leven.

Want als Helgoland compleet van de buitenwereld was afgesneden, konden de verschrikkingen waarvoor ze was gevlucht het eiland niet meer bereiken. En pas dan zou ze haar schuilplaats durven verlaten.

'Genoeg voor vandaag,' zei ze hardop en ze stond op van haar tekentafel. Al vanaf vanochtend vroeg had ze aan de scène gewerkt, de showdown waarin de amazoneachtige heldin zich op haar opponent wreekt, en nu, zeven uur later, was haar nek zo hard als beton.

Eigenlijk was er geen reden voor dat ze de laatste dagen als een bezetene had doorgewerkt.

Er was geen nieuwe opdracht, de uitgever wist niet dat ze voor het eerst aan haar eigen verhaal werkte, na altijd alleen manuscripten van andere schrijvers te hebben geïllustreerd. Verdomme, de uitgeverij wist niet eens dat ze nog bestond, nadat ze van de ene dag op de andere stilletjes van de aardbodem was verdwenen, zonder haar laatste project te hebben afgemaakt. Vermoedelijk zou ze nu, omdat ze een belangrijke deadline had laten verstrijken, nooit meer een opdracht krijgen, zodat het haar eigenlijk vrijstond te tekenen wat ze wilde. Maar telkens als ze was gaan zitten om haar creativiteit de vrije loop te laten, waren het niet haar favoriete natuurmotieven geweest, maar het beeld van de stervende man dat voor haar geestesoog verscheen. En ook al worstelde ze, zoals gewoonlijk, met de geweldsscène, toch wist ze diep in haar hart dat ze hem beslist op papier moest krijgen, als ze tenminste eindelijk weer een nacht goed wilde slapen.

Pas als dat me gelukt is, zal ik de zee schilderen. Eerst moet ik dat geweld van me af tekenen.

Linda zuchtte en liep naar de badkamer op de verdieping eronder. Aan het einde van een werkdag voelde ze zich alsof ze een marathon had gelopen. Moe, leeg en vies. Ook al had ze zich nauwelijks bewogen, toch had ze dringend een douche nodig. Het huis was nooit gerenoveerd, getuige de spartaans ingerichte badkamer: de donkergroene tegels had Linda voor het laatst in de wc van een wegrestaurant gezien, en het douchegordijn was in de mode geweest in de tijd dat telefoons nog draaischijven hadden. Toch werd het water in een paar seconden warm, en dat was heel wat beter dan Linda van de douche in haar Berlijnse flat gewend was. Onder andere omstandigheden zou ze zich in het kleine huis met de scheve muren, de kromgetrokken ramen en de lage plafonds zelfs thuis hebben gevoeld. Linda gaf niet veel om luxe en het uitzicht over zee compenseerde het bloemetjesbehang, de okerkleurige stoelovertrekken en de opgezette vis boven de kachel.

Jammer genoeg compenseerde het de duistere dromen niet, die haar uit haar slaap hielden.

Ze trok de donkere blouse die ze bij haar intrek in het huis voor de spiegel van de kast had gehangen weer recht, toen kleedde ze zich uit. Ze wist dat de laatste maanden hun sporen hadden nagelaten, en dat wilde ze niet elke dag in de spiegel zien.

Onder de douche masseerde ze shampoo in haar bruine haar, dat tot haar schouders kwam, en verdeelde de rest van het schuim over haar magere lichaam. Vroeger was ze wat te zwaar geweest, tegenwoordig zag je alleen nog aan haar brede heupen dat ze vroeger 'aardig wat vlees op de botten' had gehad, zoals Danny ooit voor de grap had gezegd. Ze huiverde bij de herinnering en draaide de warme kraan verder open. Zoals altijd probeerde ze haar gezicht bij het wassen te ontzien.

Om mijn wonden niet te hoeven aanraken.

Maar vandaag had ze niet snel genoeg gereageerd en was er wat schuim van haar haar naar beneden gelopen, over de poreuze littekens op haar voorhoofd, die je gelukkig alleen zag als haar pony per ongeluk opzij viel.

Shit.

Met tegenzin hield ze haar gezicht onder de warme straal van de douche, wat bijna nog erger was dan wanneer ze de sporen die het zuur had achtergelaten met haar eigen vingers zou hebben betast.

Linda had veel littekens. De meeste waren groter dan die op haar voorhoofd en slechter genezen, want ze bevonden zich op een plek waar geen wondzalf en geen chirurg ooit zouden kunnen komen: diep verborgen in het weefsel van haar ziel.

Nadat ze haar nek ongeveer tien minuten lang met de straal uit de douche had gemasseerd, voelde ze dat de spanning begon weg te ebben. Misschien zou een ibuprofen de ergste hoofdpijn kunnen wegnemen, als ze het tablet op tijd innam voor het slapengaan. Eergisteren had ze het vergeten en was midden in de nacht met een pneumatische boor onder haar schedel wakker geworden. Ze draaide de kraan weer dicht, wachtte tot de verkalkte douchekop niet meer druppelde en trok het douchegordijn opzij. Toen verstijfde ze.

Eerst was het alleen een onbestemd gevoel dat haar had doen aarzelen. Ze begreep nog niet wat er in de badkamer was veranderd. De deur was dicht, haar blouse hing voor de spiegel, de handdoek over de radiator. En toch was er iets anders.

Een jaar geleden zou ze nog niets hebben gemerkt, maar na alles wat haar sindsdien was overkomen, had ze zoiets als een zesde zintuig voor onzichtbare dreigingen ontwikkeld. Het waren niet alleen de videocassettes op haar nachtkastje in haar Berlijnse appartement geweest die haar zo alert hadden gemaakt. Videobanden waarop ze zelf te zien was. Gefilmd door iemand die naast haar bed moest hebben gestaan. Terwijl ze sliep!

Linda hield haar adem in, luisterde naar verdachte geluiden, maar alles wat ze hoorde waren de windstoten die het huis teisterden.

Vals alarm, dacht ze terwijl ze rustig ademde om haar hartslag weer tot bedaren te brengen. Vervolgens stapte ze rillend van de kou onder de douche vandaan en reikte naar haar handdoek.

Het was of ze een elektrische schok kreeg, want op dat moment begreep ze wat er was gebeurd.

Ze slaakte een kreet, begon over haar hele lichaam te trillen en draaide zich met een ruk om, alsof ze verwachtte dat ze elk moment van achteren kon worden aangevallen. Maar het enige wat haar bedreigde was haar eigen angst, en die liet zich niet zo gemakkelijk afschudden als de handdoek die ze van zich af had gegooid.

De handdoek... die enorme weerzin bij haar had opgeroepen toen ze hem had aangeraakt.

Want hij was nat.

Iemand moest zich ermee hebben afgedroogd terwijl ze onder de douche stond.

2

'Nee, ik heb er niets mee gedaan, verdomme. Ik weet nog precies hoe ik hem vanochtend over de verwarming heb gelegd.'

Linda voelde dat het bloed haar naar het hoofd steeg, en daar ergerde ze zich bijna nog meer aan dan aan de pogingen van haar broer aan de andere kant van de lijn om haar te sussen. Hoewel Clemens haar niet kon zien, kende hij haar goed genoeg om aan de klank van haar stem te horen wanneer ze rood aanliep – wat ze altijd deed als ze over haar toeren was.

'Rustig aan, kid,' zei hij; hij klonk als een personage uit de films over de onderwereld van New York, waar hij zo van hield. 'Ik heb alles geregeld. Je hoeft nergens meer bang voor te zijn.'

'Hah!' Ze ademde hortend en stotend. 'En hoe verklaar je die natte handdoek dan? Dat is toch typisch iets voor Danny!'

Danny. Shit, waarom noem ik die ellendeling nog steeds bij zijn koosnaam?

Inmiddels werd ze misselijk bij de gedachte dat ze met die weerzinwekkende vent het bed in was gedoken, en zelfs meer dan eens. En ze kon niet zeggen dat ze niet gewaarschuwd was. 'Zo goed als hij eruitziet, zo slecht gaat dit aflopen,' had haar moeder gesomberd. En ook haar vader had met zijn opmerking 'Ik heb het gevoel dat hij nog niet zijn ware gezicht heeft laten zien' de spijker op de kop geslagen; zoals altijd eigenlijk als het om het inschatten van andere mensen ging. Hoe wereldvreemd haar ouders, wier burgerlijke bestaan zich grotendeels tussen proefwerken en leraarsconferenties afspeelde, soms ook waren, toch was hun mensenkennis door dertig jaar lesgeven aan gymnasiasten aardig op peil. Hoewel je ook geen helderziende hoefde te zijn om te voorspellen dat hun relatie slecht zou aflopen. Tenslotte had Daniel Haag het meeste succes van alle auteurs van wie ze het werk illustreerde, en hij was dus zoiets als haar baas. En een verhouding met de baas liep meestal slecht af. Maar *hoe slecht* – daar had niemand een idee van gehad. Ook haar ouders niet.

Het was allemaal onschuldig begonnen. Waarschijnlijk was dat bij dat soort dingen altijd zo. Natuurlijk was Daniels opvliegende temperament Linda niet ontgaan, ze had aanvankelijk alleen geamuseerd geglimlacht om zijn jaloerse reacties, als hij zich bijvoorbeeld over een vrijblijvend complimentje van een kelner ergerde of haar verweet niet snel genoeg op zijn sms'jes te hebben gereageerd.

Linda was zich ervan bewust dat haar directheid veel mannen onzeker maakte. Ze vertelde graag schuine moppen, lachte graag en luid en voelde zich niet te min om in bed het initiatief te nemen. Aan de andere kant kon het haar verovering gebeuren dat hij na een nacht dansen in een club de volgende ochtend naar een museum werd meegetroond, om daar te aanschouwen hoe wildvreemde mensen aan Linda's lippen hingen terwijl ze uit de losse pols college gaf over de tentoongestelde kunstwerken. Veel van haar contacten werd het domweg te veel; ze dachten dat ze een doorgedraaide troela was, die met de ene vent na de andere het bed in dook, wat niet het geval was.

Dat haar relaties meestal van korte duur waren, kwam alleen doordat ze het met een 'standaardexemplaar' niet lang uithield; dus met een vent die haar gevoel voor humor niet deelde. Daarom had ze een eenvoudige test bedacht waarmee ze al in de eerste nacht checkte of een eventuele verhouding volgens haar toekomst had: zodra haar verovering zich slapend op zijn zij draaide, schudde ze de man wakker en vroeg hem dan zogenaamd woedend: 'Zeg op, waar heb je het geld neergelegd?'

Tot dan toe hadden maar twee mannen gelachen, en met de

eerste was ze vijf jaar samen geweest. De verhouding met de tweede, Danny, had een klein jaar geduurd maar die tijd kwam haar
nu als een eeuwigheid voor, want de maanden met hem waren de
ergste van haar leven geweest.

'Kindje, heb ik je niet beloofd dat wij hem voor onze rekening
zouden nemen?' hoorde Linda haar broer vragen, terwijl ze naakt
door de slaapkamer stapte en een spoor van druppels en vochtige
voetafdrukken op het parket achterliet. Ze had het koud, maar ze
gruwde van het idee de vochtige handdoek te moeten aanraken.

Ja, dat heb je, dacht ze, met de hoorn stevig tegen haar oor
gedrukt. *Je hebt me beloofd ervoor te zorgen dat Danny ermee ophoudt, maar misschien was dat iets te hoog gegrepen voor je?*

Linda wist dat het geen zin had die vraag te stellen. Als haar
grote broer één zwak punt had, dan was het wel dat hij zichzelf onoverwinnelijk achtte. Alleen zijn imposante verschijning
al deed de tegenstander meestal op de vlucht slaan. De enkeling
die stom genoeg was om het op te nemen tegen de bonk spieren
van een meter negentig, die in zijn vrije tijd een straatvechters-
training deed, moest zijn grootheidswaan met een ziekenhuisop-
name betalen. Na tal van confrontaties stond het fysieke geweld
Clemens in het gezicht geschreven, in de waarste zin des woords.
Hij had door een medewerker van zijn tattoostudio in Neukölln
de inslagwond van een kogel midden op zijn voorhoofd laten tatoeëren.

'Wat hebben jullie met Danny gedaan?' vroeg Linda, toen ze
voor de koffer met haar spullen stond. Ze was nu al veertien dagen hier en nog steeds had ze haar kleren niet in de kast opgeborgen. Ze pakte haar jeans en stapte er zonder slipje in. 'Ik heb er
recht op dat te weten, Clemens.'

Linda was de enige die haar broer zonder gevaar te lopen bij
zijn voornaam kon noemen. Iedereen, zelfs haar ouders, moest
hem met zijn achternaam aanspreken, omdat Kaminski volgens
Clemens veel mannelijker klonk dan de nichterige voornaam die

zijn moeder voor hem had uitgekozen. Het was een wonder dat ze nog met elkaar praatten, nadat Clemens door zijn levenswandel ongeveer alle idealen had verraden waarvoor hun ouders hun leven lang krom hadden gelegen.

'Je hoeft alleen maar te weten dat Danny je nooit meer iets zal aandoen.'

'O ja? Hebben jullie misschien de vinger gebroken waarmee hij mijn overlijdensadvertentie heeft opgesteld?' Linda sloot haar ogen en dacht aan de halve pagina in de zondagskrant; aan het zwarte kader en het keurige kruis naast haar naam. Als overlijdensdatum had Danny de dag aangegeven waarop zij het had uitgemaakt.

'Hebben jullie de ogen uitgestoken waarmee hij door de videocamera heeft gekeken?' *Waarmee hij mij filmde toen ik mijn vriendinnen ontmoette? Terwijl ik boodschappen deed? Toen ik sliep?*

'Of hebben jullie de handen afgehakt waarmee hij het zuur door mijn gezichtscrème heeft geroerd?' *Nadat ik had gedreigd hem te zullen aangeven als hij mij zou blijven lastigvallen?*

Onwillekeurig voelde ze aan de littekens op haar voorhoofd.

'Nee,' zei Clemens vlak. 'Zo gemakkelijk is die idioot niet van ons af gekomen.'

'Hij is geen idioot.'

Integendeel. Danny Haag was niet dom, en ook geen impulsief heethoofd. Hij deed niets zonder een grondige en intelligente voorbereiding, en altijd op zo'n manier dat geen van zijn handelingen tot hem kon worden herleid. Bovendien had hij er kennelijk geen moeite mee weken te wachten tot hij weer toesloeg, en daarom voelde de politie zich niet geroepen gericht actie tegen Danny te ondernemen. Naar mening van de autoriteiten wezen de voor een stalker ongewoon lange tussenpauzes waarin Linda met rust werd gelaten in de richting van meerdere daders. Waarschijnlijk had Linda gewoon pech gehad en was ze toevallig door verschillende mannen lastiggevallen (*Misschien door fanatieke le-*

zers van uw comics?') en precies die misvatting had Danny willen uitlokken. Bovendien was hij een bekende auteur, welgesteld en knap, dus iemand die *'elke vrouw krijgen kan'*, zoals de agenten bij het proces-verbaal van haar aangifte hadden opgemerkt, alsof Linda het niet waard was door Danny gestalkt te worden. Clemens had het meteen al gezegd: de wet was een aanfluiting, en zijn handhavers een lachertje. *'Dat soort dingen moet je zelf in de hand nemen.'* En daarom had haar broer haar hier naar Helgoland gebracht, zodat hij Danny tijdens haar afwezigheid in Berlijn voor zijn 'rekening' kon nemen.

'Je hebt gezegd dat ik hier veilig zou zijn,' zei Linda verwijtend.

'En dat ben je ook, kindje. Dat huis is van Olli, en je kent mijn maat. Voordat hij iets loslaat, deelt de paus condooms uit.'

'En als iemand me op de veerboot heeft gezien?'

'Dan zou die iemand geen gelegenheid meer hebben gehad het aan Danny te vertellen,' zei Clemens met zijn 'hoe duidelijk moet ik het nog uitleggen'-stem.

Linda's onderlip trilde. In de slaapkamer tochtte het door het kromgetrokken raam, en ze kreeg het met de minuut kouder. Met één hand kon ze geen pullover aantrekken. Aan de andere kant wilde ze de telefoonverbinding met haar broer onder geen beding ook maar een seconde onderbreken. Dus ging ze bij het bed staan en sloeg de deken terug, waarmee ze zich wilde toedekken.

'Zeg dat ik niet bang hoef te zijn,' zei ze, terwijl ze zich op de matras liet zakken.

'Ik zweer het je,' beloofde Clemens, maar dat kon Linda al niet meer horen, want ze had haar hoofd nog niet op het kussen gelegd of ze schreeuwde haar longen uit haar lijf.

3

'Wat is er verdomme bij jou aan de hand?' brulde Clemens in de hoorn.

Linda sprong het bed uit alsof de matras haar had gebeten.

'Kom op, zeg iets!'

Het duurde even tot ze weer genoeg was gekalmeerd om haar broer te antwoorden. Dit keer was haar weerzin nog groter. Want nu was het bewijs overtuigender dan de vochtige handdoek in de badkamer.

'Het bed,' hijgde ze.

'Shit, wat is daarmee?'

'Ik wilde erin gaan liggen.'

'Ja, en?'

'Het is warm. Verdomme, Clemens.'

Er heeft iemand in gelegen.

Ze kermde bijna en moest op haar tong bijten om het niet uit te schreeuwen.

'En het ruikt naar hem.'

Naar zijn aftershave.

'Oké, oké, oké, luister eens even. Dat verbeeld je je maar.'

'Nee, dat doe ik niet. Hij is hier geweest,' zei ze. Toen zag ze haar vergissing in.

Hij was niet hier *geweest.*

Het bed is warm. De geur is nog sterk.

Hij is nog steeds in huis!

Met die gedachte struikelde ze achterwaarts de kamer uit,

draaide zich snel om en rende de trap af naar de begane grond. Ze schoot haar rubberlaarzen bij de kapstok aan.

'Wat ben je van plan?' vroeg Clemens, die de geluiden probeerde te interpreteren die Linda maakte terwijl ze zich aankleedde.

'Ik smeer hem.'

'Maar waarheen?'

'Geen idee. Ik moet naar buiten.'

'De storm in?'

'Kan me geen reet schelen.'

Linda griste een groene regenjas van de haak, schoot hem haastig aan en duwde de deur open. Het was de eerste keer dat ze zich sinds haar aankomst op Helgoland buiten waagde, en toen was het licht en zonnig geweest.

En niet zo koud.

De wind joeg tranen in haar ogen, terwijl ze met één hand probeerde de ritssluiting van haar jas dicht te doen. Tevergeefs.

Even was ze haar oriëntatie kwijt, in de opwinding was ze door de achterdeur naast de keuken gelopen en keek over de rotstuin uit over de kolkende zee.

'Wees nou verstandig, wacht even,' hoorde ze Clemens zeggen, maar ze sloeg geen acht op hem. De snelste weg naar het dorp was een slingerpad dat van de rand van de krater in de richting van de zuidelijke haven naar zee liep.

'Ik bel je terug zodra ik onder de mensen ben, ik...'

'Nee, niet ophangen. Jezus, luister toch naar me!'

Linda had het pad bereikt en keek naar de bewolkte hemel boven de ruwe zee. Ze voelde zich geen zier beter dan in het huis. Integendeel: de stormachtige wind leek het gevoel van dreiging in haar nog aan te wakkeren.

Ook deze winter was er nauwelijks sneeuw op Helgoland gevallen, maar de met gras begroeide grond was bevroren. Buiten adem en angstig, met de geur van zijn aftershave nog steeds in haar neus, staarde ze van boven naar de zee, die zich als een dol geworden beest met een opengesperde, schuimende muil op de betonblokken langs de kust stortte.

Hij is hier. Ik voel het. Hij is hier.

Ze keek om naar het huis.

Niets. Geen man achter het raam. Geen schaduw achter de gordijnen. Alleen het licht dat ze in het atelier onder het dak had laten branden.

'Je moet me hier komen halen, Clemens,' zei ze en ze merkte hoe hysterisch ze klonk. Ze draaide zich weer naar de zee toe.

'Je bent niet goed wijs, Linda. Niemand komt het eiland nog op. Ik niet en je ex-vriend ook niet.'

Noem hem niet mijn vriend, dacht Linda, maar voor ze iets kon zeggen werd ze door een voorwerp afgeleid dat de golven voor de zeewering hadden gedeponeerd.

Tot dan toe had ze in een reflex gehandeld en was voor een gevaar gevlucht dat ze niet kon zien, maar des te beter kon voelen. Maar nu had ze een doel. Linda rende zo hard ze kon de weg naar beneden af, tot ze de oever had bereikt.

'Oké, Linda, luister. Of je staat nu in een windtunnel of in een tornado. Dat is allebei goed. Ga maar even lekker uitwaaien. Ik heb meteen al gezegd dat je op een gegeven moment doordraait als je niet af en toe naar buiten gaat.'

Door het steeds luider wordende gebulder van de wind was haar broer nauwelijks nog te verstaan. Ze stond ongeveer vijftien meter van het water, dichtbij genoeg om de vochtige adem van de golven in haar gezicht te voelen.

'Ik bel je later,' brulde ze tegen de woedende elementen in.

'Ja, doe dat. Haal maar een frisse neus, diep ademhalen.'

Linda knikte, hoewel ze al niet meer naar haar broer luisterde toen ze langzaam maar zeker naar de muur van de zeewering liep. Geïrriteerd staarde ze naar de donkere klomp die tussen de betonnen uitsteeksels van de golfbreker hing.

'En neem maar van mij aan: die hufter kan je niks meer maken. Begrijp je?' hoorde ze Clemens zeggen.

'Hij is dood,' zei ze toonloos.

'Niet over de telefoon,' antwoordde hij, zonder te weten dat ze het niet tegen hem had gezegd.

Linda zette een stap achteruit, begon te kokhalzen en wilde weglopen, maar de vreselijke aanblik verlamde haar ledematen.

Zo goed zal ik nooit worden, dacht ze. Op dat moment was de telefoon allang uit haar hand gevallen.

Later schaamde ze zich voor die gedachte, maar het eerste wat haar door het hoofd schoot toen ze naar het verwrongen gezicht staarde was dat ze de dood nooit zo perfect zou kunnen tekenen als hij zich in die seconde openbaarde. Toen begon ze te huilen. Deels vanwege de schok, maar als ze eerlijk was voornamelijk vanwege de teleurstelling omdat ze meteen al zag dat het lijk in het water Danny Haag niet was.

4

Straks krijg ik ongelooflijk op mijn bek.
Paul Herzfeld ging langzamer lopen en overwoog de straat over
te steken. Hij was nog maar een paar meter van het woonhuis
vandaan dat in de steigers stond, en het gedeelte van het trottoir
dat veiligheidshalve was afgezet. Voor de ingang van de overdekte
passage waardoor de voetgangers langs de bouwplaats moesten
lopen, stond een groepje hem op te wachten.
Vier mannen, de een nog potiger dan de ander. Die met de
hamer in zijn hand glimlachte.
Verdomme, waarom werken die vandaag eigenlijk?
Herzfeld had niet verwacht dat er in dit weer bouwvakkers de
steiger op zouden worden gestuurd. Er waren plekken op de zuid-
pool die aangenamer waren dan Berlijn in februari. Nauwelijks
zon, maar zoveel sneeuw dat de sneeuwscheppen in de bouwmarkt
waren uitverkocht. En had het weerbericht niet storm voorspeld?
Waarom waren die idioten dan weer op de bouwplaats? En nog te
vroeg ook?
De zon was nog niet opgegaan, zoals zo vaak wanneer Herzfeld
's ochtends op weg naar zijn werk ging. In de vier jaar dat hij als
hoofd Forensische Geneeskunde op de BKA werkte, de federale
recherchedienst, was Herzfeld niet één keer te laat in de snijka-
mer verschenen. En dat terwijl de eerste vroege werkbespreking
al om halfacht stond gepland, een in zijn ogen absurd tijdstip; al
helemaal voor een single, die zich na zijn gestrande huwelijk ook

graag eens in het Berlijnse nachtleven zou hebben gestort.

Alsof de lijken niet konden wachten, had hij vaak gedacht, wanneer hij zoals vandaag zijn ochtendkoffie staande achteroversloeg, voor hij naar de u-Bahn rende, de Berlijnse metro. Aan de andere kant, ook dat besefte hij, kon alleen iemand die vroeg opstond de enorme werkdruk bij de BKA aan. Alleen vandaag al lagen er zes lijken in de koelcellen. Je hoefde maar een blik in de krant te werpen om te weten dat de wereld steeds gewelddadiger werd. Daarvoor hoefde je niet aan het hoofd te staan van de speciale eenheid Extreme Delicten, een afdeling die werd ingeschakeld als er forensisch onderzoek nodig was bij bijzonder gewelddadige misdrijven tegen het leven.

En nu maak ik een goede kans op mijn eigen sectietafel te belanden, dacht Herzfeld toen hij de mannen naderde. Hij voelde zijn kuiten verkrampen en was bijna gestruikeld. Nerveus balde hij zijn vuist in zijn jaszak. De pijn in zijn knokkels riep de herinnering op aan zijn uitbarsting van gisteren, waar hij nauwelijks een verklaring voor had. Hij bewaarde altijd de zelfbeheersing die in zijn beroep noodzakelijk was. Zelfs als je met de gruwelijkste misdaden werd geconfronteerd, moest je het hoofd koel houden. Een eigenschap waarop hij zich steeds had laten voorstaan. Tot gisteren.

Het was op weg naar huis gebeurd, na een lange ochtend aan de sectietafel en een nog langere middag achter zijn bureau, waar hij het papierwerk moest afhandelen dat onvermijdelijk met de autopsie van lijken was verbonden. Herzfeld was in gedachten bij de drie maanden oude zuigeling – ze hadden tijdens de ochtenddienst met chirurgische precisie zijn ogen verwijderd om via de bloeduitstortingen in het netvlies te kunnen bewijzen dat de kleine door elkaar was geschud tot de dood erop volgde – toen een hond tussen zijn benen door liep; een zwangere bastaard, die haar lijn achter zich aan sleepte. Het teefje had zichzelf van de fietsenrekken naast de supermarkt aan de overkant van de straat losgetrokken en maakte een gedesoriënteerde indruk.

'Hallo, kleintje,' riep Herzfeld en hij ging op zijn hurken zitten om haar te lokken. Hij wilde beslist voorkomen dat het dier de drukke straat weer zou oversteken. Eerst leek hij succes te hebben. De hond was blijven staan, precies aan de andere kant van het zebrapad. Het zwarte vel glansde in de motregen, ze hijgde en knipperde angstig met haar ogen, maar ze klemde haar staart niet meer stijf tussen haar achterpoten sinds hij was begonnen haar sussend toe te spreken. 'Kom hier, kleintje.'

Eerst zag het ernaar uit alsof ze hem begon te vertrouwen. Maar toen kwam hij. De arbeider. Als uit het niets was hij verschenen, net zo groot en slank als Herzfeld, maar het gemak waarmee hij zijn buitenmaatse gereedschapskist droeg, verried dat hij wat lichaamskracht betrof in een andere categorie viel.

'Rot op,' zei de man, die op de bouw als dakdekker werkzaam was en luisterde naar de bijnaam Rocco, zoals Herzfeld later te weten zou komen. Eerst dacht hij nog dat het ordinaire bevel hem gold, maar toen gebeurde het ondenkbare: de proleet schopte de hoogzwangere teef met zijn zware, van een stalen neus voorziene bouwvakkerslaars uit alle macht in haar ronde buik.

Het dier schreeuwde het uit. Ontzettend luid en ontzettend schel, en met die kreet van pijn werd er in Herzfelds hoofd een schakelaar overgehaald, die het opschrift 'blinde woede' droeg. Van de ene seconde op de andere bevond meneer de professor zich niet langer in zijn slanke, maar ongetrainde drieënveertigjarige lichaam. Hij stond naast zichzelf, alsof hij op afstand werd bediend, zonder een gedachte aan mogelijke consequenties te verspillen.

'Hé, smerige lafbek!' hoorde Herzfeld zichzelf zeggen, net op tijd, voor de man de in het nauw gedreven hond nog een schop kon verkopen.

'Wat?' Rocco draaide zich om en staarde Herzfeld aan alsof een emmer kots hem de weg versperde. 'Wat zei je daar, mietje?'

Intussen stonden ze nog maar een kleine stap van elkaar af. In zijn handen leek de zware gereedschapskist op een lege schoenendoos.

'Welk woord van de twee heb je niet begrepen? *Smerige* of *lafbek*?'

'Wacht, ik sla de stront uit je darmen...' had Rocco willen zeggen, maar alles wat hem na *stront* over de lippen kwam, was voor de omstanders niet meer te verstaan. Herzfeld maakte gebruik van het verrassingseffect, bewoog zich als een springveer naar voren en ramde zijn voorhoofd tegen het vierkante gezicht van de dierenbeul.

Het kraakte, het bloed spoot uit zijn neus, maar Rocco gaf geen kik. Hij leek vooral verbaasd.

De hond, die gelukkig niet ernstig gewond leek te zijn, was uit de gevarenzone weggeslopen en naar haar baasje gevlucht, die weer was teruggekomen en nu samen met de andere toeschouwers de ongelijke strijd gadesloeg: Herzfeld tegen Goliath. Hersens tegen spieren. Woede tegen kracht.

Ten slotte zegevierde het geluk over de wet van de sterkste.

Herzfeld weerde één, twee klappen af, maar moest een zware treffer tegen zijn borst incasseren en wankelde al toen de bouwvakker op een bevroren stoeptegel uitgleed en met zijn achterhoofd tegen het plaveisel sloeg. Daardoor was de tegenstander weliswaar nog niet uitgeschakeld, maar hij vormde nu een makkelijk doelwit voor Herzfelds winterlaarzen. Keer op keer schopte hij de dierenbeul in zijn gezicht, zijn maag, tegen zijn borst. Keer op keer krabbelde de man op, maar steeds als hij erin was geslaagd zich af te zetten liet Herzfeld weer zijn vuist op zijn gezicht neerdalen. Hij bewerkte zijn onder-, dan zijn bovenkaak en liet de man pas met rust toen hij niet meer bewoog.

Later hoorde Herzfeld van de agent die zijn verklaring opnam dat Rocco naar het oordeel van de artsen een maand lang geen vaste voeding meer tot zich kon nemen en ternauwernood aan een zware hersenschudding was ontsnapt. Herzfelds gezwollen hand zou sneller genezen, maar het kon iets langer duren voor hij met zijn gehavende vingers weer zonder pijn zou kunnen snijden. Daaraan had hij bij zijn woede-uitbarsting natuurlijk niet gedacht, net zomin als aan het feit dat zijn bazen er niet erg blij mee zouden zijn dat er zich een afdelingschef in de gelederen bevond tegen wie strafvervolging werd ingesteld.

Om die reden had Herzfeld vanmiddag een afspraak op de afdeling Personeelszaken. Maar momenteel zag hij heel wat grotere problemen opdoemen dan een schorsing.

Nu hij voor hen stond, herkende hij de collega's van de man die hij een dag eerder het ziekenhuis in had geslagen; in gesloten formatie belemmerden ze hem de doorgang.

'Wat?' vroeg hij. Herzfelds adem vormde dampwolkjes. Opeens zat zijn boord te strak en schuurde langs zijn hals. Hij voelde de adrenaline door zijn aderen jagen, maar veel te weinig om de krachten van gisteren weer te ontketenen. Vandaag zou hij zich niet eens tegen één zo'n kerel kunnen verdedigen, laat staan tegen vier.

'Rocco heeft veel pijn,' zei de kleinste van de groep, die de hamer in zijn hand hield. Een pokdalig, pezig type met een kaalgeschoren kop.

'En?'

'En het gaat echt klote met hem, man.'

'Tja, kan gebeuren,' zei Herzfeld en hij wilde zich tussen hen door dringen, maar de kerel duwde hem ruw tegen zijn borst en zei: 'Ho, niet zo snel, professor.'

Zoekend naar bijval keek hij achterom naar zijn grijnzende collega's.

Professor? Verdomme, ze weten wie ik ben.

'We willen u alleen iets geven,' zei de aanvoerder. Het knikken en grijnzen in het groepje nam toe.

Herzfeld trok zijn schouders op, spande zijn buikspieren en

zette zich schrap voor de eerste klap. Maar tot zijn verbazing drukte de kerel hem de hamer in zijn hand. Nu pas zag Herzfeld het blauwe strikje om de steel.

'De volgende keer pakt u dit ding hier als u die hufter de schedel wilt inslaan, ja?'

De groep lachte, de een na de ander trok zijn werkhandschoenen uit en begon te klappen, terwijl Herzfeld, nog steeds met een hevig bonkend hart maar met een verbaasde glimlach op zijn gezicht, langs hen heen liep.

'Bravo!'

'Goed gedaan.'

'Het werd tijd dat Rocco de verkeerde tegenkwam,' riepen ze hem achterna.

Herzfeld was zo opgewonden dat hij hen vergat te bedanken. Het schoot hem pas te binnen toen hij een halfuur later de sectiezaal binnenkwam en met het gruwelijkste geval van zijn carrière werd geconfronteerd.

5

De onderkaak was uit het gewricht gehaald, vermoedelijk met dezelfde grove zaag waarmee de dader de bovenkaak had verwijderd. Of dat voor of na haar dood was gebeurd, kon Herzfeld pas zeggen als hij de luchtpijp en de longen van de onbekende had onderzocht.

'De dode is een Midden-Europese vrouw, geschatte leeftijd op grond van de toestand van de organen tussen de vijftig en zestig,' sprak hij in de dictafoon. 'De op de vindplaats van het lijk gemeten rectale temperatuur, die bijna gelijk was aan de omgevingstemperatuur, evenals het optreden van lijkstijfheid en lijkvlekken, wijst erop dat de dood hooguit achtenveertig en minimaal zesendertig uur geleden is ingetreden.'

Eigenlijk had Herzfeld een diepe en luide stem, waarmee hij de meest vermoeide student op de achterste rijen van de collegezaal kon wekken, maar hij had er een gewoonte van gemaakt tijdens het werk in de sectieruimte zacht te praten. Alleen al uit respect voor de doden, maar ook om het de secretaresse, die later het sectierapport moest schrijven, gemakkelijker te maken. Hoe harder je hierbeneden praatte, des te sterker was de echo die van de betegelde wanden terugkwam en de verstaanbaarheid van de opname verminderde.

'De twee takken van de onderkaak inclusief de kaakhoek zijn blijkbaar na het afstropen van de opperhuid en het onderhuidse vetweefsel losgemaakt...' Herzfeld pauzeerde even en boog zich nog eens onderzoekend over het lijk op de stalen tafel, voordat hij het rapport voor het Openbaar Ministerie verder dicteerde, 'zodat de stembanden duidelijk te zien zijn. De huid van de kin en de mondbodem hangt nu in plooien naar beneden. Geen bloeduitstortingen in het onderhuidse vetweefsel of de blootliggende mondbodemmusculatuur. Ook rond de kaakhoek geen hematoom in de omgevende, geëxposeerde weke delen.'

Het barbaars toegetakelde vrouwenlijk was door een dakloze in een verhuisdoos op het stilgelegde pretpark van het Spreewaldpark ontdekt, toen de arme man er zijn nachtbivak wilde opslaan. *'Iemand heeft het hoofd leeg laten lopen,'* had de zwerver tegen de agenten gezegd. Een verbazingwekkend rake omschrijving. Het gezicht van de dode deed Herzfeld aan een leeg masker denken. Vanwege de ontbrekende kaak was het als een verschrompelde luchtballon in elkaar gezakt.

'Is de doos waarin ze werd gevonden ook hier?' vroeg hij aan de anderen.

'Die ligt nog bij de technische recherche.'

Herzfeld opende de mondholte om die te onderzoeken op eventuele ingebrachte vreemde voorwerpen. Alleen al door de handbewegingen kromp hij ineen van pijn, maar hij had er niet zoveel last van als hij had gevreesd. Zolang hij zijn vingers bleef bewegen was het nog wel uit te houden.

'Oef... goeie genade.'

Hij trok zijn neus op onder zijn mondkapje. De dode was pas een paar minuten het koelvak uit, maar desondanks begon de zoetige geur van de beginnende ontbinding zich beneden al te verspreiden.

De sectiezaal was met vierentwintig graden weer eens veel te warm. Het viel de huismeesters van het pand gewoon niet aan het verstand te brengen dat het niet hetzelfde was of je in de kantoren op de bovenste verdiepingen werkte of helemaal beneden in de kelders van de Treptower, een markant complex van kantoorflats in de Berlijnse wijk Treptow, direct aan de oever van de Spree. Zodra de buitentemperatuur zakte, werkten de radiatoren in het hele gebouw van de BKA op volle toeren, waardoor de airconditioning van de sectiezaal steevast van slag raakte en er vervolgens de brui aan gaf.

'Beide handen zijn in het overgangsgebied tussen het uiteinde van de ellepijp en het spaakbeen en de handwortelbeentjes glad afgesneden,' dicteerde Herzfeld verder.

'Ongewoon intelligent,' was het commentaar van dr. Scherz op de uitwendige schouwing, en daarmee zei de plompe assistent-arts naast hem hardop wat Herzfeld de hele tijd al dacht: *Wie die vrouw heeft vermoord, was niet achterlijk en wist precies wat hij deed.*

Veel daders haalden hun kennis uit thrillers en Hollywood-films en dachten dat het voldoende was om de tanden van het lijk te trekken als je de identiteit van het slachtoffer wilde verbergen. Er waren weinig mensen die wisten dat zoiets de identificatie door de tandarts wel bemoeilijkte, maar niet onmogelijk maakte. Het verwijderen van boven- en onderkaak en beide handen was overduidelijk het werk van een professional.

'Voor ik het vergeet,' zei Scherz opeens, terwijl hij spottend zijn dikke lippen krulde. 'De nieuwe van de receptie vroeg me je te zeggen dat ze een grote fan van je is.'

Herzfeld sloeg zijn ogen ten hemel.

Hij had de pech dat hij als twee druppels water op een bekende acteur leek: het wat hoekige, maar symmetrische gezicht, grote donkere ogen onder een hoog door het vele nadenken gegroefd voorhoofd, licht golvend haar dat ooit ravenzwart was geweest, maar langzamerhand begon te grijzen – de gelijkenis was zo verbluffend dat hij zelf even met stomheid geslagen was toen hij de foto van de tv-ster toevallig in een tijdschrift had ontdekt. De slanke verschijning, de licht naar voren hangende schouders, de brede glimlach, zelfs de bij Wikipedia aangegeven lichaamslengte van een meter tachtig bij negenenzeventig kilogram kwam overeen. Vanaf dat moment begreep Herzfeld waarom wildvreemde

37

mensen hem keer op keer om een handtekening vroegen. Eén keer had hij zijn handtekening zelfs in het poëziealbum van een vasthoudende vrouwelijke fan gekrabbeld, gewoon om ervanaf te zijn. Tot overmaat van ramp was zijn dubbelganger sinds kort in een ziekenhuisserie te zien, waarin hij – hoe is het mogelijk! – de zonderlinge patholoog-anatoom dr. Starck vertolkte, die tijdens een autopsie naar hardrock luisterde en schuine moppen vertelde, als hij tenminste niet net een pizzakoerier naar de sectiezaal had laten komen. Het was er allemaal met de haren bij gesleept, maar ongelooflijk succesvol, en daarom ging Herzfeld ervan uit dat hij in de toekomst wel vaker handtekeningen zou moeten vervalsen. Om te beginnen waarschijnlijk voor de nieuwe bij de receptie.

'Wat laat de CT-scan zien?' vroeg hij aan dr. Sabine Yao, die tegenover hem aan de tafel stond. De Duitse van Chinese afkomst was naast dr. Scherz het derde lid van het team dat deze week dienst had, en de collega met wie Herzfeld het liefst sectie verrichtte. Alles aan haar was gecultiveerd: haar fijne, gewelfde wenkbrauwen, de doorzichtig gelakte vingernagels, haar heldere stem, de onopvallende parels aan haar oren. Hij waardeerde Yao's rustige, bedachtzame manier van doen en haar talent om altijd een stap vooruit te denken. Nu had ze de opnames van de computertomografie ongevraagd gedownload en duwde de zwenkarm met de platte monitor naar hem toe, zodat hij er een korte blik op kon werpen zonder het werk aan de borstkas te hoeven onderbreken.

'Zie je het vreemde voorwerp?' vroeg Yao. Met haar een meter zestig moest ze op een kleine verhoging naast de sectietafel staan. Herzfeld knikte.

Het object in het inwendige van de schedel moest uit ijzer, staal, aluminium of een ander materiaal bestaan dat geen röntgenstralen doorliet, anders zou het niet zo duidelijk op de computertomografie te zien zijn geweest. Het was cilindervormig en niet groter dan een pinda. Misschien een deel van een projectiel, en mogelijk een aanwijzing voor de doodsoorzaak.

Schot in het hoofd. Zou niet de eerste zijn deze week.

Scherz, die het hart er al uit had gehaald, sneed nu met vaardige hand de longen uit de borstkas en legde ze op de orgaantafel aan het voeteneind van de sectietafel.

'Er is geen bloed geïnhaleerd. Niet in de luchtpijp en niet in de longen,' constateerde Herzfeld nadat hij de bronchiën had opengesneden. Hij knikte zijn collega toe.

'Postmortale lijkschennis.'

De vrouw was al dood geweest toen ze werd verminkt. Als haar kaak was afgezaagd terwijl ze nog leefde, zou er onvermijdelijk bloed in haar keelholte en strottenhoofd zijn gelopen, en zou ze dat hebben ingeademd. Die kwelling was haar tenminste bespaard gebleven.

Scherz reageerde op de informatie met een onverschillige grijns. De dagelijkse omgang met de dood had de assistent-arts afgestompt. Ook Herzfeld slaagde er doorgaans in zijn gedachten onder het werk in een soort trance te laten overgaan, als een automobilist die een bekend traject bijna automatisch aflegt. Hij concentreerde zich op het lichaam en niet op de ziel van de persoon op wie hij sectie verrichtte. Hij vermeed elk contact met de familie, zowel voor als na de autopsie, om niet emotioneel bij de zaak betrokken te raken. Hij had een helder hoofd nodig als het erom ging juridisch steekhoudende bewijzen te verzamelen. Vorige week nog hadden de ouders van een moordslachtoffer gevraagd of ze de forensisch arts mochten spreken die hun elfjarige dochter, die slachtoffer van misbruik was geworden, had onderzocht. Herzfeld had geweigerd, zoals gewoonlijk. Want met het beeld van de huilende moeder in zijn achterhoofd was de verleiding groot om naar de veroordeling van de vermeende moordenaar toe te werken en dan een fout te maken die eventueel tot vrijspraak zou leiden. Daarom probeerde hij zijn gevoelens onder het werk zo veel mogelijk uit te schakelen. Toch was hij opgelucht dat de onbekende op zijn tafel niet levend in stukken was gezaagd.

'Vervolgens beschouwen we de maaginhoud...' zei hij, toen achter hem met veel kabaal de schuifdeur van de sectiezaal werd opengetrokken.

'Neem me niet kwalijk dat ik zo laat ben.'

Herzfeld en zijn collega's draaiden zich om naar de ingang en zagen een jongeman die haastig de ruimte in beende. Hij droeg dezelfde blauwe werkkleding als de anderen, alleen was die voor hem wat aan de krappe kant.

'En jij bent...?' vroeg Herzfeld de rijzige man, die met elke stap die hij naderbij kwam jonger leek te worden. In eerste instantie had hij hem midden twintig geschat. Nu hij vlak voor hem stond, gaf Herzfeld de bezoeker een paar jaar minder. De magere blonde man, met naar achteren gekamd, met gel gefixeerd haar, een rond brilletje op de spitse neus en een arrogant naar voren gestoken kin, herinnerde hem aan de strebers onder de eerstejaarsstudenten, die bij zijn colleges altijd op de eerste rij gingen zitten en hoopten dat het voortdurende oogcontact hogere cijfers bij de tentamens zou opleveren.

'Ingolf von Appen,' stelde hij zich voor. In alle ernst stak hij zijn hand naar hem uit.

Goed idee.

Herzfeld haalde ongegeneerd zijn vingers uit het geopende onderlichaam en pakte de hand van de bezoeker om die te schudden, zonder eerst zijn met bloed en uitscheidingen overdekte latexhandschoen uit te trekken.

Zijn gezwollen vingers schreeuwden van pijn, maar dat was het wel waard.

Een seconde raakte het gezicht van de jongen uit de plooi, maar toen speelde hij het spelletje mee en liet Herzfeld in vriendelijke bewoordingen weten dat de professor zojuist een grote fout had gemaakt door hem ten overstaan van de verzamelde aanwezigen belachelijk te maken.

6

'Prettig kennis te maken, professor. En ik dank u zeer dat u aan het verzoek van mijn vader om een gaststudent te accepteren gehoor hebt gegeven.'

Von Appen. Verdomme. Herzfeld kon zich wel voor de kop slaan.

Bij die naam had er een belletje moeten rinkelen. Vorige week nog had het hoofd van de BKA hem persoonlijk te kennen gegeven dat de zoon van de Berlijnse senator met alle egards behandeld diende te worden, koste wat kost – en nu had hij hem in de eerste seconden van zijn stage al belachelijk gemaakt! Hij overwoog of hij de zaak zou verergeren als hij de jongeman een zakdoek zou aanreiken, maar toen had Ingolf von Appen zijn hand al aan zijn schort afgeveegd en vol verwachting zijn wiebelige nikkelen brilletje rechtgezet.

'Alstublieft, mijne heren, mevrouw, laat u zich niet door mij storen,' neuzelde hij op de arrogante, zangerige toon die de spruiten van rijke ouders kennelijk al op de kleuterschool instudeerden. Volgens de kranten had Ingolfs vader het met zijn firma in alarminstallaties tot miljonair geschopt, voor hij als lid van de Berlijnse senaat zijn functie kon gebruiken om de angst van de mensen – en zodoende zijn belangrijkste activiteit – nog verder te doen groeien. Als er een mensenslag bestond dat Herzfeld meer verachtte dan snel rijk geworden politici, dan waren het wel hun kinderen, die zonder zelf iets te presteren van het geld en de status van hun ouders profiteerden. Zelf had Herzfeld op zijn zeventiende over de grens van de DDR de wijk genomen naar West-Berlijn,

wat vooral een vlucht voor zijn vader was geweest, die als partij-
getrouwe officier bij de staatsveiligheidsdienst alles belichaamde
wat Paul Herzfeld aan het systeem verfoeide. Des te meer ergerde
het hem als hij constateerde dat het er ook in een democratie om
ging op welke politieke vrienden – of liever gezegd op welke relaties – iemand kon bogen. Normale stervelingen, die geen senator
als vader hadden, kregen de kans niet om een kijkje te nemen in
een speciale BKA-afdeling.

Nou ja, hij lijkt tenminste niet misselijk te worden.

'In de maag honderdveertig milliliter grijswitte, melkachtig
aandoende, papperige inhoud met een zure geur,' zei Herzfeld
in de dictafoon die Yao nu voor hem vasthield, zodat hij beide
handen vrij had.

'Vreemd,' was het commentaar van de senatorszoon op de achtergrond.

'Vreemd?'

'Ja, er wordt hier helemaal geen muziek gedraaid.'

Herzfeld sloeg zijn ogen ten hemel.

*Dat is vandaag al de tweede fan van dr. Starck. Dat kan nog leuk
worden.*

'Nee. Geen muziek.'

In de aflevering van gisteren waren de scenarioschrijvers op het
absurde idee gekomen de patholoog naar Depeche Mode te laten luisteren. Herzfeld had de tv, zoals zo vaak, geïrriteerd uitgezet, nadat hij er al zappend per ongeluk was blijven hangen. 'De
maaginhoud moet worden geanalyseerd,' zei hij, om zich weer op
het werk zelf te concentreren. 'Net als de kruimelachtige objecten
hier in het begin van de twaalfvingerige darm. Maar nu onderwerpen we eerst het hoofd aan een nader onderzoek.'

'Wat is er eigenlijk met die vrouw gebeurd?' vroeg Ingolf. Hij
zette een stap naar voren en boog zich geïnteresseerd over het lijk.

Herzfeld zag het al aankomen en wilde hem waarschuwen,
maar het was te laat. Het vervaarlijk wiebelende nikkelen bril-

letje gleed van Ingolf von Appens neus en viel linea recta in de geopende borstkas van de dode.

'O, dat spijt me.'

Scherz, Yao en Herzfeld keken elkaar eerst verbijsterd, vervolgens geamuseerd aan toen de arme drommel probeerde zijn bril uit het lijk te vissen. Uiteindelijk gaf Herzfeld hem een pincet, maar moest zich toen, nadat Ingolf zijn bril snel weer had opgezet, van hem afwenden om niet in lachen uit te barsten. Ingolf had de glazen provisorisch met de zoom van zijn schort schoongeveegd, waardoor de met bloed besmeurde bril eruitzag als een feestartikel voor Halloween.

'Het spijt me oprecht,' zei Ingolf von Appen schuldbewust.

'Geen probleem. Probeer in het vervolg gewoon wat op de achtergrond te blijven.'

'Ik wilde me alleen nuttig maken.'

'Nuttig?'

Herzfeld, die juist een schedelbeitel had gepakt, nam Ingolf op en glimlachte geamuseerd achter zijn mondkapje. 'Prima, dan mag je een cardioversieapparaat voor me halen.'

'Een wat?'

'Ik heb nu geen tijd om het uit te leggen. Ga maar gewoon naar de eerste verdieping en vraag naar het afdelingshoofd, dr. Strohm, die begrijpt meteen wat ik bedoel.'

'Een cardioversieapparaat?'

'Ja, maar snel. Zeg dat het voor het lijk hier is, en dat elke seconde telt.'

Nauwelijks was Ingolf de sectiezaal uit gerend of Herzfelds collega's proestten het uit.

'Je weet dat dit consequenties zal hebben,' giechelde Yao, nadat haar eerste lachaanval voorbij was.

'Een cardioversieapparaat!' Ook de doorgaans nogal gereserveerde assistent-arts moest grijnzen bij het idee dat de student over een paar minuten naar een defibrillator zou vragen. En wel voor een vrouw die al minstens twee dagen dood was.

'Elke seconde telt,' citeerde hij Herzfeld. 'Ik zou dolgraag het gezicht van dr. Strohm willen zien.'

Onder normale omstandigheden viel er bij hun werk weinig te lachen, maar onder normale omstandigheden zat hun team ook niet opgescheept met zo'n onbenul van een stagiair.

'Goed, dan maken we nu gebruik van de rust voor die stuntel terugkomt,' zei Herzfeld toen de hilariteit was weggeëbd.

Hij positioneerde het hoofd van de dode zodanig dat hij de kleine spleet in de geopende mondholte kon zien die zich vlak boven de plek bevond waar de bovenkaak was afgezaagd. Daar zette hij de beitel aan om de opening te vergroten.

Vervolgens kon hij met een pincet het kleine object dat op de röntgenfoto te zien was via de geopende schedelbasis verwijderen.

'Geen projectiel. Het ziet eruit als een metalen capsule,' mompelde Yao, die over zijn schouder meekeek.

Nee. En ook geen splinter.

Herzfeld onderzocht de ovale, groene cilinder eerst met de loep en ontdekte de inkeping die als een equator in het midden van de capsule zat, die zo groot was als een erwt.

Het ziet ernaar uit dat hij hier open kan, dacht hij. Inderdaad slaagde Herzfeld erin de cilinder met behulp van een tang en een pincet uit elkaar te schroeven. In de capsule zat een piepklein briefje, niet groter dan een halve pinknagel.

'Heb je hulp nodig?' vroeg Yao achter hem, terwijl Herzfeld de vondst voorzichtig gladstreek en onder de microscoop legde.

'Ga maar verder met de buikorganen, ik red het alleen wel,' zei hij, terwijl hij het oculair scherp stelde. Op het eerste gezicht zagen de tekens op de celstof eruit als toevallige verontreinigingen. Maar toen draaide hij het papier honderdtachtig graden en ontwaarde hij de getallen die erop stonden. Ze zagen eruit als een mobiel telefoonnummer en Herzfeld wilde zijn collega's net van zijn merkwaardige ontdekking vertellen, toen hij de zes kleine letters onder de getallen ontdekte. Ze sprongen door de microscoop direct in zijn amygdala, in het deel van de hersens dat voor angstreacties verantwoordelijk is. Zijn hartslag versnelde, zweet parelde op zijn voorhoofd en zijn mond werd droog. Tegelijk had Herzfeld nog maar één gedachte: *Laat dit alsjeblieft toeval zijn.*

Want de letters op het briefje dat hij zojuist uit het hoofd van een mismaakt lijk had verwijderd, vormden een naam: *Hannah.*

De voornaam van zijn zeventienjarige dochter.

7

Herzfeld zou niet kunnen zeggen wanneer zijn vingers voor het laatst zo hadden getrild. Hij had al drie keer een verkeerde toets ingedrukt, eenmaal had hij zijn telefoon bijna uit zijn handen laten vallen.

Wat heeft dat te betekenen? Wie heeft dat briefje in het hoofd van het vrouwenlijk aangebracht?

Hij had zich op het herentoilet aan het eind van de gang ingesloten en moest voortmaken. Zijn collega's verwachtten hem over een paar minuten terug. Ze vroegen zich toch al af waarom hij tegen zijn gewoonte in de zaal tijdens de obductie had verlaten.

Eindelijk.

Hij ging over. Dankzij de talrijke versterkers was de ontvangst voor mobiele telefoons, zelfs in de kelders en de liften, in het hele gebouw uitstekend.

'Hallo?'

Shit. Verdomme.

De andere kant was vier keer overgegaan, toen klonk er een klik in de lijn en was de voicemail aangegaan. Nu hoorde Herzfeld niet de gebruikelijke mededeling, maar een melding die nog schokkender was dan de situatie die hem ertoe had gebracht dit onbekende nummer te kiezen.

Hij was er zeker van geweest dat hij op dit nummer zijn dochter zou bereiken. Het lijk was zo gruwelijk toegetakeld dat de dader het erop moest hebben aangelegd het op Herzfelds tafel te krijgen. Bij een dusdanig opvallend misdrijf werd de leider van de speciale eenheid Extreme Delicten in Berlijn automatisch ingeschakeld.

Ondanks die zekerheid was Herzfeld geschokt toen hij zijn vreselijke vermoeden bewaarheid zag worden.

'Hallo, papa?'

De stem van zijn zeventienjarige dochter was glashelder, alsof ze vlak naast hem stond. En toch klonk Hannah of ze zich in een andere, duistere wereld bevond. Oneindig ver weg.

'Help me alsjeblieft!'

Grote god. Wat is dit? Waarom spreek je op je voicemail een meldtekst in die alleen voor mij bestemd is?

Hannah klonk schor, vermoeid en buiten adem, alsof ze net de trap op was gerend, en toch klonk haar stem anders dan wanneer ze geen lucht meer kreeg.

Nog kwetsbaarder. Nog wanhopiger.

Hannah had astma. Onder normale omstandigheden waren haar regelmatig terugkerende aanvallen geen probleem. Haar inhalatiespray werkte binnen een paar seconden en stelde haar in staat een bijna normaal leven te leiden, met sport en alles wat een jonge vrouw graag doet. Het werd alleen gevaarlijk als ze haar Salbutamol niet bij zich had; zo zou ze drie jaar geleden, toen ze haar jas bij een vriendin had laten liggen, op een haar na in de U-Bahn zijn gestikt als een medereiziger die ook astma had haar niet met zijn spray te hulp was gekomen. Voor zover Herzfeld wist, was dat het laatste ernstige incident geweest, maar hij kon zich vergissen, want sinds hij was vertrokken deed zijn ex-vrouw er alles aan om het contact tussen vader en dochter tot een minimum te beperken. Laatst had ze er zelfs weer van afgezien hem uit te nodigen voor Kerstmis, om het feest met haar nieuwe vriend te kunnen vieren.

Hannah leed het meest onder de scheiding en ze had hem tijdens hun sporadische ontmoetingen ronduit gezegd dat zij hem verantwoordelijk achtte voor het stuklopen van de relatie. En dat terwijl Petra hem had bedrogen. Bij de weinige afspraken die ze de afgelopen tijd hadden gehad, was het gesprek tussen vader en dochter bijna alleen over koetjes en kalfjes gegaan. Hij wist niet of ze op het moment verliefd was, of ze haar rijbewijs had gehaald en hoe het op school ging.

Des te verschrikkelijker was het om nu na weken haar stem weer te horen, omdat hij haar schreeuw om hulp had gevonden in het hoofd van een barbaars toegetakeld lijk. En wat ze zei maakte zijn afgrijzen alleen maar groter: 'Ik ben bang om dood te gaan, papa.'

Bang? Doodgaan?

Die woorden pasten niet bij het beeld van zijn dochter in zijn hart: wild, ontembaar, vol levenslust – zo vastbesloten zich niet door het noodlot te laten kisten dat ze haar astma tartte door marathons te lopen. Van hem had ze de alerte, donkere ogen geërfd en de aanstekelijke, gulle lach; van haar moeder de volle blonde krullen. Aan haar verbeten koppigheid hadden allebei haar ouders beslist een steentje bijgedragen...

'Ik weet dat hij me wil vermoorden,' zei ze huilend op de opname. Wat daarna kwam was nauwelijks te verstaan. Hannah was radeloos, wat Herzfelds laatste beetje hoop, dat het misschien wel los zou lopen en dat het een of andere bizarre grap was, de bodem insloeg.

'Hij vermoordt me als je niet precies doet wat hij zegt. Hij volgt je op de voet.'

Herzfeld had het gevoel dat hij zijn evenwicht verloor en tastte naar de deurklink om houvast te zoeken.

'Alsjeblieft, ik weet dat je duizend mensen bij de BKA kent, maar je mag met niemand praten, begrijp je? Anders ga ik dood...' Ze stokte met verstikte stem.

Wie? Hoe? Waarom?

'Liefje, waar ben je?' vroeg hij, alsof de voicemail kon antwoorden. Herzfeld hoorde de klank van zijn eigen stem, wat hem een surrealistisch, bijna schizofreen gevoel gaf. Er waren meer kinderlijkjes in de loop van zijn carrière op zijn sectietafel beland dan hij kon tellen. En nu zou opeens het leven van zijn eigen dochter op het spel staan?

Waar is het om te doen? Geld misschien?

'Wacht op Erik,' hoorde hij haar nog zeggen, zonder te begrijpen wat ze daarmee bedoelde. 'Hij heeft nog meer instructies voor je.'

Erik? Wie is in godsnaam...?

'Geen woord, tegen niemand, papa. Anders ga ik dood.'

Ze snikte, toen hoorde Herzfeld alleen nog een langgerekte pieptoon en was de lijn dood.

8

Zijn crisis duurde maar een paar minuten. Als iemand in die tijd een blik over de rand van het toilethokje had geworpen, zou hij een op de wc-deksel zittende man hebben gezien, die wanhopig zijn knieën met zijn handen tegen elkaar drukte om ze niet ongecontroleerd tegen elkaar aan te laten slaan. Herzfeld was alleen in de sanitaire ruimte, daarom was er niemand die zijn onderdrukte gekreun en gejaagde ademhaling kon horen.

De schokgolven van het bericht namen in kracht af. Hij voelde zich nog steeds alsof hij van een rots in ijskoud water was gesprongen. Hij was er met veel geweld in gedoken en werd door een allesverstikkende, woedende draaikolk naar beneden gezogen. Maar net zo snel als hij door de tekst van de voicemail in een zee van angst was geduwd, vocht hij zich nu spartelend terug naar de oppervlakte.

Rustig. Je moet tot bedaren komen als je haar wilt helpen.

Herzfeld probeerde zijn ademhaling te controleren; hij lette op elke beweging van zijn buikspieren en concentreerde zich op de luchtstroom langs zijn neushaartjes. Het werkte. Met elke ademhaling werden zijn gevoelens minder chaotisch, en nu zijn knieën niet meer onder zijn gewicht dreigden te bezwijken, kon hij opstaan en het toilet verlaten.

Op weg naar de liften dwong hij zichzelf helder na te denken. Hij moest een plan verzinnen. In de eerste plaats moest hij zijn secretaresse vragen al zijn afspraken wegens ziekte af te zeggen.

Verkoudheid, migraine – nee, buikgriep! Dat is geloofwaardiger nadat je zo lang op de wc hebt gezeten.

Gelukkig had hij het minuscule briefje in de zak van zijn doktersjas laten verdwijnen voordat een van zijn collega's het had gezien. In het sectierapport zou het telefoonnummer van zijn dochter voorlopig niet opduiken.

Hij had tegen zijn collega's gelogen over de capsule en beweerd dat hij leeg was geweest. Vermoedelijk zouden de rechercheurs zich er het hoofd over breken wat voor motief de dader kon hebben gehad om de capsule in de schedel van het slachtoffer te plaatsen, maar Herzfeld had te veel aan zijn hoofd om zich druk te maken over dit door hem gelegde dwaalspoor.

'Geen woord, tegen niemand, papa.'

Goed, daaraan zou hij zich houden. Maar dat betekende nog lang niet dat hij gedwee moest wachten tot de ontvoerder contact met hem opnam.

'Ik ga je vinden, Hannah,' zei hij tegen zichzelf toen hij voor de deur van de lift stond. Hij probeerde tevergeefs de schrikbeelden die zich weer aandienden te verdringen. Hij wist waartoe mensen die anderen in hun macht hadden in staat waren. Hij had de gevolgen met eigen ogen gezien. Naakt, bleek en dood.

Op zijn sectietafel. Dag in, dag uit.

9

IN DE HEL

Na de zesde keer had ze haar eigen naam vergeten. Ze wist niet *wie* ze was of *waar* ze was. Even lukte het haar zelfs te verdringen wat er hier, op dit moment, met haar gebeurde. En dat terwijl de man die haar met regelmatige tussenpozen verkrachtte nog steeds op haar lag.

Haar ontvoerder sloeg haar met de zijkant van zijn hand hard in haar gezicht, en met de pijn kwam tenminste een deel van haar bewustzijn terug: de herinnering aan de verlaten parkeerplaats. Het geluid achter haar. Dat ze zich omdraaide, opeens de lap op haar mond voelde en in deze kelder wakker werd.

De eerste keer, toen ze nog bij haar volle verstand was, had ze de man gesmeekt een condoom om te doen. Dat ze nog maagd was had ze niet durven zeggen, omdat dat hem misschien nog meer zou hebben opgewonden. Ze nam de pil niet, bovendien was ze bang voor ziektes. Maar intussen was aids wel haar minste zorg.

'Maar natuurlijk doen we het veilig,' had de man gezegd terwijl hij zijn broek openmaakte. Alleen al aan zijn toon hoorde ze dat hij loog. Schor en wellustig.

Hoop om hier ooit levend uit te komen had ze niet meer. Dat het bij deze ontvoering niet om losgeld ging en dat ze moest sterven, had ze begrepen toen de naar huishoudzeep ruikende verkrachter de kous van zijn hoofd had getrokken; precies op het moment toen hij voor het eerst bij haar binnendrong.

Nu kan ik je identificeren, had ze gedacht en ze was begonnen te huilen. Vol, licht golvend zandkleurig haar, een rimpelloze huid, een kleine levervlek op de rechterwang, een iets te lange nek voor het kleine, ovale hoofd met het hoge voorhoofd.

Geen dader laat een slachtoffer gaan dat zijn gezicht kent.

Eerder, toen de man nog gezichtloos was geweest, had hij een halfuur lang de tijd genomen om elk plekje van haar naakte lichaam af te likken. Dat kon ze zich nog herinneren, in tegenstelling tot andere ervaringen uit haar verleden.

Het was bijna alsof de belangrijkste herinneringen aan haar eigen ik door haar geheugen voor pijn waren verdrongen. Van de mishandelingen die ze had ondergaan, had ze elk detail onthouden: hoe de gek met het alledaagse gezicht haar met de punt van een hobbyschaar in haar tepel had gestoken. Hoe hij de broekriem om haar hals een gaatje strakker had aangetrokken en haar een hoer had genoemd, omdat hij woedend was dat zijn lid niet sneller weer stijf werd. Toen had hij haar een tijdje alleen gelaten, en dat was bijna de grootste kwelling van haar lijdensweg geweest. Niet te weten wanneer het verder zou gaan en met welk martelwerktuig hij zou terugkomen.

Dat was allemaal drie dagen geleden begonnen.

Als mijn wc-rekensommetje klopt.

Thuis – waar dat ook geweest mocht zijn – was ze hooguit één keer per dag gegaan, en hier had ze zich al drie keer moeten ontlasten. Haar ontlasting was door de metalen veren van de brits zonder matras gevallen. Als straf had haar ontvoerder haar met een vol bierblikje in haar gezicht geslagen. Als ze de plek waar vroeger haar snijtanden hadden gezeten met haar tong aanraakte, schoot er een snijdende pijn tot in haar hersens, die daar geïsoleerde, onvolledige en totaal onbruikbare herinneringen aan haar verleden opriep: bijvoorbeeld dat ze voor haar rijbewijs spaarde, bij scheikunde op overschrijven was betrapt of zonder toestemming van haar moeder een vlinder op haar enkel had laat tatoeëren.

Het spijt me, mama. Ik hoop dat je niet boos op me bent.

Al in de eerste nacht hier in de kelder had ze gemerkt dat haar geest haar lichaam wilde verlaten. Ze was in een koortsachtige slaap gezakt en had gedroomd dat ze weer negen was en met haar vader 'als het echt moest' speelde. Het spel was tijdens de lange busritten door Berlijn ontstaan; hun toertjes, zoals ze het noemden. De weinige weekends dat haar vader niet had hoeven te werken, hadden ze elke keer een andere bus genomen en van bovenaf, op de voorste rij van de dubbeldekker, de stad verkend. Met haar vraag 'Als het echt moest, papa, zou je dan liever een liter zure melk drinken of een glas met worstwater?' was alles begonnen.

'Getver, wat vies. Geen van beide.'

'Dat geldt niet.'

'Moet ik echt kiezen?'

Ze had haar ogen ten hemel geslagen, alsof haar vader traag van begrip was. 'Daarom is het toch "als het echt moest".' En toen had hij het worstwater gekozen en moest ze giechelen. 'Bleh, wat ben jij erg.'

Haar vader glimlachte en gaf haar lik op stuk: 'Oké, als het echt moest: geef je liever Markus of Tim een zoen?' Hij wist dat ze aan allebei haar klasgenoten een hekel had, en ze had zoals verwacht haar vinger in haar mond gestoken, en het had zeker tien minuten geduurd voor ze de knoop had doorgehakt.

Maar wie was het geworden? Markus of Tim?

Ze was wakker geschrokken, en net zoals de echo's van een droom vlak na het ontwaken in het niets oplosten, verdwenen de flarden van haar herinnering met de schreeuw die ze slaakte toen ze merkte dat de psychopaat weer naar de hel was teruggekomen en opnieuw aanstalten maakte zich aan haar te vergrijpen.

10

BERLIJN

Herzfeld stond met zijn telefoon in zijn hand voor de panorama-ruit van zijn bureau op de achtste verdieping van de Treptower. Hij schonk geen aandacht aan het imposante uitzicht op de skyline van Berlijn en de met ijsschotsen bedekte Spree aan zijn voeten.

Keer op keer had hij de meldtekst van de voicemail van zijn dochter beluisterd en elke keer was zijn hoop een aanwijzing voor Hannahs verblijfplaats te vinden ijdel gebleken. Als ze al een me-dedeling in haar tekst had verborgen, dan kon hij die niet ontcij-feren. Na zijn vierde poging koos hij het vaste nummer van het huis waar ze vroeger hadden gewoond, maar in de eengezinswo-ning bij de Schlachtensee nam niemand op.

Het liefst had hij Hannah op haar eigen telefoon gebeld, maar koppig als ze was had ze na zijn vertrek een nieuw nummer geno-men, dat ze hem nog steeds niet had laten weten.

Hij slikte en koos het nummer opnieuw.

'Met de telefoon van mevrouw Schirmherr, goedemiddag?'

Normaal gesproken stak het hem als hij de meisjesnaam van zijn vrouw hoorde, die ze tijdens hun scheidingsprocedure alweer had aangenomen, nog voordat de scheiding rond was geweest. Maar dit was niet het moment voor zelfmedelijden.

'Hallo Normen, ik ben het, Paul. Ik moet Petra spreken.'

'Waar gaat het over?' vroeg de man aan de andere kant van de lijn. Ondanks de slechte verbinding was zijn spottende grijns duidelijk hoorbaar. Verdomme, niet te geloven. Belde hij zijn ex-vrouw een keer vrijwillig, nam de vent die de reden voor de scheiding was geweest persoonlijk op. Petra had Normen twee jaar geleden aan hem voorgesteld als haar rechterhand in het door haar geleide architectenbureau. Twee maanden later zat die rechterhand al in haar slipje.

'Waar is ze?'

'Petra zit helaas al in het vliegtuig. Kan ik een boodschap doorgeven?'

'In wat voor vliegtuig?' vroeg hij verward.

'Een Airbus 380,' was het arrogante antwoord. Pas nu drong het typische achtergrondgeluid van een internationaal vliegveld tot Herzfeld door: het geroezemoes, de bekende gong die voorafging aan de mededeling, die in verschillende talen werd gedaan. Petra was gespecialiseerd in de ontwikkeling van grote bouwprojecten in de hele wereld, daarom was het niet vreemd dat ze met haar privésecretaris op reis was. Maar het was nauwelijks voorstelbaar dat Petra hem haar telefoon had toevertrouwd. Waarschijnlijk had ze zijn naam op het display gezien en haar telefoon aan hem gegeven.

'Luister eens, het is uiterst belangrijk. Ik moet haar echt dringend spreken,' zei Herzfeld. Bijna was hem 'het gaat om leven of dood' ontglipt, maar dat had zijn dochter misschien in gevaar gebracht.

'Geen woord, tegen niemand!'

Norman schraapte geaffecteerd zijn keel. 'Ik zou je graag met Petra willen doorverbinden, maar ook in de eerste klas maakt Qantas geen uitzonderingen.'

Qantas?

'Is ze soms in Australië?'

Bij de vreemde beltoon had hij al vermoed dat hij internationaal telefoneerde.

'Nieuw-Zeeland, al zou ik niet weten wat jou dat aangaat.'

Het liefst zou Herzfeld de idioot met alle vloeken hebben bestookt die hem op de lippen brandden, maar dan zou de slijmjurk nog sneller hebben opgehangen dan hij toch al van plan was.

'Luister, het was leuk om even met je te kletsen, maar nu moet ik inchecken en het grondpersoneel vraagt of ik nu meteen mijn mobiele telefoon...'

'Is mijn dochter bij jullie?' onderbrak Herzfeld hem, hoewel hij dat eigenlijk aan zijn vrouw wilde vragen. Weliswaar had hij weinig hoop dat de meldtekst op de voicemail een vervalsing was, maar in het digitale tijdperk was het geen enkel probleem een authentiek aandoend bericht uit oude opnames samen te stellen. Hij moest systematisch elke twijfel aan Hannahs ontvoering uitbannen, hoe klein ook. Pas dan kon hij zich ten volle op haar bevrijding concentreren.

'Hannah?' Normen klonk oprecht verbaasd. 'Nee, ze is niet met ons meegekomen. Misschien is het je ontschoten, professor, dat je dochter thuis voor haar eindexamen moet studeren.'

Maar thuis kan ik haar niet bereiken!

'Heb jij Hannahs mobiele nummer?'

'Ja. Maar na alles wat ik heb gehoord, zou het niet in jouw belang zijn om je dat te geven. Excuseer mij.' En met die woorden hing de ellendeling dan toch op.

Woedend hield Herzfeld de telefoon in zijn vuist geklemd. Het liefst had hij het ding tegen de muur gekwakt of, beter nog, tegen de glazen vitrine met historische voorwerpen die de faculteit hem voor zijn veertigste verjaardag cadeau had gedaan. Misschien zou hij zelfs aan zijn opwelling gehoor hebben gegeven als het mobieltje niet op dat moment in zijn hand had getrild.

Hij staarde naar het display en liet het ding een paar keer overgaan, toen schakelde hij de opnamefunctie in en nam op. Hoewel de onbekende persoon met een afgeschermd telefoonnummer belde, was Herzfeld er tamelijk zeker van wie hem probeerde te bereiken.

Hij verwachtte een man met een verdraaide stem die de verbinding via een gecodeerde, in het buitenland gevestigde internetrouter liet lopen.

Hannah had gezegd dat hij zichzelf Erik zou noemen.

11

Het atelier onder het dak was de enige kamer in huis die op slot kon. Bovendien was hij in één oogopslag te overzien, er waren geen bedden waaronder iemand zich kon verstoppen, geen kasten waaruit een indringer tevoorschijn kon springen en haar in de rug kon aanvallen. Linda had de grendel van de houten deur dichtgeschoven en bovendien een stoel met een solide metalen leuning onder de deurkruk geklemd. Desondanks voelde ze zich hier op zolder niet meer veilig. Niet nadat ze gisteren had gemerkt dat iemand in haar bed had gelegen. En al helemaal niet sinds ze het huis uit was gevlucht en een lijk op het westelijke strand had gevonden.

Het was puur aan het bidden en smeken van haar broer te danken dat ze naar het huis was teruggekeerd. En dat alleen omdat het alternatief, naar de politie gaan, nog onaangenamer zou zijn.

'En wat wil je de smerissen vertellen?' had Clemens aan de telefoon gevraagd toen Linda hem gisteren, terwijl ze nog voor de strekdam stond, had teruggebeld.

'Wat denk je dat er gebeurt als je ze aan hun neus hangt dat je toevallig een waterlijk hebt gevonden? Verdomme, Linda, het laatste wat we kunnen gebruiken is aandacht.'

'Je bedoelt dat *jij* geen aandacht kan gebruiken.'

Wat hij Danny ook had aangedaan, het was vast niet de bedoeling dat de autoriteiten lucht kregen van het lot van haar stalker.

'Nee. Geloof me, kid, ik ben niet achterlijk. Mij kan niets gebeuren. Maar *jouw* naam staat al in de politiecomputer. En niet in de rubriek slachtoffers. Jij staat geregistreerd als een hysterisch wijf dat zonder reden onschuldige mannen beschuldigt. Zodra je naar de smerissen gaat, zullen ze vaststellen dat je ex al dagen van de aardbodem verdwenen is. En nu ligt er een andere man dood voor je deur? Kom nou toch. Als je de komende dagen niet in voorarrest wilt zitten, moet je je gedeisd houden.'

'Ik kan die vent hier toch niet zomaar laten liggen,' had Linda tegen de razende zee in geschreeuwd.

'En waarom niet? Hij loopt niet weg. En helpen kan je hem niet meer. Dus ga terug naar huis, doe alles op slot en wacht tot een of andere sukkel het lijk vindt. Dan zit die met de gebakken peren en niet jij. En binnenkort is de storm voorbij, en kom ik je weer ophalen.'

'Maar stel dat Danny hem heeft vermoord?' had ze angstig gevraagd.

Want hij had immers al de moord op Shia op zijn geweten. Op een dag was Linda thuisgekomen en had ze zich afgevraagd waarom haar wasmachine niet had gecentrifugeerd, hoewel ze acht uur van huis was geweest. Ze had haar kat alleen nog dood uit de wastrommel kunnen vissen. Op de ruit van de wasmachine had een Post-it gezeten. *'Als je niet meer van mij houdt, mag je nergens meer van houden.'*

'Stel dat die sadist het niet bij dieren laat?'

'Dan moet hij meer levens hebben dan jouw kat,' was Clemens' ondubbelzinnige antwoord geweest.

Ze hadden nog een tijdje gediscussieerd en uiteindelijk had haar broer haar overtuigd. Ze deed geen aangifte van haar ontdekking, hoewel ze gemakkelijk naar restaurant Bandrupp had kunnen lopen, waar, voor zover ze wist, de verzamelde gezagsdragers van het eiland de situatie met elkaar bespraken. In plaats daarvan klom Linda weer omhoog naar het huis om zich in het atelier te verschansen. Ze had de nacht doorgebracht op een lappendeken op de vloer en voelde zich of ze nog geen uur had geslapen. Nu deden al haar botten pijn en voelde ze zich afgepeigerd en rusteloos tegelijk. Alsof ze een paar nachten door had gedanst en zich alleen met stimulerende middelen op de been had gehouden.

Linda gaapte en ging bij het in ruitjes verdeelde raam staan. Ze strekte zich uit en zocht naar een opening in de dichte, donkere muur van regen voor haar ogen.

Wanneer heb ik eigenlijk voor het laatst de zon gezien?

De horizon was 's nachts nog dichter naar de rotsen van het eiland gekropen. De immer aanwezige zeevogels waren verdwenen. In plaats daarvan vloog er een eenzame plastic zak door de lucht, die door de ruziënde windvlagen alle kanten op werd geblazen en uiteindelijk buiten Linda's gezichtsveld over de klippen de zee op werd gedreven.

Linda huiverde. Niet van de kou, die ze bij het tochtige raam nog sterker voelde, maar omdat ze wist dat ze vroeg of laat de deur zou moeten opendoen en naar beneden gaan. Lang zou ze de druk op haar blaas niet meer uithouden, en ze had dorst.

En dan was er ook nog die handtas!

Haar blik dwaalde naar de plek achter het raam, waar ze bij beter weer het pad kon zien. Ze kreeg weer last van haar slechte geweten.

Daarbeneden, op een steenworp afstand van de voet van de heuvel, lag het lijk van een man die tot voor kort een gezin, collega's en vrienden had gehad, die zich nu vast zorgen maakten en hem misten. Ergens wachtte iemand op zijn terugkomst, misschien zijn echtgenote, die wanhopig werd van de verschrikkelijke onzekerheid over wat haar man zou kunnen zijn overkomen. Voor Linda was de dode een onbekende, voor Clemens een probleem; maar voor een ander een geliefd mens, die gemist werd. Die gedachte had haar gisteren al beziggehouden en daarom had ze één instructie van haar broer genegeerd. Clemens had haar bevolen het lijk onder geen voorwaarde aan te raken. Maar als ze dan toch tegen haar gevoel in handelde en de man domweg als wrakhout achterliet, wilde ze tenminste weten *wie* ze in de steek gelaten had. Misschien had Clemens gelijk. Misschien was het beter dat iemand anders het lijk zou vinden. Maar misschien kon zijn ontdekking wat worden bespoedigd als ze zijn identiteit kende? Dat was de enige reden geweest dat Linda gisteren de kleine mannenhandtas had gepakt die maar een paar meter naast de dode op de muur van de zeewering had gelegen. Tot nog toe had ze het niet aangedurfd er een blik in te werpen.

Ze draaide zich om.

Het door het water vlekkerig geworden leren etui met de bruine lus lag nog steeds onberoerd op haar tekentafel.

Kom op, waar wacht je op?

Linda ging erheen, nog altijd twijfelend of ze de tas zou openen. Gisteren had ze een stok door de lus geschoven en hem zo het huis in te kunnen dragen zonder hem te hoeven aanraken.

En nu?

Ze zuchtte en trok een paar wanten uit de zakken van haar outdoorjas, die over de stoelleuning hing.

Als ze geen vingerafdrukken wilde achterlaten zat er niets anders op dan de dikke bontwanten aan te trekken. Gewone handschoenen had ze niet meegenomen, en daarom dreigde ze bij de ritssluiting al te stranden. Ze had een paar pogingen nodig, toen kreeg ze het voor elkaar. De tas was open.

Hij had licht aangevoeld. En inderdaad was hij helemaal leeg, op een telefoon na. Geen portemonnee, geen sleutels, geen papieren.

Linda haalde het mobieltje er voorzichtig uit en legde het op tafel. Het display lichtte op in een fluorescerend groen en liet zien dat er vier gemiste gesprekken waren. Bovendien knipperde in de linkerbovenhoek het symbooltje van een doorgestreepte bel.

Het geluid is uitgeschakeld. Geen wonder dat ik hem niet hoorde overgaan.

Linda hield de handtas met de opening omlaag en schudde flink, maar er viel verder niets uit.

Oké, dan zullen we dit ding eens gaan bekijken.

De telefoon was een roze model met een groot display dat eerder bij een jong meisje dan bij een oudere man paste. Ze trok haar wanten weer uit, pakte een potlood en drukte met de stompe kant op de menutoets.

Interessant.

Alle vier de telefoontjes kwamen van hetzelfde mobiele nummer. Het eerste was een halfuur oud. De andere drie een paar minuten, allemaal vlak na elkaar. In het sms-menu zag Linda dat er geen boodschap was achtergelaten op de voicemail.

Ze noteerde het nummer op haar tekenblok en ging terug naar het hoofdmenu. Daar deed ze nog een ontdekking, een zeer merkwaardige: de vier gemiste oproepen waren de enige die waren opgeslagen. Ook bleek de bezitter er zelf niet mee te hebben gebeld. Of hij had zijn hele belgeschiedenis vlak voor zijn dood gewist; best mogelijk, maar wel vreemd.

Linda legde het potlood weg en dacht na. Het was of ze onder stroom stond, maar in tegenstelling tot de stress van de laatste paar uur gaf deze spanning haar nieuwe energie. Voor het eerst sinds lange tijd had ze het gevoel dat ze iets constructiefs deed. Ze was nogal ondernemend en het achterhalen van de identiteit van de man paste veel beter bij haar dan zich als een angsthaas voor een onbekend gevaar verstoppen.

Verder dan maar.

Linda haalde de telefoon tevoorschijn die Clemens haar had bezorgd, met een nummer dat alleen haar broer kende. Ze controleerde nog eens of de nummeronderdrukking was ingeschakeld. Toen koos ze het nummer van de beller die niet minder dan vier keer achter elkaar had geprobeerd de dode op het strand te bereiken.

Bij de eerste keer overgaan hield ze haar adem in, wat het gevoel dat haar hart uit haar borst zou springen nog eens versterkte. Al bij de derde keer was ze volledig buiten adem en hapte naar lucht. Bij de vierde keer overgaan zonk haar de moed in de schoenen. Ze wilde ophangen, maar het was te laat.

Iemand had opgenomen.

Een man.

Hij klonk gejaagd, zijn stem was schor. Linda had de indruk dat hij net zo bang was als zijzelf.

Hij zei: 'Ja, hallo? U spreekt met Paul Herzfeld.'

12

BERLIJN

'Hallo? Is daar iemand?'

De onbekende beller had nog geen woord gezegd. Maar Herzfeld kon de ander horen ademen. 'Wat wilt u van mij?' vroeg hij. Hij haalde de telefoon van zijn oor om te zien of er nog verbinding was. Zijn display liet alle balkjes van het ontvangstsignaal zien, bovendien was er ruis op de lijn.

'Erik?'

Geen antwoord. Alleen die zware ademhaling. Behalve Herzfelds beste vrienden en familieleden kende niemand zijn mobiele nummer. Geen van hen belde met een verborgen nummer. Misschien had iemand verkeerd gedraaid. Misschien durfde die iemand niet op te hangen.

Misschien. Maar het is niet erg waarschijnlijk.

'Luister, ik weet niet wie u bent. Ik weet niet wat u van mij wilt. U krenkt mijn dochter geen haar, of ik verzeker u dat het woord "pijn" een heel nieuwe dimensie voor u zal krijgen, begrijpt u dat?'

Herzfeld wist dat hij hoog spel speelde. In elk handboek over de psychologie van het onderhandelen stond boven het eerste hoofdstuk geschreven: 'Irriteer nooit de gijzelnemer.' Maar in dit geval waren de spelregels anders. Hier bestond geen standaardprocedure.

Op het moment had hij maar weinig informatie over de ontvoerder, maar wat hij wél wist sprak boekdelen. Het vrouwenlijk bijvoorbeeld – dat was kennelijk door een beroepsmoordenaar geprepareerd en zo gruwelijk toegetakeld dat de dader er zeker van kon zijn dat de dode vroeg of laat op de sectietafel van zijn speciale eenheid zou belanden. En hij wist blijkbaar ook dat Herzfeld die week dienst had.

De dader was zeer goed ingevoerd in de anatomie. Anders was het gecompliceerde inbrengen van het telefoonnummer in de schedel van het lijk onverklaarbaar. Als het niet om iets persoonlijks zou gaan, had de ontvoerder zijn eisen gewoon telefonisch kunnen stellen.

Sinds hij dat had begrepen, brak Herzfeld zich er het hoofd over wat hij een mens kon hebben aangedaan dat zo erg was dat hij een vrouw vermoordde en Hannah ontvoerde.

'Ik ga ervan uit dat u precies weet wie ik ben,' zei hij tegen de zwijgende beller aan de andere kant van de lijn. 'Dan weet u ook over welke mogelijkheden ik vanwege mijn werk bij de BKA beschik om mensen zoals u te vinden. En te doden. Maar als u verstandig bent, zal ik op elke deal ingaan die u voorstelt. Stel uw eisen, en ik zal eraan voldoen. Ik wil mijn dochter levend terugzien.' Terwijl hij die woorden uitsprak, begreep hij dat er in dit geval geen deal zou komen. Herzfeld kreeg een droge mond, hij werd onpasselijk.

Nee, het ging hier niet om geld, anders hadden ze wel contact opgenomen met Petra. Niet alleen kwam ze uit een rijke familie, ze verdiende ook drie keer zoveel als hij. Als er iemand binnen een paar uur een flink bedrag bij elkaar kon krijgen, was zij het wel. En dat zou de persoon die zijn misdaad zo nauwgezet had uitgevoerd, bij zijn voorbereidingen nauwelijks zijn ontgaan.

Herzfeld probeerde kordater te klinken dan hij zich voelde: 'Zeg wat u wilt. U krijgt het. Ik wil alleen mijn dochter terug.'

Hij pauzeerde, toen vroeg hij: 'Erik?'

Niets. Het ademen was verdwenen. Hij hoorde het niet meer. Ook de statische ruis was verdwenen.

Nee, alsjeblieft niet...

Een blik op zijn telefoon bevestigde zijn vermoeden.

Ik heb het verpest. Ik had contact, het hing aan een zijden draadje, en ik heb het verbroken.

De persoon aan de andere kant had opgehangen.

Herzfeld sloeg woedend met zijn vlakke hand op het bureau, toen dacht hij over de volgende stappen na. Het lag voor de hand het telefoontje te traceren, maar zo eenvoudig als in de film ging dat niet. Elke telefoonmaatschappij eiste een gerechtelijk bevel voor ze de gegevens verstrekten die voor het peilen van een mobiele telefoon noodzakelijk zijn.

Zou hij het aandurven er derden bij te betrekken, hoewel Hannah hem had gesmeekt dat niet te doen?

'Anders ga ik dood...'

Aan de andere kant, wat had hij voor keus als die Erik, of hoe hij ook heette, niet met hem wilde praten? Of had hij toch iemand anders aan de lijn gehad?'

Maar waarom had hij dan geen woord gezegd?

Herzfeld opende het bestand met de opname en concentreerde zich op het geluid van de ademhaling dat zijn telefoon had opgenomen. Omdat hij het volume helemaal had opengedraaid, schrok hij zich dood toen de telefoon opeens ging.

'Hallo?'

Dit keer lukte het hem niet de opnamefunctie te activeren voor hij opnam. 'Erik?'

Eerst ruiste het alleen, en Herzfeld dacht al dat de beller aan de andere kant weer zou zwijgen, maar toen hoorde hij de drie woorden die hem de volgende klap bezorgden.

Drie woorden, tot Herzfelds grote verbazing uitgesproken door een jonge vrouw, die met bijna toonloze stem zei: 'Erik is dood.'

13

Ze herinnerde zich vaag dat de waanzinnige haar een briefje met een tekst had gegeven die ze in de telefoon had moeten inspreken. Een van de weinige momenten dat hij haar niet had aangeraakt, misschien omdat hij niet wilde dat haar stem zou trillen als ze het levensteken – of wat de betekenis van die zinnen ook mocht zijn – insprak. Twee gebroken ribben en een perineumruptuur later was de pijn zo ondraaglijk geworden dat haar geest zich bijna volledig van haar lichaam had losgemaakt.

Op het ogenblik stond haar vroegere ik als een uitgerangeerde treinwagon in haar bewustzijn op een dood spoor. Niet meer dan een armzalige rest van wat haar persoonlijkheid uitmaakte zat nog in de trein, die steeds verder een tunnel van pijn in raasde.

Een kunststof spons, zo groot als een golfbal, zat in haar mond en drukte voortdurend tegen de kloppende wond op haar tandvlees. Maar de pijn was een welkome afleiding. Haar verkrachter had een nieuwe lichaamsopening in haar onderlichaam gevonden en leek die open te willen scheuren. Ze schreeuwde al tien minuten, behalve als ze moest hoesten omdat ze dreigde te stikken, maar vanwege de prop in haar mond was er nauwelijks meer dan een dof gekreun te horen.

'Dat bevalt je wel, hè? Jij kleine hoer!' hijgde hij boven haar.

Ze verkrampte, wat de pijn nog gruwelijker maakte.

Er volgde een gesmoord gegrom, ten teken dat de stoten snel heftiger zouden worden.

Maar compleet onverwacht liet het monster haar los. Opeens – ze had niet gemerkt dat hij van het bed was gestapt – stond hij naast haar en wuifde naar een camera die in de hoek van de kamer rechts boven de deur hing en onafgebroken knipperde. Dat deed hij elke keer als hij in haar was gekomen. De eerste keer had ze iets kleverigs tussen haar benen naar beneden voelen lopen, inmiddels liet die helse brandende wond daarbeneden dat soort gewaarwordingen niet meer toe.

'Ik ga er nu vandoor, kleine hoer,' hoorde ze hem zeggen. Terwijl hij praatte, sproeide zijn speeksel op haar gezicht. Ze wilde haar huid helemaal van haar lichaam krabben.

Noem me geen hoer. Mijn naam is...

Ze huilde, omdat hij haar niet meer te binnen wilde schieten.

'Op een gegeven moment kom ik terug.' Hij nam haar kin tussen duim en wijsvinger, drukte zijn vingers ruw in haar kaakbeen. 'Wil je weten wat je te wachten staat als ik terug ben?'

Ze huilde nog harder, schudde haar hoofd en smeekte hem haar eindelijk met rust te laten.

'Goed dan, het was eigenlijk een verrassing, maar ik laat het je toch zien.'

Wat? Nee, niet laten zien. Alsjeblieft niets meer laten zien...

Verstard van angst staarde ze naar een roestig mes dat hij voor haar gezicht hield. Om het heft in zijn handen was een vlekkerige zijden doek gewikkeld.

'Hiermee zal ik een vrouw van je maken.'

Hij trok vragend zijn wenkbrauwen op, alsof ze iets had gezegd wat hem verwarde. 'Of dacht je soms dat ik dat al had gedaan?' Op een of andere manier had hij nu een sigaret in zijn mond. Nadat hij hem had aangestoken, tilde hij het mes weer op. 'Nee, nee, nee. Ik heb heel goed gemerkt hoe leuk je het vond. En dat is verkeerd. Verboden. Een echte vrouw moet kuis worden gehouden, begrijp je?'

Nee. Ik begrijp helemaal niets meer. Laat me alsjeblieft gaan.

'Er bestaan allerlei methodes om van een vrouw een echte vrouw te maken,' vervolgde hij genadeloos. 'Mij persoonlijk fascineert de techniek die in Somalië wordt toegepast het meest. Daar wordt zevenennegentig procent van de vrouwen besneden.'

Besneden?

Ze rukte panisch aan haar boeien en verslikte zich doordat ze gekneveld probeerde te schreeuwen, wat de man met de sigaret in zijn mond een glimlach ontlokte.

'Rustig maar. Je weet nog helemaal niet welk ritueel ik voor je heb uitgezocht.' Hij liet het mes van de ene naar de andere hand gaan. 'Zal ik alleen je clitoris weghalen? Of behalve de buitenste ook de binnenste schaamlippen? Of zal ik, zoals in Somalië gebruikelijk, daarna je yoni dichtnaaien? Wat denk jij?'

Ze probeerde zich op te richten, trok aan de leren riemen waarmee haar handen en voeten aan de brits waren vastgesnoerd. Hij boog zich over haar gezicht en blies sigarettenrook in haar ogen. 'Wat ik ook doe...' zei hij, 'één ding staat vast: je zult het niet overleven.'

En met deze woorden deed hij iets wat ze als een weldaad ervoer – hoewel ze niet veel later besefte hoe wreed het was.

'Ik laat je nu een poosje alleen,' hoorde ze hem nog zeggen. 'Het zou prettig zijn als je de tijd die je nog hebt, goed gebruikt.'

De zware branddeur viel achter hem in het slot. En ze keek ongelovig naar haar polsen, die de waanzinnige zojuist van de boeien had ontdaan.

14

'Kan ik u een lift geven, professor?'

Herzfeld keek verbaasd op. Hij was zo in gedachten verdiept dat hij de Porsche die naast hem was gestopt niet had horen aankomen. Hij bleef op de parkeerplaats van de BKA staan. Er daalde zoveel natte sneeuw neer dat hij de bestuurder van de luxueuze terreinwagen niet meteen herkende.

'Kom, stap in alstublieft!'

Herzfeld deed een pas naar voren en tuurde met samengeknepen ogen door het halfopen raam van het rechterportier.

Ingolf von Appen. Fijn, die ontbrak er nog maar aan.

'Waarom ben je niet op het instituut?' vroeg Herzfeld wantrouwig.

'Toen u was vertrokken, ben ik tot overmaat van ramp nog misselijk geworden ook. Daarom hebben uw collega's me aangeraden de stage op te geven.' Ingolf glimlachte schuldbewust. 'Ik ben bang dat ik het heb verprutst. Maar misschien kan ik het goedmaken als ik u een lift geef?'

'Dank je, dat is niet nodig.'

'U gaat in dit beestenweer toch niet met het openbaar vervoer naar huis?'

Herzfeld maakte een afwerend gebaar en wilde naar de taxistandplaats voor de oprit van de BKA wijzen, maar die was verlaten, zag hij nu.

'Een taxi? Dan kunt u lang wachten met dit weer. Die zijn allemaal weg.'

Herzfeld aarzelde. Hij kon zo gauw geen uitvlucht bedenken. Wat voor smoes kon hij bedenken om het aanbod van de stagiair af te slaan? Hij kon hem moeilijk de waarheid vertellen.

Mijn dochter is ontvoerd, en als de vrouw die Hannahs mobieltje heeft gevonden me terugbelt, wil ik alleen zijn en vrijuit kunnen praten.

Als die vrouw al zou terugbellen.

Al tijdens haar laatste gesprek, twintig minuten geleden, had ze een paar keer willen ophangen. Eerst had Herzfeld nog gedacht dat de jonge vrouw bij de ontvoerders hoorde. Maar toen had ze vreemd genoeg van Herzfeld verlangd dat hij bewees dat hij werkelijk bij de politie zat, wat onlogisch zou zijn als ze met de dader onder één hoedje speelde.

Herzfeld had even nagedacht en haar toen gevraagd zich met een telefonische informatiedienst van haar keus te laten doorverbinden met de BKA, de federale recherchedienst bij de Elsenbrücke.

Een paar minuten later werd 'een zekere Linda' naar hem doorverbonden, die 'dringend' professor Herzfeld wilde spreken. Daarna hadden ze elk iets meer vertrouwen in de ander gehad, maar ze dansten tijdens het gesprek nog steeds als twee boksers voor het grote gevecht om elkaar heen. Geen van beiden wilde zijn dekking laten zakken. Geen van beiden wilde als eerste informatie prijsgeven voor de ander zijn vragen had beantwoord – hoewel Herzfeld ongewild al meer dan genoeg had verklapt.

Linda had uit zijn woorden gemakkelijk kunnen opmaken dat zijn dochter was ontvoerd; tenslotte had hij bij haar eerste telefoontje ene Erik met de dood bedreigd als hij Hannah niet levend en wel terug zou krijgen.

Uiteindelijk liet Linda haar afstandelijkheid varen en verraste ze Herzfeld met een monoloog die deels als een rechtvaardiging en deels als een bekentenis klonk: 'Vermoedelijk zak ik zo nog verder in de stront dan ik toch al zit, en mijn broer vermoordt me. Maar als u echt degene bent die u zegt te zijn, professor, zult u deze telefoon wel kunnen peilen of zoiets, en dan kan ik u net zo goed meteen vertellen waar ik ben. Bovendien klinkt u als iemand die hulp nodig heeft, en of u het nu gelooft of niet, dat is iets wat we gemeen hebben. Ik weet wat voor belabberd gevoel het is als je in de knel zit en iemand nodig hebt om je eruit te halen. Dus vertrouw ik gewoon maar op mijn instinct, waarvan ik niet kan beweren dat het me nooit in de steek heeft gelaten, integendeel. De laatste keer dat ik erop vertrouwde bleek ik met een psychopaat in bed te liggen, maar wat zou het, ik kan me hier sowieso niet verstoppen, en u kunt niet naar mij toe komen, dus wat heb ik te verliezen?'

En toen had ze hem over Helgoland verteld en dat ze zich op het eiland voor een stalker verstopte en in geen geval wilde dat haar verblijfplaats bekend werd, en dat ze dus niet naar de politie ging. Hij kwam alles te weten over de herenpolstas en over Hannahs telefoon. En over de man bij wie ze die twee dingen had gevonden en die Herzfeld beslist geen informatie meer zou geven: 'Hij zwijgt als het graf!'

'Waar moet u heen?' drong Ingolf aan. Intussen had hij uitnodigend het rechterportier geopend.

Zonder het te weten, stelde Von Appen de hamvraag: waarheen?

Herzfeld wist wat hem nu te doen stond. Hij had een sporenkoffer nodig. Bij de BKA moest hij daarvoor een ontvangstbewijs tekenen, maar thuis lag zijn eigen koffer met alles wat hij voor het eerste onderzoek op de plaats delict en het verzamelen van bewijs nodig had. Bovendien wilde hij thuis contant geld en schone kleren ophalen, terwijl hij wachtte tot Linda zou terugbellen.

'Ik heb een taxi gebeld en gevraagd of hij naar de standplaats komt,' loog hij tegen Ingolf, toen ging zijn telefoon.

'Linda?' Hij wendde zich van de Porsche af en concentreerde zich op de bijna onverstaanbare stem van zijn gesprekspartner.

'Ik zeg het maar meteen: dit soort shit doe ik niet nog een keer.'
Ze brulde alsof ze in een windtunnel stond. 'Ik heb gedaan wat
u wilde, ja? Ben naar het strand gegaan en heb zijn zakken doorzocht. Om precies te zijn – ik sta hier nog steeds en zou het liefst
over de golfbreker kotsen. Jezus, wat was dat walgelijk. En ik heb
hem nog niet eens aangeraakt. Hoefde ook niet. Want zijn naam
staat midden op zijn T-shirt.'

'Erik?'

'Zo is het. Dwars over zijn borst met een watervaste viltstift
geschreven. Maar zoals ik al zei: wat die vent uw dochter ook mag
hebben aangedaan, professor, u krijgt er niets meer uit.'

Daar vergis je je in, dacht Herzfeld en hij moest aan de woorden van zijn dochter op de voicemail denken. Hannah had niet
gezegd: 'Erik zal contact met je opnemen.' Niet: 'Hij zal je verdere informatie geven.' Maar: 'Wacht op Erik. Hij heeft nog meer
instructies voor je.' *Nog meer.* De eerste instructie had hij vanochtend in het hoofd van het verminkte vrouwenlijk gevonden.
Nu was er een tweede dode. Je hoefde geen genie te zijn om het
patroon te herkennen: de ontvoerder speelde een morbide vossenjacht. Hij voorzag zijn slachtoffers van aanwijzingen die Herzfeld naar zijn dochter leidden.

Of naar haar lijk.

Achter hem werd tweemaal kort getoeterd, en hij draaide zich
om naar Ingolf, die nog steeds met draaiende motor op hem
wachtte. 'Bellen kunt u ook in de auto,' riep hij lachend.

Herzfeld schudde zijn hoofd en zei weer in de telefoon: 'Bedankt
voor alles wat u tot zover voor me hebt gedaan. Nu moet ik u nog
om een laatste gunst vragen: bel het ziekenhuis van het eiland en
vertel een man met de naam Ender Mueller over de vondst van het
lijk. Het is belangrijk dat u alleen met hem praat, begrijpt u?'

*Anders wordt het officieel. En dan ressorteert het lijk onder Schles-
wig-Holstein, waar ik niet bevoegd ben. Ik zou geen toestemming
krijgen de dode open te snijden om naar aanwijzingen te zoeken...*

'Wie is Ender Mueller in godsnaam?'

'De huismeester van de kliniek, ik ken hem goed.'

'Wat toevallig,' zei Linda honend.

Helemaal niet. Eerder een bewijs dat de dader het op mij persoonlijk heeft gemunt, en wel in mijn functie van forensisch arts, dacht Herzfeld. Eerst het briefje in het hoofd van de dode, dan het tweede lijk uitgerekend op het eiland met het ziekenhuis waar Herzfeld al vaak sectie had verricht, voor zijn Berlijnse tijd, toen hij nog in de universiteitskliniek van Kiel werkte. Wie er ook achter zat, de man was uitstekend over hem geïnformeerd.

'Ik zal Ender dadelijk bellen om te zeggen dat u contact met hem gaat opnemen. Praat alstublieft met niemand anders tot ik er ben.'

'Tot u er bent?' vroeg Linda spottend. 'Hebt u niet naar me geluisterd? Orkaan Anna neemt net een aanloop voor de Olympische Winterspelen, onderdeel huizenwerpen. Het dak van het ziekenhuis is er trouwens al af, daar zal ik beslist niemand meer bereiken.'

Ingolf toeterde weer.

'Hoe lang gaat dat nog duren?' vroeg Herzfeld. Hij gebaarde de student dat hij van gedachten was veranderd.

'De stormwaarschuwingsdienst zegt minstens drie dagen,' hoorde hij Linda tegen de wind in brullen, terwijl hij in de Porsche klom. De plotselinge temperatuurstijging deed hem huiveren. Ingolf schonk hem een ietwat arrogante 'als ik het niet dacht'-glimlach en duwde het gaspedaal in zodra Herzfeld het portier had dichtgetrokken, waardoor hij in de verwarmde leren stoel werd gedrukt.

'De golven zijn metershoog, hier zou Mozes niet eens overheen komen. We zijn volledig afgesneden.'

'Ik verzin wel een manier,' verzekerde Herzfeld haar en hij beëindigde het gesprek met Linda toen ze van de parkeerplaats de straat op schoten.

Ingolf wierp hem een vragende blik toe. 'En, waar gaat de reis naartoe?'

'Helgoland,' antwoordde Herzfeld, en Ingolfs zelfgenoegzame glimlach verdween.

15

HELGOLAND

'Hé, weet je eigenlijk waarom mannen geen cellulitis krijgen?'

'Wat?' zei Linda, verward door de plotselinge verandering van onderwerp. Zojuist had Ender Mueller nog lopen jammeren dat alle verantwoordelijken – artsen, zusters en verplegers – ertussenuit waren geknepen en hem alleen in deze 'ziekenhuisruïne' hadden achtergelaten, en nu wilde de huismeester haar echt een grap vertellen?

'Cellulitis, sinaasappelhuid, je weet wel. Waarom hebben mannen dat niet?'

'Omdat het er vreselijk uitziet?' Linda kaapte zijn clou weg. Achter Enders rug fronste ze sceptisch haar wenkbrauwen. De huismeester liep twee passen voor haar en duwde een brancard door de spaarzaam verlichte ziekenhuisgang. De hoofdstroomleiding functioneerde niet meer en om het noodstroomaggregaat niet onnodig te belasten waren de lampen hierbeneden op de spaarstand gezet.

'O, je kent hem al?' Ender draaide zich even naar haar om. Zijn blik leek op die van een kind dat bij de supermarktkassa tien cent tekortkomt om kauwgum te kopen, maar Linda was niet in de stemming om hem op te vrolijken: 'Je rijdt een lijk naar de afdeling Pathologie en vertelt intussen slechte moppen? Wat mankeert jou in godsnaam?'

Ender kromp ineen als een geslagen hond, waardoor hij nog kleiner leek dan hij al was. De Duitser met Turkse achtergrond was wat Linda's broer 'een gespierde dwerg in breedbeeldformaat' noemde. Wat de huismeester aan lichaamslengte ontbeerde, probeerde hij met gewichtstraining te compenseren. Zijn bovenarmen herinnerden Linda aan de grote hammen die bij de slager aan het plafond hingen. Hij droeg een shirt met lange mouwen onder een blauwe overall, die in de wasmachine was gekrompen of met opzet zo strak zat om zijn enorme dijbenen goed uit te laten komen – Linda vermoedde het laatste.

Toch leken de spiermassa's niet alleen met anabole steroïden te zijn gekweekt, tenslotte was Ender er in zijn eentje in geslaagd in de storm het lijk van het strand in zijn elektrische wagentje te tillen. Linda had stomverbaasd toegekeken. Stom, omdat er geen woorden waren die de wending die haar leven de laatste paar uur had genomen konden beschrijven. Verbaasd, omdat die Ender Mueller werkelijk bestond en het allemaal geen slechte grap was.

Linda had de huismeester, die ze op midden, eind dertig schatte, na diverse pogingen in restaurant Bandrupp bereikt. In het ziekenhuis (voor noodgevallen hing het nummer van de kliniek aan een prikbord) had er – zoals verwacht – niemand opgenomen, en zijn privénummer stond niet in het dunne telefoonboek van het eiland. Ze had een tijdje overwogen hoe ze het gesprek met de huismeester het beste kon beginnen... 'Neem me niet kwalijk, maar ene professor Herzfeld vraagt of u even naar een lijk wilt kijken...' Maar die voorbereiding was overbodig gebleken, want intussen had Herzfeld zijn kennis al gebeld en hem precieze instructies gegeven. Een paar minuten later was Ender aan komen rijden om het waterlijk naar de kliniek te vervoeren.

'Weer zo'n geval van levensmoeheid,' had hij gezegd terwijl hij naar de dode met het ERIK-T-shirt wees, zodra ze bij de golfbreker waren aangekomen. 'Zo hebben we elkaar leren kennen, weet je. Elk jaar springt hier wel iemand van het klif. Als er twijfel is, komt Herzfeld en doet hij een autopsie in het ziekenhuis. Het is een prima vent.'

Linda had gezwegen, had niet eens de regen van haar gezicht geveegd en hoopte alleen dat de nachtmerrie snel voorbij zou gaan. Maar dat deed hij niet.

'Ik denk dat de professor gelijk heeft. Daar kan voorlopig beter niemand achter komen, nietwaar?'

Ze wist niet of de huismeester werkelijk een antwoord van haar verwachtte, en had alleen haar schouders opgehaald.

'Ik bedoel, er is geen politie meer, de artsen zijn weg – en dan ineens een lijk? Nee, nee. Daar komt maar paniek van, nu niemand hier meer van het eiland af kan.' Met die woorden rolde Ender de meegebrachte lijkenzak uit en legde hem over de dode. Gelukkig had hij haar niet gevraagd te helpen, hoewel Linda aan de afkeer op Enders gezicht meende te zien dat hij niet gewend was met doden om te gaan, wat haar enigszins kalmeerde.

'Je moet me niet voor een freak aanzien, hoor,' had hij nog naar haar geroepen, vlak voordat ze met het lijk in de zak naar de kliniek waren gereden. 'Maar als Herzfeld zegt dat het moet gebeuren, dan moet het. Ik vertrouw hem blindelings.'

Eerst had Linda geweigerd met Ender mee te gaan, maar toen was ze van gedachten veranderd. In het huis voelde ze zich niet meer veilig, ze kende niemand op het eiland, en ze was het beu zich te verstoppen. Elk gezelschap was beter dan weer alleen te zijn – zelfs als het gezelschap bestond uit een ondermaatse bodybuilder met een bizar gevoel voor humor, die ze nu naar de liften volgde om met hem naar de lijkenkelder van het ziekenhuis te gaan.

Als de noodgenerator tenminste niet de geest geeft en we hier blijven steken.

Vandaag zou Linda daar niet van opkijken.

'Ik hoop dat dit ellendige pestweer over drie dagen voorbij is.' Ender krabde de kale plek van zijn prins William-kapsel. Linda vroeg zich af waarom mannen die een markante schedel hadden zich niet meteen kaal lieten scheren als je toch al meer hoofdhuid dan haar zag.

'Waarom uitgerekend drie dagen?' vroeg ze, terwijl ze de deur voor hem opendeed.

'Anders red ik het niet meer naar DDT.'

'DDT?'

'*Deutschland Deine Talente*, die tv-show. Ik doe dit baantje niet lang meer.'

Ze waren bij dubbele deuren gekomen, waarvan het ondoorzichtige rookglas doorliep tot de vloer. 'Beheerder, dat is op den duur niets voor mij, ik ben voor grote daden voorbestemd!'

'Aha.' Linda knikte en vroeg zich af of het misschien toch niet beter zou zijn geweest thuis op zolder afleiding te zoeken in het tekenen van comics.

'Ik heb met mijn stand-upcomedy de herkansingen gehaald, maar nu steekt Anna daar een stokje voor, als je begrijpt wat ik bedoel.'

DDT! Linda herinnerde zich vaag dat ze een keer al zappend bij een castingshow was beland, waarin een hardhorende bejaarde dansjes uitvoerde die meer aan een epileptische aanval dan aan de aangekondigde breakdance deden denken. Ze werd door de niet minder zwakzinnige jury weggestemd, terwijl een vierenzestigjarige ambtenaar onder uitzinnig applaus van het publiek de volgende ronde haalde, omdat hij in luierkostuum met een speen in zijn mond zijn winden had aangestoken. Linda had zich afgevraagd wat voor idioten zich bij DDT aan de leiband door de manege lieten voeren. Het antwoord stond voor haar neus.

'Mijn act heet body-comedy. Ik verschijn naakt voor de jury, poseer met mijn spieren en vertel intussen moppen.'

Enders ogen schitterden of ze een complete kerstboomverlichting weerspiegelden. 'Nou ja. Niet helemaal naakt. Mijn grootste spier blijft altijd ingepakt.'

'Is dat een grap?'

'Nee. Maar wil je nog een goeie horen? Gisteren is boven mij een souterrain vrijgekomen.'

Hij giechelde. Linda sloeg haar ogen ten hemel. Ze verlieten de vleugel door de openslaande deuren en wachtten op de lift. Zodra Ender op de knop had gedrukt, ging zijn telefoon. De huismeester peuterde een draadloze huistelefoon uit de doorzichtige plastic hoes van zijn gereedschapsgordel, die als een patroongordel om zijn heupen hing.

'Sana-kliniek, Ender Mueller, hallo? Wat? O, ben jij het. Nee, mijn mobieltje is uit. Dat doet het toch niet in de kelder.' Hij lachte ietwat overdreven. 'Ja, alles prima bij ons. Maak je geen zorgen.'

Ender gaf Linda een samenzweerderig knipoogje. Ze dacht er ernstig over na of ze wel met deze man in de naderende lift moest stappen. Ze huiverde bij de gedachte aan de keus die ze had: terug naar huis, waar een vreemde – *Danny?* – in haar bed had gelegen; hier blijven wachten? Of meegaan naar de afdeling Pathologie, waar het beslist nog kouder was, nadat de stroomstoring ook de warmtepompen van de kliniek had lamgelegd.

'Vanaf dit moment betekent Helgoland *To-Hell-Go-Land*, als je begrijpt wat ik bedoel.' Voor de zekerheid vertaalde Ender de flauwe grap voor zijn gesprekspartner: 'Naar-hel-gaan-land. Hier vergaat de wereld, er is geen hond op straat. Ik had het lijk op een Indische olifant hiernaartoe kunnen vervoeren, dat zou niemand zijn opgevallen, Paul.'

Paul Herzfeld, dacht Linda. *Wie anders.*

Ze gingen de lift binnen. Ender, die het lijk duwde, als eerste. Gelukkig was de witte zak ondoorzichtig. Linda vond het meer dan voldoende dat ze de omtrekken van de man onder de stof kon raden.

'Ik heb de lady gezegd dat er weer een hypochonder tussenuit is geknepen en... Eh, wat zeg je?' Hij keek naar Linda. 'Ja, ze is bij me, en als ik het mag zeggen, die vrouw heeft ogen als mannenvoeten. Groot, zwart en vochtig.' Hij grinnikte, maar het lachen verging hem meteen weer. 'Wat? Nee, die is niet van Fips Asmussen. Die is van... Ja, is goed, oké. Ik luister naar je.'

Er volgde een lange pauze, die Ender af en toe met een 'Hmmm' onderbrak, tot hij luidkeels uitriep: 'Geen sprake van!'

Intussen waren de liftdeuren op de eerste kelderverdieping weer opengegaan. Ender trok de brancard achterwaarts de lift uit, en het ganglicht, schelle, flakkerende neonbuizen, ging automatisch aan. Anders dan verwacht, was het hierbeneden warmer dan boven, maar Linda kon nog steeds haar adem zien.

'Kan wel zijn dat het ontzettend belangrijk is, Paul. Maar je had gezegd dat ik alleen snel het lijk naar de afdeling Pathologie moest brengen, en dat we dan quitte staan.'

Ze bleven voor een pistachekleurige schuifdeur staan. Ender klemde de telefoon tussen kin en schouder en trok de deur met beide handen open. De ruimte die ze binnenkwamen had lage plafonds en was ongeveer zo groot als een volleybalveld. In het donker zag het vertrek er op het eerste gezicht uit als een hotelkeuken: witte tegels, grijze plavuizen, roestvrijstalen kasten en wastafels tegen de muur – als er niet die grote sectietafel was geweest, die als een slachtbank in het midden van de zaal troonde...

'Geen denken aan. Nee, man. Ik doe het al in mijn broek nu ik hier bij de afdeling Pathologie sta, man.' De huismeester drukte op twee flinke lichtschakelaars naast de deur, en een groot aantal neonbuizen begon dreigend te knipperen. Tegelijk sloegen de ventilatoren boven hun hoofd aan.

'Je verlangt echt te veel. Ik moet er niet aan denken dat ik voor jou vandaag al een lijk heb aangeraakt.' Onder het telefoneren wees Ender wild gesticulerend op de koelcellen tegen de rechtermuur. 'Ik haat het om hierbeneden te zijn.' Hij hield abrupt op met praten en draaide zich om naar Linda, die nog steeds op de drempel stond.

'Hé, wat doe je voor werk?' vroeg hij.

'Wat?'

'Je beroep! Waarmee verdien je je brood?'

'Ik schilder.'

'Muren of schilderijen?' vroeg Ender, nadat hij de informatie had doorgegeven.

'Comics,' riep ze zo luid dat ook Herzfeld het aan de andere kant van de lijn moest hebben gehoord.

Ender krabde weer zijn achterhoofd, alsof de vraag van de professor hem had verward.

'Haar ogen laten je koud, maar haar handen interesseren je opeens wel, ja?' Hij nam Linda op, toen zei hij: 'Mooie vingers. Als een pianiste. Oké, ja. Is goed.' Ender gaf haar de telefoon aan.

'Wat?'

'Hij wil met jou praten.'

Linda drukte de vochtige, warme telefoon tegen haar oren. Het zweet was de huismeester uitgebroken tijdens het gesprek. En een paar seconden later wist Linda ook waarom. Herzfeld kwam meteen ter zake: 'Ik heb informatie ingewonnen. Zoals het er nu uitziet, kan het inderdaad een tijdje duren voordat ik bij jullie op het eiland ben.' Op de achtergrond hoorde ze het geluid van een richtingaanwijzer. 'En tot het zover is, wil ik je weer om een gunst vragen.'

'Wat?' vroeg Linda. Ze had al een voorgevoel, haar maag kromp ineen.

'Je moet voor mij sectie verrichten op het lijk.'

16

'Leg de dode met de voeten naar de orgaantafel. Dat is de kleine tafel met de uitschuifbare plank onder de afvoerbak. Vlak naast de handdouche, zie je die? Daarmee kun je meteen water in de bak laten lopen. Maak hem maar helemaal vol. En nu kun je de lijkenzak weghalen.'

Herzfeld opende het portier, nog voor Ingolf voor het centraal station tot stilstand was gekomen. Tijdens de rit had hij er goed op gelet geen namen te noemen of andere informatie prijs te geven waaruit de student misschien conclusies had kunnen trekken. Blijkbaar met succes. Te oordelen naar de gelaatsuitdrukking waarmee Ingolf afscheid van hem nam, was de mislukte stagiair vooral geamuseerd over de mesjogge professor, die kennelijk ook de taak had zijn collega's telefonische bijstand te verlenen bij autopsies.

Herzfeld tikte alleen even tegen zijn hoofd. Voor een behoorlijk afscheid van Ingolf was geen tijd. Het bij hem thuis afhalen van zijn koffer met het sectiegereedschap en het instrumentarium voor de plaats delict had al veel te lang geduurd. Bovendien was het onderweg verschrikkelijk druk geweest, zoals altijd in Berlijn als het regende of sneeuwde. Of allebei tegelijk, zoals nu. Met de s-Bahn zou het beslist sneller zijn gegaan, al was het dan lang niet zo comfortabel als met Ingolf, die hem eerst naar huis en daarna naar het station had gereden.

'Doe handschoenen aan, het liefst die dikke met noppen, en

zoek een gummischort uit. Ender weet waar alles ligt, hij moet je twee orgaanmessen geven, maar geen scalpel, want dat breekt te snel af als je ongeoefend bent. Je zou jezelf kunnen bezeren. En je hebt een lange pincet en een schaar nodig om de kleren van de dode open te knippen. Het lijk moet helemaal naakt zijn.'

Drommen mensen stroomden langs Herzfeld de entreehal in.

'Ho, wacht, professor! Hebt u ze wel allemaal op een rijtje?'

Herzfeld kon de gebaren waarmee Linda haar scheldkanonnade kracht bijzette bijna voor zich zien. Hij stapte opzij voor een vrouw met twee kinderen, die hem tegemoetkwam. De glazen draaideuren die op de hal uitkwamen zaten hopeloos verstopt, en daarom bleef Herzfeld met zijn sectiekoffer in zijn hand in de luwte van een betonnen pilaar staan, waar het wel tochtig was, maar waar hij tenminste ongestoord kon praten.

'Nee, om eerlijk te zijn, Linda, heb ik ze waarschijnlijk niet meer echt op een rijtje.' Hij aarzelde en dacht nog eens na of hij het erop zou wagen een volslagen vreemde in vertrouwen te nemen. Aan de andere kant had hij eerder toch al uit de school geklapt, toen hij dacht dat hij de ontvoerder aan de lijn had – die hem trouwens eigenlijk alleen had opgedragen geen officiële instanties te waarschuwen. Dus besloot Herzfeld het risico te nemen.

'Ik heb vanochtend in het hoofd van een barbaars toegetakeld lijk een bericht gevonden. Een noodkreet van mijn dochter Hannah. Toen ik haar belde, kreeg ik haar voicemail.' Herzfeld vertelde kort wat hij had gehoord en zei ten slotte: 'Ze heeft me gevraagd er met niemand over te praten. Wat dat betreft breng ik nu Hannahs leven in gevaar door je hierin in te wijden.' *Iemand die ik niet eens ken!* 'Maar ik heb geen andere keus.'

Herzfeld had een nooduitgang gezien die de massa niet had ontdekt, waardoor hij de grote hal in glipte. Hij zocht op het informatiebord naar een geschikte trein en dacht eerst dat het ding kapot was. Toen zag hij de rij woedend gebarende mensen voor de informatiestand. Hij vermoedde het ergste.

'Heb ik het goed begrepen?' hoorde hij Linda vragen. 'Uw dochter is ontvoerd, en ik moet deze man hier opensnijden omdat u denkt dat er zich meer aanwijzingen in zijn lichaam bevinden?'

'Ja.'

Herzfeld maakte zich los van de reizigers, die deels woedend, deels gelaten over het bord met de dienstregeling discussieerden. Op de S-Bahn na waren alle treinen geannuleerd.

'Linda, luister!' Herzfeld dempte zijn stem toen twee zakenreizigers hem zo rakelings passeerden dat ze met hun laptoptrolleys bijna over zijn voeten reden. 'Ik weet dat ik veel, heel veel van je vraag, maar er is bijna geen tijd meer. Hannah heeft astma. Als haar spray op is, heeft ze nog maar een paar uur.' *En ik vrees dat dat niet het grootste gevaar is waarin ze zich bevindt.* 'Bovendien gaat het hier niet alleen om mijn dochter.'

'Maar?'

'Dit is al het tweede lijk. We hebben dus met een seriemoordenaar te maken. Stel dat de moordenaar nog op het eiland is en nog niet klaar is met zijn serie?'

Pauze. Hij voelde bijna hoe de gedachten zich in het hoofd van de jonge vrouw verdrongen. Zonder haar te hebben gezien, was hij ervan overtuigd dat hij Linda op het eerste gezicht sympathiek zou vinden. Hij mocht mensen die meer naar hun gevoel dan hun verstand luisterden. En met alles wat ze al voor hem had gedaan, moest Linda een hulpvaardig persoon zijn met een goed hart, waar hij nu een beroep op deed.

'Alsjeblieft, help me.'

'Ender denkt dat die man zelfmoord heeft gepleegd,' antwoordde Linda mat.

'Hij vergist zich. Hannah heeft gezegd dat ik van ene Erik verdere instructies zou krijgen. En opeens ligt hij dood aan het strand, met een telefoon in zijn zak die het nummer heeft dat ik vanochtend in het hoofd van een verminkt vrouwenlijk heb gevonden. Moet ik nog meer zeggen?'

Nog een pauze, dit keer langer, die Linda met een diepe zucht beëindigde. 'Ik ben al jaren vegetariër. Ik kan me niet heugen wanneer ik voor het laatst een biefstuk heb gesneden, en nu moet ik...'

'Maak je geen zorgen. Ik zal je stap voor stap begeleiden, oké? Hallo, Linda?'

Hij keek op zijn telefoon.

Verdomme.

Het display was donker. De batterij had het weer zonder waarschuwing laten afweten. Waarom had hij zich die zogenaamde smartphone toch laten aanpraten? Wat was er *smart* aan een *phone* waarvan de batterij het maar een paar uur deed, terwijl de meeste stroom verbruikt werd door apps die hij toch nooit gebruikte?

Facebook, Skype, push e-mail. *Shit.*

Herzfeld pakte zijn koffer over met zijn andere hand en liep snel door de nooduitgang de kou in. De draaideur had definitief de geest gegeven en bewoog geen millimeter meer. Ook voor het station heerste volstrekte chaos. De arriverende auto's hinderden de vertrekkende reizigers, die momenteel in de meerderheid waren. Een foutparkeerder verergerde de situatie doordat hij de wachtstrook van de taxi's blokkeerde en werd daarom op een oorverdovend claxonconcert getrakteerd: Ingolfs zwarte terreinwagen.

Met zijn hand beschermde Herzfeld zijn ogen tegen de natte sneeuw, en hij keek om zich heen. Hij hoorde hem al voor hij hem zag.

'Zo, professor?' Ingolf von Appen liep over de smalle toegangsweg die het voorplein van het hoofdgebouw scheidde en tilde zijn rechterhand op, waarin zich een gegrilde braadworst bevond. Hij trok spijtig zijn mondhoeken omlaag, wat zijn arrogante uitstraling nog versterkte. 'U bent nog hier?'

Herzfeld maakte een wegwerpgebaar. 'Geen treinen. De bovenleidingen zijn bevroren. Complete chaos. Al het treinverkeer naar het noorden is opgeschort.'

Vanuit zijn ooghoeken zag Herzfeld dat een man met een woedend gezicht uit zijn taxi sprong.

'Hé sukkel, is die bak van jou?'

'Bak?' Ingolf draaide zich verontwaardigd om. 'Dat is een Porsche Cayenne Turbo S.'

'Ik ram die Turbo S dadelijk in je reet. Je blokkeert mijn standplaats, achterlijke zool.'

De man was twee koppen kleiner, maar woog minstens het dubbele van de student. Onder het praten dreigde hij met zijn gebalde vuist.

Ingolf nam onaangedaan een hapje van zijn worst en wendde zich weer tot Herzfeld. 'Het gaat mij niet aan, maar wat ik net heb opgevangen toen u belde...' Hij slikte zijn worst door. 'U bent niet echt ziek, nietwaar?'

'Nee.'

'Hé, mietje, ben je doof?' Van dichtbij zag de chauffeur er nog bozer uit. Speekseldraden hingen uit zijn mond en bleven plakken op zijn baardje. 'Opzouten hier. En presto.'

Zonder zich om te draaien hief Ingolf gebiedend zijn hand op, als een koning die zijn onderdanen vanaf het balkon tot zwijgen wil brengen. Herzfeld verwachtte elk moment de eerste klap van de taxichauffeur.

'En die kwestie in Helgoland, wat u daar ook te zoeken hebt, is die heel belangrijk voor u?'

'Van levensbelang.'

Ingolf knikte langzaam, toen keek hij weer naar de taxichauffeur, die zijn hand al naar hem had uitgestrekt. 'We zijn zo meteen vertrokken.'

'Wat bedoel je met *zo meteen*, opgeblazen aap? Ik knal *zo meteen* die studentenbril van je harses, als je niet *als de bliksem* opsodemietert.'

Ingolf glimlachte ontspannen, greep in zijn jaszak en haalde een bundel bankbiljetten tevoorschijn. 'Zou dit het leed enigszins kunnen verzachten?'

De chauffeur verstarde, keek eerst naar Herzfeld, vervolgens naar Ingolf. Ten slotte greep hij grijnzend naar de biljetten die de student voor zijn neus hield.

'Doe er vijf bij, en ik haal nog een worst voor je.'

'Niet nodig, maar bedankt voor het aanbod.' Ingolf knikte Herzfeld toe en gebaarde naar de ingang van het station. 'Ik stel voor dat we proviand en warme dekens inslaan. In deze weersomstandigheden kan het snel onplezierig worden als we op de snelweg in een file terechtkomen.'

17

HELGOLAND

Tot hier en niet verder.

Linda hield het lipje van de ritssluiting tussen duim en wijsvinger en kon zich er niet toe zetten de lijkenzak te openen. Ender had de dode op de sectietafel getild en volgens Herzfelds instructies alle instrumenten en hulpmiddelen gehaald. De meeste hadden zich in de instrumentenladen in de sectiezaal bevonden, alleen voor de kleding had hij de ruimte even uit gemoeten, om met een zwaar gummischort terug te komen, waarin Linda zich voelde als een vleeskeurder in een abattoir. Voor zichzelf had Ender geen beschermende kleren gehaald, noch een schort, noch handschoenen, wat een duidelijk statement was. Op het ogenblik bleef hij zo ver mogelijk uit de buurt en leunde tegen een tafeltje naast de schuifdeur naar de gang.

'Kunnen we nu met de uitwendige lijkschouw beginnen?'

Herzfelds stem vulde de ruimte. Blijkbaar was het hem gelukt een stroombron voor de lege batterij van zijn telefoon te vinden. Ender had de huistelefoon hard gezet en het apparaat met gereedschapsgordel en al aan de haak van de werklamp boven de sectietafel gehangen, zodat de hoorn nu als de microfoon van een ringscheidsrechter voor Linda's neus bungelde.

Goed dan, zie het gewoon als een nieuwe ervaring, probeerde ze zichzelf voor de gek te houden. *Achtergrondonderzoek om eindelijk de geweldsscènes in mijn comics beter onder de knie te krijgen. Meer is het niet.*

Ze kwam tot het angstaanjagend heldere besef dat ze op het punt stond voor het eerst in haar leven een lijk van zeer nabij te bekijken. Buiten hadden de wind en golven een veilige afstand gecreëerd, bovendien was ze gisteren verrast door haar vondst. Dit hier was iets heel anders. Er was geen natuurgeweld dat haar afleidde, alles gebeurde in het schelle neonlicht van de betegelde ruimte, afgeschermd door dikke keldermuren. Als ze nu de lijkenzak opendeed en de dode in het gezicht keek, zou het veel directer, *veel intiemer* zijn.

En veel erger.

Linda dacht erover na hoe het mogelijk was dat je in een wereld waarin dagelijks mensen stierven zo zelden met de dood werd geconfronteerd, en op hetzelfde moment realiseerde ze zich dat ze die gedachten alleen toeliet om het onvermijdelijke uit te stellen. Er waren maar twee mogelijkheden: óf ze weigerde, óf ze geloofde het verhaal van de wanhopige vader aan de andere kant van de lijn, dat het leven van zijn dochter uitsluitend van haar hulpvaardigheid afhing.

En misschien is Hannah niet de enige die hier nu in gevaar is? Ze probeerde de herinnering aan de natte handdoek in haar badkamer en Danny's geur te verdringen. Het vrouwenlijk in Berlijn, Erik, Danny: op een of andere manier moesten ze allemaal met elkaar samenhangen, ze begreep alleen niet hoe.

'Maar ik bekijk alleen de buitenkant van die vent!' Met die woorden trok Linda aan de ritssluiting, die net als bij een koffer helemaal om het verhulde lichaam heen liep. Toen de zak in tweeën was gedeeld, trok ze met een ruk de bovenste helft weg en sloot haar ogen, wat een vergissing was, want zodoende waren haar overige zintuigen nog gevoeliger voor indrukken.

'Goeie god,' zei Ender hoestend.

Ze opende haar ogen en constateerde dat de aanblik van het lijk heel wat beter te verdragen was dan de stank. Op het eerste gezicht zag de dode eruit als een goed vormgegeven, maar onrealistisch wassen beeld. Ontzield en veel te onwerkelijk om er bang voor te zijn.

Geen schoenen!

Linda vermeed naar het gezicht van de dode te kijken, daarom had ze haar blik eerst gericht op de voeten van de man, waarvan de nagels slordig waren geknipt en bij de grote teen waren ingegroeid. De dode droeg een ribfluwelen broek, de wijde pijpen waren tot zijn knieën omhooggekropen. *Net luciferhoutjes,* dacht Linda onwillekeurig toen ze de magere, sterk behaarde kuiten zag. Ze vroeg zich af hoe die spillebenen het enorme bovenlichaam van de dode door het leven hadden kunnen dragen. Hoewel het ontbindingsproces er vast ook aan had bijgedragen, was ze er niet zeker van of dat de enige oorzaak voor de enorme, opgezette buik van de dode kon zijn, waarvan het hoogste punt bijna boven zijn gezicht uit kwam.

Over het t-shirt met de letters ERIK droeg hij noch een pullover, noch een jas of andere winterkleding. Uiteindelijk dwong Linda zichzelf het hoofd te bekijken, en ze was opgelucht dat de dode zijn ogen dicht had. Maar zijn mond stond een beetje open, wat het opgezette gezicht een ietwat verbaasde uitdrukking verleende. Zijn twee bovenste snijtanden, geel van de nicotine, lagen bloot.

'Beschrijf alsjeblieft alles wat je ziet,' vroeg Herzfeld. Linda was blij dat hij niet had gevraagd de geur van het lijk te beschrijven, want dat zou heel wat moeilijker zijn geweest. Dit was de meest weerzinwekkende stank die ze ooit had geroken. Hoewel de geur lang niet zo overheersend en intensief was als bijvoorbeeld die van een verstopt openbaar toilet hartje zomer. Toch was hij alomtegenwoordig en... en *zoetig*?

De geur bestond uit twee componenten die niet bij elkaar hoorden. Zoals een goedkope geurspray in een drukke wc bij een benzinestation.

Linda probeerde door haar mond te ademen, maar kon daarmee niet verhinderen dat haar maag in opstand kwam. Hortend en stotend deed ze verslag van haar eerste indrukken.

'Komt de dode je bekend voor?' vroeg Herzfeld toen ze klaar was met haar beschrijving.

'Nee. Ik heb hem nog nooit van mijn leven gezien.'

Als het cliché klopte en veel baasjes op hun hond leken, dan moest de man op de sectietafel een sint-bernard hebben gehad: vierkante schedel, vol haar, bijna als een vacht, en een knolneus waarvan de neusgaten met zand en snot verstopt zaten. Linda wilde niet eens raden of de man een liefhebbende huisvader of een sikkeneurige single was geweest. Of hij klassieke muziek of rock op de radio had geluisterd en op welke partij hij stemde. Zijn handen waren ruw en eeltig, wat op lichamelijke arbeid wees, en zijn duimnagels zo groot als postzegels. Zijn vaalbruine slapen waren kaalgeschoren, zijn nek kortgeleden bijgeknipt, dus ging hij weleens naar de kapper, maar wat zei dat over een mens? Hij had beslist niet veel aan sport gedaan, en veel gegeten, anders zou zijn onderkin niet net zo geprononceerd zijn geweest als zijn hele bovenlichaam.

Herzfeld meldde zich weer. 'Ik heb een volledig beeld nodig, en dat betekent dat je hem helemaal uit de lijkenzak moet halen.'

'Die vent weegt minstens honderdtwintig kilo. Dat is onmogelijk.'

'Is Ender nog in de buurt?'

'Ja, *nog* wel...' antwoordde de huismeester vanaf de deur. 'Maar niet lang meer.'

'Zeur niet en handen uit de mouwen. Of wil je doorgaan voor een watje?'

'Je weet dat ik niet tegen bloed kan,' zei Ender, maar hij maakte aanstalten om naar de tafel te komen. Herzfelds beroep op zijn machogenen leek te werken.

'Je hoeft de man alleen maar op zijn zij te draaien, zodat Linda de onderkant van de lijkenzak weg kan halen.'

'Maar nu sta jij bij me in het krijt, vriend.' Ender pakte dezelfde rubberen handschoenen als Linda, die zich uiterlijk nauwelijks van gewone huishoudhandschoenen onderscheidden.

'Jezus, wat is dat goor,' liet hij zich ontvallen toen hij zich over de sectietafel boog. Toen wendde hij zich kokhalzend af.

'Wat is er aan de hand?' vroeg Herzfeld.

'Ik denk dat uw vriend moet kotsen,' antwoordde Linda, maar de huismeester draaide zich weer naar de tafel.

'Shit, helemaal niet,' zei hij hoestend. Hij gebaarde naar het lijk. 'Maar gadverdamme, wat stinkt die.'

Buiten had die indringende lucht vast ook al rond het lichaam gehangen, alleen was die aan zee door de wind verspreid.

Het duurde even voor Ender weer moed had verzameld, toen was het moment gekomen dat Linda had gevreesd sinds ze hierbeneden in de kelder stond: eerder op het strand had ze het lijk niet hoeven aanraken. Nu zou haar dat niet langer bespaard blijven.

18

De arm voelde koud en klam aan en was nog zwaarder dan hij eruitzag. Door haar dikke handschoenen heen kon ze nauwelijks iets voelen, wat haar hersens er niet van weerhield allerlei beelden te produceren. Een kort, onwerkelijk ogenblik had Linda het gevoel of ze terug was in haar kinderjaren, toen ze haar moeder hielp het kerstdiner voor te bereiden. Destijds had ze haar wijsvinger tegen de huid van de half ontdooide kalkoenpoot gedrukt, zonder te weten dat het nauwelijks anders aanvoelde dan een menselijk lijk.

'Jullie moeten hem met zijn rechterarm naar links van de brancard de sectietafel op trekken,' zei Herzfeld, en inderdaad ging het op die manier probleemloos. Ender, die de romp van de andere kant van de tafel bij de schouder had vastgepakt om het lijk zijdelings naar boven te duwen, hield zijn ogen stijf dicht. Dat was maar beter ook, want zo ontging het hem dat de bovenlaag van de vergane, door de regen doorweekte huid onder Enders hand met een slurpend geluid van het lichaam van de dode losliet en als een verschrompeld stuk boterhampapier aan zijn handschoen bleef plakken. Linda werd kotsmisselijk, maar kon haar braakneigingen onderdrukken door zich er uit alle macht op te concentreren Eriks zware lichaam, dat nu op zijn zij lag, in evenwicht te houden. Samen met de huismeester, die zijn ogen weer had geopend, slaagde ze erin de onderkant van de ruwe kunststof zak met een paar snelle rukken onder het lichaam vandaan te trekken, zonder dat het lijk op de rug of buik kantelde. Linda gooide de zak, die van een soort zeildoek was gemaakt, achteloos bij de andere helft naast de tafel op de stenen vloer.

'En nu?' Ender had de dode weer op zijn rug laten glijden en keek walgend naar zijn handschoenen.

'Nu kun je zijn hemd en broek weghalen,' zei Herzfeld.

'Wat? Ik pieker er niet over,' protesteerde Linda.

Ender schudde afwerend zijn hoofd en deed al een stap terug.

'Daar hebben we het toch over gehad? Het lijk moet naakt zijn.'

'Daar hebben we het toch over gehad, professor: u hebt ze niet allemaal op een rijtje.' Ze schudde haar hoofd. 'Ik heb gezegd dat ik hem alleen vanbuiten bekijk.'

Herzfeld zuchtte. 'Hoe wil je hem vanbuiten bekijken als hij nog aangekleed is? Als hij gewond is, zul je dat niet kunnen zien. De hele onderneming heeft alleen zin als de dode is ontkleed.'

Terwijl de professor praatte, dacht Linda een vrouwenstem op de achtergrond te horen, als van een navigatiesysteem, maar ze was er niet zeker van. Ze voelde dat haar mond zich met speeksel vulde. Het liefst had ze geslikt, maar ze was bang dat haar spuug zou smaken naar de lijkengeur die zich in haar hersens had genesteld.

Het is maar goed dat mijn mobieltje het hier in de kelder niet doet, dacht ze, terwijl ze de schaar in de onderste zoom van het t-shirt zette. *Ik zou niet weten wat ik tegen Clemens zou moeten zeggen als hij nu belt: 'Komt niet zo goed uit, broertjelief. Herinner je je die dode vent nog, die ik aan het strand moest laten liggen? Tja, het kan raar lopen in het leven, ik sta nu net met Mister Istanbul op de afdeling Pathologie en voer zoiets als een op afstand bediende autopsie uit. Ik bel je later wel terug, als ik de borstkas heb opengelegd...'*

Linda knipte het t-shirt in het midden tussen de R en de I van het woord ERIK in tweeën. Onder de stof puilde de grijsgroene ballonbuik van de man als een worst uit het vel. In tegenstelling tot zijn benen was zijn bovenlichaam niet erg behaard. Een paar centimeter onder de navel liepen groeistrepen, zo breed als een hand, als een vlechtwerk van littekens van de ene naar de andere kant.

Hoezo, mannen hebben geen cellulitis, dacht ze, met een blik naar Ender. Het gezicht van de huismeester had inmiddels dezelfde kleur als het lijk.

'Nee, geen piercings of tatoeages,' antwoordde Linda op Herzfelds vraag naar bijzondere kenmerken. 'Alleen een klein litteken onder de linkertepel. Die ziet er zo uit als die kuiltjes op je bovenarm die je vroeger van die injecties kreeg, weet u wat ik bedoel?'

Opnieuw hoorde ze de vrouwenstem, en dit keer was het duidelijk waar die vandaan kwam, want ze adviseerde Herzfeld de volgende afslag te nemen.

'En hoe ziet het eruit in de schaamstreek?'

'Dat meent u niet!'

'Linda, denk je dat ik grapjes maak? Ik zou het niet vragen als het niet echt nodig was.'

'Ik zou nog eerder een spijker in mijn knie slaan dan daarbeneden kijken,' zei Ender achter haar. Dat was waarschijnlijk bedoeld om haar emotionele ondersteuning te bieden, maar in werkelijkheid had het het tegenovergestelde effect. Linda wist dat het kinderachtig was, maar de voornaamste reden dat het haar lukte zich over deze dingen heen te zetten was dat ze niet net zo'n angsthaas wilde lijken als de huismeester.

Ze maakte de gesp los. Toen knoopte ze de broek open. De rand van zijn witte boxershort werd zichtbaar. Linda maakte de knopen van de gulp los.

Als een ongeluk. Dit alles is net een ernstig ongeluk waar je voorbijrijdt. Je wilt niet kijken, maar je doet het toch.

'Kennelijk heeft die man zich bevuild voor hij stierf,' zei ze met verstikte stem. Ze keek naar een donkergele vlek in het kruis. *Bevuild, mijn god. Waarom zeg je het niet zoals het is? Hij heeft in zijn broek gepist.*

Herzfeld schraapte zijn keel. 'Dat is normaal. Het is het beste als je de broekspijpen met de schaar openknipt, dan kun je de kleding gemakkelijker weghalen.'

Goede tip. Op die manier hoefde ze Erik niet aan te raken. De schaar gleed moeiteloos door de stof. Op twee, drie plekken beschadigde ze de huid van het dijbeen een beetje, wat Linda verzweeg alsof ze een schoolmeisje was dat bang was haar fout aan de leraar op te biechten. Ten slotte haalde ze zo ook de boxershort weg. Ze slaagde erin zich te concentreren op de stofresten, die ze met allebei haar handen vastgreep en onder het lijk vandaan trok, zodat de man nu spiernaakt op de sectietafel lag.

Waar ben je eigenlijk naar op zoek, gek? Een eikelpiercing? Een ring in zijn zak? Een tatoeage op zijn pik? Dan moet ik je helaas teleurstellen.

Ze slikte haar woede in. 'Nee,' zei ze. Op een of andere manier voelde ze zich vernederd door de aanblik van het besneden geslachtsdeel, dat onder een dichte bos schaamhaar begraven lag.

'Zijn zijn benen gespreid?'

'Ja, een beetje. Waarom is dat belangrijk?'

'Omdat je naar de anus moet kijken, om...'

'Stop, nee, nee, NEE!' Linda lachte hysterisch en deed hoofdschuddend een stap van de tafel terug. 'Geen sprake van.'

'Kom tot bedaren, oké? Rustig maar. Ik begrijp dat het niet makkelijk voor je is. Zeg me of je wat ongewoons ziet als je tussen zijn benen kijkt.'

'Nee.'

'Nee, wat?'

'Nee, er steekt geen pijl of bijl uit zijn reet,' schreeuwde Linda al haar spanning uit haar lijf. Even was het rustig, zelfs de verkeersgeluiden aan de andere kant van de lijn leken verdwenen.

Toen liet Herzfeld weer van zich horen. 'Goed, dat was het voorlopig.'

'Voorlopig?' Linda keek zoekend naar hulp naar Ender, die zijn schouders ophaalde.

'Pak nu de pincet en draai daarmee de oogleden naar buiten,' zei Herzfeld gebiedend.

'Wat?'

'Gewoon onder het ooglid gaan en dat als spaghetti naar boven om de pincet draaien.'

'Ik heb het wel begrepen. Mijn vraag is alleen: waarom deze shit, dr. Frankenstein?'

Linda wiste zich met de rug van haar hand wat zweet van haar voorhoofd. Haar littekens van het zuur brandden toen ze met het rubber van haar handschoen in aanraking kwamen.

'Puntvormige bloeduitstortingen in het bindweefsel van de ogen kunnen op een gewelddadige dood door verstikking wijzen. En dit is de enige manier om dat te controleren. Kijk er alsjeblieft naar.'

Mooi, dat heeft zin.

Blij dat ze niet langer het onderlichaam hoefde te onderzoeken, greep ze naar de pincet. Ender kreunde, alsof hij haar handelingen aan den lijve ondervond, hoewel Linda zo voorzichtig mogelijk te werk ging, om het oog van de dode niet te beschadigen.

Geen pijn, een dode voelt geen pijn, zei ze tegen zichzelf, en toch kromp ze ineen alsof ze een schok kreeg toen ze met haar pincet uitschoot en pardoes in het ooglid van het lijk stak.

'Ja, er zijn kleine donkerrode punten in zijn ogen. Als spikkels op een duivenei.'

Herzfeld reageerde met een grom op het bericht, toen vroeg hij of er letsel op de hals zichtbaar was.

'Nee. Niets te zien.'

'En de hoofdhuid? Is daar iets opvallends?' vroeg Herzfeld.

'Er zit een beetje zand in het haar, maar het ziet er niet uit als bloed of zo, als u dat misschien bedoelt.'

'Goed, dan besparen we ons voorlopig de gebruikelijke scheerbeurt en gaan meteen naar de mondholte. Ligt daar ergens een wig van hout of metaal, die je onder de rug van het lijk kunt duwen?'

Ze draaide zich om naar Ender, die weer zijn schouders ophaalde.

Mijn steun en toeverlaat.

'Niet direct.'

'Maakt niet uit, zo moet het ook gaan. Trek het hoofd alsjeblieft zo ver mogelijk naar achteren en open de mondholte.'

'Hoe vaak moet ik het nog zeggen? Ik ga die vent niet opensnijden.'

Herzfeld klakte geïrriteerd met zijn tong. 'Dat hoeft misschien ook niet. Voorlopig is het voldoende als je met je vingers de kaken van elkaar trekt.'

Ik moet mijn verstand hebben verloren, zei Linda tegen zichzelf, niet voor het eerst sinds het begin van de sectie. Haar hand zweefde boven de mond van de dode, haar uitgestrekte vingers maar een paar centimeter van zijn paarse lippen vandaan.

'Dat is toch niet normaal!'

'Jawel, we gaan te werk als bij een doodgewone uitwendige lijkschouw. Stap voor stap, zoals we dat ook op het instituut doen. Alleen dan kan ik er zeker van zijn dat we niets over het hoofd zien.'

'Hebt u er iets aan als ik zeg dat de man een kunstgebit draagt?'

Linda verbaasde zich meer en meer over zichzelf. Het hielp nog steeds om zich voor te stellen dat ze op een eerstehulpcursus zat en reanimatiepogingen oefende op een pop. Zelfs toen ze met haar vingers de kaak optrok, bleef haar weerzin binnen de perken. Het kunstgebit liet met een langgerekt, bijna onfatsoenlijk smakgeluid los van het tandvlees; toen Linda het eruit haalde en op de orgaantafel legde, hing er een dikke slijmdraad aan. Ze dacht al dat het ergste achter de rug was, tot ze de fout maakte nog eens goed in de mond te kijken.

'Er ontbreekt wat,' kreunde ze en ze begon te trillen.

Ze voelde Ender achter haar naderbij komen en hoorde dat hij geschrokken zijn adem inhield.

'Ik hou het hier voor gezien,' hoorde ze hem zeggen, toen stierven zijn voetstappen weg.

'Wacht eens...' Opeens klonk Herzfeld hoogst opgewonden. 'Ontbreken de kaakgewrichten van het lijk misschien?'

Linda schudde haar hoofd en ging nog een keer met haar pincet de mondholte in. Haar vingers beefden, net als haar stem: 'Nee. Iemand heeft de tong van die arme stakker afgesneden.'

19

De tong?

Herzfeld keek uit het zijraam naar de voorbijschietende vangrail. Het was donker, ze waren Berlijn net via Heiligensee uit gereden, en het bleef hard sneeuwen, waardoor ze op de A24 hooguit tachtig konden rijden.

Is de ontbrekende tong misschien de aangekondigde instructie?

'Misschien heeft hij hem ingeslikt?' vroeg Linda over de telefoon.

'Nee, dat is anatomisch onmogelijk.'

Sinds Hannibal Lecter zijn celgenoot Miggs in *Silence of the Lambs* er op spectaculaire wijze toe had gebracht zelfmoord te plegen door hem over te halen zijn eigen tong in te slikken, geloofden heel wat leken dat zoiets inderdaad mogelijk was. In werkelijkheid kan de tong weliswaar verslappen, achter in de keelholte glijden en zo de luchtpijp blokkeren, maar zelfs dan zou Linda de grote tongspier in elk geval hebben moeten zien.

'Is er bloed aanwezig in de mondholte?' vroeg Herzfeld, en hij speelde in gedachten verzonken met het snoer van de oplader, die zijn telefoon met de sigarettenaansteker van Ingolfs Porsche verbond. Gelukkig had hij eraan gedacht hem van huis mee te nemen.

'Ja, een beetje maar. Hoewel het genoeg was om Ender op de vlucht te jagen.' Linda probeerde het met galgenhumor.

Herzfeld beet nadenkend op zijn onderlip.

Dit slaat allemaal nergens op.

Het ontbrekende kaakgewricht van de vrouw maakte het moeilijker haar te identificeren, maar de afgesneden tong van de man wees op een andere bedoeling van de moordenaar. Er was maar weinig bloed, daarom dacht Herzfeld dat de tong na het overlijden moest zijn verwijderd. Anders zou de hoeveelheid bloed in zijn mond veel groter zijn geweest.

Waar was het verband?

Opeens werd het beeld van de losgesneden tong door dat van zijn lachende dochter verdrongen, en Herzfeld schudde zijn hoofd om Hannah uit zijn gedachten te bannen. Omdat hij begon te transpireren, zocht hij in de armada van verlichte schakelaars op het dashboard naar de knop waarmee hij de stoelverwarming kon uitzetten. Intussen vroeg hij Linda of ze in staat was hem een foto van het lijk te sturen. Ingolf trok zijn wenkbrauwen op en trakteerde de professor op een 'veel gekker moet het niet worden'-blik.

Het was niet de eerste keer sinds ze waren begonnen aan de rit; volgens het navigatiesysteem zou het nog vier uur en zevenendertig minuten duren tot ze bij de aanlegplaats van de veerboot naar Helgoland in Cuxhaven arriveerden. Het was overduidelijk dat de student brandde van verlangen om eindelijk ingewijd te worden. Vermoedelijk had Ingolf al spijt van zijn hulpvaardigheid, maar blijkbaar hoopte hij met het aanbieden van zijn chauffeursdiensten zijn blunder van vanochtend te compenseren. Hij had meer dan eens geïnformeerd of Herzfeld hem nog een kans in de sectiezaal zou gunnen, als het weekend voorbij was. *'Dan kom ik ook met een touwtje aan mijn bril, professor. Ik zweer het.'*

'Ik heb geen mobieltje waarmee ik kan fotograferen, en ook geen ontvangst hierbeneden,' antwoordde Linda.

Goed, dan moest het maar bij deze telefonische diagnose op afstand blijven.

Voorlopig.

Herzfeld wees naar de achterlichten van een kleine auto, waar

Ingolf naar zijn mening veel te dicht achter reed, en vroeg: 'Als je met de pincet naar boven gaat, in de richting van het verhemelte, stuit je dan op een vreemd voorwerp?'

'Nee, het voelt allemaal zacht aan.'

'Begrepen.'

Anders dan bij het vrouwenlijk had de dader de schedel niet vanuit de mondholte geopend om er iets in te plaatsen. Het hoofd vertoonde geen uitwendig letsel, wat erop wees dat er niet ergens anders een gat in was geboord, vooropgesteld natuurlijk dat Linda bij haar oppervlakkige inspectie niets belangrijks over het hoofd had gezien.

'Hoe ziet het er achter in de keelholte uit?'

'Ik kan niets ontdekken, maar ik heb ook geen röntgenogen.'

'Heb je een zaklantaarn?'

'Ik heb mijn mobieltje. Het display geeft wat licht.'

'Goed, probeer het dan daarmee en ga vlak achter het hoofd staan. Dan iets door de knieën zakken en van boven in de open mond schijnen.'

'Jezus nog aan toe, niet te geloven dit...' Linda foeterde binnensmonds, maar ze leek zijn aanwijzingen op te volgen, want opeens riep ze: 'Daar zit iets!'

'Wat?'

'Geen idee. Het is geel. Ziet eruit als plastic. Zit helemaal onder in zijn hals.'

Herzfeld voelde dat zijn hart sneller ging kloppen.

'Oké, haal het er maar uit.' Pauze. Hij hoorde haar kreunen van inspanning, terwijl Ingolf van rijstrook wisselde om een strooiwagen in te halen. Even werd het gesprek geheel overstemd door het geknisper en gekraak van de tegen de auto roffelende zoutkorrels. Pas toen ze de vrachtwagen voorbij waren, kon Herzfeld weer verstaan wat Linda zei: '... gaat niet.'

'Wat gaat niet?' Hij verstijfde op zijn stoel.

'Het zit te vast. Ik glij er steeds weer af met die pincet. En om eerlijk te zijn heb ik er zo onderhand genoeg van om in de mond van een lijk rond te poken.' Linda's stem sloeg over van boosheid en weerzin.

Herzfeld dwong zichzelf kalm te blijven, hoewel hij wist dat hij letterlijk centimeters verwijderd was van de volgende aanwijzing die de ontvoerder voor hem had verstopt.

'Ik begrijp je onwil. Leg de pincet maar opzij, zo gaat het niet lukken.'

Linda klonk opgelucht: 'Bedoelt u dat we wachten tot u hier bent?'

'Nee. Ik bedoel dat je nu toch de hals moet opensnijden.'

20

HELGOLAND

'Alles wijst erop dat het voorwerp een capsule is, zoals bij het eerste lijk. Ben jij ook niet benieuwd welke boodschap erin verstopt zit?'

'Nee.'

Onder het lopen trok ze haar handschoenen uit en gooide ze in de wastafel naast de uitgang. Ender had de deur op een kier gelaten, waardoor ze nu met haar telefoon in haar hand de gang op glipte.

'Ik ga ophangen.'

'Nee, wacht. Luister naar me, alsjeblieft.'

Linda bleef staan en keek gedesoriënteerd om zich heen. Ze was even vergeten of de liften nu rechts of links van de sectiezaal lagen. 'U kunt op uw kop gaan staan, maar ik ga geen mes in die man steken.'

'Geef dan antwoord op één enkele vraag!'

'Of u uw verstand verloren hebt? Ja, overduidelijk.'

Linda zoog gretig de lucht naar binnen, maar vreemd genoeg wilde de lijkengeur niet uit haar neus verdwijnen.

Herzfeld zei: 'Stel dat de aanwijzingen mij niet naar lijken moeten leiden, maar naar mensen die nog leven? Misschien heb ik de eerste aanwijzing voor Erik gewoon te laat gevonden? Misschien wordt er een perfide en uitgekookt spelletje met ons gespeeld, en zit er in dat lijk naast jou de naam van een slachtoffer dat nog kan worden gered. En elke seconde die we hier met deze discussie verspillen, brengt die redding in gevaar. Wil je echt het risico lopen dat we te laat komen?'

'Dat is maar een hypothese.' Linda had de lift bereikt.

'De gele plastic capsule in de hals van die man is geen hypothese. Die is echt. Je kunt op je gemak wachten tot ik bij je ben. Of we gebruiken de tijd die nu verloren gaat, en redden zo misschien een mensenleven.'

Linda lachte geforceerd en drukte op de liftknop. 'Dat is toch absurd. Hou toch op me voor te liegen, professor.'

'Hoe bedoel je?'

'Het gaat niet om een of ander onbekend slachtoffer. Het gaat u enkel en alleen om uw dochter.'

Een tijdje zei Herzfeld niets, toen dacht Linda dat zijn stem trilde, maar dat kon ook aan het verkeerslawaai liggen dat met zijn vraag meekwam.

'Heb jij kinderen?'

'Ik ben vierentwintig,' zei ze met haar 'God bewaar me'-stem.

'Wil je ze misschien ooit?'

Ze snoof in de telefoon. 'Als de ware opduikt.' *En als de onware voorgoed vertrokken is.* 'Ja. Ik hou van kinderen. Ik ben er zelf nog eentje. Zou ik anders comics tekenen?'

'Oké, dan heb je dus met de gedachte gespeeld. Je weet nog niet hoe het is om moeder te zijn, maar je hebt wel een idee, klopt dat?'

Volgens de cijfers boven de deur zette de lift zich nu van de eerste verdieping in beweging.

'Ik weet waar u heen wilt, professor. En ja, in uw positie zou ik precies hetzelfde hebben gedaan als iemand mijn dochter van me had weggenomen. En toch bent u een grote klootzak dat u me zo onder druk zet om een mens open te snijden.'

'Linda?'

'Ja?'

Ze vroeg zich af met welk rammelend argument hij nu weer op

de proppen zou komen om haar over te halen terug te gaan naar de sectiezaal. Ze had alles verwacht – maar niet dat hij haar aan het lachen zou maken: 'Als ik me dan voor klootzak moet laten uitmaken, kun je me dan op zijn minst tutoyeren?'

Ze lachte, het schalde door de gang. Het was niet zo bevrijdend als ze had gewild, maar zo kwam haar opgekropte spanning er tenminste uit. Toen gingen de liftdeuren open, en haar lach ging naadloos over in een langgerekte schreeuw.

IN DE HEL

Hoe lang was hij al weg?

Ze had elk besef van tijd verloren. Ze wist niet of ze het ooit had gehad, of dat het net als de herinnering aan haar naam, haar familie en de omstandigheden van haar ontvoering was verdwenen.

'Het zou prettig zijn als je de tijd die je nog hebt, goed gebruikt,' had het monster gezegd voordat hij haar boeien had losgemaakt en haar alleen in dit ondergrondse hol had achtergelaten. Ze wist niet wat hij daarmee kon hebben bedoeld. *'Op een gegeven moment kom ik terug,'* had hij gezegd – een zo vaag mogelijk ultimatum, zodat ze elke seconde voor zijn terugkeer in angst zou zitten. Hij had haar lederen boeien vervangen door verschrikkelijke beelden in haar hoofd: van verminkte vrouwen, bloedende genitaliën en roestige besnijdingsinstrumenten.

Hoe lang is dat geleden? Hoe lang heb ik op de ijzeren brits gelegen en geprobeerd tegen mijn pijn in te ademen? Zoals papa me heeft geleerd – vroeger, toen we samen gingen joggen en ik steken in mijn zij kreeg.

Uren? Dagen? Haar beul rekte tijd, en verkneukelde zich bij de gedachte aan wat hij haar nu weer zou aandoen.

'Wat ik ook doe... één ding staat vast: je zult het niet overleven.'

Toen hij net weg was had ze zich nauwelijks bewogen. In elk geval niet met opzet, want haar benen trilden onophoudelijk, net als haar buik. Ze durfde zich niet tussen haar benen aan te raken.

Alleen al de gedachte eraan deed de pijn weer oplaaien. Bovendien zou de waanzinnige zich er beslist aan opgeilen als ze zou opstaan en naar de wastafel tegen de muur zou gaan om tenminste het bloed van haar dijen te wassen.

Bloedt het eigenlijk nog steeds? Of verbeeld ik me dat maar omdat ik voortdurend bloed in mijn mond proef?

Ze was er zeker van dat ze de drie passen van de brits naar de wastafel niet zou halen. Uiteindelijk zou de voortdurend knipperende videocamera daarboven alleen haar val in de bunker registreren.

Bunker, zo noemde ze haar kerker, vanwege de donkergrijze, kale betonnen wanden; verlicht door een enkele kale gloeilamp, die los aan een draad van een vleeshaak aan het plafond hing.

Zodra hij weg was, had ze geprobeerd haar hoofd op te tillen, maar het was haar direct zwart voor de ogen geworden. Ze probeerde het opnieuw.

De misselijkheid die bij de eerste poging was opgekomen begon weer, maar nu was het beter uit te houden, wat kon betekenen dat er al wat tijd was verstreken.

Te veel tijd?

Ze klemde haar tanden op elkaar, maar desondanks schreeuwde ze het uit toen ze eindelijk op haar voeten stond.

Haar benen waren er niet meer, zo voelde het tenminste. Ze waren gevoelloos. Om niet weer meteen te vallen, knielde ze en kroop als een baby op handen en voeten verder. De vloer rook naar stof en uitwerpselen, waarschijnlijk die van haarzelf, en ze kermde bij elke kruipbeweging, die nieuwe afdrukken in haar knieën achterliet.

Lieve God, laat hem alsjeblieft niet uitgerekend nu terugkomen, bad ze onhoorbaar. Ze dacht eraan hoe hij haar als een hond over de grond zou zien kruipen en daar opgewonden van zou raken, en ze maakte haast.

Maar waarheen?

Ze wilde in de bunker rondkijken, maar verloor haar evenwicht en schreeuwde het uit toen ze op haar gebroken ribben viel. Gek genoeg kon ze zich bijna elk detail van de verkrachtingen herinneren, maar niet hoe ze de verwondingen aan haar borstkas had opgelopen, en daarom vermoedde ze dat het bij de ontvoering was gebeurd.

Verdomme...

Toen de stekende pijn iets was weggeëbd en ze de tranen uit haar ogen had gewreven, zag ze dat ze de verkeerde kant op was gekropen.

Tot dan toe was het de uitgang geweest die haar had aangetrokken, ook al had ze gehoord dat haar beul de branddeur meer dan eens had vergrendeld.

Nu ze weer naar haar brits – *mijn sterfbed* – keek, zag ze voor het eerst de kartonnen doos. Hij stond direct onder het hoofdeind.

Wat zou daarin zitten?

Haar hoop laaide op, en ook dat gevoel deed pijn, al was het niet zo erg als de terugweg over het beton. *Want hoop is niets anders dan een glasscherf in je voet,* had ze ooit ergens gelezen, *die eeuwig pijn doet tot je hem er eindelijk uit trekt.*

Natuurlijk zou in het karton niet de sleutel naar de vrijheid liggen, dat wist ze.

Of misschien toch? Hij heeft immers mijn boeien losgemaakt?

Ze hoopte op kleren, misschien een fles water en iets te eten.

Mijn galgenmaal?

Met de hoop hadden zich ook honger en dorst weer gemeld. Allemaal gewaarwordingen waarvoor ze geen plaats had gehad toen haar wereld alleen uit pijn had bestaan.

Wie denkt er nou aan eten als hij doodgaat?

Het duurde eindeloos lang voor ze erin was geslaagd de kartonnen doos te bereiken, die hier al een hele tijd moest staan. De zijkanten waren donker verkleurd door het vocht dat van de vloer optrok. Met gehaaste bewegingen trok ze de bovenste flappen uit elkaar, opende de doos en keek erin.

Wat in godsnaam...?

Geen sleutel. Geen water. Geen kleren.

Als ze niet zo uitgeput was geweest, zou ze zijn teruggedeinsd voor de slang op de bodem van de doos. Pas toen ze nog eens keek, merkte ze dat haar op dood en verwondingen gerichte fantasie haar parten speelde. In de kartonnen doos bevond zich geen levend wezen, en al helemaal geen slang, maar...

Een touw?

Nee, corrigeerde ze zichzelf, nadat ze in de overigens lege doos had gegrepen en eraan trok. *Geen touw. Dat is een strop.*

Ze trok met allebei haar handen, net zo lang tot ze het uiteinde in haar hand hield. Toen begon ze te schreeuwen, want het zag er net zo uit als ze had gevreesd.

'Het zou prettig zijn als je de tijd die je nog hebt, goed gebruikt.' Ze herinnerde zich de laatste woorden van de man aan wie ze al dagen was overgeleverd, en keek vertwijfeld naar boven, naar de vleeshaak waar de plafondlamp aan hing.

Bij uitstek geschikt voor de strop in haar handen, waarvan het andere eind uit een lus bestond.

22

Herzfeld had geen flauw idee waar ze waren beland. Ergens in Brandenburg was Ingolf van de snelweg af gegaan om een benzinestation te zoeken, nadat er kilometers lang geen één op de borden was aangegeven. Nu stonden ze op een van die servicestations van dertien in een dozijn, die er in het hele land hetzelfde uitzagen, met een tankshop die als een supermarkt was opgezet, inclusief fastfoodbuffet en een koffiehoek, waar Herzfeld stond met een dubbele espresso, terwijl de stagiair naar de wc was. Eerder had Ingolf hem bestookt met vragen: wat dat voor ongebruikelijke zaak was waar hij nu aan werkte, en vanwaar die merkwaardige gesprekken en de rit naar Helgoland, en nog wel op een dag waarop de professor zich ziek had gemeld? Herzfeld had hem afgewimpeld door op zijn medische zwijgplicht te wijzen, maar hij wist dat hij hem vroeg of laat zou moeten inwijden, als deze waanzinnige tocht langer zou gaan duren. Maar alles op zijn tijd. Eerst moest hij weer contact met Linda opnemen.

'Wat was er bij jou aan de hand?' vroeg hij, terwijl hij oppaste niet te hard in de telefoon te praten. Herzfeld had speciaal een plek aan de zijkant uitgekozen, maar hij had Linda nog niet aan de lijn, of er ging een stelletje aan het tafeltje naast hem zitten, met niet meer dan een plastic palm tussen hen in.

'Waarom had je opgehangen? Was dat soms een gil, voordat je ophing?'

'Sorry. Ik dacht dat ik Danny zag.'

'Danny?'

'Mijn ex-vriend, hij... Ach... laat maar.'

'Wacht even, is je vriend bij je?'

'Nee. Luister eens, ik ben ietwat overspannen, ja. Mijn ex heeft zich het afgelopen jaar als stalker ontpopt, en ik ben naar dit eiland gevlucht om afstand te nemen van die ellende, wat me eerlijk gezegd niet zo gemakkelijk afgaat als ik in mijn vrije tijd lijken moet opensnijden. Dus is het geen wonder dat ik hierbeneden spoken zie. Toen de lift openging, dacht ik dat er achter mij in de spiegel een schaduw voorbijschoot. Maar dat heb ik me maar verbeeld. Zoals gezegd, mijn zenuwen zijn er op het moment niet zo geweldig aan toe.'

'Dan is het goed. Ik maakte me al zorgen. Waar ben je nu?'

'Weer in de sectiezaal.'

Herzfeld haalde opgelucht adem.

'Ik was bang en kom een mes halen,' zei Linda meteen om een misverstand te voorkomen. 'Om me te verdedigen. Niet om Erik open te snijden.'

Ruim vierhonderd kilometer in vogelvlucht van Herzfeld vandaan bekeek Linda haar spiegelbeeld in het lemmet van het ontleedmes. Als ze niet beter wist, had ze de ogen met de donkere kringen toegeschreven aan een veertigjarige vrouw.

'Je moet het niet als een potlood of een tafelmes vasthouden, Linda. Pak het met je vuist beet, zoals een dolk.'

'Je houdt wel vol, hè?'

'Je kent mijn beweegredenen.'

Ze zuchtte. Inmiddels was de aanblik van het lijk haar bijna vertrouwd. Als ze nu naar haar schrijftafel zou gaan, zou ze de zwaarlijvige man met de ooievaarsbenen uit haar hoofd tot in detail kunnen tekenen. Op een of andere manier kon ze meer afstand nemen als ze zich de dode als het abstracte onderwerp van een oefening op de kunstacademie voorstelde.

'Goed dan, gesteld dat het me lukt zonder mezelf onder te kotsen, wat zou ik dan moeten doen?'

In werkelijkheid had ze allang het besluit genomen om door te gaan, wat te danken was aan haar schrik bij de lift. Eerst had ze nog gedacht dat ze haar weerzin niet zou kunnen overwinnen, maar nauwelijks was ze de sectiezaal uit gegaan of ze was besprongen, weliswaar niet door Danny, maar door een andere, net zo gevaarlijke bekende: haar angst.

Zeker, toen ze Erik had uitgekleed en in zijn mond had gekeken, was ze misselijk geworden. Ze had afschuw en weerzin gevoeld. Maar angst? Nee. Daarvoor was geen plaats geweest. Danny was een paar uur volkomen uit haar gedachten verdwenen. En zo had die autopsie 'op afstand' iets voor elkaar gekregen wat haar de afgelopen weken en dagen zelfs in haar slaap niet was gelukt. Hoe onaangenaam het ook was om met een lijk in dezelfde ruimte te zijn, de steeds indringender wordende geur te delen – *het aan te raken!* –, elk daarmee verbonden gevoel was altijd nog beter dan die irrationele, beklemmende paniek waaronder ze nu al maanden leed en waarvoor ze zelfs naar Helgoland was gevlucht.

Liever kotsen dan vluchten.

Ze moest grijnzen toen ze bedacht dat ze die spreuk op een T-shirt zou drukken als alles hier voorbij zou zijn. Misschien zou ze die woorden zelfs haar stripheld in de mond leggen.

'Zet het mes onder de punt van de kin, druk het stevig in het vlees en trek het in één beweging tot aan het borstbeen naar beneden,' instrueerde Herzfeld.

Inmiddels had ze de handschoenen en het gummischort weer aangetrokken. Uit de handdouche in het opvangbekken aan het voeteneind liep vers water. Ze moest er niet aan denken wat er nog meer in terecht zou komen als ze de aanwijzingen zou opvolgen.

'Is dit eigenlijk wel toegestaan?' vroeg Linda zich af met een blik op de hals van het lijk. De man moest zich vlak voor zijn dood hebben geschoren, ze kon de wondjes onderscheiden die het scheermes in de grove poriën van zijn huid had achtergelaten. 'Ik bedoel, dit mag een leek toch helemaal niet doen?'

'*Ik* mag dat, Linda. Jij bent het verlengstuk van mijn arm. Maak je geen zorgen, ik neem de verantwoordelijkheid volledig op me.'

'Ook voor mijn nachtmerries?'

Herzfeld zweeg aan de andere kant van de lijn.

Ze haalde diep adem, toen zette ze kracht.

De scherpe punt van het lemmet drong ongehinderd en geruisloos door de opperhuid. Ze had bloed verwacht, op zijn minst een dun stroompje dat uit de snijwond zou komen, maar er kwam geen druppel.

Je had rustig hier kunnen blijven, lafaard die je bent, zei Linda in gedachten tegen Ender. Toen zei ze tegen zichzelf: 'Dat is geen mens. Geen huid. Het is maar een pop.' Inderdaad voelde het aan alsof er een tapijtmes door stevige plasticine ging. De huid kwam zonder problemen open te liggen, en in de snee vormden zich twee gele randen, die uiteenweken en uitzicht boden op roodbruin spierweefsel.

'Ben je er klaar voor?' vroeg Herzfeld.

'Geestelijk of lichamelijk?'

'Zodra je bij de borstkas bent, moet je opnieuw bij de kin aanzetten, maar dit keer links en rechts langs de onderkaak gaan.'

'Waarom fluister je opeens?' wilde Linda weten, en Herzfeld vertelde dat hij niet ongestoord kon praten omdat er iemand aan het tafeltje ernaast meeluisterde.

Het tafeltje ernaast? Waar hang jij uit, terwijl ik hier dit rotklusje opknap?

Linda's spanning sloeg om in woede: 'Shit, kan ik niet gewoon door de hals heen gaan en dat ding eruit snijden? Ik kan zelfs vanbuiten zien waar die capsule een bult veroorzaakt.'

'Geen sprake van. Doe alsjeblieft precies wat ik zeg. Anders kun je het ding kapotmaken en alle informatie vernietigen.'

'Momentje.' Linda legde het mes neer, waarmee ze net de huid onder de rechterkant van de onderkaak had losgemaakt. 'Kan dat ding exploderen? Ik bedoel – wat als het een bom is?'

'Dat is onwaarschijnlijk. Als de dader me op die manier had willen doden, zou hij de explosieven al in het eerste lijk hebben aangebracht.'

Herzfeld klonk vastberaden, maar niet helemaal overtuigd. Kennelijk had hij nog niet aan die mogelijkheid gedacht.

'Hopelijk vindt onze psychopaat dat ook,' zei Linda en ze ging weer aan het werk. Toen ze klaar was, vroeg ze of het een probleem was dat ze nogal grove punten had gemaakt. Links en rechts van de luchtpijp had ze twee rechthoekige driehoeken gesneden.

'Je doet het heel goed,' zei Herzfeld goedkeurend, hoewel hij het resultaat van haar werk niet kon zien.

Linda wist dat hij maar wat zei, maar toch kalmeerde zijn meelevende stemgeluid haar enigszins. 'En nou?'

'Nu heb je allebei je handen nodig. Eén hand voor het mes, de andere voor de pincet.'

Linda pakte het instrument van de bijzettafel. Ze meende door de telefoon het geluid van bestek te horen. Was die vent nou aan het *eten*?

'Doe het precies zoals daarnet bij het ooglid,' fluisterde de professor nu weer, nadat hij net wat luider had gesproken. 'Hou een huidplooi vast en ondermijn het vetweefsel met het lemmet.'

'Ondermijn?'

'Sorry. Ik wilde zeggen: trek de huid naar boven, zo ver mogelijk, en maak het vetweefsel eronder met een horizontale snee los. Je moet het lemmet vlak houden en met de snijkant naar de respectievelijke zijkanten van de borstkas toe werken. Net als met fileren.'

'Paul?'

'Ja?'

'Doe me een lol en laat vergelijkingen met levensmiddelen of kookjargon achterwege. Ik ben zo ook al misselijk genoeg.'

Herzfeld verontschuldigde zich voor de tweede maal.

Geen mens. Gewoon een pop. Je bent nu op de kunstacademie en moet later de ingewanden van die pop tekenen.

Met het mes sneed ze de huid los als een stuk tapijt van de lijm. Toen ze de onderkaak en hals op die manier had blootgelegd, kon ze onder de punt van de kin direct in de mond kijken.

'Er zit nog een stuk vlees in zijn mond,' pufte ze.

'Dat is de tongbasis, zoals dat heet. De dader zal niet de hele tong hebben afgesneden. Je kunt de stomp heel simpel...'

'... afsnijden,' vulde Linda aan.

'Nee, niet *afsnijden*. Je moet de tongbasis *eruit snijden*. Steek de punt van het mes direct van boven in de mond, in het midden van de onderkaak, ongeveer vijf centimeter diep, vlak achter de onderste snijtanden. Daarna snij je verder langs de achterkant van de twee takken van onderkaak, vlak langs het bot naar links en rechts. Met een klem of pincet pak je het restant van de tong en trekt dat naar je toe. Dan snij je met het mes door de slijmhuid van de keelholte, eenmaal door de huig. En dan kun je de rest van de tong er heel simpel uit trekken.'

Met een van weerzin vertrokken gezicht en luid kokhalzend volgde Linda stap voor stap Herzfelds aanwijzingen op, haalde de bloederige klomp van de geamputeerde tongspier uit de slokdarm van de dode en legde die op de orgaantafel. Het water in het spoelbekken was nu bleekroze, en Linda's gelaatskleur verschoot van asgrauw naar krijtwit.

Vanaf dat moment ging alles razendsnel. Herzfeld instrueerde haar het strottenhoofd van buitenaf precies in het midden in de lengterichting met de punt van het mes open te snijden en dan het kraakbeen net als bij een cocktailgarnaal uit elkaar te trekken, tot de gele capsule in haar hand viel.

Linda was veel te opgewonden om zich druk te maken over zijn nieuwe vergelijking met levensmiddelen. En toen ook de adamsappel van de dode met luid gekraak in twee helften uiteenviel en ze een geel, rond voorwerp diep in het strottenhoofd kon onderscheiden, overheersten haar nieuwsgierigheid en de spanning elk gevoel van weerzin.

'Je raadt nooit wat er in zijn keel zat,' wilde ze nog zeggen, maar daar kwam ze niet meer toe – vanwege een geluid dat ze heel even voor een explosie hield. Linda draaide zich met een ruk om; met grote ogen van angst staarde ze naar de deur. Toen ze zag wie voor de herrie verantwoordelijk was, had ze het liefst haar ontleedmes naar de huismeester gesmeten.

'Jezus, ben je helemaal van de pot gerukt?' brulde ze over het gedreun heen. Ze had zo geconcentreerd staan werken dat ze niet had gezien dat Enders was teruggekomen. Hij had een draagbare stereo-installatie met de vorm van een bierkrat de zaal in gesleept en het volume helemaal opengedraaid.

'Hallo, wat is er in godsnaam bij jullie aan de hand?' wilde Herzfeld weten, nu Ender de geluidssterkte had verminderd en het duidelijk werd dat het geen *thrash metal* was wat uit de luidsprekers schalde, maar doodgewone disco.

'Sorry, foutje. Ik wist niet dat dat ding zo hard stond.' De huismeester trok een schuldbewust gezicht en zette de cd-speler nog iets zachter. 'Ik heb het uit mijn kantoor gehaald. Dacht dat het de boel een beetje zou opvrolijken. Ik bedoel, bij dr. Starck luisteren ze toch ook altijd naar muziek?'

'Dr. *wie?*' vroeg Linda onthutst.

'Starck. Een bezopen ziekenhuisserie op tv,' antwoordde Herzfeld door de telefoon. 'En voor zover ik kan horen, is dat Lady Gaga en geen muziek.'

Linda moest lachen. 'Op dat punt zijn we het dan toch eens, professor.'

Ze bukte zich om het voorwerp op te pakken dat ze zojuist van schrik uit haar handen had laten vallen.

'Momentje. Is dat een grap? Heb je dat ding zojuist uit die man gehaald?' Ender kwam opgewonden op de sectietafel af, maar wendde zich af toen hij het bloedige water in het opvangbekken zag.

'Ja,' zei Linda. 'Een verrassingsei.'

'Een wat?' vroeg Herzfeld.

'De gele schaal van zo'n kindersurprise waarin altijd plastic speelgoed zit, om precies te zijn.'

'Of een andere verrassing,' zei Ender, zonder zich te realiseren hoe dubbelzinnig zijn opmerking was.

'Moet ik het openmaken?'

Dit keer wachtte Linda Herzfelds instructies niet af. Ze brandde van nieuwsgierigheid.

'Zou een foto kunnen zijn,' zei ze, terwijl ze het opgerolde papier eruit haalde en onder de werklamp boven haar hoofd gladstreek.

'Wat staat erop? Kun je iets zien?' Herzfeld klonk gespannen. Ze hoorde dat er een stoel verschoof, alsof hij opeens opsprong.

'Een vrouw. Grijs haar, rond gezicht. Ziet eruit als een typische oma van de reclame.' Ze haalde haar schouders op. 'Ik heb haar nog nooit van mijn leven gezien.'

'Laat mij eens,' zei Ender, en opnieuw schrok ze, omdat ze niet had gemerkt dat hij achter haar was gaan staan om ook een blik op de foto te werpen.

De huismeester kwam een stap dichterbij, hield zijn hoofd schuin en bekeek de foto. 'Krijg nou wat, als dat de oude Friederike Töven niet is,' zei hij na een tijdje.

'Ken je haar?' vroegen Linda en Herzfeld bijna tegelijk.

'Nee, niet persoonlijk.' Ender krabde zich bezorgd op het achterhoofd. 'Maar ik weet wel waar ze woont.'

23

'Hoe gaat het met u, professor?'

'Goed, eh, dat wil zeggen...' Bijna had Herzfeld vergeten dat hij zich officieel ziek had gemeld. 'Het gaat al beter, ik denk dat ik er maandag wel weer bovenop ben.'

'Goed om te horen,' zei zijn secretaresse opgelucht.

Babettes bezorgdheid was niet gespeeld. De zevenenveertigjarige vrouw, die je op het eerste gezicht voor een man zou kunnen aanzien, was de kloek van de BKA. Door de meeste medewerkers werd ze 'mams' genoemd, en dat was niet alleen een toespeling op haar zes kinderen.

'Wordt er goed voor u gezorgd? Zal ik wat kippensoep brengen?'

'Nee bedankt, heel vriendelijk van je.' Herzfeld zou willen dat hij werkelijk alleen buikgriep had. Hij zou elke ziekte op aarde voor lief nemen als dat zijn dochter zou redden.

'De voorzitter van de ondernemingsraad is in alle staten, omdat u zich ziek hebt gemeld en niet op de afspraak kunt komen, professor.'

O ja, inderdaad. Herzfeld bekeek de blauwgroen gezwollen vingers van zijn rechterhand. Niets liet hem nu zo koud als de gevolgen van zijn handgemeen met de dierenbeul. Dan gooiden ze hem er maar uit. Intussen had hij bewijs achtergehouden en een vrouw ertoe aangezet lijkschennis te plegen bij een potentieel moordslachtoffer. Redenen waren er genoeg.

'Misschien kun je iets opzoeken in mijn computer,' vroeg hij aan zijn secretaresse, terwijl hij samen met Ingolf weer in de

Porsche stapte. Naast hen probeerde een automobilist wanhopig zijn bevroren ruitensproeiers met warm water te ontdooien. Op Ingolfs voorruit bleef geen sneeuwvlokje plakken. Tijdens hun korte rustpauze had hij de interieurverwarming aan laten staan.

'U bent nog steeds ingelogd, professor,' zei Babette even later vermanend. 'Wat moet ik doen?'

'Friederike Töven. Kijk alsjeblieft na of je iets over deze vrouw in mijn gegevens kunt vinden.'

Nauwelijks had Ender de naam uitgesproken, of Herzfeld had het gevoel alsof hij voor een belangrijk tentamen was gezakt. Töven. Hij had die naam al eens gehoord of gelezen, daar was hij van overtuigd. Stom dat hij zich niet kon herinneren in welk verband.

'Ik heb een afspraak in mijn privéagenda, maar ik weet niet meer waarom,' loog Herzfeld.

'Met een umlaut of met *oe*?' vroeg Babette.

'Ik heb de naam genoteerd met een ö en een v. Het is het beste als je naar alle varianten zoekt. Het kan een patiënte zijn, een collega, een politieagente of de naam van een zaak.'

'O jee, professor. Anders bent u toch niet zo vergeetachtig. U moet er echt beroerd aan toe zijn. Weet u zeker dat ik toch niet liever met thee en warme handdoeken zal langskomen?'

Herzfeld voelde hoe hij in zijn stoel werd gedrukt, en hoopte dat Babette het motorlawaai van de Porsche niet zou opvallen, die net over de provinciale weg naar de snelweg raasde.

'Gebruik gewoon de zoekfunctie, dat zou me enorm helpen.'

'Als ik er al uw dossiers ook bij betrek, kan het wel een paar minuten duren.'

'Bel me als je zover bent, oké?'

Herzfeld hing op en wilde Ingolf erop wijzen de ruitenwissers met de hevige sneeuwregen wat meer te gebruiken, om niet ook nog een ongeluk te veroorzaken, toen er weer werd gebeld.

Eerst dacht hij dat de radio zichzelf had ingeschakeld, toen besefte hij dat de riedel die Tsjaikovski's eerste pianoconcert inleidde, de beltoon van Ingolfs telefoon was.

De student sloeg zijn ogen ten hemel en drukte met zijn duim op een knop aan het stuur.

'Hallo, papa.'

'Hallo, mijn zoon.'

Mijn zoon? Goeie genade, de senator klinkt privé bijna net zo bekakt als op tv.

Ingolf wierp Herzfeld een verontschuldigende blik toe, toen zei hij: 'Het komt nu even niet uit, ik ben onderweg en niet...'

'Bij jou komt het altijd even niet uit,' onderbrak zijn vader hem ruw. Toen werd zijn toon vriendelijker: 'Ik had zojuist een lang gesprek met Joe Harper in New York.'

'En?'

'Hij zei dat het geld nog steeds niet was overgemaakt.'

'We zijn het ook nog steeds niet eens, papa.'

Ingolf peuterde een pakje kauwgom uit de binnenzak van zijn jasje. Het viel Herzfeld op dat hij een overhemd met manchetknopen onder zijn maatpak droeg, en vroeg zich af of hij dat vanochtend ook onder zijn schort in de sectiezaal had gedragen. Waarschijnlijk ging hij in dit pak zelfs naar de universiteit. Tegelijk verwonderde Herzfeld zich over de natuur van de menselijke geest, om op de meest ongepaste momenten de meest irrelevante details te registreren.

'Jongen, ik dacht dat we het daarover hadden gehad.' De gebiedende toon van zijn vader was weer terug. Tot Herzfelds verbazing leek Ingolf zich op het aanstaande meningsverschil te verheugen. Hij ging rechtop op zijn stoel zitten. 'Dus je zet meer politie in op de stations?' vroeg hij zijn vader.

Von Appen slaakte een diepe zucht. 'Berlijn is failliet, hoe moet ik dat betalen?'

'Tja, laat me eens nadenken.' Ingolf pauzeerde even, waarbij hij met zijn vingers tromgeroffel op het stuur imiteerde. 'O, daar schiet me wat te binnen. Het toverwoord is: bezuinigen!'

'Daar begrijp jij niets van, jongen.'

'O nee? Ik zal je vertellen wat ik niet begrijp. Gisteren reed ik langs een affiche van het Berlijnse waterbedrijf.'

'En?'

'Reclame voor een monopolist? Wat is dat voor onzin? Ik heb toch helemaal geen keus wiens water er uit mijn kraan komt. Ik heb het nagerekend, en volgens mij kost die zinloze imagocampagne de belastingbetaler een paar miljoen euro.'

'Dat kan wel zijn. Maar ik heb voor meer politie op straat alleen al vijfendertig miljoen nodig. En dat elk jaar!' Zijn vader klonk nu alsof hij in een talkshowdebat verwikkeld was.

'Die affiches zijn maar een voorbeeld, papa. Jij bent de senator, wees creatief, anders...'

'Bedreig je me soms?'

'Nee, ik waarschuw je. Als jurist zou je het verschil tussen bedreigen en waarschuwen toch moeten weten.'

Stilte. Terwijl Herzfeld de dingen probeerde te begrijpen waar hij nu naar luisterde, bekeek hij Ingolfs profiel. Geen verandering. Hij zag er nog steeds jongensachtig, arrogant en vlegelachtig uit, alleen paste dat opeens niet meer bij zijn woorden.

'Je bent een vrij mens, papa. Jij hebt de keus. Óf je wilt dat ik je verkiezingscampagne met een gulle gift steun, óf...'

'Goed dan, wanneer kan ik op je geld rekenen?' onderbrak de senator hem ongeduldig. Blijkbaar had hij ingezien dat het zinloos was met zijn zoon ruzie te maken.

'Direct na de persconferentie waarop je de inzet van extra politie aankondigt. Maar maak een beetje voort. Gisteren nog werd op het U-Bahn-station Lichtenberg weer een passagier het ziekenhuis in geslagen.'

Na een halfhartig afscheid hing Ingolf op. Een flauwe glimlach speelde om zijn smalle lippen, waardoor hij nog jonger leek.

Herzfeld deed zijn mond open, maar zei een tijdje niets. Toen begon hij: 'Het gaat me niets aan, maar...'

Ingolf draaide zich naar hem toe. 'Het spijt me dat u dit moest aanhoren.'

'Het spijt je vast niet.'

De student tilde even zijn handen van het stuur, alsof hij zich wilde overgeven. 'Betrapt,' zei hij lachend. 'Maar het is mijn vaders eigen schuld. Ik wilde hem nog zeggen dat ik niet alleen ben.'

'Dat wilde je niet,' sprak Herzfeld hem opnieuw tegen.

Je wilde dat ik het zou horen.

Ingolf glimlachte nog breder. Het ontbrak er nog maar aan dat hij begon te fluiten.

Was het een grap, of zou het echt kunnen dat een melkmuil met te veel geld invloed had op de Berlijnse politiek?

'Hoe oud ben je?' vroeg Herzfeld.

'Eenentwintig.'

'En waar heb je...'

'... je geld vandaan?'

Ze wisselden van rijstrook en minderden snelheid. Vóór hen kondigde zich een file aan. Een auto verderop schakelde net zijn alarmknipperlichten in.

'Weleens van Facebook gehoord?'

Herzfeld sloeg zijn ogen ten hemel. 'Zie ik eruit als een idioot? Ik ben geen twintig meer, maar ik leef wel in deze wereld.'

Ingolf schoof zijn kauwgum van de ene mondhoek naar de andere en zei: 'Ik heb Stayclose.de opgericht.'

'Zegt me niks.'

'Zegt bijna niemand iets. Die website bestaat al jaren niet meer. Toen ik dertien was, zijn we van Hamburg naar Zehlendorf in Berlijn verhuisd. Ik was al mijn vrienden kwijt.'

'Dat moet een verdomd zware tijd zijn geweest,' was Herzfelds laconieke commentaar.

'Ja, en toen ik moederziel alleen op het schoolplein stond zonder mijn zandbakvriendjes, dacht ik: Ingolf, jongen, dit is beslist iets wat veel anderen ook meemaken. Dus begon ik een website waarop scholieren met elkaar contact konden houden.'

'Stayclose.de,' zei Herzfeld.

'Het was gewoon een openbaar poëziealbum. Je zet er je foto op, je vrienden vinden je en kunnen wat op het prikbord schrijven. Natuurlijk was ik niet het enige genie dat de tijdgeest had aangevoeld. Later schoten schülerVZ, studiVZ, wkw, Facebook en al die andere sociale netwerken als paddenstoelen uit de grond.'

'Wat een pech!'

'Nee. Wat een geluk! Op mijn site hadden zich al veertigduizend scholieren geregistreerd, toen ik een e-mail van de concurrentie kreeg.'

'Laat me eens raden. Je hebt je site voor een miljoen verkocht?'

Zijn speelse glimlach was weer terug. 'Vermenigvuldig dat maar met veertien.'

'Veertien miljoen euro?' Herzfeld perste zijn lippen op elkaar om te voorkomen dat zijn mond openviel.

Ingolf lachte opnieuw. 'Overgemaakt op mijn veertiende verjaardag. Onnozel van me, ik weet het, maar mij beviel die symboliek wel.'

'En met dat geld financier je nu de verkiezingscampagne van je vader?'

Ingolf schudde zijn hoofd. 'Papa krijgt alleen de rente. Harper heeft het merendeel van het geld goed belegd – in tegenstelling tot mijn vader. Die heeft zijn vermogen met onrendabel vastgoed en waardeloze investmentfondsen niet laten groeien, maar in rook doen opgaan.'

Voordat Herzfeld er nog langer over kon nadenken of hij in de maling werd genomen of niet, bracht Babettes telefoontje hem terug in de werkelijkheid. Hij staarde naar zijn mobieltje, en voelde er veel voor om niet op te nemen.

Even was hij helemaal van de zaak afgeleid geweest, nu moest hij weer aan zijn dochter denken en aan het beeld van de afgesneden tong, dat hij gewoon niet uit zijn hoofd kon krijgen.

'Ja?' vroeg hij. Zijn hart begon sneller te kloppen, in tegenstelling tot de Porsche, die steeds langzamer ging.

'Hebbes,' zei ze vrolijk, terwijl Herzfeld zich afvroeg of hij eigenlijk wel wilde weten wat ze had ontdekt. Ze vertelde het en al na de eerste zin schoot hem weer te binnen in welk verband hij de naam Friederike Töven eerder had gehoord, of liever gezegd gelezen. Hij had gehoopt dat hij nooit door deze verschrikking uit zijn verleden zou worden ingehaald. Hij had zich vergist.

Herzfeld sloot zijn ogen. Hij dacht aan de nachtmerrie van vier jaar geleden, waarvan de naschokken hem nu hadden bereikt, en wist dat de toestand van zijn dochter uitzichtloos was.

BERLIJN

Op die dag, toen de dingen allang uit de hand waren gelopen en het leven van dr. Sven Martinek het niet meer waard was geleefd te worden, scheen de zon door het bovenlicht van het Forensisch Instituut in de Turmstrasse. Het was even voor achten, de ochtendbespreking was net achter de rug, en Herzfeld had die dag eigenlijk helemaal niet in de dependance van het Charité-ziekenhuis moeten zijn. De koffers voor de korte vakantie met Petra waren gepakt: een 'laten we het nog een keer proberen'-weekend in Barcelona, bij wijze van uitzondering zonder Hannah. Herzfeld had nog twee uur voor het vliegtuig vertrok, onder zijn schort droeg hij een bermuda en een t-shirt. Als het niet uitgerekend zijn oude vriend en mentor professor Biel zou zijn geweest die hem als collega had gevraagd hem uit de brand te helpen, had hij al in de taxi naar het vliegveld gezeten. Dus was Petra in haar eentje vooruitgereden (wat later een slecht voorteken zou blijken) en stond Herzfeld voor de sectietafel met het mannenlijk zonder hoofd.

'We zitten echt met de handen in het haar, Paul,' zei de oude professor. Hij wreef zich in zijn vermoeide ogen. Biel had wallen onder zijn ogen zo groot als theezakjes. Hij slofte in halfopen gezondheidsschoenen rond de tafel.

Twee jaar hadden ze elkaar niet meer gezien, maar toen hij zijn oude promotor weer ontmoette, had Herzfeld het gevoel dat er een veel langere periode verstreken moest zijn. Biel oogde ouder dan vierenzestig, zij het dan heel wat levendiger dan het lichaam voor hem op de tafel.

'De dode werd in zijn auto gevonden?'

'Ja. Hij zat met zijn gordels om op de bestuurdersstoel met beide handen aan het stuur. Het voertuig werd onder een boom langs een allee in Brandenburg gevonden. Geen deukje of krasje.'

'Dus het was geen ongeluk?'

'En toch...' Biel wees naar een tweede sectietafel ernaast, waarop een afgehouwen mannenschedel lag. *Toch heeft iets de bestuurder de kop gekost,* voltooide Herzfeld de zin van de ervaren forensisch arts in gedachten.

'We hebben het hoofd op de achterbank gevonden,' zei Biel. 'Het patroon van bloedsporen in het voertuig laat er geen twijfel over bestaan dat zijn hoofd is afgehouwen toen hij op de bestuurdersstoel zat. Bloedspatten op de achterkant van de stoel en op de vloer erachter. Heel fijne druppeltjes op de bekleding van de achterbank, in overeenstemming met de positie waarin we het hoofd hebben gevonden.'

Herzfeld kwam bij de tafel staan, die in tegenstelling tot de rechthoekige roestvrijstalen blokken bij de BKA uit een zandkleurige marmeren plaat bestond. Hier werd nog sectie verricht op de originele werkbladen, die al ten tijde van Rudolf Virchow werden gebruikt.

Als een guillotine, dacht Herzfeld toen hij de snijwond inspecteerde. Het hoofd was met een scherpe, gave snee iets onder het strottenhoofd verwijderd.

'Wat zegt de technische recherche?'

'Geen vreemd DNA, geen ongewone textielvezels, voet- of vingerafdrukken. De man, een vierenvijftigjarige huisvader, zat op het moment van zijn onthoofding waarschijnlijk alleen in de auto.'

Herzfeld bekeek opnieuw de romp van het lijk, waar de organen al uit waren gehaald.

'Zat hij misschien in een cabriolet? En was de kap open?'

Biel, die nog even een blik in het proces-verbaal wierp, keek op. 'Hoe weet je dat?'

In plaats van te antwoorden knikte Herzfeld alleen. Langzamerhand kon hij zich een beeld vormen. 'Is er misschien een afscheidsbrief?'

De wallen onder Biels ogen begonnen te trekken, zoals altijd als hij nerveus werd. 'Denk je aan zelfmoord?'

Herzfeld knikte opnieuw. 'Als ik jou was zou ik in de buurt van die plek naar een boom of ander vast object zoeken. Kijk eens of je daaraan of in de buurt restanten van een lange, stevige lijn, bijvoorbeeld van staal, kunt vinden.'

Het bizarre sterfgeval deed hem aan de vondst van een lijk in de vs denken. Iemand die een eind aan zijn leven wilde maken had een stuk dun staaldraad aan de stam van een eik bevestigd en het andere eind in een strop om zijn hals gelegd. Toen was hij op zijn motorfiets gestapt, had gas gegeven en zichzelf met de strop onthoofd. De motorfiets was na de dood van de bestuurder verder gerold en zonder een krasje midden op het veld omgevallen. Het hoofd had er een paar meter achter gelegen.

Hij wilde zijn gedachten juist met Biel delen, toen de deur van de sectiezaal open werd gerukt en een collega binnenstormde wiens gezicht Herzfeld de laatste paar weken voortdurend in de krant had zien staan.

'Sven, wat is er aan de hand?' kon hij nog juist zeggen, voordat hij de eerste klap moest afweren.

Dr. Sven Martinek had hem niet al te hard met zijn vuist op zijn bovenarm geslagen. Eigenlijk had hij op Herzfelds kin gemikt, maar die had zijn hoofd op tijd kunnen wegdraaien. Nu was hij naar de andere kant van de sectietafel gevlucht. Biel, die de aanval eerst sprakeloos had aangezien, deinsde ook terug toen de man een autopsiemes greep.

'Drieënhalf jaar,' schreeuwde Martinek. Het speeksel droop

schuimend uit zijn mond, als bij een dolleman. Hij droeg een gekreukt pak, zijn slordig gestrikte das slingerde als een sjaal om zijn nek. 'Ze hebben hem drieënhalf jaar gegeven.'

'Het spijt me.'

'Het spijt je? En wat ga je nu zeggen? Dat je weet hoe ik me voel?'

Herzfeld schudde droevig zijn hoofd. 'Nee. Dat zou gelogen zijn. Ik heb geen idee hoe erg de pijn is die je nu hebt.'

Maar wel de woede, de onmacht. En zijn zucht naar wraak. Hij had het zelf gevoeld, op het moment dat hij een jaar geleden het telefoontje had gekregen met het bericht wie er op zijn sectietafel lag: Lily Martinek, veertien jaar, vermoeden van lustmoord. Toen hij haar naakt voor zich had zien liggen, haar misbruikte lichaam als een aanklacht voor hem, haar ontzielde ogen star naar het plafond gericht, had hij in een eerste impuls zijn sectiemes niet in Lily's lichaam, maar in het monster willen steken dat haar dat had aangedaan: Jan Sadler, een wegens exhibitionisme en ongewenste intimiteiten bij herhaling veroordeelde pedagoog. Bij zijn arrestatie hadden ze video's gevonden waarop was te zien hoe hij de veertienjarige ontvoerde en verkrachtte.

Uit de dagboeknotities die Sadler na zijn daad had geschreven bleek overduidelijk dat hij Svens dochter na de ontvoering uiteindelijk had willen vermoorden. Zover kwam het niet. Lily slaagde erin zich van haar boeien te bevrijden. De sadist had, ook dat viel uit zijn dagboek op te maken, Lily van tevoren elke stap van haar lijdensweg, elke kwelling die haar boven het hoofd hing tot in alle perverse details beschreven.

Daarvoor had hij op weerzinwekkende wijze haar lichaam geheel afgelikt. Martineks dochter wist wat haar te wachten stond. En omdat ze geen mogelijkheid had om te vluchten, zag ze maar één manier om aan de verschrikkingen te ontsnappen: ten einde raad hing ze zich met haar eigen boeien op aan een dakbalk.

'Je hebt mijn leven verwoest. Ik heb je op mijn knieën gesmeekt het niet in je rapport te zetten,' schreeuwde Martinek tegen hem. Het ontleedmes trilde in zijn hand.

Inderdaad had hij er sterk bij hem op aangedrongen het sectierapport te vervalsen. Omdat hij als vader partijdig was, werd Martinek van de autopsie uitgesloten, en tot op de dag van vandaag betreurde Herzfeld dat hij het onderzoek op Lily niet ook vanwege emotionele betrokkenheid had geweigerd.

Hij had het moeten zien aankomen. Uit de diagnose bleek onomstotelijk dat Lily zichzelf om het leven had gebracht, en Martinek vroeg hem die uitkomst te verzwijgen. Want alleen als Sadler zelf de handeling van het doden had voltrokken, kon hij worden aangeklaagd wegens moord.

'Schuif het dat varken in de schoenen, ik smeek het je. Hij was het. Hij heeft haar opgeknoopt. Als bekend wordt dat ze zelfmoord heeft gepleegd, komt hij er met doodslag van af.'

'Ik kon het rapport niet vervalsen,' zei Herzfeld en hij hoorde zelf hoe goedkoop het klonk, ook al was het de waarheid. Voor hem stond een vader die alles had verloren en hij discussieerde met hem over moraal en voorschriften. 'Begrijp het toch: eerst was ik ook razend. Als ik de kans had gehad, zou ik hebben geholpen dat varken te vermoorden.'

'En waarom heb je me dan verraden?' schreeuwde Martinek, verteerd door pijn. 'Ik wilde toch alleen dat je het rapport veranderde?'

'Dat zou beslist zijn uitgekomen, en dan hadden we Sadlers advocaat een kans voor open doel gegeven.' Herzfeld liet zijn stem dalen. 'Ik vind het zelf ook moeilijk me aan de regels te houden. Maar als ik het niet had gedaan, zouden de gemanipuleerde bewijzen zijn doorzien en zou Sadler er misschien zelfs met vrijspraak vanaf zijn gekomen. Je weet toch hoe dat gaat.'

'Drieënhalf jaar.' Martinek keek hem met ogen rood van het huilen aan. Zijn onderlip trilde. 'Die oude heks heeft hem drieenhalf jaar gegeven – voor het feit dat hij mijn Lily heeft verkracht en mishandeld en de dood in heeft gedreven. Mijn alles.'

Herzfeld knikte. Hij was er al bang voor geweest. Als je in Duitsland de belasting ontdook, belandde je tot je pensioen in de bak. Als je een kind verkrachtte, maakte je een goede kans vrijuit te gaan of er met een voorwaardelijke straf vanaf te komen.

Martinek snikte. 'Ze hebben zijn dagboek niet als bewijs toegelaten.'

'Het spijt me heel erg.'

'Mevrouw de rechter is zelfs onder de voorgestelde strafmaat van de verdediging gebleven, omdat ze de dader de kans wil geven te resocialiseren.' Martinek wankelde. Hij zocht houvast bij de marmeren plaat van de sectietafel. 'Resocialisatie?' brulde hij toen. 'Dat uitvaagsel mag verder leven terwijl de maden uit Lily's ogen kruipen?'

Op het laatst had hij zo hard geschreeuwd dat zijn woorden nauwelijks te verstaan waren. Maar opeens werd hij rustig. Zo plotseling dat Herzfeld de echo van zijn stem nog meende te horen. Hoewel Martineks blik tot dan toe ietwat glazig was geweest, werd hij nu helder. Hij staarde Herzfeld woedend aan. 'En dat is jouw schuld.' Het mes in zijn hand beefde niet meer. Hij kwam een stap dichterbij.

'Sven...'

'Je zegt dat je niet weet hoe ik me voel?'

'Luister naar me. Alsjeblieft, Sven.'

Martinek kwam nog dichter bij Herzfeld staan. Opeens liet hij het mes vallen. 'Nee, ik luister niet. Nu luister jij een keer naar mij, klootzak.'

Tot Herzfelds ontzetting pakte Martinek het afgehouwen hoofd bij het haar en tilde het van de sectietafel. 'Je had maar beter op je eerste impuls kunnen afgaan. Fuck de regels! Fuck het systeem! Doordat je je ondanks alles aan de regels hebt gehouden, heb je Lily opnieuw vermoord, Paul. En daarvoor zul je boeten. Het kan best zijn dat je nu nog niet weet hoe het voelt als je het belangrijkste in je leven verliest. Maar vanaf vandaag zal ik elke dag bidden dat je dat ooit een keer zult meemaken.'

Met die woorden smeet hij het hoofd naar Herzfeld, die veel te ontdaan was om het te ontwijken. De schedel raakte hem vol op de borst, kneusde twee ribben en viel met het geluid van een bowlingbal op de stenen vloer, waar hij na een paar omwentelingen tot stilstand kwam.

Niemand hield Martinek tegen toen hij de sectiezaal uit rende. Niemand maakte melding van het incident. Daar was geen aanleiding voor. Na zijn bijzondere verlof, dat hij in verband met het proces had aangevraagd, kwam Sven Martinek nooit meer terug naar de BKA.

Herzfeld had hem later nog geprobeerd te bellen, hij was drie keer naar zijn huis in Lichterfelde gereden, maar had steeds voor een dichte deur gestaan. Ten slotte hoorde hij van een buurvrouw dat zijn collega naar zijn ouderlijk huis in Mecklenburg-Vorpommern was verhuisd. Via het kadaster kwam hij achter het adres, maar in het stadje met de naam Zarrentin had hij al evenmin succes. Het oude herenhuis aan de Schaalsee maakte al van verre een kille en onbewoonde indruk. Hij sprak met de buren, de postbode en de werknemers van de onvermijdelijke supermarkt aan de rand van het plaatsje – niemand had Martinek gezien. Sinds zijn vrouw aan kanker was overleden had de forensisch arts al een teruggetrokken bestaan geleid. Nu, na de moord op zijn enige dochter, leek hij zich volledig voor de buitenwereld te hebben verborgen.

Tijdens zijn zoektocht naar zijn voormalige collega ontmoette Herzfeld ook de advocaat die Martinek als civiele partij bij de rechtszaak tegen de moordenaar van zijn dochter had vertegenwoordigd. De man verwonderde zich er niet over dat zijn cliënt van het toneel was verdwenen. 'Ik zou het zelfs kunnen begrijpen als hij de wereld waarin dat soort vonnissen mogelijk zijn, voorgoed heeft verlaten.'

De advocaat had hem een afschrift van het dossier van het proces in handen gedrukt. Toen hij het las, kwam Herzfeld keer op keer de naam van de persoon tegen die Sven Martinek als 'die oude heks' had aangeduid: de presidente van het rechtscollege. Haar achternaam was Erlang. Het was haar laatste vonnis geweest voor ze met pensioen ging en haar meisjesnaam weer aannam, toen de berichtgeving van de media rond haar persoon en het schandalige vonnis waarvoor ze verantwoordelijk was haar begon te irriteren.

Tegenwoordig noemde ze zich Töven. Friederike Töven.

24

Het met leisteen beklede huis met het platte dak stond op de rand
van het hoge gedeelte van het eiland. Het voorste gedeelte stond
op palen, waardoor de veranda als een springschans half over de
rotsachtige klip hing. 's Zomers was de heuvel met groen mos
bedekt. Nu strekte de kale aardbodem zich als een smerig tafelkleed uit over de helling naar zee. Dankzij Enders elektromobiel
hadden ze maar een paar minuten nodig gehad om het aan het
eind van de doodlopende weg gelegen huize Töven te bereiken.
Te voet zou Linda het korte stukje nauwelijks hebben kunnen
afleggen, de wind vormde een betonnen muur voor iedereen die
zich naar buiten waagde. In de voortuin had de storm al een paar
bloembakken omvergeblazen, en zelfs een grote, in de open carport geparkeerde paardentrailer wankelde vervaarlijk wanneer de
wind vat kreeg op de huif.

'Eens kijken of die tante nog op het eiland is,' brulde Ender en
hij hamerde met zijn knuist op de voordeur. Op de rit hiernaartoe had hij Linda verteld dat 'die tante', die hij eind zestig, begin
zeventig schatte, een paar jaar geleden naar het eiland was gekomen en een zeer teruggetrokken leven leidde, zonder noemens-
waardig contact met de eilandbevolking. Eén keer had hij haar
met zijn elektromobiel afgehaald om haar voor onderzoek naar
het ziekenhuis te brengen; blijkbaar had ze vocht in de benen en
kon niet meer goed lopen. Hij had geprobeerd een gesprek met
haar te beginnen, maar ze had al zijn vragen ontweken. Linda kon

zich nauwelijks voorstellen dat een oudere dame de oproep van de stormwaarschuwingsdienst zou negeren, temeer omdat haar huis vlak naast de afgrond stond. Uit de verte deed huize Töven haar denken aan een vogelnest tegen de rotsen van de steile kust. Je moest groot vertrouwen in de architect hebben als je dat huis zelfs niet verliet wanneer er een orkaan dreigde.

'Hallo, mevrouw Töven. Bent u thuis?'

Linda vroeg zich af wat ze de oude dame eigenlijk wilde vertellen, mocht ze op Enders roepen en kloppen reageren. *Neem me niet kwalijk, maar we hebben uw foto in de hals van een lijk gevonden.*'

'Niemand thuis,' brulde Linda na een tijdje. 'Laten we gaan.' De ingang van het huis was maar door een klein afdakje beschut en bood weinig bescherming tegen de sneeuwjacht, die uit alle richtingen kwam. Intussen was Linda door en door verkleumd en had ze geen zin meer om te schreeuwen.

'Niet zo snel,' riep Ender terug en hij haalde een zware sleutelring tevoorschijn, waaraan niet alleen een heleboel sleutels van de kliniek hingen, maar ook een professionele loper. Het duurde geen tien seconden voor de deur open was.

'We kunnen toch niet zomaar...'

Voor ze het woord 'inbreken' kon zeggen, was Ender al in de hal verdwenen.

Er zat voor Linda niets anders op dan hem te volgen. In de kou daarbuiten hield ze het geen seconde meer uit, en de open elektromobiel was geen alternatief.

In het smalle huis was het verbazingwekkend licht. Overal bevonden zich grote ramen, die al het sombere winterse licht opvingen dat door het wolkendek heen kwam. Een eenzame donkerblauwe loden jas hing in de hal aan een kleerhanger, daaronder stond een respectabele collectie wandelschoenen. Aan het sleutelbord naast de kapstok hingen sleutels, die zorgvuldig naar grootte waren gerangschikt. Allemaal waren ze van een opschrift voorzien, geen haakje was onbezet. Vanwege het plotselinge temperatuurverschil begon haar neus te lopen.

'Hallo, mevrouw Töven?' riep Linda en ze trok haar handschoenen van haar vingers om aan de radiator te voelen.

Lauw.

Boven haar hoofd hoorde ze zware voetstappen op de planken vloer. Blijkbaar had Ender de trap al genomen om op de bovenverdieping rond te kijken.

Linda trok de voordeur dicht en liep langzaam de gang door. Eerst kwam ze langs de keuken, die in tegenstelling tot de rest van het huis, dat er heel modern uitzag, nogal ouderwets was ingericht. Allerlei pannen en koekenpannen hingen in een creatieve chaos aan het plafond boven een keukenblok. Onvermijdelijk moest Linda aan de sectietafel denken, ook omdat de zoetige geur nog altijd in haar neus zat, en dat terwijl ze buiten in de wind behoorlijk was uitgewaaid.

Het huis ziet er bewoond uit. Maar het voelt leeg.

Linda zag een opengeslagen krant op een tafeltje naast het keukenblok. Ze liep de keuken in en keek naar de datum. Het was de zondagskrant van afgelopen week, wat niets te betekenen had, omdat ook de post nog maar onregelmatig langskwam sinds de storm was begonnen. MILDE RECHTER, was de kop boven een artikel van twee pagina's. In de eerste alinea werd de naam Friederike Erlang genoemd in samenhang met een zekere Jan S.

Linda hoorde een geluid achter zich en draaide zich om, omdat ze dacht dat Ender naar beneden was gekomen, maar er was niemand.

'Hallo?'

Van het ene moment op het andere voelde ze zich weer zoals bij de lift van de pathologieafdeling. Ze was bang. Linda greep haar telefoon vast alsof het een wapen was waarmee ze zich in geval van nood kon verdedigen, en riep Ender.

Geen antwoord.

Opeens vibreerde het mobieltje in haar hand, ze liet het bijna vallen. Terwijl ze probeerde rustig genoeg te worden om op te nemen, las ze op het display dat een paar mensen haar steeds weer hadden geprobeerd te bereiken.

Verdomme. Zeven gemiste oproepen. Vier van haar broer.

Buiten had ze de beltoon in de bulderende orkaan waarschijnlijk niet gehoord.

'Ja, hallo?'

'Waar zijn jullie?' Herzfeld klonk nog nerveuzer dan bij hun eerdere gesprekken.

'Wist je dat je vriend ook bij de sleuteldienst werkt?' vroeg Linda bewust ironisch, ook om haar angst met een geestige opmerking te verdrijven. 'Wij hebben het huis van die Friederike Töven gevonden, maar er lijkt niemand thuis te zijn.'

'Niet naar binnen gaan. Ga onder geen beding het huis van de rechter in!'

Aha. Ze is dus rechter.

Linda was de keuken weer uit gegaan en keek door de gang in de richting van de woonkamer, waar juist een staande klok drie keer sloeg, hoewel het beslist nog niet zo laat was.

Geen Ender. Geen mevrouw Töven. Niemand.

'Niet naar binnen gaan? Echt man, nou breekt mijn klomp. Je vindt het geen probleem als ik een lijk met een mes bewerk, maar bij huisvredebreuk doe je het in je broek?'

Linda sprak bewust harder dan nodig, zodat Ender haar kon horen en eindelijk een teken van leven zou geven. Waar zat die kerel nou?

'We kijken hier alleen even rond en dan gaan we weer. Wat is het probleem?' wilde ze weten. En voor Herzfeld haar kon antwoorden, opende ze de deur naar de huiskamer en zag ze het.

'Het probleem' lag geboeid in een plas bloed op het parket en kreunde met gesloten mond.

25

'Ender! Eéénder!?' Als in slow motion stapte Linda de huiskamer in, en ze legde haar telefoon op een donkerbruine secretaire. Als ze niet gehoord had dat de oude dame nog leefde, was ze het liefst gillend het huis uit gerend.

Help! Die vrouw heeft hulp nodig, dacht ze en opnieuw riep ze de huismeester.

Grijs haar, rond gezicht. *Zoals op de foto in het verrassingsei.* Geen twijfel mogelijk, dit was Friederike Töven.

De vrouw lag met opgetrokken knieën en gekromde rug op haar zij, voor een glazen vitrine, haar handen met een touw aan haar enkels gebonden.

Linda knielde naast haar, niet wetend wat haar het eerst te doen stond. De verplichte cursus eerste hulp van de rijschool was lang geleden, ze kon zich nog maar vaag herinneren dat je bij een levenloos lichaam eerst de ademhaling moest controleren.

En dit lichaam was opeens verdomd levenloos!

Daarnet had Linda de vrouw luid en duidelijk horen kreunen, maar nu bewoog haar borstkas geen millimeter meer.

Mevrouw de rechter was bijzonder corpulent, een crèmekleurige blouse spande over haar reusachtige boezem. Ze droeg een wijde rok met een bloemmotief, waarvan de achtergrond ooit wit was geweest maar die nu vanaf de heupen een roestbruine kleur had aangenomen. Het leek bijna alsof ze zich opzettelijk in de plas bloed onder haar lichaam had rondgewenteld. Op het eerste gezicht kon Linda geen open wond ontdekken. Het ronde hoofd, het gezicht, het omvangrijke bovenlichaam – er leken geen verwondingen te zijn.

Oké, wat had de cursusleider destijds gezegd? *'Je eigen wang is het gevoeligst.'*

Linda bracht haar gezicht vlak bij dat van de vrouw.

Niets.

Ze bespeurde niet het minste zuchtje adem.

Goed dan. Reanimatie.

'Shit, wat is hier aan de hand?' hoorde ze Ender achter haar roepen. Eindelijk was hij naar beneden gekomen. Het volgende moment begon de huismeester al te puffen. Blijkbaar had hij de bloedplas gezien waarin Linda knielde.

Concentratie. Laat je niet afleiden.

Ze moest de luchtwegen vrijmaken, maar hoe? Normaal gesproken had ze de gewonde vrouw daarvoor op haar rug moeten draaien, maar dat was vanwege de boeien zo goed als onmogelijk. Linda moest ermee volstaan het hoofd van mevrouw Töven op te richten door het eerst opzij en vervolgens achterover te duwen.

'Ze is dood,' stotterde Ender.

'Toen ik binnenkwam leefde ze nog,' zei Linda; toen merkte ze dat de huismeester niet tegen haar praatte, maar zijn telefoon had gepakt om Herzfeld te informeren, want hij zei: 'Ik denk dat ze mond-op-mondbeademing probeert.'

Inderdaad hield Linda met duim en wijsvinger de neus van de rechter dicht en haalde ze diep adem. Toen drukte ze haar lippen stevig tegen de nu rood besmeurde mond. Het bloed op het parket, waarop Linda zich steeds moest afzetten en dat ze bij haar reddingspogingen over het lichaam en de kleding van de vrouw verspreidde, voelde stroperig aan.

Een-en-twin-tig.

Een seconde lang perste Linda uit alle macht de lucht uit haar longen het andere lichaam in. Toen draaide ze zich opzij om in te ademen en zag Ender met zijn telefoon aan het oor. Hij had iets tegen Herzfeld gezegd wat ze vanwege haar reanimatiepogingen niet had gehoord.

Toen ze weer diep had ingeademd, draaide Linda zich naar de vrouw toe en stelde tot haar ontzetting vast dat haar borstkas niet was gedaald.

Verdomme!

Linda trok de blouse uit en trok resoluut de vleeskleurige bh van de borsten.

'Steek de handen eens uit de mouwen!' brulde ze, maar Ender maakte geen aanstalten haar te helpen de rechter op haar rug te draaien.

'De vlekken,' zei hij alleen, en nu vielen ze haarzelf ook op.

Hoe... hoe is dat mogelijk?

Ze had het met hart-longmassage willen proberen, maar nu schrok Linda ervoor terug haar huid aan te raken. Het gebied rond de linkerborst was aan de zijkant van het lichaam donkerpaars verkleurd.

'Dat zijn lijkvlekken,' legde Ender ten overvloede uit. Die had Linda eerder in de sectiezaal meer dan genoeg op Eriks lichaam gezien.

Maar dan moet ze al een tijdje dood zijn!

'Herzfeld vraagt of je de lijkvlekken nog kunt wegdrukken.'

'Wat?'

'Als je er met je vingers op drukt, wordt de huid dan bleker?'

Linda, die de schok van de onverwachte aanblik nog niet helemaal te boven was, drukte met haar wijsvinger op de donkerpaarse verkleuring van de huid. Eerst voorzichtig, toen iets doortastender. Tegelijk reikte ze naar de telefoon die Ender haar aangaf, zonder zich naar de huismeester om te draaien. Anders dan in de sectiezaal droeg ze nu geen handschoenen, en daarom was de aanraking van de naakte huid van het afgekoelde lichaam directer en op een of andere manier intiemer. En veel onaangenamer dan bij Erik in het felle neonlicht van de sectiezaal. Het voelde alsof ze haar vingers tegen een koud gelkussen aan duwde.

'Het gaat niet,' zei ze buiten adem. Ze wist dat dat geen goed nieuws was. *Het opdrogende bloed op de grond, de koude lippen bij de mond-op-mondbeademing en nu de lijkvlekken.* 'Ze blijven donker. Ik kan ze bijna niet wegdrukken.'

'Dan is mevrouw Töven al meer dan tien uur niet meer in leven, Linda,' constateerde Herzfeld.

Al meer dan tien uur?

'Maar ik heb haar daarnet nog horen kreunen?' Linda vroeg het meer dan dat ze het vaststelde.

'Ademhalingsgeluiden bij doden komen vaker voor, als er bij voortschrijdende ontbinding lucht uit de longen ontsnapt,' legde Herzfeld uit. Op de achtergrond hoorde ze auto's toeteren, wat haar op dit moment als een levensteken uit een ander sterrenstelsel voorkwam. In haar universum, op dit van God en alle mensen verlaten, door de storm geteisterde eiland, was er geen enkel teken van menselijke beschaving. Alleen geweld, pijn en dood.

'En nu?' vroeg Linda vermoeid. Ze stond op, keek omlaag naar zichzelf. Haar handen, haar trillende knieën – alles zat onder het bloed.

Mijn god. En overal mijn vingerafdrukken! In een huis waarin we hebben ingebroken.

'Ender zegt dat de moordenaar daar niet meer is. Toch vind ik het geen goed idee dat je het in het huis doet.'

'Wat zou ik moeten doen?' vroeg Linda geïrriteerd, maar toen begon ze het te snappen.

'Nee, o nee,' zei ze, maar Herzfeld negeerde haar protesten.

'Breng de dode naar de afdeling Pathologie. Ik meld me weer als ik een bezoekje heb afgelegd bij een vroegere collega van me.'

26

'Zarrentin?' zei Ingolf. 'Nooit van gehoord.' Ze hadden verschillende verkeersovertredingen moeten begaan om uit de file op de snelweg te ontsnappen. Het begon ermee dat Ingolf achteruit de vluchtstrook af was gejakkerd om de tweehonderd meter achter hen liggende afrit voor werkverkeer te bereiken. Nu reden ze op een provinciale weg met bomen aan weerszijden en haalden elk voertuig in dat zich aan de maximumsnelheid hield.

'Een gat met vijfduizend inwoners aan de Schaalsee. Het is een omweg van hooguit tien minuten.'

'Volgens de navigatie, maar ik denk dat het in vijf gaat lukken. Maar wat hebben we daar eigenlijk te zoeken?' vroeg Ingolf.

'Daar woont Martinek.'

'En wie is dat nu weer?'

Herzfeld zuchtte. 'Ik denk dat het beter is als je zo weinig mogelijk te weten komt.'

Ingolf wierp hem een snelle blik toe, toen concentreerde hij zich op de scherpe bocht voor hem, waarvoor een normale bestuurder ook zonder gevaar voor ijzel zou hebben geremd.

'Professor Herzfeld, ik ben misschien jong, maar ik ben niet gek. Ik weet nu toch ook al meer dan u voor raadzaam hield. Uw dochter is in gevaar, vermoedelijk is ze ontvoerd.'

Hij presteerde het zelfs in de bocht nog te accelereren.

'Ik kan er nog geen chocola van maken waarom u telefonisch zoiets als een op afstand bestuurde autopsie laat uitvoeren, en wel, zoals het mij in de oren klinkt, door een vrouw met bijna of helemaal geen vakkennis, maar omdat er één of zelfs meerdere lijken blijken te zijn, is of zijn de ontvoerder of ontvoerders blijkbaar zeer gevaarlijk. Weliswaar ben ik een beschaafde jongeman, die zijn medemens graag behulpzaam is, maar als tegenprestatie, denk ik, heb ik toch een kleine tegemoetkoming verdiend, als ik me dan toch samen met u in gevaar begeef.'

Herzfeld draaide zich naar hem toe. 'Je wilt informatie?'

'Dat zou buitengewoon fideel van u zijn!'

'Heeft iemand je al eens gezegd dat je praat alsof je een stok in je reet hebt?' Herzfeld dwong zichzelf te glimlachen, om de scherpe kantjes van zijn woorden af te halen.

Ingolf grijnsde. 'En heeft iemand u al eens gezegd dat u een tamelijk puberaal gevoel voor humor hebt? Een stagiair de eerste dag om een defibrillator sturen...'

Even dacht Herzfeld weemoedig terug aan de autopsie van een paar uur geleden en aan het feit dat zijn grootste problemen op dat moment bestonden uit een luidruchtige verwarmingsradiator in zijn slaapkamer, een vergeten verjaardag van een oude schoolvriend, een krantenabonnement dat hij weer eens had vergeten op te zeggen, en de eerste grijze haren bij zijn slapen. En niet te vergeten natuurlijk zijn scheiding, de dreigende intrekking van zijn toelating als arts en de radiostilte tussen hem en zijn dochter Hannah.

Wat zou hij er niet voor overhebben als alles weer bij het oude zou zijn!

'Waarom help je mij?' vroeg hij aan Ingolf, nadat ze een tijdje zwijgend hadden gereden. Het was bijna twaalf uur 's middags, maar buiten zag het eruit alsof de zon op het punt stond onder te gaan. De xenonkoplampen van de Porsche uitschakelen zou gelijkstaan aan zelfmoord. Ze reden juist door een gebied met veel meren, waardoor er tot overmaat van ramp ook nog mist kwam opzetten. Gelukkig was het niet zo druk op de provinciale weg als op de A24.

'Waarom doe je alsof je mijn chauffeur bent?'

Ingolf krabde zich op zijn vooruitstekende kin en leek opeens nerveus te zijn. 'Toen ik u in de natte sneeuw buiten zag staan, wilde ik eerst voorkomend zijn. Toen merkte ik dat u in moeilijkheden zat, en omdat ik dit weekend niets hoef te doen, kwam het me niet helemaal slecht uit...'

Herzfeld tilde zijn hand op. 'Bla, bla, bla. Ik geloof er geen woord van. Je hoeft me niet de kont te likken. Je bent de zoon van de belangrijkste Berlijnse senator, en bovendien heb je in de familie kennelijk de broek aan. Eén telefoontje en je krijgt elke stage ter wereld.'

Ingolf knikte. 'Dat zou kunnen kloppen. Maar ik wil niet *elke* stage. Ik wil alleen die bij u.'

'Waarom?'

'Het lijkt mij gezien de huidige ontwikkelingen werkelijk niet het juiste moment om mijn verzoek kenbaar te maken.'

'*Wat* wil je van mij?' Heel even daagde bij Herzfeld het inzicht dat Ingolfs hulpvaardigheid misschien net zomin toeval was als de omstandigheid dat ze elkaar uitgerekend vandaag hadden leren kennen, en toen deed de student zijn wantrouwen nog toenemen door te zeggen: 'Ik wil u een deal voorstellen, professor Herzfeld.'

'Een deal?'

'Ja. Het is uiterst lucratief, de jaarwinst ligt naar verwachting wellicht rond de vierhonderd miljoen dollar, en dat is de pessimistische schatting in het businessplan.'

'Dat is een grap.'

'Nee, het gaat om een product op de wereldmarkt voor veiligheidstechnologie dat enig is in zijn soort. Een verdere ontwikkeling van de PetSave-One.'

'PetSave-One?' echode Herzfeld argwanend.

'Ik heb het patent uitgewerkt nadat Misty ervandoor was gegaan, onze kat. We hebben twee weken gezocht en haar ten slotte teruggevonden in de leegstaande villa naast de onze, waar ze tijdens de controle van de veiligheidsdienst naar binnen was geglipt. En toen bedacht ik hoeveel moeite we ons bij het zoeken hadden kunnen besparen als Misty een gps-ontvanger in haar halsband had gehad.'

'De PetSave-One?'

'Precies. Inmiddels zijn die dingen zo klein dat je ze zelfs onder het vel kan implanteren. Het mooie is dat je met die gps-modules de kat via je iPhone kunt lokaliseren. Zelfs als het dier niet kwijt is, blijkt het enorm interessant om te zien waar de vagebond de hele dag uithangt. Je kunt elke stap op Google Maps nagaan.'

'Maak het een beetje.' Herzfeld kon er met zijn verstand niet bij. 'Mijn dochter is ontvoerd, en jij wilt mij in alle ernst een investering voor een zoeksysteem voor weggelopen katten aanpraten?'

Ingolf trok een berouwvol gezicht. 'Ik zei toch dat dit niet het juiste moment is. En nee, het gaat niet om huisdieren. Dat patent heb ik allang weer verkocht.'

Herzfeld wilde niet weten voor hoeveel miljoen. Hij wilde helemaal niets meer uit de mond van deze omhooggevallen vlegel vernemen. Het liefst zou hij direct zijn uitgestapt en in zijn eentje achter de ontvoerders van zijn dochter aan zijn gegaan. Hij overwoog serieus Ingolf bij de eerste de beste gelegenheid de Porsche uit te gooien en in zijn eentje verder te rijden.

'Ik heb een gloednieuw, revolutionair idee. Een verdere ontwikkeling van PetSave-One, maar ik zou nu echt graag van onderwerp veranderen en veel liever iets over het doel van onze reis horen. Die Martinek, is hij een vriend?'

Herzfeld keek strak voor zich uit naar een plaatsnaambord.

'Niet buiten het werk.'

'Dan was het voor uw collega een hele reis naar zijn werk.' Ingolf wees op het bord. Ze reden Zarrentin binnen, 229 kilometer van Berlijn vandaan.

'Martinek had een appartement in Lichterfelde, tot...'

... tot dat met Lily gebeurde.

Hij gaf er de voorkeur aan te zwijgen, tot Ingolf vroeg: 'En hij zal u helpen uw dochter te vinden?'

'Nee.'

Als hij aan Martineks laatste woorden terugdacht, moest hij eerder van het tegendeel uitgaan: *'Het kan best zijn dat je nu nog niet weet hoe het voelt als je het belangrijkste in je leven verliest. Maar vanaf vandaag zal ik elke dag bidden dat je dat ooit een keer zult meemaken.'*

Martineks gebeden leken te zijn verhoord. En hoogstwaarschijnlijk had hij een handje geholpen.

Herzfeld was dankbaar dat zijn sombere gedachten door de monotone vrouwenstem van het navigatieapparaat werden onderbroken. Ze hadden hun doel bereikt.

'Niemand thuis,' mompelde hij toen ze stilstonden voor het scheve houten hek dat het perceel omgaf. Een paar decennia geleden zou het vrijstaande herenhuis vast de blikvanger van het plaatsje zijn geweest. Tegenwoordig was de grijze gevel met de vermolmde vensterluiken hooguit nog een inspiratiebron voor griezelverhalen.

'Doet denken aan een spookhuis. Daar aanbellen is voor de dorpskinderen vast de favoriete manier om hun moed te bewijzen,' merkte Ingolf op. 'Tot zover het thema economische stimulering van Oost-Duitsland.'

Hij wilde de oprit in draaien, maar zag er vanwege de dikke laag sneeuw van af en parkeerde schuin op de stoep. 'Geen licht, geen rook uit de schoorsteen,' zei hij en hij schakelde het grote licht in om de gevel beter te belichten.

'Zelfs het dak is bouwvallig. Lieve hemel, als hier iemand woont, trek ik de jungle in.'

'Veel plezier in Australië dan,' zei Herzfeld en hij wees naar het raam op de eerste verdieping, waarachter juist een gordijn bewoog.

27

Herzfeld was er zeker van dat ze werden gadegeslagen. Alleen al de Porsche op het trottoir moest bij bewoners van de ook al verwaarloosde huizen rondom opzien hebben gebaard. En het onwaarschijnlijke duo al helemaal, dat tot hun enkels in de sneeuw zonk terwijl ze door de tuin liepen. Herzfeld zag er met zijn laarzen, zwarte jeans en donzen jack in bijpassende kleur nogal onopvallend uit, maar Ingolf viel hier volledig uit de toon. Al na een paar meter had hij een van zijn speciaal gestikte leren schoenen verloren en ruïneerde zijn kasjmier jas toen hij bij zijn pogingen de schoen uit de sneeuw te vissen languit op de grond viel.

'Grand malheur,' foeterde hij, wat vermoedelijk gelijkstond aan een woede-uitbarsting. Voor hij de sneeuwblubber van zijn jas en pak klopte, fatsoeneerde hij bedaard zijn haar.

'Ik blijf erbij,' riep Ingolf Herzfeld achterna, terwijl hij met natte sok en al in zijn handgemaakte schoen gleed. 'Het pand is onbewoond.'

De professor was vooruitgelopen en stond onder aan de trap die naar een imposante voordeur leidde. Ook hij had het gemerkt toen hij dichterbij was gekomen: het raam op de eerste verdieping stond op een kier. Het gordijn bewoog in de wind.

Nadenkend bekeek Herzfeld een groene kist van weerbestendig plastic onder de luifel, waarin vermoedelijk ooit de kussens waren opgeborgen van de tuinmeubels, die nu op het voorste gedeelte van het terrein onder een grote linde verpieterden. Nu stonden er een paar fabrieksnieuwe, bruine werklaarzen op. Herzfeld pakte ze op. *Maat vierenveertig,* constateerde hij verwonderd. Martinek was tien centimeter korter dan hij. Hadden ze werkelijk dezelfde schoenmaat? Peinzend opende Herzfeld de deksel van de kist, waarin hij geen kussens maar een grijze kartonnen doos ontdekte.

'*Gezwind met Schwintowski.*' Ingolf las hardop de reclameslogan van het verhuisbedrijf op de deksel. Met een zakdoek wreef hij de regen van zijn brillenglazen en kneep zijn bijziende ogen tot spleetjes boven de schouder van de professor.

Net als de laarzen moest de doos al geruime tijd in de kou hebben gestaan. Het karton was oud en vochtig en bij het openen scheurden de kleppen.

'Hee poppelepee.' Ingolf floot bewonderend tussen zijn tanden door en wees met een pootje van zijn bril naar de geopende doos. 'Ik zou zeggen dat het uitstapje heeft geloond.'

De bovenste laag in de kartonnen doos bestond uit contant geld: dikke bundels met banderollen bijeengehouden bankbiljetten. Herzfeld haalde er een stapel uit en liet het geld door zijn vingers gaan.

'Dat is minstens honderdduizend euro,' schatte Ingolf.

'157.560 euro,' bevestigde Herzfeld. Hij schudde gelaten zijn hoofd.

Verdomme, Sven.

'Bent u ook nog een soort Rain Man, hoe kunt u dat in één oogopslag zo precies zien?' Ingolf keek heen en weer tussen het geld en Herzfeld.

'157.560 euro. Dat is het bedrag dat Martinek mij destijds heeft geboden als ik de bewijzen zou vervalsen.'

Hij legde Ingolf zo kort mogelijk uit wat er tussen hem en zijn collega was gebeurd.

'En u hebt geweigerd?'

Herzfeld knikte en legde de bundel terug bij de andere. 'Ja. Het was precies het bedrag dat hij na een erfenis op zijn rekening had staan. Zoals je ziet, is het na de dood van zijn dochter niets meer waard voor hem.'

Herzfeld duwde het geld opzij en stuitte eronder op een in een wollen deken gewikkelde bijl.

'Hé, voorzichtig,' zei Ingolf toen Herzfeld het gloednieuwe werktuig met een korte steel eruit haalde. 'Hoort zoiets ook bij de standaarduitrusting van een forensisch arts?'

Herzfeld schudde zijn hoofd. 'Nee. Bij die van een inbreker.'

Hij wees naar het hangslot waarmee de voordeur was afgesloten en liet Ingolf zien wat Martinek met viltstift op de steel van de korte bijl had geschreven: *Dit zul je nodig hebben, Paul.*

'Het lijkt erop dat ik word verwacht.'

Herzfeld ging bij de deur staan, nam het slot keurend in zijn hand, identificeerde de zwakke plek en hakte met een snelle, doelgerichte slag een verroeste schakel in de ketting doormidden, waarbij hij op zijn lip moest bijten om het niet uit te schreeuwen van de pijn die door zijn gekneusde vingers schoot.

De deur had geen deurknop meer, maar ging zonder problemen open.

'Jij blijft hier!' zei Herzfeld op een toon die geen tegenspraak duldde, maar Ingolf was niet in het minst onder de indruk. Hij legde een hand achter zijn oor en vroeg: 'Hoort u dat?'

Verdomme, hij heeft gelijk. Wat is dat in vredesnaam?

Er bruiste en ruiste iets binnen in het huis, en het werd luider toen ze naar binnen gingen. Maar dat was niet het enige wat bevreemdend was.

Op de drempel al bespeurde Herzfeld een onverwachte, heel onnatuurlijke warmte, heel anders dan je in een te warme woning in de winter zou verwachten. Het was veel vochtiger, bijna als in een broeikas.

'Het is hier nauwelijks te harden,' pufte Ingolf achter hem. Toen Herzfeld zich omdraaide, zag hij dat zijn metgezel zijn boordenknoopje losmaakte. Ook Herzfeld begon te zweten. Hij tastte naar een lichtschakelaar naast de lege kapstok, maar alle gloeilampen in de armaturen aan het plafond ontbraken.

'Sven?' riep hij, hoewel hij vermoedde dat hij geen antwoord zou krijgen. Zelfs als zijn vroegere collega zich hier ergens verstopte, zou Herzfeld het antwoord bij deze herrie nauwelijks kunnen horen.

Of het moet zijn dat hij vlak achter me staat.

Herzfeld werd overmand door een irrationele angst en hij draaide zich om, maar het was Ingolf maar, die nu tegen hem op liep.

'Voorzichtig, alstublieft. U bent bewapend,' zei hij met een blik op de bijl die Herzfeld nog steeds in zijn hand hield.

Herzfeld knikte alleen en keek om zich heen.

Het pand had de opzet van een klein stadspaleis. Direct achter de ruime vestibule lag een atrium, een grote open ruimte van twee verdiepingen hoog, waar een gebogen dubbele trap naar de hoger gelegen vertrekken leidde. Links en rechts van de twee trappen bevonden zich brede doorgangen. In de prospectus van een makelaar zou het beslist hoogdravend zijn beschreven; in werkelijkheid zag het er somber en triest uit, wat ook kwam doordat er nergens meubels of schilderijen waren, alleen de lege muren met verbleekt, vlekkerig behang.

'Ik zei het toch: hier woont niemand meer,' hield Ingolf vol.

'En wie is er dan verantwoordelijk voor die herrie?' Herzfeld wees naar links. 'Jij wacht hier, heb je dat begrepen?'

Ingolf knikte en zette zijn bril weer op; de glazen besloegen meteen.

Het ruisen leek uit de doorgang aan Herzfelds linkerhand te komen, dus liep hij daarheen. De smalle, sombere gang deed hem aan een hotel denken, omdat er verschillende kamers op uitkwamen. Op één deur na zaten ze allemaal op slot. Hoe verder Herzfeld kwam, hoe luider het werd.

En warmer!

Herzfeld bereikte een openstaande deur die bij een kleine kamer hoorde en ontdekte daarin de bron van het lawaai: het heteluchtkanon op de vloer had een roestvrijstalen pijp met de diameter van een handbal en moest al uren, zo niet dagen, in bedrijf zijn. De brander stond roodgloeiend, en het rook naar verbrand plastic. Het verwarmingstoestel was krachtig genoeg om een kleine opblaashal van warme lucht te voorzien, voor de smalle gang naar de eetkamer was het veel te groot.

Herzfeld pakte het snoer en trok het uit het stopcontact. Op slag werd het kouder, maar er was nog steeds lawaai, al was het dan een eindje verderop.

'Er moeten nog meer ventilatorkachels zijn.' De stem achter hem deed hem schrikken.

Hij draaide zich woedend om. 'Ik heb toch gezegd dat je vóór op me moest wachten.'

'Heb ik ook, en intussen heb ik dit hier ontdekt.'

Ingolf stak met een schuldbewust gezicht een smalle ordner naar hem uit.

Herzfeld legde de bijl neer om zijn handen vrij te hebben, toen klapte hij de kartonnen flap open. Snel las hij het vertrouwde formulier van een autopsierapport door, terwijl Ingolf hem in de schemerige gang met het display van zijn telefoon bijlichtte.

* Gescheurd maagdenvlies met recente bloeduitstorting, de vrouw/het meisje was tot op heden maagd
* Gebroken nek
* Resten van vreemd speeksel op de huid, over het hele lichaam, in het bijzonder in de schaamstreek

'Waar heb je dat vandaan?' vroeg Herzfeld terwijl hij in de kolom voor de persoonlijke gegevens naar naam en leeftijd van het slachtoffer zocht. Beide categorieën waren niet ingevuld.

In plaats daarvan bevond zich op de laatste bladzijde van het rapport één enkele losse foto. De polaroid liet een jonge vrouw op een sectietafel zien. Martinek boog zich over haar heen en opende juist de borstkas met een Y-vormige incisie.

Nee. Dat is onmogelijk.

Het gezicht van de vrouw stond niet op de foto, maar wat lichaamsgrootte en gestalte betrof...

... zou het kunnen.

Bij de gedachte aan zijn dochter gleed de ordner uit Herzfelds handen.

'Het dossier lag helemaal onder in de doos.' Ingolf raapte de map weer op. 'Ziet u enige samenhang tussen al deze dingen? Het rapport? Het geld? Het heteluchtkanon?'

'Ik ben bang van wel,' antwoordde Herzfeld zacht.

Wat was het levensmotto ook alweer dat je in je Facebookprofiel hebt gezet, Sven? 'Niets aan het toeval overlaten'?

'Martinek weet precies wat hij doet,' zei Herzfeld en hij wees naar het verwarmingstoestel. 'Hij heeft akoestische wegwijzers voor ons neergezet.'

'En waarheen moeten die ons leiden?'

'Daar zullen we zo achter komen.'

Herzfeld snoof de lucht op. Nu de stank van de oververhitte kunststof wat was geweken, vingen zijn neustrilhaartjes een andere kwalijke geur op.

'Ruik jij dat ook?' vroeg hij aan Ingolf en hij keek naar de glazen deur aan het eind van de gang. Zonder het antwoord af te wachten zette hij zich in beweging, trok de schuifdeur open en ontdekte daarachter de volgende ventilatorkachel. Ook dat apparaat gloeide al vanwege de overbelasting, en ook nu onderbrak hij de stroomtoevoer. Het duurde even voor Herzfeld aan de plotselinge stilte en het schemerige licht was gewend, en hij meer kon onderscheiden dan alleen contouren.

De eetkamer was een gelambriseerde zaal met een hoog stucplafond en een glazen uitbouw die op de tuin uitkwam. Net als in de andere kamers waren ook hier de muren kaal, maar hier kon je aan de zwarte randen op het hout zien dat er enige tijd geleden een schilderij ter grootte van een wandtapijt tegenover de eettafel moest hebben gehangen. Hoewel 'tafel' als aanduiding voor het meubelstuk, het enige in de zaal, bepaald een understatement was. Rond het monster van rood-zwart mahoniehout zou gemakkelijk een bruiloftsgezelschap kunnen zitten. In het oude herenhuis moesten dat soort feesten in een ver verleden liggen, alleen al naar de toestand van de kroonluchter te oordelen, die vol zat met spinnenwebben en nog maar aan twee van de zes schroeven aan het plafond hing. Maar noch de tafel, noch de kroonluchter was het meest opvallende voorwerp in de zaal.

'Lieve god, wat is *dat*?' bracht Ingolf uit en hij wees naar het midden van de tafel; hij hield zijn neus en mond dicht.

Herzfeld deed een stap naar voren en hij begon te trillen.

Ik ben bang om het hardop te zeggen.

Op de eettafel, midden onder de oude kroonluchter, lag een...

... een homp? Een lichaam?

Het was niet goed te zien, want over het vormloze object was een witte doek gelegd.

Opeens wilde Herzfeld dat de herrie van het heteluchtkanon weer terugkwam, in de irrationele hoop dat het lawaai zijn reukzin zou uitschakelen. Wat er ook onder de doek op hem lag te wachten, het verspreidde de onmiskenbare geur van ontbinding. En alsof dat niet genoeg was – het dunne linnen leek te bewegen.

'Het leeft nog,' zei Ingolf kokhalzend, maar Herzfeld wist wel beter. Alsof zijn grootste vrees bewaarheid werd, kronkelde er een witte made onder de lap vandaan, en kromde zich op het tafelblad.

Te klein. Dat kan geen compleet lijk zijn, dacht hij en die gedachte maakte het voor hem nog ondraaglijker.

Ik kan dat niet.

Er klonk een gezoem in zijn oren, alsof er geen kevers en maden maar wespen aan het rottende vlees onder de afdekking vraten.

Vandaar die hoge temperaturen. Daarom die luchtvochtigheid.

Martinek wilde het ontbindingsproces versnellen.

De tranen sprongen Herzfeld in de ogen toen hij zijn hand naar de bewegende stof uitstrekte, maar het was onmogelijk.

Dat red ik niet.

Hij had in zijn leven al duizenden doden in het gezicht gezien, maar wat hij vreesde nu te moeten aanschouwen, ging zijn krachten ver te boven.

Herzfeld voelde het zweet in zijn nek lopen, sloot zijn ogen en deed een stap opzij omdat hij zijn evenwicht dreigde te verliezen.

Tot dan toe had hij Ingolf het uitzicht op de tafel ontnomen, maar nu kon ook hij zien wat de professor zo had geschokt. Het waren niet de stank en de maden die hem ervan weerhielden de lijkwade weg te trekken, maar de astmaspray die voor Herzfelds ogen op tafel lag.

28

'Waar zat je eigenlijk al die tijd, daarnet bij Töven?' wilde Linda weten toen ze met de lift naar de afdeling Pathologie afdaalden.

Terwijl ze het zei, viel het haar op dat ze Ender op een gegeven moment ongemerkt was gaan vertrouwen.

Waanzin verbroedert. Ook een goede tekst voor op een t-shirt.

'Het kostte me moeite het luik naar de zolder open te krijgen, het slot klemde en zelfs mijn loper deed het niet. Ik had het ding net kleingekregen toen ik je beneden hoorde roepen.'

De ruime liftcabine kwam met een schok tot stilstand, de deuren gingen open.

'Denk je dat Herzfelds dochter nog leeft?' Linda hield de wanstaltige rol tapijt vast aan het eind, om hem bij het verlaten van de lift niet van het ziekenhuisbed te laten rollen. Sinds ze in het huis van de rechter het bloed waarin ze zich had afgezet, van haar handen had geprobeerd te schrobben, voelden die vreemd gevoelloos aan. Ze hadden besloten voor het transport het Perzische tapijt te gebruiken dat voor de bank lag. Aanvankelijk had Linda het vuile werk in haar eentje moeten opknappen, omdat Ender had geweigerd mee te helpen zolang er nog bloed te zien was. Maar nadat het lijk in het tapijt was gerold had hij het wel eigenhandig naar de auto gedragen, om het – zoals Herzfeld had opgedragen – hier naar de kliniek te brengen.

'Of denk je dat ze Hannah allang hebben vermoord?'

'Geen idee,' antwoordde Ender. Ze duwden het rollende bed

de sectiezaal in en werden verwelkomd door de geur waarvan Linda wist dat ze er in geen duizend jaar aan zou wennen.

'Ik weet alleen dat er binnenkort geen tafel meer over is als dit zo doorgaat.'

Ender rolde het bed naar de tweede sectietafel, drie meter van de eerste, waarop Eriks opengesneden lijk lag te stinken. En dat terwijl het hierbeneden dankzij de defecte verwarming nog geen negentien graden was – wat overigens heel wat beter was dan de kou die buiten de kliniek heerste. Door de storm had je buiten het gevoel in een ijskast te lopen, met als prettige bijkomstigheid dat er onderweg niemand was die hen het lijk door de achterdeur van de kliniek naar binnen had zien dragen.

'Op drie,' zei Ender en hij beduidde Linda het andere eind van de tapijtrol te pakken. Vervolgens verplaatsten ze mevrouw de rechter naar haar nieuwe locatie.

Toen de inspannende actie achter de rug was, merkte Linda dat de handen van de huismeester trilden. Ze raakte zacht zijn bovenarm aan. 'Ben je bang?'

Hij keek haar met een vermoeide blik aan. 'Jij niet soms?'

'Natuurlijk. Ik bedoel, wie is er blij met twee lijken op één dag?'

'Een begrafenisonderneming,' zei Ender bij wijze van kwinkslag. Intussen was het hem duidelijk aan te zien dat het slecht met hem ging. Linda pakte zijn hand, maar hij trok hem terug.

'Aan de slag,' zei hij. Verlegen schraapte hij zijn keel. 'We hebben niet veel tijd.'

Linda probeerde het nog een keer, dit keer kreeg ze hem te pakken. Zijn hand was nat van het zweet.

'Nee,' zei ze.

'Hoezo nee?'

'Nee, wij gaan hier niets doen voordat ik precies weet wat er met je aan de hand is.'

Ender stiet een nerveus lachje uit en wreef met zijn andere

hand langs zijn overall. 'Wat zou er met mij aan de hand moeten zijn?'

Hij probeerde nonchalant over te komen, maar zijn lichaamstaal verried hem. Elke spier in zijn hals stond gespannen, alsof hij voor een bodybuildingwedstrijd poseerde.

'Luister,' zei Linda en ze liet hem weer los om een scalpel te pakken. 'Ik doe alleen mee met deze onzin omdat ik doodsbang ben dat er echt een seriemoordenaar op het eiland rondloopt, en ik niet wil dat iemand anders de volgende keer een verrassingsei uit *mijn* hals haalt.'

'En je wilt Hannah redden,' stelde Ender.

'Klopt, en daar gaat het om. Toen je een tijdje terug naar mijn huis kwam, wist je toen dat Herzfelds dochter was ontvoerd?'

Ender schudde zijn hoofd. 'Nee. Dat heb ik pas later van jou gehoord.'

'En toch heb je de professor geholpen, voordat je enig idee had wat er allemaal op het spel stond. Waarom?'

Ender zuchtte. Toen hij geen antwoord gaf, zette Linda allebei haar handen in haar zij.

'Omdat Paul mij ook een keer uit de brand heeft geholpen,' fluisterde hij ten slotte. Hij pauzeerde even en ging verder: 'Toen ik hier twee jaar geleden begon, was ik zo'n fiftyfiftyfiguur. De ene helft van het personeel mocht me, de andere wist niet wat te denken van een Turkse Popeye als huismeester.'

Voor het eerst moest Linda om een opmerking van Ender glimlachen.

'Nou ja, in het begin ging het niet al te best, dat moet ik toegeven. De eerste werkdag al was een complete ramp.'

'Hoe dat zo?'

'Ik heb de geneesheer-directeur mijn lievelingsmop verteld.'

'Die van de cellulitis?'

'Nee, die van het kind dat thuiskomt en tegen zijn vader zegt: "Papa, Markus vertelt iedereen op school dat ik homo ben." Zegt zijn vader: "Nou, dan sla je hem toch op zijn bek." ' Ender glimlachte al voor de clou. 'Zegt zijn zoon: "Nee, hij is zo lief." '

Linda gniffelde. 'Laat me eens raden, de geneesheer-directeur was ook homo?'

Ender grijnsde. 'Nee, dat zouden we dan met elkaar gemeen hebben.'

O ja?

Ze fronste en vroeg zich af waarom haar gaydar haar in de steek had gelaten. Normaal gesproken kon ze de seksuele geaardheid van haar gesprekspartners in één oogopslag zien. Een paar van haar beste vrienden waren homoseksueel.

'Ik ben er nog niet helemaal uit,' zei Ender, alsof hij haar gedachten had geraden. 'Hoe het ook zij, de grap viel niet zo goed, omdat de zoon van de arts pas een week geleden uit de kast was gekomen en een enorm familieschandaal had veroorzaakt, dat op Helgoland niet onopgemerkt is gebleven. En vanaf dat moment zal ik wel op dezelfde zwarte lijst hebben gestaan als die ontspoorde spruit van hem.'

'En Herzfeld heeft je weer van die lijst gehaald?' vroeg Linda.

Ze sloeg een punt van het tapijt om en begon het lijk van de rechter uit te pakken. Ender schraapte zijn keel opnieuw en kuchte. Blijkbaar vond hij het onaangenaam om over het verleden te praten.

'Meer dan dat. Anderhalf jaar geleden heeft iemand hier zelfmoord gepleegd. Een patiënte, die ik regelmatig buiten in haar rolstoel heb rondgereden. Na haar hersenbloeding kon ze niet meer lopen. In elk geval heb ik me om haar bekommerd. De mensen die me niet mochten, maakten me uit voor een Anatolische erfenisjager. En uiteindelijk was ik inderdaad als laatste met haar op het terrein gezien, voor ze zich met rolstoel en al van de klip stortte.'

'Werd jij daarvan verdacht?' vroeg Linda ten overvloede.

Ender wuifde haar woorden weg, alsof hij het er verder niet

over wilde hebben, maar zei toen: 'Alleen de geneesheer-directeur verdacht me. Voor hem was ik Ender Bin Laden. Staatsvijand nummer één.'

Linda trok aan het losse eind van het tapijt en vroeg Ender op te passen dat het lijk bij het afrollen niet van tafel viel. Haar aanpak was ongetwijfeld onorthodox en onhandig, *maar verdomme, Paul, meer kun je van een striptekenaar niet verwachten.*

'En Herzfelds obductie heeft je vrijgepleit?' vroeg ze. Het lijk was al een slag om zijn as gedraaid, maar was nog helemaal in het tapijt gehuld.

'Beter nog,' antwoordde hij. 'Paul heeft de afscheidsbrief van de vrouw op de oever gevonden.' Ender keek haar veelbetekenend aan. 'Dat was eigenlijk helemaal niet zijn taak, de plaatselijke politie had er met de pet naar gegooid. Maar het liet hem niet los. Toen iedereen mij al op de korrel had, ging hij er nog eens alleen op uit en vond de brief, die me vrijpleitte.' Hij glimlachte. 'Daarvoor ben ik Paul eeuwig dankbaar, en daarom help ik hem met deze waanzin en hoop...'

Ender kwam er niet meer aan toe zijn zin af te maken. De plotseling invallende duisternis slokte zijn laatste woorden en de hele sectiezaal op.

29

ZARRENTIN

De stank was niet te harden. De aanblik van de wriemelende maden die uit de oogkassen puilden was gruwelijk. En de schreeuw van Herzfeld, die zich eindelijk had vermand en het doek van het vormloze lijk had weggetrokken, weerkaatste schril van de kale wanden van de eetzaal. Toen begon hij te lachen.

Allejezus nog aan toe...

'Godzijdank,' zei Ingolf, maar de blijdschap stond niet zo duidelijk op zijn gezicht te lezen als bij de professor. De stagiair wees naar de kop van het kadaver dat Herzfeld zojuist had blootgelegd. 'Ik denk dat deze symboliek niet al te lastig te interpreteren is.'

Herzfeld knikte. 'Voor Martinek ben ik een walgelijk varken.'

En vermoedelijk heeft hij gelijk. Misschien heb ik zijn dochter inderdaad voor de tweede keer vermoord omdat ik me destijds aan de voorschriften heb gehouden.

'Ik ben een varken,' herhaalde hij fluisterend.

'Fijn,' neuzelde Ingolf, die zijn neus stevig met zijn vuist had omklemd. 'Nu we dit hebben opgehelderd, maakt het u vast niets uit als we ons naar een ruimte begeven die wat minder olfactorische gewenning vereist? Hallo?'

Herzfeld negeerde hem; hij liep langzaam om de tafel heen. 'Sven Martinek was gespecialiseerd in rituele moorden,' zei hij nadenkend, meer tegen zichzelf dan tegen Ingolf.

'En dat wil zeggen?'

'Hij was een meester in symboliek. Een tandenstoker in het haar van een dode, post mortem geknipte teennagels, een emmer tapijtreiniger naast een lijk – hij herkende het patroon en meteen ook de relevante aanwijzingen achter elke schijnbaar nog zo absurde daad. Als hij niet zo'n briljante patholoog-anatoom was geweest, had hij ook forensisch psycholoog kunnen worden.'

'Ik snap nog steeds niet waarom dat ons ervan weerhoudt de frisse lucht in te gaan.' Ingolf wipte ongeduldig van het ene been op het andere, alsof hij naar de wc moest.

'We moeten niets overhaasten,' zei Herzfeld vermanend en hij ging op zijn hurken zitten om het rottende varkenskadaver uit een ander perspectief te bekijken.

Ingolf kreunde. 'U overweegt toch niet serieus het beest aan een autopsie te onderwerpen?'

Herzfeld maakte een afwerend gebaar en stond erop. 'Nee. Waarschijnlijk is dat tijdverspilling. Martinek was zeer nauwgezet, hij heeft altijd vaste procedures gevolgd, dus zullen we de belangrijke aanwijzingen alleen in menselijke lijken vinden.'

'Denkt u soms dat die hier ook ergens liggen?' Ingolf werd nog bleker.

'Ik weet niet waar de wegwijzers ons zullen brengen.'

Hopelijk niet naar Hannah.

'Wegwijzers?'

'Ja, natuurlijk.' Herzfeld keek Ingolf kort in de ogen voor hij zich weer naar de tafel toe draaide. 'De bijl, het geld, de astmaspray – het heeft allemaal betekenis, net als de hitte, het sectierapport en het kadaver.'

'En?'

'We hebben iets over het hoofd gezien. Denk na, Von Appen. Wat zijn wij op het terrein het eerst tegengekomen?'

'Sneeuw.'

Herzfeld fronste geïrriteerd zijn wenkbrauwen. 'Ik heb het over de rubberlaarzen.'

Hij oogstte een argwanende blik. 'Bedoelt u dat die ook iets te betekenen hebben?'

'Alles heeft een reden,' citeerde Herzfeld Martinek, die in de sectiezaal altijd met aforismen had gestrooid als hij iets vreemds had ontdekt.

Het is geen toeval dat die laarzen mij passen.

'En wat betekenen die lelijke stappers dan?' wilde Ingolf weten.

'Dat is precies de goede vraag.'

Herzfeld draaide zich om naar de erker achter de tafel en gebaarde Ingolf hem te volgen. Toen hij zo dicht bij het raam naar de tuin stond dat de ruit door zijn adem besloeg, hief de professor zijn arm op en wees naar buiten.

'Die staan voor plassen, regen, nattigheid, voor water in het algemeen.' Hij wees naar een klein botenhuis aan de oever van het meer, dat onder aan de glooiing van het besneeuwde terrein lag. Een vaal lichtschijnsel schemerde door de gaten in het karton waarmee het enige raam van de grijze houten schuur was afgedekt.

30

Het was de werkkamer van een bezetene. Herzfeld was er niet zeker van of Martinek het had gedecoreerd om bewust de volgende aanwijzing te geven, of dat zijn collega de laatste paar weken compleet mesjogge was geworden.

Het enige wat nog aan de oorspronkelijke bestemming van het botenhuis herinnerde, was een oude roeispaan naast de ingang. Voor de rest leek de vierkante ruimte, waar vroeger ooit roeiboten, reserveonderdelen, schoonmaakmiddelen en zeildoek lagen opgeslagen, op een bizar oord voor rituelen.

Het eerste wat je bij binnenkomst zag was de schrijn. Die stond achter in de schuur, voor een metalen rolluik dat vermoedelijk op het meer uitkwam en waardoor de boten naar binnen en naar buiten konden.

De foto met Martineks dochter Lily, die probeerde veertien verjaardagskaarsjes in één keer uit te blazen, stond in het centrum van het kleine, door kerstboomlichtjes omzoomde altaar. Het was de enige lichtbron in de ruimte, afgezien van de oplichtende led van de kleine elektrische olieradiator. In tegenstelling tot de enorme ventilatorkachels in het huis was deze verwarming op de laagste stand gezet en voelde je alleen wat warmte als je er vlak naast stond.

Herzfeld zette een stap dichterbij en bekeek de talloze persoonlijke snuisterijen die Martinek als aandenken aan zijn dochter om de foto had gerangschikt. Op de houten richel van het altaar lagen een scholierenkaart, een opbergdoos voor een beugel, een briefkaart, pennen, snoepgoed, knikkers en een pluchen ezel, die tegen Lily's communiekaars aan leunde. Die was pas voor een derde opgebrand. Herzfeld stelde zich voor hoe Martinek hier had geknield en de kaars had aangestoken om eenzaam en alleen om de dood van zijn dochter te rouwen. Op deze plek moest zijn woede over het vonnis hem hebben vergiftigd.

Hier heeft hij het plan opgevat om me met gelijke munt terug te betalen. Mij te laten merken hoe het is om je dochter te verliezen.

'Beetje morbide,' mompelde Ingolf achter hem. Daarmee bedoelde hij niet de schrijn, maar de foto's. Ze waren overal. Op de planken, de stellages, zelfs tegen het plafond van het botenhuis had Martinek de opnames met een pneumatische nietmachine vastgemaakt. Op de meeste was Sadler te zien, heimelijk gefotografeerd van grote afstand, op de dag waarop hij uit de gevangenis was ontslagen. Hoe hij in de ingang van een u-Bahn verdween. Bij het openmaken van zijn voordeur. Op een paar foto's zag je de kinderverkrachter in zijn vrije tijd, bij een bezoek aan een videotheek, transpirerend op een loopband, genomen vanuit het gebouw dat tegenover de fitnessstudio moest liggen. Op één foto nam Sadler met een innige omhelzing afscheid van een tiener op een speelplaats. Veel foto's waren vergroot; vooral die waarop de moordenaar lachte.

Een doodgewone lach, dacht Herzfeld en hij pakte een grofkorrelige opname. *Niets waarvoor je je kinderen kunt waarschuwen.*

Hij zag de datum op de rand van de foto. Het kiekje was pas een paar weken geleden gemaakt, getuige de sneeuw op het trottoir.

Martinek had een enorme klus geklaard. Mogelijk had hij de moordenaar van zijn dochter vierentwintig uur per dag geschaduwd, misschien zelfs dagen achtereen.

Geen wonder dat je doorgedraaid bent, Sven.

Temeer daar Martinek drieënhalf jaar had moeten wachten om deze foto's te kunnen nemen.

'Waarom bent u eigenlijk het doelwit van zijn wraak?' vroeg

Ingolf op zijn typische hoogdravende manier. Hij hield een krantenartikel omhoog dat hij op de grond had gevonden. Het moest door de wind op de vloer zijn gewaaid toen ze het botenhuis binnenkwamen. In de kasten stonden stapels met kisten vol uitgeknipte krantenberichten, die op het eerste gezicht allemaal over de verkrachter en kindermoordenaar gingen.

Herzfeld keek in Ingolfs richting en werd door een lichte reflectie in de kast achter de stagiair afgeleid. Langzaam liep hij langs hem heen, schoof een schoenendoos met foto's opzij en kneep zijn ogen samen. De letters op de sticker waren in de schaduw lastig te lezen, daarom droeg hij zijn vondst naar de schrijn.

'Ik bedoel, zou Martinek zich niet eerder met die Sadler moeten bezighouden dan met u?' hield Ingolf aan.

Herzfeld knikte, toen zei hij: 'Ik ben er zeker van dat mijn collega dat stadium van wraak allang achter zich heeft gelaten.'

'Hoe komt u daar zo bij?'

'Omdat ik het bewijs nu in mijn hand heb.' Hij reikte Ingolf het glazen potje aan dat hij net uit de kast had gehaald.

Ingolf las het opschrift hardop voor: *Jan Erik Sadler.*' Herzfeld huiverde toen hij de tweede voornaam van de moordenaar hoorde.

'Is dat wat ik denk dat het is?' vroeg Ingolf en hij keek vol afkeer naar de inhoud van het glas.

'Een menselijke tong,' bevestigde Herzfeld en hij pakte zijn telefoon. 'Ik laat Linda weten dat we het raadsel van Eriks identiteit in elk geval hebben opgelost.'

31

HELGOLAND

Aan. Uit. Pauze. En weer aan.

'Wat is hier aan de hand?' vroeg Linda toen ze even iets kon zien. Toen ging het licht weer uit.

'Misschien de noodstroomvoorziening.' Ender fluisterde bezorgd, alsof hij het onheilspellende licht-donkerstaccato waaraan ze opeens waren blootgesteld nog erger zou maken als hij op normaal volume zou praten.

Of Ender denkt dat we niet meer alleen zijn.

'Kan zijn dat het aggregaat het begeeft.'

De huismeester klonk niet erg zeker van zijn zaak. Tijdens de laatste lichtfase was Ender naar de lichtschakelaars bij de deur gelopen, die hij nu de een na de ander uitprobeerde – zonder resultaat.

Aan. Uit. Pauze.

Grandioos, een lichtorgel in de sectiezaal.

Linda overwoog of ze haar plaats naast de sectietafel met Töven niet beter kon verlaten en zich met een van beide messen zou bewapenen, die drie meter verder op de bijzettafel lagen. Ze kreeg kippenvel.

Het luide gekraak was nog onaangenamer dan de steeds terugkerende inktzwarte duisternis. Elke keer als het licht uitviel, klonk het alsof de ruggengraat van een monster op zijn plaats werd geduwd. De geluiden kaatsten van de betegelde muren tegen de roestvrijstalen tafels en mengden zich met een onaangenaam, elektrostatisch gezoem.

'Waar ga je heen?' vroeg Linda. Het licht brandde weer drie seconden, en Ender stond al met één voet in de gang.

'Naar de kamer met de hoofdschakelaars. Ik ben zo terug.'

Ja hoor. Laat mij maar alleen in de disco van de duivel, dacht Linda en toen werd ze misselijk. Ze kon nauwelijks haar evenwicht bewaren. Ze had de fout gemaakt om naar de sectietafel te kijken toen de werklamp erboven even was aangegaan, en nu het weer donker was, danste de beeltenis van de dode rechter op Linda's netvlies. Toen ze het stoffelijk overschot op de tafel hadden gehesen, was het tapijt afgerold. Inmiddels lag het lichaam helemaal bloot.

Friederike Tövens lijk lag op de buik, haar rok tot over haar heupen naar boven geschoven, zodat er nu vrij uitzicht was op de gescheurde en met bloed doordrenkte katoenen onderbroek...

... en op de stok. Shit, Ender, kom terug alsjeblieft!

Linda kneep haar ogen stijf dicht om de details niet te hoeven zien, maar het haalde niets uit. De aanblik van de afgebroken bezemsteel, die tussen de brede dijen direct uit de schaamstreek van de rechter stak, had zich in haar bewustzijn geprent – en wel tot in alle eeuwigheid, vreesde Linda.

Het licht floepte weer aan, een seconde maar, en ze voelde een onweerstaanbare drang om te braken. De oorzaak van het massale bloedverlies was duidelijk: de moordenaar had Friederike Töven gespietst.

Boing.

Ze verstijfde van schrik. Dit keer had het geluid waarmee de lampen uitgingen een ander karakter. Luider, met een langere echo, maar zonder gekraak.

Waarschijnlijk had Ender de hoofdschakelaars bereikt en het aggregaat helemaal stilgezet, want ze hoorde het zoemen van de airconditioning niet meer, en het bleef donker.

Maar nu begon het ergens te rinkelen.

Linda's blik dwaalde naar het zwakke groene schijnsel dat

boven Eriks lijk danste. De huistelefoon van de kliniek zat nog steeds in de gereedschapsgordel aan de lamp en rinkelde elke seconde luider.

Ze bewoog zich op de tast naar de andere sectietafel, en toen ze die bereikt had, gebeurde er een aantal dingen razendsnel achtereen: eerst verstomde het gerinkel, en met het display doofde ook het laatste restje licht. Ze hoorde een kletterend geluid, dat haar aan vroeger deed denken, toen ze haar moeder had geholpen het afgewassen bestek in de keukenla te sorteren. En toen de telefoon boven de buik van het lijk opnieuw tot leven kwam, ontsnapte haar een hoge, schelle kreet – vanwege een aanraking, die aanvoelde als een koude kus in haar nek.

32

'Ik kan haar niet bereiken.'

Herzfeld keek naar Ingolf, die met zijn handen in zijn zij pein-zend voor het altaar stond dat Martinek ter nagedachtenis van zijn dochter in het botenhuis had opgesteld.

De nagedachtenis van een waanzinnige.

'Hebt u dit al gezien?' vroeg de student. Eigenlijk had Paul de kliniek weer willen bellen, maar nu kwam hij met zijn telefoon in zijn hand nieuwsgierig dichterbij. 'Dat is de foto van Lily.'

'Dat bedoel ik niet.'

Ingolf tilde het smalle tafelkleed op waarop Martinek de kost-baarheden had uitgestald die hem aan zijn dochter moesten her-inneren – *souvenirs van de dood,* schoot het door Herzfelds hoofd –, waardoor de communiekaars begon te wankelen.

'Voorzichtig,' zei hij. Hij wilde de kaars vasthouden, toen hij het toetsenbord zag dat Ingolf had blootgelegd.

Het morbide altaar was om een laptop heen gebouwd, bedekt met lappen en servetten, die voor de oppervlakkige beschouwer onzichtbaar was. Lily's foto in A4-formaat was niet op een hou-ten paneel vastgemaakt, zoals Herzfeld had gedacht, maar op een platte computermonitor.

Opeens hoorde hij zacht gezoem, toen begon het beeld van het lachende meisje spookachtig van kleur te veranderen.

'Er zit nog leven in de laptop,' constateerde Ingolf. Herzfeld legde zijn telefoon naast de computer, hij ademde op zijn van kou verstijfde vingers en trok de foto los van de monitor, die hun gezichten met een koud, blauw licht bescheen.

Er verscheen een vakje waarin je een wachtwoord moest intypen. Zonder na te denken typte Herzfeld de voornaam van Martineks dochter in, en het volgende moment zag hij het bureaublad van een pc. De desktop zag er bijzonder sober uit, bijna leeg. Naast de gebruikelijke pictogrammen voor tekstverwerkings- en mailprogramma's, browsers en een belastingprogramma, waren er geen opvallende bestanden of snelkoppelingen die de moeite van het openen waard leken, temeer omdat Herzfeld geen idee had waarnaar hij op de harde schijf zou moeten zoeken.

'Kijk eens in de geschiedenis,' suggereerde Ingolf en Herzfeld volgde zijn slimme advies op door bij 'Onlangs geopende items' in het startmenu de namen van de bestanden te bekijken die Martinek de laatste tijd had geopend.

Het verbaasde hem niet dat hij maar één enkele vermelding vond; te oordelen naar de extensie ging het om een video:

•••*seethetruth.mp4*•••

'Zie de waarheid?' vertaalde Ingolf, terwijl Herzfeld zich weer voelde als een paar minuten geleden, toen hij op het punt had gestaan de doek van de vleesklomp af te trekken.

En helaas was hij ervan overtuigd dat het dit keer geen varkenskop was die hij te zien zou krijgen.

Martinek had de video de laatste paar weken een aantal malen bekeken en bewerkt.

De klok tikt.

In weerwil van het stemmetje in zijn hoofd dat hem waarschuwde het niet te doen, klikte Herzfeld op het bestand en keek naar wat er op het scherm veranderde.

Het duurde geruime tijd tot er in het grijze venster, dat niet groter was dan een YouTubevideo, iets te zien was.

Je zag meteen dat het een amateuristische opname was: over-belicht, onscherp en bewogen, maar de getoonde beelden waren er niet minder intens om, hoewel je eerst moest raden wat de camera precies registreerde. Pas toen de opnames wat scherper werden, kwam de oplossing van het raadsel.

'Voeten?' veronderstelde Ingolf. Hij vroeg Herzfeld de video groter te maken, maar blijkbaar had de videoplayer geen moge-lijkheid van weergave op een volledig scherm. Wel was het moge-lijk het beeldscherm van het toetsenbord af te halen, zoals Herz-feld zag toen Ingolf twee hendels aan de zijkant van de laptop bediende en hem de losse monitor aanreikte. Intussen was op de video een vrouwenlichaam te zien, het gezicht had de cameraman buiten beeld gelaten.

Gladde, jeugdige huid; naar lengte en postuur te oordelen een meisje tussen dertien en zeventien jaar oud.

Om zich voor de gruwelijke video af te sluiten, was Herzfeld in zijn professionele autopsieroutine vervallen.

Ze ligt in een geopende lijkenzak op een tafel die gelijkenis ver-toont met die in de eetkamer van het herenhuis. Haar heupen zijn smal; geschoren of geëpileerde bikinizone, geen bijzondere uiterlijke kenmerken, afgezien van een tatoeage op de linkerenkel, verdomme...

De tatoeage rukte Herzfeld los uit zijn rol van neutrale waarne-mer en maakte hem weer tot angstige vader.

Is dat Hannah?

Hij kende die tatoeage niet, maar dat hoefde niets te bete-kenen. Misschien had ze die kortgeleden laten aanbrengen. En bovendien, hoe zou hij op een slechte, op het formaat van een bierviltje afgespeelde video zijn dochter hebben kunnen identifi-ceren?

Opeens was het lijk van het meisje niet meer het enige in beeld. Martinek, die er kennelijk niet voor terugschrok zijn gezicht te laten zien, ging voor de camera staan en keek droevig in de lens. In de ene hand hield hij een scalpel, in de andere iets wat er eerst uitzag als een ijzeren staaf maar zich vervolgens als het eind van een bezemsteel ontpopte. Herzfeld kon een paar inkervingen in het hout onderscheiden, die Martinek met het mes in de stok moest hebben gekrast.

'En nu?' vroeg Ingolf naast hem, toen de opname afgelopen leek te zijn, want het beeldscherm in Herzfelds handen was weer zwart. Even was er alleen sneeuw te zien, maar toen ging de opname verder vanuit een ander perspectief. Martinek had het statief waarop de camera stond gedraaid, zodat het nu opzij van de tafel stond. Je kon zien hoe hij de borstkas van het meisje opensneed.

'Nee!' riepen Ingolf en Herzfeld bijna gelijktijdig, als bioscoopbezoekers die sidderen van angst voor de volgende horrorscène, met het verschil dat de steeds grotere wond geen special effect was.

Ik hou van je, papa,' hoorde Herzfeld zijn dochter in gedachten zeggen en hij wilde zich afwenden, omdat hij, als hij dan tussen twee kwaden moest kiezen, liever onwetend zou sterven dan te moeten zien hoe Martinek het lichaam van zijn dochter opensneed. Maar dat was niet nodig. De opname stopte voordat het scalpel de navel van het meisje had bereikt.

'Wat doet hij?' vroeg Ingolf. Voor de volgende serie opnames had Martinek de camera zelf ter hand genomen. De witte lijkenzak zat weer dicht en was aan de buitenkant hier en daar met bloed besmeurd. Op een snijplank aan het hoofdeind van de tafel lagen de uit de jonge vrouw verwijderde organen, en pas nu was, dankzij een korte camerabeweging naar de vloer, te zien dat de hele ruimte met een waterdicht zeil was bedekt.

Tot dan toe had Martinek zonder geluid gefilmd, maar nu hoorde je geritsel van plastic, toen de forensisch arts de lijkenzak over de tafel trok. Martinek legde de camera even neer om zijn handen vrij te hebben, en in een ondersteboven gefilmd fragment kon Herzfeld in een hoek van het beeld zien dat zijn voormalige collega de zak in een gereedstaande kruiwagen tilde. Toen kwam de volgende scène, en er volgde een beeldwisseling naar buiten.

'Hij brengt haar hierheen, naar het botenhuis,' zei Ingolf ten overvloede. Martinek moest de camera aan een riem om zijn nek hebben gehangen, want het toestel bevond zich ter hoogte van zijn borst en filmde vanuit dat perspectief het gedeelte van de tuin achter het herenhuis inclusief het botenhuis, de steiger en het meer.

Afgezien van de hijgende ademhaling en het knerpen van de sneeuw was er op de schommelende video-opname niets te horen. Het wiel van de kruiwagen had de steiger, die het bevroren meer in stak, bereikt.

'Wat is hij van plan?' mompelde Ingolf net toen Herzfeld met beeldscherm en al de loods uit liep. Buiten was het grijs maar nog niet donker, en daarom was het voor hem geen probleem de actie op het scherm te volgen en zich tegelijk in de omgeving te oriënteren, om de opnames met de huidige situatie te vergelijken. De steiger lag drie meter naast het botenhuis. Er bevond zich een smalle trailerhelling op de oever, waarlangs rietstengels als vingers boven de sneeuw uitstaken.

Toen hij dichterbij kwam zag Herzfeld een klein VERBODEN TE BETREDEN-bordje aan een paal, dat hij negeerde, net als Martinek op de video deed.

Op de opname had zijn collega het eind van de steiger al bereikt. Het water moest op dat moment hoger hebben gestaan; Martinek hoefde maar een kleine stap omlaag te zetten of hij stond al met de kruiwagen met lijkenzak op het ijs.

Vanaf dat moment liep de opname ononderbroken door. Martinek beende doelgericht met gelijkmatige stappen het meer op, terwijl de schommelende camera voortdurend gericht bleef op het besneeuwde ijs en delen van de lijkenzak.

'Is dat een boei?' vroeg Ingolf en hij drong zich langs Herzfeld heen toen ook zij aan het einde van de steiger waren gekomen en zich voor hen alleen nog de ijsvlakte van het meer uitstrekte. De sporen van de kruiwagen waren niet meer zichtbaar. Hierbuiten, ruim twintig meter van de oever, waaide de wind nog harder en sneed als een scalpel in de vingers waarmee Herzfeld de monitor vasthield.

'Zou kunnen.' Hij kon niet onderscheiden wat er ongeveer in het midden van het meer in de schemering op de ijsvloer stond. Het licht was ten tijde van de video-opname heel wat beter geweest dan nu, maar op de camera was het donkere object niet te zien.

'Ik ga even kijken,' zei Ingolf, en voor Herzfeld hem kon tegenhouden, stapte hij van de rand op het ijs.

'Wacht nog even,' wilde hij roepen, maar toen had de stagiair zich al glibberend in beweging gezet.

'De zon is bijna onder,' riep hij. Zonder zich om te draaien wees hij naar boven, naar het gesloten, grijszwarte wolkendek. 'Nog een paar minuten en we zien hier geen steek meer.'

'Blijf staan!' waarschuwde Herzfeld opnieuw en hij wilde het beeldscherm al op de steiger leggen om Ingolf te volgen, toen Martineks stem hem weerhield.

'Hallo, mijn beste.'

Het klonk hartelijk, bijna plechtig; er lag een weemoedige ondertoon in de opname, en daarom wist Herzfeld dat de woorden niet aan hem waren gericht, nog voor hij de grote hand van de andere man zag, die in beeld verscheen. Er volgde een lange, ferme handdruk.

'Ziet eruit als een kruis,' hoorde hij Ingolf roepen, maar Herzfeld had alleen oog voor de gebeurtenissen op het beeldscherm.

'Dus zo moet het zijn?' vroeg Martinek, nadat hij de hand van de onbekende weer had losgelaten.

De lichaam- en gezichtloze vriend zei geen woord. Vermoedelijk knikte hij, want nu pakte Martinek de kruiwagen weer, draaide hem negentig graden en tilde hem aan de handvatten op.

Herzfeld herinnerde zich de meldtekst van de voicemail. *'Hij vermoordt me als je niet precies doet wat hij zegt. Hij volgt je op de voet.'*

Had ze hem daarmee te kennen gegeven dat Martinek een medeplichtige had? Een partner, die op het moment dat de opname werd gemaakt naast Martinek stond en toekeek terwijl de lijkenzak langzaam van de kruiwagen gleed en met een zware plons in het zojuist uitgehakte wak viel?

'Nee,' schreeuwde Herzfeld, terwijl de zak in het zwarte water verdween.

Ik heb toch gedaan wat jullie wilden!

Ingolf, die er ten onrechte van uitging dat de schreeuw hem gold, bleef tien meter van de steiger staan.

'Wacht,' schreeuwde Herzfeld opnieuw en hij legde het beeldscherm op de planken van de steiger. Ingolf had het kruis bereikt.

'Je staat te dichtbij.'

'Wat doe ik?' vroeg Ingolf en toen gebeurde het.

Het kraakte zo hard alsof een jager aan de andere oever een geweer had afgevuurd, toen zakte Ingolf von Appen door het ijs, en hij zonk net zo snel de diepte in als vlak daarvoor de lijkenzak op de video.

33

Ondanks de bijna Siberische kou was het ijs nog niet dik genoeg, wat kon liggen aan de warme stromingen in het meer waarover Martinek hem ooit enthousiast had verteld. Anders kon Herzfeld niet verklaren waarom het ijs onder Ingolfs gewicht was bezweken. Tergend langzaam verstreken de seconden waarin de stagiair onder water bleef.

'Help,' schreeuwde Herzfeld, terwijl hij voorzichtig op handen en voeten naar de scherpe rand van het wak kroop. Het meer en de oever waren uitgestorven, redding was niet in zicht, en toch wilde hij niets onbeproefd laten om de aandacht te trekken. Hij tastte naar zijn telefoon.

Verdomme, ik heb hem op de schrijn laten liggen.

Wanhopig vroeg Herzfeld zich af of hij genoeg tijd had om over de steiger naar de oever en het botenhuis terug te rennen, om daar naar dingen te zoeken die hij bij zijn reddingspoging zou kunnen gebruiken: zijn telefoon, een touw, de roeispaan of een ladder waarop hij kon liggen om zijn gewicht beter over het ijs te verdelen. Hij besloot het niet te doen.

Als medicus wist hij dat er bij iemand die in ijskoud water is beland meteen een ademhalingsreflex optreedt, die op zichzelf al tot dood door verstikking vanwege verkramping van de stembanden kon leiden. Ingolf was beslist in shock vanwege de kou, en met elke seconde die verstreek zou het hem meer moeite kosten zijn spieren te bewegen. Mocht het hem desondanks lukken zich op eigen kracht naar de oppervlakte te worstelen, en er zou niemand in zicht zijn, dan zou de stress hem definitief de das omdoen. Herzfeld slaagde er al nauwelijks in om niet in paniek te raken.

Hij dacht dat zijn handen vast zouden vriezen, elke keer als hij ze tegen het ijs aan duwde wanneer hij zich vooruit bewoog. Maar de pijn in zijn gezwollen vingers werd tenminste verdoofd door de kou.

Hij bewoog een paar meter verder naar opzij en schoof in een scherpe hoek met de steiger naar de plek waar hij Ingolf het laatst had gezien.

'Ingolf,' schreeuwde hij een paar keer achtereen. Hij was bang naar beneden te kijken, omdat hij verwachtte dat er elk moment een gezicht onder de ijsvloer kon opduiken; die angst was tenminste ongegrond, want opeens hoorde hij luid geplons. Ingolf was weer aan de oppervlakte gekomen, roeide met zijn armen en zoog gretig lucht naar binnen.

'Hé, hier. Achter je.'

De student hoorde hem niet. En helaas deed hij bij zijn hulpeloze poging om zichzelf te redden alles fout wat je maar fout kunt doen: hij verspilde zijn krachten aan de kant van het wak die van de oever af lag, waardoor hij geen oogcontact had. Bovendien probeerde hij zich op de rand af te zetten alsof het een zwembad was, in plaats van zichzelf op zijn buik of zijn rug uit het water te manoeuvreren. Maar waaraan had hij zich moeten vasthouden? Het ijs waarop hij houvast zocht, brak af, wat ertoe leidde dat het gat steeds groter werd. En Herzfelds uitgestrekte arm was uit het zicht en buiten bereik.

'Ingolf, wacht!' schreeuwde hij uit alle macht. Tegelijk hoorde hij het onder zich kraken, en bad tot God dat hij zijn gewicht beter had verdeeld dan Ingolf. Hij tijgerde inmiddels als een grondsoldaat op het wak af.

'Rustig, niet bewegen,' brulde Herzfeld en eindelijk was hij zo dichtbij dat Ingolf hem hoorde. De stagiair draaide zich om zonder zijn bedrieglijke houvast aan de getande rand van het gat op te geven. Zelfs de kleine beweging van zijn hoofd leek hem oneindig veel moeite te kosten. Herzfeld zag zijn gezicht en dacht daarin al de eerste voorbode van de dood te zien: de lichtblauwe verkleuring van de gezichtshuid en lippen was bijna identiek aan die van de lijken op zijn sectietafel. 'Kerkhofrozen,' hadden de oude forensische artsen dat genoemd.

'Maak je geen zorgen, ik haal je eruit,' beloofde hij, zonder een flauw idee hoe hij het moest aanpakken.

Ingolf haalde moeilijk adem en keek hem met grote ogen aan. Zijn eerder zo accuraat met gel gemodelleerde haar lag nu als zeewier over zijn voorhoofd. Hij klappertandde.

'... spijt me,' bracht hij uit.

'Pak mijn arm,' beval Herzfeld energiek. Lang zou Ingolf zichzelf niet meer boven water kunnen houden.

'Lukt het u om iets dichter naar mij toe te komen?'

Herzfeld betwijfelde het, maar Ingolfs leven hing ervan af dat hij zich om zou draaien. Als Herzfeld zou proberen rond het gat naar de plek toe te kruipen waar Ingolf zich zo goed en zo kwaad als het ging boven water hield, zou hij zelf door het ijs dreigen te zakken of veel te veel tijd verliezen.

'... weet... niet,' steunde Ingolf en hij draaide zich nog om en strekte nu ook een arm uit, maar begreep zelf ook dat het zo niet kon lukken. De afstand was gewoon te groot als hij zich niet zou afzetten en naar de andere kant zou zwemmen.

Ingolf probeerde het. En faalde.

Hij was niet tot ook maar één zwembeweging in staat, zijn spieren waren als verlamd door kou en uitputting, en binnen een seconde was hij onder water verdwenen.

'Nee,' schreeuwde Herzfeld. Hij bracht zichzelf in levensgevaar door zich ver vooraver te buigen en als een kind dat een vis wil vangen met zijn blote handen in het ijzige water te slaan. In de schemering zag de oppervlakte van het water eruit als olie.

Herzfeld had gehoopt dat de student tenminste nog zijn hand

omhoog zou steken, maar daartoe ontbrak hem de kracht. Toch was de actie van de professor niet vergeefs, want hij kreeg Ingolf aan zijn haar te pakken, wat voldoende was om hem weer naar de oppervlakte te trekken. Zodra hij het hoofd boven water kon houden, tastte Herzfeld naar de schouders, tot hij eindelijk een arm had gevonden.

'Blijf ademen, hoor je?' schreeuwde hij. Doordat hij Ingolf met een hand bij zijn haar en met de andere aan zijn bovenarm had gepakt, kon hij weliswaar niet meer zinken, maar ook niet uit het water worden getrokken.

Oké, denk na. Herzfelds hersens werkten op volle toeren, en intussen spoorde hij Ingolf aan er de moed in te houden; hij had nog wel zijn ogen open, maar maakte een allengs apathischer indruk. Door de volgezogen kleren en de ontbrekende spierkracht in zijn lichaam voelde Ingolf aan als een levend lijk. Maar hij probeerde tenminste nog te communiceren.

'Het lukt... me... niet,' mompelde hij vermoeid.

'Jawel, echt waar. Niet opgeven, je kunt het.'

Maar hoe dan, verdomme?

Herzfeld voelde hoe ook bij hem de kou steeds dieper in zijn huid sneed naarmate hij langer op zijn buik lag. Sommige delen van zijn bovenlichaam waren gevoelloos, andere brandden als vuur. Bovendien sloeg er steeds meer ijswater over de rand, en ook zijn kleren raakten nu doorweekt.

'Niet flauwvallen, hoor je?'

Ingolf had nog niet het bewustzijn verloren, maar zijn bewegingen werden steeds trager, als de onbewuste bewegingen van iemand die droomt. Zijn vingers werden slap en dreigden zich los te maken van die van Herzfeld.

Herzfeld beet zijn tanden op elkaar, verslapte zijn greep en nam het risico dat de student weer onder water zou verdwijnen, wat snel een vergissing bleek te zijn. Want nog voor Herzfeld zijn laatste wanhopige plan kon uitvoeren en zich op zijn zij kon draaien, was Ingolf hem opnieuw ontglipt, en dit keer schoof hij met zijn hoofd vooruit onder het ijs.

34

Het licht in de sectiezaal was weer aan, maar dat maakte de zaak er niet beter op. Het gevaar dat Linda voelde was als radioactiviteit. Onzichtbaar en toch alomtegenwoordig.

Nog steeds brandde haar huid op de plek waar iemand haar in het donker had aangeraakt. Nog steeds voelde Linda de aandrang wild om zich heen te slaan, zoals ze een paar minuten geleden had gedaan.

Toen het licht was uitgevallen.

Toen ze zich in het wilde weg in de duisternis had geprobeerd te verdedigen, had ze alleen de tafel met instrumenten geraakt, die met veel kabaal omviel nadat ze er in een vluchtreflex tegenaan was gelopen. Ze was met tafel en al op de grond beland.

Het was een oorverdovende herrie geweest, die nog steeds naklonk in haar oren. *Geen geluid ter wereld kan angstaanjagender zijn,* had Linda gedacht, tot ze het gekraak had gehoord – het typische geluid van leren zolen op een harde ondergrond.

Linda had aan haar vader moeten denken, die weinig geld aan kleren uitgaf, maar voor schoenen een uitzondering maakte: *'Want aan zijn schoenen is te zien hoe stevig een man in het leven staat, meisje.'*

En te horen hoe dichtbij een moordenaar in het donker is.

Het gekraak was eerst zachter geworden, toen kwam het weer terug, en Linda had er niet lang bij stilgestaan hoe ze zich moest gedragen. Angst is als een slecht gedresseerde vechthond, die je niet aan de lijn kunt houden als hij bloed ruikt. Hij rukt zich los, oncontroleerbaar en intens als een natuurkracht zodra je voelt dat de dood nabij is, en in die extreme situatie zijn er maar twee mogelijkheden: aanvallen of vluchten. Linda koos voor het laatste. Zonder op te staan was ze al zittend naar achteren geschoven. Weg, weg van de knerpende schoenen, die steeds dichterbij kwamen... *ver, ver weg...* tot ze niet meer verder achteruit kon, omdat ze met haar rug tegen de verwarming aan stootte. Op dat moment ongeveer verdween het geluid. In de sectiezaal heerste diepe stilte. Zelfs het elektrostatische gezoem van de lampen was verdwenen.

'Kijk een man niet in de ogen; kijk naar zijn voeten als je zijn karakter wilt zien.'

Er kwam nog een herinnering bij Linda op, dit keer aan een citaat van haar moeder, die nu waarschijnlijk de boterhammen smeerde die haar vader elke zaterdag bij het sportprogramma voor de televisie verorberde.

Waarom ben ik zo weinig bij hem gaan zitten, schoot haar door het hoofd, met een mengeling van wanhoop en melancholie; een onzinnige gedachte in een surrealistische situatie: alleen, in diepe duisternis zittend tussen twee lijken op de vloer van een stilgelegde pathologische afdeling.

En toen had ze de aftershave geroken. Dezelfde aftershave als gisteren op het kussen in haar bed. O god, was dat echt gisteren pas gebeurd? Het enige verschil was dat de geur zich vandaag met die van de lijken op de sectietafels mengde.

Danny?

Ze had de reflex onderdrukt om de naam van haar stalker hardop te schreeuwen, hoewel ze zeker wist dat degene die hier met haar in de sectiezaal was precies wist waar hij zijn slachtoffer kon vinden. Met haar hand op haar mond en met ingehouden adem had ze op de geluiden gelet, die nu niet meer te horen waren, maar de geuren werden intenser, hoewel dat ook verbeelding kon zijn geweest; een zinsbegoocheling, veroorzaakt door de archaïsche angst voor het onzichtbare. Haar knieën begonnen te beven, zo sterk dat haar linkerbeen zich strekte voor ze het kon bedwingen, en daarom was ze er niet zeker van of zij het was geweest of de onzichtbare man die het mes met de voet had aangeraakt.

Vanaf dat moment verloor ze alle voorzichtigheid uit het oog en probeerde bij het wapen te komen.

Ze verplaatste haar gewicht naar haar knieën, tastte in het donker met haastige, ongecoördineerde bewegingen over de vloer naar het mes en sneed zich in de muis van haar hand toen ze het eindelijk aan het lemmet te pakken kreeg, maar dat kon haar op dat moment weinig schelen.

'Pak het met je vuist beet, zoals een dolk,' had Herzfeld haar daarnet aangeraden, en zo hield ze het nu ook vast. Hier, op dit moment, nu het licht precies in deze seconde was aangegaan, toen ze net wilde uithalen om te steken omdat ze zeker wist dat het gezicht van haar aanvaller maar een paar centimeter van het hare af was. Maar toen het uiteindelijk zover was, toen het licht weer aanging, was het gevaar verdwenen.

Niets.

Geen leren schoenen. Geen aftershave. Geen Danny.

Niemand.

Ze was alleen met de geur en de doden en haar angst, die maar niet minder wilde worden en die – sterker nog – alleen maar toenam toen ze na een tijdje voor het eerst weer naar de vloer keek.

Op het eerste gezicht zou ze niet kunnen zeggen waarom haar maag zo samentrok, tot ze de fout in het plaatje zag: beneden, op de tegels, lagen twee pincetten, een schaal, rubberen handschoenen en andere benodigdheden voor de autopsie. Haar mes hield ze in haar hand, daarom kon dat niet tussen de wirwar van instrumenten liggen.

Maar waar was het tweede mes?

Linda bukte zich kort, even maar, uit angst dat ze de deur waardoor het gevaar de zaal moest hebben verlaten, te lang uit het oog zou verliezen, maar ze kon het niet vinden. Het tweede autopsiemes was verdwenen, net als de huismeester, die er verrekte lang over deed om van de hoofdschakelaars terug te komen.

Verdomme, Ender, waarom ben je er steeds niet als ik je nodig heb, dacht Linda nog; toen hoorde ze hem opeens met zijn laarzen door de gang sloffen.

'Ender?' riep ze opgelucht, omdat ze dacht zijn voetstappen te herkennen, al leken ze dan wat langzaam. Haar opluchting sloeg om in blijdschap toen hij inderdaad in de deur verscheen.

'Godzijdank!' Ze wilde hem al verwijten dat hij haar zo lang alleen had gelaten, *alleen met het onzichtbare gevaar*, toen ze het tweede autopsiemes ontdekte.

Het stak uit Enders hals.

35

ZARRENTIN

Met elke stap liet Herzfeld het wak in het ijs verder achter zich. Hij wist dat hij niet mocht stoppen, niet pauzeren, want als hij eenmaal tot stilstand zou zijn gekomen, zou hij zichzelf nooit meer in beweging kunnen zetten, nooit meer tegen de pijn in zijn armen en benen en tegen de kou kunnen vechten. En hij zou het veilige botenhuis nooit bereiken, maar uitgeput op de steiger in elkaar zakken en doodvriezen.

Samen met Ingolf.

'Volhouden,' zei hij hijgend, meer tegen zichzelf dan tegen de last op zijn schouders. Hij droeg Ingolfs slappe lichaam als een zak kolen; zijn jas had hij als nutteloze ballast op de plaats des onheils achtergelaten. De zoon van de senator was gelukkig niet zo zwaar als zijn lengte deed vermoeden, maar alleen al de tegenwind maakte de tocht tot een beproeving. Herzfelds jas, zijn broek, zijn schoenen – alles was doorweekt van het ijskoude water en dreigde vast te vriezen op zijn huid als ze niet maakten dat ze uit deze polaire windtunnel wegkwamen. Het botenhuis lag nog zo'n tien meter verderop en dus onbereikbaar ver weg.

Herzfeld had nooit geweten dat kou zoveel pijn kon doen; nu pas begreep hij de berichten over bergbeklimmers die een paar passen van hun basiskamp waren doodgevroren in de sneeuw. Hij zag de houten hut, wist dat de beschutting binnen bereik was, en toch had hij het bijna onweerstaanbare verlangen gewoon op de grond te gaan liggen en het hoofd in de schoot te leggen.

'... aaapen.'

'Wat?'

Ingolf kreunde, vermoeid als hij was, iets wat als 'slapen' had geklonken, maar misschien had Herzfeld zich vergist.

'Niet opgeven!' bracht hij uit. Ook al kostte elk woord hem moeite, hij moest Ingolf wakker zien te houden. Anders zou alle moeite vergeefs zijn geweest. Hij mocht niet wegzakken.

Niet nu. Niet nu we al zo ver zijn gekomen.

De stagiair was daarnet volledig onder het ijs verdwenen en dus eigenlijk reddeloos verloren geweest als Herzfeld niet op het nippertje zijn schoen te pakken had gekregen, juist op het moment dat hij zich op zijn zij had willen draaien, om met zijn andere hand zijn broekriem los te maken.

Mijn riem, waarom heb ik daar niet eerder aan gedacht?

In de stresssituatie bij het wak had Herzfeld zich er het hoofd over gebroken hoe hij aan een pikhouweel, een ladder of een zak kon komen, en intussen had hij de reddingslijn die hij om zijn heupen droeg bijna vergeten.

Uiteindelijk was het hem niet alleen gelukt om zijn broekriem uit de lussen te trekken zonder Ingolf los te laten, bovendien was hij erin geslaagd hem om de enkel van de drenkeling te leggen. Vanaf dat moment moest alles razendsnel zijn gegaan. Zo snel dat Herzfeld zich de afzonderlijke handelingen niet meer kon herinneren die er ten slotte toe hadden geleid dat Ingolf, naar adem happend als aangeschoten wild, gekromd naast hem op het ijs had gelegen. Het was duidelijk dat het ijs niet onder zijn reddingspoging was bezweken, hoewel Herzfeld naar de andere kant van het gat had moeten kruipen, zodat de riem in het verlengde van Ingolfs been zou liggen en hij de student op zijn buik over de rand kon trekken.

'Zijn er zo,' hijgde Herzfeld, en inderdaad zou het onder normale omstandigheden geen drie seconden hebben geduurd. Het werd hem zwart voor ogen, zijn bevroren, om warmte en rust schreeuwende spieren weigerden dienst en deden hem op de laatste, steile meters voor de loods wankelen. Alleen het feit dat ze de deur daarnet niet achter zich hadden dichtgetrokken voorkwam dat het ergste gebeurde. Anders zouden Ingolf en hij voor de ingang in elkaar zijn gezakt, maar nu struikelden ze het botenhuis in, als een liefdespaar dat geen seconde meer kan wachten, en vielen samen op de grond.

Gelukt. Bijna.

De plotselinge windstilte was een godsgeschenk. Geen herrie in zijn oren, geen klauwen meer die in zijn huid sloegen en, dankzij de radiator, een kamertemperatuur vlak boven het nulpunt. Aan de andere kant – Ingolf lag als een natte zak dwars over hem heen en benam hem de adem.

Herzfeld dacht niet dat hij nog tot enige krachtsinspanning in staat was, maar ten slotte had hij geen andere keus dan onder de student vandaan te kruipen, als ze dit tenminste wilden overleven. Vooral Ingolf moest zo snel mogelijk uit zijn natte kleren, anders was een longontsteking nog het minste wat hem te wachten stond. Herzfeld bleef een tijdje op handen en knieën staan en probeerde in deze positie tot bedaren te komen.

Zijn tanden klapperden nog steeds luid, en de pijn in zijn spieren was door de warmte eerder erger dan minder geworden, want nu begon zijn bloedsomloop langzaam op gang te komen, en dat voelde alsof er een legioen mieren door zijn aderen kroop.

Toen de flitsen voor zijn ogen verdwenen en zijn ademhaling iets kalmer was, pakte hij het snoer van de olieradiator en probeerde de verwarming naar zich toe te trekken. Zodra het apparaat onder handbereik was, zette hij de blazer op de hoogste stand en schoof het ding naar Ingolf, die eruitzag of hij met een epileptische aanval kampte. Hij rilde over zijn hele lichaam.

'We moeten het huis weer in,' zei Herzfeld en hij probeerde Ingolfs hemd open te knopen. De jongen zag eruit als een geest, zijn lippen waren tot een nauwelijks zichtbare donkerblauwe streep gereduceerd. Zijn lichaamstemperatuur moest extreem laag zijn, maar hij leek tenminste geen water in zijn longen te hebben gekregen, omdat Herzfeld hoorde dat zijn jachtige ademhaling niet vergezeld ging van verdachte borrelende of klokkende geluiden.

Als hij erin zou slagen Ingolf van zijn kleren te bevrijden voordat ze allebei van uitputting in slaap zouden vallen, zouden ze het misschien redden.

Herzfeld trok Ingolfs knopen met een ruk van zijn hemd, omdat het met zijn trillende ijskoude vingers niet anders ging.

'Meteen bij het eerste afspraakje al?' fluisterde de stagiair; hij schoof zijn hand opzij. Zijn poging tot een grijns verzandde in een grimas.

Herzfeld schudde resoluut zijn hoofd. 'Dit is niet het moment voor valse schaamte.'

Ik heb waarachtig wel genoeg naakte mensen gezien. De meesten waren dood, net als jij straks als die kleren niet snel uitgaan.

Maar Ingolf wilde zich onder geen beding laten uitkleden en weerde Herzfeld steeds fanatieker af, terwijl hij zo ver overeind kwam dat hij met zijn rug tegen de verwarming kon leunen.

'Dat lukt me zelf ook wel,' zei hij, wat nauwelijks te verstaan was, omdat Herzfelds telefoon ging. Ingolf tilde zijn wijsvinger op en wees naar de schrijn, waarop het rinkelende mobieltje vibrerend ronddraaide.

Herzfeld knikte. Hij kroop op handen en voeten naar de stellingkast, en trok zichzelf op aan de planken.

'Hallo?'

Hij moest zijn telefoon met beide handen vastgrijpen en tegen zijn oor drukken om hem niet te laten vallen. De stem aan de andere kant was zo luid en doordringend dat zelfs Ingolf hem kon horen. Hij keek geschrokken op en staakte zijn pogingen zich uit zijn overhemd te worstelen.

'Wat zeg je daar?' vroeg Herzfeld ontzet in de eerste pauze die Linda in haar woordenstroom liet vallen. Hij voelde zich weer net zo vertwijfeld als een paar minuten eerder op het ijs.

'Hoe kon *dat* nou gebeuren?'

Linda was er met haar nauwelijks verstaanbare, hysterisch uit-gespuwde woorden in geslaagd zijn toch al ijzige binnenste verder te verkillen. Om er zeker van te zijn dat hij haar niet verkeerd had begrepen, vroeg hij nog eens: 'Ender is dood?'

36

'Geen idee,' riep Linda in de telefoon en terwijl ze naast hem knielde, voelde ze nog eens de pols van de huismeester, die met zijn rug tegen de muur en uitgestrekte benen bij de schuifdeur lag. 'Het licht ging uit, Ender was weg, het licht ging weer aan en hij stond voor me. Met het mes in zijn nek.'

Inderdaad kon ze alleen nog het lichtblauwe rubberen handvat zien. Het leek erop dat Ender van achteren was aangevallen en zich op het laatste moment naar zijn aanvaller had omgedraaid. Het mes stak scheef in zijn hals en was van opzij, zo'n twee centimeter van zijn nek, binnengedrongen. Zo te zien was het nergens naar buiten gekomen.

'Maar Ender kon nog lopen?'

Herzfeld klonk vermoeid, bijna onverschillig, en Linda vroeg zich af of de professor misschien had gedronken. Ze had de indruk dat hij zich op elk woord moest concentreren. 'Twee stappen, toen is hij in mijn armen in elkaar gezakt. Wat moet ik nou doen?'

Verdomme, Paul, je hebt me alleen laten weten hoe je mensen opensnijdt, niet hoe je ze moet repareren.

'We hebben geen andere keus, je moet meteen hulp halen,' hoorde ze hem zeggen.

'Hoe dan? Er zijn geen artsen meer op het eiland, voor zover ik weet tenminste. Bovendien ben ik als de dood dat de moordenaar terugkomt.'

Ze moest aan Danny denken, aan de vochtige handdoek, aan de dode kat in haar wasmachine en de video's die hij van haar had gemaakt terwijl ze sliep, en vroeg zich af hoe de gekte van haar verleden met de waanzin van het heden samenhing. Hoe langer ze erover nadacht, des te erger beefde de hand waarmee ze de telefoon vasthield.

'Kun je je daarbeneden insluiten?' vroeg Herzfeld.

'Al gebeurd. Enders sleutel zit aan de binnenkant. Als die gek niet door de ventilatieschacht komt of zo zijn we veilig, maar ik weet niet hoe lang Ender het nog volhoudt.'

'Ademhaling?'

'Geen idee, hij beweegt niet.'

'Pols?'

Ze duwde haar wijs- en middelvinger tegen Enders halsslagader en wist niet of ze wel iets voelde.

'Als die er is, dan is hij heel zwak.'

'Bloed?'

'Weinig.'

'Wat betekent weinig?' Herzfeld klonk alsof hij geen lucht kreeg, of ook hij een mes in zijn hals had.

'Er zit wat bloed op zijn overall, maar het spuit nergens uit.'

'Dan hebben we misschien geluk...'

'GELUK?'

'... en zijn er geen belangrijke bloedvaten geraakt. Als hij nog kon lopen, lijkt het ruggenmerg intact te zijn.'

Als hij nog leeft, tenminste.

'Ik weet niet, hij is echt lelijk toegetakeld, Paul.'

Linda voelde onder haar haargrens een zweetdruppel naar beneden komen, en dat herinnerde haar weer aan Danny en de littekens die hij met zijn zuuraanval had veroorzaakt.

Verdomme, Clemens. Je hebt gezegd dat je hem zou aanpakken. En nu?

Linda kreunde en veegde met haar vlakke hand het zweet van

haar voorhoofd. 'Zal ik het mes eruit trekken?'

'Onder geen beding. Hij mag zich ook niet bewegen! Hou hem warm, wikkel dekens om hem heen en...' Te oordelen naar de geluiden op de lijn opende Herzfeld, waar hij ook mocht zijn, een krakende houten deur en liep hij naar buiten. Het laatste deel van zijn zin werd compleet overstemd door de bulderende wind.

'En wát?' vroeg ze, terwijl ze opstond en erover nadacht hoe ze aan warme dekens kon komen zonder de sectiezaal uit te gaan.

'Geef me vijf minuten!' Herzfeld klonk nu niet alsof hij had gedronken, maar alsof hij pijn verbeet, het leek of het telefoongesprek een loodzware last voor hem was waaronder hij algauw zou bezwijken. De gierende wind op de achtergrond werd steeds luider.

'Alles oké bij jou?' vroeg Linda, maar ze kreeg geen antwoord meer.

'Shit, ik praat tegen je!' brulde ze, hoewel ze wist dat de professor het gesprek gewoon had afgebroken. Omdat ze merkte dat haar gebrul hielp tegen de opkomende paniek, ging ze door met in de telefoon schelden, tot haar stem het begon te begeven.

'En wat moet ik nu beginnen, achterlijke klootzak?'

Er waren beslist dekens en kussens in overvloed in het ziekenhuis. *Alleen niet hierbeneden in de lijkenkelder.*

Haar ogen dwaalden naar een rood-groen pictogram boven de wastafel. IN GEVAL VAN NOOD RUSTIG BLIJVEN, adviseerde het bordje in drukletters. Linda lachte hysterisch.

Dat kan alleen een idioot hebben geschreven die nog nooit een echte noodsituatie heeft meegemaakt.

'Rustig blijven, baarlijke nonsens.'

Geldt dat ook voor stalkingslachtofers die zich met een opengesneden waterlijk, een gespietste rechter en een stervende huismeester op de afdeling Pathologie van een stilgelegde kliniek voor een psychopaat moeten verstoppen?

Ze keek naar de sectietafels. Opeens voelde ze zich doodmoe.

De geestelijke inspanningen van de laatste uren hadden het uiterste van haar gevergd. Linda onderdrukte een geeuw, en toen schoot haar de brancard te binnen waarmee ze de rechter de sectieruimte in hadden gerold.

De matras. Precies!

Ze ging naar de brancard en trok haastig het hoeslaken van de matras. De stof rook weliswaar muf maar was redelijk schoon; het moest voorlopig toereikend zijn.

'Iets warmers heb ik jammer genoeg niet,' fluisterde ze Ender in zijn oor nadat ze het laken een paar keer had dubbelgevouwen en het over hem had uitgespreid. Daarna trok ze de latex matras van de brancard en schoof hem met enige moeite naar de deur. Herzfeld had weliswaar gezegd dat Ender niet mocht worden verplaatst, maar aan de andere kant kon hij ook niet zo lang op de koude tegels blijven liggen.

Als hij de kou tenminste nog voelt, dacht Linda, en vanaf dat moment werd alles erger.

Om te beginnen sperde Ender zijn ogen open, hapte naar lucht, en Linda kreeg al hoop, toen de levensgeesten hem van het ene op het andere moment weer verlieten. En dit keer, leek het, definitief.

Alle lucht ontsnapte uit de longen van de huismeester, als uit een opengesneden autoband. Enders laatste woord was: 'Help!' Toen was er van zijn ogen alleen nog het wit te zien, voordat hij letterlijk instortte.

'Nee, niet doen. Je mag niet doodgaan!' wilde Linda schreeuwen, maar ze bracht niet meer uit dan verstikt gekras, en dat was misschien haar geluk.

Als ze haar wanhoop luid had uitgeschreeuwd, had ze zich vermoedelijk verraden en zou ze niet zijn gewaarschuwd door het geluid: iemand stond achter de deur van de sectiezaal en stak een sleutel in het slot.

37

O nee, hij draait mee.

Van haar ouders, trotse bezitters van een eigen huis, had Linda geleerd altijd de sleutel aan de binnenkant te laten zitten.

'Dat biedt bescherming tegen inbrekers. Je weet nooit wie er stiekem een kopie van de sleutel heeft laten maken,' preekte haar moeder tot vervelens toe, voordat ze elke avond voor het slapengaan de voordeur controleerde. Inderdaad was het bij haar ouders onmogelijk geweest binnen te komen als het slot van binnenuit was geblokkeerd. Maar wat destijds in een rijtjeshuis aan de rand van de stad had gewerkt, bleek hierbeneden op de afdeling Pathologie een nutteloze veiligheidsmaatregel. Voor Linda was er maar één verklaring: de schuifdeur moest met een veiligheidsslot zijn uitgerust, waarbij het niet uitmaakte of iemand van binnenuit het sluitmechanisme blokkeerde of niet.

Wie het ook was daarbuiten, het was duidelijk dat hij de sleutel van de sectiezaal had en hem zonder problemen kon gebruiken.

Want hij draait rond, verdomme.

De cilinder van het slot bewoog met de wijzers van de klok mee, en daarmee de sleutel aan Enders sleutelring, waarmee Linda een paar minuten geleden de schuifdeur met twee slagen had dichtgedraaid.

Wat moet ik nou doen?

Als verlamd staarde ze naar de langzaam draaiende cilinder. Het liefst had ze geschreeuwd en zich tegen de handgreep van de deur schrap gezet. Tegelijk was er iets in haar wat zich ertegen verzette om zich kenbaar te maken en kracht te verspillen.

Dus dan maar vechten?

Ze keek naar het autopsiemes op de grond, dat ze had laten vallen toen Ender in haar armen in elkaar was gezakt. Het lag maar een paar centimeter naast het dijbeen van de huismeester, in wie nu geen greintje leven meer leek te zitten.

Ik ben alleen, realiseerde Linda zich op dat moment in paniek. *Alleen in de sectiezaal!*

Voor haar geestesoog verscheen een plaatje uit een comic – ze zag zichzelf in een tekening met een spreekballon boven haar hoofd, waarin een engeltje en een duiveltje ruzie met elkaar maakten.

'*Ik kan toch niet in mijn eentje met een moordenaar vechten!*'
'*Wie zegt dat het een moordenaar is die achter de deur staat?*'
'*Wie anders?*'
'*Geen idee. Misschien iemand die je wilt helpen?*'
'*O ja. Zoals hij Ender, Erik en de rechter heeft geholpen?*'

Linda vocht haar innerlijke strijd uit, terwijl voor haar ogen de sleutel in het slot steeds verder ronddraaide. De persoon die hier naar binnen wilde nam er uitgebreid de tijd voor, alsof hij geen geluid wilde maken en zo stilletjes mogelijk binnen wilde komen.

Nog een draai van driehonderdzestig graden en de matglanzende stalen deur kon probleemloos open worden geduwd.

'*Door iemand die te hulp komt.*'
'*Door mijn moordenaar!*'

Ze wist dat ze nog maar weinig tijd had – en dat ze iets moest ondernemen, anders zou haar de beslissing uit handen worden genomen.

Afwachten? Vechten? Of...?

Linda koos voor het *of* en rende naar de kast tegenover de sectietafels. Halverwege draaide ze zich nog een keer om, griste het mes van de vloer en haastte zich weer naar de koelvakken, waarin de overleden patiënten werden bewaard.

Er waren er maar twee; vermoedelijk verwachtte het kleine eilandziekenhuis niet meer sterfgevallen tegelijk.

Tja, zo zie je maar, een mens kan zich vergissen.

Linda opende een van de vakken en trok zo zacht mogelijk de rails met het platform eruit.

Snel, sneller...

Zonder na te denken stopte ze het heft van het mes tussen haar tanden, trok zich op aan de bovenkant van het lijkenkoelvak en werkte zich met haar voeten vooruit de schacht in. Daar ging ze op haar rug liggen en trok zichzelf, met haar handpalmen stevig tegen de metalen wanden van de schacht aan gedrukt, met platform en al, als een bobsleeër die in zijn slee springt, *het donkere hol in.*

38

Net als de hele uitrusting in de sectiezaal was ook het lijkenvak nieuw en ongebruikt. Linda drukte tegen het deurtje dat ze net achter zich had dichtgetrokken, en constateerde opgelucht dat ze het ook van binnenuit kon openen. Net zo opgelucht was ze over het feit dat het koelvak blijkbaar niet op het circuit van het noodaggregaat was aangesloten. Het was vreselijk klein, maar tenminste niet koud.

Zal ik hier ook de sleutel vanbinnen laten zitten, mammie, dacht ze toen het luik definitief dichtzat, en ze moest zichzelf dwingen om daar in het donker niet in een hysterische lachbui uit te barsten.

Pas nu merkte ze dat ze het heft van het mes nog steeds tussen haar tanden geklemd hield. Ze pakte het en hield het tegen haar borst, haar vingers vast om het heft.

Hij komt!

Ze hoorde een langdurig, slepend geluid, daarna voetstappen. De geluiden die tot haar doordrongen klonken gesmoord, maar waren toch verbazend goed te horen, wat waarschijnlijk lag aan het feit dat haar gehoor in de koude duisternis, die geen andere waarnemingen toeliet, scherper was dan anders. Het leek of de indringer vlak voor het koelvak stond en zwaar ademde, wat haar in een soort shocktoestand bracht. Ze hield er rekening mee dat het luik elk moment kon worden opengerukt en ze oog in oog zou staan met de moordenaar.

Met moeite bedwong Linda haar impuls de deur op een kier te zetten om tenminste een glimp van de persoon te kunnen op-vangen die nu met slepende tred door de sectiezaal dwaalde. Nu leek hij zich weer van het koelvak te verwijderen, en paradoxaal genoeg deed dat haar angst toenemen, omdat ze ten onrechte veronderstelde dat de waanzinnige een aanloop nam om haar uit haar schuilplaats te trekken.

Verdomme, waar ben ik nu weer in verzeild geraakt? Twee lijken, eentje door mij half opengesneden, het andere met een stok in haar anus en een huismeester met een autopsiemes in zijn hals. En ik zit hier vast in een lijkenkoelkast!

Ze moest denken aan het bloed in de afvoerbak, sporen van een gevecht, instrumenten op de grond – de in de gereedschapsgordel vastgeklemde huistelefoon, die boven het opengesneden lijk bungelde, zou in haar nachtmerries opduiken, net als het gekreun toen de bedorven lucht uit het lichaam van Friederike Töven ontsnapte.

Op het moment bleven haar dergelijke gruwelijke geluiden bespaard, en Linda wist niet zeker of het een goed of een slecht teken was dat het buiten het koelvak opeens doodstil was geworden op de afdeling Pathologie.

Geen hijgen, geen slepend geluid. Geen voetstappen of gerammel met sleutels.

'Hij is weg,' zei het duiveltje, nadat ze een tijd lang geen vin had verroerd.

'En hoe kom jij aan die wijsheid?'

'Als hij had geweten dat jij hier in de val zit, had hij je er allang uit gehaald.'

'Goed punt.'

'Zeg ik toch. Weg hier.'

Linda haalde diep adem, ze legde haar handen tegen de binnenkant van het luik achter haar hoofd en wilde het al behoedzaam openen, maar aarzelde.

Binnen ben ik veilig. Buiten zal ik sterven.

Ze wist zelf hoe dwaas die gedachte was, net zo lachwekkend

als de veronderstelling van een klein kind dat het onzichtbaar is zolang het zijn hand voor zijn ogen houdt.

Maar hierbinnen, in de met staal omgeven duisternis, voelde ze zich minder kwetsbaar. Het was een fragiele bescherming, een cocon, die ze niet wilde verlaten omdat ze bang was dat zodra ze de deur opendeed, niet alleen de lijkengeur zich weer meester van haar zou maken, maar ook de angst.

Koude, naamloze, verlammende angst voor de moordenaar die al die lijken op zijn geweten had: Erik, Töven. En misschien Ender. Voor de waanzinnige die het eiland en waarschijnlijk ook de kliniek onveilig maakte. En voor Danny.

Het liefst had ze gehuild bij de gedachte dat misschien een en dezelfde persoon verantwoordelijk was voor de doodsangst die haar teisterde: één persoon, die Herzfelds dochter had ontvoerd, de lijken had geprepareerd en Ender een mes in de hals had geramd.

Maar waarom?

Linda beet op haar onderlip, probeerde al haar moed te verzamelen, en vatte het rinkelen van de telefoon uiteindelijk op als het teken om haar schuilplaats te verlaten – zonder te vermoeden dat er zich een paar meter van haar vandaan een man in de aardedonkere zaal tussen de sectietafels verborg.

39

ZARRENTIN

De tweede etappe was nog zwaarder dan de eerste, en al die tijd was Herzfeld er zeker van dat ze het nooit zouden halen, en dat hoewel hij de kortste route had gekozen.

Ingolf, met wie het in het botenhuis met de minuut beter was gegaan, had voor de Porsche gepleit: 'Standkachel... staat aan... stoelverwarming... hem meteen smeren.'

Maar Herzfeld had voet bij stuk gehouden en was op weg gegaan naar het huis, wat uiteindelijk de beslissing bleek te zijn die hun het leven redde, want Ingolf had zichzelf overschat. Met zijn ontblote bovenlichaam, waaromheen hij provisorisch de vilten deken had gewikkeld die bij wijze van isolatie tegen de deur gespijkerd had gezeten, had hij op eigen kracht geen twee stappen kunnen zetten. Hij zakte door zijn knieën zodra ze de beschutting van de loods hadden verlaten. Herzfeld hees Ingolf opnieuw op zijn rug en moest hem meermalen neerzetten voor ze de tuindeur van het herenhuis hadden bereikt.

Vergeleken met eerder, bij hun aankomst, was het inwendige van het pand merkbaar afgekoeld, maar in de eetzaal heersten nog steeds tropische temperaturen, wat eerst een weldaad, maar in tweede instantie een kwelling bleek te zijn. Het bloed zette uit in hun aderen, en Herzfeld moest op zijn tong bijten om het niet uit te schreeuwen van de pijn. Het was paradoxaal. Vlak daarvoor had hij nog gedacht dat hij zou bevriezen. Nu verlangde hij alweer naar frisse lucht, zozeer spande zijn huid zich door de plotselinge warmte. Toch had Herzfeld, zodra hij ertoe in staat was, de blaaskachel in de eetzaal aangezet, hoewel daardoor ook de stank van het ontbindende varken weer door de lucht werd gemengd. Hun lichaam had dringend behoefte aan warmte, ook al voelde het niet zo.

'Bedankt,' zei Ingolf na een tijdje, zonder Herzfeld aan te kijken. Hij moest luid spreken om boven de herrie uit te komen.

Ze hadden zich allebei helemaal uitgekleed en knielden nu, gehuld in de warme wollen dekens die Herzfeld in een kist in de gang had gevonden, al een tijdje bij de kachel.

Herzfeld schudde zijn hoofd.

'U hebt me het leven gered.' Ingolf glimlachte mat, toen slikte hij. 'Tjonge jonge, ik had nooit gedacht dat ik dat versleten cliché zelf nog eens zou gebruiken.'

Herzfeld wilde iets terugzeggen, maar het kostte hem moeite zich te concentreren. Tijdens de korte tocht naar het huis had hij alleen gedacht aan overleven. Nu dwaalden zijn gedachten weer af naar Hanna. En naar Linda.

Hij keek naar de eettafel, waarop zijn telefoon lag.

'Maar het klopt,' hoorde hij Ingolf volhouden. Zijn stem was veranderd. Hij klonk dof en werd schor. 'Ik sta diep bij u in de schuld.'

Herzfeld wierp hem een fletse blik toe en bleef nog tien seconden in de buurt van de warme luchtstroom staan, voor hij het erop waagde naar zijn mobieltje op tafel te kruipen.

'Je staat pas bij me in de schuld als je niet ophoudt als een acteur in een derderangssoap te klinken,' zei hij en hij stond op.

Ingolf glimlachte weer. 'À propos acteur. Heeft iemand u eigenlijk ooit gezegd dat u eruitziet als die arts, hoe heet hij ook...'

'Stop!' onderbrak Herzfeld hem ruw, maar met een schertsende ondertoon in zijn stem.

'Nee, zo heette hij niet,' zei Ingolf, in een poging grappig te zijn. 'Maar u hebt gelijk, het begint met een s.' Hij giechelde te luid en te lang voor zo'n zouteloze dialoog, en ook Herzfeld was het liefst in lachen uitgebarsten; niet omdat hij het zo leuk vond, maar om van het beklemmende gevoel af te komen dat hij had sinds ze aan de dood waren ontsnapt. In tegenstelling tot Ingolf ontbrak hem de energie voor overbodige emoties. Hij moest zich er volledig op concentreren de eettafel te bereiken zonder over zijn deken te struikelen.

Hannah, dacht hij toen de stank van het ontbindende kadaver weer sterker werd, nu hij dichter bij de tafel kwam.

Onderweg voelde Herzfeld pas hoe uitgeput hij was. De warmte was nu aangenamer en deed niet meer zoveel pijn, maar nu had ze het effect van een slaapmiddel. Gelukkig had hij niet de typische apathie van veel koudeslachtoffers, die langzaam de geest geven als hun onderkoeling niet tijdig wordt behandeld. Als de lichaamstemperatuur eenmaal onder een kritische waarde is gezakt, zijn alle ventilatorkachels ter wereld zinloos.

Herzfeld voelde zich stijf, alsof hij overal in zijn lichaam spierpijn had, maar dat was het beste bewijs dat hij deze dag zou overleven. Mensen die bevriezen, stond in de leerboeken, voelen vanaf een bepaald moment geen enkele pijn meer. Integendeel, ze ontwikkelen blijkbaar in hun door de meest uiteenlopende hormonen en neurotransmitters gebombardeerde hersens zoiets als een laatste euforie vlak voor hun dood.

Maar wie weet dat nou zeker, dacht Herzfeld en hij pakte zijn telefoon, die door het trilalarm bijna van tafel schoof.

Hij dacht dat er vermoedelijk nooit een overledene was teruggekeerd om zich voor medisch onderzoek aan te melden, en wilde opnemen – toen hij merkte dat dat niet mogelijk was.

Geen oproep.

Zijn piepende mobieltje herinnerde hem aan een afspraak.

NAAR PERSONEELSZAKEN
(Vechtpartij)

Hij zette het alarmsignaal uit en de afspraak verdween net zo snel van het display als uit zijn bewustzijn. Slechts een paar uur geleden had hij zich nog zorgen gemaakt om zijn baan, maar dat was nu van geen belang. Het enige wat ertoe deed was zijn dochter. Als het Hannah niet was geweest die Martinek onder het ijs in het meer had laten zakken – dus als ze nog leefde – dan had hij de volgende aanwijzing voor haar verblijfplaats misschien in het lijk van de rechter aangebracht.

Herzfeld drukte op de herhaaltoets om Linda in de kliniek te bellen.

Nadat de telefoon minstens twintig keer was overgegaan, ging de kiestoon over in een snelle bezettoon, en hij probeerde het nog eens. En nog eens.

Met elke nieuwe poging nam zijn wanhoop toe. Hij hoorde Ingolf hoesten en zijn neus ophalen, maar die geluiden leken van ver te komen, alsof hij niet meer in dezelfde kamer was.

Neem op. Alsjeblieft, Linda, neem op!

Hij stond op het punt op te hangen en de telefoon door de eetzaal te smijten, toen er eindelijk werd opgenomen.

'Linda?' riep hij zo hard dat Ingolf achter hem schrok.

En ritselde iets.

'Hallo, hoor je me?' vroeg Herzfeld.

Iemand kuchte in de hoorn. Herzfeld was er niet zeker van of het lachen of hoesten was. Maar het geluid volstond om hem te laten weten dat het niet Linda was die had opgenomen.

Het was een man.

En te oordelen naar de bezettoon die Herzfeld nu weer hoorde, had de onbekende opgehangen.

40

Linda's hart stond stil.

Niet in overdrachtelijke zin, zoals weleens wordt gezegd als iemand schrikt, maar letterlijk. Haar hartkleppen hielden er even mee op, haar bloedsomloop kwam tot stilstand, en voor het eerst in haar leven had Linda de symptomen van een aanval van claustrofobie.

Doorgaans had ze geen moeite met hoogtes of benauwde ruimtes. Ze hield van sporten die de meeste mensen als extreem beschouwden: parachutespringen, duiken in grotten, bungeejumpen. Het idee in een lift vast te zitten bezorgde haar geen nachtmerries. Maar sinds de telefoon in de sectiezaal voor het eerst had gerinkeld, had ze het gevoel alsof ze in een stortkoker voor vuilnis zat, waarvan de wanden zich langzaam maar zeker naar elkaar toe bewogen. Tegelijk steeg de druk binnen in haar, ze voelde zich alsof er een manchet steeds strakker om haar hart spande naarmate de telefoon langer ging.

En dat terwijl ze zichzelf bij het horen van de eerste beltoon eindelijk had vermand, klaar om uit haar schuilplaats te klimmen. Maar Linda had de deur van het koelvak nog niet op een kier gezet, of haar ergste vrees werd bewaarheid: ze werd besprongen. Door de stank. Door de geluiden. Door de angst.

De indringer was er nog, en ze mocht van geluk spreken dat de telefoon hem had afgeleid en hij haar niet had gehoord. Verstijfd van ontzetting had ze naar de geluiden in de sectiezaal geluisterd en een vergeefse poging gedaan zichzelf voor de gek te houden: *Misschien droom ik dit allemaal maar? Misschien heb ik nooit een lijk gevonden, laat staan opengesneden? Ik lig niet in een koelcel voor een dode, maar in mijn bed?*

Was het maar waar, Linda zou er alles voor hebben overgehad; maar het was waarschijnlijk niet zo, anders zou het mes in haar hand niet zo echt aanvoelen.

Ze had haar duim tegen het lemmet geduwd en was er pas mee gestopt toen ze een scherpe pijn voelde.

Geen droom, inderdaad. Shit.

Linda had haar duim in haar mond gestoken, er als een baby op gezogen, het bloed geproefd en aan haar moeder moeten denken, die haar vroeger had getroost als ze bang was geweest in het donker.

'Sssj, er ligt niemand onder je bed, lieveling.'

'Nee, niet onder mijn bed, maar...'

... maar in de sectiezaal, daar kon geen twijfel over bestaan: wat ze had gehoord waren voetstappen geweest, niet het geluid van de ventilatie. Het waren lichtreflecties van een zaklantaarn geweest die door de zaal flitsten, het was geen zinsbegoocheling. Ze zat vast in een koelvak en niet in een of andere dagdroom.

Iemand, een persoon van vlees en bloed, had de telefoon opgenomen. Iemand had opgenomen en...

Gehoest!

Ze had het gehoord, iets tussen hoesten en lachen, alsof de man zich vrolijk maakte over de beller. Nu, een tijdje nadat hij zwijgend had opgehangen, hoorde Linda opnieuw het geluid van slepende voetstappen. Eerst hadden ze zich van de koelvakken verwijderd, maar nu kwamen ze langzaam naderbij.

Grote god, help, schreeuwde Linda, al was het dan in gedachten, en toen maakte ze de fout het heft van het mes, dat nat was van het zweet, aan haar broek af te vegen, om het in het uiterste geval beter vast te kunnen houden. Ongelukkig genoeg gleed het mes uit haar gevoelloze vingers en verdween kletterend tussen de spijlen van het platform.

Ze had niet lang de tijd om zichzelf verwijten te maken en erover na te denken of de onbekende iets kon hebben gehoord, want op dat moment werd de deur van haar schuilplaats opengerukt.

41

'Jij?'

Voor de zoveelste keer sinds Linda uit het koelvak was geklauterd vroeg ze zich af of ze hallucineerde. Ze was zo verbluft dat ze de lijkengeur even vergat.

'Ender?'

De zaklamp scheen niet meer direct in haar gezicht, maar naar het plafond, waardoor de hele sectiezaal in een spookachtig schemerlicht was gedompeld.

Nu Linda nog maar één stap van hem vandaan stond, moest ze haar hand tegen haar mond drukken om het niet uit te schreeuwen. Ender zag er luguber uit.

Net als de lijken op de roestvrijstalen tafels vertoonde ook de huismeester gelijkenis met een wassen beeld uit een gruwelkamer. Zijn lichte, warrige haar stond aan alle kanten van zijn hoofd af, zijn gezicht en handen waren net als zijn overall overdekt met bloed, en het heft van het sectiemes in zijn hals rees en daalde bij elke ademhaling.

'Hoe... Waarom... Voel je dan niet...?' begon ze keer op keer, niet in staat haar vragen af te maken.

Hoe is het mogelijk?

Ender haalde zijn schouders op en keek haar aan, meer verwonderd dan geschrokken. Hij opende zijn mond en wilde kennelijk iets zeggen, maar vanwege zijn verwonding kwamen er alleen nauwelijks verstaanbare klanken uit zijn mond.

Twee dingen waren zonneklaar: Linda had zich vergist – de huismeester was niet dood geweest, maar weggezakt in een diepe bewusteloosheid; en hij was in shock sinds hij weer bij kennis was. Ze moest aan een reportage over Irak denken, waarin over slacht- offers van zelfmoordaanslagen werd bericht. Een groenteman had na de explosie naar zijn zoontje gezocht en pas gemerkt dat zijn linkerarm er bij de schouder af was gerukt toen hij het kind onder het wrakhout van de marktkramen vandaan wilde trekken.

Ook Ender moest een dergelijk trauma hebben, anders was het niet te verklaren dat hij doodkalm voor haar stond en zich hoege- naamd niet over zijn situatie leek te verbazen.

Hij trok zijn wenkbrauwen op en zei met krassende stem iets wat klonk als: 'Wat is er aan de hand?'

Linda schudde ongelovig haar hoofd.

Ongelooflijk. Hij voelt het mes niet.

Blijkbaar produceerde zijn lichaam wagonladingen endorfine, die de pijn en bepaalde herinneringen onderdrukte.

'Ben... verkou...' neuzelde hij, terwijl hij zijn keel betastte.

Inderdaad, ja. Je hebt iets te pakken. Geen virus, maar een mes!

'Nee, niet doen!' riep Linda toen Ender aanstalten maakte zijn hoofd opzij te draaien, vermoedelijk om zijn stijve nekspieren los te maken. Hij wierp haar een vragende blik toe, alsof zij het was die met een autopsiemes in haar lijf voor hem stond, en niet om- gekeerd.

'Geen abrupte bewegingen,' zei ze tegen hem.

Linda wist niet zeker of ze de situatie niet zou verergeren als ze Ender op de hoogte zou stellen. Eén verkeerde draaibeweging, één foute stap en hij kon voor altijd verlamd zijn, zo niet erger. Aan de andere kant parelde er zweet op Enders voorhoofd, zijn handen trilden licht. Vroeg of laat zou de shock wegebben en de pijn terugkomen – en dan zou hij de situatie begrijpen. Linda moest er niet aan denken hoe Ender zou reageren als hij het mes in zijn hals ontdekte.

'We zijn overvallen,' begon ze, in een eerste poging hem de waarheid te vertellen.

'Wie?' bracht Ender uit. Met elk woord sprak hij iets verstaanbaarder.

'Ik denk door de persoon die ook deze mensen op zijn geweten heeft.' Ze wees in de richting van de sectietafels.

'Versjtopt?'

'Ja, ik heb me verstopt.'

Zo ongeveer.

Ender richtte de lichtbundel op de uitgang en de matras op de grond, daarna op de vloer, om Linda niet te verblinden. Intussen merkte hij dat de veters van zijn rechterlaars los waren gegaan. Hij wilde zich bukken.

'Nee, niet doen.'

'Wat?' vroeg Ender.

'De moordenaar heeft je ernstig verwond.'

Linda besloot tot een leugentje om bestwil. 'Ik ben bang dat je een schedelbreuk hebt of zo. Je moet rustig aan doen, je mag geen plotselinge bewegingen maken, niet bukken en jezelf al helemaal niet aanraken, hoor je? Zeker niet je nek of je hoofd.'

'Nek?' vroeg Ender, en toen was het te laat. Voor Linda het kon verhinderen had hij zijn arm al opgeheven en bij zijn poging zijn nek te betasten het heft van het mes aangeraakt.

'Wat in godsnaam...' waren zijn laatste, verbazend duidelijke woorden, voor hij begon te schreeuwen. Eerst geluidloos, met opengesperde mond, zoals een man die tegen zijn testikels is geschopt en bij de eerste golf pijn niet genoeg lucht krijgt om te schreeuwen. Vervolgens luid en diep uit zijn keel.

Linda's waarschuwingen ten spijt tuimelde hij zijdelings naar de wastafel naast de deur waarvoor hij daarnet nog had gelegen, en richtte de bundel van de zaklantaarn op de spiegel erboven.

'Voorzichtig,' riep Linda een laatste keer – tevergeefs.

Ender zag zijn spiegelbeeld en hij begreep wat hij daarnet met zijn vingers had aangeraakt. Zijn lippen vormden een verbaasde o. Hij knipperde, alsof er iets in zijn oog was gekomen, toen viel de zaklantaarn uit zijn hand. De lamp maakte een hol, krakend geluid toen hij op de tegels sloeg, vlak voor Enders verslapte lichaam omviel en hetzelfde deed.

42

'Dit is de versie met alle opties,' zei Ingolf met gesmoorde stem. Vanuit de passagiersstoel drukte hij op een knop aan het stuur. De motor sloeg aan. 'Honderdvijfendertigduizend euro catalogusprijs, dus rij alstublieft...'

'Voorzichtig, ja ja,' zei Herzfeld en hij ramde de versnellingspook in de achteruit en schoot met slippende banden achteruit de straat op.

'Stop!' riep Ingolf en hij hield zich vast aan de handgreep boven de deur. 'Niet zo snel!'

Herzfeld schakelde de wagen met een gierend geluid naar de eerste versnelling.

'En waarheen gaat de reis?' was Ingolfs terechte vraag.

Nu we weten wie er achter deze waanzin zit?

Herzfeld raasde over de provisorisch sneeuwvrij gemaakte weg het stadje uit en staarde met lege blik door de gedeeltelijk beslagen voorruit. Het was weer begonnen te sneeuwen.

Hij rilde van de kou, ondanks de standkachel en de stoelverwarming, maar lang niet zo erg als de senatorszoon naast hem.

Ingolf had last van regelmatig terugkerende koude rillingen, hij klappertandde aan één stuk door en hijgde onder het praten als een hond die uren in de zon heeft gelegen. Bovendien kon hij zijn opgezwollen vingers, die twee keer zo groot waren geworden als normaal, niet meer bewegen.

'We hebben veel te veel tijd verloren,' zei Herzfeld ontwijkend en hij accelereerde op een recht stuk.

Ze hadden het herenhuis al geruime tijd geleden achter zich gelaten, nadat hun ondergoed, dat ze op de pijp van de blaaskachel hadden gelegd, eindelijk droog was geworden. Ingolf droeg nu een donkerblauw trainingspak dat Herzfeld in een sporttas in de bagageruimte had gevonden, en had de warme deken omgeslagen die ze op het station met vooruitziende blik tegelijk met de proviand voor de reis hadden gekocht. Herzfeld had zijn jeans weer aangetrokken, hoewel die hier en daar nog vochtig was, maar hij riskeerde liever een longontsteking dan iets van Martineks spullen te dragen, de kleren van een ontvoerder.

Van een moordenaar?

'Ik heb de oplaadkabel nog eens nodig,' zei Herzfeld. Zijn stem klonk monotoon, afgemat van de gebeurtenissen die hen allebei tot de rand van de dood hadden gebracht. En tot een vermoeden zo verschrikkelijk dat alleen al de gedachte eraan onverdraaglijk was: *Hannah is dood.*

Ingolf gaf hem de kabel aan, en na een paar vergeefse pogingen slaagde Herzfeld erin al rijdend de adapter in de sigarettenaansteker te duwen. Vroeger, toen mobieltjes vooral werden gebruikt om te telefoneren, kon je meteen verder bellen als het toestel aan de lader hing. Tegenwoordig moest je minutenlang wachten tot de smartphone het weer deed. Die tijd gebruikte Herzfeld om zijn sombere gedachten op een rij te zetten, terwijl ze terugreden naar de snelweg.

Enerzijds leed het geen twijfel dat Martinek achter de verschrikkingen zat. Zijn voormalige collega had eerst de hoofdschuldigen voor de dood van zijn eigen dochter laten boeten, als eerste Jan Erik Sadler. Voor hij hem vermoordde, had Martinek de tong van de psychopaat afgesneden, waarmee hij Lily van top tot teen had afgelikt voor hij haar had verkracht. Daarna had mevrouw de rechter eraan moeten geloven.

En nu is het mijn beurt.

De auto reed door een wolk opwaaiende sneeuw en Herzfeld remde instinctief.

Nu moet ik meemaken wat het betekent je enige dochter te verliezen, omdat ik hem destijds niet heb geholpen het bewijs te manipuleren.

De kans was groot dat Hannah niet meer in leven was. Tenslotte had hij gezien hoe Martinek het lichaam van een jonge vrouw had opengesneden en in het meer had gegooid.

Aan de andere kant... Hij zocht naar een tak waaraan hij zich in het kreupelhout van zijn wanhoop kon vastklampen.

... past dat niet bij Sven. Hij loopt over van haat en wraakgevoelens, maar ik heb zijn dochter niets aangedaan. En Hannah draagt al helemaal geen schuld; er is geen enkele rechtvaardiging voor de kwellingen die ze ondergaat.

Natuurlijk kon hij door Lily's dood zijn verstand hebben verloren. Maar dat was in tegenspraak met de geraffineerde planning van zijn acties.

Trouwens, als Hannah al dood is, waarom zou ik de politie dan niet mogen waarschuwen?

Was dat alleen een bijkomend sadistisch spelletje? Of was er nog een kans om Hannah te redden als hij zich aan de regels hield? Maar wie was het dode meisje dan dat Martinek in het meer had gegooid? En wie was zijn handlanger? Een beroepsmoordenaar kon het niet zijn, die zou het geld in de verhuisdoos hebben gewild. Dus wie werkte mee aan de bloedige – en zeer persoonlijke – wraakactie van de forensisch arts?

Veel te veel vragen. Geen antwoorden. Herzfeld moest hoesten en zijn been deed pijn, hij had weer kramp in zijn kuit.

Ook dat nog.

Hij verslikte zich bij zijn poging de hoestprikkel te onderdrukken. Inmiddels lag Zarrentin al twee dorpen achter hen, en de batterij van zijn telefoon had nu genoeg stroom, zodat hij zijn pincode kon intoetsen. Toen de smartphone verbinding maakte met het netwerk klonk er een kakofonie van pieptonen, die elk een gemiste oproep signaleerden.

Hij drukte op nummerherhaling en had Linda al aan de lijn voor hij de telefoon aan de andere kant hoorde overgegaan.

'Eindelijk,' foeterde ze woedend. Haar stem kwam niet uit de telefoon, maar door de luidsprekers van de Porsche.

Herzfeld wierp een snelle blik zijn passagier, die alleen mismoedig zijn schouders ophaalde. Nu was Herzfelds mobieltje automatisch via bluetooth met de handsfree-installatie verbonden. Hij twijfelde even of hij het gesprek zou wegdrukken, maar besloot toen dat het hem inmiddels niets meer kon schelen of Ingolf meeluisterde of niet. Bovendien leek zijn vermoeidheid door de temperatuur in de auto erger te worden, het was slechts een kwestie van tijd voor hij in slaap zou vallen.

'Waar zit je?' wilde Linda weten. Haar stem echode en klonk alsof ze een eindje van de telefoon af stond.

Voor Herzfeld kon antwoorden, hoorde hij een rammelend geluid op de achtergrond, alsof iemand een vuilnisbak op straat omvergooide.

'Wat is er in godsnaam bij jou aan de hand?'

'Als je het per se wilt weten...' Linda's stem was weer dichterbij gekomen. '... het is me eindelijk gelukt de voorraadkast om te duwen.'

'Waarom heb je dat gedaan?'

'Om de ingang te blokkeren,' zei ze geïrriteerd, alsof ze het hem al duizend keer had uitgelegd. 'Nu moet ik dat kloteding nog tegen de deur aan kantelen.'

Herzfeld voelde de achterbanden op een glad weggedeelte slippen, en hij voelde zich alsof hij zelf ook zijn houvast verloor.

Waarom barricadeert ze de deur op de afdeling Pathologie?

'Ik dacht dat je een sleutel had?' vroeg hij.

'Ja, professor Bolleboos, die heb ik inderdaad. Maar kennelijk ben ik niet de enige. En bovendien is die vervloekte deur ook vanbuiten te openen als je hem vanbinnen hebt afgesloten. En omdat ik niet nog eens in de lijkenkoelkast wil kruipen als hier iemand binnenwandelt, tref ik mijn maatregelen totdat er hulp komt.'

'Dat kan nog wel even duren,' mompelde Ingolf op de passagiersstoel naast hem. Herzfeld knikte en zette de ruitenwissers in de snelste stand, maar zelfs zo lukte het nauwelijks de voortjagende sneeuw van de voorruit te wissen.

'Luister eens, Linda, je zegt zelf dat de moordenaar nog in de buurt kan zijn. Ik denk dat de sectiezaal nu geen veilige plek meer voor je is.'

'Echt waar? En ik had het hier nog wel zo naar mijn zin.'

'Je moet maken dat je daar wegkomt.'

'En Ender alleen laten?'

O ja, inderdaad. Ender!

'Hoe is het met hem?'

'Klote. Hij was even bij bewustzijn, maar is toen gevallen. Gelukkig viel hij met zijn buik op de matras die ik naast de deur had gelegd. Geen idee of hij er nu erger aan toe is. Het is hier stervensdonker sinds de moordenaar in het hele gebouw de stroom heeft uitgeschakeld. Maar ik denk dat hij nog ademt.'

'Hij moet dringend worden geopereerd,' dacht Herzfeld hardop.

'Ik heb al gebeld, dat kun je vergeten.'

Herzfeld was verbaasd. '*Wie* heb je gebeld?'

'De Duitse meteorologische dienst. Ik heb gevraagd wanneer het vliegverbod naar Helgoland wordt opgeheven. De meteorologen verwachten over vijf uur een korte periode waarin de storm gaat liggen. Op dit moment zouden de rotorbladen van een reddingshelikopter eraf worden gerukt.'

Vijf uur? Dat was te lang. Veel te lang.

Zowel voor Ender als voor Hannah, als ze nog in leven was.

'Jij bent toch een smeris, Paul. Kun jij geen speciale helikopter organiseren of zo?' vroeg Linda.

Herzfeld schudde zijn hoofd en gaf richting aan om op de snelweg in te voegen. 'Geloof me, ik zeg het niet alleen omdat mijn dochter me heeft gevraagd de politie erbuiten te houden. Maar het is niet zo eenvoudig. Er is geen hotline naar de helikopter-brigade die ik even kan bellen. De BKA is een enorm instituut. Bureaucratie, voorschriften.'

Hij liet erop volgen: 'Maar ik zal het proberen.'

'Goed, want ik heb geen zin om toe te kijken hoe Ender dood-gaat. Ik doe het al in mijn broek bij het idee dat die gek terug-komt om mij als volgende te spietsen, net als die oude vrouw hier.'

Dit keer was het Ingolf die naast hem instinctief met zijn voe-ten meeremde, omdat Herzfeld te snel een bocht in vloog.

'Wat zei je daarnet?' vroeg hij aan Linda. Hij voelde dat het bloed hem naar het hoofd steeg.

Linda zuchtte. 'Ik wil hier geen seconde langer blijven dan no-dig, dus bel je politievriendje en zeg dat...'

Hij onderbrak haar opgewonden. 'Nee, ik bedoelde dat met het spietsen.'

'Ja, wat is daarmee?'

De Porsche ontketende formidabele krachten toen Herzfeld op de invoegstrook het gaspedaal intrapte.

'Wil je daarmee zeggen dat er bij Friederike Töven een lang-werpig voorwerp is ingebracht?' vroeg hij, nu iets harder, om bo-ven het motorgeluid uit te komen.

'Nee. Ik wil daarmee zeggen dat iemand met een stok haar reet heeft opengescheurd,' schreeuwde Linda terug, nog woedender dan daarnet. 'Verdomme nog aan toe, dat speelt nu toch geen rol?'

'Trek hem eruit!' beval Herzfeld, toen ging hij over twee rij-banen direct naar de inhaalstrook. De toerenteller schoot in het rood.

'Ben je nou helemaal van de pot gerukt?' vroeg Linda, nadat ze een tijdje niets had gezegd. 'Mijn leven was al een hel voor ik jou kende. En nu is het helemaal naar de knoppen. Als ik je niet had geholpen, zou ik nu niet zitten wachten op een arrestatieteam dat me hier hopelijk op tijd uit krijgt.'

'Let op, Linda. Bij alles wat me lief is, zweer ik dat ik een manier zal vinden om binnen twee uur bij je te zijn.'

Ingolf wierp hem een twijfelende blik toe.

'Voordat het zover is, heb je de keus om de lijken aan te staren, of me te helpen zoeken naar mijn dochter.'

Herzfeld vertelde Linda wat hij op Martineks laptop aan het begin van de opname had gezien: de stok in de hand van zijn voormalige collega, het mes waarmee de forensisch arts de stok had ingekerfd. Nu kreeg die scène een gruwelijke betekenis.

'Tot nog toe heeft Martinek in elk lijk een bericht achtergelaten. Ik vrees dat hij het volgende in de stok heeft gekrast.'

'En ik vrees dat je mijn rug op kunt,' zei Linda en ze hing op.

Verdomme.

Herzfeld sloeg met zijn vuist op het met leer beklede stuur.

'Hmmm,' gromde Ingolf, met wie het inmiddels iets beter leek te gaan. Zijn tanden klapperden tenminste niet meer onder het praten. 'Twee uur?'

Hij wees naar het beeldscherm van het navigatiesysteem, waarop werd aangegeven dat het alleen al zo lang zou duren om naar de kust te rijden.

'Zelf als we dit tempo kunnen volhouden...' Herzfeld had de richtingaanwijzer voortdurend aanstaan om de auto's vóór zich van de linkerbaan af te jagen, '... is dat godsonmogelijk.'

Hij keek naar Herzfeld, die in het adresboek van zijn telefoon naar een nummer zocht en intussen moeite had het voortrazende vehikel op koers te houden.

'Of het moet zijn dat u het nummer van Superman in uw contacten hebt opgeslagen.'

'Zoiets,' zei Herzfeld, nadat hij eindelijk het telefoonnummer had gevonden.

Hij drukte op de toets met het groene hoorntje en vroeg zich af of hij daarmee niet definitief het doodvonnis van zijn dochter had getekend.

43

'Levenstekens?'

'Geen, behalve Hannahs meldtekst op de voicemail.'

'Dag van ontvoering?'

'Geen idee.'

'Bewijzen voor Martineks betrokkenheid?'

De weinig mededeelzame medewerker die Herzfelds telefoontje al na de eerste keer overgaan had opgenomen, heette Florian Leuthner, een commandant van de BKA.

'De doden moeten door een professional zijn geprepareerd,' antwoordde Herzfeld zijn collega. 'De in de lijken verstopte aanwijzingen hebben me op het spoor gebracht, en ik heb videoopnames gezien die zijn betrokkenheid bewijzen.'

Herzfeld had het karige woordgebruik van de BKA-inspecteur overgenomen, en hij merkte dat de nuchtere weergave van de feiten hem hielp afstand van de gruwelijke gebeurtenissen te nemen. 'De computer met de opname waarop Martinek een illegale autopsie uitvoert, bevindt zich echter niet meer in mijn bezit.'

Het beeldscherm van de laptop ligt nog steeds op de steiger bij het meer, om precies te zijn.

'Voorwaarden?'

'Werden niet gesteld. Ik vermoed dat het een wraakactie is.'

'Klinkt niet goed,' mompelde Leuthner, bijna meevoelend voor zijn doen.

Herzfeld en hij konden elkaar niet luchten of zien, wat vooral kwam doordat Leuthner een fervente Ossi-hater was. De chef van de afdeling Mensensmokkel en Gedwongen Prostitutie stak zijn afkeer van alles en iedereen uit de voormalige DDR niet onder stoelen of banken. Hij vond het een beproeving in Treptow te moeten werken, ging nooit vrijwillig naar een wijk in Oost-Berlijn, had persoonlijk een petitie tegen de solidariteitsheffing ten behoeve van de Duitse eenwording ingediend en beschouwde die als een grotere catastrofe dan Tsjernobyl en Fukushima bij elkaar. Eerst had hij in Herzfeld een bondgenoot gezien, nadat hij had gehoord dat de forensisch arts nog voor de val van de Muur naar het Westen was vertrokken. Maar toen hij had gemerkt dat Herzfeld niet was geïnteresseerd in botte borrelpraat, of in het filosoferen bij een biertje na het werk over de ondankbare Oost-Duitsers en de ondergang van de D-mark, was zijn aanvankelijke sympathie omgeslagen in het tegendeel. Privé zouden ze elkaar niet eens een hand geven. Maar in hun werk waren hij en Leuthner hoogst professioneel, elk bereid de persoonlijke geschillen buiten beschouwing te laten tot de klus was geklaard. Daarom verbaasde het hem ook niet dat zijn collega een nuchtere en professionele kijk had op de zaak, waarvan Herzfeld de details zo bondig mogelijk had weergegeven: van het telefoonnummer in het hoofd van het vrouwenlijk, via Hannahs ontvoering en de op afstand uitgevoerde obductie, tot de aanval op Ender, die nu dringend medische hulp van een specialist nodig had.

'Op Helgoland?' informeerde Leuthner nog eens.

'Ik weet niet zeker waar Hannah naartoe is gebracht.'

'Naar het buitenland misschien?'

Herzfeld had wel zo'n idee waarom hij dat vroeg. De BKA was niet verantwoordelijk voor kidnapping, behalve als het een internationale kwestie was. Leuthner wilde hem dus tegemoetkomen.

'Nee. Om eerlijk te zijn denk ik dat Hannah nog in Duitsland is, als ze nog leeft. Maar ik heb je niet gebeld om de officiële weg te bewandelen, Leuthner.'

'Waarom dan?'

Herzfeld ging van de inhaalstrook naar de rechterbaan en min-derde vaart om niet zo hard boven het geluid van de motor uit te hoeven schreeuwen. Naast hem zat Ingolf te knikkebollen van vermoeidheid.

'Je voert toch wel vaker geheime operaties uit. Ik dacht dat jij misschien een vliegtuig of helikopter kon regelen, zonder papierwinkel.'

'Geheimhouding en helikoptervluchten gaan normaal gesproken niet samen,' zei Leuthner; het was de langste zin die hij tot dusverre had uitgesproken.

'Normaal gesproken,' herhaalde Herzfeld met nadruk.

Gezien hun wederzijdse antipathie leek Leuthner wel de minst geschikte persoon die hij om een gunst kon vragen. Aan de andere kant was het zijn specialiteit mensen in het diepste geheim en onder strenge veiligheidsmaatregelen uit de klauwen van gewelddadige criminelen te bevrijden. Een week eerder had zijn team met behulp van een infiltrant nog een bende mensenhandelaars opgerold. Omdat de spion een hoerenloper had moeten vermoorden om zijn valse identiteit aan de handelaars te bewijzen, was die actie zonder medeweten of goedkeuring van Leuthners superieuren uitgevoerd. De directie-etage werd pas geïnformeerd toen de missie met succes was volbracht.

'Vanwaar dat geheimzinnige gedoe?' vroeg Leuthner aan Herzfeld, die net vluchtig naar Ingolf had gekeken. Óf zijn passagier was in slaap gevallen, óf hij luisterde met zijn ogen dicht naar het gesprek, met zijn hoofd tegen het raam geleund.

'Hannah zei op haar voicemail dat ze zou worden vermoord zodra ik de politie zou inschakelen. En als Martinek hierbij betrokken is, kent hij de officiële procedures, en kunnen we ervan uitgaan dat hij als ex-BKA-man een systeem heeft opgezet waardoor hij wordt gewaarschuwd als ik me niet meer aan zijn instructies hou.'

'En waarom leg je dat alles nu toch naast je neer?'

'Omdat ik geen andere keus heb. Het eiland is afgesneden, en intussen is niet alleen het leven van mijn dochter in gevaar.'

Leuthner gromde ontstemd. 'Je had me beter via een beveiligde verbinding kunnen bellen.'

'Ook dat risico moet ik nemen. Ik heb geen tijd om een satelliettelefoon te regelen. De huismeester sterft als hij niet onmiddellijk naar de intensive care wordt gebracht. Momentje alsjeblieft.'

Herzfeld hoorde een onderbroken pieptoon en zag op het display van de boordcomputer op het dashboard dat er een tweede telefoontje binnenkwam. Aan het nummer te zien was het ook uit een kantoor van de Berlijnse BKA-dependance afkomstig. Hij verontschuldigde zich kort tegenover Leuthner, zette hem in de wacht en beantwoordde het tweede gesprek.

'Ja?'

'Sorry dat ik stoor,' zei Yao, de assistent-arts met wie hij vanochtend nog de sectie op het verminkte vrouwenlijk had uitgevoerd.

Hij voelde een nerveuze spanning in zijn maag en vroeg zich af wat ze wilde. 'Is er een probleem?'

'Je wilde toch dat wij de maaginhoud zouden onderzoeken?'

De tabletten, inderdaad. Dat had hij helemaal vergeten.

'De uitslag van het laboratorium is net binnen. Er is sprake van een cyaankaliderivaat.'

'Dus de vrouw is vergiftigd?'

'Nee. Het was zelfmoord.'

'Zelfmoord?' herhaalde Herzfeld zo luid dat Ingolf naast hem uit zijn halfslaap opschrok. Hij moest aan het gruwelijk toegetakelde lijk denken en schudde zijn hoofd. 'De kaak van de onbekende is verwijderd en haar handen zijn afgesneden. Hoe komen jullie in godsnaam op het idee dat het zelfmoord is?'

'Ze heeft een boodschap achtergelaten waarin ze afscheid neemt.'

Herzfeld liet de informatie even bezinken terwijl ze onder een viaduct door reden, toen zei hij: 'Die afscheidsbrief moet een vervalsing zijn.'

'Het is geen brief, het is een video,' zei Yao. 'En die vrouw is nu geen onbekende meer.'

Herzfeld was te perplex om op de twee berichten te reageren, wat Yao de kans gaf hem met verdere informatie te verwarren. 'Vanmiddag is een particuliere veiligheidsdienst een penthouse in Charlottenburg binnengegaan, nadat het alarm was afgegaan,' begon Yao. 'Het luxeappartement had een uitzonderlijk alarmsysteem, dat ook aanslaat als er lange tijd geen bewegingen worden geregistreerd. Toen de bewaker het appartement binnenkwam, ontdekte hij bloedsporen en een paar afgesneden vingers op het witte tapijt. Hij lichtte de politie in, en de technische recherche vond een dvd in de speler.'

'Haar testament?'

'Meer dan dat. De vrouw had de complete toedracht gefilmd. Hoe ze in de keuken zit en de tabletten inneemt, en ondertussen in haar videoboodschap afscheid neemt van familie en vrienden.'

'Weten we waarom ze dat zichzelf heeft aangedaan?' vroeg Herzfeld met een blik in de achteruitkijkspiegel.

Hoewel het pas even na vieren was, was het al aardedonker. Maar het sneeuwde niet meer, en het was niet zo druk als aan het begin van de reis.

'Op de opname zegt ze duidelijk dat haar leven geen zin meer heeft en dat de hele waarheid vroeg of laat aan het licht zal komen.'

'En hoe verklaren jullie de verminkingen?'

'Die verklaart ze zelf. Letterlijk zegt ze, en ik citeer...' Herzfeld hoorde Yao met papieren ritselen. ' "... na mijn dood dient mijn stoffelijk overschot nog één doel. Mijn lichaam zal er daarna net zo verschrikkelijk uitzien als mijn ziel zich nu voelt. Maar ik laat hierbij weten dat ik met alle handelingen die tot de verwondingen na mijn zelfgekozen dood leiden, van tevoren heb ingestemd, en dat zeg ik in het volle bezit van mijn geestelijke vermogens." '

Herzfeld schudde zijn hoofd en zwenkte de linkerrijbaan op,

om een stationwagen in te halen die een hevig slingerende cara-van achter zich aan sleurde.

'Waarom zijn jullie er zo zeker van dat er niemand met een wapen achter de camera staat die haar tot die uitspraken dwingt?'

'Je moet de video met eigen ogen zien, Paul. Honderd procent zeker is het natuurlijk nooit, maar ik heb zelden iets gehoord wat zo authentiek en oprecht overkomt als de laatste woorden van mevrouw Schwintowski.'

De adem stokte Herzfeld in de keel. 'Sorry, wat zei je?'

'Oprecht. Het klonk geen seconde gespeeld of afgedwongen...'

'Nee, dat bedoel ik niet. Hoe heette ze?' Hij knipperde een paar keer met zijn ogen en dacht aan de tekst op de verhuisdoos die ze naast Martineks voordeur in de kist voor de kussens had-den gevonden.

'Sybille Schwintowski, geboren Thron. Getrouwd met verhui-zer Philipp Schwintowski. Samen hadden ze een dochter, Rebec-ca, zeventien jaar oud. Beiden zijn spoorloos verdwenen.'

Gezwind met Schwintowski!

Naast hem had Ingolf de naam ook opgevangen en hij wierp hem een vragende blik toe, voordat hij gaapte en zijn ogen weer sloot.

'Wat betekent dat allemaal?' fluisterde Herzfeld, zo zacht dat Yao hem niet over de handsfree-installatie kon horen.

'Zei je iets?'

'Wat? Eh, nee.'

Een onherkenbaar verminkt lijk, maar er is zelfmoord in het spel. Hannahs ontvoering. Martinek. De begrafenis op het meer en een verhuizer die met zijn dochter verdwijnt – hoe hangt dat alles samen?

'Wat weten we over die man?' vroeg hij, en Yao begon opnieuw met haar documenten te ritselen.

'Philipp Schwintowski is geen onbeschreven blad,' zei ze. 'In de jaren tachtig stond hij terecht wegens moord; destijds was hij zesentwintig. Hij zou zijn vermogen met illegale gokpraktijken en later als woekeraar hebben vergaard. De pers noemde hem de Boeddhamoordenaar, wat met zijn zwaarlijvige gestalte te maken had. Met een bewakingscamera is gefilmd dat hij een klant met een betalingsachterstand van een brug over de snelweg door de stad gooide, waarna de man door een vrachtwagen werd overreden.'

Herzfeld vertrok zijn gezicht.

'Maar de aanklacht werd ingetrokken nadat de opnames onder mysterieuze omstandigheden bleken te zijn gewist. Vijftien jaar later zat hij dan toch vast in het huis van bewaring in Tegel, wegens zware mishandeling. Hij had een uitsmijter voor een bordeel, die hem niet wilde binnenlaten, met een boksbeugel in elkaar geslagen. Daarvoor kreeg hij tweeënhalf jaar. Na negen maanden stond hij weer op straat.'

'Goed gedrag, wed ik.'

'Correct. In de gevangenis papte hij aan met een sociaal werkster, die hem wilde betrekken bij een project waarin jeugdige delinquenten bekeerd moesten worden.'

'En die sociaal werkster...'

'Heette Sybille Thron. In de gevangenis was ze al zwanger van Rebecca. Na zijn ontslag kwam de bruiloft en daarna leek het er inderdaad op dat Schwintowski het rustiger aan ging doen. De laatste paar jaar is er geen sprake geweest van fysiek geweld, niet eens een caféruzie, waar hij vroeger berucht om was. Maar de recherche gaat ervan uit dat hij nog steeds goede connecties in de onderwereld heeft en dat zijn verhuisbedrijf voornamelijk een witwasorganisatie is.'

'Is die man in staat zijn vrouw post mortem te verminken?' wilde Herzfeld weten.

'Gezien zijn gewelddadige verleden wel, maar de rechercheurs betwijfelen het. De belastingdienst heeft hem een halfjaar laten schaduwen, en alle opsporingsambtenaren waren het erover eens dat ze zelden zo'n zorgzame huisvader hadden gezien. Hij heeft een jaar lang niet gewerkt om samen met zijn vrouw voor de baby te kunnen zorgen. De twee hebben regelmatig hun trouwbelofte hernieuwd, voor het laatst zes maanden geleden in Las Vegas. En hoewel Sybille Thron ten tijde van de bruiloft bijna geen cent had, zijn er geen huwelijkse voorwaarden. Integendeel, toen zijn vrouw nog leefde heeft Philipp de helft van zijn vermogen op haar naam gezet, voor het geval dat hem iets zou overkomen, inclusief het penthouse, een paar spaarrekeningen en een zeewaardig jacht.'

'Jacht?'

Er begon een adertje in Herzfelds ooglid te trillen, zonder dat hij er iets tegen kon doen.

'Ja, de Rebecca 1, genoemd naar zijn dochter. Schwintowski staat bekend als een enthousiaste zeezeiler. Twee jaar geleden heeft hij de Family Cruiser Cup gewonnen.'

'Welke route heeft hij genomen?'

'Waarom is dat belangrijk?'

'Alsjeblieft!' drong Herzfeld aan. Het trillen werd erger.

'Momentje.' Hij hoorde Yao op een toetsenbord tikken, toen gaf ze antwoord: 'De Cruiser Cup wordt regelmatig gehouden in het kader van de Noordzee-weken.'

'En de route?'

'Die bestaat uit drie etappes rond Helgoland.'

44

'Eindelijk,' blafte Leuthner, nadat Herzfeld het gesprek met Yao had beëindigd en weer naar zijn collega had overgeschakeld. Hoewel de stem van de commandant heel wat luider was dan die van Yao, drong hij niet tot Ingolf door, die met zijn hoofd tegen de ruit eindelijk in slaap leek te zijn gevallen.

'Het spijt me dat ik je heb laten wachten,' zei Herzfeld schor. Hij was als verdoofd. Een paar minuten geleden had hij nog geloofd dat hij een deel van het raadsel rond Martinek had opgelost, maar nu was de zaak onduidelijker dan ooit.

Waarom heeft Sybille Schwintowski zelfmoord gepleegd en zich daarna laten verminken? Door wie? En als ze op die afscheidsvideo inderdaad de waarheid heeft gezegd, waarom heeft ze haar lichaam dan voor deze waanzinnige puzzeltocht beschikbaar gesteld? Wat voor connectie bestaat er tussen haar en Martinek? En Sadler? En mij?

Tussen al die variabelen leek er maar één constante in deze hele waanzin te zijn. En die heette Helgoland. Leuthner accepteerde Herzfelds verontschuldiging met een norse grom, toen zei hij: 'In de tussentijd heb ik hier en daar mijn licht opgestoken. Er is inderdaad een vliegtuig dat ik buiten de Dienst om zou kunnen organiseren. Een Cessna, persoonlijk eigendom van een goede vriend van me, met wie we vorige maand vier kinderen van een bordeel bij de Poolse grens hebben overgevlogen. Maar daar heb je niets aan.'

'Waarom niet? Over een paar uur komt er rustiger weer,' zei Herzfeld en hij wees door de voorruit, alsof Leuthner in staat was te bevestigen wat hij zag. Het was inderdaad opgehouden met sneeuwen, en het waaide niet meer zo hard.

'Misschien in jouw regio. Aan de kust woedt een storm. Op Helgoland een orkaan.'

Ondanks die slechte tijdingen klonk Leuthner niet alsof hij alle hoop had laten varen, daarom vroeg Herzfeld: 'Wat stel je voor?'

In plaats van te antwoorden zei de commandant alleen: 'Geef me een halfuur.'

'Waarvoor?'

'Dat vertel ik je als ik een oplossing heb.'

Als?

'En als je geen oplossing vindt?'

Op de passagiersstoel naast hem kreunde Ingolf met zijn ogen dicht.

'Dan heeft dit gesprek nooit plaatsgevonden,' hoorde hij Leuthner zeggen. Toen was de lijn dood.

45

In luttele uren was de kelder van de kliniek van een steriele, brandschone sectiezaal in een abattoir veranderd. Als Linda de chaos van bloed en pijn die zich ontrolde had moeten tekenen, zou ze haar werk van de titel 'Werkplaats van de waanzin' hebben voorzien. Maar ze betwijfelde of de details haar goed gelukt zouden zijn, omdat ze zo haar problemen met expliciete geweldsscènes had.

Het van de muren weerkaatsende, indirecte licht van de zaklantaarn, die ze naast de afvoerbak met de straal naar boven had neergezet, stelde haar slechts in staat een schemerig verlicht gedeelte van de ruimte te zien, maar wat Linda kon onderscheiden deed haar maag omdraaien: twee lijken in ontbinding op de sectietafel, het halfopen koelvak, een omgevallen instrumentenkast voor de ingang; daarnaast, op een matras, een stervende man met een mes in zijn hals... *en ik ermiddenin.*

Linda hield nog steeds de huistelefoon vast, hoewel het al een kwartier geleden was dat ze Herzfeld aan de lijn had. Ze wist niet of het haar met de omgevallen kast werkelijk gelukt was een voor de moordenaar onneembare barrière voor de ingang op te werpen. Eigenlijk betwijfelde ze dat. Ze kon alleen maar hopen dat degene die het op haar had gemunt inmiddels de belangstelling voor zijn slachtoffers in de sectiezaal had verloren. En dat Herzfeld snel een manier zou vinden om een einde te maken aan deze verschrikking.

Wat een doffe ellende. Als anderen erover klagen dat ze zich met de verkeerde mannen inlaten, gaat het over mislukte afspraakjes en slippertjes. En bij mij?

Ze controleerde het hoeslaken nog eens, dat ze provisorisch over Enders bovenlichaam had gedrapeerd, en bij de gedachte dat een ander laken zijn gezicht waarschijnlijk binnenkort zou bedekken, ging er een steek door haar hart.

Van alle negatieve emoties die ze op het moment doormaakte, was het gevoel van hulpeloosheid het sterkst. Als het alleen om haar leven zou gaan, zou ze meteen uit de kliniek zijn gerend en in restaurant Bandrupp alarm hebben geslagen. Maar ze kon Ender niet zomaar achterlaten, en bovendien was dat het risico niet waard. Zelfs als ze erin zou slagen de kliniek ongezien uit te komen, had ze daarmee nog niets bereikt. Op het geëvacueerde eiland bevond zich geen ervaren chirurg die Ender van het mes kon verlossen. Om van een anesthesist maar te zwijgen.

Aan de andere kant kan ik hier niet werkeloos toezien hoe hij doodgaat.

Ze pakte de zaklantaarn, richtte hem op de sectietafel met Tövens lijk en sloeg geschrokken haar hand voor haar mond: er was iets anders aan het lijk.

Iemand had aan het lijk gezeten.

De laatste keer dat ze een blik op de rechter had gewaagd, had ze haar ontblote achterste gezien. Nu had iemand in de tijd dat ze zich in het koelvak had verstopt haar rok weer naar beneden getrokken.

Linda draaide zich om naar Ender, wiens lichaam op de matras in het schemerige licht maar vaag te zien was. Ze betwijfelde dat de huismeester het lijk had gemanipuleerd toen hij in shocktoestand over de afdeling Pathologie rondzwalkte. Hoewel, hij had ook de telefoon opgenomen.

De telefoon...

Ze bekeek het toestel in haar handen en besloot het weer in

de gereedschapsgordel boven Eriks lijk te steken, zodat ze beide handen vrij had.

Op het ogenblik heerste in de ware zin des woords doodse stilte binnen en buiten de sectiezaal. Sinds de elektriciteit definitief was uitgevallen – *of uitgezet?* – ruiste zelfs het ventilatiesysteem niet meer, en Linda moest er niet aan denken wat dat binnenkort voor consequenties voor de lucht hierbeneden zou hebben. Ze draaide zich weer naar de tweede sectietafel toe, veegde het zweet van haar handen aan haar schort af en haalde diep adem.

Vooruit dan maar. Op naar de volgende ronde.

Langzaam tilde ze de grove linnen rok op en trok hem over de melkwitte dijen van de vrouw naar boven. Op een of andere manier kwam deze handeling haar nog weerzinwekkender en obscener voor dan het opensnijden van Eriks onderbroek, misschien omdat dit slachtoffer een vrouw was; bovendien, een oudere dame help je met oversteken en je draagt haar boodschappen het huis in, *maar je ontbloot niet haar onderlijf!*

Met elke centimeter die ze blootlegde, groeide Linda's onwil.

Waarom doe ik dit eigenlijk, vroeg ze zich af.

Een innerlijke stem antwoordde: *Omdat je een einde wilt maken aan deze puzzeltocht.*

Door de rust van de doden te schenden?

Door de professor de volgende aanwijzing te geven, die hem naar de moordenaar leidt. En op die manier mensenlevens te redden.

Of ze een wisse dood in...

Je zou die mensen op zijn minst kunnen waarschuwen.

Maar als ze nu de burgemeester zou informeren, zou ze hooguit haar eigen huid redden en met zekerheid paniek onder de resterende bewoners van Helgoland zaaien, die zich op het door het noodweer afgesneden eiland overgeleverd zouden zien aan een seriemoordenaar.

Herzfeld heeft gezegd dat het een persoonlijke wraakactie was tegen hem en iedereen die iets met een oude zaak te maken had.

O ja, en waarom is Ender dan ook slachtoffer geworden?

Omdat hij zich ermee heeft bemoeid, net als ik. Als ik die mensen waarschuw voordat Herzfeld de moordenaar heeft ontdekt en zijn dochter heeft gevonden, breng ik haar eerder in gevaar dan dat ik haar help.

Linda trok haar schouders op en liet ze met een zucht weer zakken. Ze kon dit zelfgesprek in gedachten zo lang voeren als ze wilde, maar ze zou steeds op een en hetzelfde punt uitkomen: hier blijven bracht haar eigen leven in gevaar, en vluchten dat van Herzfelds dochter. Om Ender te redden en de rest van de bevolking te beschermen was er hulp van buitenaf nodig, en die had Herzfeld beloofd, binnen de komende twee uur.

Goed dan, professor. Twee uur, hoe je dat ook voor elkaar denkt te krijgen. Zo lang help ik je nog, maar daarna ben ik hier weg.

Linda hield haar horloge schuin in het licht van de zaklantaarn om de wijzers te kunnen zien. Heimelijk was ze blij dat de plafondverlichting was uitgevallen en dat de huiveringwekkende aanblik van de sectietafel, die ze nu alleen kon vermoeden, haar bespaard bleef.

De wasachtige huid. De lijkvlekken. De met bloed overdekte binnenkant van de dijen. De stok met gestold bloed...

Intussen had ze de rok tot de heupen omhooggeslagen. De houten steel stak ongeveer vijftien centimeter uit de anus. Hij voelde ruw en stug aan toen Linda hem beetpakte, en pas toen merkte ze dat ze had vergeten haar handschoenen weer aan te trekken.

Doet er niet toe.

De kans op een splinter was nu wel haar minste zorg. Linda voelde een onverwacht grote weerstand bij haar eerste, zij het ietwat aarzelende poging de stok eruit te trekken. Met tegenzin begon ze er met op- en neerwaarste bewegingen aan te trekken, om de vanwege de lijkstijfheid verstarde sluitspier op te rekken. De geluiden die ze daardoor veroorzaakte klonken alsof ze de laatste restjes uit een lege fles met douchegel probeerde te knijpen.

Linda pauzeerde even, wachtte tot haar hortende ademhaling weer wat tot bedaren was gekomen en trok het moordwapen er met een ruk uit.

Net het potlood van een reus, schoot het door haar hoofd toen ze de punt aan het eind zag. Wat een beestachtige manier om iemand te vermoorden.

Linda rilde, toen ontdeed ze de stok van het slijm door hem zonder omhaal aan haar schort af te vegen. Daarna richtte ze de zaklantaarn direct op het hout en las het bericht, dat onbeholpen in het hout was gekerfd.

46

'53666 435 736 490.' Herzfeld herhaalde de lange cijferreeks die Linda zojuist aan hem had doorgegeven, zodat Ingolf de getallen kon noteren. Ze hadden de A24 verlaten en raasden langs Hamburg over de A1 verder naar de Noordzeekust. Sinds kort was Ingolf weer aanspreekbaar. Hij knipperde met zijn vermoeide ogen, en elke paar minuten probeerde hij tevergeefs een geeuw te onderdrukken. De naweeën van de onderkoeling en de shock waren nog niet overwonnen.

'Het zou een buitenlands telefoonnummer kunnen zijn,' zei Herzfeld en hij knipperde met zijn koplampen om een voorligger van de linkerbaan te verjagen.

'Heb ik al geprobeerd.' Linda klonk moedeloos. 'Onbekend nummer. Misschien ontbreekt de bijpassende landcode. Ik hoor steeds een bezettoon. Bij de tweede reeks gebeurt hetzelfde.'

'Martinek heeft nog een ander getal in de stok gekrast?'

'Ja, aan het eind dat in het lichaam zat,' antwoordde ze vol weerzin. 'De cijfers, voor zover ik kan zien, zijn: 908920 705 318 451.'

'Heb je dat?' vroeg Herzfeld zacht aan Ingolf, die vermoeid knikte. Zonder zijn bril, die hij in het meer had verloren, en met zijn warrige, plat tegen zijn hoofd plakkende haar leek hij nog meer op een schooljongen die zich verslapen heeft. Het in leer gebonden notitieblok in zijn hand versterkte die indruk nog.

'Het kan van alles zijn,' zei Linda. 'Een creditcard, een rekeningnummer, een bankkluisje of een wachtwoord.'

'Punten,' zei Ingolf naast hem.

'Wat?' vroegen Herzfeld en Linda tegelijk.

De stagiair onderstreepte de twee getallenreeksen op zijn blocnote.

'Wie praat daar?' wilde Linda weten, en Herzfeld realiseerde zich dat hij nog niets over zijn reisgenoot had gezegd.

'Ingolf von Appen. Hij werkt bij mij op het instituut en is mijn chauffeur,' deelde hij haar mee op een toon die verried dat hij zijn tijd niet wilde verdoen met tekst en uitleg.

'En wat heeft hij gevraagd?' vroeg ze.

Herzfeld keek naar Ingolf. Blijkbaar had hij moeite zich te concentreren, want de woorden kwamen hortend en stotend uit zijn mond.

'Punten. Staan er punten?'

'Waar?'

Ingolf sloeg zijn ogen ten hemel, toen zei hij langzaam: 'Tussen de cijfers.'

'Moment,' zei Linda, die nu van de telefoon weg leek te lopen. Er klonk het geluid van stromend water, toen hoorde Herzfeld haar van een afstand roepen: 'Ik maak de stok nog een keer schoon in de afvoerbak.'

Herzfeld draaide zich vragend om naar Ingolf, die zich met een van pijn vertrokken gezicht op zijn stoel voorover probeerde te buigen.

'Waar heb je het over?'

'PetSave-One,' steunde hij. Maar voordat Herzfeld kon vragen waarom hij daar in vredesnaam weer over begon, slaakte Linda opeens een kreet.

'Dat kan niet waar zijn!' Haar stem klonk nu weer dichtbij. 'Hoe wist je dat? Er staan inderdaad punten tussen.'

Ingolf dwong zichzelf tot een matte glimlach. 'Eentje per segment, neem ik aan. Het eerste begint met 53 punt 666, de tweede met 9 punt 08, nietwaar?' Hij leek langzamerhand weer op krachten te komen.

'Ja. Wat betekent dat?'

In plaats van te antwoorden opende Ingolf het handschoenen-kastje, haalde er een smalle maar lijvige leren map uit en gooide die in Herzfelds schoot.

'Wat moet dat?'

'Dat is het instructieboek van de Cayenne.'

'Dat zie ik. Maar wat heeft dat met die getallen...'

'Ik ben te moe. Zoek het alstublieft voor me op.'

'Wat dan?' vroeg Herzfeld ongeduldig. En Linda vroeg opnieuw wat de punten te betekenen hadden.

'Navigatiesysteem. Trefwoord: coördinaten.'

Ingolf wees naar het handboek, en Herzfeld begon te begrijpen waar hij naartoe wilde.

'Je bedoelt...'

'Ja. PetSave-One, het systeem dat ik heb ontwikkeld, alweer vergeten? Dat werkt met gps-gegevens, en die herken ik als ik ze zie. De eerste reeks slaat op de lengte-, de tweede op de breedte-graad. Maar u moet de punten niet vergeten.'

'En die kun je gewoon in dat ding intypen?' vroeg Herzfeld, in de hoop dat hij daarmee een geweldige stap in de richting van de schuilplaats van zijn dochter zou zetten.

'Ja.' Ingolf knikte slaperig. Zijn ogen begonnen weer dicht te vallen, en hij had ze al gesloten toen hij zei: 'Maar niet *gewoon*. Ik heb geen flauw idee hoe het moet...' Hij gaapte nog hartgrondiger dan eerst en wilde nog iets zeggen, maar de vermoeidheid dreigde hem opnieuw te overmannen.

Snel zei Herzfeld tegen Linda dat hij terug zou bellen en hing op. Na een korte blik in de achteruitkijkspiegel stak hij twee rij-banen over en reed de vluchtstrook op, waar hij naast een kilome-terpaaltje tot stilstand kwam.

Het duurde tergend lang voor hij in de handleiding van het luxueuze voertuig, die zo dik was als een telefoonboek, het hoofd-stuk over de programmering van het satellietgestuurde navigatie-systeem had gevonden.

Uiteindelijk lukte het hem, en hij wist niet of hij moest lachen of huilen toen de boordcomputer Ingolfs vermoeden bevestigde.

Martinek had inderdaad de coördinaten van een geografische locatie gekrast in de stok waarmee de rechter was doodgemarteld.

Een locatie die volgens het display van het navigatiesysteem midden in een bos in de regio Cuxhaven lag.

Onbereikbaar over de weg.

Mijlenver van de bewoonde wereld.

47

Anderhalf uur later ploegden de brede banden van de terreinwagen over het besneeuwde bospad.

De laatste kilometer meldde het navigatieapparaat dat ze zich niet meer op een berijdbare weg bevonden, sinds ze de provinciale weg ter hoogte van Hemmoor hadden verlaten en het bos in waren gereden. De Noordzeekust lag minstens twintig kilometer verder, maar ook hier had de wind de afgelopen uren een spoor van verwoesting achtergelaten. Takken waren afgeknapt, ze waren juist nog om een ontwortelde boom heen gereden. Bovendien kreeg de wagen een windstoot te verduren die zelfs de loodzware kolos opzij had geduwd, zodat Herzfeld het stuur met beide handen had moeten vasthouden om niet van het steeds smaller wordende pad te worden geblazen.

Verdomme, hoe zal het er dan niet op volle zee uitzien? Aan een overtocht viel inderdaad niet te denken.

De kronen van de bomen zwiepten wild boven hun hoofd heen en weer. Ze hadden de sneeuw die hun takken moest hebben verzwaard allang verloren. Af en toe waaide er wat poedersneeuw tegen de voorruit.

Voor zover Herzfeld door het raam van het schuifdak kon zien, was de hemel nog steeds bewolkt, desondanks sneeuwde het al een tijd niet meer. Maar het werd wel snel donker, hoewel de zon pas over een paar uur zou ondergaan.

Hij moest aan mevrouw Schwintowski denken, die haar zelfmoord blijkbaar had gefilmd voor ze door iemand anders verminkt en in een verhuisdoos afgevoerd was.

Het was maar een paar uur geleden dat hij die ochtend de autopsie op haar had uitgevoerd. En toch leek het hem wel een eeuwigheid.

'Waar zijn we?' vroeg Ingolf gapend naast hem. Hij had de hele rit geslapen en werd langzaam wakker.

'Dat zou ik ook weleens willen weten.'

Op het beeldscherm van het navigatiesysteem was een vlag te zien, ten teken dat ze over een paar meter hun doel zouden bereiken. Toch zag Herzfeld niets anders dan ver uit elkaar staande bomen, hoofdzakelijk dennen en berken. Ze reden nog een minuut verder, toen begon de zwart-wit geblokte racevlag op het display te wiebelen, en bracht Herzfeld de auto tot stilstand.

'U hebt uw bestemming bereikt,' mompelde hij bij zichzelf.

Midden in de pampa.

'Misschien heeft Linda de coördinaten in het donker niet goed gelezen,' opperde Ingolf. Hij had zijn reservebril uit het handschoenenvak gehaald en keek om zich heen.

Ze stonden op een splitsing waarvandaan één weg naar een open plek voerde. Afgezien van een wegwijzer voor wandelaars en een besneeuwde stapel omgehakte boomstammen verderop was er niets te zien.

'Oké, Von Appen, jij blijft in de auto. Ik kijk hier even rond,' zei Herzfeld en hij liet de motor draaien, zodat het grote licht aan bleef en het terrein bescheen.

'Bent u er zeker van dat u er alleen opuit wilt?' vroeg Ingolf.

'Wat kan er gebeuren? Als Martinek ons had willen vermoorden, had hij dat allang kunnen doen.'

'En het is hem nog bijna gelukt ook,' zei Ingolf. 'Stel dat u hier in een valkuil loopt?'

Herzfeld schudde zijn hoofd. 'Ik denk dat we op het meer een ongeluk hebben gehad. Dat hoop ik tenminste. En mocht dat niet zo zijn, dan is dat voor jou reden te meer om in de auto te blijven, zodat je me in geval van nood te hulp kunt komen.'

Herzfeld keek de stagiair streng aan. 'Heb je dat begrepen?'

'*Aye aye, sir,*' zei Ingolf en hij salueerde. 'Nog één ding.'

Herzfeld had zijn hand al op de deurgreep. 'Wat?'

'Brandt het daar?'

Herzfeld keek in de richting waarin Ingolfs wijsvinger wees...
Inderdaad!

Nu de netjes opgestapelde boomstammen direct door de xenonkoplampen werden verlicht, was er geen twijfel mogelijk.

'Daarachter stijgt rook op,' bevestigde Herzfeld. Vanwege de wind kostte het hem moeite het portier open te duwen. Een woedende windvlaag drukte ertegenaan en blies de grijze rookpluim weg die hij net nog boven de boomstammen uit zag komen.

De kou die de auto binnenstroomde bevestigde het weerbericht op de radio, dat temperaturen van twaalf graden onder nul had voorspeld.

Herzfeld sprong van zijn stoel en zonk tot aan zijn enkels in de sneeuw. Hij sloot het portier en ploeterde naar de open plek. Al na een paar meter zag hij waar de rook vandaan kwam: een dikke walm, grijs als beton, steeg op uit een scheve schoorsteenpijp op het dak van een bouwwagen van houthakkers.

Onder zijn voeten brak een besneeuwde tak, en Herzfeld bleef instinctief staan. Hij wilde net verder lopen, toen het achter hem opeens licht werd.

'Ik zei toch dat je in de auto moest blijven,' riep hij. Hij draaide zich om, maar verstijfde toen.

Het rechterportier stond op een kier, de binnenverlichting van de Porsche brandde, en daarom kon Herzfeld in één oogopslag zien dat de zoon van de senator verdwenen was.

'Ingolf?'

Herzfelds maag kromp ineen.

Hij keek beurtelings naar de bouwwagen en naar de Porsche. Ondanks de rook boven de eerste en de binnenverlichting in de laatste, leken beide voertuigen geheel verlaten te zijn.

Herzfeld wilde weer naar de auto lopen, maar toen bedacht hij zich en ging door zijn knieën.

Niets.

Hij was bang geweest dat hij Ingolf naast de auto roerloos op de grond zou zien liggen, maar daar was hij niet.

'Ingolf,' riep hij opnieuw. Geen antwoord.

Wat is hier verdomme aan de hand?

Hij sloop behoedzaam terug naar de Porsche.

Hij liep om de motorkap heen en stond nu aan de rechterkant, maar tegen zijn verwachting in werd hij niet aangevallen of overmeesterd.

En van de student ontbrak nog steeds elk spoor.

'Ingolf?'

De ventilator van de terreinwagen klikte toen Herzfeld de gesloten achterklep naderde. Door de getinte ruiten kon Herzfeld alleen de lege achterbank zien.

Hij pakte de deurgreep van het achterportier, klemde zijn vingers stevig om het handvat en rukte het met een harde schreeuw open. Maar er was niemand die hij met zijn gebrul had laten schrikken. Geen gevaar dat in zijn gezicht sloeg.

En geen Ingolf.

Het interieur van de Cayenne was leeg.

Herzfeld draaide zich om. 'Waar zit je?' fluisterde hij ten einde raad in de richting van het donkere bos.

In het licht dat nu uit de auto naar buiten viel, zag hij diepe voetafdrukken in de sneeuw. Voor zover Herzfeld kon zien, liep het spoor van de auto rechtstreeks naar een klein groepje bomen naast de weg, waaronder zich ook een flinke eik bevond.

'Waar ben je?' riep Herzfeld opnieuw en hij volgde de sporen.

Wat is Ingolf van plan? Waarom is hij zonder iets te zeggen het bos in gelopen?

Hoe dichter hij bij de bomen kwam, des te donkerder werd het. Voor het eerst in zijn leven wenste hij dat de forensisch artsen van de BKA ook met een dienstwapen werden uitgerust.

En hij vervloekte zichzelf dat hij niet naar zijn instinct had geluisterd. Van meet af aan had hij vermoed dat er met die Ingolf iets niet in de haak was, ook al was hij de zoon van de senator. Wie reed zijn professor nu dwars door heel Duitsland, alleen om een stageplaats veilig te stellen?

Commercieel idee? Flauwekul!

Twijfelend of hij naar Ingolf zou zoeken of liever naar de auto zou teruggaan bleef hij staan, ongeveer een meter van de eik.

En nu?

Hij keek naar de auto, toen naar het groepje bomen waarachter het spoor leek dood te lopen, en toen hij naar beneden keek, merkte hij het.

Verdomme.

Hij had er meteen op moeten komen. De voetsporen die hij was gevolgd. In de sneeuw. Ze waren te diep.

Veel dieper dan de mijne.

Alsof Ingolf iets zwaars had gedragen.

Of...

Op het moment dat de waarheid tot Herzfeld doordrong, stapte er een schim achter de boom vandaan.

... alsof iemand Ingolf uit de auto heeft gedragen.

Voor hij kon zien wie de vochtige lap tegen zijn mond drukte, was Herzfeld al bewusteloos.

48

Hij was weer op het meer. Alleen was het ditmaal niet Ingolf, maar hijzelf die door het ijs was gezakt en met zijn hoofd onder water voor zijn leven vocht. Herzfeld wilde zijn hand omhoogbrengen om bij de rand van het wak te komen, maar de kracht ontbrak hem. Weliswaar voelde hij het water of de kou niet, maar wel het verlammende, loodzware gewicht dat hem naar beneden trok; het donker in, waar zijn longen onder de druk van het water zouden bezwijken. Hij wist dat zijn longen zich met water zouden vullen als hij inademde.

Maar hoe moest hij zijn onweerstaanbare behoefte aan zuurstof weerstaan? Hij kon zijn ademreflex niet meer controleren, en uiteindelijk maakte het niet uit of hij met of zonder water in zijn longen zou verdrinken. Hij sperde zijn ogen open en zag de scheur vlak boven hem. Het ijs was zo dichtbij dat hij het met zijn tong kon aanraken.

Opeens bewoog het bevroren wateroppervlak zich van hem af, alsof het beledigd was dat hij zijn tong ernaar had uitgestoken. Hij gleed verder naar beneden, en toen de druk zo groot werd dat zijn hele lichaam dreigde te exploderen, liet hij alle hoop varen. Hij dacht een laatste keer aan Hannah en opende zijn mond.

Zijn schreeuw om lucht was zo luid dat Herzfeld er zelf van wakker schrok.

Goddank...

Opgelucht dat het maar een nachtmerrie was geweest, bleef hij nog even amechtig brabbelen, alleen om zijn eigen stem te horen, het bewijs dat hij nog leefde.

In werkelijkheid was het heel wat donkerder dan in zijn droom. Eerst was Herzfeld er niet zeker van of zijn ogen eigenlijk wel open waren. Hij voelde dat er druppels van zijn neus vielen, zijn overhemd plakte tegen zijn borst; niet vanwege het water van het meer, maar door het angstzweet dat hem was uitgebroken. Herzfeld wilde over zijn voorhoofd vegen en had een déjà vu.

Opnieuw was hij niet in staat zijn handen te bewegen, dit keer omdat ze achter zijn rug waren vastgebonden.

Wat gebeurt er met me?

Verward draaide hij zijn hoofd alle kanten op en zag nog steeds niets anders dan streepjes licht in de duisternis.

Hij slikte en proefde bloed, en daarna drong de stekende pijn in zijn hoofd en zijn nek tot zijn bewustzijn door. Herzfeld knipperde een paar keer met zijn ogen. Langzaam raakte hij gewend aan het schemerdonker, waarin maar één nietig lichtpuntje te bekennen was. Een rode led, twee passen van hem vandaan, verspreidde een zwak maar gelijkmatig schijnsel, en hoe langer Herzfeld ernaar keek, des te duidelijker werden de contouren van de videocamera waar het vandaan kwam. Lange tijd leek die op magische wijze in de ruimte te zweven, toen zag hij de driepoot waarop hij stond, met de lens precies op Herzfeld gericht.

Waar ben ik in godsnaam?

Onwillekeurig kwam bij Herzfeld de gedachte aan video's van terroristen op, waarin ze voor een draaiende camera hun gijzelaars onthoofdden, en hij vroeg zich af of er achter zijn rug misschien een spandoek met Arabische letters hing.

Hij probeerde zich om te draaien, wat hem vanwege de pijn niet erg goed afging, toen zijn blik op het gebogen dak van golfplaat viel dat zich boven de ruimte welfde, en hij begreep waar hij gevangen werd gehouden.

Ik ben in de bouwwagen.

Toen hij dat besefte kwam zijn herinnering terug aan de laatste minuten voor hij bewusteloos was geraakt en in zijn nachtmerrie was weggezakt: de rook uit de kachelpijp achter het hout, Ingolf die verdwenen was, de doek op zijn mond.

Opnieuw wilde hij met zijn handen naar zijn hoofd gaan, dit keer om zijn kloppende slapen te masseren, en opnieuw werden zijn armen tegengehouden.

De stoel waarop hij zat had een metalen rugleuning; de poten waren op de vloerplanken vastgeschroefd. Een ruw touw was een paar keer om Herzfelds handen geslagen.

Hoewel hij zich realiseerde dat hij de huid boven zijn polsslagaderen zou afschaven, moest hij op zijn minst proberen zich van de boeien te ontdoen. Maar nog voor hij daarmee kon beginnen, ging er opeens een deur open en kwam Sven Martinek met een golf Siberische kou de bouwwagen in.

Hij hield een elektrische lantaarn in zijn hand, een waarschuwingslamp van het soort dat bij wegwerkzaamheden wordt gebruikt, en zwaaide die in Herzfelds richting. Intussen knikte hij hem toe, zoals je naar een buurman knikt die je toevallig tegenkomt als je de vuilniszak buitenzet. Hij sloot de deur, schoof een kleine grendel dicht en ging vlak voor Herzfeld staan.

Ziek, was het eerste woord dat de professor door het hoofd schoot toen hij zijn voormalige collega voor het eerst sinds lange tijd terugzag.

Hij ziet er ziek uit.

En dat in het flatterende gele licht van de lamp.

Goeie god, Sven. Wat is er van je geworden?

Martineks uiterlijke verschijning was het spiegelbeeld van zijn verscheurde ziel. Hij was volledig kapot, zowel psychisch als fysiek. Zijn kleren leken al weken niet meer te zijn gewassen en stonken naar zweet, vuil en natte hond. De laarzen, waarvan de zolen aan de punten loslieten, waren net zo vlekkerig als zijn met baardstoppels overdekte gezicht. Hij was minstens tien kilo afgevallen, waardoor zijn kleren veel te groot leken. Zijn haar was net zo lang niet geknipt als zijn nagels.

Je bent in de vernieling geraakt, dacht Herzfeld en hij wist niet wat hij moest zeggen tegen de man die ooit zoveel zorg aan zijn uiterlijk had besteed, maar nu nauwelijks van een zwerver was te onderscheiden.

Martinek verbrak het stilzwijgen nadat hij de bouwlamp aan een haak naast een geblindeerd raam rechts van Herzfeld had gehangen.

'Eindelijk dan.' Hij keek op zijn horloge. 'Je hebt er alle tijd voor genomen. Ik dacht dat je nooit meer wakker zou worden.'

Hij draaide zich om, liep naar een weinig comfortabel uitziende zithoek en klapte een kist onder de bank open.

'Maar ik ben blij dat je bij me bent,' zei hij, met zijn rug naar Herzfeld, waardoor de professor weer een paar seconden kon proberen zijn polsen uit de boeien te wurmen.

Toen hij zich weer had omgedraaid, had Martinek een fles water in zijn hand. 'Dat meen ik oprecht. Ik ben blij dat je me hebt gevonden.' De klank in zijn stem was net zo droevig als de blik in zijn ogen.

Hij kwam dichter bij Herzfeld staan, die van het ene moment op het andere kookte van woede.

'Waar is Hannah?' vroeg hij met een heftigheid die hij zelf niet voor mogelijk had gehouden, omdat hij zich nog steeds half verdoofd voelde. Alleen die vraag deed ertoe. De rest kon hem gestolen worden. 'Leeft ze nog?'

Martinek fronste zijn voorhoofd. 'Waar zie je me voor aan?' vroeg hij vermoeid. Hij nam een slok uit de fles en zette hem op de grond. Toen haalde hij ergens diep uit zijn jaszak een halfautomatisch pistool tevoorschijn.

'Ik heb je met veel moeite een lesje geleerd; denk je nou echt dat ik nu rekenschap aan jou ga afleggen?'

Hij tikte met de loop van het wapen tegen zijn voorhoofd.

Herzfeld sloot even zijn ogen en dwong zichzelf niet te schreeuwen. 'Lesje? Jij vermoordt mensen. Je speelt met het leven van mijn dochter, Sven. Hannah is ziek. Ze gaat dood als ze zo lang geen medicijnen krijgt.'

'Astma, weten we.'

'*We?* Met wie werk je samen?'

Zijn voormalige collega trok zijn mondhoeken naar beneden. 'Zo werkt dat niet, Paul. Dit hier is geen showdown waarin de moordenaar om op te scheppen zijn motieven prijsgeeft, om de held de tijd te geven zichzelf te bevrijden.' Hij pauzeerde even. 'Maar één ding kan ik je gerust vertellen. Op je telefoon is een sms binnengekomen. Had ik je niet verboden de BKA erbij te betrekken? En dan nog uitgerekend Leuthner? Ik dacht dat jullie elkaar niet konden uitstaan! Hij schrijft dat de orkaan volgens het laatste weerbericht even gaat liggen. Vroeger dan verwacht. Een korte luwte, waarin een vlucht van twintig minuten naar Helgoland eventueel mogelijk is. Hij heeft een piloot gevonden die op een sportvliegveld in de buurt van Cuxhaven op je wacht en die, ik citeer, "gek genoeg is het risico te nemen".'

Martinek glimlachte cynisch. 'Onze collega heeft het bij het rechte eind. Maar helaas is de weersverbetering maar van korte duur en treedt ze al over een halfuur in, zodat je er niet veel aan zult hebben. Daarom ben ik zo vrij geweest een sms'je terug te sturen waarin ik hem bedank en de vlucht annuleer. Toen heb ik je mobieltje vernield en in het bos begraven.'

Waarmee je niet alleen mijn telefoon, maar ook mijn enige kans naar het eiland te komen hebt gesaboteerd.

'Overigens, je zou het noodweer wel dankbaar mogen zijn.'

'Hoezo?'

'Helgoland ligt buiten jouw jurisdictie, Paul. Ik weet niet hoe het je is gelukt aan de informatie te komen die je uiteindelijk hier naar mij heeft gevoerd, maar ik veronderstel dat er iemand ter plaatse is die je helpt; klopt dat?'

Herzfeld knikte onbewust.

'Die huismeester, neem ik aan. Nou ja, maakt niet uit. In elk geval zou je zonder de orkaan geen mens zover hebben gekregen dat smerige klusje voor je op te knappen. Als het ziekenhuis op het eiland niet geëvacueerd was geweest, zou een officier van justitie officieel opdracht tot autopsie hebben gegeven. En zodra de relatie tussen Hannah en de dode was uitgekomen, zou je van verder onderzoek zijn uitgesloten. Komt die situatie je bekend voor?'

Dus dat was het plan, dacht Herzfeld. Destijds had Martinek niet mogen deelnemen aan de sectie op zijn eigen dochter, en nu moest Herzfeld dezelfde verschrikkingen doorstaan en zich desnoods met geweld toegang tot de onderzoeksresultaten verschaffen om zijn dochter te redden.

'De orkaan heeft je in staat gesteld in je eentje te opereren, anders had je nooit zoveel vooruitgang geboekt,' zei Martinek.

Herzfeld hield zijn adem in en staakte zijn poging zich van de boeien te ontdoen. Zijn voormalige collega had niet erg zijn best op de knoop gedaan, vermoedelijk had hij weinig ervaring met het vastbinden van mensen.

Hij heeft beslist het vuile werk door zijn handlanger laten opknappen. De man op de video, die hem heeft geholpen het lijk in het meer te gooien. Iemand die niet in staat is een fatsoenlijke knoop te leggen, wordt nooit een koelbloedige gijzelnemer, laat staan een seriemoordenaar. Herzfeld bad in stilte dat in dit geval de wens niet de vader van de gedachte was.

'Ik begrijp het allemaal niet, Sven. Jij bent toch geen moordenaar.' Hij zocht oogcontact met Martinek, die naast de camera was gaan staan.

'Weet je dat zeker?'

'Ja, dat weet ik zeker. Je mag misschien de aanwijzingen hebben voorbereid, en wellicht heb je ook de lijken geprepareerd. Misschien, maar daar heb ik grote twijfels over, komt het hele plan van jou. Het spietsen van de rechter was in elk geval een duidelijke verwijzing naar een zedendelict.'

'Ik wist dat je het zou begrijpen,' zei Martinek met een zweem van een droevige glimlach.

'Nee. Ik mag dan je aanwijzingen hebben ontcijferd, begrijpen doe ik het niet, Sven. Waarom doe je dit allemaal?'

Waarom doe je me dit aan?

Martinek beet op zijn gebarsten onderlip en liet het pistool van de ene naar de andere hand gaan. Toen stelde hij een wedervraag. 'Wist je dat de rechter Sadler waarschijnlijk alleen zo'n lichte straf heeft gegeven omdat haar man ooit een proces vanwege ongewenste intimiteiten aan zijn broek had gekregen?'

Herzfeld schudde zijn hoofd.

'Magnus Töven was dirigent, en een jonge vrouw, een celliste, wilde wraak op hem nemen omdat hij haar uit het orkest had gegooid wegens te laat komen. Later trok ze haar beschuldigingen in, maar de reputatie van de man was geruïneerd. Tot hij relatief jong aan een hartaanval overleed, vond hij geen werk meer.'

Herzfeld zuchtte. 'Dan weet je zelf waartoe blinde wraakzucht kan leiden, Sven. Töven wreekt zich met milde vonnissen op de vrouw die haar man heeft aangeklaagd, of liever op de maatschappij waarin zoiets mogelijk is. Maar jij maakt mijn gezin kapot, hoewel ik jouw dochter niet op mijn geweten heb.'

'Zie je dat zo?' vroeg Martinek. Hij klonk ietwat teleurgesteld.

'Ja. Ik ben Sadler niet. *Ik* heb je dochter niet verkracht en vermoord.'

'Nee.' Martinek was even stil. Hij staarde peinzend naar het wapen in zijn hand en zei toen: 'Lily heb je niet vermoord. Haar niet.'

Haar niet?

'Waarom leg je zo de nadruk op "haar"?'

Martinek hief zijn wapen op, draaide zijn hand een kwartslag, net als in een Amerikaanse bioscoopfilm, en richtte het pistool op Herzfelds borst. 'Zoals ik al zei, dit is geen showdown uit de film.'

Zonder te kijken greep hij naar de camera naast hem, drukte op een knop aan de zijkant en trok iets met het formaat van een postzegel uit een vak, dat met een langgerekte pieptoon was opengegaan.

'Wat ben je van plan?' vroeg Herzfeld, die de bui al zag hangen, maar Martinek liet niet zien wat hij in zijn vuist had. Hij stond nu tussen Herzfeld en de camera in en keek hem strak aan met een blik die met de seconde uitdrukkingslozer werd.

'Je hebt gelijk, Paul. Ik ben geen moordenaar. Daar heb ik het lef niet voor.' Hij haalde zwaar adem. 'Maar het gaat hier niet alleen om jou of om je dochter. Het gaat om heel veel meer, dat heeft hij mij duidelijk gemaakt.'

Hij?

'Wie is hij?'

'Je zult hem vast gauw leren kennen, denk ik. Heb vertrouwen. Hij is een goede man.'

Ontzet begreep Herzfeld dat de tragedie met Lily Martineks verstand moest hebben vergiftigd. Hij was volkomen buiten zichzelf, zijn woorden waren net zo schokkend als zijn daden. Hij drukte zijn handpalm tegen zijn mond. Herzfeld zag alleen nog Svens adamsappel door zijn moeizame slikbewegingen als een lift op en neer gaan.

'Wat heb je gedaan?' riep hij. Wanhopig rukte hij aan zijn boeien. Een paar seconden nog, dan zouden ze losgaan, daar was hij zeker van. Maar die tijd gunde Martinek hem niet, en hij tilde zijn wapen weer op.

'Je zei dat je blij was dat ik ben gekomen,' zei Herzfeld, in een laatste poging hem van zijn voornemen af te brengen. 'Waarom?'

Martinek knipperde met zijn ogen, alsof hij serieus over de vraag nadacht. Toen zei hij zacht: 'Om aan het eind niet alleen te hoeven zijn.'

Hij keek Herzfeld met ogen nat van tranen aan en duwde het wapen tegen zijn voorhoofd.

'Ik heb niemand anders meer die me begrijpt.'
Toen haalde hij de trekker over.

De kracht van de explosie was zo groot dat er delen van de schedel en de hersenmassa in Herzfelds gezicht spatten. Een paar keer nog voer er een stuiptrekking door Martinek, nadat hij tegen de vloer van de bouwwagen was geslagen. Maar dat waren alleen nog de onwillekeurige reflexen van zijn stervende zenuwstelsel.

49

Herzfeld schreeuwde. Uit wanhoop. Vanwege de schok. Om hulp.

Hij brulde Martineks naam, zelfs toen diens ledematen allang niet meer bewogen en alle leven uit het lichaam was geweken. Toen riep hij Ingolf, en ten slotte schreeuwde hij van pijn toen hij zijn polsen abnormaal ver uitrekte om ze uit de boeien te kunnen draaien.

Nog meer dan zijn tot bloedens toe geschaafde polsen deed hem het bittere besef pijn dat Martinek hem niet had verdoofd en vastgebonden om hem iets aan te doen. Martinek had hem daar vastgehouden zodat hij de zelfmoord van zijn gebroken collega niet kon verhinderen.

Gelukt!

Met een laatste ruk had Herzfeld zijn boeien losgemaakt, was hij van de stoel opgesprongen en bukte zich enigszins duizelig over het lijk heen, toen de deur openzwaaide en Ingolf naar binnen strompelde.

Zijn jas zat vol sneeuw. Vermoedelijk had hij verdoofd in het bos gelegen.

Hij leunde tegen de wand en boog zich hoestend voorover, zodat Herzfeld al dacht dat de stagiair vanwege de aanblik van Martinek moest overgeven. Maar toen Ingolf weer opkeek, begreep hij dat het de zoon van de senator al zijn kracht moest hebben gekost om de bouwwagen te bereiken. Net als hij had ook Ingolf bebloede polsen, wat erop wees dat ook hij zich moest hebben bevrijd om hem te hulp te komen.

'Stop, blijf staan,' riep Herzfeld, en pas toen zag Ingolf de plas bloed op de vloer, waar hij bijna in was gestapt.

'Ach, lieve hemel, is dat...?'

'Ja, Martinek.'

'En hebt u...?'

'Nee. Dat was hijzelf. Haal mijn koffer.'

'Ja,' zei Ingolf en hij knikte, maar maakte geen aanstalten in beweging te komen. Het zien van de dode had hem gehypnotiseerd. Als verlamd staarde hij naar het lichaam.

'Hé, wakker worden. We mogen geen tijd verliezen,' blafte Herzfeld. Pas toen hij het herhaalde, drong zijn stem tot Ingolf door.

'Sorry, wat zei u?'

'Mijn koffer. Haal mijn sectiegereedschap.'

'Waarom moet dat?' Ingolfs gezicht werd nog een paar tinten bleker.

Herzfeld wees naar de nog steeds rood knipperende camera boven zijn hoofd.

'Martinek heeft voor zijn zelfmoord een geheugenkaartje ingeslikt. Dat moet ik er zo snel mogelijk uit halen, voor het wordt aangetast door het maagzuur.'

50

'Hartelijk gefeliciteerd, professor Herzfeld! Als u tot hier bent gekomen, bent u een heel snelle leerling.'

Paul had de zwaarlijvige man die hem bijna vertrouwelijk met zijn naam aansprak nooit eerder gezien.

'Wie is dat?' wilde Ingolf weten. Hij had zich verbazend snel hersteld en had zich tegen de verwachting in bijzonder nuttig gemaakt. Niet alleen omdat hij de koffer met autopsie-instrumenten had gehaald; hij had ook bij het openen van de buikholte van Martinek geholpen, wat vanwege het recente tijdstip van overlijden en de omstandigheden waaronder de gedeeltelijke sectie op de vloer van de bouwwagen moest worden uitgevoerd heel wat bloediger was geweest dan gebruikelijk.

Om de geheugenkaart uit Martineks maag te kunnen halen, hadden ze hem moeten uitkleden en op zijn rug moeten draaien, iets waar Ingolf zich niet te goed voor had gevoeld, hoewel je aan zijn trillende onderlip kon zien dat hij onder grote druk stond. Zowel lichamelijk als geestelijk. Op het meer had hij de dood in de ogen gezien, een ervaring die hij nog lang niet had verwerkt, en nu moest hij toezien hoe Herzfeld in minder dan vijf minuten het lichaam van een man van zijn nek tot aan het schaambeen opensneed, de in de ijskoude bouwwagen dampende, van bloed druipende buikwand openklapte, de maag van de dode tussen de lever en de milt uit de diepte van de buikholte trok en die vervolgens opensneed om daarin naar het kaartje te zoeken. In de haast had hij zelfs geen handschoenen aangetrokken.

Later zou Herzfeld huiveren als hij aan dat onwerkelijke moment in de bouwwagen terugdacht, maar op dat moment had zijn bezorgdheid voor Hannah alle andere emoties verdrongen.

Hij dacht er niet over na dat hij een mens had opengesneden met wie hij zich verbonden had gevoeld. Zijn gedachten draaiden alleen om wat hij in de maag vreesde te zullen aantreffen. Hij gruwde bij de gedachte aan de opname die hij op de kaart vermoedde, maar bad toch dat de video niet door het maagzuur zou zijn aangetast.

En zijn gebeden werden verhoord.

Zonder de fles water die Martinek voor zijn dood had klaargezet, hadden ze de bloed- en uitscheidingsresten niet zo snel kunnen verwijderen van de geheugenkaart, die nu weer in de camera zat. Omdat de zijwaarts uitgeklapte monitor niet groter was dan de handpalm van een volwassene, moesten Herzfeld en Ingolf zich tegen elkaar aan drukken om iets te kunnen zien. Ze hadden Martineks lijk naar het achterste gedeelte van de bouwwagen naast de gedoofde kachel getrokken en provisorisch een deken over hem heen gelegd.

'Het lijkt erop dat u zich dit keer niet aan de voorschriften hebt gehouden,' sprak de man in de camera. De onbekende met de onderkin liet een vreugdeloos lachje horen. Hij stond zo dicht bij de lens dat alleen zijn gezicht in beeld was, van zijn haargrens tot zijn hals. De belichting was weinig flatteus, en omdat hij van onderaf was gefilmd, zag de vreemde er nog pafferiger uit dan hij al was. Onder het praten ontblootte hij gele, door sigarettenrook aangetaste tanden.

'Om zo ver te komen, moest u belangrijk bewijs achterhouden dat u bij de secties hebt ontdekt. Merkwaardig. Toen Sven dat van u verlangde, hebt u zijn verzoek afgewezen.' Opnieuw klonk het vreugdeloze lachje. 'Maar dit keer gaat het ook om uw eigen dochter. Het hemd is nader dan de rok, waar of niet?'

'Wie ben jij?' fluisterde Herzfeld, en alsof de man op de video hem had gehoord, stelde hij zich voor.

'U zult zich wel afvragen wie ik ben. Mijn naam is Philipp Schwintowski, en u zou maar al te graag weten wat voor rol ik bij dit alles speel, nietwaar?'

Herzfeld knikte onbewust.

'Dat is eenvoudig uit te leggen: ik ben de vader van het meisje dat u hebt vermoord.'

Ingolf draaide zich met een ruk om naar Herzfeld, die zijn vragende blik negeerde.

'Hebt u de foto's in het botenhuis gezien?'

De foto's die Martinek van Sadler had genomen toen hij hem schaduwde?

Herzfeld voelde zich opeens alsof hij op een deinend scheepsdek stond.

'Als Sven die ellendeling niet na zijn ontslag uit de gevangenis had gevolgd, zou ik Rebecca nooit hebben gevonden.'

Rebecca?

Vaag herinnerde hij zich de samenvatting van de gezinssituatie die Yao hem eerder had doorgegeven: *Sybille Schwintowski... getrouwd met verhuizer Philipp Schwintowski. Samen hadden ze een dochter, Rebecca, zeventien jaar oud. Beiden zijn spoorloos verdwenen.'*

'De rechter meende dat een kinderverkrachter kan worden geresocialiseerd. Denkt u dat ook, professor? Ik zal u vertellen hoe er volgens mij met veroordeelde misdadigers moet worden omgegaan.'

Even was alleen een grote hand te zien, toen was de camera verduisterd. Toen Herzfeld weer iets anders dan schaduwen zag, was het objectief opnieuw ingesteld, en zat Schwintowski op een stoel die niet op zijn gewichtsklasse berekend leek te zijn. Om zijn kolossale bovenlichaam spande een muisgrijze wollen pullover met v-hals.

'Ik vind dat iedere dader even lang moet lijden als zijn slachtoffer. En even lang als diens naaste familie. Wat in mijn geval zou betekenen: Sadler moet tot aan zijn dood de ergste kwellingen doorstaan.'

Schwintowski. Lily. Rebecca. Sadler.

Herzfeld begon de omvang van de verschrikkingen te begrijpen.

'Mensen zoals Sadler zijn niet behandelbaar. Zodra ze de kans krijgen, zoeken ze hun volgende slachtoffer. Nauwelijks was het monster de gevangenis uit of hij sloeg toe. En dit keer greep hij mijn Rebecca.'

De tranen liepen over Schwintowski's wangen.

'Hij heeft haar naar een voormalige vleesfabriek in Hohenschönhausen ontvoerd. Daar heeft hij haar twee dagen lang verkracht.' Zijn stem brak, en ook Herzfeld kreeg tranen in zijn ogen.

'Dat is vier weken geleden. Sven had Sadlers *minivan* tot de parkeerplaats voor het sportterrein in Westend gevolgd. Rebecca was een goede voetbalster, moet u weten. Die avond hadden ze een grote overwinning gevierd, en het was al laat toen ze bij het fietsenrek afscheid van haar vriendinnen nam. Sven lette even niet op. Hij had Sadler al uren gevolgd en was in slaap gevallen. Toen hij weer wakker werd, was Sadlers minivan verdwenen. De parkeerplaats was leeg, op één fiets na. De fiets van Rebecca. Ze had zo'n mand op haar bagagedrager voor haar sportspullen. Die had dat varken achtergelaten.'

Schwintowski boog voorover en schoof zijn stoel naar de camera. Hij vouwde zijn handen in zijn schoot.

'Weet u, ik kan me niet meer heugen wanneer ik voor het laatst heb geslapen sinds Martinek bij me aanbelde – met Rebecca's scholierenkaart in zijn hand.'

Zijn stem was onvast.

'Die had hij in haar sporttas gevonden. Ik heb meteen geprobeerd haar op haar mobieltje te bereiken. De sadist heeft haar een tekst op haar voicemail laten inspreken, een laatste tekst voor de ouders. Daarna heb ik niet de fout gemaakt om de politie in de arm te nemen. En zeker niet nadat ik had gehoord welk recht Martinek is wedervaren. Als u zich met mijn biografie bezighoudt, zult u geruchten horen die kunnen bevestigen dat ik een man ben die de zaken graag zelf ter hand neemt. Sadler heeft het verkeerde slachtoffer uitgezocht.'

Herzfeld knikte instemmend en dacht aan Yao's persoonsbeschrijving: *'Philipp Schwintowski is geen onbeschreven blad. (...) De pers noemde hem de Boeddhamoordenaar, wat met zijn zwaarlijvige gestalte te maken had. Met een bewakingscamera is gefilmd dat hij een klant met een betalingsachterstand van een brug over de snelweg door de stad gooide, waarna de man door een vrachtwagen werd overreden.'*

'Martinek heeft me helpen zoeken. We zijn alle plekken afgegaan waar hij Sadler in de weken ervoor had geschaduwd. Bij nummer zeven was het raak. Maar helaas kwamen we te laat. Rebecca was al dood toen we haar vonden.'

Daarom de opname van het lijk van de jonge vrouw op Martineks laptop.

Herzfeld haatte zichzelf om het gevoel van opluchting dat over hem kwam toen hij zich realiseerde dat het niet Hannah was geweest, *maar Rebecca*, die Martinek samen met haar vader naar haar laatste rustplaats in het meer had gebracht. De eerder uitgevoerde en op video geregistreerde autopsie had de daden aan het licht moeten brengen die Sadler had begaan.

'Maar desondanks...' Schwintowski haalde zijn neus op en veegde zijn tranen weg met de rug van zijn hand. 'Desondanks kregen wij Sadler te pakken. We vonden hem in de kelder ernaast, toen hij net naar de opnames zat te kijken die hij had gemaakt terwijl hij Rebecca folterde. Zijn broek hing op zijn enkels. Hij was gemakkelijk te overmeesteren, omdat hij zich net aan het...' Schwintowski slikte. 'Weet u dat de verkrachting voor hem maar bijzaak was? Hij wilde zich afrukken, omdat hij erop geilde hoe hij Rebecca de dood in had gedreven.'

Dat was dus de aanpak en het doel van de sadist, dacht Herzfeld. In wezen was Sadler een laffe hond. Het zou vast blijken dat hij vroeger vaak mishandeld en vernederd was, en de zedendelinquent beschouwde zichzelf vast al sinds zijn kindertijd als het stuk stront dat hij was – alleen in de paar seconden waarin hij de macht voelde die hij over het leven van andere mensen had, kreeg hij een gevoel van eigenwaarde en voelde hij zich machtig. En omdat die seconden zo zelden voorkwamen, was hij ertoe overgegaan ze op video vast te leggen.

Grote god. Geen wonder dat Schwintowski was doorgedraaid en dorstte naar wraak op iedereen die ook maar in de verste verte iets met de beestachtige moord op zijn dochter te maken had. Töven en Sadler had hij al uitgeschakeld, samen met Martinek.

En nu ben ik aan de beurt. Met het verschil dat hij mij niet wil vermoorden, maar wil laten lijden. Hij wil me met gelijke munt terugbetalen.

Herzfeld werd misselijk toen hij eraan dacht hoe onwaarschijnlijk het was dat twee vaders die hun dochter hadden verloren Hannah in leven zouden laten.

Het volgende moment bekroop Herzfeld weer het griezelige gevoel dat het leek of Schwintowski zijn gedachten kon lezen: 'Ik weet dat u in wezen geen slecht mens bent, professor. U hebt mijn dochter niet aangerand of een te mild oordeel geveld. Mijn wraakzucht gold aanvankelijk alleen mevrouw de rechter. En natuurlijk ook Sadler, wiens tong ik nog ter plekke heb afgesneden, waarmee hij Rebecca...' Schwintowski's stem brak opnieuw, en het lukte hem niet het onzegbare uit te spreken.

... waarmee hij haar heeft afgelikt voor hij haar verkrachtte.

'Mijn eerste impuls was Sadler dood te martelen en mijn mensen op de rechter af te sturen. Maar toen liet Martinek me inzien dat het niet alleen om ons gaat.'

Hij leunde vermoeid achterover in zijn stoel, en voor het eerst richtte Herzfeld zijn aandacht op de ruimte waarin Schwintowski zich bevond. Naar de bruine houten balken te oordelen bevond hij zich in een lege zolder. Opzij van hem moest een klein raam zijn, waardoor het voor de opname noodzakelijke licht viel.

'Het gaat om het hele systeem, dat van slachtoffers daders maakt,' verklaarde Schwintowski. 'Om de politie, die het veel te druk heeft om bij elke aangifte van vermissing een zoekactie te starten. Het gaat om rechtbanken, die belastingontduikers harder straffen dan kinderverkrachters. Om psychologen, die verkrachters vrijpleiten zodra ze een trauma in hun kindertijd ontdekken, terwijl men mij voor mijn illegale casino's het liefst in een isoleercel zou opsluiten. En natuurlijk gaat het om het forensisch apparaat als onderdeel van de zogenaamde rechtsstaat, die uiteindelijk alleen in het voordeel van de daders werkt en de slachtoffers voor de tweede keer straft.'

Schwintowski kneep zijn ogen samen en hief een worstvinger. 'We hebben gewacht tot Sadlers wond was genezen. Martinek heeft de stomp van zijn tong gehecht, om het varken niet te laten doodbloeden. En daarna, toen hij genezen was, hebben wij hem het vuile werk laten opknappen.'

Dus Sadler heeft de lijken verminkt? De rechter gespietst?

Herzfeld vroeg zich af hoe ze het monster daartoe hadden kunnen dwingen, en kwam zelf op het antwoord: de beloning die ze hem hadden beloofd, was Hannah. Nu was hij het die tranen in zijn ogen kreeg.

'Ik geef toe dat de vossenjacht die u naar uw dochter brengt misschien wreed is. Maar de aanwijzingen zijn verborgen in de lichamen van mensen die de dood hebben verdiend. U hebt nog steeds een kans om uw dochter te redden. Onze gezinnen hebben alles al verloren wat hun leven zin gaf.'

Vandaar de zelfmoord van Schwintowski's vrouw. Dus het klopte inderdaad: Sybille Schwintowski werd niet gedwongen de tabletten in te nemen of haar afscheidsvideo te maken, die de technische recherche in het penthouse had gevonden. 'Zo, nu bent u bijna aan het eind van uw reis naar inzicht, meneer Herzfeld. Ik zou natuurlijk kunnen verklappen waar wij uw dochter hebben verborgen. Maar zo gemakkelijk wil ik het u niet maken. Zoals gezegd blijkt uit mijn onderzoek dat u een goed mens bent. Maar ook goede mensen maken fouten, en die hebt u te verantwoorden.'

Hij veegde een traan uit een ooghoek.

'Ik zit anders in elkaar dan Sven. Pathetisch gedoe ligt me niet. Daarom zal ik u de laatste tip mondeling geven: we hebben Hannah met Sadler alleen gelaten.'

O god.

Diep in Herzfelds hart ging een donkere deur open.

'Hannah is dicht bij me in de buurt. Volg het witte licht van Alcatraz, als u haar wilt vinden.'

'Wat bedoelt hij daar in godsnaam mee?' vroeg Ingolf, wiens aanwezigheid Herzfeld volkomen was vergeten.

'Als ik u was zou ik haast maken, als u Hannah niet voorgoed wilt verliezen.' Dat waren Schwintowski's laatste woorden. Hij stond op. Eerst verdween zijn hoofd uit het blikveld van de camera. Daarna waren alleen nog zijn benen te zien, want hij was op de stoel geklommen waarop hij al die tijd had gezeten.

'Nee,' schreeuwden Herzfeld en Ingolf tegelijk, maar toen had Schwintowski de stoel al met één been naar achteren geschopt.

Zijn vrouw had voor pillen gekozen. Martinek voor een pistool. Schwintowski voor de strop.

Herzfeld kromp ineen toen hij zag hoe Schwintowski's lichaam hevig begon te spartelen aan het touw, tot de om zijn hals gesnoerde strop de bloedtoevoer naar zijn hersens volledig tot stilstand had gebracht. En terwijl Herzfeld verstijfd van ontzetting naar de voor de camera bungelende voeten staarde, realiseerde hij zich dat met Philipp Schwintowski de laatste persoon was gestorven die hem had kunnen vertellen waar zijn dochter zich bevond.

51

'We hebben Hannah met Sadler alleen gelaten.'

Herzfeld wist dat die woorden hem eeuwig zouden achtervolgen als hij er niet in slaagde Schwintowski's laatste raadsel op te lossen. Eigenlijk had hij opgelucht moeten zijn, want Sadler lag dood op de sectietafel op de afdeling Pathologie van de eilandkliniek, wat betekende dat Hannah niet langer in zijn macht kon zijn. Maar misschien betekende dat alleen dat het voor haar allang te laat was. En zelfs als Hannah de martelingen van de sadistische dader tot nog toe had overleefd, bevond ze zich nu in een kerker, alleen en zonder de medicijnen die voor haar onontbeerlijk waren.

'Volg het witte licht van Alcatraz.'

'Ik neem aan dat hij daarmee niet het gevangeniseiland voor San Francisco bedoelt?' opperde Ingolf.

'Nee, dat sloeg waarschijnlijk alleen op een gevangenis op een eiland. Hoogstwaarschijnlijk lopen alle sporen naar Helgoland.'

Herzfeld had de verhuisondernemer al minuten geleden naar zijn dood zien springen, en nog steeds kon hij zich niet van de langzaam heen en weer slingerende voeten losmaken. Volgens de tijdbalk aan de rand van het scherm duurde de opname nog een kleine drie kwartier.

Hoewel Herzfeld het liefst nog zo lang in de bouwwagen zou zijn gebleven om te kijken of er nog bruikbare aanwijzingen in de opname voorkwamen, wist hij dat ze daar geen tijd voor hadden.

We hebben geen veertig minuten om de video helemaal te zien. Verdomme, we hebben niet eens veertig minuten om naar het eiland te komen.

Hij wilde de video stopzetten, toen een laatste blik op de tijd-code hem weerhield.

'Wat is er?'

'Er klopt iets niet,' fluisterde Herzfeld. Hij raakte het touch-screen aan.

Het beeld stond stil, en hij wees op de linkerbenedenhoek van de monitor.

'Wat zou er moeten zijn?' vroeg Ingolf, terwijl hij zijn nek mas-seerde. Om iets te kunnen zien, moest de opgeschoten stagiair zich weer naar het schermpje van de camera vooroverbuigen.

'Volgens deze tijdcode heeft Schwintowski al drie dagen ge-leden zelfmoord gepleegd. De laatste veerboot ging eergisteren. Vanaf dat moment moet Martinek in elk geval op het vasteland zijn geweest.'

'Wanneer werd Sadlers lijk op Helgoland gevonden?' vroeg In-golf.

'Linda heeft het gisteren aan de kust gevonden, maar het kan er langer hebben gelegen.'

'Goed, Schwintowski heeft Sadler alias Erik daar gedumpt. Dat was drie dagen geleden, vlak voor hij zichzelf ophing.' In-golf fronste argwanend zijn wenkbrauwen. 'Maar wat gebeurde er daarna?'

De professor knikte. 'Goede vraag! Wie heeft Ender daarnet het mes in zijn hals geplant, als Sadler en Schwintowski dood waren en Martinek niet op het eiland was?'

'U bedoelt...?'

'Ja. Er moet nog een derde medeplichtige zijn.'

Herzfeld raakte opnieuw het beeldscherm aan en ging terug naar de scène waarin Schwintowski zijn stoel wegtrapte.

'Zou gemanipuleerd kunnen zijn,' veronderstelde Ingolf, die op het laatste moment zijn blik afwendde om de verschrikkelijke beelden niet opnieuw te hoeven zien. 'Maar waarom zou Marti-nek zelfmoord plegen en Schwintowski...'

'Ssst!' onderbrak Herzfeld hem en hij legde zijn wijsvinger tegen zijn lippen. 'Hoorde je dat?'

'Nee. Wat?' Ingolf draaide zich weer naar de camera.

Herzfeld spoelde nog eens terug en draaide het volume helemaal open.

Inderdaad. Ik heb me niet vergist.

Ingolf knikte opgewonden. 'Is dat een gong of zo?' Het geluid kwam nauwelijks boven de achtergrondruis uit, en daarom hadden ze het eerst niet gehoord, maar nu Herzfeld wist waar hij op moest letten, twijfelde hij niet. 'Nee, geen gong. Dat is een klok.'

En die heb ik vandaag al eens gehoord.

'Klopt,' viel Ingolf hem bij. 'Zo'n oud ding staat bij ons thuis in de bibliotheek.'

'En ergens op Helgoland.'

Herzfelds hart ging sneller kloppen. Tot nu toe had hij alleen een vermoeden gehad dat Hannah op het eiland werd vastgehouden. De vindplaats van de lijken hoefde niet de plek te zijn waar ze was ondergebracht, en bovendien had hij de eerste aanwijzing op zijn sectietafel in Berlijn gevonden. Maar nu was er eindelijk een concreet spoor naar Helgoland. Een paar uur geleden nog had hij een staande klok horen slaan terwijl hij met Linda had gebeld. Hij wist alleen niet meer precies waar ze toen op het eiland was geweest.

'Geef me je telefoon,' zei hij.

Ingolf schudde spijtig zijn hoofd en haalde zijn mobieltje uit de zak van zijn trainingsbroek. 'Die doet het niet meer,' zei hij. 'Martinek heeft de batterij en de simkaart eruit gehaald toen ik buiten westen was.'

Verdomme. Dat was te verwachten.

'Dan moeten we naar een telefooncel rijden.'

Herzfeld wilde net de camera van het statief af halen om hem als bewijsmateriaal mee te nemen, toen Ingolf hem bij zijn arm greep.

'Wat is er?'

'Wilt u niet eerst testen of de internetverbinding nog bestaat?'

'Hoe bedoel je?'

Ingolf tikte met zijn wijsvinger op de rode led. 'Ik heb de indruk dat uw collega een techniekfreak was. Eerst een tablet-pc waar het beeldscherm af kan, nu een camera met internetverbinding.'

'Betekent dat dat alles wat we hier hebben gezien, online staat?'

De bekentenis, de beschuldigingen, de zelfmoord?

'Nee. Maar op een of andere manier moet dat videobestand van het eiland hier naar de bouwwagen zijn gekomen. Ik doe maar een gooi, maar ik denk dat Schwintowski zijn zelfmoord via een videochat direct in het geheugen heeft gezet. Technisch gezien zou dat bij dit model in elk geval mogelijk moeten zijn.'

Ingolf vroeg Herzfeld opzij te gaan en drukte op een paar knoppen aan de zijkant van de camera. Schwintowski's bungelende lichaam maakte plaats voor allerlei getallen en gegevens.

Ingolfs handen trilden, en zijn vingers lieten vochtige plekken achter op het beeldscherm, maar hij had niet veel tijd nodig om tot een eerste conclusie te komen: 'Precies zoals ik dacht.' Hij draaide zich om naar Herzfeld, die tevergeefs probeerde te begrijpen wat de student zojuist had gedaan.

'Schwintowski heeft een anoniem chataccount gebruikt, en zijn camera op het eiland dus als beeldtelefoon gebruikt. En Martinek heeft de opname met deze camera hier geregistreerd en opgeslagen.'

'En?'

'Helaas is er geen *en*. De verbinding bestaat al dagen niet meer, en daarom heb ik geen...' Ingolf stokte midden in zijn zin en reageerde niet toen Herzfeld hem vroeg naar het waarom. In plaats daarvan hield hij de camera nu met beide handen vast en benam Herzfeld het zicht, zodat die niet zag welke instellingen hij veranderde.

'Ha,' riep hij ineens opgewonden en toen hij van het statief terugtrad, stond er iets tussen euforie en angst op zijn gezicht te lezen.

'Wat is er?'

'Zoals gezegd is de chatruimte met Schwintowski allang gesloten. Maar ik zie in het protocol dat Martinek de afgelopen paar dagen voortdurend een andere verbinding heeft opgebouwd.'

Voor Herzfeld iets kon vragen, had Ingolf al een link op het touchscreen aangeklikt, en nu werd een draaiende zandloper in het midden van het beeldscherm zichtbaar. Het duurde nog geen tien seconden, of een luide toon signaleerde dat er verbinding was. Tien seconden, tot de eerste wazige beelden verschenen.

En Herzfeld een gesmoorde kreet slaakte toen hij de bunkerachtige kelder zag.

52

IN DE HEL

Het was gemakkelijker geweest dan ze had gedacht. Haar ijzeren bed had precies onder de gloeilamp gestaan en dus ook direct onder de vleeshaak. Het duurde even voor ze genoeg krachten had verzameld om op het bed te klimmen, maar toen het uiteindelijk was gelukt en ze enigszins stabiel op de verende ondergrond stond, kon ze moeiteloos de kabel van de haak nemen en in plaats daarvan de strop aanbrengen.

'Zo, is dit wat je wilt?' vroeg ze koppig aan de camera. Ze nam een besluit. Niet dat ze zou sterven. Dat had ze allang besloten. Ze zou zichzelf liever vrijwillig de dood in jagen dan haar meest gevoelige plek aan de waanzinnige met het besnijdingsmes prijsgeven.

Nog meer pijn verdraag ik niet.

'Bovendien zal ik dit toch niet overleven,' zei ze tegen zichzelf. Aan de belofte die de moordenaar haar had gedaan, had ze niet de minste twijfel. De uitdrukking in zijn ogen terwijl hij haar verkracht, geslagen, geschopt en met de schaar mishandeld had, was keihard en niet mis te verstaan: voor hem was ze geen mens, maar een hoer, een wegwerpartikel. Zodra hij met haar klaar was – *zodra hij mij heeft besneden* – zou hij zich van haar ontdoen. De enige keus die ze had, was het tijdstip en zodoende de omstandigheden van haar dood zelf te bepalen.

En dat tijdstip was nu aangebroken.

Ze zou springen. Maar eerst moest ze nog één ding doen.

Haastig, iets te snel en daarom onhandig, stapte ze van het bed en verzwikte haar enkel. Die nieuwe, bijkomende pijn maakte haar woedend, en ze begon weer te huilen, vooral omdat ze wist dat ze nu een tijdje moest uitrusten voor ze weer kon staan – en dat kostte tijd, tijd die ze niet had.

Want straks komt hij terug.

'Op een gegeven moment,' had hij gezegd. Maar wanneer was een gegeven moment?

Ze trok haar knieën op tot haar kin en wreef haar enkel op de plek waar haar tatoeage zat, streelde de vlinder en wilde dat ze kon vliegen.

Maar zelfs daar zou ik nu niets meer aan hebben, nietwaar?

Toen de pijn was weggeëbd en haar enkel alleen nog zacht klopte, probeerde ze voorzichtig op te staan, maar het ging niet. Op zichzelf was de blessure onschuldig, vergeleken met alles wat ze tot nog toe had moeten ondergaan. Maar alles bij elkaar was de verstuikte voet de druppel die de emmer met kwellingen deed overlopen. Op dit moment zou ze het in elk geval niet voor elkaar krijgen het bed naar de hoek van de bunker te slepen om van daaruit de camera kapot te slaan.

Ze vermoedde, nee, ze *wist* dat haar moordenaar alleen zo lang was weggebleven omdat het hem opwond te zien hoeveel macht hij over haar had. Waarschijnlijk zat hij de hele tijd naar haar te kijken. Vermoedelijk zou hij een stijve krijgen als hij later naar de video keek waarop ze haar dood tegemoet sprong. Maar dat genoegen gunde ze hem niet. Als ze stierf, dan zonder publiek.

Alleen, hoe verniel ik die camera voordat hij terugkomt?

Ze kroop naar de hoek waar het gestaag knipperende apparaat met een simpele, maar praktische constructie met dubbelzijdig plakband was vastgemaakt. De camera werkte op een accu en via een draadloze verbinding, in elk geval kon ze geen snoer zien waaraan ze het ding gewoon omlaag had kunnen trekken.

Te oordelen naar de hoek was ze op dit moment, nu ze vlak

onder de lens zat, niet of maar gedeeltelijk te zien, en het besef dat ze nu al uit het blikveld van de waanzinnige was verdwenen, vervulde haar met een irrationele blijdschap, die echter van korte duur was en plaatsmaakte voor grote neerslachtigheid.

Hij kan me niet zien. Maar ik kan mezelf ook nooit meer in de spiegel aankijken.

Ze sloot haar betraande ogen en probeerde uit de diepte van haar geheugen wanhopig de herinneringen aan haar eigen identiteit naar boven te halen, maar ze zag alleen een paar onsamenhangende fragmenten:

* haar vader op een fiets;
* een paar verhuisdozen, zoals die waarin ze de strop had gevonden;
* haar moeder op een vliegveld;
* de tatoeëerder, die haar ervoor waarschuwde dat het op die plek veel pijn deed.

Ze herinnerde zich dat ze haar eindexamen wilde doen en goed in wiskunde en sport was – maar dat was niet genoeg voor haar.

'Ik wil niet dood!' fluisterde ze en ze slikte hevig. 'Niet zonder te weten waarom.'

Ze wiste de tranen uit haar ooghoeken, toen zei ze wat luider: 'En niet zonder te weten wie ik ben.'

Toch krabbelde ze weer overeind en strompelde terug naar de brits. Het was beter dat ze zich weer liet zien, voor die gek zou terugkomen. Door op de koude vloer te blijven liggen zou haar herinnering niet terugkomen. Nadenken kon ze ook met een strop om haar nek.

53

'Dit gaat niet lukken,' protesteerde Ingolf, die moeite had hem bij te houden. Herzfeld beende haastig over de open plek door de enkelhoge sneeuw terug naar de Porsche. De ijlings van het statief af geschroefde videocamera droeg hij onder zijn donsjack, maar hij constateerde dat het een overbodige voorzorgsmaatregel was.

Leuthner had gelijk gekregen. Het weer was nu heel wat beter, alsof het hen wilde bespotten, en er was weinig kans dat de camera door wind of sneeuw schade zou oplopen. De storm was nog maar een stijve bries en alle voorspellingen ten spijt vielen er zelfs een paar stralen van de avondzon door het opengebroken wolkendek.

'Voortmaken,' riep Herzfeld en hij keek even achterom om te zien waar Ingolf bleef. De stagiair wreef huiverend over zijn armen, die hij stijf tegen zijn bovenlichaam gedrukt hield. Met zijn donkere trainingspak was hij bijna onzichtbaar tegen de achtergrond van het donkergrijze bos en de gevelde boomstammen achter hem.

'We kunnen niet rijden,' hijgde hij, en Herzfeld werd bekropen door een duister voorgevoel. 'Heeft hij de sleutel afgepakt?'

'Ja, maar dat is het probleem niet. Ik heb een reservesleutel in de auto verstopt.'

'Oké, vooruit dan met de geit.' Herzfeld zette de pas er weer in en liep in de richting van de Porsche, waarvan de binnenverlichting nog steeds brandde omdat er drie deuren openstonden.

'We moeten in het volgende dorp hulp halen.'

Herzfeld had geen idee hoe het weer buitengaats was, maar hij nam aan dat een reddingshelikopter onder deze omstandigheden nog wel toestemming zou krijgen om op te stijgen. Om het even of het Leuthner, de BKA, de politie of een reddingsorganisatie was – hij moest beslist iemand zien te bereiken voordat het weer omsloeg.

En voor mijn dochter haar toevlucht zoekt tot de dood.

Hij had alleen een lege bedspiraal en kale muren gezien, meer niet, omdat ze was weggekropen in de achterste hoek van de kelder, zoals hij uit het geluid van haar ademhaling kon opmaken. Maar de strop aan de vleeshaak sprak boekdelen. Die gaf aan dat Hannah op het punt stond het lot van Martineks dochter te delen. Schwintowski had hem de ogen geopend. Sadlers methode was om zijn slachtoffers zo lang te kwellen tot ze voor het oog van de camera uit angst voor verdere martelingen besloten er een eind aan te maken. Weliswaar lag Sadler al een dag lang dood op Linda's sectietafel, maar wat had die sadist haar allemaal aangedaan voor hij was vertrokken? Welke verschrikkingen had hij haar in het vooruitzicht gesteld? En hoe lang had ze eenzaam en alleen in haar hol zitten wachten op de onvoorstelbare pijn die komen ging? Wie weet lang genoeg om haar psychisch te breken.

Sadler leefde niet meer, maar het zaad waarmee hij Hannahs geest had vergiftigd nog wel. En dat was de reden dat Schwintowski hem had aangezet tot spoed.

Het was nog maar een kwestie van minuten tot Hannah haar laatste beslissing zou nemen.

En zou springen.

'Waar ligt die reservesleutel precies?' informeerde Herzfeld toen hij de bosweg had bereikt. Onder de sneeuw was de aarde door de aanhoudende vrieskou zo hard als beton en het zou voor de terreinwagen geen probleem zijn geweest. Als hij tenminste niet...

'Nee, nee, nee!' schreeuwde Herzfeld en hij sloeg met beide handen tegen zijn slapen. Ingolf, die hem had ingehaald, knikte verslagen en maakte alles alleen maar erger toen hij zei: 'Het spijt me zo.'

O ja? Spijt het je zo dat mijn dochter zich nu op Helgoland ophangt terwijl wij hier machteloos in het bos zitten? Zonder telefoon? Zonder auto?

Hun situatie was uitzichtloos, en dat alleen door banale pesterij: Martinek had alle banden lek gestoken. Zelfs als ze op de velgen de provinciale weg zouden halen, zou dat veel te veel tijd kosten, tijd die ze niet hadden.

Uitzinnig van woede, bezorgdheid en teleurstelling schopte hij tegen een van de platte banden en smeet keihard het rechterportier dicht.

'Jammer genoeg hebben we maar één reserveband,' zei Ingolf en hij opende de achterklep, boog zich voorover in de kofferbak en peuterde een sleutel onder het reservewiel vandaan.

'Daar hebben we nu ook niets meer aan.' Herzfeld leunde verslagen met zijn hoofd tegen de ruit van het portier linksvoor. Zijn blik viel op de in leer gebonden handleiding van de Cayenne, die op de mat voor de passagiersstoel was gevallen. Hij kromp ineen of hij een elektrische schok kreeg. Toen rukte hij de deur open, stapte in en deponeerde de camera op de achterbank.

'Kom, kom, kom,' riep hij naar Ingolf, die juist de achterklep weer wilde dichtdoen en hem nu verward aankeek.

'Wat bent u van plan?'

'De reservesleutel, geef op.'

Ingolf deed de kofferbak dicht, maar maakte niet veel haast om in de passagiersstoel te klimmen. 'Zo komen we niet erg ver,' zei hij bedrukt toen hij Herzfeld de sleutel gaf.

'We zijn er zo.'

'Zo? Het dichtstbijzijnde dorp is tien minuten verderop. Gezien de toestand van mijn wagen betekent dat... Wohoaaa!'

Ingolf hield met één hand de greep boven de deur vast, met de andere zocht hij steun tegen het handschoenenvakje op het

dashboard om zich schrap te zetten tegen de middelpuntvlie-
dende kracht waaraan hij werd blootgesteld, omdat Herzfeld het
gaspedaal had ingetrapt. De combinatie van de lege banden en de
hobbelige bosweg zorgde ervoor dat de Porsche niet meer als een
luchtgeveerde luxe limousine maar als een bokkend wild paard
aanvoelde en Ingolf beurtelings met zijn hoofd tegen de ruit en
het plafond werd gekwakt.

'Heb je je gordel om?' was het laatste wat Herzfeld zijn passagier vroeg, die schreeuwde dat ze de verkeerde kant op gingen.
Inderdaad bewogen ze zich dieper het bos in en niet in de richting
van de hoofdweg. Herzfeld had steeds meer moeite de wagen op
het smalle weggetje te houden.

'Wilt u ons dood hebben?'

Ik kom eraan, kleintje.

Met een snelle blik vergewiste Herzfeld zich ervan dat zijn gordel vastzat, toen sloot hij zijn ogen en gaf een ruk aan het stuur.

De Porsche schampte een met sneeuw bedekte zwerfkei en had
daarom bijna het doel gemist. Maar na een korte draai sloeg hij
in volle vaart tegen een tweehonderd jaar oude eik, waarvan de
stam als een mes door de grille sneed, de motorruimte tot aan het
dashboard in tweeën spleet en de carrosserie dusdanig vervormde
dat alle ruiten aan de voorkant van de auto als confetti uit elkaar
spatten.

54

HELGOLAND

Hoe kouder het beneden op de afdeling Pathologie werd, des te luider werd het gerommel. Enders pogingen adem te halen – of liever gezegd, de pogingen van zijn bewusteloze lichaam – klonken alsof iemand met een rietje de laatste druppels uit een plastic bekertje zoog.

Linda zat geknield naast hem sinds hij had geprobeerd zich in zijn slaap om te draaien. Voor die ongecontroleerde beweging hadden zijn benen even gebeefd, maar nu lagen ze weer stil. Anderzijds bewogen zijn ogen onder de gesloten oogleden onrustig van links naar rechts.

'Wees niet bang, alles komt goed,' zei Linda nog een keer, een tekst waarin ze allang niet meer geloofde en die ze alleen voortdurend herhaalde omdat er niets anders te doen viel. Van de twee uur die Herzfeld van haar had gekregen, waren nog maar een paar minuten over, en ze had weinig hoop dat de professor zich aan zijn belofte zou houden en professionele hulp zou sturen. Keer op keer had ze geprobeerd hem te bereiken. Eerst was zijn telefoon eindeloos lang overgegaan, later kreeg ze meteen zijn voicemail.

'De persoon die u probeert te bellen is momenteel niet bereikbaar. U kunt een bericht...'

Linda slaakte een wanhopige zucht.

'Nog een kwartier, dan ga ik er zelf opuit,' beloofde ze Ender, wiens koude, vochtige hand ze stevig vasthield, zodat hij tenminste onbewust zou registreren dat hij niet alleen was.

Terwijl ze met haar knieën op de matras voor de huismeester leunde, worstelde ze met verschillende gevoelens tegelijk, het ene nog ongepaster dan het andere. Maar langzamerhand werd alles overheerst door de drang naar de wc te gaan.

Ze was voor het laatst in het strandhuis gegaan, en dat was een eeuwigheid geleden. Weliswaar had ze de afgelopen uren nauwelijks iets gedronken, maar nu dreigde haar blaas te exploderen. Ze had al overwogen een emmer te gebruiken, maar een loodzware vermoeidheid stond dat in de weg.

De laatste paar minuten was ze een paar keer kort ingedommeld. Tot overmaat van ramp had ze honger, ondanks de onappetijtelijke omgeving. Ze had het gevoel dat haar bloedsuikerspiegel te laag was, en zou nauwelijks meer in staat zijn haar arm op te tillen als ze niet snel iets at.

Dus daar komt het woord 'galgenmaal' vandaan, was een van haar laatste absurde gedachten toen haar hoofd vooroverzakte en ze indutte. Ze voelde dat ze haar evenwicht verloor, maar het maakte haar niet uit dat ze opzij tegen de betegelde muur naast de matras aan viel. Desondanks wilde ze het contact met Ender niet verliezen, en daarom hield ze zijn hand stevig vast toen ze in een droomloze slaap wegzakte. Helaas was die maar van korte duur.

De donderslag die haar terug naar het heden katapulteerde was zo oorverdovend dat ze zichzelf slaperig probeerde wijs te maken dat ze het had gedroomd. Maar toen klonk er weer zo'n geluid, alsof Linda onder een kerkklok stond waar iemand met een hamer tegenaan sloeg.

Iemand moest uit alle macht tegen de deur zijn gesprongen, anders kon Linda de trillingen en de echo niet verklaren.

Aan het schemerige licht van de op het plafond schijnende zaklantaarn was niets veranderd, maar Linda was ervan overtuigd dat de staalplaat aan de buitenkant van de deur een deuk moest hebben opgelopen. Het zou haar niets verbazen als de binnenkant ook vervormd was.

Opnieuw kwam er een stomp voorwerp (een voet? een li-chaam?) tegen de deur aan, en dit keer deed Linda wat ze tot dan toe van schrik had nagelaten: ze schreeuwde en liet Enders hand los.

De honger, de volle blaas en de vermoeidheid waren vergeten. Ze krabbelde op en staarde naar de deur, waarachter de geluiden niet waren verstomd. Weliswaar wierp niemand zich er meer te-genaan, maar nu hoorde Linda een metalig gekletter. En toen zag ze het.

Het licht.

Koud en scherp als een mes viel het door de langzaam breder wordende spleet van de deur, wat betekende dat iemand zich met al zijn kracht tegen het handvat moest afzetten om hem open te schuiven. Het was alleen aan de omvergegooide instrumenten-kast te danken dat de indringer niet al in de ruimte stond.

'Wie is daar?' schreeuwde Linda. Geen antwoord.

Het gerammel aan de deur hield aan, ook al werd de spleet voorlopig niet breder. Zoals haar bedoeling was geweest, blok-keerde de zijkant van de kast de handgreep, waardoor de deur niet verder open kon. Maar nu veranderde de indringer zijn aanpak en probeerde niet langer de deur opzij te schuiven, maar beukte ertegenaan om het obstakel met het geweld van de slagen op te schuiven.

Linda handelde instinctief door Ender eerst met matras en al uit de gevarenzone te slepen. Toen zette ze zich schrap tegen de kast om te verhinderen dat hij van de deur los zou komen. Als die aan de rechterkant tegen de muur en links tegen de handgreep aan zou komen, kon de moordenaar de deur onmogelijk open-schuiven.

Of hij moet een andere manier vinden om bij me te komen.

Ze tuurde naar het plafond, maar kon in het flauwe schijnsel boven haar hoofd geen afdekplaat van een ventilatieschacht ont-dekken, wat niet betekende dat die er niet was. Maar de indringer leek zijn strategie niet te willen veranderen. Integendeel. Keer op keer gooide hij zich tegen de schuifdeur, en elke keer slaagde Linda er met een enorme krachtsinspanning in de wegspringende instrumentenkast weer naar voren te duwen. Ze wist dat het een kwestie van tijd was voor haar verzet gebroken zou zijn.

Of het moet zijn dat...

Panisch keek ze om zich heen en probeerde de tijd in te schatten die ze nodig had om extra barricades aan te voeren.

De twee zware sectietafels stonden een paar meter verder en waren dus onbereikbaar, nog afgezien van het feit dat ze in de vloer waren verankerd en dus niet konden worden verplaatst.

Maar de brancard wel!

Linda maakte van de rustpauze die de onbekende voor de ingang blijkbaar nodig had gebruik om de brancard te pakken waarmee ze de rechter hadden vervoerd. Zonder er lang bij stil te staan of het echt iets zou uithalen, zette ze de brancard overeind en liet hem languit tegen de deur vallen. Daardoor ging een la van de instrumentenkast open en vielen er allerlei voorwerpen uit. Behalve plastic slangen, houten spatels en elastiek zag Linda twee lange, puntige metalen stangen, die er als ijspickels uitzagen en die haar voorkwamen als een geschenk uit de hemel.

Onder het gedreun van de slagen die opnieuw van buitenaf de stalen deur deden trillen, pakte Linda een van de pickels en klom op de instrumentenkast. Daardoor kon ze het bovenste deel van de schuifdeur met haar handen aanraken. Ze tastte de rails koortsachtig af, tot ze had gevonden wat ze zocht.

Een schroef!

'Wat wil je van me?' schreeuwde ze, zonder antwoord te krijgen.

Het geweld van de slagen deed de deur trillen, en elke keer kromp Linda geschrokken ineen; daarom had ze een paar pogingen nodig voor ze de punt van de ijzeren staaf in de juiste positie had gebracht.

Uitzinnig van angst sloeg ze met haar blote hand vertwijfeld tegen het rubberen handvat van de pickel, zette opnieuw kracht en dacht te voelen dat ze de schroef daadwerkelijk en beetje los had gedraaid. Ze stelde zich voor dat ze een tand uit het gebit van de moordenaar daarbuiten moest wrikken, drukte de punt nog verder in de rail – *in het tandvlees* – en trok toen het handvat naar boven.

Is het gelukt? Komt de schroef nu zo ver naar buiten dat de rail is geblokkeerd?

Linda wist het niet. Ze had ook geen idee waarom het lawaai in de gang voor de sectiezaal opeens was verstomd, vlak nadat ze van de instrumentenkast af was gestapt.

Trillend over haar hele lichaam, met een hand om de ijspickel geklemd en de andere in haar haar, staarde ze naar de deur, die niet meer bewoog.

De tranen sprongen haar in de ogen toen ze besefte dat ze ergens tussen haar poging een extra barrière op te werpen met de brancard en het losdraaien van de schroef de controle over haar blaas moest hebben verloren. De vlek tussen haar benen werd langzaam koud en voegde aan het palet van vreselijke gevoelens nog dat van schaamte toe.

En nu?

Linda geloofde dat ze hoogstens uitstel van executie had bereikt. En het zou haar zonder hulp nooit lukken hier nog uit te komen. Het laatste beetje kracht dat ze had gehad, was nu verbruikt. Uitgeput gleed ze met haar rug langs de muur naar de vloer en begroef haar gezicht in haar handen. Het ruisen in haar oren was zo luid dat ze haar eigen hijgende ademhaling niet eens hoorde.

Laat staan de zachte klik waarmee de deur van de tweede lijkenkoelcel openging, vlak nadat Linda haar ogen had gesloten om over haar uitzichtloze situatie na te denken.

55

Het eerste wat Linda registreerde was de stem, die haar zowel vertrouwd als onwerkelijk voorkwam. Toen deed ze haar ogen open en merkte dat er enige tijd verstreken moest zijn, want het noodaggregaat deed het weer en daarmee ook de plafondlampen.

Ze had geen tijd meer erover na te denken waarom ze de man, die haar als een bankschroef vastklemde, niet had horen aankomen. De vraag of ze werkelijk van vermoeidheid in slaap was gevallen was onbelangrijk, gezien de pijn die ze kon verwachten.

Gezien mijn naderende dood.

'Herken je me niet?' neuzelde de psychopaat, wie Linda geen naam wilde geven, niet eens in gedachten. Want zijn naam noemen betekende het einde accepteren.

Ze wilde opstaan, maar dat liet de man niet toe, want hij hield haar vast bij haar bovenarmen en drukte haar tegen de muur.

'Ik ben een beetje veranderd sinds we elkaar voor het laatst hebben gezien,' zei de man. Het klonk of hij met volle mond sprak, hoewel zijn gezicht eruitzag alsof het tegendeel waar was. Want daarin ontbrak de helft van zijn onderkaak, en in zijn linkerwang gaapte een onregelmatig gevormd gat. De bron van de bedorven adem die met elk woord dat hij sprak in Linda's gezicht waaide. En de reden waarom elk woord uit zijn mond gepaard ging met gesis.

'Ik ben het, Danny, je liefste.'

Danny.

Nu kon Linda de waarheid niet meer negeren. De moordenaar was geen vreemde meer. Het gevaar had een naam. En het kwam ook niet van buiten, maar had zich al die tijd vlak bij haar verborgen gehouden.

In het koelvak vlak naast mij, begreep ze.

Dan had ze zich toch niet vergist en was het geen inbeelding geweest toen ze eerder had gedacht dat ze zijn schaduw in de spiegel van de geopende lift langs had zien glijden. Was hij daarna bij haar in de sectiezaal geweest? Linda sperde haar mond open en probeerde van Danny weg te komen, toen deze onverwacht zijn greep liet verslappen.

'Rustig maar, lieveling. Niet bang zijn!'

Danny Haag, de stalker, van wie haar broer haar eens en voor altijd had willen verlossen – de man voor wie ze naar Helgoland was gevlucht, alleen om hem hier weer in de hel tegen te komen – die man probeerde te glimlachen, zodat zijn verwrongen grimas nog grotesker werd

Hij stak zijn hand naar haar uit, alsof hij haar overeind wilde helpen.

'Je broer Clemens wilde ons uit elkaar drijven,' zei hij moeizaam. Linda bleef op de grond gehurkt zitten en keek ontzet omhoog naar Danny, die tranen in zijn ogen had.

'Hij is tegen onze liefde, kleintje. Zo erg dat hij heeft geprobeerd me te vermoorden. Wist je dat?'

Als in trance schudde Linda haar hoofd.

Ze registreerde dat Danny's haar, ooit de trots van de ijdele kunstenaar, niet was geknipt of gewassen.

'Eerst hebben ze me in elkaar geslagen, je broer en zijn getatoeeerde vrienden. Toen hebben ze me in het bos achtergelaten. En opeens duikt dat meisje op. Hij had haar verteld waar ze me kon vinden.'

Hij sprak langzaam, deed zijn best verstaanbaar te praten, wat hem vanwege zijn verwondingen niet gemakkelijk afging. Veel woorden hadden geen begin en geen eind, gingen slissend in elkaar over.

Danny trok zijn neus op. Zijn stem kreeg een huilerige klank.

'Bijna waren we voor altijd van elkaar gescheiden geweest, lieveling. Je hebt geen idee wat ik heb doorgemaakt. Halfdood, in een kofferbak in het bos. Alleen de herinnering aan jou en onze liefde heeft me in leven gehouden. Ik heb gebeden dat je langskwam, mijn engel, om me te redden. Maar in plaats daarvan kwam de duivel. Ik dacht, die kleine komt me te hulp, en dan pakt ze een pistool dat je broer in de auto voor haar had klaargelegd en schiet me in mijn gezicht.'

Linda tastte verdwaasd met haar linkerhand rond op de vloer, in de hoop een van de instrumenten te vinden die zojuist uit de kast waren gevallen.

De ijspickel misschien, het liefst een autopsiemes. Verdomme, waar heb ik dat mes gelaten?

'Ik denk dat het meisje nog niet eens strafrechtelijk aansprakelijk was,' zei Danny, en in haar angst had Linda bijna vergeten over wie hij het had. 'Zodat ze de gevangenis niet in hoeft als ze wordt gepakt. Maar het is haar niet gelukt, zoals je ziet. Ze heeft niet gecontroleerd of ik echt dood was. Anders zou ze hebben gemerkt dat ik mijn hoofd net op tijd had weggedraaid.'

Hij liet Linda zijn door de kogel verminkte onderkaak zien. Ze stond op. Ondanks alles voelde Linda iets van medelijden met Danny, bij wie het speeksel oncontroleerbaar langs de randen van de wond omlaag druppelde.

'Ik geef toe dat ik meteen daarna vol haat was. Ik wilde me wreken. Op je broer, op het meisje en, ik geef het toe, ook op jou, want jij hebt me niet eens gebeld. En ik kon je op je nummer niet meer bereiken. En toen ik thuis lag, mezelf met pijnstillers volstopte en tevergeefs op je telefoontje wachtte, heb ik bedacht wat ik jullie allemaal zou aandoen.' Hij grijnsde zijn bloedstollende glimlach, en Linda's medelijden veranderde in pure weerzin. 'Hoe heb je me gevonden?' bracht ze uit.

'Via je e-mails. Gelukkig had je me je wachtwoord gegeven.'

Gegeven? Dat heb je zelf uitgevist! Net als de toegangscode van mijn voicemail en alle andere dingen waarmee ik mijn privacy probeerde te beschermen!

'Ik heb de mail van Clemens gelezen. Hij schreef dat hij het huis op Helgoland voor je had geregeld, en je leek daarmee akkoord te gaan. Ik heb de laatste veerboot genomen voordat de storm losbarstte.'

Linda kon zich levendig voorstellen hoe Danny onherkenbaar vermomd van boord was gegaan. Met zijn sjaal om zijn hoofd gewikkeld, zoals zoveel andere passagiers die hun gezicht tegen de kou wilden beschermen. Alleen moest zijn sjaal zijn verwonding verbergen.

Maar als je vanwege mij hier bent, wat heb je dan met Herzfelds dochter te maken? Waarom al die doden? En wie is er daarnet op de gang zo tekeergegaan?

Danny maakte aanstalten haar gezicht aan te raken, maar ze ontweek hem.

'Wat heb je toch, schatje?' Hij spreidde uitnodigend zijn armen. 'Ik heb toch gezegd dat ik niet meer boos op je ben. Dat is voorbij. Een tijd lang werd ik verteerd door haat, ja, dat geef ik toe; zelfs op de eerste dag nog, toen ik hier op het eiland aankwam. Ik wilde je bang maken, ben in je bed gaan liggen, heb je handdoeken gebruikt. Maar toen hoorde ik je met je broer aan de telefoon. Je wilde weten wat hij mij had aangedaan. God, Linda, je was zo woedend, zo bezorgd om me! Toen wist ik dat hij je had gedwongen de stad te verlaten en dat je nog altijd van me houdt. Dat doe je toch, nietwaar?'

Linda werd onpasselijk, maar ze wist dat ze ten koste van alles moest voorkomen dat de zaak weer zou escaleren. 'Ja, Danny,' kraste ze daarom. Ze krabbelde overeind.

'Kijk me aan!' zei hij en hij kwam een stap dichterbij. Linda zette haar opties op een rij en kwam tot de conclusie dat die er niet waren. Ze was ongewapend, haar enige helper was dood of lag op sterven, en ze had zichzelf ingesloten.

'Zeg me dat je van me houdt.'

'Ik hou van je,' loog ze.

'Ik hoor twijfel in je stem.'

En in de jouwe hoor ik pure waanzin.

'Omdat ik niet begrijp waarom je je hier verbergt,' probeerde ze de komedie vol te houden. 'Waarom heb je je niet eerder laten zien?'

'Ik schaamde me, Linda. Dat begrijp je toch wel? Toen ik kwam, zon ik op wraak. Toen ik je zag, wilde ik alleen nog maar bij je zijn. Maar hoe kon ik je zo onder ogen komen?'

Hij wees op zijn geschonden gezicht. 'Ik was bang dat je me niet meer wilde. Dus hield ik me gedeisd. Maar ik was steeds bij je in de buurt, al helemaal toen ik merkte dat je hier in de problemen zat.' Hij slikte moeizaam, alsof hij een brok in zijn keel had. 'Ik ben je beschermengel.'

'Je bent dus niet gekomen om me pijn te doen?' vroeg Linda, die haar lippen tot een potsierlijke glimlach had vertrokken. Lang zou ze die rol niet meer volhouden. In elk geval kreeg ze het voor elkaar om niet achteruit te deinzen toen Danny haar haren aanraakte.

'Ik zal je nooit iets aandoen, dat weet je.'

Je hebt mijn voorhoofd met zuur bewerkt en mijn kat afgemaakt!

'En waarom heb je *dat* dan gedaan?'

'*Wat* gedaan?' Hij klonk oprecht verbaasd.

'Al die mensen. Wat hebben ze misdaan?'

'Die daar?' vroeg hij, haar blik volgend, die eerst naar Ender op de grond en toen naar de ene en de andere sectietafel dwaalde. Hij schudde zijn hoofd. 'Daar heb ik niets mee te maken.'

Niets mee te maken? Was dat mogelijk?

'Dat is iemand anders, dat zweer ik. Ik heb geen idee wat hier aan de hand is. Ik dacht dat jij me dat kon uitleggen. Heeft Clemens je gedwongen die lijken open te snijden?'

285

'Nee,' antwoordde ze. Meteen had ze spijt van haar onbezonnenheid. Clemens was de gehate persoon op wie Danny alles projecteerde, en dat had ze moeten uitbuiten.

'Wie dwingt je dan?'

'Dat leg ik je uit als we hieruit zijn, Danny.'

Ze wilde zich naar de deur omdraaien, maar hij hield haar vast aan haar hand.

'Linda?'

Ze draaide zich naar hem om en huiverde. Hoewel het haar ergens speet dat hij slachtoffer was geworden van het geweld, kon ze zich niet aan de gedachte onttrekken dat Danny's uiterlijk voor het eerst overeenkomst vertoonde met zijn gestoorde geest.

'Wat?' vroeg ze.

'Kus me!'

'Pardon?'

De angst snoerde haar keel dicht.

'Een verzoeningskus. Zodat ik weet dat ik me niet in je heb vergist.'

Hij tilde zijn hoofd op; van zijn kin daalde een druppel speeksel neer als een spin aan zijn draad.

Nee, alsjeblieft niet. Dat niet.

Ze sloot haar ogen, wat hij opvatte als een uitnodiging. Toen hij haar tegen zich aan trok, moest ze zichzelf dwingen niet te schreeuwen.

'Ik weet dat ik voor de anderen lelijk ben. Maar jij kijkt naar me met de ogen van de liefde. Dat is toch zo, Linda?'

'Ja.'

Ze deed haar ogen dicht en voelde zijn natte mond tegen de hare drukken; hoe zijn tong probeerde haar gesloten lippen uit elkaar te duwen. Ze slikte moeizaam om niet te hoeven kotsen.

Hij duwde steeds harder, maar na een tijdje liet hij haar los, zo abrupt dat ze dreigde haar evenwicht te verliezen, nu hij haar niet meer vasthield.

'Wat is er?' vroeg ze. Het antwoord las ze in zijn ogen. Er flikkerden haat, woede en teleurstelling in. Linda kende zijn aanvallen, de driftbuien die hem tot het uiterste dreven.

Verdomme, ik heb het verpest.

Danny tilde zijn hemd op, en tussen zijn buik en broeksband zag ze het autopsiemes dat ze had gezocht.

'Slet die je bent,' fluisterde hij. Toen sloeg hij haar met zijn vlakke hand in haar gezicht. Linda wilde over haar brandende wang wrijven toen de volgende pijnscheut door haar hoofd schoot. Danny had haar opeens aan haar haren gepakt. 'Dacht je dat ik niet in de gaten heb dat je me voorliegt?'

Nu stond hij achter haar en drukte het mes tegen haar keel. Opnieuw rook ze zijn aftershave, en dit keer werd ze er nog misselijker van dan van de alomtegenwoordige stank van de lijken.

'Je walgt van me.'

'Nee, Danny.'

'Ik voel dat je niet meer van me houdt.'

'Jawel hoor.'

'Heb je een ander?'

'Wat? Nee, ik zweer...'

Danny pakte een van haar armen, boog die achter haar rug omhoog en duwde haar naar voren. Samen struikelden ze naar een van de tafels met de lijken toe.

'Alsjeblieft, Danny, laten we het nog een keer proberen. Ik hou van je.'

'Jouw leugens zitten me tot hier.'

Hij bleef staan en trok haar hoofd aan haar haar opzij, zodat ze Ender een laatste keer kon zien, die nog steeds niets merkte van de gebeurtenissen om hem heen. Danny had de zaklantaarn in de buurt van de matras laten liggen, daarom was Enders omgeving veel beter verlicht dan de plek waar zij nu stonden.

'Had je wat met hem?' wilde Danny in alle ernst weten.

Linda wist niet hoe ze op die waanzin moest reageren. Hij

duwde haar weer naar voren, en Linda had een akelig voorgevoel waarheen haar gedwongen mars door de sectiezaal zou leiden.

'Of word je geneukt door de vent met wie je de hele tijd hebt gebeld?'

Ze hadden de afvoerbak bereikt, en zoals verwacht ontspande Danny zijn greep om de kraan te kunnen opendraaien.

De straal kletterde met veel lawaai in het bekken, dat sinds de obductie al halfvol met bloedig water stond, en Linda dacht koortsachtig na wat ze kon zeggen of doen om het onvermijdelijke af te wenden. Er schoot haar niets te binnen en op het moment dat het waterniveau het overloopgat had bereikt, ging alles razendsnel. Linda had niet eens meer tijd om een laatste keer in te ademen, en zoog een golf koud water naar binnen toen Danny haar met haar hoofd in de bak duwde.

'Als ik jou niet krijg, krijgt niemand je!' schreeuwde hij.

Rustig aan. Er is nog niets verloren, dacht ze. Ze wilde tegelijk schreeuwen, huilen en... *ademhalen.*

In een strip die ze jaren geleden had getekend, was de heldin haar moordenaar te slim af omdat ze zich op tijd dood hield, lang voordat ze werkelijk zuurstofgebrek had. Maar nu besefte Linda hoe onrealistisch die scène was.

Toen ze eenmaal onder water was geduwd, had ze geen controle meer over haar bewegingen. Instinctief sloeg en schopte ze om zich heen. Nu al, een paar tellen nadat ze was ondergedompeld, dacht ze geen seconde meer zonder zuurstof te kunnen. Haar huid prikte alsof hij met jeukpoeder was ingewreven. In die toestand kon ze haar spieren onmogelijk bewust ontspannen om Danny te laten denken dat ze al dood was, zodat hij haar te vroeg zou loslaten.

Ik ga dood.

Haar handen sloegen tegen de stalen rand van de sectietafel.

Ender. Opstaan. Mes. Help.

Haar laatste gedachten bestonden alleen uit losse woorden. Nu joegen ze nog door haar hoofd, maar ze zouden al snel vervagen. En haar handen zouden niet lang meer tegen de zijkant van de afvoerbak slaan.

Ze hoorde een gedreun dat steeds luider werd, alsof ze in een startend vliegtuig zat. Bliksemschichten dansten voor haar ogen, waarvan ze niet meer wist of ze open of dicht waren.

Ik. Wil. Niet. Sterven.

Linda sloeg met haar knie tegen de onderkant van de afvoerbak, maar Danny hield haar nek in een ijzeren greep.

Het gedreun in haar hoofd was overgegaan in ritmisch gezoem. Haar bewegingen werden trager, en nu dreigde haar lichaam te verslappen, niet omdat ze simuleerde, maar omdat ze werkelijk op het punt stond dood te gaan.

Neeeee!

Ze balde haar hand een laatste keer tot een vuist, ook al wist ze dat ze de kracht niet meer had om naar achteren te slaan; tegen het gezicht van de stalker, die met zijn hele gewicht op haar leunde.

Maar...?

Linda opende haar vingers, om ze meteen weer te sluiten.

Wat... is... dat?

Een herinnering uit haar kinderjaren maakte zich kenbaar onder het zoemen in haar schedel. Ze moest aan een boswandeling denken en aan een steenslinger die haar vader uit een tak voor haar had gesneden, en ze kon er eerst geen betekenis in ontdekken, tot ze besefte wat ze daar toevallig op de sectietafel had aangeraakt.

Ik...

Linda verstevigde haar greep...

Ik wil...

... en slingerde, in een laatste poging zich te verzetten tegen de dood, haar arm omhoog, naar de plek waar ze het hoofd van de stalker vermoedde.

...niet sterven...

En ze had geluk.

Een ander had misschien meer afstand gehouden. Had in de laatste seconden van de doodsstrijd zijn greep laten verslappen. Maar Danny wilde zo dicht mogelijk bij Linda zijn wanneer ze doodging. Daarom bevond zijn gezicht zich vlak boven het water en met de punt van de stok waarmee Friederike Töven was gespietst raakte ze zijn rechteroog.

Linda voelde de loodzware druk op haar lichaam wegvallen en ze gooide haar hoofd omhoog. Ze hoestte en schreeuwde tegelijk, en daarom kreeg ze niet genoeg lucht in haar longen toen ze naast de afvoerbak op de grond viel.

Ze wist dat ze daar niet zo mocht blijven liggen, ze zou zich op zijn minst moeten strekken om niet alsnog te stikken, maar in plaats daarvan trok ze haar knieën op tot haar borst en had het gevoel dat haar hoofd in een plastic zak zat. Elke ademhaling was een kwelling die een bijna bovenmenselijke inspanning vergde.

Ik red het niet.

Ze verspilde er geen gedachte aan wat er met Danny was gebeurd en of hij op dat moment misschien weer zou aanvallen, nu ze op de grond hulpeloos naar zuurstof hapte. De pneumatische hamer in haar hoofd, die steeds luider werd, verpulverde elke gedachte, op één na: *lucht!*

Het ging zo tekeer in haar schedel dat ze niets anders meer hoorde.

Zoals Danny's gerochel naast haar, of het luide gekners en gekraak van de deur, waarachter iemand een breekijzer hanteerde om zich eindelijk een weg te banen naar het inwendige van de afdeling Pathologie.

56

'Waar staat de klok?'

Linda opende haar ogen, maar ze dacht dat ze droomde en sloot ze weer.

'Hé, nee, nee, nee. Niet in slaap vallen!'

Ze voelde trillingen – zoals in een auto die over kinderhoofdjes rijdt, alleen was het of ze niets met het lichaam dat door twee sterke mannenhanden werd vastgehouden te maken had. Alsof het iemand anders was bij wie de even markant als vermoeid uitziende man het haar uit het gezicht streek.

'Wie ben jij?' vroeg Linda met een nasaal stemgeluid, dat aardig leek op dat van haar stalker. Haar tong voelde gezwollen en gevoelloos aan.

'Ik ben het,' antwoordde de man niet al te snugger, toen schreeuwde hij iets naar achteren, naar de anderen die daar in de weer waren.

Zijn ze nou met een heel leger aangerukt om me de genadeslag te geven?

Linda's hoofd zakte voorover op de borst van de vent met het donsjack. Voor het eerst sinds lange tijd voelde ze zich geborgen, hoewel ze er nog steeds van uitging dat ze tegen de moordenaar leunde die verantwoordelijk was voor de lijken die niet op het conto van haar ex-vriend kwamen.

'Danny,' bracht ze ontzet uit, toen ze zich realiseerde dat ze niet wist wat er met hem was gebeurd.

'Geen paniek,' zei de onbekende sussend met zijn sonore stemgeluid, dat haar steeds bekender voorkwam. 'Je hebt hem een oog uitgestoken, hij is flauwgevallen van de pijn en opgesloten. Hij kan je niets meer doen.'

Ze zou bijna weer zijn weggezakt als de man haar niet heen en weer had geschud. Maar van de woorden die hij nu tegen haar zei werd ze pas echt wakker: 'Ik ben het, Linda. Paul Herzfeld.'

Ze sperde haar ogen open, knipperde een paar keer en schudde ongelovig haar hoofd, dat opeens helemaal leeg leek te zijn.

'Paul?' vroeg ze, alsof ze de naam nog nooit had gehoord. 'Dus het is je gelukt?'

'Ja. Je hoeft niet bang meer te zijn. Alles komt goed.' Hij pakte haar gezicht met beide handen vast en keek haar diep in de ogen. 'Ik moet alleen weten waar je precies was toen die staande klok sloeg!'

57

'Huize Töven. Waar is dat?' vroeg Herzfeld de potige man die hem voor de uitgang van het ziekenhuis de weg versperde.

De landing van de reddingshelikopter op de parkeerplaats van de kliniek had een drom mensen aangetrokken, onder wie ook een onbehouwen woesteling, die zich met sonore stem als de burgemeester van het eiland voorstelde. 'Mijn naam is Till Bandrupp, en ik wens eindelijk te horen wat hier aan de hand is.'

De achterdocht stond op zijn gezicht te lezen, en daar kon Herzfeld wel in komen. In de kleren die hij nu droeg, beantwoordde hij eerder aan het cliché van een seriemoordenaar dan dat van een professor in de forensische geneeskunde. Zijn jas was met bloed besmeurd, net als zijn handen, de veiligheidsgordel van de Porsche had hem bij de botsing in zijn hals gesneden, zijn haar stond alle kanten op, en zijn gezicht was overdekt met het poeder uit de opengebarsten airbag. Alleen Ingolf, die volledig uitgeput in het ziekenhuis was achtergebleven, had er bij aankomst minder vertrouwenwekkend uitgezien.

'Mijn naam is Paul Herzfeld, ik sta aan het hoofd van een speciale eenheid van de BKA,' zei hij. Hij liet de burgemeester zijn identiteitskaart zien. Tegelijk beduidde hij de arts en de piloot die hen hiernaartoe had gevlogen hem te volgen, maar de twee mannen bleven besluiteloos staan toen Bandrupp afwerend zijn hand hief.

'Wacht eens even. U kunt hier niet zomaar even langskomen om...'

'Ja, dat kan ik wel. En ik beloof dat ik alles zal uitleggen, maar nu heb ik daar geen tijd voor.'

Herzfeld keek de man met het door weer en wind getaande gezicht diep in de ogen en voelde dat hij niet met een muggenzifter te maken had die naleving van de regeltjes eiste als het erom ging te handelen.

'Alstublieft!' zei hij met nadruk. 'We moeten snel in actie komen, het leven van mijn dochter Hannah staat op het spel.' Bandrupp aarzelde nog even, toen zette hij een stap opzij en zei met een korte hoofdknik: 'Goed dan. Ik breng u erheen. Maar ik hoop dat u onderweg een verdomd goede verklaring voor mij hebt.'

Hij liep voorop en bracht hen naar een elektromobiel, die hij vlak naast de reddingshelikopter had geparkeerd. Een krachtige windstoot deed de wagen schudden, maar het was niet te vergelijken met de storm van een paar uur eerder, ook al duidden de donkere wolken boven de Noordzee erop dat de korte pauze snel voorbij zou zijn.

Bandrupp keek naar de hemel, toen naar Herzfeld, die met zijn sporenkoffer op schoot op de passagiersstoel was gaan zitten, en zei ten slotte tegen de piloot en de arts op de achterbank: 'Er moet echt een steekje bij jullie loszitten, dat jullie het hebben aangedurfd hiernaartoe te komen.'

De mannen knikten.

Als Ender en Hannah deze dag zouden overleven, zouden ze dat uiteindelijk aan een gebruiksaanwijzing te danken hebben. Toen Herzfeld een paar uur eerder had willen nalezen hoe het navigatiesysteem van Ingolfs auto moest worden geprogrammeerd, had hij ook een alinea doorgenomen waarin de veiligheidsmodule met gps van de Porsche werd beschreven. Op dat moment had hij alleen een ongeduldige frons overgehad voor de informatie over het geïntegreerde reddingssysteem bij ongevallen. Hij wilde weten hoe het ding van coördinaten kon worden voorzien, niet wat er gebeurde als de airbags bij een botsing werden opgeblazen. Volgens de fabrikant zou de alarmcentrale dan binnen tien minuten de peilzender van het wrak lokaliseren en een reddingsteam naar de plaats des onheils sturen.

Wat de tijdsindicatie betrof waren de ingenieurs te bescheiden geweest. Het duurde zeven minuten, wist Herzfeld nu. En ze hadden geen ambulance gestuurd, nadat hij de auto opzettelijk tegen de boom had gereden, maar een helikopter.

De arts en zijn assistent die op de open plek waren geland, waren eerst blij geweest hun patiënten ongedeerd naast de compleet vernielde terreinwagen aan te treffen. Maar toen ze hoorden wat Herzfeld en Ingolf van hen verlangden, vermoedden ze dat de twee een ernstige shock hadden opgelopen. Pas toen Herzfeld hun zijn BKA-pasje had laten zien en erop stond met een collega, Leuthner genaamd, te worden verbonden, begonnen ze te begrijpen dat de twee warhoofden het blijkbaar serieus meenden en *werkelijk* naar een particulier vliegveld in de buurt van Cuxhaven wilden worden gevlogen, waar schijnbaar een piloot met een Cessna op ze wachtte.

Toen het reddingsteam hoorde dat er een man met een ernstige steekwond in de hals in het eilandziekenhuis lag en dringend naar het vasteland moest worden getransporteerd, checkten ze de weersomstandigheden en besloten de zaak zelf af te handelen.

Om de voorschriften niet te overtreden, stond de arts erop eerst Ingolf en Herzfeld naar de dichtstbijzijnde eerste hulp te vliegen, voor ze verder naar Helgoland zouden gaan. Maar toen stelde hij verbaasd vast dat de jongste van de twee slachtoffers de zoon was van de belangrijkste senator van Berlijn, een politicus wiens biografie hij had gelezen en voor wie hij sindsdien groot respect had. De doorslag om hen mee te nemen gaf uiteindelijk een plastic zak, die Ingolf uit een geheim vak in de kofferbak onder het reservewiel haalde en met de woorden 'Ziet u dat maar als slechtweertoeslag' aan de twee redders overhandigde.

Herzfeld wilde niet weten hoeveel contant geld de stagiair bij zich had, maar toen de twee in de zak keken, spraken hun gezichten boekdelen.

En zo was het gekomen dat het reddingsteam na overleg met de centrale van de korte weersomslag gebruik had gemaakt om koers naar Helgoland te zetten. Ze bereikten het eiland na twintig minuten van hevige turbulentie, die er de oorzaak van was dat Ingolf meer dan eens had moeten overgeven. Momenteel zat de student als een hoopje ellende ineengedoken op een bed in de kliniek.

Twintig minuten.

Sneller dan Herzfeld had durven dromen.

En waarschijnlijk toch te laat.

Op weg naar het huis op de klip gaf hij de burgemeester een korte samenvatting met de belangrijkste feiten: dat zijn dochter door een paar wanhopige vaders was ontvoerd, die zich het slachtoffer van een gerechtelijke dwaling voelden en zich wilden wreken op de mensen die volgens hen voor hun misère verantwoordelijk waren.

'En de ontvoerders zijn allemaal dood?' vroeg Bandrupp ongelovig toen ze bij de steile kust voor Tövens huis stopten.

'Ja. Ze hebben zelfmoord gepleegd nadat ze hun missie hadden volbracht.'

Sadler, Töven, mijn dochter. De slachtoffers van hun wraakactie liggen nu op de afdeling Pathologie... of zijn ernaartoe op weg.

'En hoe zijn de moordenaars op het eiland gekomen zonder dat wij het hebben gemerkt?' vroeg Bandrupp, maar Herzfeld wilde geen tijd meer aan verdere uitleg verspillen, ook al lag het antwoord wat hem betrof voor de hand, toen hij bij aankomst de paardentrailer in de carport van de rechter zag: *Gezwind met Schwintowski.*

De vertrouwde reclameslogan op het klapperende zeildoek bezorgde hem een schok.

Gezwind, anders sterft je kind.

Hij durfde er zijn hoofd om te verwedden dat het schip van de ondernemer, waarmee hij zijn als verhuisboedel gedeclareerde 'vracht' naar het eiland had verscheept, in een van de twee havens lag aangemeerd. 'Hé, wacht op mij,' hoorde hij de burgemeester roepen, die een zaklantaarn onder zijn stoel tevoorschijn haalde, maar toen was Herzfeld de auto al uit gesprongen en had hij de voordeur bereikt.

De deur zat niet op slot. Hij stormde het huis in, rende de trap op naar de eerste verdieping en van daaruit de smalle wenteltrap omhoog naar de zolder.

Hij knipte het licht aan. De zolder zag er precies zo uit als hij zich van de video herinnerde: de schuine wanden met wit rauhfaser behangen, het dakraam, de omgevallen stoel... *en de strop aan de balk daarboven.* Herzfeld voelde zich alsof hij door een werkelijkheid geworden nachtmerrie wandelde. De opname had zich gematerialiseerd en was in al zijn gruwelijkheid realiteit geworden. Zo echt dat hij Schwintowski's stem weer dacht te horen, die tegen hem zei: *'Hannah is dicht bij me in de buurt.'*

Geen twijfel mogelijk. Hij had de plek bereikt waar de ondernemer zich had opgehangen.

Er was maar één ding dat aan dit gruwelijke beeld niet klopte: de strop was leeg.

Schwintowski hing er niet meer.

58

Herzfelds eerste impuls was naar beneden te rennen en elke kamer van het huis naar zijn dochter af te zoeken.

'Hannah is dicht bij me in de buurt.'

Maar toen herinnerde hij zich dat Ender dat al had gedaan,
een paar uur eerder, toen Linda het lijk van de rechter in de huiskamer had ontdekt. Bovendien was hier geen kelder, verzekerde
Bandrupp hem. En hij had duidelijk betonnen muren op de video gezien.

Betonnen muren en een strop, net zoals hier op zolder.

Herzfeld moest aan een uitspraak van Martinek denken, dat je
in een storm nooit een besluit moest nemen, maar hij wist niet
hoe hij een eind kon maken aan de orkaan, die nu niet op het
eiland, maar des te heviger in hemzelf woedde.

Wat was er met Schwintowski's lijk gebeurd? En wat had hij
met zijn laatste raadsel bedoeld?

'Volg het witte licht van Alcatraz.'

Herzfeld liep naar het dakraam en deed het kleine venster
open. De koude wind bracht hem tranen in de ogen.

Hij hoorde de golven tegen de steile klip slaan, rook de zilte
zeelucht en staarde in de schemering. De zon was nog niet onder,
maar inmiddels was het wolkendek zo dicht dat het eiland was
vervaagd tot een landschap van schaduwen.

'Hier ligt bloed,' hoorde hij iemand zeggen; hij herkende de
stem niet, omdat de man tot dan toe nauwelijks een woord had
gezegd. Herzfeld draaide zich om naar de piloot, die inmiddels
ook naar de zolder was geklommen en een donkere vlek op de

houten vloer inspecteerde. 'Het is al droog, dus het is niet zo vers meer.'

Bandrupp haalde twijfelend zijn schouders op. De burgemeester moest zijn vierkante kop intrekken om hem niet tegen de dakbalken te stoten. Toen hij zag dat de gloeilamp aan het plafond genoeg licht gaf, deed hij zijn zaklantaarn uit.

'Dat bloed klopt niet,' mompelde Herzfeld diep in gedachten.

'Wat zegt u?'

'Schwintowski heeft zich opgehangen, hij heeft geen mes gebruikt.'

'Wie is Schwintowski?' wilde Bandrupp weten.

Ook de arts en de piloot keken vragend op.

'Hij heeft mijn... Hij is...' Herzfeld maakte een wegwerpgebaar. 'Dat verhaal duurt veel te lang.'

'Nou, misschien kunt u eindelijk eens beginnen het te vertellen, als we u verder moeten helpen.'

'Helpen?' schreeuwde Herzfeld bijna. Hij moest hoesten, wat het beeld van zijn stikkende dochter nog levendiger maakte, en daardoor verloor hij alle zelfbeheersing. 'U wilt me helpen? Goed dan. Pas een uur geleden heb ik een opname gezien waarop een man zich op deze zolder heeft opgehangen. Vlak daarvoor zei hij tegen me dat mijn dochter bij hem in de buurt was. Ik moest gewoon het witte licht van Alcatraz volgen. Weet u misschien wat die waanzinnige daarmee bedoelt?'

Tot Herzfelds verbazing knikte Bandrupp bedachtzaam; hij beduidde met zijn zaklamp hem te volgen en draaide zich om.

'Hé, waar gaat u heen?'

De burgemeester antwoordde niet, en Herzfeld moest een paar treden tegelijk nemen om niet achter te blijven. Aangekomen op de benedenverdieping beende hij achter Bandrupp aan, tot hij hem vlak voor het einde van de gang inhaalde. De burgemeester deed de deur naar buiten open. Herzfeld volgde hem de kou in.

In het zwakke schijnsel dat uit het huis viel, zag het terras eruit als een vlot. Een aantal grote planken vormden een over de klip overhangend vierkant. De touwen die bij wijze van balustrade aan de rand waren gespannen, deden aan een boksring denken. Bandrupp ging er vlakbij staan en wees met zijn zaklantaarn naar het zuiden, naar het hoger gelegen deel van het eiland. De lichtbundel werd al na een paar meter opgeslokt.

'Ziet u dat daar?'

Herzfeld kneep twijfelend zijn ogen samen. 'Geen idee. Ik denk... Ja!'

Inderdaad. Dat was een flits.

Langzaam tekende zich de omtrek van een toren in de duisternis af.

'Wat is dat?'

Bandrupp keek hem aan. 'Onze vuurtoren. En het lichtsignaal komt om de vijf seconden.'

Als op commando bevestigde de hoekige, uit baksteen opgetrokken toren de woorden van de burgemeester. 'Hetzelfde licht en hetzelfde ritme als de vuurtoren van Alcatraz.'

'En zit er ook een kelder onder die toren?' vroeg Herzfeld, die door de nieuwe hoop onder hoogspanning stond.

'Zou je kunnen zeggen,' antwoordde Bandrupp weinig enthousiast.

'Goed, laten we gaan!' Herzfeld stond op het punt te vertrekken, maar de burgemeester bleef hoofdschuddend staan.

'Dat heeft geen zin, professor.'

'Hoezo?'

'Onder de toren ligt een twintig kilometer lang bunkercomplex van de nazi's uit de Tweede Wereldoorlog. We hebben de hoofdingang jaren geleden afgesloten, nadat twee kinderen er waren verdwaald.' Zijn gezicht betrok. 'We hebben ze dagen later gevonden. Toen waren ze dood.'

59

IN DE HEL

Toen ze de geluiden achter de deur hoorde, besefte ze dat haar laatste uur had geslagen.

Snel. Voor hij hier is.

Lang, veel te lang probeerde ze haar evenwicht te bewaren. De spiralen van het bed boorden zich in haar blote voeten, de ruwe strop schuurde langs haar hals. En ze was moe.

Levensmoe.

Nu kon ze niet meer terug. Ze moest handelen, ook al was ze nog steeds haar geheugen kwijt.

Hoe zou ik dat ook kunnen vinden, als elke ademhaling pijn doet?

Ze hoefde maar diep in te ademen of ze had het gevoel dat ze zou exploderen. Als ze zich niet vergiste, was het tussen haar benen ook weer begonnen te bloeden. Ze wilde het niet onderzoeken. Alleen het idee al zichzelf daarbeneden aan te raken deed pijn.

De geluiden achter de deur werden luider, en ze sloot haar ogen.

Kom op. Waar wacht je op? Wil je meemaken hoe hij je clitoris met een glasscherf afsnijdt? Wil je dat roestige mes tussen je schaamlippen voelen?

Ze haalde haar neus op, vocht niet meer tegen haar tranen, ook al werd alles nu gefilmd omdat het haar niet was gelukt de camera te vernielen.

Wat zou het. Dan zijn er tenminste bewijzen, als dat varken ooit wordt gepakt.

Een laatste maal opende ze haar ogen en liet haar door tranen vertroebelde blik door de bunker dwalen. De gloeilamp, de wastafel, het bed – hier was niets waarvan ze afscheid kon nemen.

Niets, behalve...

Haar blik gleed weer naar de vloer naast het bed. Naar de plek waar de kartonnen doos stond waaruit ze de strop had gehaald.

De geluiden achter de deur werden luider. Dadelijk zou ze zich laten vallen. En toch dwong ze zichzelf in alle rust haar laatste gedachte te volgen. Tegelijk voelde ze dat alle paniek en stress van haar af gleed, want die laatste blik op de doos had iets teruggebracht wat ze voorgoed dacht te hebben verloren: haar geheugen.

60

'Snel. Ik moet naar binnen.'

'Dat is echt zinloos,' bromde de burgemeester en hij probeerde de branddeur met een andere sleutel van de bos open te maken. De toegang tot het bunkercomplex uit de Tweede Wereldoorlog bevond zich in de muur die aansloot op de sokkel van de vuurtoren en iets weg had van een dijk. Hij deed denken aan de tunnel in een voetbalstadion waardoor de spelers uit de catacomben het veld op lopen.

'Het is lang geleden dat ik deze sleutel heb gebruikt,' zei Bandrupp verontschuldigend. Herzfeld wiebelde ongeduldig met de zaklantaarn die de burgemeester hem in de hand had gedrukt – de enige lichtbron die ze hadden, afgezien van de lichtbundel van de vuurtoren, die om de vijf seconden vlak boven hun hoofd de duisternis verdreef.

'Is er nog een andere manier om binnen te komen?'

'Eén?' Bandrupp zocht een andere sleutel uit. 'Dit is een enorm doolhof, nauwelijks onderzocht. Veel gangen komen uit op geschutstellingen in het rotsgesteente van de kust. Dus eerlijk gezegd...' Hij schudde spijtig zijn vierkante hoofd. 'We hebben honderd man nodig om dat alles te doorzoeken.'

'Verdomme!' Herzfeld schreeuwde zijn wanhoop uit, schopte woedend tegen de deur.

Alle moeilijkheden overwonnen. Zo dicht bij het doel. En toch gestrand.

'Hé, wat is er aan de hand? Waarom houdt u op?' vroeg hij de burgemeester, die zich van de deur had afgewend.

'Het is toch zinloos ze allemaal te proberen,' antwoordde hij mistroostig. Hij borg zijn sleutelbos weer op. 'Op een minuut meer of minder komt het nu niet meer aan. Laten we op de jongens van de brandweer wachten, die hebben de benodigde uitrusting...'

'Geen denken aan,' zei Herzfeld en hij griste de sleutels uit zijn hand.

61

IN DE HEL

De metalige geluiden achter de deur waren een tijdje verstomd, vlak nadat iemand ertegenaan had geschopt.

Het varken wil me bang maken. Hij is aan het tijdrekken.

Ze reikte omhoog, hield zich met allebei haar handen vast aan de strop, die de huid van haar hals tot bloedens toe had geschaafd. Nu kon het niet meer lang duren. Nu zou de gek met zijn spelletjes ophouden, de goede sleutel in het slot steken en de kerker binnenkomen.

Maar daarvoor was ze niet bang meer. Ook niet voor de dood. Niet nu ze haar eigen ik had teruggevonden, uitgerekend in een oude verhuisdoos. Ze wist niet waarom de doos niet eerder de bal van haar herinneringen aan het rollen had gebracht. Maar nu loonde het de moeite niet daar nog over na te denken. Nu moest ze in actie komen, voordat het te laat was. Voordat de waanzinnige met zijn besnijdenismes tegenover haar stond, haar van de strop sneed, om zich nogmaals aan haar te vergrijpen. Om haar beestachtig te martelen. Te vermoorden.

Nee. Dat is nu voorbij. Geen pijn meer.

Opnieuw hoorde ze gerammel. Opnieuw sloeg de sleutelbos van buitenaf tegen de branddeur.

Ze keek voor het laatst in de camera en stak haar middelvinger op naar de moordenaar.

'Nu weet ik wie ik ben,' zei ze met een tevreden glimlach.

'Ik ben geen hoer, klootzak.'

Toen schreeuwde ze haar naam naar de camera en sprong.

Toen de branddeur opensprong en de mannen naar binnen stormden, was ze al dood.

62

'Hannah,' brulde Herzfeld en hij hoorde zijn kreet twee, drie keer terugkomen. De schreeuw naar zijn dochter echode door de gangen van het bunkercomplex. Direct vóór hem splitste de hal zich in twee tunnels, die in tegenovergestelde richtingen liepen. Alles wat Herzfeld in het schijnsel van zijn zaklamp kon zien, waren grijze muren. Dikke waterdruppels welden op uit de poriën van het metselwerk en verzamelden zich in plassen op de licht aflopende bodem.

'Hannah, ben je hier?' probeerde Herzfeld nog eens. Iets harder. Veel wanhopiger.

Al na een paar passen werd hij bevangen door de kou, wat hem aan de gebeurtenissen op het meer en zodoende aan de dood herinnerde.

'Hannah? Kleintje?'

'Hier is iemand,' hoorde hij Bandrupp zeggen, die op de splitsing achter de ingang de andere tunnel in was gelopen. Hij bevond zich in een van de talrijke ruimtes zonder deur die op onregelmatige afstanden van elkaar op de tunnel uitkwamen. Ook zijn stem galmde door het labyrint, zodat het Herzfeld moeite kostte de richting te bepalen terwijl hij naar de ingang terugliep.

'Waar?' riep hij en hij haastte zich terug door de gang.

Zijn vraag was overbodig. Bandrupp en de arts stonden voor de ingang naar een smalle, vierkante kamer, waaruit een flakkerend, door elektrostatisch gezoem begeleid licht scheen. Hij werkte zich langs de twee mannen en begreep waarom zijn compagnons even hadden geaarzeld voor ze de ruimte binnengingen.

Ze waren bang geweest alleen nog de dood van het meisje te kunnen constateren.

Hannah!

Met een gesmoorde snik rende Herzfeld de kamer in, knielde voor de bank waar ze ineengedoken op lag, pakte haar slappe hand en drukte, toen hij had gezien dat ze geen teken van leven vertoonde, haar lichaam tegen het zijne, hield haar stevig vast en huilde in haar loshangende, naar stof en zweet ruikende haar.

'Ik ben bij je, kleintje. Het is voorbij. Ik ben bij je, Hannah.'

Hij voelde dat iemand een hand op zijn schouder legde, maar wilde zich niet naar de burgemeester en zijn meevoelende stem omdraaien. In plaats daarvan nam hij Hannahs hoofd in zijn handen, controleerde haar ademhaling, probeerde haar hartslag te voelen aan een halsslagader.

'Cortison,' schreeuwde hij naar achteren, en de arts, die nu ook naast hem knielde, schudde zijn hoofd.

'Ik denk niet dat ze dat nog nodig heeft.'

'Wat?' Herzfeld staarde hem woedend aan.' Mijn dochter heeft astma, dus klets geen onzin, maak liever de injectie klaar.'

'Dat is niet nodig.' De dokter wees naar Hannah. 'Kijk maar.'

En toen zag Herzfeld het ook: de inhalator in haar hand. Haar vlakke, maar regelmatige ademhaling.

'Ze heeft geen aanval,' zei de arts zacht. 'Ze...'

Herzfeld knikte en maakte zijn zin af: 'Ze verkeert in shock.'

Op dat moment sperde Hannah haar ogen open, die tot dan toe gesloten waren geweest. Een fractie van een seconde keek ze naar haar vader, maar ze gaf geen blijk van herkenning. Erger nog, haar glazige blik was volkomen uitdrukkingsloos, ze staarde langs hem heen, de leegte in.

'Hannah, kleintje. Ik ben hier,' begon Herzfeld, maar ze knipperde niet eens met haar ogen toen hij pal voor haar pupillen met zijn vingers knipte. Opeens, toen Herzfeld juist haar haar uit haar gezicht veegde, opende ze haar mond.

'Wat zei ze?' vroeg de arts naast hem toen ze de naam had gepreveld, maar ook Herzfeld had het niet verstaan. Iets wat als 'stekker' of 'bakker' klonk.

Of 'slachter'?

Hannah probeerde het nog eens, maar kon geen woord uitbrengen. Tegelijk tilde ze haar arm op. Herzfeld draaide zijn hoofd opzij, keek in de richting waarin zijn apathische dochter wees. Bandrupp had de televisie op het campingtafeltje meteen al gezien, hij was vermoedelijk door het flakkerende schijnsel in de tunnel de goede kant op gelopen. Nu stond hij vlak naast het ouderwetse ding, waarvandaan een elektriciteitskabel naar een aantal met elkaar verbonden autoaccu's liep.

Herzfeld pakte Hannahs krachteloze handen. Hij wreef haar koude vingers, terwijl hij naar de televisie staarde. Hij had in zijn leven al veel gezichten van de dood gezien, maar nooit had iets hem zo geraakt als de beelden van het naakte, met bloed besmeurde meisje dat aan een strop boven een ijzeren bed bungelde.

Wie is dat?

Hoewel hij het gezicht van de jonge vrouw nooit eerder had gezien, ontroerde het hem, alsof hij in een onbekend fotoalbum een vreemd vertrouwde foto tegenkwam. Op het beeldscherm was een bunkerachtige ruimte te zien, dezelfde als op de videocamera in de bouwwagen.

Als door een onzichtbare hand bewogen, draaide de veel te jonge dode aan de strop om haar as. Herzfeld slaakte een verstikte kreet toen hij de tatoeage van de vlinder op de enkel van het meisje herkende.

Nee!

Langzaam, alsof hij werd voortgetrokken door de veiligheidslijn van een bergbeklimmer, verliet hij zijn plek naast Hannah en wankelde naar de televisie.

'Niet aankomen,' schreeuwde hij tegen Bandrupp, maar het was al te laat. De burgemeester had de dvd-speler onder de campingtafel uitgezet, en de reden daarvoor stond in zijn ogen te lezen toen hij zich naar Herzfeld omdraaide. Hij had de beelden niet langer kunnen verdragen.

Maar ik moet het zien, dacht Herzfeld, wetend dat de opname die Hannah al die tijd dat ze hier opgesloten had gezeten had moeten verdragen, eigenlijk voor hem was bedoeld.

Hij duwde de burgemeester opzij, negeerde het principe dat je op een plaats delict niets mag aanraken en knielde voor de televisie.

Ik moet het zien. Daarom ben ik hiernaartoe geloodst.

Hij drukte op de play-toets, en de dvd werd afgespeeld vanaf het punt waar hij het laatst was gestopt.

Naar de aanklacht tegen mij.

Naar de plaats waar de jonge vrouw nog op de spiraal van haar bed stond waarop ze zonder enige twijfel beestachtig was verkracht; op een ijzeren brits in een kelder die nog troostelozer was dan het hok waar ze Hannah in hadden gegooid, waar hij nu knielde om getuige te zijn van een daad van pure wanhoop.

'U kunt daar beter niet naar kijken,' zei Bandrupp met onvaste stem; hij had zijn blik allang afgewend. Herzfeld kroop er nog dichter naartoe. Het knisperde toen hij met zijn vinger het gezicht van het onbekende en toch vertrouwde meisje natekende. Vreemd genoeg leek het alsof er een krachtige schok door heel haar lichaam voer, vlak nadat ze een laatste keer om zich heen had gekeken en haar blik op een kartonnen doos naast het bed viel. De opname was haarscherp en in kleur, van veel betere kwaliteit dan een normale bewakingsvideo.

Iemand heeft de moeite genomen haar lijdensweg op te nemen.

En er was geluid!

Nu was er alleen geruis te horen, maar toen tilde de jonge vrouw haar hoofd op. Een glimlach verdreef de machteloosheid en paniek uit haar betraande gezicht. Daarna stak ze haar middelvinger op tegen de camera en riep met onverwacht krachtige stem: 'Nu weet ik wie ik ben. Ik ben geen hoer, klootzak.' Ze glimlachte nog steeds. 'Mijn naam is Rebecca Schwintowski.'

En met die woorden sprong Jan Sadlers laatste slachtoffer, het zeventienjarige meisje dat hij al weken geleden had ontvoerd en gefolterd, haar dood tegemoet.

Herzfeld deinsde achteruit, kroop naar Hannah, die nog steeds als gehypnotiseerd naar het beeldscherm staarde. Huilend hield hij zijn hand voor haar gezicht en zorgde ervoor dat ze niet nog een keer hoefde te zien wat de camera daarna had geregistreerd: de deur van de kelder sprong open en twee mannen stormden binnen die Herzfeld direct herkende: de een was zijn voormalige collega Sven Martinek, de tweede had hij pas op een video gezien.

Philipp Schwintowski had zijn dochter Rebecca gevonden.

En voorgoed verloren.

63

'Paul Herzfeld?' vroeg de jonge vrouw die met een rugzak om haar schouders uit het donker was gestapt.

'Linda?'

Herzfeld keek omhoog en kwam moeizaam overeind uit de ongemakkelijke plastic bank voor de ingang van de eilandkliniek. Tevergeefs probeerde hij een geeuw te onderdrukken. Hij was doodmoe. Hij hoopte dat Hannah weer wakker zou worden, voor de politie van het vasteland zou komen om haar mee te nemen voor verhoor. Toen ze haar weghaalden, weg van de bunker, was ze al in zijn armen in slaap gevallen. Nu lag ze op de tweede verdieping van het ziekenhuis, ingepakt in warme dekens, en met een infuus dat haar lichaamsvocht op peil moest brengen. Tot zo'n tien minuten geleden had hij voortdurend haar hand vastgehouden, maar nu was hij even naar buiten gegaan, de frisse lucht in, om niet zelf in de warme kamer in slaap te vallen.

'Waar zat je? Ik heb je gezocht, Linda, maar je was nergens te vinden.'

'Heb mijn spullen gepakt. Ik zie geen reden om op dit eiland te blijven,' zei ze. 'Ik vertrek met de eerste de beste veerboot.'

Herzfeld knikte en er viel een ongemakkelijke stilte omdat hij niet wist wat hij tegen de jonge vrouw, die haar leven voor hem had gewaagd, moest zeggen.

Eerder in de sectiezaal, na haar gevecht met Danny, had hij zich kort over haar heen gebogen. Nu zag hij Linda voor het eerst bewust in de ogen en constateerde dat hij zich haar heel anders had voorgesteld. Zoals zo vaak als je alleen iemands stem kent, kwam de werkelijkheid niet overeen met het beeld dat zijn fantasie van die persoon had gevormd. Herzfeld had een sympathieke maar al in haar jonge jaren afgeleefde vrouw verwacht. Interessant, maar geen schoonheid. Een kunstenares die het belangrijker vond hoe haar werk eruitzag dan zijzelf. Nu stond er een zelfverzekerde, intelligente vrouw voor hem, die niet leek te beseffen hoe aantrekkelijk ze was. Met haar brede heupen zou ze nooit een contract als model krijgen, maar daarin was ze waarschijnlijk even weinig geïnteresseerd als in een herhaling van de gebeurtenissen van de afgelopen uren.

'Ik, ik...' Herzfeld merkte dat hij begon te stotteren, omdat hij nog steeds niet wist hoe hij haar fatsoenlijk kon bedanken voor alles wat ze voor hem had gedaan.

'Je hebt mijn dochter gered,' zei hij ten slotte.

Linda's reactie trof hem als een emmer water in zijn gezicht. Alleen harder. Ze haalde uit en gaf hem een klinkende oorvijg.

'Twee uur, heb je gezegd,' siste ze woedend en opnieuw haalde ze uit. 'Twee uur maar, en dan zou je me eruit halen.'

Haar adem vormde dampwolken.

Herzfeld wreef met één hand over zijn brandende wang en hield de andere voor zijn gezicht om verdere klappen af te weren.

'Shit, ik had dood kunnen zijn als je er nog langer over had gedaan.'

'Het spijt me.'

'Je kunt mijn rug op.'

Ze liet haar arm zakken, zuchtte en frommelde een pakje sigaretten uit haar jas. Herzfeld zag even aan hoe ze worstelde met haar aansteker en vormde daarna met zijn handen een kom, zodat ze in de luwte haar sigaret kon aansteken.

'Bedankt.' Ze nam hem op en verontschuldigde zich voor de klap. 'Maar je hebt hem verdiend.'

Herzfeld knikte. *Vermoedelijk meer dan dat.*

Drie zelfmoorden, een beestachtig afgeslachte rechter, een geëxecuteerde sadist en een vermoedelijk voor de rest van haar leven getraumatiseerde dochter – als hij destijds naar Martinek had geluisterd en de bewijzen had vervalst, zou dat alles niet zijn gebeurd.

Hij had Linda niet hoeven dwingen lijken open te snijden, en Ender zou nu niet voor zijn leven vechten. Waarschijnlijk zou Linda zelfs de worsteling met de stalker in de donkere pathologieafdeling bespaard zijn gebleven, ook al waren zijn daden niet door Herzfeld uitgelokt.

'Behoorlijk druk hier,' zei Linda met een blik op de hel verlichte ingang van het ziekenhuis. 'Ik geloof dat de elektriciteit het weer doet.'

Herzfeld knikte.

Het door geld en goede woorden geïnspireerde reddingsteam was een geschenk uit de hemel en had de kliniek samen met de burgemeester, een fysiotherapeute en een paar vrijwilligers – ongeschoold maar hulpvaardig en opofferingsgezind – omgetoverd in een deugdelijk veldziekenhuis, tenminste de delen van het gebouw die niet door de storm waren beschadigd.

Ender en Danny waren gestabiliseerd en met de reddingshelikopter naar het vasteland gevlogen. Herzfeld had aangeboden bij de twee mannen, indien nodig, nog op het eiland een noodoperatie te verrichten, maar toen was het weer nog verder opgeklaard. Er konden nog geen schepen uitvaren, maar voor reddingshelikopters waren start en landing nauwelijks nog een probleem.

'Waar heb je je assistent eigenlijk gelaten?' vroeg Linda en ze blies wat rook onder haar pony. Herzfeld was er niet zeker van, maar hij dacht op haar voorhoofd een paar slecht genezen littekens te hebben gezien.

'Hij voelt zich al beter.'

Inderdaad had Ingolf bij de burgemeester al naar een sushibezorgdienst geïnformeerd, in zijn optiek een gat in de markt op een door de zee omgeven eiland. Ook zijn zeeziekte na de stormachtige overtocht bleek hij dus te hebben doorstaan.

'Geef mij er ook eentje,' zei Herzfeld, maar hij kwam er niet meer toe van Linda de eerste sigaret sinds zijn studietijd te bietsen. De schuifdeuren van de kliniek waren opengegaan en een van de vrijwillige verpleegsters stelde zich voor met haar naam, die hij meteen weer vergat nadat ze hem had verteld dat Hannah zojuist wakker was geworden.

64

Toen Herzfeld de smalle kamer binnenkwam, had hij verwacht dat zijn dochter afgemat zou zijn en half in slaap, aangeslagen door de verschrikkingen van de afgelopen dagen. Hij had zich vergist. Ze was klaarwakker.

En woedend.

'Wat moet je?'

Drie woorden. Vol bittere vijandigheid.

'Ik ben gekomen om...' begon Herzfeld en hij stokte toen Hannah met fonkelende ogen in haar ziekenhuisbed rechtop ging zitten. Ze was bleek, haar wangen waren ingevallen, maar in haar blik lag een vuur dat alleen tomeloze woede kon voortbrengen.

'Waarom? Zodat ik je als mijn redder kan bejubelen?'

Terwijl ze zat, maakte ze een kleine buiging en een handgebaar alsof Herzfeld een koning was en zij zijn onderdaan.

Hij wilde een houten stoel van de tafel naar zich toe trekken, maar besloot te blijven staan.

'Ik wilde gewoon zien hoe het met je gaat.'

'Hoezo?'

Hij keek haar verbaasd aan. Hannah deed demonstratief haar armen over elkaar. 'Ja, dat wil ik weten. Waarom juist nu?'

Nooit had hij haar zo vijandig meegemaakt. Tegenover hem noch anderen.

'Aha.' Haar gezicht werd nog strakker. 'Ik begrijp het al. Er moet me eerst iets overkomen voor je je een keer vertoont.' De tranen schoten haar in de ogen. Ze maakte geen aanstalten ze af te vegen, ze liet ze gewoon lopen.

'Het spijt me zo dat je dat moest doormaken.'

'Het spijt je zo?' Ze kneep haar vuisten zo hard dicht dat haar knokkels wit werden. 'Het *spijt* je zo?' Ze schreeuwde bijna. 'Ik heb haar zien doodgaan, papa. Dat meisje was net zo oud als ik en ik heb verdomme tot in detail gezien wat dat monster haar heeft aangedaan.'

Ik weet het, kleintje. En ik kan niets doen om dat ongedaan te maken.

'Het was echt. Ik heb in haar ogen gekeken en wist wat ze dacht. Wat ze voelde terwijl hij...'

Ze stokte met verstikte stem, sloot haar ogen en Herzfeld had het vermoeden dat de gruwelijkste scènes van Rebecca's martelgang aan haar geestesoog voorbijtrokken.

'Je had dat niet mogen zien.' Hij ging bij haar bed staan. Ze begon over haar hele lichaam te trillen, zo hevig dat Herzfeld bang was dat zijn dochter de slang van het infuus van haar arm zou afschudden.

'De beelden waren verschrikkelijk. Maar dat was niet het ergste,' zei Hannah met trillende onderlip. 'Wat hij zei, was nog erger. Wat die Sadler haar zou aandoen als hij terugkwam. Geloof me, papa, ik zou mezelf ook hebben opgehangen.'

Ze opende haar ogen weer, keek hem met een heldere, koude blik aan, die hij nooit eerder bij zijn dochter had gezien.

'Mocht je de video niet stopzetten?' vroeg Herzfeld. 'Waarmee hebben ze je gedreigd als je niet zou kijken?'

Het antwoord trof hem als een zweepslag.

'Ze hebben helemaal niet gedreigd.'

'Hoe bedoel je?'

'Zoals ik het zeg: ik stond niet onder dwang. Ik heb er vrijwillig naar gekeken.'

Herzfeld knipperde verward met zijn ogen. 'Maar waarom in godsnaam, kleintje?'

'Omdat ik het wilde.'

'Niemand wil zoiets zien, lieveling.'

'Jawel hoor, hij heeft het me uitgelegd. Je collega, die me hier-naartoe heeft gebracht en me de dvd gaf. Hij zei dat ik als ik hem had bekeken, zou begrijpen waarom ze jou een lesje wilden leren. Waarom ze het hele systeem een lesje wilden leren.'

Martinek, vuile klootzak.

'Het gaat hier niet om ons, papa. Morgen al staan er schreeu-wende koppen in de krant, en dan weet iedereen dat in onze zo-genaamde rechtsstaat de slachtoffers geen kans maken en de da-ders alle rechten hebben.'

Herzfeld sloot een moment zijn ogen. Het was duidelijk dat Hannah alleen de kreten napraatte die de ontvoerders er bij haar in hadden gepompt, en hij wist niet hoe hij moest reageren zon-der haar nog meer tegen zich in het harnas te jagen.

'Het belangrijkste is nu dat het weer goed met je gaat, lieve-ling.'

'Maar het ging nooit slecht.'

'Sorry?'

'Ze hebben me goed behandeld. Ik had genoeg te eten en te drinken. Ze hebben zelfs aan mijn astmaspray gedacht.'

'Goed behandeld? Ze hebben je ontvoerd en opgesloten.'

Hannah sloeg haar ogen ten hemel, alsof haar vader traag van begrip was. 'Je snapt er niets van. Mij zou nooit een haar worden gekrenkt. Ik was geen moment in gevaar. In het begin, toen ik de voicemail moest inspreken, was ik bang. Onterecht, bleek later. De dikke, die Schwintowski, heeft goed voor me gezorgd.'

'En als ik niet op tijd zou zijn gekomen?'

'Zou je over twee dagen een e-mail met een plattegrondje heb-ben gekregen. Ik heb zelf gezien hoe Schwintowski de timer op zijn mobieltje heeft ingesteld. Zo, daar sta je van te kijken, hè?' Ze lachte hem honend uit.

Verdomme, Martinek. Waarom heb je haar dat aangedaan?

Niets was zo gemakkelijk te manipuleren als de geest van een

318

tiener. Zelfs sterke persoonlijkheden neigen ertoe onder extreme druk de kant van hun ontvoerder te kiezen.

Herzfeld wist dat, maar hoewel hij duidelijk symptomen van een stockholmsyndroom bij zijn dochter zag, kon hij niets met die wetenschap beginnen.

'Dat zou allemaal niet zijn gebeurd...' zei ze luid.

Herzfeld hief zijn hand, wilde zich verdedigen. 'Nee, schat, je vergist je...'

'Als je hem destijds zou hebben geholpen...'

'Dat zou niets hebben uitgehaald.'

Hij wilde haar uitleggen dat hij de bewijzen niet kon manipuleren omdat het zijn werk was objectief en onafhankelijk te zijn, en dat je juist in zijn beroep alleen de waarheid mocht laten gelden, maar hij kon niet tot haar doordringen.

'En mama had ook gelijk...'

'Sadlers verdedigers zouden korte metten met een gemanipuleerd rapport hebben gemaakt, en hij zou misschien zelfs vrijgesproken zijn.'

'Je bent weerzinwekkend. Jouw werk is weerzinwekkend...'

'En het zou de dood van Martineks dochter niet hebben kunnen verhinderen...'

'Maar wel die van Rebecca. Jij bent ook alleen maar een geolied radertje dat het systeem in stand houdt.'

Ze praatten wild door elkaar heen, hun woorden werden steeds luider, verdrongen elkaar en versmolten tot een onbegrijpelijk geschreeuw. Geen van beiden luisterde nog naar de ander, tot Herzfeld een laatste poging deed en de hand van zijn dochter vastpakte.

Hannah slaakte een gil, net zo luid en scherp als de zwangere hond die de bouwvakker in zijn buik had geschopt, en Herzfeld deinsde achteruit.

'Hannah, alsjeblieft, het spijt me,' begon hij nog een keer, maar het was zinloos.

Ze wilde niets meer van hem horen en trok de deken over haar hoofd.

Hij bleef een tijdje naast haar bed staan, hoorde haar schreeuwen, telde haar gesmoorde snikken tot die zachter en onregelmatiger werden. Toen ging hij de kamer uit met het gevoel in zijn hart dat hij het belangrijkste in zijn leven voorgoed had verloren.

'Ze bedaart wel weer,' zei Ingolf, die voor de kamer had staan wachten en alles blijkbaar had gehoord. 'Het is gewoon de shock.'

'Wat weet jij er nou van?' siste Herzfeld en hij had op hetzelfde moment spijt. Ingolf had hem alleen willen helpen.

Maar ik ben niet meer te helpen.

'Ik ben er zeker van dat ze morgen al berouw heeft van haar woorden en haar tong zal willen afbijten.'

'Bedankt, maar ik wil nu...'

Herzfeld bleef staan, keek om naar de deur waarachter Hannah lag, toen naar Ingolf. 'De tong...'

Hij kon niet zeggen waarom uitgerekend die woorden van Ingolf hem zo onaangenaam hadden getroffen, zo erg dat hij dacht dat hij geen lucht meer kreeg.

'Waar wilt u nu weer naartoe?' riep de stagiair hem verbaasd achterna, maar Herzfeld handelde als in trance en gaf geen antwoord.

'... haar tong zal willen afbijten...'

Flarden herinnering dwarrelden als confetti op de grond, maar vormden geen duidelijk beeld. Hij dacht aan het botenhuis bij Martinek, aan de pot met de tong, aan Sadler. En aan wat Linda tijdens haar eerste autopsie tegen hem had gezegd.

En terwijl de herinneringen in zijn hoofd rondspookten, liep hij steeds sneller, ging over tot een snelle draf, tot hij ten slotte door de gang van het ziekenhuis naar het trappenhuis holde, de trap af naar de afdeling Pathologie, waar hij wilde nagaan of zijn vreselijke vermoeden juist was.

65

'Ontbreken de kaakgewrichten van het lijk misschien?'

'Nee. Iemand heeft de tong van die arme stakker afgesneden.'

Met Linda's stem in zijn achterhoofd en de herinnering aan hun eerste gezamenlijke, telefonisch geleide obductie ging hij tussen de sectietafels staan. Iemand had allebei de lichamen in witte lijkenzakken gestopt. Maar dat was de enige poging geweest om de chaos van de laatste uren uit de weg te ruimen, want de afdeling Pathologie bevond zich in een rampzalige toestand: alle hulpvaardige lieden die uit het plaatsje naar het ziekenhuis waren gekomen, hadden hun sporen achtergelaten. Er stonden overal voetafdrukken met natte sneeuw op de vloer, waar nog steeds instrumenten, plastic handschoenen en ook de smerige matras rondslingerden. De kast en de brancard stonden weliswaar weer overeind, maar waren lukraak neergezet.

Herzfeld opende de rits van de eerste lijkenzak. Omdat het lichaam merkwaardig genoeg met de voeten vooruit lag, ontblootte hij eerst de benen en de romp van de rechter. Zelfs hij voelde weerzin toen hij de met bloedkorsten overdekte, door lijkengas opgeblazen blaren op de dijen bekeek. Hoe moest het Linda dan zijn vergaan, als je bedacht dat er ook nog een stok in de anus van het lijk had gezeten?

Hij deed de zakken weer dicht en ging naar Sadler op de tafel ernaast, wiens opengesneden T-shirt hij op het tafeltje had ontdekt.

Jan *Erik* Sadler.

'Is er bloed aanwezig in de mondholte?'

Herzfeld aarzelde even voor hij de ritssluiting weer opentrok om Sadlers lijk nader te inspecteren.

Hij sloot zijn ogen, probeerde zich het gezicht van Sadler nog eens voor te stellen, dat hij op ontelbare foto's in Martineks botenhuis had gezien. Toen opende hij de lijkenzak.

Geen twijfel mogelijk.

De man op de sectietafel zag er precies zo uit als hij hem in herinnering had. Herzfeld zou hem ook zonder de beelden van de bewakingscamera hebben herkend. Sadlers foto had in de aanloop naar het proces wekenlang in de media gecirculeerd. Zijn haar was nu iets langer, maar zelfs de uitgesmeerde bloedvlekken in zijn gezicht konden het niet verdoezelen: hier lag de moordenaar van Martineks dochter Lily.

De moordenaar van Schwintowski's dochter Rebecca.

Herzfeld boog voorover om beter in de wijd geopende mondholte van Sadler te kunnen kijken. Met een balpen, die hij uit de binnenzak van zijn jas had getrokken, constateerde hij zoals verwacht dat die leeg was. De tong was verwijderd zoals Linda hem had verteld en Schwintowski op de video had bekend: *'Mijn wraakzucht gold aanvankelijk alleen mevrouw de rechter. En natuurlijk ook Sadler, wiens tong ik nog ter plekke heb afgesneden, waarmee hij Rebecca...'*

'Maar hoe valt dat te rijmen?' fluisterde Herzfeld tegen zichzelf.

Hoezo had Linda bloed in de mondholte ontdekt?

Herzfeld verstijfde. Nu wist hij wat hem zo verontrustte. Hij zag Schwintowski's videotestament weer voor zijn geestesoog: *'We hebben gewacht tot Sadlers wond was genezen. Martinek heeft de stomp van zijn tong gehecht, om het varken niet te laten doodbloeden. En daarna, toen hij genezen was, hebben wij hem het vuile werk laten opknappen.'*

'Hoe is dat mogelijk?' fluisterde Herzfeld opnieuw, terwijl hij langzaam de lijkenzak verder opende boven de borstkas van het lijk. Als Sadler al weken geleden was verminkt, zou Linda een naad, draden of korsten hebben moeten vinden.

Maar geen bloed.

Hij boog zich over het lichaam heen en toen merkte hij het. Onder normale omstandigheden, als hij niet zo doodmoe en verstrooid was geweest, zou het hem meteen zijn opgevallen. Linda had de mondholte van het lijk opengesneden, zijn hals geopend en een capsule uit het strottenhoofd gepeld, dacht hij nog in de seconde waarin Sadler zijn rechterarm ophief en een sectiemes in Herzfelds buik plantte.

66

Fuck.

Het liefst zou hij hem nog eens hebben gestoken, maar nu moest hij er als de sodemieter vandoor. Wegwezen hier. Snel.

Fuck. Fuck. Fuck.

Sadler sprong van de sectietafel.

Wat een klotezooi!

Afgelopen. Uit.

Zijn plan – zijn enige kans om ongemerkt van dat kankereiland af te komen – verziekt. Alleen omdat die stomme eikel lont had geroken en was teruggekomen.

Verdomme, wat had hij allemaal niet moeten doormaken!

Eerst die martelingen. Die vette Schwintowski had zijn tong afgesneden. Met een broodmes. Zomaar. Alleen omdat die domme slet van een dochter van hem zich had opgehangen, dat waardeloze stuk stront. Hij had nooit een wijf gehad dat beroerder neukte dan zij.

Geen idee hoe ze Rebecca hadden gevonden. Geen idee hoe ze *hem* hadden gevonden. Op een of andere manier had hij aan zijn water gevoeld dat hij werd achtervolgd sinds hij was vrijgelaten. Vast en zeker door die andere schooier, die Martinek, zijn dochter was veel lekkerder geweest. *Veel jonger.*

Ze hadden hem ontvoerd, de schoften. In een kist, met een verhuiswagen. Ergens naar het oosten, die stomme klootzakken, naar een huis aan een meer. Eerst dacht hij dat ze hem daar definitief van kant zouden maken. Het was al een wonder dat hij niet in zijn eigen bloed was gestikt nadat die dikke zijn tong had afgesneden. Maar toen had dat mietje van een arts hem een deal aangeboden.

De rechter in ruil voor een laatste nummertje.

Hij had er geen woord van geloofd. Alsof ze hem werkelijk bij die Hannah zouden laten als hij dat rotklusje voor ze zou opknappen. Maar wat voor keus had hij? Als hij had geweigerd, zou Schwintowski hem dood hebben gemarteld, zoveel was zeker. Dan liever tijd zien te winnen en een geschikt moment afwachten om te vluchten. Bovendien was het wel lollig geweest om die ouwe taart van een rechter te spietsen. Drieënhalf jaar had ze hem aangesmeerd, die hoer.

Sadler sloop voorzichtig naar de uitgang van de sectiezaal. Herzfeld, die achter hem op de grond lag, rochelde niet meer. Mooi zo.

Was die schooier in zijn eentje hierheen gekomen?

Allemaal sukkels. Net als Martinek. Als die vette verhuizer er niet was geweest, had hij zich allang kunnen bevrijden. Maar Schwintowski was uit ander hout gesneden dan zijn armzalige maat. Martinek zou nooit de kloten hebben gehad om zijn tong af te snijden. En in zijn eentje zou het hem nooit zijn gelukt hem naar het eiland te krijgen. Verdoofd en in een paardentrailer gedouwd, op een vrachtboot van zijn verhuisbedrijf geladen. Samen met Hannah. Verdomme. Hij had haar nooit gezien, maar hij wist dat ze hier op het eiland zat. Hij had wel haar stem gehoord toen ze in de kelder ernaast met die vette kankerlijer had gepraat. Schijnheilig stuk vreten, hoe normaal ze geklonken had, alsof die dikzak haar beste kameraad was.

Toen hij klaar was met mevrouw de rechter, gebeurde er wat gebeuren moest. Zoals verwacht. Ze probeerden hem te vermoorden. Of liever gezegd: Schwintowski probeerde het. De ander was op de wal gebleven, om wat voor reden dan ook.

Klote, nietwaar? Was nou maar meegekomen.

Schwintowski had hem met blote handen willen wurgen.

Martinek was dokter. Hij zou de hartslag niet aan zijn pols, maar aan zijn hals hebben gevoeld. Schwintowski was het wat verleerd. Vroeger had hij de mensen van wie hij geld kreeg misschien de keel dichtgeknepen, maar dat moest jaren geleden zijn. Die idioot was te vroeg gestopt, en toen Sadler weer bijkwam, lag hij met alleen een T-shirt aan en een gruwelijk gepiep in zijn oren op de oever. Hij dacht dat zijn hoofd elk moment kon exploderen, en zijn keel brandde of hij zoutzuur had ingeslikt. Hij wilde om hulp roepen, maar toen hij zijn eigen gesmoorde gegrom hoorde, schoot hem te binnen dat hij geen tong meer had. In plaats daarvan lag er iets anders, iets vreemds in zijn mond. Iets van plastic, wat Schwintowski erin moest hebben gedaan en wat hij rochelend in het zand spuugde toen hij overeind krabbelde.

Hoorde hij iets?

Sadler bleef bij de halfgeopende schuifdeur staan, gluurde vanuit de sectiezaal de gang in en dacht aan het moment waarop hij op de oever wakker was geworden. Half verlamd van de kou. Schwintowski, dat varken, had hem zijn winterjas uit- en een dun T-shirt aangetrokken, waarop hij met viltstift zijn tweede voornaam had geschreven: ERIK.

Hoezo?

In de storm was Sadler naar het huis van de rechter teruggestrompeld, om de rat die hem had willen wurgen zijn ballen af te snijden. Maar dat plezier was hem niet gegund. Hij had Schwintowski op zolder gevonden. Bungelend aan een strop, pal voor een draaiende videocamera. De idioot had zich van kant gemaakt.

En nou?

Sadler had zich willen wreken, maar nu was er niets anders meer voorhanden dan lillend dood vlees. Hij werd razend. Haalde Schwintowski eerst van de strop en sneed hem toen zijn vette leugenaarstong uit.

Oog om oog. Tong om tong. *Jammer dat die ouwe zak het niet meer heeft gevoeld.*

Het had iets rustgevends gehad om Schwintowski's tong in zijn handen te hebben. Iets reinigends. Opeens had Sadler weer helder kunnen denken.

Hij herinnerde zich de gesprekken tussen Hannah en Schwintowski, die hij in de cel ernaast had afgeluisterd. Over hun plan het systeem een lesje te leren en dat soort onzin. Sadler had er nauwelijks iets van begrepen, maar één zin was hem bijgebleven. Schwintowski had hem twee keer herhaald; één keer toen hij al in de gang van die ellendige bunker had gestaan, voor hij Hannahs celdeur dichtdeed. *'Wees niet bang, meisje. De lijken van de moordenaars zullen je vader naar je toe leiden.'*

Nu begreep hij wat hij bedoelde. Herzfeld was een lijkensnijder, net als de vader van Lily. En zijn lijk had als wegwijzer moeten dienen.

Maar dan zijn jullie midden in de stront gestapt, jongens. Zoiets laat ik me niet flikken.

Toch beviel het idee hem wel om Hannah en zodoende zijn beloning te vinden. Omdat hij de kerker met een zak over zijn hoofd was binnengekomen en er ook op die manier weer uit was geloodst, wist hij niet waar ze gevangen hadden gezeten. Maar met wat geluk zou haar vader, de lijkensnijder, hem naar zijn dochter voeren. Alles wat hij moest doen was ervoor zorgen dat de puzzeltocht verderging. Meer dan afwachten en toekijken kon hij in dit pokkenweer toch niet. Wie weet zat er toch nog een bonusnummertje in.

Sadler had zowat een uur nodig gehad om Schwintowski het Erik-t-shirt aan te trekken, dat verschrikkelijk strak zat, hoewel het al maat xxl was. *Vet varken.* Maar het was kinderspel geweest om het lijk naar het strand beneden te slepen en op dezelfde plaats te dumpen waar hij zelf had moeten liggen. Hij had de plek teruggevonden door de lelijke mannenhandtas die Schwintowski op de betonnen pijler had gezet. Alleen het gele plastic ding had hij bijna vergeten. Schwintowski had het hem los in zijn mond gelegd, maar hij ramde het uit alle macht de keel van die schooier in, zo ver mogelijk. Vanaf dat moment had Sadler nieuwsgierig toegekeken. Zag hoe de slet met de dikke reet en de dunne armpjes het lijk vond. Hoe ze hectisch telefoneerde. En hoe ze Schwintowski de volgende ochtend met de Turk naar de kliniek bracht.

Van de meeste dingen die hij stiekem gadesloeg, werd hij goed geil: hoe het meisje opeens het lijk begon uit te kleden. En zelfs open te snijden! De vent aan de andere kant van de lijn die haar aanwijzingen gaf was gegarandeerd Hannahs vader geweest. Maar wie was die gek met de verminkte kop in godsnaam, die hier ook door de donkere gangen sloop en het rare gedoe in de sectiezaal leek te bespioneren?

Toen was het noodaggregaat uitgevallen, en de geitenneuker was hem in de armen gelopen toen hij op weg ging om het ding te repareren.

Gelukkig had hij het mes uit de sectiezaal meegenomen, anders had de Turk beslist alarm geslagen.

Vanaf dat moment wilde hij geen risico meer nemen. Misschien was het toch niet zo'n goed idee om naar Hannah te zoeken. Meisjes genoeg.

Om een helder hoofd te krijgen, zocht hij een bed in een uithoek van het ziekenhuis en ging eerst even liggen. Heerlijk. Weliswaar retekoud, maar na weken eindelijk eens een echte matras. Toen hij weer wakker werd, had hij willen kijken hoe het op de afdeling Pathologie ging. Misschien had die Linda al iets over Hannah ontdekt? En zo niet, dan zou hij zich met haar kunnen bezighouden. De kleine was wel te oud, maar best leuk, en hij had hem al een tijd nergens meer in geslingerd, dus was hij niet zo kieskeurig. De slet had geluk dat ze de zaak had gebarricadeerd en het hem niet lukte bij haar te komen voordat het in de kliniek opeens een gekkenhuis was. Er landde een helikopter, allerlei mensen renden het ziekenhuis in, overal stemmen. Een wonder dat ze hem niet hadden ontdekt.

Hij had gewacht tot de eerste chaos voorbij was en met de gedachte gespeeld uit het ziekenhuis weg te gaan. Maar waarheen? En zelfs als hij een goede schuilplaats vond, hoe had hij dan van dat pesteiland af moeten komen? Hij kreeg een idee, maar dat had alleen kans van slagen als hij zich nog één keer in het hol van de leeuw zou wagen. In de sectiezaal.

In tegenstelling tot de rest van de kliniek was de ruimte merkwaardig genoeg uitgestorven. Iemand had die hoer van een rechter en de opengesneden vetzak in lijkenzakken gestopt.

Helemaal niet zo'n slecht idee.

Zonder er veel gedachten aan te wijden hoeveel kans zijn plan maakte, had hij Schwintowski met zeil en al van tafel getrokken en hem bijna moeiteloos – nu hij was uitgerust – in een van de twee koelvakken geduwd. Toen had hij een nieuwe lijkenzak gepakt, die op de sectietafel uitgespreid, en was er zelf in gaan liggen. Het was helemaal niet zo eenvoudig geweest de ritssluiting van binnenuit dicht te krijgen, maar uiteindelijk was het hem gelukt.

Fuck! Het was bijna perfect geweest.

Als iemand alleen vluchtig naar hem keek, liep hij geen gevaar. Als die idioot van een Herzfeld hem niet zo grondig had gecontroleerd, zouden ze hem samen met Töven als lijk van het eiland hebben gekard. Op een of andere manier zou hij zich hebben kunnen bevrijden. Op het vasteland zou hij degene die de zak openritste het mes dat nu uit de buik van de dode professor stak, in het gezicht hebben geramd.

Man, het zou te gek zijn geweest in zijn ogen te kijken toen hij het mes voelde en wist dat zijn laatste uur geslagen had.

Sadler had nog steeds een stijve.

Hij bevond zich nu halverwege de sectiezaal en de liften. Vanuit het trappenhuis klonken er zware voetstappen, maar die leken zich te verwijderen. Toch verschool hij zich achter een medicijnkast in de gang. Hij had geen idee waar hij naartoe moest. Hier in de kliniek, zoveel was zeker, kon hij in geen geval blijven. Net nog had de politie op alle vragen antwoord gekregen: Töven? Dood! Sadler? Dood.

Twee lijken op de afdeling Pathologie: check!

Iemand die de video van Schwintowski's zelfmoord had gezien, vroeg zich misschien af waarom die schooier niet meer aan de balken onder het dak van de rechter hing. Maar het was wat anders of de smerissen het eiland naar een verdwenen lijk afzochten of naar een ontsnapte moordenaar. En dat zouden ze doen zodra ze Herzfelds lijk in de sectiezaal hadden ontdekt.

Fuck.

De voetstappen werden zachter, maar de lift had zich in beweging gezet.

Ging hij naar boven of naar beneden?

Sadler had geen tijd meer om naar het lichtbord te kijken. Er zat niets anders op dan achter de medicijnkast vandaan te komen. Als hij niet in de val wilde zitten, moest hij het trappenhuis bereiken voordat de deuren opengingen.

Vooruit dan maar.

Hij wilde net wegrennen toen hij iets warms in zijn nek voelde.

Adem.

Wat, verdomme nog aan toe... dacht hij nog. Hij draaide zich om, en meteen explodeerde zijn schedel.

67

Dit keer was het anders dan het gevecht met de bouwvakker. Dit keer brak hij ook zijn eigen neus.

De pijn die Herzfeld voelde toen zijn neusbeen versplinterde, nadat hij zijn hoofd tegen Sadlers gezicht had gebeukt, was heel wat beter te verdragen dan wat hij vlak daarvoor had gevoeld toen hij zonder nadenken het mes uit zijn buik had getrokken.

In plaats van te schreeuwen was hij flauwgevallen, een paar seconden maar. Toen was het alsof er een schakelaar in zijn hoofd werd omgezet, en een oncontroleerbare woede die alle handelingen en gevoelens in de schaduw stelde, had hem nieuw leven ingeblazen.

Een woede, wild en sterk als een vulkaanuitbarsting. Gezien de hoeveelheid bloed die hij verloor had Herzfeld met de seconde zwakker moeten worden, maar zijn razernij gaf hem nieuwe kracht. 'Ik vermoord je!' zei hij hijgend. Hij schopte de verkrachter in zijn maag.

Sadler kromde zich. Een onduidelijke klank kwam uit zijn tongloze mond. Na de eerste klap op zijn hoofd was hij achterovergetuimeld, had nergens houvast gevonden en was op de grond gevallen. Dikke bloeddruppels kwamen uit zijn scheve neus. Hij staarde omhoog naar Herzfeld, alsof die uit de doden was opgestaan. Toen trof Herzfelds laars opnieuw doel, en Sadler sloeg met zijn hoofd tegen de muur.

Het kraakte alsof er een droge tak knapte, maar dat kon Herzfeld vanwege de herrie in zijn hoofd niet meer horen.

Te veel stemmen riepen in zijn innerlijk door elkaar. Hij hoorde Martinek, die hem verweet Lily voor de tweede keer te hebben vermoord en wenste dat Paul ooit zou voelen wat het betekende om je dochter te verliezen.

'*O ja, Sven. Jij hebt het me laten voelen.*'

Herzfeld schopte Sadler in zijn maag en hoorde Rebecca haar eigen naam schreeuwen, terwijl ze uit angst voor de verschrikkingen haar dood tegemoet sprong.

Hij trok de sadist aan zijn haar omhoog en ramde zijn knie in zijn gezicht. Sadlers geschreeuw, dat diep uit zijn keel kwam, overstemde dat van Hannah niet: '*Ik haat je.*'

Hij drukte het achterhoofd van het varken tegen zijn borst, zette hem het mes op de keel en maakte de fout een keer diep adem te halen. Op dat moment trok het waas voor zijn ogen op en stonden ze opeens allemaal voor hem: Linda, Ingolf, Bandrupp.

Ze waren met twee agenten in hun kielzog uit de lift gestapt. Vermoedelijk om de politiemannen, wie het eindelijk was gelukt vanaf het vasteland het eiland te bereiken, naar de lijken op de afdeling Pathologie te brengen.

Geen idee hoe lang ze er al stonden. Hem aangaapten. Op hem inpraatten. Een van beide agenten had zijn dienstpistool getrokken en op hem gericht. Hij brulde: 'Laat vallen! Meteen laten vallen!'

Herzfeld keek hem aan, voelde dat zijn woedeaanval op het punt stond weg te ebben en de pijn weer de overhand zou krijgen.

'Dat kan ik niet,' zei hij met krassende stem.

Welke straf staat een misdadiger nou helemaal te wachten die tot zijn moorden is gedwongen?

In gedachten zag hij Schwintowski hem toeknikken. Hij had zijn lesje geleerd. Soms moet je de regels overtreden om het goede te doen.

'Alstublieft. Doet u het niet!' Ingolf.

'U verwoest uw eigen leven.' Bandrupp.

De laatste zin kwam van Linda: 'Laat maar, het is nergens goed voor. Je zult je daarna niet beter voelen.'

'Ik weet het.' Herzfeld knikte en hij dacht aan Rebecca's gekwelde gezicht. Aan het bloed tussen haar benen en de uitdrukking in haar ogen toen ze begreep wie ze was en dat haar maar één mogelijkheid restte om een einde aan de zaak te maken. Net als hij, hier en nu.

Met de echo van de dode kinderstemmen in zijn hoofd sneed hij Sadler de keel door.

EPILOOG

DRIE WEKEN LATER

Hoe duurder het hotel, des te dikker de tapijten.

Paul Herzfeld had het gevoel dat hij over een spons wandelde. Toen hij door de gang liep zakten zijn schoenen geluidloos in de vloerbedekking weg, die zo hoogpolig was dat hij zijn voeten als een wadloper bij elke stap moest optillen. Intussen begon hij te transpireren, niet door de fysieke inspanning, maar vanwege het litteken dat hij aan Sadler te danken had. De artsen hadden gezegd dat hij zijn leven lang last zou blijven houden van de pijn: telkens als hij zware dingen droeg, de trap op liep, aan sport deed – of, zoals nu, alleen ademhaalde.

Herzfeld bleef staan en drukte zijn hand tegen de plek waarachter het kloppende litteken van de operatie boven zijn navel zat. Het liefst was hij omgekeerd.

De blinkend gepoetste messing bordjes aan de muur hadden hem al gewaarschuwd. Kamer 4011 van het Hyatt-hotel aan de Potsdamer Platz bevond zich helemaal aan het eind van de gang. Hij mocht van geluk spreken dat hij geen koffer bij zich had. De wieltjes zouden onverbiddelijk in het hoge tapijt blijven steken.

4003, 4005, 4007... Herzfeld had zich de moeite kunnen besparen op de kamernummers te letten. De deur die hij zocht was niet te missen. Hij leek mijlenver van de lift vandaan te liggen, was dubbel zo groot als de andere en de enige waar aan weerszijden een vaas met bloemen stond.

335

Herzfeld rook aan een roos, die geen kans maakte tegen het aroma van tropische houtsoorten dat aan de ventilatielucht was toegevoegd; een exotische geur die je op straat voor het hotel al tegemoet sloeg. Hij wilde net aankloppen, toen de ronde knop op de deur hem opviel, vlak naast de sleuf voor de elektronische sleutelkaart. Hij drukte hem in en hoorde binnen een gedempt gezoem.

'Fijn dat het u gelukt is, professor!'

Ingolf von Appen moest vlak achter de deur hebben gewacht, zo snel had hij opengedaan.

Hij schudde Herzfelds hand, straalde over zijn hele gezicht en had vlekken van opwinding op zijn wangen. Als hij een hond was geweest, dacht Herzfeld, zou hij ter begroeting tegen zijn been zijn opgesprongen en blij hebben gekwispeld.

'Wilt u uw jas uitdoen?' vroeg Ingolf nog in de hal. Herzfeld keek verbaasd om zich heen.

De hal was groter dan die van menige eengezinswoning.

Geen twijfel mogelijk. Kamer 4011 was geen kamer maar een suite. Alleen het woongedeelte al waar Ingolf hem naartoe bracht was twee keer zo groot als een normale hotelkamer; met een eettafel, zithoek en een tv met plasmascherm, waarop je gemakkelijk tafeltennis had kunnen spelen als je hem plat had gelegd. Op het moment was er een geluidloze bierreclame achter het ontspiegelde matglas te zien.

Herzfeld telde vier deuren die op de huiskamer uitkwamen, waarvan er een openstond en naar een badkamer leidde, een Romeinse consul waardig. Crèmekleurig marmer, passend bij de kleur van het interieur.

'Waarom al dat gedoe?' vroeg hij.

Ingolf keek hem niet-begrijpend aan, terwijl hij Herzfelds oude winterjas in een verzonken garderobe liet verdwijnen. Overeenkomstig zijn stand droeg de zoon van de Berlijnse senator een donkerblauwe blazer met gouden knopen en een pochet, daaronder een grijze flanellen broek en handgemaakte gaatjesschoenen. Van een das had hij afgezien, vermoedelijk omdat de teugels in het weekend wat konden worden gevierd. Maar elk haartje op zijn hoofd zat vastgeplakt, en Herzfeld vroeg zich af hoe lang de jongen onder de douche zou moeten staan om al die gel er weer uit te spoelen.

Zelf beantwoordde hij momenteel eerder aan het cliché van de verstrooide professor. Zijn bruine pullover met v-hals paste noch bij zijn versleten corduroy jasje, noch bij zijn tennisschoenen. Hij had zich al dagen niet geschoren en daarom leek zijn gezicht onder de jukbeenderen diep in de schaduw te liggen.

'Wat bedoelt u met gedoe?' vroeg Ingolf, terwijl hij met hem door de suite liep.

Herzfeld trok een gevoerde envelop met het familiewapen van de Von Appens uit zijn achterzak en hield hem omhoog als een scheidsrechter een rode kaart. 'Ik bedoel deze uitnodiging hier. Je schreef dat we een keertje koffie zouden moeten drinken. Waarom huur je daarvoor de presidentiële suite in een vijfsterrenhotel?'

Even zag Ingolf er nog verwarder uit dan eerst, toen moest hij hartelijk lachen. 'Nee, dat is een vergissing, professor. De suite heb ik niet speciaal voor onze afspraak gehuurd.'

'Maar?'

'Ik woon hier.'

Herzfeld keek opnieuw om zich heen. 'Dat meen je niet.'

'Jawel hoor. Al een halfjaar. Ik hield het thuis bij mijn ouweheer niet meer uit, en toen moest ik snel een oplossing zien te vinden. Het is weliswaar nog wat onpersoonlijk ingericht, maar tijdens mijn studie bedrijfseconomie wil ik mezelf de stress van een binnenhuisarchitect besparen, zoals u begrijpt.'

'Natuurlijk,' zei Herzfeld droogjes. 'Welke student kent dat probleem niet?'

Hij keek naar de tot de vloer reikende panoramaruiten, waardoor je een indrukwekkend uitzicht over de Berliner Philharmonie tot aan Tiergarten had.

'U beschouwt mij als decadent, dat weet ik. Maar deze suite is maar half zo groot als die van de rockzanger boven mij, en bovendien krijg je korting als je twee jaar vooruitbetaalt.'

'Een koopje dus.'

Ingolf leek immuun voor zijn sarcasme, want hij somde op: 'En dat is inclusief alles: elektriciteit, water, verwarming, schoonmaakster, fitnessstudio, zelfs het zwembad.'

'En niet te vergeten de douchegel,' zei Herzfeld met een stalen gezicht. 'Anderen betalen daarvoor een vermogen bij de drogist, maar hier staat het allemaal gratis en voor niks in de badkamer.'

Als op commando werd er een toilet doorgetrokken, toen ging vlak naast hem een deur open die hij nog niet had gezien.

'Is de reclame al afgelopen?' vroeg Ender, die gebogen over de wastafel in het gastentoilet met zijn rug naar hem toe water in zijn gezicht gooide. Toen hij opkeek, ontdekte hij Herzfeld in de spiegel.

'Paul!'

Hij draaide zich met een ruk om, blijkbaar iets te snel, want hij greep met een van pijn vertrokken gezicht naar zijn vleeskleurige halskraag. De malloot had nog meer geluk dan spieren. De artsen op het vasteland hadden wonderen verricht en in een drie uur durende operatie het sectiemes verwijderd, bloedvaten gerepareerd en de wond genaaid. Als hij het de komende weken rustig aan deed, hoefde hij niet bang te zijn voor blijvende gevolgen.

'Mooi om je een keer zonder lijk te zien. Of heb je misschien je werk meegenomen?' Ender grijnsde nog breder dan Ingolf bij zijn begroeting. 'Kom, dit moet je zien.'

Herzfeld dacht dat Ender hem een bijzondere attractie van de suite wilde tonen, maar hij duwde hem voor de televisie. De reclame was afgelopen en het logo van een amusementsprogramma, ongeveer zo subtiel als dat van de *Bild,* schoof over het scherm.

'*Deutschland Deine Talente!*' zei Ender, alsof Herzfeld niet kon lezen. Op een of andere manier had hij een vuistdikke afstandsbediening in zijn klauwen gekregen, waarmee hij het geluid aanzette.

'Wat is dit voor waanzin?'

Ingolf legde het achter hem uit: 'Bij die *waanzin* heeft uw vriend op een haar na zijn reputatie te grabbel gegooid.'

'Mijn wat?' vroeg Ender, zonder zijn ogen van het scherm af te wenden. Een als een randdebiel in de camera blikkende man met een matrozenmuts eiste al zijn aandacht op.

'Die hufter heeft mijn plek ingepikt,' jammerde hij, terwijl hij met de afstandsbediening rondzwaaide alsof hij een degen vasthield. 'Eigenlijk had *ik* daar moeten optreden. *Ik* zat in de herkansing met mijn comedyact. Alleen omdat ik op Helgoland vastzat, hebben die idioten deze afgezaagde slapjanus genomineerd.'

'Waarom?' vroeg Herzfeld walgend. 'Zodat hij voor de draaiende camera zijn gebit uit zijn mond kan halen?'

'Goedkoop hè? Dat doet hij alleen als gag,' zei Ender. 'Nummertje oud-Frans, weet je wel: pijpen zonder tanden.'

'Heel komisch.'

'Dat zeg ik. Zijn grappen zijn niet half zo goed als de mijne. Verdomme.'

'Ik weet zeker dat je volgend jaar de kans van je leven krijgt,' zei Ingolf en hij klopte Ender van achteren op zijn schouder.

Het gebaar en zijn intonatie herinnerden Herzfeld aan een psychiater die zijn patiënt zegt dat alles in orde komt, zolang hij zijn pillen maar slikt.

'We kunnen er samen later naar kijken. Maar nu iedereen er eindelijk is, stel ik voor dat we beginnen.'

Het was niet zozeer een voorstel als wel een beslissing, want Ingolf beende zonder het antwoord van zijn gasten af te wachten dwars door de suite en opende een van de vier deuren. 'Wilt u mij alstublieft naar mijn werkkamer volgen?'

Hij bleef even op de drempel staan en stapte toen de ruimte in, waar Herzfeld nog een bekend gezicht ontdekte.

'Linda.'

'Paul.'

Wat Ingolf zijn *werkkamer* noemde, zou elders een *vergaderzaal* worden genoemd.

Linda zat aan een lange tafel en onderbrak haar werk aan een tekening, die ze blijkbaar had gemaakt om de tijd te doden. Het was een schets van een stervende man, liggend in een plas bloed. Ondanks of juist dankzij het brute, gewelddadige karakter van de scène kon Herzfeld niet anders dan Linda's talent bewonderen.

'Goed je te zien.'

Linda stond op en omhelsde Herzfeld alsof hij een uit de oorlog teruggekeerde soldaat was. Ze had haar met kunstbont gevoerde leren jas aangehouden, en haar kraag kietelde zijn oor. Ze rook aangenaam, pittig en fruitig tegelijk, hoewel Herzfeld er zeker van was dat ze geen parfum droeg.

'Voelt beter dan die klap van laatst,' fluisterde hij toen ze zich van hem losmaakte.

Toen knikte hij de man toe die op de stoel tegenover Linda was gaan zitten en die, afgezien van Ingolf, de enige was die zich in dit soort vertrekken op zijn gemak leek te voelen: maatpak, das met grote knoop, gemanicuurde nagels en tanden wit als Tipp-Ex. Je kon zien hoeveel moeite het dit prototype van een bedrijfsadviseur kostte de uitdossing van de bodybuilder te negeren die zich in trainingspak op de stoel naast hem liet vallen. Herzfeld ging met een van pijn vertrokken gezicht zitten, met een hand op het drukverband over zijn maag.

Ingolf von Appen begon met zijn presentatie zonder de onbekende voor te stellen. Hij had het vertrek verduisterd en een beamer aangezet, die op een scherm aan het eind van de ruimte gericht stond.

'Ik heb jullie allemaal gevraagd vandaag naar mijn appartement te komen omdat ik jullie hulp nodig heb.'

'Dat zei Herzfeld ook toen hij mij laatst belde, en we weten allemaal wat daarvan kwam,' zei Linda droog.

Ender was de enige die lachte.

'Wees maar gerust. Waar ik jullie voor nodig heb is heel wat minder riskant, maar des te profijtelijker voor jullie.'

Ingolf liet zijn eerste powerpointdia zien, die alleen uit een simpele tekst bestond: G.P.SAVE.

'Wat moet dat voorstellen?'

'Dat, beste professor, is de werkelijke reden dat ik de stage bij u wilde doen. U herinnert zich toch dat ik u over PetSave heb verteld?'

'Over de kat, ja. Je hebt een gps-chip ontwikkeld waarmee je weggelopen dieren kunt terugvinden.'

Ingolf grijnsde. 'Precies. En G.P.SAVE...' Hij wees met een laserpointer op het logo op de muur. '... is gebaseerd op het idee van PetSave. Alleen op een hoger niveau van ontwikkeling.'

'Wilt u vermiste mensen zoeken?' vroeg Ender.

Ingolf lachte. 'Nee. Ik wil voorkomen dat ze worden ontvoerd.'

Hij keek weer ernstig en richtte zich tot Herzfeld. 'Ik heb ooit in een tijdschrift een artikel van uw hand gelezen, professor. Daarin schrijft u dat er zesenvijftig plekken zijn waar je met een microchirurgische ingreep dingen in een lichaam kunt verbergen zonder zichtbare littekens achter te laten.'

In de *National Geografic*. Herzfeld knikte zwijgend.

'Denkt u zich eens in hoeveel leed we families en nabestaanden zouden besparen als we tijdig een gps-zendertje konden implanteren bij personen die het risico lopen ontvoerd te worden.'

Er verscheen een nieuwe dia. Een grafiek.

'Elke zestig seconden wordt er alleen al in Zuid-Amerika iemand ontvoerd. In Duitsland komt het natuurlijk veel minder voor, maar toch neemt de angst onder de bevolking toe. Over de hele wereld.'

Hij nam iedereen afzonderlijk op, en in zijn ogen stond te lezen: *En niet pas sinds de zaak-Sadler.*

'Mijn analisten voorspellen een potentiële groeimarkt van meer dan twintig miljoen geïnteresseerde klanten. Dat komt zelfs in de meest conservatieve schatting overeen met een jaaromzet van 1,4 miljard dollar. Daarvan bedraagt de winst vierhonderddertig miljoen. Als het slecht verkoopt.'

Hij liet zijn woorden bezinken.

'De markt is gigantisch, er zijn talloze klanten: ondernemingen die hun topmanagers in de derde wereld voor veel geld tegen ontvoering moeten verzekeren. De staat, die geïnteresseerd is in een kostenbesparende enkelband voor gedetineerden. Maar hoofdzakelijk ouders, die willen weten waar hun kind is. Als we de operatie vlak na de geboorte zouden uitvoeren, kan een bezorgde moeder die zich afvraagt waarom haar kind niet allang terug is van de speelplaats gewoon de computer aanzetten om te zien waar het zich bevindt.'

'Wacht even, heb ik iets gemist of zei je net dat je een chip bij mensen wilde implanteren?' vroeg Linda.

'Ja. Zodra er een concrete verdenking bestaat, kan een speciale eenheid worden gestuurd om de ontvoerde te zoeken. De techniek is geperfectioneerd, onze juristen hebben de randvoorwaarden onderzocht. Als we de ingreep door een arts laten uitvoeren en alle betrokkenen akkoord gaan, bestaan er geen juridische bezwaren.'

'En ethische?' vroeg Linda verontrust.

'Ik zie geen probleem,' schoot Herzfeld Ingolf te hulp. Hij hief zijn hand. 'Ik begrijp je wel, Linda. Gegevensbescherming, persoonlijkheidsrecht, allemaal heikele thema's, maar voornamelijk theorie. Als je het me een halfjaar geleden had gevraagd, zou ik zo'n idee verontwaardigd van de hand hebben gewezen. Maar nu? Na alles wat we hebben doorgemaakt?' Hij haalde zijn schouders op. 'Ik zou er mijn rechterarm voor hebben gegeven als ik Hannah via een satelliet had kunnen lokaliseren.'

'Dan zou u g.p.save dus eventueel kunnen ondersteunen?'
Ingolfs ogen schitterden.

'Nee.'

'Maar...' Von Appen leek verward. 'Zei u niet...'

'Ik zei dat ik geen ethische bezwaren tegen je idee heb. Maar
ik wil er niet aan meewerken.' Herzfeld maakte aanstalten op te
staan.

'Ho, wacht even, professor. Ik heb u niet nodig als arts, als u
dat mocht denken. U hoeft niemand open te snijden. U zou alleen als adviseur fungeren. Jullie allemaal...' Ingolf liet zijn blik
langs de aanwezigen dwalen. '... jullie zullen allemaal in het team
werken. Linda, jij bent handig en hebt een groot tekentalent. Je
zou de marketing voor je rekening kunnen nemen. Dat je kritisch
tegen de zaak aan kijkt, is een goed uitgangspunt. En Ender...'
Hij knikte hem toe. 'Jij hebt organisatietalent en kunt de afdeling
Verkoop organiseren.'

'Ik?' Ender wees ongelovig op zichzelf. 'Ik ben alleen huismeester geweest. En die baan heb ik voor mijn comedycarrière aan de
wilgen gehangen.'

'Mooi, dat betekent dat jullie allemaal op het moment niet zijn
gebonden aan een werkkring. Ook u hebt momenteel verlof, professor.'

Ja, zo kun je het ook noemen.

'Komaan, hak de knoop door. Alleen al van de garantiebonus
in het eerste jaar kan ieder van jullie zijn eigen Porsche tegen een
boom rijden.'

Zelfs Herzfeld moest erom glimlachen. Tot op heden had Ingolf de verzekering niet eens gemeld dat zijn Cayenne total loss
was.

'Waarom vertel je ons niet de waarheid, Ingolf? Vierhonderd
miljoen winst? Wij zijn het perfecte team? Bullshit.' Linda snoof,
ze streek haar haar van de littekens op haar voorhoofd. 'Er is maar

één reden waarom je ons hebt laten komen. Niet omdat wij zulke geweldige experts zijn.' Ze wees naar Herzfeld. 'Nou ja, afgezien van hem dan, misschien.'

'Maar?'

'Maar omdat we een ontvoerd meisje hebben teruggevonden en een eind hebben gemaakt aan een serie moorden. Wij zijn de grote mediahype van het jaar. Je hebt ons nodig als uithangbord.'

'En als dat waar zou zijn?' Ingolf glimlachte.

'Dan ben je een idioot.' Herzfeld nam het woord. 'Alweer vergeten? Ik ben alleen vrijgelaten op borgtocht. Over een halfjaar begint mijn proces wegens moord met voorbedachten rade.'

'En op dit punt komt dr. Torben Ansorge in beeld,' zei Ingolf met een brede glimlach.

De man met das naast Ender voelde aan zijn boord, schraapte zijn keel en knikte gewichtig.

'Dr. Ansorge is een van de beste strafpleiters van het land en is ervan overtuigd dat hij u voor het grootste onheil kan behoeden, professor.'

De advocaat knikte zelfgenoegzaam.

'Is dat zo?' vroeg Herzfeld aan de man. 'Denkt u dat u mij uit de gevangenis kunt houden?'

'Nou, het zal niet gemakkelijk zijn,' zei Ansorge met een verrassend hoge stem. 'Maar als er een manier is, dan vinden wij die.'

Wij? Sprak die blaaskaak over zichzelf in koninklijk meervoud?

'En tenslotte hebt u niet de winnaar van de Nobelprijs voor de Vrede gedood, maar Jan Sadler.'

'Nou, dat is dan prima in orde,' zei Herzfeld. 'Ik heb maar één vraag.'

'En die is?' Het rechterooglid van de advocaat trilde vol verwachting.

'Hebt u in al die jaren dat u nu strafpleiter bent weleens een cliënt verdedigd die zonder twijfel schuldig was?'

Ansorge aarzelde, maar Linda maakte gebruik van de gelegenheid om de vraag te beantwoorden.

'Hij verdedigt mijn broer. Die had geprobeerd me die stalker van het lijf te houden. Clemens bedoelt het goed. Maar zijn methodes deugen van geen kant. Hij is beslist schuldig, net als zijn vriend Sandro, die een minderjarig meisje heeft gebruikt om Danny uit te schakelen.'

Herzfeld knikte. Hij had over de dertienjarige Fiona en de problemen die justitie had om haar voor haar daad verantwoordelijk te stellen in de krant gelezen.

'En toch verdient uw broer door het systeem te worden beschermd,' vulde Ansorge aan. 'Een van de meest verheven beginselen van onze grondwet is dat ieder mens recht heeft op de best mogelijke verdediging.'

'Mooi, en zat er tussen al die schuldige mensen ook weleens een verkrachter of kindermoordenaar?'

'Daarvoor zou ik eerst mijn dossiers...'

'Kom nou toch, dr. Ansorge. De beste strafpleiter van Duitsland zal toch een goed geheugen hebben. Geen enkel geval van verkrachting of kindermishandeling?'

'Ik denk het wel, ja. Maar in die zaken hebben wij geen vrijspraak bereikt, maar...'

'... hebt u alleen de waarheid aan het licht gebracht en bent ervan uitgegaan dat het recht zijn loop neemt. Ik weet het.'

Herzfeld zei het zonder weerzin. Niet opstandig. En zonder Ansorge te veroordelen. Ooit had hij precies zo gehandeld. Voordat zijn dochter was ontvoerd.

Hij had zich aan de spelregels gehouden en op het systeem vertrouwd. Hij was ervan uitgegaan dat er een scheidsrechter was die de feiten correct zou interpreteren. En waar had het toe geleid? Sadler was belachelijk snel vrijgelaten. En een volgend gezin werd in het ongeluk gestort en ging toen compleet te gronde. Tal van mensen hadden moeten sterven.

'Bedankt, nee, ook dat aanbod wijs ik van de hand.' Herzfeld stond op en liep de vergaderruimte uit, zonder zich nog eenmaal om te draaien.

'Hé, wacht even.'

Ingolf rende achter hem aan en hield hem tegen in de hal. 'U maakt een fout als u zich niet door hem laat verdedigen.'

Herzfeld opende de garderobe en pakte zijn jas. 'Laat maar. Je bent een fatsoenlijke kerel. Een beetje zonderling misschien, maar ik mag je graag, dat meen ik.'

'Zonderling? Wie van ons beiden is hier zonderling? U hebt uw baan verloren, uw titel zal u worden ontnomen, uw reputatie is naar de maan, en nu verdwijnt u ook nog jarenlang achter de tralies. Ik heb u zojuist de mogelijkheid geboden dat alles te voorkomen. U verdient miljoenen en hoeft niet naar de gevangenis.'

'Dat is allemaal niet zo belangrijk voor me, Ingolf.'

'Geld en vrijheid? Wat is er belangrijker dan uw toekomst?'

'Het heden.' Herzfeld glimlachte droevig. 'Ik heb eerst mijn vrouw, en nu ook nog mijn dochter verloren. Ik moet het beetje tijd dat ik nog heb gebruiken om mijn relatie met Hannah te herstellen. Die ga ik niet met powerpointpresentaties en onderhandelingsstrategieën verdoen.' Herzfeld liep naar de deur, deed hem open en draaide zich nog een laatste keer om toen hij in de gang stond. 'Kop op. Kijk niet zo sip. Ik weet dat je hier het beste met me voorhad. Maar je hoeft me geen wederdienst te bewijzen, alleen omdat ik je uit het meer heb gehaald. Je hebt me bijzonder geholpen. We staan quitte.'

Hij reikte hem de hand. 'En maak je geen zorgen. Ik heb geen belasting ontdoken, alleen iemand vermoord. Wat stelt dat nou helemaal voor?'

De terugweg leek niet meer zo lang. Het tapijt leek minder dik en de geur was nog maar half zo doordringend als daarnet. Zelfs zijn pijn leek niet meer zo hevig, maar Herzfeld wist natuurlijk dat het allemaal maar inbeelding was. Over een paar uur al zou het alarm van zijn horloge hem eraan herinneren dat het tijd was zijn medicijnen in te nemen. En uiteindelijk, als hij straks nog eens zou proberen Hannahs voicemail te bereiken, zou het gevoel van welbehagen verdwijnen. Maar nu, op dit moment, koesterde hij voor het eerst sinds lange, lange tijd de vage hoop dat er dingen konden veranderen. En dat gevoel bleef nog een hele poos bestaan. Vier verdiepingen lang, het hele traject van de lift tot aan de lobby beneden, en het was pas weer verdwenen toen Paul Herzfeld het hotel uit liep, de regen in, om op het trottoir in de anonieme massa op te gaan.

Hij heeft een vierjarig kind misbruikt en mag in hetzelfde huis als zijn slachtoffertje blijven wonen: Andreas S. werd afgelopen week in Dresden weliswaar tot **22 maanden gevangenisstraf** veroordeeld, maar de rechters maakten er een voorwaardelijke straf van omdat Andreas S.' advocaat een deal met de officier van justitie en de rechtbank had gesloten: Andreas S. bekende schuld en kreeg daarom **geen gevangenisstraf**.

Bron: *Stern* van 13 april 2011

De ondernemer Stefan W. heeft (...) miljoenen aan inkomsten verzwegen. Toen de belastingdienst hem op het spoor kwam en zijn woning en het kantoor van zijn belastingadviseur doorzocht, zei de fiscus (...) dat de belastingaangiftes met de gecorrigeerde, juiste gegevens al waren voorbereid. De rechtbank vond dat niet opwegen tegen het feit dat W. zichzelf niet had aangegeven. De arrondissementsrechtbank van München veroordeelde hem wegens belastingontduiking en beleggingsfraude tot **zeven jaar gevangenisstraf**.

Bron: *Basler Zeitung* van 2 juli 2010

Instituut voor Forensische Geneeskunde
Speciale eenheid voor Extreme Delicten
Autopsierapport

Sectie op: 26-09-2012 **Naam:** Afgesneden, geen voornaam **Beroep:** thriller	Rapport nr: 666
Overleden op: Tijdstip van overlijden onbekend, vermoedelijk laat in de avond na urenlang voorafgaande inwerking deels van stomp geweld, deels van een scherp trauma op het gevoelsleven (heftig geblader).	**Lijkschouwers:** 1. Mr. Sebastian Fitzek 2. Prof. dr. Michael Tsokos
Geboortedatum: Voorjaar 2011	**Sectieassistenten:** Hans-Peter Übleis (uitgever van alle autopsierapporten bij Droemer), Carolin Graehl en Regine Weisbrod (stijl-, zin- en woordsectie), Sabrina Rabow (bewijspresentatie in de openbaarheid), Fritz Breitenthaler en Frank Hellberg (piloten van de vlucht Berlijn-Helgoland-Berlijn ten behoeve van verzamelen bewijsmateriaal m.b.v. luchtfoto's), Lars Carstens (waterpolitie Helgoland), Sibylle Dietzel (prepareren van het te obduceren object), Roman Hocke (contractueel overeengekomen verzamelen van bewijzen), Christian Meyer (overbrenging en transport van de forensisch arts), Helmut Henkensiefken (fotograaf plaats delict), Noomi Rohrbach (organisatie van de wetenschappelijke varianten), Monika Neudeck (contact misdaadverslaggevers), Manuela Raschke (quick-out-hersenen v. Fitzek), Karl Raschke (fysieke tuchtiging v. Fitzek), Freimut Fitzek (vaderlijke bijstand), Sandra Fitzek (echtelijke ondersteuning), Anja Tsokos (veel geduld met een maniak).

Binnengekomen als: Duidelijk geval van misdaad vanachter bureau.	
Voorgeschiedenis: Psychothrillerauteur ontmoet non-fictieschrijver en forensisch arts bij televisieopname in 2009; interesse in elkaars werk en wederzijdse sympathie; weerzien 2010; idee van een gemeenschappelijk boekproject tijdens verorberen van steaks (bloedig).	**Doodsoorzaak:** Uitgelezen. **Diagnose:** Boek met afmetingen 13,5 x 21 x 3 cm, paperback, gewicht 476 g, 352 pagina's, macroscopisch geen duidelijke beschadigingen vast te stellen; slechts een incidenteel ezelsoor. Diverse vingerafdrukken van een tot dusverre niet geïdentificeerde lezer over het gehele boekobject. Lijkvlekken duidelijk aanwezig op de achterkant van het boek, met sterke druk van de vingers niet te verdrijven. Op de rug van het boek een spoor van een bloedige vloeistof met in etiologisch opzicht onduidelijk aandeel van afscheidingen. Bewerkelijke autopsie, omdat het object onder hoogspanning staat.
Aanwezige bewijsstukken: zie formulier (bijl).